Insights to Performance Excellence 2009–2010

Also available from ASQ Quality Press:

The Making of a World-Class Organization
E. David Spong and Debbie Collard

The Executive Guide to Understanding and Implementing the Baldrige Criteria: Improve Revenue and Create Organizational Excellence
Denis Leonard and Mac McGuire

Homeland Security Assessment Manual: A Comprehensive Organizational Assessment Based on the Baldrige Criteria
Donald C. Fisher

On Becoming Exceptional: SSM Health Care's Journey to Baldrige and Beyond
Sister Mary Jean Ryan, FSM

Transformation to Performance Excellence: Baldrige Education Leaders Speak Out
Sandra Cokeley, Margaret A. Byrnes, Geri Markley, and Suzanne Keely, editors

The Principal's Leadership Counts!: Launch a Baldrige-Based Quality School
(also available in audio book)
Margaret A. Byrnes with Jeanne C. Baxter

Business Performance through Lean Six Sigma: Linking the Knowledge Worker, the Twelve Pillars, and Baldrige
James T. Schutta

There is Another Way!: Launch a Baldrige-Based Quality Classroom
Margaret A. Byrnes with Jeanne C. Baxter

Charting Your Course: Lessons Learned During the Journey Toward Performance Excellence
John G. Conyers and Robert Ewy

From Baldrige to the Bottom Line: A Road Map for Organizational Change and Improvement
David W. Hutton

The Executive Guide to Understanding and Implementing Lean Six Sigma
Robert M. Meisel, Steven J. Babb, Steven F. Marsh, and James P. Schlichting

To request a complimentary catalog of ASQ Quality Press publications, call 800-248-1946, or visit our Web site at http://qualitypress.asq.org.

Insights to Performance Excellence 2009–2010

An Inside Look at the 2009–2010
Baldrige Award Criteria

Mark L. Blazey

ASQ Quality Press
Milwaukee, Wisconsin

American Society for Quality, Quality Press, Milwaukee 53203
© 2009 by ASQ
All rights reserved. Published 2009
Printed in the United States of America

14 13 12 11 10 09   5 4 3 2

ISBN-13: 978-0-87389-755-6

No part of this book may be reproduced in any form or by any means, electronic, mechanical, photocopying, recording, or otherwise, without the prior written permission of the publisher.

Publisher: William A. Tony
Acquisitions Editor: Matt Meinholz
Project Editor: Paul O'Mara
Production Administrator: Randall Benson

ASQ Mission: The American Society for Quality advances individual, organizational, and community excellence worldwide through learning, quality improvement, and knowledge exchange.

Attention bookstores, wholesalers, schools, and corporations: ASQ Quality Press books, videotapes, audiotapes, and software are available at quantity discounts with bulk purchases for business, educational, or instructional use.

For information, please contact ASQ Quality Press at 800-248-1946, or write to ASQ Quality Press, P.O. Box 3005, Milwaukee, WI 53201-3005.

To place orders or to request a free copy of the ASQ Quality Press Publications Catalog, including ASQ membership information, call 800-248-1946. Visit our Web site at http://www.asq.org or http://www.asq.org/quality-press.

 Printed on acid-free paper

Quality Press
600 N. Plankinton Avenue
Milwaukee, Wisconsin 53203
Call toll free 800-248-1946
Fax 414-272-1734
www.asq.org
http://www.asq.org/quality-press
http://standardsgroup.asq.org
E-mail: authors@asq.org

This book is dedicated to the memory of my father, Everett,
who taught me the value of continuous improvement,
and to my family members, who provide support for the
continuous search for excellence: my mother, Ann L. Blazey,
who at 81 continues to strive to improve
everything she does; my brothers Scott, Brian, and Brent;
my children Elizabeth and Mark; and most of all,
my lifelong partner and loving wife Karen.

Contents

Foreword .... *xi*

Preface .... *xiv*

Acknowledgments .... *xv*

Introduction .... *xvi*

Insights to Performance Excellence 1

Preface: Organizational Profile 77
    P.1 Organizational Description 78
    P.2 Organizational Situation 81

Category 1—Leadership 83
    1.1 Senior Leadership 84
    1.2 Governance and Societal Responsibilities 93

Category 2—Strategic Planning 103
    2.1 Strategy Development 105
    2.2 Strategy Deployment 115

Category 3—Customer Focus 125
    3.1 Customer Engagement 126
    3.2 Voice of the Customer 134

Category 4—Measurement, Analysis, and Knowledge Management 147
    4.1 Measurement, Analysis, and Improvement of Organizational Performance .. 148
    4.2 Management of Information, Knowledge, and Information Technology 158

Category 5—Workforce Focus 165
    5.1 Workforce Engagement 166
    5.2 Workforce Environment 181

Category 6—Process Management 189
    6.1 Work Systems 190
    6.2 Work Processes 197

Category 7—Results 207
    7.1 Product Outcomes 209
    7.2 Customer-Focused Outcomes 213
    7.3 Financial and Market Outcomes 217
    7.4 Workforce-Focused Outcomes 221
    7.5 Process Effectiveness Outcomes 226
    7.6 Leadership Outcomes 230

Contents

Tips on Preparing a Baldrige Award Application	**235**
Scoring System	**247**
Clarifying the Baldrige Scoring Requirements	**255**
Self-Assessments of Organizations and Management Systems	**299**
The Site Visit	**317**
Clarifying Confusing Terms	**341**
Glossary	**345**
About the Author	*359*
Index	*361*

CD-ROM Contents

Insights to Performance Excellence 2009–2010 contains a companion CD-ROM, located on the inside back cover, with the following contents:

2009 CD-ROM Contents *(PDF and Word)*

2009 Baldrige Process Calendar *(PDF and Word)*

2009 Business
- 2009–2010 Baldrige Business Criteria and Applications
    - *2009–2010 Baldrige Business Criteria Booklet (PDF)*
    - *2009–2010 Baldrige Business Criteria – Categories only (PDF and Word)*
    - *2009 Baldrige Award Application Forms Booklet (PDF)*
    - *2009 Baldrige Award Application Form (Word)*
    - *2009 Eligibility Certification Forms (Word)*
    - *2009–2010 Optional Worksheet - Business (PDF and Word)*
- 2009 Baldrige Business Scoring Calibration Guide *(PDF and Word)*
- 2009 Baldrige Business Application Development Templates *(Word)*
- ISO 9001 and Baldrige 2009 Comparison
    - *2009 Baldrige or ISO 9001 (PDF)*
    - *ISO 9001 and Baldrige 2009 Comparison Matrix (PDF and Excel)*

Alignment of Baldrige With Six Sigma, Lean Thinking, and Balanced Scorecard *(PDF)*

Additional Materials from the Baldrige Award Web Site
- A Baldrige Perspective *(PDF)*
- Are We Making Progress As Leaders? *(PDF)*
- Are We Making Progress? *(PDF)*
- Baldrige Frequently Asked Questions *(PDF and Word)*
- Getting Started *(PDF)*
- How Do You Know? *(PDF)*
- Improvement Act of 1987 *(PDF)*
- Why Apply *(PDF)*
- Why Baldrige *(PDF)*

Some files on this CD-ROM require Microsoft Word or Microsoft Excel.

PDF files may be opened using Adobe Reader 6.0 or higher or Adobe Acrobat 6.0 or higher. Adobe Reader may be downloaded free of charge from the Adobe Web site at http://www.adobe.com.

All original materials on this CD-ROM ©2009 by ASQ Quality Press and Quantum Performance Group. All rights reserved.

To place orders or to request a free copy of the ASQ Quality Press Publications Catalog, including ASQ membership information, call 800-248-1946. Visit our Web site at http://www.asq.org or http://www.asq.org/quality-press.

Foreword

LEADERSHIP CHALLENGES

This year the Baldrige National Quality Award celebrates its twentieth year answering the question, "What drives success in organizations?" Some specific drivers have changed over time but the fundamental drivers are the same. These fundamental drivers of excellence have proven to be the same for all types of organizations whether in the private sector, education, health care, or government. Dr. Mark Blazey is the leading expert in the application of the Baldrige Criteria to help organizations improve and achieve outstanding levels of performance. He provided extremely valuable insight—through his writings and personal consulting—to help Xerox develop world-class management systems that led to Xerox Business Services being recognized as a 1997 recipient of the Baldrige Award. He has helped many other organizations increase their performance and earn the Baldrige Award and similar state awards as well. Dr. Blazey provides many valuable insights to help leaders make the changes needed to achieve the highest levels of performance excellence—many of which are highlighted in this introduction.

To be successful, organizations must engage their customers—although they may choose to call them many names, such as clients, students, patients, families, constituents, communities, voters, rate-payers, or passengers, to name a few. The nomenclature changes depending upon the language of the organization, but it is these customers who make decisions about whether they will continue to be loyal or go elsewhere. Organizations that can keep customers loyal and attract new ones will thrive. Strange as it may seem, there are organizations that have not put delighting customers at the top of their priority list (or anywhere on the list). Delighted customers are five times more likely to continue to use an organization or recommend that organization to others, than those who are simply satisfied. On the other hand, 80 percent of dissatisfied customers are likely to walk away without a word to the offending organization.

They are, however, likely to tell at least 20 of their friends, while only five will hear of the startling news associated with delight. Worst of all, it costs 10 times as much to regain a lost customer as it does to retain a current one. With the large number of Internet-based consumer buying sites in place today, dissatisfied customers can easily tell thousands about their bad experiences. The 21st century has evolved a more demanding customer-driven economy. If organizations intend to thrive, the workforce and leaders must understand the requirements and expectations of their customers.

Being customer-focused and understanding their requirements are necessary for success, but not sufficient. Organizations must consistently deliver value to the customers they want to serve. This requires that key work processes produce desired results every time. That is why a process orientation is important. Too many people in nonmanufacturing disciplines, such as sales, education, or health care, believe that using process discipline to carry out work is an idea that does not apply in their professional-driven world. The recipients of the Baldrige Award would not agree with this view. They demonstrate clearly that a customer-focused process orientation is critical for success in manufacturing as well as nonmanufacturing (such as health care and public school systems) and in large and small organizations.

Unfortunately, even when organizations begin to execute processes consistently, their leaders may find that excellence and optimum performance continue to elude them. Organizations can fail to satisfy customers even when key work processes function as designed—if the design was not based on customer requirements. Internally focused processes are too often driven by designers—without regard for customer concerns. The resulting organizational arrogance—the belief that we know better than the customer—is almost certain to bring about customer dissatisfaction and ultimately revolt, causing customers to demand change or leave.

Foreword

To be successful, organizations must consistently understand and precisely execute those processes that deliver the four or five characteristics—the vital few—that are critical to customer delight. The winners in a highly competitive environment are the organizations that listen to the voice of the customer to understand their preferences and requirements and then design and execute work processes aimed at delighting them better than anyone else.

Many leaders find it difficult to determine what customers want, fend off the competition, satisfy workers, and operate within a constrained budget. That is why the development and execution of strategy is essential. Strategy development demands:

- Understanding the direction in which customers are moving, the direction in which the competition is moving, and the direction in which the market is moving
- Coupling that information with the capabilities and desired direction of the organization
- Identifying the few things that are critical to the future success of the organization
- Defining, in measurable, outcome-oriented terms, what the organization must actually achieve to be successful in the future
- Converting those strategies into action to align and focus the work of the organization at all levels.

Managing the implementation of strategy and related actions requires clear directions and effective monitoring at all levels, which is facilitated by a dashboard showing key performance and process measures throughout the organization. No one would think of driving a car on a trip or getting on an airplane if the instrument panel was missing. Yet unsuccessful leaders often make critical decisions based on intuition and inadequate measures.

A good dashboard provides measures of leading indicators to help leaders understand what is important to customers, how well it is delivering on those things that are important, the reaction of its customers, and the capacity of its work processes and delivery systems. With this advance knowledge, leaders can make better decisions about the actions needed to be successful, bring more value to the marketplace, and respond effectively to changing circumstances and new opportunities.

While customer focus, strategic planning, and data to support effective decision making are critical components of the successful organization, these factors combined are still not sufficient to ensure success. Every high-performing organization must acquire good people, train them, motivate them, and retain them. To be successful today, organizations must develop an engaged workforce that contributes its utmost to the success of the organization and its customers. Workers must have the competencies to use facts and information to make good decisions, and to continue learning and contribute to their own growth and development. In a world where product and service superiority lasts only a short time, it is the capabilities and commitment of the workforce that drive ongoing excellence and differentiation. No longer are top performing organizations simply looking for workers with the right skills. Today, successful organizations need workers who are data-driven, customer-focused, and process-oriented—engaged people who promote improvement and innovation.

The responsibility of leadership is to make this system come together and work harmoniously. Basically, leadership has two functions: first, to set the direction very clearly, based on a strategy that brings value to its customers and the marketplace; and then to establish the environment in which that direction is carried out consistently.

Some leaders find it difficult to establish and articulate a clear vision and role model a set of values that lead to success. Without a clear direction, the people in an organization are forced to substitute their own ideas about the right direction. When many do this, the organization finds itself pulled in different directions. Leaders cannot expect people to know what to do if they have not established and continuously reinforced the norms of desired behavior. Great leaders lead by example—role modeling the desired behaviors that are expected of all.

The best organizations in every sector have demonstrated that all parts of the system must be effectively integrated to optimize performance. It is not possible to achieve excellence by only doing the things that are easy and ignoring the rest.

With his best-selling series and his personal involvement, Dr. Blazey has been helping leaders and organizations of all types and in all sectors achieve success and develop enviable performance levels. He has helped them develop practical approaches for continuous improvement that serve as the cornerstone for leadership and organizational success. Blazey's personal insight and clear explanations help make complex Baldrige concepts much simpler. That is what makes this book a best-seller. *Insights to Performance Excellence 2009–2010* is a book for beginners as well as experts in the field of organizational development and operational excellence. The book delivers the lessons, provides the insights, and sets the framework for a successful journey to performance excellence.

John Lawrence
Retired Vice President of Quality
Xerox Business Services
1997 Baldrige Recipient

Preface

A substantial portion of my professional life has been spent helping people understand the power and benefits of this integrated management system and become examiners for many performance excellence awards. These people come from all types of organizations and from all levels within those organizations. Participants include CEOs, generals, admirals, corporate quality directors, planners, state organization chiefs, small-business owners, heads of hospitals, teachers, professors, medical doctors, and school superintendents, to name a few.

This book was originally developed for them. It was used as a teaching and reference text to guide their decisions and deliberations as they provided feedback to organizations that documented their continuous improvement efforts using Baldrige Award-type management systems. Many examiners who used this text, especially Tom Kubiak, asked me to publish it in a stand-alone format. They wanted to use it to help their own organizations, customers, and suppliers guide and assess their continuous improvement efforts.

These two groups of readers—examiners of quality systems and leaders of organizations seeking high levels of performance—can gain a competitive edge by understanding not only the parts of a high-performance management system, but also how these parts connect and align. My goal for this book is that readers will understand more fully what each area of the performance excellence system means for organizations and find the synergy within the six major process-oriented parts of the system—leadership; strategic planning; customer and market focus; measurement, analysis, and knowledge management; workforce focus; and process management—that lead to excellent performance results.

Leaders report that this book provides a valuable, step-by-step approach to help identify and put in place properly focused continuous improvement systems. As progress is made, improvement efforts in one area will lead to improvements in other areas. This process is similar to experiences we have all encountered as we carry out home improvement: improve one area, and many other areas needing improvement become apparent. This book will help identify areas that need immediate improvement as well as areas that are less urgent but, nevertheless, vitally linked to organizational and operational excellence.

I am continually looking for feedback about this book and suggestions about how it can be improved. Please contact me via e-mail at authors@asq.org.

Acknowledgments

Harry Hertz, Curt Reimann, and the dedicated staff of the Malcolm Baldrige National Quality Award office have provided long-standing support and guidance in promoting performance excellence. Karen Davison, April Corniea, John Lawrence, and Paul Grizzell provided substantial editorial and analytical assistance. They have all contributed to analyses that are a part of this book.

I also greatly appreciate the work of Scott Blazey of Enterprise Design and Publishing for working with me every step of the way to prepare this book for publication. Without his efforts, this book would not exist.

Many others have helped shape my thinking about performance excellence and refine this book, including Joe Sener, Olga E. Soroka Striltschuk, Gary Floss, Rosye Faulk, John Barnette, Roy Bourne, Deborah Cremeans, Jeff Calhoun, Brian Lassiter, Jean Bronk, Rob Ecklin, Rob Marchelonis, Harry Zechman, Al Aycock, Kathy Ahsing, Ernestine Tyler, Chad Cloud, Christina Chonka, Cynthia LeFebvre, Wanda Thurmond, Stephen Milne, Gerald Winters, Mickey Mayland, Mary Gamble, Sylvia Rolfs, Patrick O'Boyle, Maggie Cronin, Norma Krech, Barbara Risser, Angie Germain, Orland Pitts, Ed Hare, April Umluf, Debra Danziger-Barron, Jim Shipley, Tom Kubiak, Thad Allen, Christine Wehrenberg, Kory Brendsel, Doug Borden, Rich Harris, Ginger Baker-Betz, Patricia Billings, Wendy Brennan, Gerald Brown, Beverly Centini, Sheryl Billups, Joe Kilbride, Linda Vincent, Jim Percy, Elizabeth Hale, Joan Wills, Steve Hoisington, Liz Menzer, Brett Remington, John Gustafson, Jack Evans, Arnie Weimerskirch, Marty Mariner, Jerry Holt, Bill MacLachlan, Doug Green, John Riabov, Paul Kuchuris, Carol Ganster Fisher, Bob Ewy, Jo-Ann Kratz, Sandra Cokeley, Gary Jones, Bill Smith, Mike Smith, Janice Weinman, Peggy Siegel, Norm Ridder, Chuck McCausland, Ann Galbraith, Bob Griswold, Harry Burt, Paul Schindler, Steve Uebbing, Lynn Erdle, Brian Dunster, Robert Frisina, James Miller, Jack Smith, Fred Smith, Dennis Nystrom, Rich Rose, Kathy Malcolm, Harold Stafford, Annie Norman, Roberta Early, Judd Prozeller, Dan Thorpe, Ed Bergin, Linda Watson, Diane Rivers, Michael Chapman, Linda Janczak, Judith Cherrington, Laurie Emerson, Patricia Stevens, Charlie Blass, Kelly Gilhooly, Pat Webb, Annemieke Hytinen, and George Raemore.

I would also like to thank Christina Perrin and Liz Blazey for typing, background research, and proofreading.

The chapter on site visits, including the Expected Results Matrix, the Criteria model and integrated management systems analysis, the management and performance excellence surveys, the performance standard for leadership, the sections concerning the potential adverse consequences of not doing what the Criteria require, the application preparation files, the Item flow diagrams, the engagement questions, and the Scoring Calibration Guides are used with permission of Quantum Performance Group. I would also like to recognize and thank Brian Lassiter, April Corniea, Jean Bronk, and Mike Reagan for helping to expand the Expected Results Matrix into its current form and, together with Sylvia Rolfs and Jeff Calhoun for helping to edit the Scoring Calibration Guides.

The analysis of Six Sigma, Lean, and Balanced Scorecard is used with permission of Paul Grizzell and Quantum Performance Group. The Core Values, Criteria, selected glossary terms, award recipients, and background information in this book are drawn from information in the public domain supplied by the Malcolm Baldrige National Quality Award program. Kevin Hendricks and Vinod Singhal provided research results that were used in this book from their extensive study of financial performance. Data from the Economic Evaluation of the Baldrige National Quality Program by Albert Link and John Scott was prepared for the National Institute of Standards and Technology (NIST) in October 2001. The "Excellence equals Managing Change at an Accelerated Rate" formula is used with permission from Quantum Performance Group.

Mark Blazey

Introduction

The Malcolm Baldrige National Quality Award (MBNQA) 2009–2010 Criteria for Performance Excellence and scoring guidelines are powerful assessment instruments that help leaders identify organizational strengths and key opportunities for improvement. The primary task of leaders is then to use the information to improve work processes and achieve higher levels of performance.

Building an effective management system capable of driving performance improvement is an ongoing challenge because of the intricate web of complex relationships among management, labor, customers, stakeholders, partners, and suppliers. The best organizations have put in place a management system that improves its work processes continually. They measure every key facet of business activity and closely monitor organizational performance. Leaders of these organizations set high expectations, value workers and their input, communicate clear directions, and align the work of everyone to optimize performance and achieve organizational goals.

The Baldrige Criteria for Performance Excellence were first launched over 20 years ago, in 1987-1988. Since then, organizations of all types and sizes have learned that the disciplined approach to continuous improvement required by the Criteria has helped them keep up with the competition and succeed. In the 1980s, continuous improvement was rare. With even modest efforts, an organization committed to improvement could beat its competitors. Today, however, with more and more organizations striving to improve their key processes, programmatic improvement has become common. No longer is routine improvement sufficient to create a competitive advantage. The best competitors now know that long-term sustainability and market superiority require that they get better at getting better. The best organizations not only make improvements, but they improve their rate of improvement. They get better faster than their competition.

Einstein explained the relationship of mass and energy with the formula $E=mc^2$. We can borrow the formula and adapt it to describe what top managers must do to thrive in today's economic and competitive climate. Energy becomes Excellence, Mass becomes the ability to Manage organizational change, and the speed of light becomes the accelerated rate of Change, or Change squared. Therefore, Excellence equals Managing Change at an accelerated rate or $E=mc^2$. Not a scientific formula for physics, but a practical formula for success.

> **Excellence equals Managing Change at an accelerated rate: $E=mc^2$**

Unfortunately, because of the complexity of modern management systems, the criteria used to examine them are also complex and sometimes difficult to understand. *Insights to Performance Excellence 2009–2010* helps performance-excellence examiners and organization-improvement practitioners to understand the 2009–2010 Baldrige performance excellence criteria and the linkages and relationships among the Items.

Six types of information are provided in this book for each of the Items in Categories 1 through 6:

1. The actual language of each Item, including Notes (presented in the shadow box). [Author's note: The information in these shadow boxes presents the official Baldrige Criteria and serves as the only basis for the examination.]

2. A plain-English explanation of the requirements of each Item with some suggestions about the

rationale for the Item and ways to meet key requirements.

3. A summary of the requirements of each Item in flowchart form. The flowcharts capture the essence of each Item and isolate the requirements of each Item to help organizations focus on the key points the Item is assessing. Note that most boxes in the flowcharts contain an Item reference in brackets [ ]. This indicates that the criteria require the action. If there is no Item reference in brackets, it means the action is suggested but not required. Occasionally a reference to *[scoring guidelines]* is included in a box. This means that the authority for the requirement comes from the scoring guidelines.

4. The key linkages between each Item and the other Items. The major or primary linkages are designated using a solid arrow (⟶). The secondary linkages are designated using a dashed arrow (--▶).

5. An explanation of some potential adverse consequences that an organization might face if it fails to implement processes required by each Item. (Examiners may find this analysis useful as they prepare relevant feedback concerning opportunities for improvement. However, these generic statements should be customized—based on key factors, core values, or specific circumstances facing the organization being reviewed—before using them to develop feedback comments supporting opportunities for improvements in Categories 1 through 6.)

6. Examples of effective practices that some organizations have developed and followed consistent with the requirements of the Item. These samples present some ideas about how to meet requirements. (Remember, examiners should not convert these sample effective practices into new requirements for organizations they are examining.)

Changes to this 2009–2010 edition include:

- New information from the Baldrige 2009–2010 Criteria for Performance Excellence to help leaders focus on priority opportunities for improvement and better understand the role they must play in refining their management systems and processes.

- The CD-ROM included with this book has been modified to bring templates and related analyses up to date with the changes in the Criteria.

Reading *Insights to Performance Excellence 2009–2010* will strengthen your understanding of the Criteria and provide insight on analyzing your organization, improving performance, and applying for the award.

Insights to Performance Excellence

This book provides information for leaders who seek to transform their organizations to achieve performance excellence. This section:

- Presents a business case for using the Baldrige Criteria to improve organizational performance

- Describes the core values that drive organizational change to high levels of performance and underlie the Baldrige Criteria

- Provides practical insights and lessons learned—ideas on transition strategies to put high-performance systems in place and promote organizational learning

This section emphasizes themes driven by the 2009–2010 Criteria and Core Values. It also includes suggestions about how to start down the path to systematic organizational improvement, as well as lessons learned from those who chose paths that led nowhere or proved futile despite their best intentions.

The designers of the U.S. national award wanted to avoid problems inherent in both approaches. Accordingly, the principle was adopted that the Criteria must be continually refreshed and be based on the verified management practices of the world's best-performing companies that enabled them to achieve such high levels of performance, productivity, customer satisfaction, and market dominance.

To ensure that the Baldrige Criteria for Performance Excellence continue to be relevant, the U.S. Department of Commerce, National Institute of Standards and Technology (NIST) reviews the drivers of high performance each year. Based on these analyses, the Criteria for the Malcolm Baldrige National Quality Award are validated and refined.

In spite of this ongoing renewal, some critics of the Baldrige Criteria argue that the Baldrige standards are *outdated* and *passé*. These critics often ask, "If the Baldrige Criteria are updated each year, why don't they reflect the newest management techniques?" Early critics, pointing to the rising success of e-commerce and the dot-coms, seemed to prefer to employ unproven theories of what is needed to be successful in the global market. None of these critics, however, were able to offer any performance-based evidence to support their opinions. In fact, the collapse of thousands of badly managed dot-coms and other organizations seems to indicate that unproven theories and management fads do no more to build solid performance today than they did in prior decades.

The main reason why the Baldrige Criteria do not require the use of the latest management fads is because a management practice must be a proven driver of high performance before the practice is included as a requirement. Such *proofs* require strong evidence of widespread practice and related performance outcomes.

A new management practice might work well for one organization but not for another. Fact-based evidence must demonstrate that the practice leads to high performance in many types of organizations, including small and large, manufacturing and service, union and nonunion, and public and private.

Because it usually takes two or more years for a *promising practice* to prove its value, the Baldrige Criteria will lag behind the newest, unproven fads. However, the rigor of the Baldrige review is part of the value the Baldrige Criteria add to business excellence. The Criteria help leaders sort out the fads from the proven techniques. *The Baldrige Criteria reflect leading-edge, validated management practices essential to achieving optimum performance.*

Finally, it is important to mention that the Baldrige Criteria were never intended to limit improvement, innovation, and creativity—in fact, the Criteria require those traits in all process Areas. Specifically, the Criteria require leaders to develop and enhance their personal leadership skills, to participate in organizational learning [1.1a(3)], and to improve their own effectiveness [1.2a(2)] and promote innovation and an environment for learning throughout the organization [1.1a]. The Criteria require, in many areas, that the organization keep work processes current with changing business needs, including:

- Identifying and innovating product offerings and providing customer support [3.1a(1)]
- Creating a customer-focused culture and building customer relationships [3.1b(3)]
- Determining customer satisfaction, dissatisfaction, engagement, and the use of customer data [3.2c(4)]
- Keeping performance-measurement systems current [4.1a(3)]
- Using performance review findings for continuous and breakthrough improvement and innovation [4.1c]
- Ensuring availability of software and hardware systems and information [4.2b(3)]
- Evaluating and improving workforce and leader development systems [5.1b(3)]
- Improving key work processes [6.2c]

In addition, the Scoring Guidelines require effective, fact-based systems in place to evaluate and improve processes required by the Items in Categories 1 through 6 in order to score at the 50 to 65 percent level. This requirement was strengthened in the 2008 Scoring Guidelines. Now to score in the 60 to 65 percent level, organizations must show that improvement has led to meaningful change (innovation).

The best leaders use the principles described by the Baldrige Criteria as the fundamental way they manage the organization, and then search for methods to refine and enhance their work systems to provide even more competitive advantage. They experiment with new techniques and are not content to simply follow a management cookbook. However, they install a solid management system first, then experiment and improve—not the other way around.

Many of these top leaders use the Baldrige principles and management systems to achieve high performance without any public announcements or fanfare. They have never applied for the award and do not intend to do so. They are content to achieve excellence and win in the business world.

Nearly all business leaders and managers who reject the value of the Criteria out of hand do not understand the principles they contain, even those who claim to have "tried Baldrige." The system that effectively drives top performance in organizations is complex. After all, if it was easy to achieve excellence, everyone would do it. The landscape is littered with organizations that never understood or failed to continue using the validated, leading-edge management practices defined by the Baldrige Criteria. This book is for those leaders who are willing and able to commit to becoming great leaders, optimizing performance, and sustaining the excellence they have helped to achieve.

THE BUSINESS CASE FOR USING THE BALDRIGE PERFORMANCE EXCELLENCE CRITERIA

All leaders know that change is not easy. They will be asked and perhaps be tempted to turn back many times. They may not even be aware of these temptations or of the backsliding that occurs when their peers and subordinates sense their commitment is wavering. Leaders who are dedicated to achieving high performance appreciate examples of success from organizations that are ahead of them on the journey. These excellent leaders have held the course despite nagging doubts, organizational turbulence, and attempts at sabotage.

The following section of the book:

- Summarizes research on financial performance of approximately 400 firms that were recognized by local, state, or national awards for quality management practices. (Research results are reported with permission of Dr. Vinod R. Singhal. Research was conducted by Kevin B. Hendricks and Vinod R. Singhal.)

- Describes public- and private-sector organizations that have gained ground and made rapid strides forward on their journeys, having achieved recognition as recipients of the MBNQA. It then identifies the core values that have guided these organizations to achieve high levels of performance excellence.

VALUE OF BALDRIGE CRITERIA AND AWARDS

In a report entitled "The Nation's CEOs Look to the Future," 308 CEOs from large, small, and several noncorporate organizations described what they believe lies ahead for business in the United States and the value of the Baldrige Criteria and Award. These trends relate in many ways to the 2009–2010 Criteria and are considered as the Criteria are revised to reflect the current business environment and the most effective management practices for that environment.

The vast majority (67 percent to 79 percent) of the CEOs believe that the Baldrige Criteria and Awards are very or extremely valuable in stimulating improvements in quality and competitiveness in U.S. businesses. More than 51 percent of the CEOs reported the following trends as major directions that will be likely to affect business in the years ahead. These include (from most cited, 69 percent, to least cited, 52 percent):

- Developing new workforce relationships based on performance
- Improving human resources management
- Improving the execution of strategic plans
- Developing more appropriate strategic plans
- Measuring and analyzing organizational processes
- Developing a consistent global corporate culture
- Outsourcing of manufacturing
- Creating a learning organization

As part of the survey, CEOs were asked to reflect on their own skills and their peer group's skills and to report on which skills were most in need of improvement. The skills cited in the following list were thought by more than 50 percent to need "a great deal" of improvement. They are key to addressing the major business trends reported earlier in this section. The skills include:

- The ability to think globally and execute strategies successfully
- Flexibility in a changing world
- The ability to develop appropriate strategies and rapidly redefine their business
- The understanding of new technologies

Another 40 to 50 percent of CEOs believe that these skills also need to improve "a great deal." Skills needing improvement include the ability to:

- Work well with different stakeholders
- Create a learning organization
- Make the right bets about the future
- Be a visible, articulate, charismatic leader
- Be a strong enough leader to overcome opposition

When asked which required more improvement—the development or execution of appropriate strategies, CEOs selected *execution* by about a three-to-one margin. This means that alignment of work and realistic action plans needs to be improved along with accountability. If the organization is pulling in different directions, it is more difficult to accomplish individual unit or division priorities—energies and resources are being drained, execution is flawed, and results are suboptimized.

Research Supports the Business Case

Two researchers, interested in quality award winners, wanted to determine the extent (if any) quality management impacted business performance. The research of Dr. Kevin B. Hendricks from the College of William and Mary, School of Business, and Vinod R. Singhal from the Georgia Institute of Technology, Dupree College of Management is the basis for the following evidence that supports the use of the Baldrige Criteria. Their research looked beyond hype and the popular press to the real impact of quality management and examined the facts surrounding performance excellence. The research was based on about 600 recipients of various quality awards and similar recognition. The recognition provided to these organizations was based upon similar core values and concepts. Companies were mostly manufacturing firms (75 percent). All were publicly traded companies. Although Hendricks and Singhal did not find that quality management turned "straw into gold," their research added significantly to the business case for using the Criteria as a tool to enhance performance.

Hendricks and Singhal examined the following efficiency or growth measures:

- Percent change in sales
- Stock price performance
- Percent change in total assets
- Percent change in number of employees
- Percent change in return on sales
- Percent change in return on assets

Implementation Costs Do Not Negatively Impact the Bottom Line

The research examined two five-year periods during the quality management implementation cycle. The first period can be called beginning implementation. This period started six years before and ended one year before the receipt of a first award. During this period, organizations are implementing quality management and incurring associated costs of implementation, such as training, communications, and production and design changes. The researchers found no significant differences in financial measures between these companies (winners) and the control group of companies (nonwinners but similar in other respects) for this period. This is important because of the costs (both direct and indirect) associated with implementing quality management systems. The research suggests that the significant cost savings identified during this period of intensified focus on cycle time, time to market, and other factors pay for the implementation costs.

Improved Financial Results Can Be Expected with Successful Implementation

The study then examined results of companies from one year before winning the award to four years after the award was given. This period can be called mature implementation and it is in this period that one would expect the improved management to bear fruit. This was the case with this research. There were significant differences in financial performance between award winners and controls (nonwinners). For example, the growth in operating income averaged 91 percent for winners contrasted to 43 percent for non-award winners. Award-winning companies reported 69 percent growth in sales compared with 32 percent for the control group. The total assets of the winning companies increased 79 percent compared to 37 percent for the controls. Winners had significantly better results than the control group. The graphs in Figures 1 and 2 represent the study findings. Researchers found that award-winning companies outperformed control firms (non-award-winning companies) at least two-to-one, as Figure 1 indicates.

Hendricks and Singhal also found that there was no significant difference between the companies prior

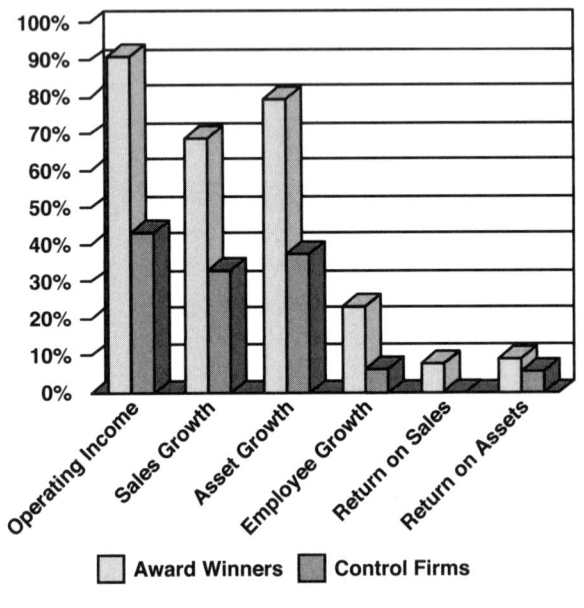

Figure 1 Comparison of award-winning and control firms.

Insights to Performance Excellence

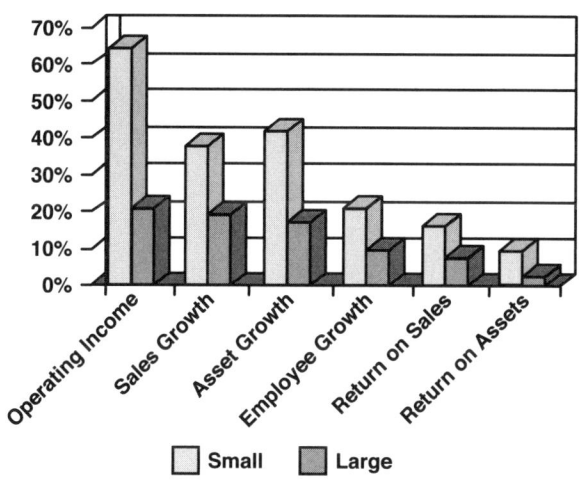

Figure 2 Comparison of large and small award-winning companies.

to the period of implementation of these quality principles. Performance of the award-winning firms was significantly better after implementation, suggesting the difference was due to the performance excellence systems that they installed.

In addition, Hendricks and Singhal found that small companies did significantly better than large companies in implementing the quality principles. This is depicted in Figure 2. Although large companies may have more resources with which to implement these systems, small companies may have an easier time deploying these systems fully throughout the organization and achieving maximum benefit.

Although both small (less than $600 million) and large firms benefited, small firms did even better. Small winners outperformed the control counterparts by 63 percent, whereas large firms outperformed their controls by 22 percent. A similar profile existed for low capital- versus high capital-intensive award winners.

Baldrige Processes Drive Improved Performance Outcomes

One of the key management practices that has been a part of the Baldrige Award criteria for many years is the use of business results to analyze and subsequently improve organizational performance. James R. Evans and Eric P. Jack conducted an extensive correlational study to examine 20 hypothesized linkages between various Baldrige-required management practices and organizational results [Evans, James R. and Eric P. Jack, "Validating Key Results Linkages in the Baldrige Performance Excellence Model." *Quality Management Journal*, 10.2 (April 2003): 7–24]. The first 10 hypotheses in their study represent linkages among the endogenous (internal system) variables as follows [Note: The strikethrough hypotheses (H3, H4, and H10) were not supported by the data. All other hypotheses were supported.]:

H1: Employee satisfaction has a positive impact on process performance

H2: Work system improvement has a significant impact on productivity

~~H3: Work system improvement has a significant impact on employee satisfaction~~

~~H4: Work system improvement has a significant impact on process performance~~

H5: Process performance has a significant impact on productivity

H6: Employee satisfaction has a significant impact on service quality

H7: Employee satisfaction has a significant impact on product quality

H8: Process performance has a significant impact on service quality

H9: Process performance has a significant impact on product quality

~~H10: Supplier performance has a significant impact on product quality~~

The next 10 hypotheses evaluate the direct linkages between the exogenous (external) variables and the exogenous results as follows:

H11: Employee satisfaction has a significant impact on market performance

H12: Service quality has a significant impact on customer satisfaction

H13: Product quality has a significant impact on customer satisfaction

H14: Product quality has a significant impact on financial performance

H15: Supplier performance has a significant impact on financial performance

H16: Process performance has a significant impact on financial performance

H17: Productivity has a significant impact on financial performance

H18: Customer satisfaction has a significant impact on market performance

H19: Market performance has a significant impact on financial performance

H20: Customer satisfaction has a significant impact on financial performance

The study's empirical results support the overall hypothesis that improving internal management practices leads to improvements in external results (Evans and Jack, p 18):

> "Consider the relationships among endogenous variables in the Baldrige results Category, such as between employee satisfaction and process performance, and between work system improvement and productivity. Strong correlation among these latent variables suggests the importance of many fundamental management practices that are embedded in the Baldrige requirements, such as a focus on employee well-being and motivation, and attention to the design of work systems and their linkage to other categories, such as process management. By strengthening the practices that lead to improved levels of internal performance, the analysis indicates that improved performance of production/delivery processes will likewise occur. Second, high levels of the endogenous variables are correlated with exogenous performance results as measured by market share, customer satisfaction, and financial performance. This provides evidence that improving the performance of endogenous variables will positively impact the most important external business performance measures. Thus, this research provides new evidence of the validity of the Baldrige model and its examination/self-assessment process that seeks to validate strong business results as an outcome of high-performance management practices."

The following is a summary of the study findings:

- Employee satisfaction is driven by process performance and product quality. (This is consistent with observations from many Baldrige Award winners that increased employee satisfaction leads to higher performance.)

- Process performance is correlated significantly with employee satisfaction as a dependent variate, and with product quality and market performance as an independent variate.

- Customer satisfaction is driven by product quality, service quality, and work-system improvement. Customer satisfaction is a more significant indicator of satisfaction than customer retention. Customers may indeed be satisfied but still switch allegiance based on other factors. Thus, customer retention is not necessarily a reliable indicator of satisfaction.

- Product quality is driven by employee satisfaction, work-system improvement, and process performance. Product quality drives customer satisfaction and financial performance.

- Service quality is correlated significantly only with customer satisfaction. On-time delivery dominates the relationship.

- Work-system improvement drives product quality, customer satisfaction, and financial performance.

- Financial performance is driven by productivity, market performance, work-system improvement, and product quality. From a practical perspective, this suggests that quality-related initiatives do have a significant impact on financial performance, as many studies have shown (for example, Hendricks and Singhal (1997) and the National Institute of Standards and Technology's continuing study of Baldrige recipients). Cost of quality, prevention cost, and warranty cost are the major contributors to productivity and product quality. Return on assets (ROA) and growth in ROA are the major contributors to market performance.

- Productivity is correlated significantly with financial performance. Rework and scrap contribute strongly to the relationship.

- Market performance is correlated significantly with process performance and financial performance.

Performance Excellence Is a Long-Term Solution

Companies that expect immediate gains from performance-enhancing systems are likely to be disappointed. It took years to create the culture you have today; it can take years to change it. Nevertheless, this research, combined with other results, makes a solid business case for using Baldrige-based management Criteria as the way to run a thriving organization.

High-Performing Organizations

High-performing organizations outrun their competition (or potential competition) by delivering value to stakeholders through an unwavering focus on customers and improved organizational capabilities. Examples of improved capabilities have occurred in all sectors of the economy, not just the private sector. These results range from time and cost savings to customer retention and loyalty.

Many examples of significant improvements from using the Baldrige-based management system are evident. Consider findings of the Baldrige Board of Examiners from the three 2008 Baldrige Award recipients: Cargill Corn Milling North America, Poudre Valley Health System, and Iredell-Statesville Schools.

Cargill Corn Milling North America (CCM), a 2008 manufacturing recipient, is a manufacturer of corn- and sugar-based products serving food, feed, and fermentation markets. CCM's products include corn syrup, high-fructose corn syrup, sugar, corn oil and dry corn ingredients; gluten feed and meal; and ethanol, acidulants, and industrial starches. CCM delivers 60-plus products to more than 3000 customers. Headquartered in Wayzata, Minnesota, CCM has revenues of more than $1 billion, and a workforce of 2321 employees. CCM has nine manufacturing facilities in eight states (Alabama, Illinois, Indiana, Iowa, Nebraska, North Dakota, Ohio and Tennessee), eleven distribution terminals in seven states (California, Florida, Maryland, Massachusetts, Tennessee, Texas and Washington), and sales offices in Coral Gables, Florida, and Naperville, Illinois.

- CCM's selling, general, and administration expense per gross profit—the cost of doing business—improved from about 35 percent in FY 2005 to 30 percent in FY 2008, exceeding competitive benchmarks by at least 5 percent for the FY 2005–2007 period.

- CCM's Earnings After Tax nearly tripled from FY 2003 to FY 2007.

- CCM's compound annual growth rate (growth over a year for a specific business element) with strategic customers has increased significantly in recent years, including:
  – Sugar, 44 percent from FY 2002 to 2008
  – Corn oil, 28 percent from FY 2003 to 2008
  – Dry corn, 20 percent from FY 2002 to 2008
  – Branded feed, 19 percent from FY 2003 to 2008
  – Ethanol, 28 percent from FY 2002 to 2008
  – Specialty starches, 15 percent from FY 2004 to 2008

- CCM maintained an error-free delivery rate of about 99 percent from FY 2005 to 2008.

- CCM's team-based culture and matrix organization foster an environment of cooperation, communication, skill sharing, and leveraging of diverse ideas.

- Since 2001, CCM has measured workforce engagement and satisfaction through a nationally administered Employee Engagement Survey. From FY 2004 to 2008, CCM increased its overall Engagement Score from approximately 37 percent to 65 percent. CCM also increased the engagement scores for each of its workforce segments.

- CCM strives for a safety standard of "excellence" rather than "compliance" and has an explicit goal to achieve an injury-free environment. To reach this standard, CCM utilizes a nationally administered Behavioral-Based Safety process (BBS) and an Error Cause Removal process. This is reinforced through safety teams at each manufacturing facility.

- CCM's senior leaders create a focus on the organization's mission and strategic objectives through the CCM Scorecard. Reviewed and posted on the employee intranet monthly, the scorecard leads to corrective actions for any performance below expectation.

- CCM's Best Practice Model is used by employee teams to design and innovate key work processes and, in turn, to address efficiency, effectiveness, agility, and cost control requirements. It entails identifying potential opportunities for improvement or innovation, selecting and standardizing key measures, and evaluating the opportunities using the measures. The model also includes documenting those improvements or innovations that are determined to be best practices, sharing these practices throughout CCM, and continuing to evaluate and refine the best practices as needed.

- CCM continually strives to improve its operational reliability and effectiveness through real-time and predictive monitoring of equipment health, stringent maintenance, and careful energy usage. As a result, CCM was able to maintain steady per-bushel costs from FY 2006 to 2008 even though energy costs increased 50 to 80 percent, chemical costs rose 30 percent, and maintenance costs increased 10 percent.

- A prime example of CCM's commitment to community was the company's efforts to rebuild its Cedar Rapids, Iowa, facility after severe floods in June 2008 completely shut down the plant. CCM moved quickly to implement disaster recovery processes, rebuild and restore the plant, assist employees and the community, and minimize operational and customer impacts. Most importantly, CCM employed its workforce through the entire period.

Poudre Valley Health System (PVHS), a 2008 health care recipient, is a locally owned, private, not-for-profit health care organization serving residents of northern Colorado, western Nebraska, and southern Wyoming. PVHS provides a full spectrum of health care services through two hospitals (Poudre Valley Hospital in Fort Collins, Colorado, and the Medical Center of the Rockies in Loveland, Colorado), and a network of clinics and care facilities. PVHS has revenues of $330.5 million and a workforce totaling 4082.

- PVHS patient loyalty ranks in the top 1 percent of U.S. hospitals, according to the U.S. Centers for Medicare and Medicaid Services.

- Avatar honored Poudre Valley Hospital with its Five Star Inpatient Care Award for the highest inpatient satisfaction score among 300 hospitals nationally. In 2007, Avatar named the Medical Center of the Rockies the Exemplary Service Overall Best Performer and ranked it among the top 12 nationally for customer satisfaction.

- PVHS demonstrates high levels of performance in many process measures for clinical assessments, care, and discharge. PVHS is consistently in or near the top 10 percent of national performance standards for treating acute myocardial infarction, heart failure, and pneumonia.

- PVHS has consistently maintained competitive health care costs when compared to local competitors who have a similar patient base and to the average health care costs in the Denver metropolitan area, which is the PVHS secondary service area. In 2006, the average PVHS charge was $2,000 lower than its main competitor and $7,000 lower than the Denver metro rate.

- The PVHS score on the Financial Flexibility Index (a composite of seven financial ratios measuring financial stability) determined by Ingenix, a provider of comparative clinical and financial results, has approached or surpassed the top 10 percent nationally for six years.

- Overall physician satisfaction ranks in the national 99th percentile, according to Gallup.

- A community case management program that pairs advance practice nurses and social workers with high-risk, chronically ill patients decreased emergency visits annually by 50 percent and resulted in more than $850,000 savings for the past three years.

- PVHS extensively involves customers and stakeholders through a systematic voice-of-the-customer process to provide guidance for strategic planning, goal setting, and improvement initiatives. For example, significant community, staff, and stakeholder input was incorporated into the planning and building of Poudre Valley Health System's newest hospital, the Medical Center of the Rockies. This included aspects such as the layout of the emergency rooms, the views from the patient room windows, healing gardens, and family amenities such as showers and kitchens.

- On a monthly basis, PVHS collects and analyzes input from various customer groups and multiple listening methods for use in strategy development, measuring performance, and identifying opportunities for improvement. Care units utilize patient feedback for goal setting and performance measurement, and post the comments on the PVHS intranet to engage the entire workforce.

- PVHS works with local community leaders and customers to identify and address specific health needs in the region. Among the community wellness, education, and preventive health programs in action are ones for heart disease, prenatal issues (such as low birth weight), child safety, and injury avoidance. Total community support surpassed $110 million—or greater than 25 percent of net patient revenue—in 2007.

- PVHS senior leaders and Board of Directors use the Global Path to Success (GPS) model to deploy the system's mission, vision, and values. Direct, two-way communication between management and staff includes an open door policy, access to management home phone numbers, and an exceptionally high level of face-to-face contact with leadership. Senior leaders maintain a culture of celebration to reinforce high performance, customer focus, and achievement of organizational goals.

- In 2008, PVHS received the Peak Performance Award, Colorado's highest award for performance excellence, marking the second time in five years for the honor. Also in 2008, Modern Healthcare Magazine named PVHS as one of "America's 100 Best Places to Work in Healthcare."

- The American Nurses Credentialing Center (ANCC) awarded Poudre Valley Hospital its "Magnet Designation for Nursing Excellence" in 2000 and again in 2004. The hospital was the first in the Rocky Mountain region and the 18th nationally to receive this designation. Based on its National Database of Nursing Quality Indicators, the American Nurses Association named Poudre Valley Hospital the nation's number one hospital for nursing quality.

- In March 2008, Thomson Reuters, a national health care consulting firm, named Poudre Valley Hospital as a "100 Top Hospital" for the fifth year in a row.

Iredell-Statesville Schools (I-SS), a 2008 education recipient, is a K–12 public school system located in southwestern North Carolina within a diverse community and economy. I-SS offers a variety of courses and educational programs to meet student needs, including heterogeneously grouped classrooms, two at-risk/behavior schools, and virtual and early college settings. The system also offers dual enrollment courses in partnership with a local community college and short-term alternative site placement programs. I-SS has four central offices and 35 schools, including 19 elementary schools, seven middle schools, five high schools, two alternative/at-risk schools, and two early colleges. Its budget is $160 million and its workforce of 3416 includes 1661 faculty and 1254 staff.

- In spite of a lower budget and per-pupil expenditure (ranked 107 out of 115 in North Carolina), I-SS has outperformed comparative districts at the state and national level. Student achievement rose from 55th to 9th, out of North Carolina's more than 100 school districts, during the period 2002–2008. Iredell-Statesville's total average SAT score at 1056 in 2008 was better than peer district (995), state (1007, rising from 57th to 7th), and national (1017) averages.

- The district has provided teachers with both face-to-face and virtual opportunities to collaborate on improving student learning. The initiative transformed the school system's culture from a "focus on teaching" to a "focus on learning."

- I-SS has steadily improved reading proficiency. For example in 2006–2007, the district:
  - Achieved a 90.6 percent proficiency on the state reading assessment
  - Closed the reading proficiency gap between African-American children and all students from 23 percent to 12.3 percent
  - Decreased the reading proficiency gap between exceptional children and all students from 42 percent to 21 percent

- Cohort graduation rates (the percentage of ninth graders who graduated from high school four years later) have steadily increased from approximately 61 percent in 2002–2003 to 81 percent in 2007–2008.

- At the district, school, and classroom levels, I-SS is using a "Raising Achievement, Closing the Gap" model to focus staff on what students should know and be able to do. When performance does not meet targets, the gap is addressed through the use of a "Plan-Do-Study-Act" (PDSA) cycle to identify and implement improvement opportunities. As a result:
  - SAT performance at Iredell-Statesville Schools during the past five years has improved by over 60 points to 1056 while national averages have seen a 9-point decline to 1017
  - Twenty-nine percent of I-SS students achieve a score of 3 or higher on at least one Advanced Placement exam during their high school career, almost double the national rate of 15 percent

- I-SS has outperformed comparable districts in the state of North Carolina in the following areas: attendance (96 percent versus 94 percent), dropout rate (3.5 percent versus 5.3 percent), and teacher turnover rates (10 percent versus 12 percent).

- In I-SS classrooms, fact-based, data-driven decision making supports learning and continuous improvement. Data are reviewed at the class and individual student level, where they are used to assess progress toward goals and modify PDSAs.

- To meet its strategic priority of "Quality Teachers-Administrators-Staff" and embrace the state mandate of "21st century skills for leaders and teachers," I-SS implemented evaluation rubrics that have led to an improvement in staff and stakeholder capability. As a result:
  - The percentage of highly qualified teachers in I-SS schools has increased from 84 percent to 96.5 percent over the last four years
  - The percentage of faculty certified by the National Board for Professional Teaching Standards has increased by 50 percent in the last four years

- I-SS utilizes a multi-faceted recruitment program that has increased both the number of applicants and the minority workforce during recent years. I-SS started the last two years with 100 percent of staff positions filled.

- I-SS has been used as a best practice case study by the American Productivity Quality Council, the American Society for Quality, TeachScape, and Follett.

Although the success of current Baldrige recipients is extraordinary, the performance and work processes of earlier award recipients are just as strong.

PRO-TEC Coating Company, a 2007 small business recipient, in Leipsic, Ohio, provides world-class, hot-dipped galvanized coated sheet steel primarily to the automotive market. Established in 1990 as a joint venture between United States Steel and Kobe Steel of Japan, PRO-TEC has revenues of $846 million and employs 236 associates. A team of experts from both companies designed the original production facility with a state-of-the-art, hot-dip continuous galvanizing/galvannealing line. Improvements to the line and its processes have allowed PRO-TEC to set numerous world production records. A second galvanizing line added in 1998 established PRO-TEC as the largest hot-dip galvanizing/galvannealing plant in North America.

PRO-TEC has been continuously profitable for 12 years in an industry that has been undergoing widespread bankruptcies and consolidations. Over the past five years, profits have doubled.

PRO-TEC is the industry leader in advanced high-strength steel coating and ultrahigh-strength steel coating, supplying about 15 percent of all hot-dipped galvanized steel to the automotive market. PRO-TEC produces in excess of 100 percent of design capacity in a 24/7 operation.

PRO-TEC proactively addresses potential concerns with its operations above compliance to ISO 9001, ISO/TS 16949, and ISO 14001 standards. This is done through voluntary participation and acceptance in EPA's National Environmental Performance Track (NEPT) and OSHA's Voluntary Protection Program (VPP) Star site status. PRO-TEC was the first steel processing plant to have earned both the VPP Star and NEPT recognition at the same time.

PRO-TEC's first priority is safety, and it operates to a standard that exceeds safety and environmental regulatory compliance of OSHA and the EPA.

Mercy Health System (MHS), a 2007 health care recipient headquartered in Janesville, Wisconsin, is a vertically integrated health system that serves more than one-million people a year through its 64 facilities in southern Wisconsin and northern Illinois. With over 4000 employee partners including 285 physicians, Mercy operates three hospitals and multiple clinics, specialty centers, and community outreach centers; MercyCare Insurance Company; Mercy Assisted Care; and Mercy Harvard Hospital. Mercy's gross revenues have steadily climbed from $33 million in 1989 to $833 million in fiscal year 2007. Total patient visits have increased tenfold.

Over the past five years, Mercy has implemented performance improvement initiatives resulting in increased patient and customer satisfaction in all core service areas. Results for inpatient satisfaction in 2007 attained the 81st percentile ranking with Press Ganey while the Emergency Department satisfaction improved from the 63rd to the 84th percentile ranking. Outpatient physician clinic satisfaction was in the top quartile of the American Group Management Association (AMGA) for the last three years.

The overall risk-adjusted mortality rate was among the top 15 percent of hospitals in the nation. MercyCare Insurance Company enrollees benefit from a childhood immunization project that has been recognized by the National Committee for Quality Assurance as a best practice. Mercy's proven medication safety practices include an automated medication management system that allows for 24-hour-a-day, seven-day-a-week pharmacist review of medication orders prior to administration at all hospital locations. Mercy was ranked number one in the nation on the 2006 American Association of Retired Persons (AARP) Top Employers for Workers Over Age 50 list, and was named one of the "100 Best Companies in Which to Work" by *Working Mother* magazine.

Sharp HealthCare, a 2007 health care recipient in San Diego, California, is an integrated regional health care delivery system that includes four acute care hospitals, three specialty hospitals and three medical groups, plus a full spectrum of other facilities and services and a health insurance plan. With 2600 physicians on hospital medical staffs, 1500 physicians in affiliated medical groups, over 14,000 employees, and licensed to operate 1870 beds, Sharp provides a wide range of health care services to more than 27 percent of the San Diego market. At the end of the 2006 fiscal year, Sharp reported $1.3 billion in assets and $1.8 billion in net revenues.

All four of Sharp's acute-care hospitals are at or approaching top 10 percent in performance nationally for non-intensive care unit community-acquired pneumonia patients, with sustained improvement year over year. Sharp benchmarks with the National Cancer Institute for survival rates of cancer in all of Sharp's cancer programs. Sharp meets or exceeds the five-year survival rate of all the major cancers listed. Bloodstream infection prevention is a key concern at Sharp, with the surgical intensive care units (ICUs) across the system outperforming the top quartile of the National Healthcare Safety Network (NHSN).

Sharp Hospitals exceed Agency for Healthcare Research and Quality patient safety indicators for inpatient care. Inpatient and outpatient satisfaction scores approach the top quartile in Press Ganey rankings. The patient loyalty index demonstrates top quartile performance. Sharp's vacancy rates and leader and clinical staff retention exceed the California benchmarks. Sharp has consistently performed better than the California benchmark in annual turnover.

Management donation of hours toward community programs increased from 10,000 hours to almost 60,000 during the period 2003–2006. Financial support for San Diego's vulnerable population, health research efforts, and the broader community increased from approximately $4 million to approximately $6.5 million during the period 2001–2006.

City of Coral Springs, Florida, a 2007 nonprofit recipient, is a municipal corporation—a city government following a corporate management model. Coral Springs is the 13th largest city in Florida, with over 130,000 residents. With a median age of 36.2, Coral Springs is a city of young families. The city's budget is $135 million and it employs 771 full-time employees, 295 part-time and temporary employees, 106 volunteers providing supplemental emergency response, and 700 occasional volunteers. The city's major facilities include City Hall, City Hall South, City Hall in the Mall, Public Safety Building, Public Safety Training and Technology Center, five fire stations, four police substations, three regional parks, 732 acres of neighborhood parks, sports, and aquatic facilities, a conference center, a middle/high charter school, and a Center for the Arts.

The city demonstrates a consistently high level of financial performance, including a AAA bond rating from the major rating agencies and zero findings on external audits for 11 years. Employee satisfaction and willingness to recommend the city as a place to work have been 90 percent or higher for 10 consecutive years.

The city's improvements to public safety have resulted in crime rate incidents per 100,000 decreasing by nearly half over the last 10 years. This is the lowest crime rate in the state and the fourth lowest in the nation for cities of this size.

The city is committed to customer focus. Senior leaders communicate the city's strategic priorities, goals, and plans to customers, and report on progress through multiple mechanisms.

Department-level improvement initiatives are triggered by ideas from empowered employees, complaint tracking data, information on innovations in other communities, and new developments in a field. Process Improvement Teams produce a cross-fertilization of ideas by having staff from Information Systems, Human Resources, and Financial Services collaborate with departmental staff on major process improvement initiatives.

U.S. Army Armament Research, Development and Engineering Center (ARDEC), a 2007 nonprofit (government) recipient located at Picatinny Arsenal, New Jersey, is the Army's principal researcher, developer, and sustainer of current and future armament and munitions systems. ARDEC provides 90 percent of the Army's suite of armaments and is responsible for several hundred programs in the acquisition process. ARDEC employs approximately 3000 civilians and several hundred contractors across five sites. It has one of the highest numbers of training hours and annual investment in training per employee in the country based on an American Society for Training and Development benchmark.

Efforts to diversify ARDEC's revenue stream have led to a growth in non-Army revenue from about $60 million in FY 2001 to $140 million in FY 2007. Results for workforce engagement were more than 84 percent positive and job satisfaction increased from about 87 percent positive in FY 2004 to 92 percent positive in FY 2007.

At all ARDEC locations, 100 percent of employees are trained in anti-terrorism, ethics, information assurance and protection, personnel recovery, safety, and security. ARDEC was selected by APQC in FY07 as one of several best-in-class benchmarks for Business Process Management.

ARDEC's customer support process provides a mechanism to listen and learn from the voice of the customer. Market Development Teams coupled with Integrated Product Teams, maintain a constant interface with customers. ARDEC is a best value to its customers by consistently having one of the lowest man-year costs to customers. Customer funding increased almost 40 percent since FY01 and customer satisfaction is at an all time high.

ARDEC was selected as the Army's leader in Knowledge Transformation in 2006. The award program recognizes breakthrough initiatives that provide critical knowledge sharing and collaboration solutions to improve situational awareness and organizational decision making.

MESA Products, a 2006 small business recipient headquartered in Tulsa, Oklahoma, designs, manufactures, and installs cathodic protection systems that control the corrosion of a metal surface. Products and materials are sold to a variety of contractors, end-users, and resellers across the United States, while technical and installation services are provided primarily to the mid-continent, southwest, and southeast United States. Mesa has a workforce of 70 with locations in Oklahoma, Texas, and Florida. Annual revenues are $25 million.

MESA Products demonstrated sustained sales growth, increasing from less than $6 million in 1985 to over $25 million in 2006. This growth came primarily through gains in market share from its competitors. Return on equity exceeded industry competitors by 20 percent.

MESA's performance in all 17 areas of satisfaction on its third-party Customer Satisfaction Survey exceeded that of its best competitor.

Results from MESA's employee satisfaction survey showed performance levels for the 17 surveyed attributes were 20 percent or more above the industry normative comparisons, and most met or exceeded the top 10 percent of the group of companies included in the survey.

Premier of San Diego, California, a 2006 service recipient, is a health care strategic alliance entirely owned by not-for-profit hospitals and health system organizations. The 200 owners operate or are affiliated with more than 1500 hospitals and thousands of non-hospital sites such as nursing homes and ambulatory centers. Premier's three business units provide group purchasing and supply chain management, insurance and risk management, and informatics and performance improvement. Premier's workforce includes 932 employees at locations in California, North Carolina, and Washington, D.C. Annual revenues are $500 million.

As an indirect measure of customer-perceived value, retention of hospital members increased from 94 percent in 2002 to approximately 97 percent in 2006. Premier utilizes systematic approaches to focus on career development of employees, including the Ph.D. Program, The Leadership College, and tuition reimbursement.

Premier's Informatics Business Unit market share, as measured by number of clients, was more than double that of its nearest competitor, making it the largest provider in the nation for comparison data for hospitals and related organizations.

North Mississippi Medical Center (NMMC) in Tupelo, Mississippi, a 2006 health care recipient, is the largest rural hospital in the country, and is also Mississippi's largest community-owned hospital. NMMC provides a wide array of services and has dedicated facilities to provide women's health, behavioral health, cancer treatment, and rehabilitation services. NMMC has a workforce of 3875 and annual revenues of $460 million. In 2006, NMMC provided community services to 156,750 people. Charitable donations, charity care, medical cost savings, and volunteer services total about $70 million annually.

A care-based cost management approach has provided cumulative gains of $11.1 million since 1999. NMMC had $56.5 million in revenue over expenses for 2006, an increase of $29 million over 2005.

In 2006, physician overall satisfaction and ease-of-practice scores were at 99 percent and the leadership score was at 98 percent. Since 2000, overall employee satisfaction has exceeded the 90th percentile benchmark levels from Human Resources. Inpatient satisfaction demonstrated consistent improvement since 2004. "Likelihood to Recommend" scores approached the Press Ganey 90th percentile in 2006.

Recipients prior to 2006 include the following:

Sunny Fresh Foods (now Cargill Kitchen Solutions), 2005 manufacturing and 1999 small business

DynMcDermott Petroleum Operations, 2005 service

Park Place Lexus, 2005 small business

Richland College 2005 education

Jenks Public Schools, 2005 education

The Bama Companies, 2004 manufacturing

Bronson Methodist Hospital, 2005 health care

Texas Nameplate Company, 1998 and 2004 small business

Kenneth W. Monfort College of Business, 2004 education

Robert Wood Johnson University Hospital Hamilton, 2004 health care

Medrad, 2003 manufacturing

Boeing Aerospace Support, 2003 service

Caterpillar Financial Services Corporation U.S., 2003 service

Stoner Solutions, 2003 small business

Community Consolidated School District 15, 2003 education

Baptist Hospital, 2003 health care

Saint Luke's Hospital of Kansas City, 2003 health care

Motorola Commercial, Government, and Industrial Solutions Sector, 2002 manufacturing

Branch-Smith Printing Division, 2002 small business

Sisters of Saint Mary Health Care, 2002 health care

Clarke American Checks, 2001 manufacturing

Chugach School District, 2001 education

The Pearl River School District, 2001 education

The University of Wisconsin-Stout Campus, 2001 education

Pal's Sudden Service, 2001 small business

Dana Corporation—Spicer Driveshaft Division, 2000 manufacturing

KARLEE Company, 2000 manufacturing

Los Alamos National Bank, 2000 small business

Operations Management International, 2000 service

BI, 1999 service (a training organization)

STMicroelectronics, 1999 manufacturing

The Ritz-Carlton Hotel Company (now part of Marriott International), a service recipient in 1999 and 1992

Boeing Airlift and Tanker, 1998 manufacturing

Solar Turbines, 1998 manufacturing

3M Dental Products Division, 1997 manufacturing

Merrill Lynch Credit Corporation, 1997 service

Solectron Corporation, 1997 and 1991 manufacturing

Xerox Business Services, 1997 service

ADAC Laboratories of California, 1996 manufacturing

Custom Research, 1996 small business

Dana Commercial Credit Corporation, 1996 service

Trident Precision Manufacturing, 1996 small business

Armstrong World Industries, Building Products Operations, 1995 manufacturing

Corning, Telecommunications Products Division, 1995 manufacturing

AT&T Consumer Communications Services (now Consumer Markets Division), 1994 service

Verizon Information Services (formerly GTE Directories Corporation), 1994 service

Wainwright Industries, 1994 manufacturing

Ames Rubber, 1993 small business

Eastman Chemical Company, 1993 manufacturing

AT&T Network Systems Group, Transmissions System Business Unit, 1992 manufacturing

AT&T Universal Card Services (now part of Citigroup), 1992 service

Granite Rock Company, 1992 small business

Texas Instruments, Defense Systems and Electronics Group, 1992 manufacturing

Marlow Industries, 1991 small business

Zytec Corporation (now part of Artesyn Technologies), 1991 manufacturing

Cadillac Motor Car Company, 1990 manufacturing

Federal Express Corporation, 1990 service

IBM Rochester, 1990 manufacturing

Wallace Company, 1990 small business

Milliken and Company, 1989 manufacturing

Xerox Corporation, Business Products and Systems, 1989 manufacturing

Globe Metallurgical, 1988 small business

Motorola, 1988 manufacturing

Westinghouse Electric Corporation, Commercial Nuclear Fuel Division, 1988 manufacturing

Through 2008, 79 Award recipients have been selected across six categories: 27 manufacturing companies, 15 service companies, 18 small businesses, eight education organizations, nine health care organizations, and two nonprofit organizations.

Economic Impact of the Baldrige National Quality Program

In October 2001, Albert N. Link, Department of Economics, University of North Carolina at Greensboro, and John T. Scott, Department of Economics at Dartmouth College reported on a study they completed that examined the economic impact of the Baldrige National Quality Program. Specifically, their study examined the net private benefits associated with the Baldrige National Quality Program to the U.S. private and public sector and the relationship between economy-wide net benefits and the social costs associated with operating the program.

Based on information collected from a mail survey of the U.S. organizational members of the American Society for Quality (ASQ), the conservative estimate of the value (in constant 2000 dollars) of the net private benefits associated with the Baldrige National Quality Program was $2.17 billion. Conservatively, Link and Scott estimated the value (in constant 2000 dollars) of social benefits associated with the Baldrige National Quality Program to be $24.65 billion. Based on information provided by the Baldrige National Quality Program, the value (in constant 2000 dollars) of social costs associated with the program to date was $119 million. Therefore, from an evaluative perspective for the economy as a whole, the benefit-to-cost ratio characterizing the Baldrige National Quality Program was conservatively 207 to 1.

The Worldwide Use of the Baldrige Criteria

As indicated, the performance of U.S. companies using the Baldrige principles has steadily increased since the launch of the Baldrige Award in 1987. U.S. companies began to recapture market share lost to international competition. When the reason for the increased success of U.S. companies became apparent, other countries throughout the world began to create their own national quality awards based on the Baldrige Criteria. Although the U.S. Congress may not have intended the Criteria to benefit companies throughout the world, that is precisely what has happened. After all, the Criteria are not secret. Millions of copies of the Criteria are distributed freely through the World Wide Web.

According to the U.S. Department of Commerce, more than 60 countries throughout the world have adopted the Criteria as a basis for their own quality awards in an effort to improve the competitiveness of organizations in their own countries.

THE INTEGRATED MANAGEMENT SYSTEM

Ingredients to Optimum Performance

Clearly, in today's highly competitive economy, past success means nothing. Desire, without disciplined and appropriate action, also means nothing. However, it is just as clear that implementing a disciplined approach to performance excellence based on the Baldrige Criteria produces winning levels of performance. The key to the success of the Baldrige Criteria has been the identification of the key drivers of high performance. The National Quality Award Office within NIST ensures that each element of the Baldrige Criteria is necessary, and that together they are sufficient to achieve the highest levels of performance. Many management practices of the past have proven to be necessary ingredients of high performance. However, taken piecemeal, these practices by themselves have not been sufficient to achieve optimum performance.

Achieving winning levels of performance requires that each component of the organization's management system be optimized. In many ways, optimizing the performance of an organization's management system is like making an award-winning cake. Too much or too little of any key ingredient suboptimizes the system. For example, a cake may require eggs, flour, sugar, butter, and cocoa. A cake also requires a specific level of heat for a certain time in an oven. Too little or too much of any ingredient, including oven temperature, and the system (in this case the cake) fails to achieve desired results. The same principle applies in an organization. A successful organization requires a strong customer focus, skilled workers, efficient work processes, fact-based decision making, clear direction, and continuous improvement. Organizations that do not focus on all of these elements find that their performance suffers. Focusing on only a few of the required ingredients, such as reengineering to improve work processes or training to improve worker skills, is necessary but not sufficient by itself to drive high levels of performance.

The following figures depict the elements necessary and sufficient to achieve high levels of performance in any organization or part of an organization. The elements apply to any managed enterprise, regardless of size, sector, product, or service.

Get Results, Produce Value. (Figure 3) In the first place, in order for an organization, team, or individual to stay in business (or keep a job) for any length of time, it must produce desired results. The work results must be valued. History has demonstrated that people, organizations, or even governments that failed to deliver value eventually went away or were overturned. Value can be measured in a variety of ways, including fitness for use, return on assets, profitability, reliability, and durability, to name a few.

Engaged Customers. (Figure 4) Understand and meet their requirements—engage them. We have learned that it makes no difference if the producer of the goods or services believes they are valuable if the customer or user of the goods or services believes they are not. The customer is the best entity to legitimately judge the value of the goods or services its suppliers produce. It is the customers who finally

Building the Integrated Management System

Figure 3   Get results, produce value.

Building the Integrated Management System

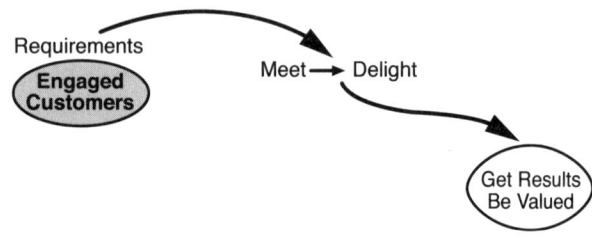

Figure 4   Customer requirements.

decide whether the organization, team, or government continues to stay in business. Imagine that you go to a restaurant, order seafood, and find that it tastes awful. Upon complaining about the bad-tasting meal, you are not impressed with the chef's claim that "only the finest ingredients were used." It also does not help if the chef claims that he likes the taste of the fish. It still tastes bad to you. At this juncture the restaurant has an opportunity to recover customer confidence and build loyalty to better engage the customer. Unless the chef is willing to make an adjustment, you are not going to be satisfied and are unlikely to return. If enough customers find the food or service offensive and do not return, the restaurant goes out of business. On the other hand, by properly managing the complaint and taking steps to promptly resolve the problem *to the satisfaction of the customer,* the restaurant can not only recover but enhance loyalty and better engage its customers so they become active supporters.

Accordingly, it is very important for the organization to obtain feedback from the customers after they have had an opportunity to experience its products or services. The failure to understand the requirements of the customers may cause the organization to deliver the wrong thing, creating customer dissatisfaction, delay, or lower value. Every time our organizations fail to meet customer requirements, value suffers. In order to consistently produce value, therefore, organizations must accurately determine the requirements of their customers and consistently meet those requirements and, if possible, exceed expectations. This creates the initial value chain that provides the competitive advantage for any organization or part of an organization.

To ensure that the customer is satisfied and likely to return (or recommend a service or product to others), it is important to determine if the customer received appropriate value. If the customer is dissatisfied, you have an opportunity to correct the problem and still maintain customer loyalty. In any case, it is important to remember that it is the customer and not the marketing, engineering, or manufacturing departments or the service provider that ultimately judges value received and determines satisfaction.

Engaged Workers. (Figure 5) Engaged workers are key to the next part of the management system to ensure optimum performance and value. In any organization or part of an organization, people do the work that produces customer value. As described previously, if the work is not focused on customer requirements, customers may be dissatisfied. In order to satisfy customers, work may have to be redone, adding cost and suboptimizing value. In order to optimize output and value, people doing the work must have the willingness and desire to work. The best workers contribute their *utmost* for the success of the organization and its customers. Disgruntled, disaffected, unwilling workers hurt productivity.

However, *motivated workers* means more than simply possessing the willingness to work. Workers must also possess the knowledge and skills to carry out their jobs effectively. In leading-edge technologies such as microelectronics engineering, the half-life of useful knowledge is about 11 months. That means that one-half of the relevant knowledge of a microelectronics engineer becomes obsolete within 11 months. In 1989 the half-life was 18 months, approximately 50 percent greater. As new knowledge is created at an accelerating rate, it is more critical than ever to have effective training systems in place to ensure workers stay current and can effectively apply the new knowledge.

In addition, in order to optimize output, people must be free from bureaucratic barriers and arbitrary restrictions that inhibit work. Every minute that work is delayed while waiting for an unnecessary approval adds cost but not value. Every minute that work has to be redone because of sloppy performance of a

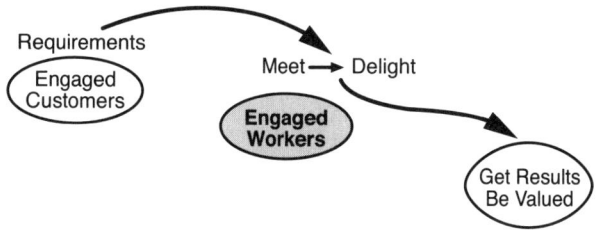

Figure 5 Engaged, motivated people.

coworker adds cost but not value. Every minute that work has to be redone because of inadequate knowledge or ability adds cost but not value.

Remember that one person cannot produce optimum levels of performance. However, one person can prevent optimum levels of performance, and may not be aware that he or she is doing so. The question that should concern management is, "In your organization, how many people are disgruntled, discouraged, underskilled, or prevented from working effectively so that they suboptimize the organization's performance?"

Efficient Processes. (Figure 6) Even the most highly skilled, knowledgeable, and willing workers will fail to optimize value if asked to do stupid things. Over time, even the most efficient processes can become suboptimal and inefficient. Business process Lean Enterprise and Six Sigma reengineering have been seen by some as a panacea for organizational optimization. Certainly these tools allow organizations to redesign and quickly eliminate much of the bureaucratic silliness and inefficiency that grow up over time. However, how long does it take for the newly reengineered process to lose efficiency? Even new processes must be evaluated periodically and improved or they eventually become suboptimal and obsolete. Ensuring that processes are optimal requires ongoing, fact-based evaluation and meaningful improvement.

Every process in the organization has the potential for increasing or decreasing the value provided to customers. Obviously, key work processes are perhaps the most important. However, frequently the core processes of an organization are disrupted because of failed support processes or supplier failure. For example, production can come to a halt if key materiel from the procurement office is not available on time. Production can also be disrupted if key workers that were supposed to be provided by the personnel office are not available. Performance suffers if the transportation provider is always late.

As discussed above, failures must be addressed to satisfy customers. Fixing a problem constitutes rework. Any time an organization engages in rework, value for the customer is suboptimized. To make matters worse, if the need to engage in rework is not discovered until the product or service is complete, the cost of correction is higher, driving value lower. It is important, therefore, to uncover potential problems as early as possible, rather than wait for the end result to determine if the product or service is satisfactory. In order to uncover potential problems early we must be able to predict the outcomes of our work processes. This requires *in-process* measures. Through the use of these measures, organizations can determine if the product or service is likely to meet expectations. Consider the two examples that follow:

- Example one: A customer comes to the "Wait-And-See" coffee shop and orders a cup of coffee. The coffee is poured and delivered to the customer. The customer promptly takes a sip and informs the server that the coffee is too cold, too bitter, too weak, and has a harsh aroma. Furthermore, the customer complains that it took too long for the coffee to be served. The server, in an effort to satisfy the customer, discards the original coffee, brews a fresh pot, and delivers a new cup of coffee to the customer at no additional charge. This problem happens frequently. As a result, the "Wait-And-See" coffee shop has been forced to raise the price of coffee in order to stay in business and has noticed that fewer customers are willing to pay the higher price. Many customers have stopped coming to this coffee shop entirely. The customers that continue to buy coffee from this shop are subsidizing the sloppy performance and poor quality.

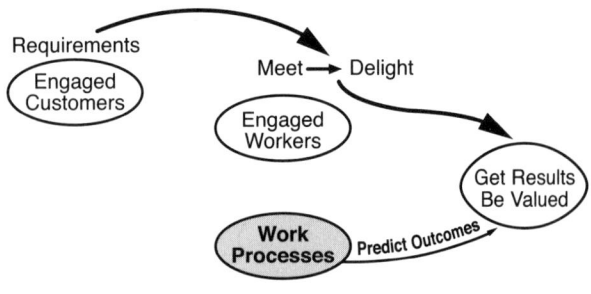

Figure 6 Efficient, effective processes.

- Example two: In order to increase the likelihood that its customers will like the coffee it serves, the "In-Process-Measure" coffee shop has asked its customers key questions about the quality of coffee and service that they expect. The "In-Process-Measure" coffee shop has determined through testing and surveys that its customers like coffee served hot (between 76° and 82° Celsius); not too bitter or acidic (pH > 7.4); strong, but not too strong (75 grams of super-fine grind per liter of filtered water); and fresh (served within five minutes of brewing). By checking these measures, this coffee shop can predict that nearly all customers will be satisfied with the quality and service it delivers. Since the "In-Process Measure" coffee shop can consistently deliver coffee within these customer-defined specifications, its customers like the coffee. No rework is required, no coffee is discarded, the price is lower, the value is higher, the store is profitable, and it is taking customers from the "Wait-And-See" coffee shop down the street.

Data and Dashboard to Monitor Progress. (Figure 7) Data and information help the organization and its workers make better decisions about their work. This enables them to spot problems more quickly and take actions to improve performance and correct or minimize non-value-added costs. Without appropriate measures, organizations and their workers must rely on intuition to determine whether customers are likely to be satisfied and willing to return.

One of the problems in basing decisions on intuition or best guess is that it produces highly variable decisions. The guess of one worker is not likely to be consistent with the guess of another. Appropriate data, therefore, are critical to increase decision-making consistency and accuracy. In order for data to be used correctly to support decision making, organizations must develop a system to manage, collect, analyze, and display the results.

If the data that drive decision making are not accurate or reliable, effective decision making suffers. More mistakes are made, costs increase, and value is suboptimized. Furthermore, in the absence of relevant data and supporting analyses, leaders are generally unwilling to allow subordinates to substitute their intuition for that of the leader. As a result, decisions tend to get pulled to higher and higher levels in an organization, further suboptimizing the contribution of workers who are generally closest to and know the most about the work they do. Failure to fully utilize the talents of workers, as discussed previously, further reduces efficiency and morale and suboptimizes value production.

The system described in Figure 7, which includes engaged customers, motivated people, efficient processes, and a dashboard to monitor progress leading to desired results and value, applies to any managed enterprise. It applies to whole corporations as well as departments, divisions, teams, and individual work.

The system applies to schools, classrooms, government agencies, and health care organizations. In each case, in order to produce optimal value, the requirements of customers must be understood and met. Workers must be motivated, possess the skill and knowledge needed to do their work, and be free from distractions in order to contribute their utmost. The organization must develop efficient work processes and monitor effectiveness of work to make adjustments in an effort to maximize value.

Leadership. (Figure 8) What makes an organization unique is the direction that top leaders set for it. Leaders must understand the requirements and expectations of customers and the marketplace to decide what direction is necessary to achieve success. However, it is not enough simply to understand customer requirements and expectations. Leaders must also understand organizational capabilities and the

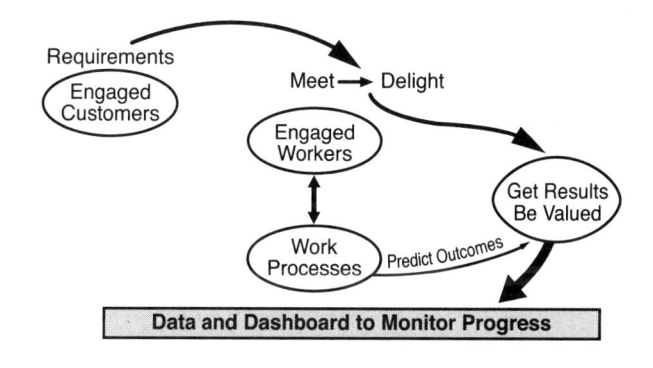

Figure 7 Information and data dashboard.

capacity and capabilities of the workforce, partners, and suppliers of critical goods and services.

Strategy. (Figure 9) Effective leaders use the process of strategy development to determine the most appropriate direction for the organization and identify the level of performance in key areas that are critical for success. Strategic objectives must define, in outcome-oriented terms, what the organization must actually achieve to be successful in the future. Once strategic direction and strategic objectives are defined, leaders identify the people and the processes that must be in place to produce desired results and be valued by customers. Leaders must then communicate with the workforce, suppliers, partners, and customers.

If leaders are not clear about the strategy and actions that must be taken to be successful, they force subordinates to substitute their own ideas about the proper direction and actions. This creates inefficiency within an organization. People come to work and want to be successful. Without direction from the top, they will still work hard but often at cross-purposes. Unless everyone is pulling in the same direction, processes, products, and services will not be optimized and value to customers will be reduced.

The Integrated System. Leaders cannot eliminate a single part of this management system and still expect to produce optimum value. Each part is necessary. Furthermore, studies repeatedly demonstrate that when these processes are integrated and used to manage work, they are sufficient to achieve high levels of performance. Imagine what might happen if one or more of the pieces of the integrated management system described previously were missing. The following table provides some suggestions.

Building the Integrated Management System

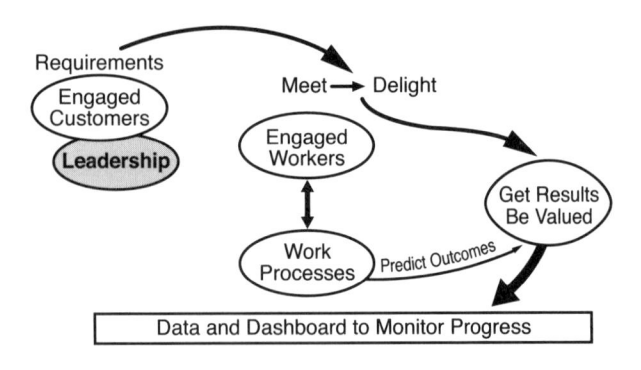

Figure 8 Leadership.

The Integrated Management System

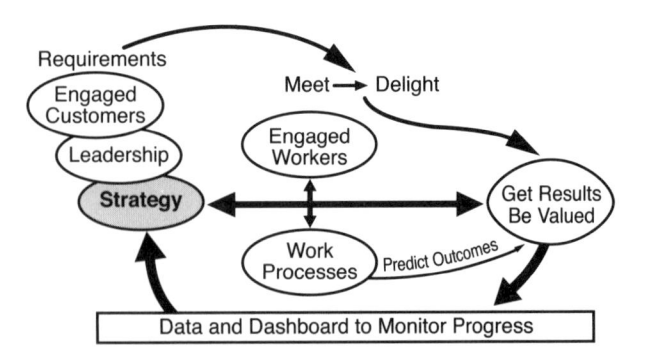

Figure 9 Strategy development and execution.

MISSING ELEMENT	ADVERSE CONSEQUENCE LEADING TO SUBOPTIMUM PERFORMANCE
Systems to understand customer requirements and expectations	Designing, building, and delivering an unsatisfactory product or service. Adds delay. Increases cost due to rework. Wastes resources on low-priority work that does not optimize customer value.
Poor worker skills, minimal initiative or self-direction	Limited expansion opportunities. Unable to keep up with changing technology. Requires close monitoring. Difficulty in finding better ways to carry out work. Ultimately reduces morale, motivation, and performance.
Data about customer engagement, satisfaction, key-process performance, and overall organizational performance do not exist or are incomplete	Makes it difficult to engage employees in decision making about their work. Forces decisions to be made at higher levels on the basis of intuition or guesswork. Reduces decision accuracy and increases incorrect decisions. Makes it difficult to allocate resources appropriately or determine the best use of limited resources. Makes accountability difficult to achieve
Leaders do not clearly set direction, performance expectations, vision, or values	Causes subordinates to invent their own ideas and substitute them for a common set of performance expectations, vision, and values. Creates significant inefficiencies as people throughout the organization begin to work at cross-purposes, suboptimizing organizational performance. Makes it difficult to establish accountability for achieving results.
Plans do not contain measurable outcome-oriented objectives and a time line for accomplishing each objective	Leaders, managers, and employees do not know what level of performance is expected at any given time, making it difficult or impossible to effectively monitor progress.
Leaders do not make it clear that customers are the key to success—they do not create a focus on customers or a customer culture	If managers and employees do not focus on customers, they become internally focused. Managers, engineers, or marketers drive the business, not customers. Customers and their requirements lose importance.
Top leaders do not encourage employees to develop and use their full potential	Employee engagement and satisfaction become optional. Some managers encourage employee participation, innovation, and creativity; most do not. The organization risks losing its best employees to competitors, and gets sub-optimal performance from those who stay.
Customer comments and complaints are not encouraged. If a complaint is received it is not resolved promptly. The root cause of complaints is not identified	Failure to capture customer comments and complaints, identify the root causes of the complaints, and work to prevent the problems from happening again makes it difficult to learn about problems quickly and dooms the organization to repeat its failures. Failure to resolve complaints promptly increases customer dissatisfaction and reduces loyalty.
Poor two-way communication exists between leaders and employees	Unclear top-down communication makes it difficult to ensure alignment and focus throughout the organization, reducing teamwork and increasing bureaucratic stagnation. Poor upward communication maintains organizational fragmentation and prevents problems and barriers to effective work from being discussed and resolved.

THE CORE VALUES TO ACHIEVE PERFORMANCE EXCELLENCE

The Criteria are built upon a set of interrelated Core Values and Concepts, which are embedded beliefs and behaviors found in high-performing organizations. They are the foundation for integrating performance excellence requirements that create a basis for action and feedback within a results-oriented framework.

The 2009–2010 Core Values and Concepts follow. The text in the box presents the exact wording of the Baldrige core values and concepts.

Visionary Leadership

Every system, strategy, and method for achieving excellence must be guided by visionary leadership.

- Effective leaders convey a strong sense of urgency to counter the natural resistance to change that can prevent the organization from taking the steps that these Core Values for success demand.

- Such leaders serve as enthusiastic role models, reinforcing and communicating the Core Values by their words and actions.

- Words alone are not sufficient. The actions of great leaders match their words.

Visionary Leadership

Your organization's senior leaders should set directions and create a customer focus, clear and visible values, and high expectations. The directions, values, and expectations should balance the needs of all your stakeholders. Your leaders should ensure the creation of strategies, systems, and methods for achieving performance excellence, stimulating innovation, building knowledge and capabilities, and ensuring organizational sustainability. The defined values and strategies should help guide all of your organization's activities and decisions. Senior leaders should inspire and encourage your entire workforce to contribute, to develop and learn, to be innovative, and to embrace change. Senior leaders should be responsible to your organization's governance body for their actions and performance. The governance body should be responsible ultimately to all your stakeholders for the ethics, actions, and performance of your organization and its senior leaders.

Senior leaders should serve as role models through their ethical behavior and their personal involvement in planning, communicating, coaching the workforce, developing future leaders, reviewing organizational performance, and recognizing members of your workforce. As role models, they can reinforce ethics, values, and expectations while building leadership, commitment, and initiative throughout your organization.

Customer-Driven Excellence

This value demonstrates a passion for making the organization customer-driven. Without loyal customers, little else matters. Customers are the final judges of how well the organization did its job, and what they say counts. It is their perception of the service and product that will determine whether they remain loyal or constantly seek better providers.

- The organization must focus on systematically listening to customers and acting quickly on what they say.

- The organization must build positive relationships with its customers through focusing on accessibility and management of complaints.

- Dissatisfied customers must be heeded most closely, for they often deliver the most valuable information.

- If only satisfied and loyal customers (those who continue to do business with us no matter what) are paid attention, the organization will be led astray. The most successful organizations keep an eye on customers who are not satisfied and work to understand their preferences and meet their demands.

Customer-Driven Excellence

Performance and quality are judged by an organization's customers. Thus, your organization must take into account all product features and characteristics and all modes of customer access and support that contribute value to your customers. Such behavior leads to customer acquisition, satisfaction, preference, and loyalty; to positive referrals; and, ultimately, to business expansion. Customer-driven excellence has both current and future components: understanding today's customer desires and anticipating future customer desires and marketplace potential.

Value and satisfaction may be influenced by many factors throughout your customers' overall experience with your organization. These factors include your organization's customer relationships, which help to build trust, confidence, and loyalty.

Customer-driven excellence means much more than reducing defects and errors, merely meeting specifications, or reducing complaints. Nevertheless, these factors contribute to your customers' view of your organization and thus also are important parts of customer-driven excellence. In addition, your organization's success in recovering from defects, service errors, and mistakes is crucial for retaining customers and engaging customers for the long term.

A customer-driven organization addresses not only the product and service characteristics that meet basic customer requirements but also those features and characteristics that differentiate the organization from its competitors. Such differentiation may be based on innovative offerings, combinations of product and service offerings, customization of offerings, multiple access mechanisms, rapid response, or special relationships.

Customer-driven excellence is thus a strategic concept. It is directed toward customer retention and loyalty, market share gain, and growth. It demands constant sensitivity to changing and emerging customer and market requirements and to the factors that drive customer engagement.

It demands close attention to the voice of the customer. It demands anticipating changes in the marketplace. It demands a customer-focused culture. Therefore, customer-driven excellence demands organizational agility.

Organizational and Personal Learning

The most potent value is organizational and personal learning. High-performing organizations are learning organizations—they evaluate and improve everything they do. They strive to get better at getting better.

- A culture of continuous improvement is essential to maintaining and sustaining true competitive advantage.

- Without systematic improvement and ongoing learning, organizations will ultimately face extinction.

- With systematic, continuous, organizational improvement, time becomes a powerful ally. As time passes, the organization grows stronger and smarter.

- Leaders embed this value by linking rewards, recognition, and incentives for workers, supervisors, and managers at all levels to innovation, improvement, and learning. Otherwise, people do not think continuous change is important.

- Personal learning that is shared widely becomes organizational learning. Individuals can improve processes they own, but maximum organizational benefit does not occur unless these learnings (improvements) are shared/adopted throughout the organization.

Organizational and Personal Learning

Achieving the highest levels of organizational performance requires a well-executed approach to organizational and personal learning that includes sharing knowledge via systematic processes. Organizational learning includes both continuous improvement of existing approaches and significant change or innovation, leading to new goals and approaches. Learning needs to be embedded in the way your organization operates. This means that learning (1) is a regular part of daily work; (2) is practiced at personal, work unit, and organizational levels; (3) results in solving problems at their source

Continued

> *Continued*
>
> ("root cause"); (4) is focused on building and sharing knowledge throughout your organization; and (5) is driven by opportunities to effect significant, meaningful change and to innovate. Sources for learning include employees' and volunteers' ideas, research and development (R&D), customers' input, best-practice sharing, and benchmarking.
>
> Organizational learning can result in (1) enhancing value to customers through new and improved products and customer services; (2) developing new business opportunities; (3) developing new and improved processes or business models; (4) reducing errors, defects, waste, and related costs; (5) improving responsiveness and cycle time performance; (6) increasing productivity and effectiveness in the use of all your resources; and (7) enhancing your organization's performance in fulfilling its societal responsibilities.
>
> The success of members of your workforce depends increasingly on having opportunities for personal learning and for practicing new skills. Leaders' success depends on access to these kinds of opportunities, as well. In organizations that rely on volunteers, the volunteers' personal learning also is important, and their learning and skill development should be considered with employees'. Organizations invest in personal learning through education, training, and other opportunities for continuing growth and development. Such opportunities might include job rotation and increased pay for demonstrated knowledge and skills. On-the-job training offers a cost-effective way to cross-train and to better link training to your organizational needs and priorities. Education and training programs may have multiple modes, including computer- and Web-based learning and distance learning.
>
> Personal learning can result in (1) a more engaged, satisfied, and versatile workforce that stays with your organization; (2) organizational cross-functional learning; (3) the building of your organization's knowledge assets; and (4) an improved environment for innovation.
>
> Thus, learning is directed not only toward better products but also toward being more responsive, adaptive, innovative, and efficient—giving your organization marketplace sustainability and performance advantages and giving your workforce satisfaction and the motivation to excel.

Valuing Workforce Members and Partners

Organizations must invest in their people to ensure they have the skills for today and to do what is necessary to succeed in the future. This core value has broadened from employee participation and development to valuing workers and partners. In high-performing organizations, the people who do the work of the organization should make most of the decisions about how the work is done. A significant barrier exists, however, that limits worker decision making—access to data and poor data-based decision-making skills.

Organizations cannot effectively push decision making down to the level where most of the work is done unless those doing the work have access to the necessary data and are skilled at making fact-based decisions. As mentioned previously, leaders are unwilling to let subordinates make decisions based on intuition—they reserve that type of decision for themselves. Therefore, access to data and developing skills to manage by fact are prerequisites for optimizing workforce contributions to the organization's success.

> ### Valuing Workforce Members and Partners
>
> An organization's success depends increasingly on an engaged workforce that benefits from meaningful work, clear organizational direction, and performance accountability and that has a safe, trusting, and cooperative environment. Additionally, the successful organization capitalizes on the diverse backgrounds, knowledge, skills, creativity, and motivation of its workforce and partners.
>
> Valuing the people in your workforce means committing to their engagement, satisfaction, development, and well-being. Increasingly, this involves more flexible, high-performance work practices tailored to varying workplace and home life needs. Major challenges in the area of valuing members of your workforce include (1) demonstrating your leaders' commitment to their success, (2) providing recognition that goes beyond the regular compensation system, (3) offering development and
>
> *Continued*

Insights to Performance Excellence

> *Continued*
>
> progression within your organization, (4) sharing your organization's knowledge so your workforce can better serve your customers and contribute to achieving your strategic objectives, (5) creating an environment that encourages risk taking and innovation, and (6) creating a supportive environment for a diverse workforce.
>
> Organizations need to build internal and external partnerships to better accomplish overall goals. Internal partnerships might include labor-management cooperation. Partnerships with members of your workforce might entail developmental opportunities, cross-training, or new work organizations, such as high-performance work teams. Internal partnerships also might involve creating network relationships among your work units or between employees and volunteers to improve flexibility, responsiveness, and knowledge sharing.
>
> External partnerships might be with customers, suppliers, and education or community organizations. Strategic partnerships or alliances are increasingly important kinds of external partnerships. Such partnerships might offer entry into new markets or a basis for new products or customer support services. Also, partnerships might permit the blending of your organization's core competencies or leadership capabilities with the complementary strengths and capabilities of partners to address common issues. Such partnerships may be a source of strategic advantage for your organization.
>
> Successful internal and external partnerships develop longer-term objectives, thereby creating a basis for mutual investments and respect. Partners should address the key requirements for success, means for regular communication, approaches to evaluating progress, and means for adapting to changing conditions. In some cases, joint education and training could offer a cost-effective method for workforce development.

Agility

Agility is a value usually driven by customer requirements and the desire to improve operating efficiency and lower costs.

- Except for a few pleasurable experiences, everyone wants things faster.

- Organizations that develop the capacity to respond faster by eliminating activities and tasks that do not add value find that productivity increases, costs go down, and customers are more loyal.

- Analyzing and improving work processes enable organizations to perform better, faster, and cheaper.

- To improve work processes, organizations must focus on improving design quality and preventing problems. The cost of preventing problems and building quality into products and services is significantly less than the cost of taking corrective action later.

- It is critical to capture learning from other design projects.

- Use information concerning customer preference, competitors' products, cost and pricing, marketplace profiles, and research and development (R&D) to optimize the process from the start, and avoid delay and rework.

- Public-responsibility issues and factors, including environmental demands, must be included at the design stage.

> ### Agility
>
> Success in today's ever-changing, globally competitive environment demands agility—a capacity for rapid change and flexibility. Organizations face ever-shorter cycles for the introduction of new/improved products, and nonprofit and government organizations are increasingly being asked to respond rapidly to new or emerging social issues. Major improvements in response times often require new work systems, simplification of work units and processes, or the ability for rapid changeover from one process to another. A cross-trained and empowered workforce is a vital asset in such a demanding environment.
>
> A major success factor in meeting competitive challenges is the design-to-introduction (product or service feature initiation) or innovation cycle time. To meet the demands of rapidly changing markets,
>
> *Continued*

> *Continued*
>
> organizations need to carry out stage-to-stage integration (such as concurrent engineering) of activities from research or concept to commercialization or implementation.
>
> All aspects of time performance now are more critical, and cycle time has become a key process measure. Other important benefits can be derived from this focus on time; time improvements often drive simultaneous improvements in work systems, organization, quality, cost, supply-chain integration, and productivity.

Focus on the Future

To remain competitive, every organization must be guided by a common set of measurable outcome-oriented goals and a focus on the future.

- These outcome-oriented goals, which emerge from the strategic planning process, help to align the work of everyone in the organization and serve as a basis for factual monitoring of progress.

- Measurable goals allow everyone to know where they are going and when they deviate from their path.

- Without measurable goals, everyone still works hard, but they tend to focus on the things they believe are important, not the direction set by top leaders. As a result, they can easily go in different directions—suboptimizing the success of the organization.

- Focusing on the future requires the organization's leaders to consider new, even revolutionary, ideas. Strategic objectives should reflect this future focus.

> ### Focus on the Future
>
> Creating a sustainable organization requires understanding the short- and longer-term factors that affect your organization and marketplace. The pursuit of sustainable growth and sustained performance leadership requires a strong future orientation and a willingness to make long-term commitments to key stakeholders—your customers, workforce, suppliers, partners, and stockholders; the public; and your community.
>
> Your organization's planning should anticipate many factors, such as customers' expectations, new business and partnering opportunities, workforce development and hiring needs, the increasingly global marketplace, technological developments, changes in customer and market segments, new business models, evolving regulatory requirements, changes in community and societal expectations and needs, and strategic moves by competitors. Strategic objectives and resource allocations need to accommodate these influences. A focus on the future includes developing your leaders, workforce, and suppliers; accomplishing effective succession planning; creating opportunities for innovation; and anticipating societal responsibilities and concerns.

Managing for Innovation

The accelerating rate of change today demands ever-increasing innovation. Such innovation cannot be random. It must be focused on factors that are essential to organizational success. To be focused, innovation must be managed. Innovation should focus on changing products, services, and processes to create more value for the organization's stakeholders, employees, and customers. The winners in the highly competitive race to innovate will be the organizations that uncover new paradigms of breakthrough performance. To begin to optimize this breakthrough capacity, everyone in the organization needs to be involved. The more brain power, the better. *Requirements for innovation should be a part of every employee and managerial performance plan and appraisal.* Just like continuous improvement, innovation must be embedded in the culture and fabric of daily work. The best organizations are not satisfied to just *improve* or *innovate*. The best organizations work hard at increasing the speed at which they improve and innovate. Anything less allows competitors to overtake them. Anything less allows customer expectations to exceed the speed of change, causing the customers to look elsewhere.

Managing for Innovation

Innovation means making meaningful change to improve an organization's products, services, programs, processes, operations, and business model to create new value for the organization's stakeholders. Innovation should lead your organization to new dimensions of performance. Innovation is no longer strictly the purview of research and development departments; innovation is important for all aspects of your operations and all work systems and work processes. Organizations should be led and managed so that innovation becomes part of the learning culture. Innovation should be integrated into daily work and should be supported by your performance improvement system. Systematic processes for innovation should reach across your entire organization.

Innovation builds on the accumulated knowledge of your organization and its people. Therefore, the ability to rapidly disseminate and capitalize on this knowledge is critical to driving organizational innovation.

Management by Fact

Management by fact is the cornerstone value for effective planning, operational decision making at all levels, employee involvement and empowerment, and leadership.

- People make decisions every day. However, without data, the basis for decision making is usually intuition—gut feel. Although intuition can be valuable at times, it introduces too much variation into the decision-making process. Intuition is not consistent person-to-person or time-to-time. It is also difficult to explain the rationale for decisions based on intuition. That makes communication more difficult within the organization. Finally, if the decision must be made on the basis of intuition, it is usually the boss' intuition that drives the decision. Because of this phenomenon, issues are pulled to ever-higher levels for resolution. As a result, excessive reliance on intuition minimizes employee empowerment.

- Most drivers decide when to fill their fuel tanks based on data from the fuel gage and get very uncomfortable if the gage is broken. Yet people routinely make decisions of enormous consequence about customers, strategies, goals, and employees with little or no data. This is a recipe for disaster, not one designed to ensure optimization.

Management by Fact

Organizations depend on the measurement and analysis of performance. Such measurements should derive from business needs and strategy, and they should provide critical data and information about key processes, outputs, and results. Many types of data and information are needed for performance management. Performance measurement should include customer, product, and process performance; comparisons of operational, market, and competitive performance; supplier, workforce, partner, cost, and financial performance; and governance and compliance outcomes. Data should be segmented by, for example, markets, product lines, and workforce groups to facilitate analysis.

Analysis refers to extracting larger meaning from data and information to support evaluation, decision making, improvement, and innovation. Analysis entails using data to determine trends, projections, and cause and effect that might not otherwise be evident. Analysis supports a variety of purposes, such as planning, reviewing your overall performance, improving operations, accomplishing change management, and comparing your performance with competitors' or with "best practices" benchmarks.

A major consideration in performance improvement and change management involves the selection and use of performance measures or indicators. *The measures or indicators you select should best represent the factors that lead to improved customer, operational, financial, and societal performance. A comprehensive set of measures or indicators tied to customer and organizational performance requirements provides a clear basis for aligning all processes with your organization's goals.*

Continued

> *Continued*
>
> Measures and indicators may need to support decision making in a rapidly changing environment. Through the analysis of data from your tracking processes, your measures or indicators themselves may be evaluated and changed to better support your goals.

Societal Responsibility

Every high-performing organization practices good public responsibility and citizenship.

- Organizations must determine and anticipate any adverse effects to the public of their products, services, and operations. Failure to do so can undermine public trust and distract workers, and also adversely affect the bottom line. This is true of both private and public organizations.

- During the last few years we have seen several examples of companies that have been seriously hurt by failing to practice good citizenship or protect the interests of the public from risks they created. Enron and Arthur-Anderson are well-known examples. Even when unintended, failure to protect stakeholder interests can cripple companies. Consider Dow-Corning and the silicone breast implants, banks sued because they failed to provide adequate security for automatic teller machines (cash machines), or Exxon for the massive oil spill in the Pacific.

- Safety and legal requirements need to be met beyond mere compliance. The best organizations stay ahead of minimum requirements and actually lead efforts to raise the bar. In this manner, when regulatory agencies increase requirements, the best organizations are not caught off guard and may even be able to place their competitors at a disadvantage.

> ## Societal Responsibility
>
> An organization's leaders should stress responsibilities to the public, ethical behavior, and the need to consider societal well-being and benefit. Leaders should be role models for your organization in focusing on ethics and the protection of public health, safety, and the environment. The protection of health, safety, and the environment includes your organization's operations, as well as the life cycles of your products. Also, organizations should emphasize resource conservation and waste reduction at the source. Planning should anticipate adverse impacts from production, distribution, transportation, use, and disposal of your products. Effective planning should prevent problems, provide for a forthright response if problems occur, and make available the information and support needed to maintain public awareness, safety, and confidence.
>
> For many organizations, the product design stage is critical from the point of view of public responsibility. Design decisions impact your production processes and often the content of municipal and industrial waste. Effective design strategies should anticipate growing environmental concerns and responsibilities.
>
> Organizations should not only meet all local, state, and federal laws and regulatory requirements, but they should treat these and related requirements as opportunities for improvement "beyond mere compliance." Organizations should stress ethical behavior in all stakeholder transactions and interactions. Highly ethical conduct should be a requirement of and should be monitored by the organization's governance body.
>
> "Societal well-being and benefit" refers to leadership and support—within the limits of an organization's resources—of publicly important purposes. Such purposes might include improving education and health care in your community, pursuing environmental excellence, being a role model for socially important issues, practicing resource conservation, performing community service, improving industry and business practices, and sharing nonproprietary information. Leadership as a role-model organization also entails influencing other organizations, private and public, to partner for these purposes.
>
> Managing societal responsibilities requires the organization to use appropriate measures and leaders to assume responsibility for those measures.

Focus on Results and Creating Value

A results focus and an emphasis on creating value help organizations communicate requirements, monitor actual performance, make appropriate adjustments in priorities, and reallocate resources effectively. Without a results focus, organizations can become fixated on internal, self-directed processes and lose sight of the important factors for success—such as customers and their requirements.

Strategic objectives should be results- or outcome-oriented, not activity-oriented. When the focus shifts from achieving outcomes to completing activities, accountability erodes. Many times managers and workers carry out assigned tasks but the required outcome or benefit has not occurred.

> **Focus on Results and Creating Value**
>
> An organization's performance measurements need to focus on key results. Results should be used to create and balance value for your key stakeholders—your customers, workforce, stockholders, suppliers, and partners; the public; and the community. By creating value for your key stakeholders, your organization builds loyalty, contributes to growing the economy, and contributes to society. To meet the sometimes conflicting and changing aims that balancing value implies, organizational strategy explicitly should include key stakeholder requirements. This will help ensure that plans and actions meet differing stakeholder needs and avoid adverse impacts on any stakeholders. The use of a balanced composite of leading and lagging performance measures offers an effective means to communicate short- and longer-term priorities, monitor actual performance, and provide a clear basis for improving results.

Systems Perspective

Taken together, the Baldrige Criteria promote a systems perspective and define the processes required to achieve optimal organizational performance. As with any system, no part can be ignored and the whole still be expected to perform at peak levels. When part of a well-functioning system begins to underperform or work in a manner that is inconsistent with system requirements, the performance of the whole system suffers.

The same is true of a management system. If leaders are ambiguous, if plans are not clear, if work processes are not consistent, if people are not able to do the work they are asked to do, and if it is difficult to keep track of progress and make appropriate adjustments, it will be impossible for the organization to achieve maximum levels of performance. For most of the 20th century, a long list of management gurus has suggested a variety of quick and simple remedies to enhance organizational performance. By itself, each quick fix has failed. Hopefully we have learned that no single solution is sufficient to optimize performance in a complex system. Leaders who approach management from a systems perspective are more likely to optimize organizational performance than leaders who continue to take a piecemeal approach to organizational management. There is no magic potion for excellent management to achieve high performance.

There are always better ways to do things. The challenge is to find them, but we are not likely to find them alone. We must create an environment—a work climate where better ways will be sought out, recognized, and put in place by everyone.

> **Systems Perspective**
>
> The Baldrige Criteria provide a systems perspective for managing your organization and its key processes to achieve results—and to strive for performance excellence. The seven Baldrige Criteria Categories, the Core Values, and the Scoring Guidelines form the building blocks and the integrating mechanism for the system. However, successful management of overall performance requires organization-specific synthesis, alignment, and integration. Synthesis means looking at your organization as a whole and builds on key business attributes, including your core competencies, strategic objectives, action plans, and work systems. Alignment means using the key linkages
>
> *Continued*

> *Continued*
>
> among requirements given in the Baldrige Criteria Categories to ensure consistency of plans, processes, measures, and actions. Integration builds on alignment, so that the individual components of your performance management system operate in a fully interconnected manner and deliver anticipated results.
>
> These concepts are depicted in the Baldrige Criteria framework on page 68. A systems perspective includes your senior leaders' focus on strategic directions and on your customers. It means that your senior leaders monitor, respond to, and manage performance based on your results. A systems perspective also includes using your measures, indicators, core competencies, and organizational knowledge to build your key strategies. It means linking these strategies with your work systems and key processes and aligning your resources to improve your overall performance and your focus on customers and stakeholders.
>
> Thus, a systems perspective means managing your whole organization, as well as its components, to achieve success.

PRACTICAL INSIGHTS

Connections and Linkages

A popular children's activity, connect the dots, helps them understand that, when properly joined, apparently random dots create a meaningful picture. In many ways, the seven Categories, 18 Items, 36 Areas to Address, and 82 subparts in the Baldrige Criteria are like the dots that must be connected to reveal a meaningful picture. With no tools to connect the dots, workforce activities are not aligned to strategic planning; measurement, analysis, and knowledge management are isolated from process management; and improvement efforts are disjointed, fragmented, and do not yield robust results. This book describes the linkages among and between each Item. The exciting part about having them identified is that you can look for these linkages in your own organization and, if they don't exist, start building them.

Transition Strategies

Putting high-performance management systems in place involves a major commitment. Achieving excellence is an outcome that will not happen quickly or easily. At the beginning, you will need a transition strategy to get you across the bridge from management by opinion or intuition to more data-driven management. The next part of this section describes one approach that has worked for many organizations in various sectors: creating a performance improvement council.

Performance Improvement Council

Identify a top-level executive leadership group of six to eight members. Each additional member beyond this number will seem to double the complexity of issues and render decision making much more cumbersome. The executive leadership group could send a message to the entire organization by naming the group *the performance improvement council*—reinforcing the importance of continuous performance improvement to the future success of the organization.

The performance improvement council should be the primary policy-making body for the organization. It should spawn other performance improvement councils at lower levels to share practices and policies with every employee in the organization as well as to involve customers and suppliers. The structure permeates the organization as members of the performance improvement council become area leaders for major improvement efforts and sponsors for several process or continuous improvement task teams throughout the organization. The council structure, networked and cascaded fully, can effectively align the work and optimize performance at all levels and across all functions.

Council Membership

Selecting members for the performance improvement council should be done carefully. Each member should be essential for the success of the operation, and together they must generate a synergy sufficient for success. The most important member is the senior leader of the organization or unit. This person must participate actively, demonstrating the kind of leadership that the Baldrige Criteria require and all should emulate. Of particular importance is a commitment to consensus building as the *modus operandi* for the council. This tool, a core of performance improvement programs, is often overlooked by leadership. Other council members selected should have leadership responsibility for broad areas of the organization such as human resources, operations planning, customers, and data systems.

Council Expertise

The performance improvement council should be extremely knowledgeable about high-performance management systems. If not, as is often the case, performance improvement council members should be among the first in the organization to learn about continuous improvement tools and processes.

To be effective, every member of the council (and every member in the organization) must understand the Baldrige Criteria, because the Criteria describe the components of the entire management system. Participation in examiner training has proved to be a great way to understand the complexities of the system needed to achieve performance excellence. Any additional training beyond this should be carried out in the context of planning—that is, learn tools and use them to plan the performance improvement implementation, practices, and policies.

The performance improvement council should:

- Develop a business plan that integrates continuous improvement and strategic performance improvement.

- Create the web (communication plan and infrastructure) to transmit performance improvement policies, practices, and priorities throughout the organization.

- Define the roles of workers, including new recognition and reward structures, to cause needed behavioral changes that are aligned with strategic objectives and action plans.

- Develop a workforce and leadership development system. Assess skills needed and compare with skills that are in place. Involve team representatives in planning so they can learn skills close to when they are needed. Provide training and development and close the skill gaps.

- Launch improvement projects that will produce both short- and long-term successes. Improvement projects should be clearly defined by the performance improvement council and aligned with strategic priorities. Typical improvement projects include important human resource processes such as career development, performance measurement, and diversity, as well as improving operational products and services in the line areas. Become a leader in the use of tools such as Lean Enterprise and Six Sigma, but be sure to focus those tools on areas of importance to strategic plans, business plans, and human resource and workforce plans.

- Develop a plan to communicate the progress and successes throughout the organization. Through this approach, the need for—and successes of—performance improvement processes are consistently communicated to workers, partners, suppliers, collaborators, and customers. Barriers to optimum performance are weakened and eliminated.

- Create champions to remove barriers to performance excellence through the Categories of the Baldrige Criteria.

- Most important—make business transformation, continuous improvement, and performance excellence a requirement and not an option.

Category Champions

This section describes the responsibilities of Category champions. The people in the administrative or leadership cabinet should each be the champion of a Category and have appropriate staff support.

Organizational Leadership Champion

The *organizational leadership champion* is a senior executive who, in addition to other executive duties, works to coordinate and enhance leadership effectiveness and alignment throughout the organization. It is both a strategic and an operational activity.

From the strategic side, the champion should focus on ensuring that all senior leaders:

- Understand what is expected of them as leaders of organizational change and make sure their actions and words support this change.

- Ensure that effective governance systems are in place to protect the interests of all stakeholder groups and maintain organizational integrity and ethical behavior.

- Consistently speak with one voice as a senior leadership team.

- Serve as role models of performance excellence for managers and workers at all levels of the organization.

- Develop future leaders (succession planning) throughout the organization.

- Create measurable outcome-oriented performance expectations and monitor performance to achieve the key improvements and strategic objectives of the organization. This means that necessary data and analyses must be coordinated to ensure appropriate information is available for the champion and the entire senior leadership team.

- Review (conduct independent audits) ethical and legal behavior of all leaders and managers and hold them accountable for their actions

- Evaluate, develop, and enhance their personal leadership skills

The champion should coordinate the activities involving the review of organizational performance and capabilities:

- Define key performance outcome and in-process measures.

- Install systems to review organizational success, performance, and progress relative to outcome-oriented goals and strategic objectives.

- Use performance-review findings to identify priorities for improvement. Communicate those priorities to all units that have responsibilities for making the improvements, including suppliers and partners.

- Systematically use performance-review findings, together with employee feedback, to assess and improve senior leadership (including the chief executive) effectiveness and the effectiveness of managers throughout the leadership system.

From the operational side, the champion should work to identify and eliminate both individual and system deficiencies, territorial conflicts, and knowledge shortfalls that limit leaders' ability to meet expectations and goals consistently.

The champion should be the focal point in the organization to ensure all parts of the organization have systematic processes in place so they fully understand leadership and management requirements.

A process should exist to monitor ongoing initiatives to ensure leaders effectively set and communicate organizational values to employees:

- Create a culture than focuses on delivering value to customers and other stakeholders

- Aggressively reinforce an environment that promotes engagement (empowerment and innovation) throughout the workforce

- Review policies, systems, work processes, and the use of resources to ensure sufficient data are available to assist in workforce decision making

The champion must work as part of the senior leadership team to help coordinate all facets of the management system to drive high performance. This involves teaching the team about the requirements of effective and consistent leadership at all levels and its impact on organizational performance. The senior leader of the organization usually serves as the organizational leadership champion and leads this council.

Finally, the senior leader champion must ensure that everyone in a leadership position supports the values and activities critical to achieving performance excellence. Implement policies of zero tolerance for managers who do not support these efforts fully. To be successful, implementing the system to achieve performance excellence cannot be seen as optional. This is essential to ensure the systems and processes required to achieve optimum performance are launched and sustained.

Strategic-Planning Champion

The *strategic-planning champion* is a senior executive who, in addition to other executive duties, works to coordinate and enhance strategic planning and action-plan alignment throughout the organization. It is both a strategic and an operational activity.

From the strategic side, the champion should ensure that the focus of strategy development is on sustained competitive leadership, which usually depends on achieving revenue growth, as well as consistently improving operational effectiveness. The strategic-planning champion should help the senior leadership team acquire a view of the future and provide clear strategic guidance to the organization through goals, objectives, action plans, and measures.

From the operational side, the champion should work to ensure sufficient data are available regarding:

- The organization's operational and workforce strengths and weaknesses (including core competencies)

- External opportunities, risks, and threats that may arise from customers, competitors, supplier weaknesses, regulatory changes, economic conditions, and financial, technological, ethical, and societal risks

- The competitive environment and other challenges that might affect sustainability and future success, including encroachment on core competencies

The champion should be the focal point in the organization to ensure all parts of the organization have systematic processes in place so they fully understand the implications of strategy on their daily work.

The champion should ensure that strategy is customer- and market-focused and is actually used to guide ongoing decision making and resource allocation at all levels of the organization:

- All strategic objectives or goals should define, in measurable terms, the *outcomes* the organization must actually achieve to be successful in the future. *Activities are not strategic objectives. Enablers are not strategic objectives.*

- A process should exist at each level of the organization to convert measurable, outcome-oriented strategic objectives into actions, which are aligned and used to achieve goals necessary for business success. These actions may define the activities believed to be critical to achieving desired outcomes, but may not substitute for the outcomes.

- Every employee should understand his or her role in carrying out actions to achieve the organization's goals.

- Rewards, recognition, incentives, and compensation should be aligned to support strategic objectives, action plans, and customer and business success.

The champion should coordinate the work of strategy development and deployment to:

- Acquire and use various types of forecasts, projections, scenarios, or other techniques to understand the plausible range of future options.

- Determine how the projected performance of competitors is likely to compare with the projected performance of the organization in the same time frame in order to set goals to ensure competitive advantage.

- Define the expected path which growth and performance are likely to take for each strategic objective. Time lines (the schedule) of projected future performance should match the frequency of organizational performance reviews.

- Determine what changes in services or products might be needed as a part of strategic positioning and direction. Strategy should define what the organization must achieve to be successful in the future, not simply justify a continuation of current activities.

- Ensure a system is in place to develop action plans and activities that address strategic goals and objectives. Ensure those action plans and activities are understood throughout the organization, as appropriate.

- Determine what capabilities must be developed within the organization to achieve strategic goals and coordinate with other members of the senior leadership team and Category champions to ensure those capabilities are in place. Ensure a system is in place to identify the human resource requirements necessary to achieve strategic goals and objectives. This may include training, support services for employees, reorganization, and new recruitment, to name a few.

- Ensure a system is in place to allocate resources throughout the organization sufficient to accomplish the action plans.

- Coordinate with the leadership system during performance reviews to help ensure that priorities for improvement and innovation at different levels throughout the organization are aligned with strategy and action plans.

- Ensure the process for strategic planning, plan deployment, the development of action plans, and the alignment of resources to support actions is systematically evaluated and improved each cycle. Also evaluate and improve the accuracy of determining the projected performance of competitors for use in goal setting.

Finally, the champion must work as contributing member of the senior leadership team to help coordinate all facets of the management system to drive high performance. This involves teaching the team about the requirements of strategic planning and its impact on organizational performance.

Customer-Focus Champion

The *customer-focus champion* is a senior executive who, in addition to other executive duties, coordinates and enhances customer engagement, satisfaction, relations, and loyalty throughout the organization. It is both a strategic and an operational activity.

From the strategic side, the champion should focus on ensuring that the drivers of customer satisfaction, customer engagement, and related market share (which are key factors in competitiveness, profitability, and organizational sustainability) are considered fully in the strategic planning process. This means that necessary data and analyses must be coordinated to ensure appropriate information is available for the executive planning councils.

From the operational side, the champion should work to identify and eliminate system deficiencies, territorial conflicts, and knowledge shortfalls that limit the organization's ability to engage customers consistently.

The champion should be the focal point in the organization to ensure all parts of the organization have systematic processes in place so they fully understand key customer, market, and operational requirements as input to customer satisfaction, market goals, and customer engagement.

A process should exist to monitor ongoing initiatives to ensure they are aligned with the customer aspects of the strategic direction. This may involve:

- Reviewing policies, systems, work processes, the use of resources, and the availability of workers who are knowledgeable and focus on customer engagement and building relationships

- Ensuring sufficient data are available to assist in decision making about customer issues

- Ensuring that strategies and actions relating to customer issues are aligned at all levels of the organization from the executives to the work unit or individual job level

The champion should coordinate the activities involving understanding customer requirements for products and support, as well as managing the interaction with customers, including how the organization determines customer satisfaction and satisfaction relative to competitors. (Satisfaction relative to competitors and the factors that lead to customer preference are of increasing importance to managing in a competitive environment.)

- The champion should also examine the means by which customers have access to seek information, assistance, or comment and complain.

- The champion should coordinate the customer support requirements (sometimes called customer-service standards) and the deployment of those requirements to all points and people in the organization that interact with customers.

- The champion should ensure that systems exist to respond quickly and resolve complaints promptly to recover customer confidence that might be otherwise lost.

- The champion should ensure that workers responsible for the design and delivery of products and customer support services receive information about customer complaints so they may eliminate the causes of these complaints.

- The champion should work with appropriate managers to help set priorities for improvement projects based on the potential impact of the cost of complaints and the impact of customer dissatisfaction and attrition on the organization.

- The champion should be charged with coordinating activities to build engagement (loyalty and positive referral), as well as evaluating and improving customer relationship-building processes throughout the organization.

Finally, the champion must work as contributing member of the senior leadership team to help coordinate all facets of the management system to drive high performance. This involves teaching the team about the requirements of customer and market focus and its impact on organizational performance.

Measurement, Analysis, and Knowledge-Management Champion

The *measurement, analysis, and knowledge-management champion* is an executive-level person who, in addition to other executive duties, coordinates and enhances information, analysis, and knowledge management systems throughout the organization to ensure they meet the decision-making needs of managers, workers, customers, partners, collaborators, and suppliers. It is both a strategic and an operational activity.

From the strategic side, information and analyses and the resulting knowledge can provide a competitive advantage. The champion should focus on ensuring, to the extent possible, that timely and accurate information and analyses are available to enhance knowledge acquisition and the development and delivery of new and existing products and customer support services to meet ongoing and emerging customer needs and expectations.

From the operational side, the champion should work to ensure that information and analyses are available throughout the organization to aid in decision making at all levels. This means coordinating with all other champions to ensure data are available for day-to-day review and decision making at all levels for their areas of responsibility.

The measurement, analysis, and knowledge-management champion has responsibility for the information infrastructure as well as ensuring the appropriate use of data for decision making. The champion should coordinate activities throughout the organization involving data collection, accuracy, analysis, retrieval, and use for decision making and improvements. The champion should ensure:

- Complete data are available and aligned to strategic goals, objectives, and action plans to ensure performance against these goals, objectives, and action plans can be effectively monitored.

- Systems are in place to collect and use comparative data and information to support strategy development, goal setting, and performance improvement.

- Data and information throughout the organization are complete, accurate, and reliable to enhance fact-based decision making.

- Data and information are used to support a better understanding of the cost and financial impacts of various improvement options.

- Appropriate correlations and performance projections are available to support strategic planning and operational decision making.

- The performance-measurement system is evaluated and improved to ensure it continues to meet organizational needs—even as those needs change.

- Data analysis supports the senior executives' organizational performance review and organizational planning and helps leaders set priorities for meaningful change.

- Data analysis addresses the overall health of the organization.

- Information, data, and supporting analyses are available to workgroup, functional-level operations, partners, and suppliers to support decision making at those levels.

- Data analysis supports daily decisions regarding operations throughout the organization to ensure actions align with plans.

- Information management systems, including hardware and software, are easy to use, reliable, and regularly updated to keep them current with changing decision-making needs. Data in these systems are correct (accurate), consistent (reliable), complete (integrity), free from tampering or inappropriate disclosure (secure and confidential), and available when needed (timely).

Finally, the champion must work as part of an organization-wide council to help coordinate all facets of the management system to drive high performance.

Workforce-Focus Champion

The *workforce-focus champion* is an executive-level person who, in addition to other executive duties, coordinates and enhances systems to enable workers (including managers and supervisors at all levels, permanent, temporary, and part-time personnel, and contract employees and volunteers supervised by the organization) to develop and utilize their full potential, consistent with the organization's strategic objectives. This includes building and maintaining a work environment conducive to full employee participation and growth. It is both a strategic and an operational activity.

From the strategic side, the workforce constraints of the organization must be considered in the development of strategy, and subsequently eliminated to ensure the workforce is capable of achieving the strategies necessary for business success.

From the operational side, the champion should ensure that the work climate enhances workforce satisfaction and engagement and that work is organized and jobs are designed to enable workers to contribute their utmost to achieve optimum levels of performance.

The workforce-focus champion has responsibility for ensuring that workers' needs are met to enable them to contribute fully to the organization's goals and objectives. The champion should ensure:

- A culture of workforce cooperation, collaboration, individual initiative, innovation, and flexibility.

- An environment in which workers are motivated to do their utmost for the benefit of the organization and its customers.

- An effective system to provide compensation, reward, recognition, and incentives to enhance performance and achieve strategic objectives. This includes systems to identify skill gaps.

- Support for business objectives and actions to build workforce knowledge, skills, capacity, and capabilities to enhance career progression and performance. This includes ensuring workers understand tools and techniques of performance measurement, performance improvement, quality control methods, and benchmarking. This also includes ensuring that managers and supervisors reinforce knowledge and skills on the job.

- A healthy, safe, and secure work environment with measurable performance measures and targets for each key factor affecting the workplace.

- The assessment of workforce engagement and satisfaction, and prompt actions to improve conditions that adversely affect morale, motivation, productivity, and other related performance results.

Finally, the champion must work as part of an organization-wide council to help coordinate all facets of the management system to drive high performance.

Process-Management Champion

The *process-management champion* is an executive-level person who, in addition to other executive duties, coordinates and enhances all aspects of the organization's core competencies and related systems to manage and improve work processes to meet the organization's strategic objectives and action plans. This includes activities and processes to create value for customers and other stakeholders. It is both a strategic and operational activity.

From the strategic side, rapid and accurate design, development, and delivery of products and services create a competitive advantage in the marketplace. From the operational side, the champion should work to ensure all key work processes are examined and optimized to achieve higher levels of performance, reduce cycle time and costs, and subsequently contribute to organizational success and sustainability.

The process-management champion has responsibility for creating a fact-based, process-management orientation within the organization. Since all work is a process, the process-management champion must ensure that the process owners (including other champions) systematically design, examine, improve, and execute their processes consistently error-free. The champion should ensure:

- Systematic continuous improvement activities are embedded in all processes, which lead to ongoing refinements and higher performance and productivity.

- Initial and ongoing customer requirements are incorporated into all product and service designs, production and delivery systems, and processes.

- Design, production, and delivery processes are structured and analyzed to reduce cycle time; increase the use of learning from past projects or other parts of the organization; reduce costs; increase the use of new technology and other effectiveness or efficiency factors; and ensure all products and services meet or exceed performance requirements.

- The work system and workplace are prepared for disasters and emergency situations. Prevent potential problems and/or manage them to ensure work continues.

Finally, the champion must work as part of an organization-wide council to help coordinate all facets of the management system to drive improvement and innovation throughout the organization.

Results Champion

The *results champion* is an executive-level person who, in addition to other executive duties, coordinates the *display* of the organization's performance results. This champion has substantially different work than the champions for Categories 1 through 6. No actions leading to or resulting from the performance-outcome data are championed by the results champion. Those actions are driven by process champions because they have responsibility for taking action to implement and deploy procedures necessary to produce the desired results. For example, the measurement, analysis, and knowledge management champion (Category 4) is responsible for collecting data that reflect all areas of strategic importance leading to desired results. The measurement, analysis, and knowledge management champion is also responsible for ensuring data accuracy, reliability, integrity, accessibility, and availability.

The results champion is responsible, however, for ensuring that the organization reports results required by Category 7 to provide evidence of the organization's performance improvement in key areas and facilitate monitoring by leaders and others in the workforce. These include product and service performance, customer satisfaction, financial and marketplace performance, workforce performance results, operational performance, and leadership results.

Results must be broken out by appropriate segment and group, such as different customer groups, market segments, workforce groups, or supplier/partner groups. Appropriate comparison data must be included in the results display to judge the relative *goodness* or *strength* of the results achieved. Senior leaders use these results to monitor organizational performance and competitiveness.

Finally, the results champion must work as part of an organization-wide council to help coordinate all facets of the management system to drive high performance. For example, if the organization is not collecting data necessary for inclusion in the business results report card, the results champion coordinates work with the other champions on the council to ensure those data are available, used for decision making, and included in appropriate reports.

LESSONS LEARNED

General Lessons

Twenty years ago the fierce global competition that inspired the quality movement in the United States was felt primarily by major manufacturers. Today, all sectors are under intense pressure to "be the best or be history." The demand for performance excellence reaches all corners of the economy, from manufacturing and service industries to professional services, education, health care, public utilities, and government. All of these segments have contributed valuable lessons to the quality movement and have played an important part in our recovery from the economic slump of the 1970s caused by poor service and products. Some insights and lessons learned from leaders of high-performing organizations are worth highlighting.

Desire and History Are Not Enough

> While using the Baldrige Criteria can help an organization reach high levels of performance, leaders cannot expect to sustain those levels of performance without continuing to use the Criteria as the way they run the business.

It is important to point out a fact that may be obvious to most: *To optimize organizational performance, organizations must actually use the principles contained in the Baldrige Criteria.* It is not enough to think about them. It is not enough to have used them in the past and no longer continue to do so. It is not enough to use a part but not all of the Criteria. To leave out any part suboptimizes the organization's performance.

The experience of Xerox provides a useful example. Xerox won the Baldrige Award in 1989. They demonstrated significant performance improvement through the 1980s and continued to grow substantially through the 1990s. Top leaders used the Baldrige Criteria as the way they ran their business, not just a list of additional activities they would do if they felt like it. They were absolutely customer-focused. They made decisions based on data, and fully engaged and involved their workforce. They continuously evaluated and improved their effectiveness in every aspect of their work. In fact, one business unit, Xerox Business Services (XBS), which made copies of and managed documents, won the Baldrige Award again in 1997. The performance of XBS was similar to Xerox as a whole. In 1989, XBS, with a few hundred employees, generated approximately $300 million in annual revenue. They worked so efficiently and satisfied customers so well that their market revenue grew from $300 million in 1989 to approximately $2 billion in 1997 and to approximately $6 billion in 2000.

However, a new Xerox CEO, Richard Thoman (a transplant from IBM who replaced Paul Allaire), did not use the Baldrige Criteria to provide the leadership needed to maintain the customer focus and bring the company into the emerging digital market. Within a year and a half under Thoman's direction, Xerox performance plummeted. So did its stock price, losing approximately 80 percent of its value. The Xerox board of directors, after firing Thoman and rehiring the previous CEO and other senior leaders, has been struggling to rebuild the processes and systems that led Xerox to high levels of performance excellence in the past. However, it will take the company years to recover.

The Xerox story points out an important lesson. While using the Baldrige Criteria can help an organization reach high levels of performance, leaders cannot expect to *sustain* those levels of performance without continuing to use the Criteria as the way they run the business. High-performing athletes of all types know this lesson well. To continue to win, they cannot rest on the success of the past. To continue to win, world-class athletes must continue to follow the discipline of training, diet, and effective coaching, and take advantage of technological advances in equipment. The same is true in any competitive environment.

A Tale of Two Leaders

It was a time of turbulence; it was a time of peace. It was a time of growth and streamlining. It was the happiest of times; it was also the most painful of times. Most of all it was a time that demanded change—although it was more comfortable to consider it a time for the status quo.

The following tales are of two leaders. One is consistent and persistent in communicating the direction and message that will bring about excellent results and high performance. Another is uncertain and vague. He does not wish to push his people into anything, let alone the significant commitment required to use the Baldrige Criteria as the way to run the business. After all, the business is still profitable and healthy. Why rock the boat? You may know these people or someone who reminds you of them. If so, you will understand the reason for this section.

There is no lonelier, more challenging, yet critical and rewarding job than that of the leader. I work with many, many leaders who listen to advice carefully. They really want to know the best approaches to optimize their organizations. Yet what they do with the advice and counsel is always interesting and unpredictable. This section is intended to help those leaders go resolutely down the right path.

Neither leader exists in real life, but both leader profiles are based on actual events and observations of different people in leadership positions.

Tale One

John was the CEO of a *Fortune 500* manufacturing company that was slowly but surely losing market share. Shareholders and employees were happy because profits and growth, although slower, were still hearty. However, their business that once enjoyed a near monopoly position was rapidly facing more and more competition. Customers who had to beg and plead for limited products and service over the years were happily turning to competitors that were trying in earnest to meet their needs and even delight them. In such an environment, aggressive, customer-focused companies were winning the hearts, minds, and pocketbooks of John's customers. After working with a consulting firm or two and studying the work of W. Edwards Deming, John decided that performance excellence was urgently needed to keep the company in business more than five years.

The First Message to the Leadership Team

John called an urgent meeting of his senior team. Many members of this team had been there since the company began its 20-year growth spurt and had been good soldiers in times of runaway growth and profit. John was wondering how many members of the senior staff would welcome the message he was about to send. The meeting was scheduled the next week for five days at the corporate headquarters. Short of an emergency illness, attendance was required.

During the next few days, John received 20 phone calls from secretaries who informed John their bosses could not attend because of other priority commitments. Priorities were quickly realigned when they were informed that attendance was not optional.

The week-long meeting began with training—the kind of training in which the group was required to participate, listen, and discuss the content. The training was presented by an outside firm with frequent discussions of company-wide application and emphasis presented by John. At the end of three days, John took over the meeting and asked for input on how best to apply these principles to the organization at all levels. The leadership group voiced resistance to change, some more than others. They basically voiced concern that "this performance excellence stuff with all of its requirements for empowerment and data" would get in the way of their doing business and was not needed.

John clarified the objectives of the group by walking to the white board and writing: "This new program, performance excellence, is in the way of doing business effectively." The senior staff pretty much agreed.

John responded by placing a large *X* through the word *in*. The statement now read, "Performance excellence is the way of doing business effectively." John notified the attendees, "I will negotiate an exit package with anyone who does not understand the implications of this message, and who does not want to be part of this new way of doing business." John learned that day that to institute meaningful change, it may be necessary to fire someone he liked. He also realized that to ignore the challenges and lack of commitment would be seen by everyone as tacit approval and send the message that the new way of doing business was *optional*.

The Next Steps

John focused on two next steps: (1) making sure his top team role-modeled behavior that would facilitate the needed changes; and (2) planning and implementing a company-wide training requirement to communicate the new skills and performance expectations. John started to change his behavior and the behavior of his top staff, feeling that *walking the talk* would signal the importance of new behaviors more than any speech or videotaped presentation. The next top staff meeting was called within a week to plan the design and rollout of training corporate-wide, including all foreign and domestic sites. The top staff had very little interest in training, feeling largely that this was a human resource function and should be delegated to that department. Based on the advice of external advisors, John informed the staff that it was now their job to plan, design, and execute this training. A *core design team* was formed with senior leaders and expert-content and course-design specialists to design the training within one month and present it to the senior corporate leaders.

In spite of prior agreements to manage their meetings effectively, to be on time, not interrupt, and follow the agenda, most continued to ignore the rules.

Behaviors of the top leadership group at this meeting included the usual set of interruptions, "I told you so's," and everyone talking at the same time. John, whose goal was to create a listening and learning environment, challenged the group to "ante up." He asked that all top leaders bring 50 $20 bills to the meeting. John introduced new meeting ground rules. They were simple. Interruptions, put downs, blocking behaviors, and talking over someone else were violations of meeting ground rules. On the other hand, building on ideas, clarifying ideas, supporting, and disagreeing respectfully were good meeting behaviors. Every violation was worth a $20 bill. Good meeting behaviors were rewarded, although they did not materialize until several meetings had been completed.

At first, it seemed that the pot would win big time—no one took John seriously. After about the third meeting, with penalties piling up, leadership group participants' behavior actually changed. Other meeting-management skills were slowly introduced, such as time-frame limits and action planning. Then John was confident his team could role-model this behavior to others. He ordered that, "This is the way we treat each other at all meetings, including staff meetings, communication forums, and all company business meetings." A core value and new behavior of courtesy and professionalism became deployed company-wide through the senior management team.

Training and the Change Process

Each five-day, high-performance management course was identical, ensuring that a uniform message and set of skills were communicated. Each course was eventually taught by two instructors, a shop supervisor and a manager, so that management and the workforce would both be involved. John personally taught the top leadership team the entire five-day course, assisted by a member of the design team, and this tale spread across the organization like wildfire. It became the thing to be invited to take part in this instruction because their leader had done it. The core skills became part of the fabric of the organization—the way to conduct business. They included fact-based decisions, a focus on customers, and using and improving processes. Also included was a way to solve problems continually with a well-defined process at the level the problem was occurring.

The focus had shifted from status quo to a thirst for improvement. Improvement began to bring rewards whereas the status quo was disdained. A comprehensive business evaluation was conducted and improvement targets were identified. Clear assignments with reasonable but aggressive goals were cascaded to all levels of the organization. Performance planning, goals, compensation, and recognition were aligned to support the overall business strategy, especially the need to focus better on satisfying internal and external customers. Managers who did not work to meet these new goals, who did not role-model the behaviors necessary to achieve high performance, were reassigned to jobs that did not require their management skills. New role models emerged to lead the organization at all levels. Within three years the company regained market share, improved profitability, expanded its employee base, and became, once again, one of the world's most admired companies.

Tale Two

Victor was the CEO of a West Coast manufacturing company that also was a proud member of the *Fortune 500*. Company performance had been uneven over the past few years. Profits were low this year relative to previous years, but the company still met financial targets. Product demands were high and the outlook was fairly good for the next quarter. The industry as a whole was fairly evenly matched as far as management problems. Trends for return on investment were also uneven, and other indicators such as sales volume and net profit were up and down. Investors were not happy, especially when other companies consistently outperformed theirs. Victor thought it was time to do something different. Victor consulted several valuable and trusted advisors and then decided that high-performance excellence might be worth considering.

The First Message to the Leadership Team

Victor scheduled a series of weekly dinner meetings over the next month (January) and engaged several top consultants to talk to the group about the business case for using high-performance management. He invited 50 top-level managers from across the country to attend. Most top leaders attended the meetings, enjoyed the dinners, and Victor attended most but not all of them. The sessions were interesting—the top leaders found the meetings were a great forum for politicking, posturing, wining and dining, and trying to sharpshoot the consultant. Victor asked his top leaders to come together for a half day in the spring to discuss the content and direction of the high-performance initiative, being convinced intellectually by the dinner discussions that this was the right direction for the company. At the half-day meeting, it was obvious that about half of the group agreed with the CEO and about half were uncertain or downright resistant, particularly one very senior vice president. Victor left the team with this message, "Let me take your comments under advisement and think about them as we go forward." Later, at the consultant's suggestion, he conducted an organizational assessment to identify problems that might be contributory to the uneven, up-and-down performance. The assessment uncovered several serious problems that required change, yet the senior leaders continued to resist.

The Next Steps

Victor finally hired one of the external advisors who had withstood the test of several dinner meetings and the challenges of his threatened senior management team. Victor asked the advisor to speak to the top leaders of the entire company about what a great group they were and how important the performance excellence initiative was going to be for the company. The advisor closed by telling them that only the best go after high performance; if they did not, their competitors would. During the following discussion sessions, Victor's chief operating officer (COO) announced to the group that he was far from convinced and stated he was not going to change the way he did business. That comment went unchallenged by Victor or anyone else in the company. Frustration continued to build.

In an effort to regain momentum, Victor wanted to create a change team. He asked each division to send a person to *facilitate* the initiative and receive appropriate training in managing change. The people selected were far from the best each division could offer, since no selection criteria had been provided and many thought this was a waste of time and talent. The division leaders supplied people who were expendable. The people who formed the facilitator group, for their part, were very enthusiastic but not particularly respected or credible. Because they were given absolutely no relief from any regular duties, they were stretched very thin. Also, the division heads were not supportive in any way of their participation, so they were almost punished for participating on this team. As the facilitators worked to please the demands of the CEO, there was no clear charter or mission as to what they were actually supposed to accomplish—no way to assess their performance or keep track of progress.

The power struggle intensified between the COO (who thought this was not the way to go and would have none of it) and the CEO. The CEO and the top management team arranged to travel to a leadership conference where they could hear presentations from high-performance organizations that had used the performance excellence techniques successfully. The CEO made it a priority to plan only morning presentations so everyone could play tennis or golf together each afternoon. Tennis and golf, not the need for better management systems, was the main topic of discussion at the evening dinners. A good time was had by all, but no consensus around change developed or was even discussed.

Training and the Change Process

Still, Victor wanted the facilitators to continue their work to assist change. The internal facilitators were placed in charge of conducting training for the entire organization. After the initial training was designed, a date was set to present a half-day version to the senior staff. Although the training designed for employees and lower-level managers was a four-day course, the senior staff did not feel they needed the same intense training or skills as the workforce. However, Victor made it a high priority for his direct reports to attend. At the last minute, Victor had to attend a function related to the board of directors and did not attend the training.

The training was, to put it mildly, a disaster. The executives, prompted by the snide comments of the COO, never gave it a chance. They concluded that the training was not effective and should not be rolled out to the employees. In the face of compelling opposition, Victor quietly diverted his attention elsewhere.

Leadership Style Summary

It is probably obvious what is the current state of John's high-performance *way to run the business* versus the high-performance *initiative* at Victor's company. Perhaps you could spot some of the problems each type of leader addressed and solutions they supported.

Using symbols and language to manage the change to high performance is tricky and usually demands that some external person be involved who can provide good sound advice, based on experience and expertise, to the CEO. Using power constructively is absolutely critical, since failure of the top leader to use all forms of power and influence available will intensify conflict and power struggles that act as a *de facto* barrier to change.

Motivating people to act constructively, and not feel threatened, is another challenge. Providing a clear focus on the future state, while rewarding behavior that facilitates the transition, will work to ensure the change actually happens. Victor's vision was unclear. He did not act as a leader. He ensured his facilitators would never succeed by never championing their work in any way. The next time Victor gets a new idea, these people (if they are still employees) will take a nosedive rather than be at the forefront of the initiative.

John never lost his vision or influence as CEO. He ensured his management team was supportive by first defining and clarifying organizational values, direction, and expectations; encouraging them to climb on board; and ensuring they acquired the skills and support to spread the approaches throughout the company.

Leadership Lessons

Based on the organizational performance research cited earlier, coupled with the relentless pace of change in all sectors and increasingly global competition, there are several strong messages leaders need to understand. Then they must be willing to take the necessary steps to change. This will require an assessment of current management systems and a willingness to drive the necessary adjustment. Once the assessment is complete and priorities are agreed upon, line up plans and resources and support the change wholeheartedly. Focus on the marketplace for your cues to change. Ask, for example:

- Is your competition growing weaker?
- Is the economy more stable and secure?
- Are the demands of your customers declining?
- Do you have all of the resources you need to meet your current and future goals?
- Do you believe your employees will be willing or able to continue working at the pace you have set for them? Will they do more?

If the answer is no to any of these questions, read on. Assess management systems and launch improvements. This will require your organization to assess its management systems against the Baldrige Criteria. After the assessment is complete, identify the vital few next steps, assign responsibility, make improvements, and reevaluate.

Great Leaders Are Great Communicators Who Lead by Example

One characteristic of a high-performance organization is outstanding performance results. How does an organization achieve such results? How does it become world-class? We have found unanimous agreement on the critical and fundamental role of leadership. There is not one example of an organization or unit within an organization that achieves superior levels of performance without the personal and active involvement of its top leadership. Similarly, in all cases where an organization has not been able to achieve or sustain high performance, the cause can be traced to leadership failures.

Top leaders in high-performing organizations create a powerful vision that focuses and energizes the workforce. They engage workers to drive change and innovation. Everyone is pulling together toward the same clearly defined goals and objectives. An inspired vision, combined with appropriately aligned recognition and reward, is the catalyst that builds trust and launches initiatives to overcome the organizational *status quo*.

Great leaders also communicate clear objectives. They assign accountability, ensure that employees have the tools and skills required, and create a work climate where individual initiative and the transfer of learning thrive. They reward teamwork and data-driven improvement. Practicing what they preach, they serve as role models for continuous improvement, consensus building, and fact-based decision making their actions match their words. They push authority and accountability to the lowest possible levels.

One lesson from great leaders is to refrain from the use of the word *quality*. Unfortunately, the use of the word quality can create an unintended barrier of mistrust and negativism that leaders must overcome before even starting on the road to performance excellence. Too often, when skilled, hard-working, dedicated employees are told by leaders, "We must improve quality," they conclude that their leaders believe their work is poor. They frequently retort with, "We already do quality work!" Registered professionals (engineers, chemists, psychologists, physicians, teachers, to name a few) often exacerbate the communication problem by arguing that they, not customers, are the best ones in a position to know and define quality. These messages confuse the workforce.

Instead, we advise leaders to create a work climate that enables employees to develop and use their full potential, to improve continually the way they work—to seek higher performance levels and reduce activities that do not add value or optimize performance. Most employees readily agree that there is always room for improvement—all have seen work that does not add value.

The use of the word *quality* can also open leadership to challenges as to what definition of quality the organization should use. This leads to our second lesson learned. Leaders will have to overcome two organizational tendencies—to reject any management model or approach *not invented here* and to think that there are many equally valid models. Quality differs from a decision tree or problem-solving model where there are many acceptable alternatives. The Baldrige model—and the many national, state, and organization assessment systems based on it—is accepted as *the* standard for defining performance excellence in organizations worldwide. Its criteria define validated, leading-edge practices for managing an organization to achieve peak performance.

Over twenty years of extraordinary business results shown by Baldrige Award recipients and numerous state-level, Baldrige-based Award recipients have helped convince those willing to learn and listen.

To be effective, leaders must understand the Baldrige model of performance excellence and communicate to the workforce and leadership system their decision to use that model for assessment and improvement. Without clear, unwavering leadership commitment to achieving the requirements of the comprehensive Baldrige model, resources may be wasted chasing fads, special projects, and isolated strategies. Although programs such as activity-based costing, management by objective, reengineering, project management, quality circles, balanced scorecards, Six Sigma, Lean Enterprise, and ISO 9000 certification, to name a few, have produced some good results, unless leaders focus on the entire system, performance is not optimized.

Without clear leadership there will be many *hikers* walking around but no marked trails for them to follow. Unless leaders understand the entire system and take their responsibility for transforming the workplace, performance optimization is not attainable. This brings us to our third leadership lesson learned.

A significant portion of senior leaders' time—as much as 60 to 80 percent—should be spent in visible Baldrige-related leadership activities such as goal setting, planning, reviewing performance, recognizing and rewarding high performance, improving their personal leadership skills, and spending time understanding and communicating with customers and suppliers, not micromanaging subordinates' work. In setting goals, planning, and reviewing performance, senior leaders must look at the inside from the outside. Looking at the organization through the critical eyes of external customers, suppliers, and other stakeholders provides a vital perspective.

A key role of the effective senior leader is to focus the organization on engaging customers. Leaders must champion change and ensure actions focus on creating customer value and exceeding their expectations. Leaders must role-model the tools of performance excellence and ensure the organization focuses on its vision, mission, and strategic direction to keep customers loyal.

Listen

Successful leaders know the power in listening to their people—those they rely on to achieve their goals. One vital link to the pulse of the organization is employee feedback. It is important to check with workers to determine whether what you have said has been understood, ask for feedback and then listen carefully. To know whether what you have outlined as a plan makes sense or has gaping faults, ask for feedback and then listen. Your leadership system cannot improve without evaluating and acting on employee feedback. In fact, the 2009 Baldrige Criteria [Item 1.2a(2), Note 3] expect that leaders use workforce and other stakeholder feedback in assessing and improving their effectiveness and the effectiveness of managers at all levels.

Manage and Drive Change

Leaders of all types of organizations can count on relentless, rapid change being part of their world. The rate of change confronting organizations today is far greater than ever before. Skills born out of the Industrial Revolution carried our parents through a 40-year work life. Human knowledge now doubles every five years, instead of the 40 years it took in the mid- to late-twentieth century. Today, our children are told to expect *at least* five career (not job) changes during their work life.

There are several lessons for leaders that arise from this condition today. Change may not occur on the schedule set for it. It is often too fast or too uneven to predict. Also, change driven by leaders is often resisted by their most successful followers—they have difficulty seeing the need to change. Take, for example, a school district that scheduled a Baldrige-based improvement workshop for its middle school faculty. The day before the training, the district leadership received a letter protesting the workshop on the grounds it was not needed. The letter was signed by the 20 best teachers in the school. To the credit of the school district leadership, they held the workshop anyway, and the truly outstanding teachers saw the value in continuous improvement once they began to listen and made changes that helped their students.

Leaders who share the values of high performance will need to drive change to make the necessary improvements. Change will not happen naturally. It is rarely driven by those at the bottom (except for revolutionaries and terrorists). Embracing the concepts of organizational (not just individual) learning will facilitate change in the organization. Leaders will need to develop a system that drives new knowledge throughout the organization.

Strategic Planning Lessons

Deploy through People Not Paper

Strategic planning helps leaders examine the factors that will affect an organization's future. The resulting strategic objectives must define the things the organization must accomplish or achieve to be successful in the future. The planning process should begin by ensuring that all contributors agree on terminology. Otherwise the strategic plan may be incomplete—a marketing plan, a budget plan, or a financial business plan, depending on who is leading the team. The resulting goals or strategic objectives *must* be defined in measurable, outcome-oriented terms. Strategic objectives describe desired outcomes, not enablers or activities that are necessary to achieve outcomes.

Developing separate plans for each aspect of business success is counterproductive. This approach almost guarantees a nonintegrated and short-lived fragmented performance-improvement effort. Therefore, leaders should concentrate on the few critical improvement goals in the strategic plan necessary for organizational success, such as improving customer loyalty or becoming a performance leader. The well-developed strategic plan also:

- Documents the financial and market impact of achieving these objectives.

- Details actions to support the objectives.

- Considers the competitive environment.

- Specifies, in measurable terms, the expected performance milestones that must be met to achieve the goals. The milestones (or time lines) match the leaders' cycle for reviewing progress (that is, if leaders review progress quarterly, then the plan should predict quarterly outcome-oriented milestones).

A critical lesson learned when it comes to strategic plans is that there can be no rest until everyone in the organization understands their role in the plan and how their contribution will be measured and rewarded. The goals, actions, measures, and milestones need not be complex. For every unit, they can be presented as a one-page electronic scorecard, to which senior leaders refer each month during performance reviews. Everyone at all levels should be able to use a personal one-page scorecard to display the plan, define actions needed, and monitor actual progress against expected progress.

Customer-Focus Lessons

Customers Expect Solutions to Problems They Don't Know They Have

The high-performing organization systematically determines its customers' short- and long-term service and product requirements. It does this based on information from former as well as current and potential customers. It builds relationships with customers and continuously obtains information, using the data to improve its service and products and better understand customer preferences.

The 2009–2010 Criteria require organizations to listen to the "voice of the customer" to prevent misunderstanding or inadvertently changing their requirements. When customer service representatives, sales personnel, engineers, and others fail to keep the voice of the customer intact it is easy to misrepresent the customer and fail to design and deliver the right products, programs, and services.

The smart organization prioritizes the drivers of satisfaction and loyalty of its customers, compares itself to its competitors (or organizations providing similar products or services), and continuously improves customer satisfaction and loyalty.

As the organization becomes more systematic and effective in determining customer needs and expectations, it learns that there is high variation among customer groups and segments. The more sophisticated the measurement system, the more variation will be revealed. It is particularly important that organizations focus on this vital process and make it a top priority that their customers have access to people to make known their requirements and their preferences. This helps modern organizations ensure they are building solid and positive relationships with their customers. After all, few of us have storefront windows on Main Street where our customers come and chat regularly.

One specific lesson learned comes from voice mail—a big step forward in convenience and efficiency that, if used poorly, can be a big step backward in customer relationship building. For example, a major international financial institution put its highest priority customers on a new voice-mail system. Customers were never informed about the system and one day called their special line to find rock music and a multi-tiered voice-menu system instead of their personal financial account manager. Even though the phone was answered on the first ring, these preferred customers were furious. This is a good example of a step in the wrong direction—customers were never asked about their requirements and preferences, and the organization lost accounts and created many frustrated customers.

Another important lesson is to segment customers according to their needs and preferences and do what is necessary to build strong, positive relationships with them. More and more customers are looking for service providers to help define their unique needs and respond to those unique needs. In short, customers are expecting solutions to problems that they, the customers, have not yet realized.

Organizations that make it easy for customers to complain are in a good position to hear about problems early so they can fix them and plan ahead to prevent them. If organizations handle customer complaints effectively at the first point of contact, customer loyalty and satisfaction will increase. When organizations do not make it easy for customers to complain, when finally given the chance to provide feedback customers may not bother to complain, but simply no longer do business with these organizations.

The next lesson has to do with educating the organization's leadership in the fundamentals of customer engagement and customer-satisfaction research models before beginning to collect customer-satisfaction data. Failure to do this may affect the usefulness of the data as a strategic tool. At the very least, it will make the development of data-collection instruments a long, misunderstood effort, creating rework and unnecessary cost.

Do not expect everyone in your organization to welcome customer feedback—many fear accountability that such feedback can force. Time and time again, the organizations most resistant to surveying customers, conducting focus groups, and making it easy for customers to complain are the same organizations that do not have everyday contact-handling systems, customer support standards, or trained and empowered front-line employees to serve customers and resolve their concerns promptly. Front-line employees who do not have sufficient decision-making authority and are not ready to acknowledge customer concerns are not capable of assuming responsibility to solve customer problems.

No single customer-feedback tool is sufficient by itself. A mail-based survey does not take the place of personal interviews. Focus groups do not replace surveys. The high-performance organization uses multiple listening posts and trains front-line employees to collect customer feedback and improve those listening posts. In the high-performance organization, for example, even an accounts-receivable system is viewed as a listening post.

Do not lose sight of the fact that the best customer-feedback method, whether it be a survey, focus group, or one-on-one interview, is only a tool:

- Make sure the data gathered are actionable
- Aggregate the data from all sources to permit complete analyses
- Use the data to improve work processes and strategic planning

Finally, be aware that customers are not interested in your problems. They merely want products or services delivered as promised. They become loyal when consistent value is provided that sets you above all others. Merely meeting their basic expectations brands you as marginal. To be valued you must consistently delight and exceed the customers' expectations.

Measurement, Analysis, and Knowledge-Management Lessons

Data-Driven Management and Avoiding Contephobia

The high-performance organization collects, manages, and analyzes data and information to drive excellence and improve its overall performance. Said another way, information and data are used to drive actions and build accountability. Using data and information as strategic weapons, effective leaders constantly compare their organization to competitors, similar service providers, and world-class organizations. They identify shortfalls in their own organization as a result, and take action to close the gaps.

While people tend to think of data and measurement as objective and hard, there is often a softer by-product of measurement. That by-product is the basic human emotion of fear. This perspective on data and measurement leads to the first lesson learned about measurement, analysis, and knowledge management. Human fear must be recognized and managed to practice data-driven management.

This fear can be found in two types of people. The first are those who have a simple fear of numbers—those who hated mathematics in school and probably stretch their quantitative capabilities to balance their checkbook. These individuals are lost in numerical-data discussions. When asked to measure or when presented with data, they can become fearful, resistant, or even angry. These reactions can undermine improvement efforts.

The second type of individual, who may be comfortable with numbers, realizes that numbers can impose higher levels of accountability. The fear of accountability, *contephobia* (from 14th-century Latin *to count,* modified by the French *to account*), is based on the fear of real performance failure that numbers might reveal or, more often, an overall fear of the unknown that will drive important decisions. Power structures can and do shift when decisions are data driven.

Fearful individuals can undermine effective data-driven management systems. In managing this fear, leaders must demonstrate that system and process improvement is the goal, not punishing individuals.

A mature, high-performance organization will collect data on competitors and similar providers and benchmark itself against world-class leaders. Some individuals may not be capable of seeing the benefit of using this type of process-performance information. The process of collecting these types of data is known as benchmarking. The focus is on identifying, learning from, and adopting best practices or methods from similar processes, regardless of industry or product similarity. Adopting the best practices of other organizations has driven breakthrough improvements and provided great opportunities for gaining a competitive advantage.

Lesson number two, therefore, is that an organization that has difficulty comparing itself with dissimilar organizations is not ready to benchmark and is not likely to be able to optimize or even improve its own performance as a result.

The third lesson in this area relates to not being a DRIP. This refers to a tendency to collect so much data (which contributes to contephobia) that the organization becomes data rich and information poor. This is wrong. Avoid wasting capital resources by asking this question: "Will these data help us make better decisions?" If the answer is no, do not waste time collecting, analyzing, or trying to use the data. Ideally, data should not be collected unless it supports decision making.

Workforce-Focus Lessons

Workforce Engagement: Getting Workers to Contribute their Utmost

Personnel departments have been renamed in many organizations to *human resources*. This name change is intended to draw attention to the fact that workers are valuable resources of the organization, not just dispensable commodities to be hired, commanded, and fired. Now, however, the leap made by successful organizations is that the capability and capacity of the workforce need to be part of every strategic and operational decision of the organization. This focus goes far beyond the purview of the former departments of human resources. In high-performing organizations, workers are treated as a valuable asset—where investment and development are critical to optimize the asset.

One of the valuable lessons learned in this regard is not to let an out-of-date or territorial personnel or human resources director use archaic rules to stop your performance-improvement program. Although many human resources professionals are among the brave pioneers in high-performance organizations, others have tried to keep compensation and promotions unrelated to performance but instead tied to length of service, seniority, or tenure. This approach can stop progress in its tracks or slow it significantly.

The Big Challenge Is Engagement

The most powerful drivers of workforce engagement relate to workers feeling valued by their supervisors and organization, and workers feeling involved. The high-performing organization values its workers and demonstrates this by enabling them to develop and realize their full potential while providing them appropriate rewards and incentives to do so. The organization that is focused on workforce excellence builds and maintains a climate that builds trust. Trust is essential for employee engagement, personal and professional growth, and high organizational performance.

The first human resource lesson is perhaps the most critical one. That is, revise—overhaul, if necessary—recognition, compensation, promotion, and feedback systems to align with and support high-performance work systems, a customer focus, and strategic objectives. If leaders personally demonstrate all the correct leadership behaviors, yet continue to recognize and reward *fire-fighting* performance, offer pay and bonuses tied only to traditional bottom-line results, and promote individuals who do not represent high-performance role models—engagement will suffer and their organization-wide improvement effort will be short lived.

Compensation, incentives, recognition, and rewards must be tied to the achievement of key high-performance outcomes, such as customer satisfaction, innovation, performance improvement, and other business results. The compensation/recognition tool is a powerful lever to assist in aligning, or misaligning, the work of the organization.

Developing and Maintaining Skills

A second human resource lesson learned relates to building capacity and capabilities. Training is not a panacea or a goal in itself. The organization must define the skill, competency, and staffing gaps related to performance gaps. Then the organization must take steps to close the gaps. Training, as a tool to close capability and capacity gaps, must be part of an overall business strategy. If not, money and resources are probably better spent on a memorable holiday party.

Timing is critical. Broad-based workforce skill training should not come first. Many organizations rush out and train their entire workforce only to find themselves having to retrain months or years later. Key participants should be involved in developing training plans and schedules to ensure workers develop important skills just in time to use them in their assignments.

Effective skill development requires management support to reinforce the use of new skills on the job. Training must be offered when an application exists to use and reinforce the skill. Otherwise, most of what is learned will be forgotten. The effectiveness of training must be assessed based on the extent of learning and impact on the job, not merely the likability of the instructor or the clarity of course materials.

Leadership development at all levels of the organization is an indispensable component to high performance. New technology has increased training flexibility so that all knowledge does not have to be transferred in a classroom setting. Consider many options when planning how best to update skills.

Assessing Engagement and Satisfaction

Questions used to assess engagement should examine the following topics: personal contribution; personal capabilities; reward, recognition, compensation; manager attributes; improvement, initiative, innovation; and workplace climate. Sample questions are provided on page 169, as a part of the analysis of Item 5.1.

Engaged, satisfied workers enhance organizational productivity, customer satisfaction, and financial success. Workplace surveys are often used to measure and identify weaknesses in workforce engagement and satisfaction that disrupt productivity.

Organizations have success in improving workforce engagement and satisfaction by conducting routine work-climate surveys, promptly meeting with employees to plan improvements, and tying improvements in ratings to managers' compensation/recognition.

Empowerment to Make Work-related Decisions

Two final workforce excellence lessons have to do with engaging workers in decisions about their work. Engaging workers in decision making without the right skills or a sense of direction produces chaos, not high performance.

- First, leaders who empower workers before communicating and testing that a sense of direction has been fully understood and that the necessary skills are in place will find that they are managing chaos—workers moving in different directions, working at cross-purposes.

- Second, not everyone wants to be empowered to make decisions about their work, and to do so may represent a barrier to high performance. While there may be individuals who truly seek to avoid responsibility for making improvements, claiming "that's management's job," these individuals do not last long in a high-performing organization. They begin to stick out like a lone bird during a cold and snowy winter. Team members who want the organization to thrive do not tolerate such people their team for long.

The bigger reason for individuals failing to *take empowerment and run with it* is management's mixed messages. In short, management must convince workers that they (managers) really believe that workers know their own processes and, with proper training and support, are best suited to make decisions about their work. Consistent leadership is required to help workers overcome legitimate, long-standing fear of traditional management practices used so often in the past to control and punish.

Remember, aligning compensation, incentives, and reward systems to reinforce performance plans and core values is one of the most critical means to enhance organizational performance; however, getting workers to believe their leaders really trust them to contribute their utmost and make decisions to improve their own processes is difficult.

Process Management Lessons

Listen to Process Owners and Keep Them Engaged

Process management involves the continuous improvement of processes required to meet customer requirements and deliver quality products and services. Virtually every high-performance organization identifies its key work processes and manages them to ensure that customer requirements are met consistently and performance is improved continuously.

The first lesson learned has to do with the visibility of processes. When processes are hard to observe, as so many are in the service sector (for example, service design or customer response), they are hard to improve. The simple exercise of drawing a process-flow diagram with people engaged in a process can be a struggle, but also a valuable source of information that can help identify process shortfalls and improvement opportunities. With no vantage point from which to see work as a process, many people never think of themselves as engaged in a process. Some even deny it. The fact that all work—visible and invisible—is part of a process should be understood before employees can begin to execute and improve key processes consistently.

Once this is understood, a second process management lesson comes to light. Process owners are the best ones, but not the only ones, to improve their processes. They should be part of process-improvement teams, but outsiders should be involved as well. Effective process-improvement teams are often made up of carefully selected cross-discipline, cross-functional, multilevel people who bring detailed inner knowledge and fresh insight to the examination of a process. Consultants, such as Six Sigma Black Belts, can provide important insights to process owners. However, be careful not to lose sight of the process owner—the person with expert knowledge of the process who should be accountable for long-term improvement to it. In a misguided effort to ensure that all of its process-improvement teams were cross-functional and multilevel, one organization enlisted volunteers to join process-improvement teams. Using this democratic process, one marketing process-improvement team ended up with no credible marketing expertise among its members. Instead, a group of frustrated support and technical staff members, who knew nothing about marketing, wasted time and money redesigning a process that was doomed to fail.

The third process management lesson learned involves an issue mentioned earlier. When focusing too closely on internal process data, there is a tendency to lose sight of external requirements. Organizations often succeed at making their processes better, faster, and (maybe) cheaper for them, but not necessarily for the betterment of their customers. When analyzing work processes, someone must stubbornly play the role of advocate for the customers' perspective, ensuring the voice of the customer is heard. Ensure that process changes will help make improvements for customers, key financials, employees, or top result areas. Avoid wasting resources on process improvements that do not appropriately benefit customers, employees, or the key performance objectives of your organization.

A fourth lesson involves design processes, an important but often neglected part of process management. The best organizations have learned that improvements made early in the process, beginning with design, save more time and resources than those made farther *downstream*. To identify how design processes can be improved it is necessary to include ongoing evaluation and improvement cycles. Create a series of in-process measures to help spot and fix process failures early. Remember the lesson taught by one of the founding fathers of the United States, Benjamin Franklin, "A stitch in time saves nine." To save resources, find the hole and fix it quickly.

Results Lessons

The Right Activities Lead to Desired Results

Results fall into six equally important categories:

1. Product performance, including health care outcomes and student achievement

2. Customer-focused, such as customer engagement, satisfaction, dissatisfaction, and customer-perceived value

3. Financial and market performance

4. Workforce performance, including development, engagement, and retention

5. Organizational effectiveness, such as key design, production, delivery, and support performance

6. Leadership effectiveness, such as the extent to which the following were achieved: strategic objectives, regulatory and legal compliance, ethics, and fiscal accountability

Product performance outcomes provide critical information on key measures of the product or service itself. This information allows an organization to predict whether customers are likely to be satisfied—without asking them. One important lesson in this area is to select measures that correlate with, and predict, customer preference, satisfaction, and loyalty.

Some organizations have found it beneficial to have their customers analyze some of their business results with the idea of learning from them as well as building and strengthening relationships. This may or may not be appropriate for your organization, but many successful enterprises have shared results with key customer groups at a level appropriate for their specific organization.

Systems must exist to make sure that results data are used at all levels to plan, monitor progress, identify gaps, and make improvements. Customer-satisfaction data are particularly important. Remember that when customers are asked their opinion, an expectation is created in their minds that the information will be used to make improvements that benefit them. Do not ask for customer feedback without committing to improve.

Financial and market performance is a key to survival. Organizations that make improvements that do not ultimately improve financial performance are wasting resources and growing weaker financially. This is true for for-profit and not-for-profit, education, health care, and government organizations. It is important to avoid overreliance on financial results. Financial results are the lagging indicators of organization performance. Leaders who focus primarily on lagging financial indicators often overlook problems or are not alerted in time to be able to respond to changing business needs. Focusing on finances to run the business—to the exclusion of leading indicators such as operational performance and employee satisfaction—is like driving your car by looking only in the rear-view mirror. You cannot avoid potholes and turns in the road.

Workforce performance results provide earlier alerts to problems that may threaten success. Absenteeism, turnover, accidents, low morale and engagement, grievances, poor skills, or ineffective training suboptimize organizational effectiveness. By monitoring performance in these areas, leaders can adjust more quickly and prevent minor problems from overwhelming the organization.

Organizational effectiveness and operational and service results pertain to measures of internal effectiveness that may not be of immediate interest to customers, such as cycle time (how long it takes to brew a pot of coffee), waste (how many pots you have to pour out because the coffee sat too long), and payroll inaccuracy (which may upset the affected workers). Ultimately, improving internal work-process efficiency can result in reduced cost, rework, waste, scrap, and other factors that affect the bottom line, whether profit-driven or budget-driven. In either case, customers are indirectly affected. To stay in business, to remain competitive, or to meet increased performance demands with fewer resources, the organization will be required to improve processes that enhance operational and support service results.

Regulatory and legal compliance, and citizenship, including behaving ethically as an organization and as individuals, have proven critical to long-term organizational survival. Just think of Enron and the problems that poor ethics and inadequate governance have caused the entire U.S. economy.

No single process leads to winning levels of performance. No single result can alert you to areas that need attention. The most important lesson is that every element of the entire Baldrige management system is required to achieve and sustain peak performance.

LEADERSHIP SUMMARY: SEVEN MUST-DO PRACTICES

Keys to Optimizing Performance

There is no evidence of an organization optimizing performance and achieving Baldrige or top state-level recognition without enhancing the entire management system, from leadership and planning to customers, people, and processes. Although all of these factors are critical in the long term, top leaders have the responsibility to set the direction, values, and expectations that drive change and create a sense of urgency. Leader actions absolutely determine the speed and success of the effort to optimize organizational performance. If leaders fail to take the following actions, the transformation to a high-performing organization will be seriously delayed and most likely not take place at all.

1. *Role-model effective leadership practices.* Like it or not, leader example drives the actions of others far better than words. Rhetoric without appropriate action is virtually worthless and may be counterproductive. Do not expect anyone else to do the things you will not. The concept of "do as I say, not as I do" has never worked to guide or change behavior.

- If you do not aggressively drive performance excellence in word and deed, others will think it is optional. When change is perceived as optional it is not likely to occur.

- If you do not have time to innovate, no one else will think innovation is important and it is not likely to occur.

- If you do not engage the employees with whom you work, other managers will follow your lead and fail to engage their employees.

- If you do not seek improvement ideas from your subordinates, they will not seek them in turn and people will not think of ways to improve.

- If you do not hold managers accountable for empowering their subordinates, they will believe empowerment is optional. (See the first bullet.)

- If you do not learn new things, you may not keep up with important changes affecting your business and others will not see the value in learning.

Develop a list of attributes you want to role-model in addition to those listed. Check how you are perceived on these leadership attributes from peer, subordinate, and employee feedback. Change where you are role-modeling the wrong things.

2. *Favor actions based on fact rather than intuition.* The lack of facts and data forces leaders to default to intuition as the basis for decision making. Many great leaders have relied on intuition when facts were unavailable. However, no great leader relied only, or even mostly on intuition in the face of valid facts. The best leaders make consistently good decisions, which require reliable, accurate, valid, and timely facts and data.

We rarely have access to all of the information we want prior to making decisions. However, we will surely not have enough fact-based information unless we prepare in advance. To make consistently better decisions, the best leaders drive fact-based diagnoses of organizational performance that focus on closing the gaps in areas critical to success. This information must be available when needed and easy to understand.

3. *Learn constantly.* Great leaders recognize that current knowledge limits their capabilities and success. You may think you have all of the knowledge and skills you need, but how do you know what you do not know? Do not expect your subordinates to learn for you because they suffer from the same limits. Considering the pace of change and the speed with which human knowledge is doubling, unless you aggressively pursue new knowledge, you will most certainly become obsolete or less effective faster.

Identify and list the things you must learn and the behaviors you must change to become a better leader. Ask your subordinates to give you feedback to help you complete the list. Set learning goals and time lines to monitor the pace of new learning. Make adjustments to stay on track.

4. *Share knowledge*. Enhance the impact of your new knowledge by sharing it with others. By teaching others and answering their questions, your understanding becomes stronger and you can apply new knowledge faster and better. It is also a good way to

role-model the value of learning. Set a schedule to teach others about performance excellence systems and processes at least two to four times each year, and stick to it.

5. ***Require other leaders in the organization to do the same.*** The performance of individuals drives the performance of the organization. If your performance is suboptimal because you lack certain knowledge, skills, and abilities, the same is certainly true for your subordinates and their employees. After they see the value you place in role-modeling effective practices, learning, and coaching, make it clear you expect them to do the same. It is critical to clearly set this expectation for learning, as well as set clear, measurable expectations for work after they complete the training.

Discuss your concerns and expectations, and answer their questions. You will have to do this very often at first. Be consistent. Those who resist change look for loopholes and ways to avoid change. Do not create loopholes for them. Permit no excuses for those who refuse to learn. Champion the requirements leading to optimum organizational performance. Be prepared to remove leaders who do not support continuous improvement and performance excellence systems.

6. ***Align expectations, measures, rewards, and recognition.*** The system you have in place is perfectly suited to produce the results you are currently getting. If you want to change the outcomes, you must change the people and processes that produce them. Training is only a part of the change process.

- Express new expectations for both individual and group performance in measurable, outcome-oriented terms.
- Measure progress regularly and give prompt feedback.
- Visibly reward and recognize the desired behavior.
- Find other work for those who cannot or will not do the things needed for driving high performance. By rewarding those who achieve desired results and removing those who do not, you make it clear that performance excellence is crucial to success—it will not be perceived as optional. If you keep a manager in place who has not taken the necessary steps to improve, you must realize that the subordinates of that manager will conclude that such performance must be acceptable in your eyes. Your failure to act sends the wrong message.

To enhance desired performance outcomes, ensure that goals, strategic objectives, actions, measures, analysis, training, compensation, incentives, reward, and recognition are completely aligned. Remember, *what gets measured gets done. What gets rewarded gets done first.* If achieving strategic objectives is truly critical to your future success, be sure to assign actions, make sure your people have the skills they need to do the work, measure and monitor progress, and reward desired behavior and outcomes.

7. ***Use training and development as a tool to enhance skills and inform—not as a substitute for personal leadership direction.*** Employees desire and expect important information to come from their leaders. Do not simply tell employees to do something new and different and expect it will be done. You must check understanding, measure and monitor progress, and provide appropriate incentives to actually get the desired behavior.

- Sending subordinate managers and employees to training and expecting the trainer to give the new management directions will rarely produce the desired results. It usually produces high skepticism and hostility, and reinforces the idea that leaders are not serious and committed to the new program or change—otherwise they would introduce it themselves. It also makes the trainer and the curriculum the target of criticism and blame:
  - "This class is a waste of time."
  - "The trainer should tell us what to do when we get back to the office."
  - "I do not know why I am here."
  - "Just how serious is management about these changes/programs? Have they taken this training?"
  - "What resources is management going to commit to this effort?"

Before anyone is sent to training, participants need to understand and *be able to describe* why they are there and what they are expected to get out of the training. These expectations should be set by the leaders who send the participants, not the trainers. Leaders could ask trainers to pretest the class to determine the extent to which participants understand why they are there. Those who are not prepared should be sent back. It should be the job of the sending managers to provide the proper foundation and preparation for their subordinate employees prior to training.

If you do not do the seven listed activities, you are by your actions telling your workers and subordinate managers and other workers that performance excellence is optional—something to do if they feel like it. In that event, you and your organization will most certainly fail to achieve the desired change and improvement.

LEADING THE CHANGE TO HIGH PERFORMANCE

Changing organizational culture is not easy and requires dedicated and unwavering consistency in support of the *new way* or *desired way* of behaving and believing. The following actions are usually critical to change culture in an organization:

- *Establish clear goals and a clear direction.* Explain clearly what will be required of workers and how the new requirements are different from the old. If you do not know what new behaviors are required, find out. Talk to leaders who have successfully engineered this kind of improvement in the past (such as leaders of Baldrige recipients). Leaders who are not clear invite confusion and inaction.

- *Show unwavering commitment.* Leaders are pivotal to the success of the enterprise—workers watch them closely. Don't blink in the face of setbacks—quitting is easy and doing so will make workers more cynical and demoralized. When leadership commitment and support are seen as tentative, subordinate managers and other workers will perceive the changes as optional, take-or-leave suggestions. Considering the profound ability most people have to resist change, this creates more support for doing nothing.

- *Prove you will change.* If leaders do not *walk the talk* and demonstrate their eagerness to operate differently, others once again conclude that the leaders are not serious and the new requirements are optional.

- *Keep the energy level high and focused on both process improvements and better performance outcomes.* Select improvements that are easy as well as difficult. Small successes are needed to keep the energy and support for performance excellence high. Larger improvement projects take longer to carry out but usually bring greater benefit. Celebrate process improvements as well as better performance outcomes.

- *Encourage people to challenge the status quo when doing so is consistent with enhancing customer value and achieving organizational goals.* Do not tolerate system craziness—break old bureaucratic rules and policies that prevent or inhibit high-performance work toward goals. Free your people from bureaucratic silliness and you will find great energy and support from the workforce.

- *Change rewards to make them consistent with goals and objectives.* Make following the new culture and achieving goals worthwhile by rewarding desired behaviors and making the continued use of the old ones unpleasant. All employees must understand that the rewards are issued for behaving in a certain way and for achieving desired results. Rewards, including compensation and incentives, should not be considered an entitlement of employment. It is important to test the effectiveness of rewards and recognition. Remember, just because you value a reward does not mean that workers will do the same.

- *Measure progress against desired outcomes.* When leaders use measurements to track progress, people think they are serious about the outcome. If you do not bother measuring, employee productivity is usually lower. In addition, measurements help identify those who should be rewarded and those who should not. Finally, keep measurements simple and efficient. Do not allow the measurement process to divert energy and focus. Stop collecting data that no longer support effective decision making.

- *Communicate, communicate, communicate.* Communication cannot replace an inspiring vision and sound goals, but poor communication can scuttle them. People perform better when they understand the logic and rationale behind the vision and goals. Leaders must tell them what's coming, how they will be affected, and what's expected of them. Remember to take every opportunity to communicate your desires—once is not enough. The opponents of change will work nonstop to undermine the new goal, vision, and culture; communicate consistently to overcome this resistance. Also remember that even motivated and supportive people forget; remind them often of the vision and new expectations. Leaders who do not communicate effectively invite the rumor mill to fill in the blank spaces by default. Bad news, bad rumors, and outright lies frequently fill the communication gap leaders might inadvertently leave.

- *Engage everyone.* Remember, this is not *optional* activity. People who do not actively support change oppose it, perhaps reflexively. Insist on full involvement and define a role for everyone. Find ways to make everyone accountable for transforming the culture and improving performance. If a manager fails to support the changes needed to improve performance, it is probably a good idea to encourage that person to find other work—preferably with a competitor.

- *Start fast, then go faster.* Slow progress, which the opponents of change like to see, creates a self-fulfilling prophecy—that the proposed changes will not be effective. However, speed creates a sense of urgency that helps overcome organizational inertia, achieve stunning results, and defeat the gloom and pessimism of naysayers.

Remain steadfast in support, walk the talk, involve everyone, communicate, achieve quick results, measure, and reward progress.

Improve Performance, Efficiency, and Timeliness

What Does It Mean?

- Includes but is not limited to process identification, analysis, and ongoing improvement. We must define and measure process cycle time and defects and reduce them consistently.

What Is the Leader's Responsibility?

- Set an example—ask for data/measurements on cycle time and defects
- Make time available
- Make training available
- Ensure that records discipline exists
- Charter teams
- Set high goals, get high performance
- If you do not tell workers what you expect, do not be surprised if they do not get where you want them to go

Create a Participative, Cooperative Workplace

What Does It Mean?

- Includes but is not limited to setting boundary conditions and relevant goals, then moving decisions to the lowest possible level, using work teams for planning and process improvement, and creating a *family-friendly* work environment. Leaders motivate people, provide training for managers and workers, encourage the development of self-directed work teams, delegate authority and decision making downward, empower people to focus on achieving mission and vision, value diversity, provide open communication in all directions, and measure and improve workers well-being, motivation, and satisfaction.

What Is the Leader's Responsibility?

- Coach and counsel, rather than control
- Encourage participation with the goal of achieving better decision quality and better performance—make better use of human resources

- Create and build a highly motivated and satisfied workforce

Taking Action

- All leaders have a responsibility for communicating the mission, vision, strategic objectives, and enabling activities to all workers.

- It is very important that leaders and workers understand and agree fully with the planned objectives. It is even more important that they carry out the actions needed to actually achieve the objectives. The plan-deployment process cascades from top management to all locations and levels of the organization. Top managers do not micromanage the process. This means that the top leaders determine the objective or target and an action officer determines the means. This then sets the target for the next level to determine means. Figure 10 provides one example of this effect.

Personal Management Effectiveness —The Use of Upward Evaluations

Formal upward evaluations have been used for more than 50 years to help assess job performance of leaders. As organizations become committed to improving labor relations and manager effectiveness, upward evaluation has become a widely used tool that more and more leaders value.

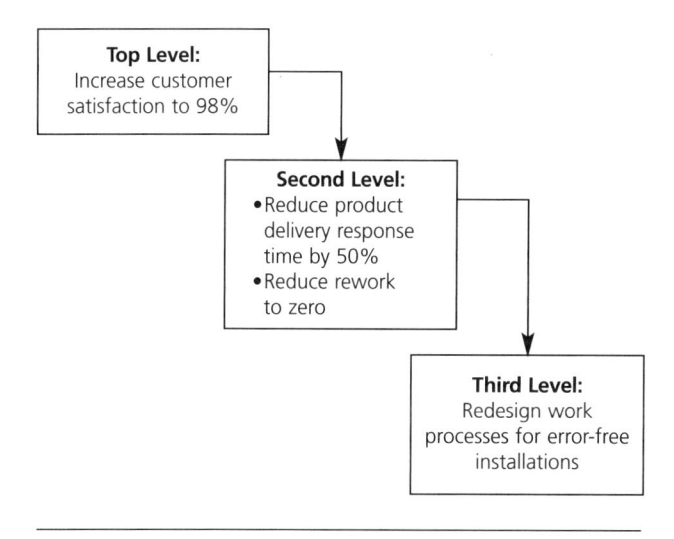

Top Level: Increase customer satisfaction to 98%

Second Level:
- Reduce product delivery response time by 50%
- Reduce rework to zero

Third Level: Redesign work processes for error-free installations

Figure 10 Deploying strategic objectives.

Three reasons why upward evaluation and the resulting feedback are beneficial include:

1. *Validity.* Subordinates interact regularly with their managers and have a unique vantage from which to assess manager style.

2. *Reliability.* Confidential feedback from numerous subordinates provides the best chance for accurate data. Workers who are hurt by poor management hope their feedback brings change.

3. *Involvement and morale.* Asking people to comment on the effectiveness and style of their managers boosts morale and sends a clear message that the organization is serious about increasing workers involvement—but only if the manager takes action to improve; otherwise, morale and motivation can get worse.

Before managers take action to change the way they manage, they should gather facts about their current style. They need to know what aspects of their style are considered strong and should not be changed. The starting point for improving management style, therefore, is an honest assessment of each manager's current behavior by subordinates, peers, and supervisors. This is also called a 360-degree evaluation.

The Feedback Process

1. Leaders solicit feedback on how they perform against specific behaviors that are characteristic of an effective manager. The Baldrige Criteria provide examples.

2. They use this information to plan personal improvement strategies.

3. They share the results of the survey with their workers and discuss possible improvement actions, then refine their plan.

4. They make improvements as planned and start the process again no more than one year later.

Figure 11 maps the process.

This process enables workers to help their manager understand how he or she is perceived, as well as identify areas of strength on which the manager can build. However, some important procedures should be in place to prevent improper use of the tool:

Insights to Performance Excellence 2009–2010

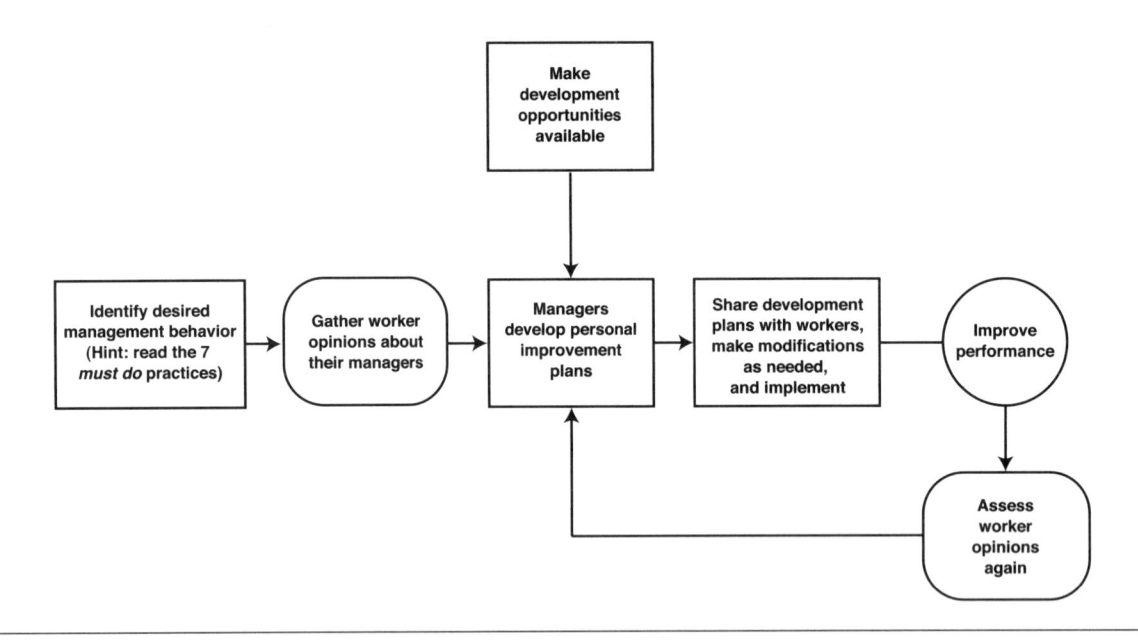

Figure 11 Improving leadership effectiveness.

- Feedback should always be used and interpreted in the spirit of continuous personal improvement. Personally identifiable results should go only to the manager who was rated and should not be used as a basis for performance ratings, promotion, assignments, or pay adjustments (unless, of course, the manager refuses to work to improve).

- Anonymity for those completing questionnaires should be carefully protected. No one other than the worker should see the actual completed questionnaire. To further protect anonymity, questionnaires should be summarized and reported to the manager in cases where fewer than five workers completed the questionnaire.

- Personally identifiable results should be provided only to the manager named on the questionnaire. When the managers receive the results, they review their own ratings to determine their strengths and opportunities for improvement. Then they take steps to improve.

Aggregate data should be reported to top leadership to monitor as part of an organization-wide improvement priority. If the average scores do not improve appropriately, then the leaders may elect to see personally identifiable data of low-performing managers to encourage them to do more.

The Management Effectiveness Survey in Figure 12 and Supervisor Management Survey in Figure 13 (©/courtesy of Quantum Performance Group) can provide information that might help leaders and managers at all levels determine areas to address to strengthen their personal effectiveness. It represents one set of questions to examine leadership communication, openness, and effectiveness. Certainly other questions may be asked as circumstances change. In fact, in order to determine if any survey is asking the correct questions, the survey itself should be evaluated. This can be done by using open-ended questions and asking workers to identify other issues that are of concern to them and should be included in the survey. Also, ask if some of the questions are not relevant or important and should be eliminated; then adjust the survey accordingly.

In addition to aggregating scores from workers, it is also useful to compare the perceptions of workers with the perception of the leader or manager who is the target of the assessment. Many times, workers identify a specific weakness that the leader believes is much stronger. These differences, together with key areas where both parties agree that a weakness exists, could be targeted for specific improvement. By aggregating the assessment data for all managers and making the overall results available to individuals, managers can determine how their stage of development compares with other managers in the office.

Insights to Performance Excellence

SAMPLE SCORED SURVEY – 10 workers completed the instrument

	#	1	2	3	4	Mean
1. My supervisor keeps me well informed about what's going on.	10	3	5	1	1	(2.0)
2. My supervisor clearly explains the reasons for decisions.	10		2	5	3	3.1
3. I am satisfied with my involvement in decisions that affect me.	10		5	5		2.5
4. My supervisor delegates the right amount of responsibility to me and does not micromanage.	10	2	3	3	2	2.5
5. My supervisor gives me honest feedback on my performance.	10	4	2	3	1	2.1
6. I have confidence in my supervisor's decisions.	10		5	5		2.5
7. My supervisor has the knowledge he/she needs to do the job.	10		5	5		2.5
8. I can depend on my supervisor to honor the commitments he makes to me.	10			2	8	3.8
9. My supervisor treats people fairly and with dignity and respect.	10		3	3	4	3.1
10. My supervisor is straightforward and honest with me.	10	2	7	1		1.9
11. My supervisor is committed to resolving the concerns that are identified in this survey and has made improvements based on past surveys (if applicable).	10	3	4	2	1	1.9
12. My supervisor strongly supports doing the right thing for the customer and all other stakeholders.	10			6	4	3.4
13. The communication process in my unit is effective. I always understand what is being communicated. (Unit refers to the level in the office your supervisor heads.)						0
14. In my unit, there is an environment of openness and trust.						0
15. I feel free to speak up when I disagree with a decision.						0
16. I feel I can elevate issues to higher-level supervisors without fear of reprisal.						0
17. The people I work with cooperate to get the job done.						0
18. In my unit, we are simplifying the way we do our work.						0
19. We have an effective process for preparing people to fill open positions.						0
20. All employees have fair advancement opportunities based on skills and abilities.						0

My supervisor frequently . . .
21. provides me with honest feedback on my performance. — 0
22. encourages me to monitor my own efforts. — 0
23. encourages me to make suggestions to improve work processes. — 0
24. ensures I have the knowledge, information, facts, and analysis I need to make decisions about my job — 0
25. defines his/her requirements of me in clear, measurable terms. — 0
26. acts as a positive role model for performance excellence. — 0
27. ensures that organizational goals/strategic objectives and related actions are understood at all levels — 0
28. favors facts before making decisions affecting our customers, workers, partners, and organization. — 0
29. identifies and removes barriers to getting work-done. — 0
30. encourages people in our unit to work as a team. — 0
31. makes me want to do my very best work to help my unit be the best. — 0
32. encourages me to ask questions and creates an environment of openness and trust. — 0
33. behaves in ways that demonstrate respect for others. — 0
34. ensures regularly scheduled reviews of progress toward goals using accurate performance-outcome measures. — 0
35. monitors my progress and compares it against goals using accurate performance-outcome measures — 0
36. ensures that rewards and recognition are fairly applied and closely tied to strategic goals, objectives, and required action plans. — 0
37. sets work plans based on strategic objectives and customer requirements. — 0
38. expects me to improve the way I do my works. — 0
39. uses a disciplined, fact-based process to make business and operational decisions and solve problems. — 0
40. treats performance excellence as a basic operating principle. — 0

Please list on the back of this form additional questions that the survey should ask about your supervisor. Also tell us which questions already on the survey are not very important and should be removed. In this way we can improve the effectiveness of the survey and better identify areas most needing improvement.

Callouts:
- *If the supervisor's self score of 4 is higher than the workers', it may indicate a possible failure to recognize a problem* (pointing to item 1, mean 2.0)
- *Relatively strong* (pointing to item 8, mean 3.8)
- *Relatively weak* (pointing to item 10, mean 1.9)

Figure 12 Sample Management Effectiveness Survey partially scored.

SUPERVISOR MANAGEMENT SURVEY

The following questionnaire lists some key indicators to help you self-assess your effectiveness in several key areas. Enter 1 for strongly disagree, 2 for disagree, 3 for agree, and 4 for strongly agree. If you cannot answer a question leave it blank.

General

1. I keep my staff well informed about what's going on in the office. — 1 2 3 4
2. I clearly explain to my staff the reasons for decisions that affect their work. — 1 2 3 4
3. My staff are satisfied with their involvement in decisions that affect their work. — 1 2 3 4
4. I delegate the right amount of responsibility to my staff and I do not micromanage. — 1 2 3 4
5. I give my staff honest feedback on their performance. — 1 2 3 4
6. My staff has confidence in my decisions. — 1 2 3 4
7. My staff believe that I have the knowledge I need to be effective. — 1 2 3 4
8. My staff can depend on me to honor the commitments I makes to them. — 1 2 3 4
9. I treat my staff and others fairly and with dignity and respect. — 1 2 3 4
10. I am straightforward and honest with my staff. — 1 2 3 4
11. My staff believe that I am committed to resolving the concerns that may be identified in this survey and that I have made improvements based on past surveys or feedback (if applicable). — 1 2 3 4
12. My staff believe that I strongly support doing the right thing for the customer and all other stakeholders. — 1 2 3 4
13. My staff believe that the communication process in my unit is effective. My staff believe that I always understand what is being communicated. (Unit refers to the level in the office you head.) — 1 2 3 4
14. In my unit, my staff believe that there is an environment of openness and trust. — 1 2 3 4
15. My staff feel that they are free to speak up when they disagree with my decisions. — 1 2 3 4
16. My staff believe that they can elevate issues to higher-level supervisors without fear of reprisal. — 1 2 3 4
17. My staff believe that they cooperate and work well together to get the job done. — 1 2 3 4
18. In my unit, my staff believe that we are simplifying the way we do our work. — 1 2 3 4
19. My staff believe that we have an effective process for preparing people to fill open positions. — 1 2 3 4
20. My staff believe that all employees have fair advancement opportunities based on skills and abilities. — 1 2 3 4
21. My staff believe that I provide them with honest feedback on my performance. — 1 2 3 4
22. My staff believe that I encourage them to monitor my own efforts. — 1 2 3 4
23. My staff believe that I encourage them to make suggestions to improve work processes. — 1 2 3 4
24. My staff believe that I ensure they have the knowledge, information, facts, and analysis support they need to make decisions about their job. — 1 2 3 4
25. My staff believe that I understand their requirements of me in clear, measurable terms. — 1 2 3 4
26. My staff believe that I act as a positive role model for performance excellence. — 1 2 3 4
27. My staff believe that I ensure that organizational goals/strategic objectives and related actions are understood at all levels. — 1 2 3 4
28. My staff believe that I favor facts before making decisions affecting our customers, workers, partners, and organization. — 1 2 3 4
29. My staff believe that I identify and remove barriers to getting work done. — 1 2 3 4
30. My staff believe that I encourage people in our unit to work as a team. — 1 2 3 4
31. My staff believe that I make them want to do my very best work to help my unit be the best. — 1 2 3 4
32. My staff believe that I encourage them to ask questions and create an environment of openness and trust. — 1 2 3 4
33. My staff believe that I demonstrate respect for others. — 1 2 3 4
34. My staff believe that I ensure regularly scheduled reviews of progress toward goals using accurate performance-outcome measures. — 1 2 3 4
35. My staff believe that I monitor our organization's progress, compare it against goals using accurate performance-outcome measures, and take steps to close gaps to be successful. — 1 2 3 4
36. My staff believe that I ensure that rewards and recognition are fairly applied and closely tied to strategic objectives and action plans. — 1 2 3 4
37. My staff believe that I set work plans based on strategic objectives and customer requirements. — 1 2 3 4
38. My staff believe that I expect them to improve the way they do their work. — 1 2 3 4
39. My staff believe that I use a disciplined, fact-based process to make business and operational decisions and solve problems. — 1 2 3 4
40. My staff believe that I treat performance excellence as a basic operating principle. — 1 2 3 4

Please list on the back of this form additional questions that the survey should ask about your supervisor. Also tell us which questions already on the survey are not very important and should be removed. In this way we can improve the effectiveness of the survey and better identify areas most needing improvement.

Figure 13 Sample Supervisor Management Survey.

Create Performance Excellence Standards for Managers—A Key Job Element

Virtually every organization has the ability to determine what performance requirements are critical for the success of employees and managers. These critical performance requirements are usually included as a key element in performance plans and appraisals. If performance excellence is critical to the success of the organization, a specific key performance requirement can be included in the performance plan (sometimes these are called personal commitment plans, personal improvement plans, personal management objectives, or individual development plans, to name a few) and evaluation of managers and leaders. Using this approach, every manager and supervisor begins to take performance excellence more seriously.

- Using the following performance standards as an example, in order for a manager to receive a rating at a particular level, that manager must have accomplished all of the activities described for that rating level. If all are not met, the rating goes to the lowest level at which all are met.

- The writer of the performance appraisal should cite measurable examples in the performance appraisal for actions listed under the rating level.

- Supervising reviewers must verify that these actions have indeed been taken. Under this system, managers are strongly encouraged to keep accurate records of activities that might exemplify compliance with these standards.

Overall Performance Standard for Leadership

The individual visibly demonstrates adherence to the high personal standards and characteristics of leaders in a high-performing organization. The individual:

- Understands the business processes of the unit.

- Focuses on customers and is customer-driven.

- Demonstrates a firm commitment to the principles of customer satisfaction. Understands customer requirements and consistently works to meet and exceed them.

- Understands and personally uses performance excellence principles and tools for decision making and planning:
  - Favors the use of data and facts to drive decisions and ensures that employees and subordinate managers do the same
  - Ensures that organizational goals/strategic objectives are converted to appropriate actions to align work within the organizational unit
  - Measures and monitors progress toward achieving the goals/strategic objectives within the organizational unit

- Demonstrates a firm commitment to the principles of workforce engagement and satisfaction:
  - Promotes flexibility, individual initiative, and innovation
  - Encourages and supports the personal and professional development of self and workers
  - Supports effective training aligned to support action plans and reinforces the use of new skills on the job
  - Ensures compensation is aligned to support high-performance business objectives and a customer focus
  - Rewards and recognizes workers who achieve objectives and incorporate the principles of performance excellence in their day-to-day work
  - Fosters an atmosphere of open, honest communication and knowledge sharing among workers and business units throughout the organization

- Rigorously drives the systematic, continuous improvement of key work processes to promote innovation, including personal self-improvement as an effective leader.

- Achieves consistently improving performance outcomes in customer satisfaction, worker engagement, motivation, and satisfaction, operational excellence, and financial (cost/budget) performance.

Rating No. 1: Performance is unsatisfactory. The individual frequently fails to meet the performance standard for leadership.

- Does not fully understand the business processes of the unit.
- Consistently disregards the needs of customers.
- Does not tolerate or care for customers well.
- Does not understand and has not taken steps to implement performance excellence (may even work against the changes needed).
    - Intuition, not data or facts, tends to dominate decision making
    - Organizational goals and actions are not aligned to actions within the unit
    - May measure and monitor some performance outcomes (such as budget tracking), but most measures are not aligned to organizational goals
- Does not effectively promote workforce engagement, motivation, and morale.
    - Tends to micromanage—does not delegate decision-making authority to the lower levels except as directly instructed to do so
    - Rarely listens to workers or cares what they think
    - Does not consistently promote flexibility and individual initiative
    - Does not consistently encourage and support the personal and professional development of self and workers
    - May send workers to training but does not consistently reinforce the use of new skills on the job
    - Has not taken effective steps to ensure that compensation and other rewards or recognition are aligned to support business strategies and actions
    - Reward and recognition are not aligned to support organizational goals or the principles of performance excellence or customer satisfaction
- Does not communicate effectively or foster an atmosphere of knowledge sharing among workers and business units.
- Does not regularly assess or improve work processes, including his or her personal effectiveness as a leader.
- Does not achieve consistently improving performance outcomes in customer satisfaction; workforce engagement and satisfaction; operational excellence; and financial (cost/budget) performance.

Rating No. 2: Performance is minimally acceptable. Individual occasionally fails to meet the performance standard for leadership. Performs higher than indicated by level one but does not meet all level-three requirements.

Rating No. 3: Performance is acceptable. Individual basically meets the performance standard for leadership.

- Is considered to be a capable leader.
- Understands the key business processes of the unit.
- Is customer-driven and promotes customer-focused values throughout the unit.
    - Demonstrates a commitment to the principles of customer satisfaction
    - Develops systems to understand customer requirements, strengthen customer relationships, resolve customer problems and prevent them from happening again, and obtain information about customer satisfaction and dissatisfaction
- Personally uses many performance excellence principles and tools for decision making and planning.
- Visibly supports performance excellence within the organization. Usually uses data and facts to drive decisions and ensures that many workers and subordinate managers do the same.
- Ensures that key organizational goals are converted to appropriate actions to align most work within the organizational unit. Most goals and

actions have defined measures of progress and time lines for achieving desired results.

- Demonstrates some commitment to the principles of worker empowerment and satisfaction. Is well-regarded by workers for:
    - Involving the workforce in identifying improvement opportunities and developing improvement plans
    - Valuing worker input on work-related matters
    - Promoting flexibility and individual initiative and ensuring that many subordinate managers do the same
    - Encouraging and supporting the personal and professional development of self and workers
    - Supporting effective training and reinforcing the use of new skills on the job
    - Ensuring compensation is aligned to support business strategies and actions
    - Rewarding and recognizing workers who incorporate the principles of performance excellence in their day-to-day work
- Fosters an atmosphere of open, honest communication and knowledge sharing among workers and business units throughout the organization.
- Visibly drives continuous improvement of many work processes, including personal effectiveness as a leader.
- Achieves consistently improving performance outcomes in customer satisfaction, workforce engagement, motivation, and satisfaction, operational excellence, and financial (cost/budget) performance.
- The levels of performance outcomes are better than average when compared with organizations providing similar programs, products, or services.

Rating No. 4: Performance is very good. Individual occasionally exceeds the performance standard for leadership. Performs higher than indicated by level three but does not meet all requirements of level five.

Rating No. 5: Performance is superior. Individual consistently exceeds the performance standard for leadership. *Is considered a role model for leadership.*

- Understands the business processes of the unit in great detail.
- Is customer-driven and actively promotes customer-focused values throughout the unit.
    - Demonstrates a firm commitment to the principles of customer satisfaction
    - Develops effective systems to understand customer requirements, strengthen loyalty and customer relationships, resolve customer problems immediately and prevent them from happening again, and obtain timely information about customer satisfaction and dissatisfaction
    - Advocates the needs of customers through the collection and use of information on customer satisfaction, dissatisfaction, and product performance
- Personally uses performance excellence principles and tools for decision making and planning.
    - Serves as a performance excellence champion within the organization and as a resource within the work unit, providing guidance, counsel, and instruction in performance excellence tools, processes, and principles
    - Acts as a role model for using data and facts to drive decisions and ensures that workers and subordinate managers do the same
    - Ensures that all organizational goals are converted to appropriate actions to align work within the organizational unit
    - Defines measures of progress and time lines for achieving desired results of each goal and action
- Demonstrates a firm commitment to the principles of workforce engagement and satisfaction. Is highly regarded by workers for:
    - Involving the workforce in setting standards of performance, identifying improvement opportunities, and developing improvement plans

- Seeking and valuing worker input on work-related matters
- Promoting flexibility and individual initiative and ensuring that subordinate managers do the same
- Encouraging and supporting the personal and professional development of self and workers
- Supporting effective training and reinforcing the use of new skills on the job
- Ensuring compensation is aligned to support business strategies and actions
- Rewarding and recognizing workers who incorporate the principles of performance excellence in their day-to-day work

• Fosters an atmosphere of open, honest communication and knowledge sharing among workers and business units throughout the organization.
- Checks the effectiveness of nearly all communication and makes changes to improve

• Rigorously drives the systematic, continuous improvement of all work processes, including personal self-improvement as an effective leader.
- Develops personal action plan and always incorporates results of 360-degree feedback to continuously improve personal leadership effectiveness and ensures subordinate managers do the same

• Achieves consistently improving performance outcomes in customer satisfaction; workforce engagement, development, motivation, and satisfaction; operational excellence; and financial (cost/budget) performance.
- The levels of performance outcomes are among the highest in the organization/nation/state and are also high when compared with organizations providing similar programs, products, or services

The following tables display some of the performance excellence ratings listed on pages 59–62 side by side to make it easier to see the progression from poor (1) to excellent (5).

Performance Excellence Standards Table

Level 1	Level 2	Level 3	Level 4	Level 5
Performance is unsatisfactory: Individual frequently fails to meet the performance standard for leadership. Is considered a poor leader.	Better than level 1 and some of level 3.	**Performance is acceptable:** Individual basically meets the performance standard for leadership. Is considered to be a capable leader.	All of level 3 and some of level 5.	**Performance is superior:** Individual consistently exceeds the performance standard for leadership. Is considered a role model for leadership.
• Does not fully understand the key business processes of the unit		• Understands the key business processes of the unit		• Understands the business processes of the unit in great detail
• Does not tolerate or care for customers well; consistently disregards the needs of customers		• Is customer-driven and promotes customer-focused values throughout the unit – Demonstrates a commitment to the principles of customer satisfaction – Develops systems to understand customer requirements, strengthen customer relationships, resolve customer problems and prevent them from happening again, and obtain information about customer satisfaction and dissatisfaction		• Is customer-driven and actively promotes customer-focused values throughout the unit – Demonstrates a firm commitment to the principles of customer satisfaction – Develops effective systems to understand customer requirements, strengthen loyalty and customer relationships, resolve customer problems immediately and prevent them from happening again, and obtain timely information about customer satisfaction and dissatisfaction – Advocates the needs of customers through the collection and use of information on customer satisfaction, dissatisfaction, and product performance

Performance Excellence Standards Table

Level 1	Level 2	Level 3	Level 4	Level 5
Performance is unsatisfactory: Individual frequently fails to meet the performance standard for leadership. Is considered a poor leader.	Better than level 1 and some of level 3.	Performance is acceptable: Individual basically meets the performance standard for leadership. Is considered to be a capable leader.	All of level 3 and some of level 5.	Performance is superior: Individual consistently exceeds the performance standard for leadership. Is considered a role model for leadership.
• Does not understand and has not taken steps to implement performance excellence (may even work against the changes needed) − Intuition, not data or facts, tends to dominate decision making − Organizational goals and actions are not aligned to actions within the unit − May measure and monitor some performance outcomes (such as budget tracking) but most measures are not aligned to organizational goals		• Personally uses many performance excellence principles and tools for decision making and planning − Visibly supports performance excellence within the organization − Usually uses data and facts to drive decisions and ensures that many workers and subordinate managers do the same − Ensures that key organizational goals are converted to appropriate action to align most work within the organizational unit − Most goals and actions have defined measures of progress and time lines for achieving desired results		• Personally uses performance excellence principles and tools for decision making and planning − Serves as a performance excellence champion within the organization and as a resource within the work unit, providing guidance, counsel, and instruction in performance excellence tools, processes, and principles − Is a role model for using data and facts to drive decisions and ensures that workers and subordinate managers do the same − Ensures that all organizational goals are converted to appropriate actions to align nearly all work within the organizational unit − Defines measures of progress and time lines for achieving desired results for each goal and action

Insights to Performance Excellence

Performance Excellence Standards Table

Level 1	Level 2	Level 3	Level 4	Level 5
Performance is unsatisfactory: Individual frequently fails to meet the performance standard for leadership. Is considered a poor leader.	Better than level 1 and some of level 3.	**Performance is acceptable: Individual basically meets the performance standard for leadership. Is considered to be a capable leader.**	All of level 3 and some of level 5.	**Performance is superior: Individual consistently exceeds the performance standard for leadership. Is considered a role model for leadership.**
• Does not effectively promote workforce engagement, motivation, and morale – Tends to micromanage; does not delegate decision-making authority to the lower levels except as directly instructed to do so – Rarely listens to workers or cares what they think – Does not consistently promote flexibility and individual initiative – Does not consistently encourage and support the personal and professional development of self and employees – May send workers to training but does not consistently reinforce the use of new skills on the job – Has not taken effective steps to ensure compensation and other rewards or recognition are aligned to support business strategies and actions – Reward and recognition are not aligned to support organizational goals or the principles of performance excellence or customer satisfaction		• Demonstrates some commitment to the principles of employee empowerment and satisfaction. Is well-regarded by employees for: – Involving the workforce in identifying improvement opportunities and developing improvement plans – Valuing worker input on work-related matters – Promoting flexibility and individual initiative and ensuring that many subordinate managers do the same – Encouraging and supporting the personal and professional development of self and workers – Supporting effective training and reinforcing the use of new skills on the job – Ensuring compensation is aligned to support business strategies and actions – Rewarding and recognizing workers who incorporate the principles of performance excellence in their day-to-day work		• Demonstrates a firm commitment to the principles of workforce engagement and satisfaction. Is highly regarded by employees for: – Involving the workforce in setting standards of performance, identifying improvement opportunities, and developing improvement plans – Seeking and valuing worker input on work-related matters – Promoting flexibility and individual initiative and ensuring that subordinate managers do the same – Encouraging and supporting the personal and professional development of self and workers – Supporting effective training and reinforcing the use of new skills on the job – Ensuring compensation is aligned to support business strategies and actions – Rewarding and recognizing workers who incorporate the principles of performance excellence in their day-to-day work

Performance Excellence Standards Table

Level 1	Level 2	Level 3	Level 4	Level 5
Performance is unsatisfactory: Individual frequently fails to meet the performance standard for leadership. Is considered a poor leader.	Better than level 1 and some of level 3.	**Performance is acceptable:** Individual basically meets the performance standard for leadership. Is considered to be a capable leader.	All of level 3 and some of level 5.	**Performance is superior:** Individual consistently exceeds the performance standard for leadership. Is considered a role model for leadership.
• Does not communicate effectively or foster an atmosphere of knowledge-sharing among workers and business units		• Fosters an atmosphere of open, honest communication and knowledge sharing among workers and business units throughout the organization		• Fosters an atmosphere of open, honest communication and knowledge sharing among workers and business units throughout the organization – Checks the effectiveness of nearly all communication and makes changes to improve
• Does not regularly assess or improve work processes, including his or her personal effectiveness as a leader		• Visibly drives continuous improvement of many work processes, including personal effectiveness as a leader		• Rigorously drives the systematic, continuous improvement of all work processes, including personal effectiveness as a leader – Develops personal action plan and always incorporates results of 360-degree feedback to continuously improve personal leadership effectiveness and ensures subordinate managers do the same
• Does not achieve consistently improving performance outcomes in customer satisfaction; workforce engagement, motivation, and satisfaction; operational excellence; and financial (cost/budget) performance		• Achieves consistently improving performance outcomes in customer satisfaction; workforce engagement, motivation, and satisfaction; operational excellence; and financial (cost/budget) performance – The levels of performance outcomes are better than average when compared with organizations providing similar programs, products, or services		• Achieves consistently improving performance outcomes in customer satisfaction; workforce engagement, development, motivation, and satisfaction; operational excellence; and financial (cost/budget) performance – The levels of performance outcomes are among the highest in the organization/nation/state and are also high when compared with organizations providing similar programs, products, or services

Lessons Learned Conclusions

Successful leaders will create a customer focus and a context for action at all levels of the organization. Effective leaders will distribute authority and decision making to all levels of the organization. Nearly instantaneous, two-way communication will permit clear strategies, measurable outcome-oriented objectives, and priorities to be identified and deployed organization-wide. Problems will be identified and resolved with similar speed. Success in this environment will demand different skills of employees and managers. Unless all managers and employees understand where the organization is going and what must be done to beat the competition, it will be difficult for them to make effective decisions consistent with overall direction and strategy. If employees at all levels are not involved in decision making, organizational effectiveness is reduced—making it more difficult to win in a highly competitive arena.

In closing this section, I would like to suggest that the scenario previously described is already happening today among the world's best-performing organizations.

- These organizations have effective leadership at all levels, with a clear strategy focused on maximizing customer value. Middle-level managers support, rather than block, the values and direction of the top leaders.

- They have developed ways to challenge themselves and improve their own processes when doing so promotes customer value and improves operating effectiveness.

- They engage workers fully and promote organizational and personal learning at all levels. They ensure that knowledge is shared within the organization to avoid duplication of effort.

- They have created effective data systems to enhance decision making at all levels.

- They have developed and aligned reward, recognition, compensation, and incentives to support the desired customer-focused behavior among all leaders, managers, and employees.

- They have found ways to design effective work processes and ensure that those processes are executed consistently and improved continuously.

- They closely monitor their performance and the performance of their principal competitors. They use this information to adjust their goals/objectives and their work and they continue to improve faster than ever.

These organizations are among the best in the world at what they do and they will continue to win, as long as they continue to apply the current principles of performance excellence.

AWARD CRITERIA FRAMEWORK

Organizations must position themselves to respond well to the environment within which they compete. They must understand and manage threats and vulnerabilities as well as capitalize on their strengths and opportunities, including the vulnerabilities of competitors. These factors guide strategy development, support operational decisions, and align measures and actions—all of which must be done well for the organization to succeed. Consistent with this overarching purpose, the Award Criteria contain the following basic elements: Driver Triad, Work Core, Brain Center, and Results/Outcomes (Figure 14).

The Driver Triad

The Driver Triad (Figure 15) consists of the categories of Leadership, Strategic Planning, and Customer Focus. Leaders use these processes to set direction and goals, monitor progress, make resource decisions, and take corrective action when progress is not achieved according to plan. The processes that make up the Driver Triad require leaders to set direction and expectations for the organization to meet customer requirements and fully empower the workforce (Category 1), provide the vehicle for determining the short- and long-term strategies for success as well as communicating and aligning the organization's work (Category 2), and produce information about critical customer requirements and levels of satisfaction and strengthen customer relations and loyalty (Category 3).

The Work Core

The Work Core (Figure 16) describes the processes through which the primary work of the organization takes place and consists of Workforce Focus (Category 5) and Process Management (Category 6). These Categories recognize that the people of an organization are responsible for doing the work. To achieve peak performance, these people must possess the right skills and must be allowed to work in an environment that promotes initiative and self-direction. The work processes provide the structure for continuous learning and improvement to optimize performance.

Results/Outcomes

The processes defined by the Driver Triad, Work Core, and Brain Center produce the Results (Category 7).

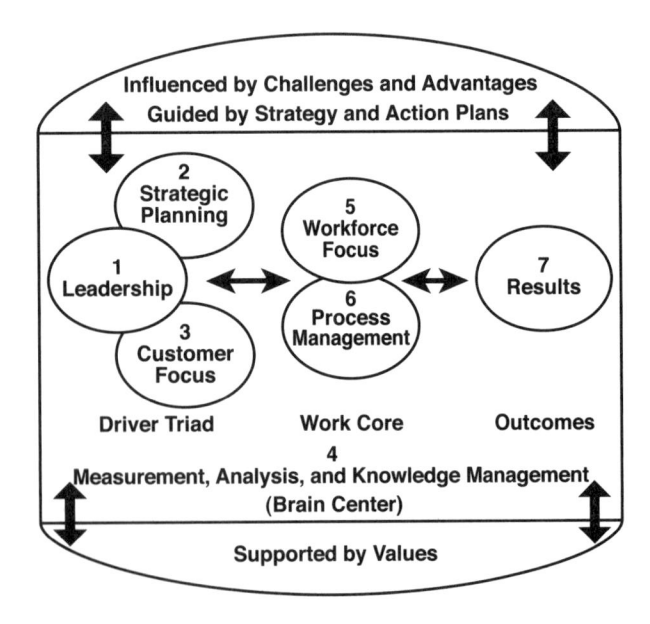

Figure 14 Performance excellence framework.

Figure 15 Driver Triad.

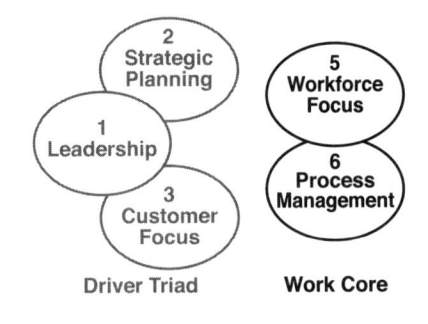

Figure 16 Work Core.

Insights to Performance Excellence

Results (Figure 17) reflect the organization's actual performance and serve as the basis for leaders to monitor progress against goals and make adjustments to increase performance. These Results include customer focus, financial and market performance, workforce performance, and internal operating effectiveness.

Brain Center

Measurement, Analysis, and Knowledge Manage-Ment (Category 4) provides data and analyses to support decision making at all levels. These processes (Figure 18) capture, store, analyze, and retrieve information and data critical to the effective management of the organization and to a fact-based system for improving organization performance and competitiveness. Rapid access to reliable data and information systems is especially critical to enhance effective decision making in an increasingly complex, fast-paced, global competitive environment.

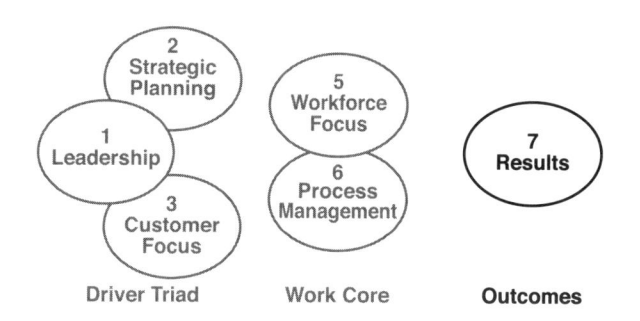

Figure 17 Outcomes.

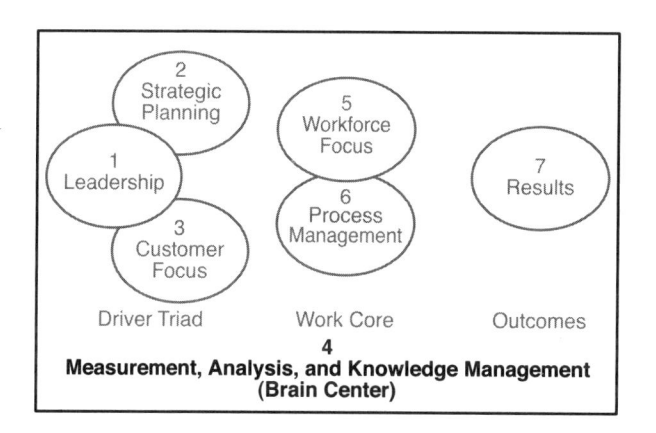

Figure 18 Measurement, Analysis, and Knowledge Management (the Brain Center).

Core Values and Concepts

The core values and concepts support the beliefs and behaviors of high-performing organizations (Figure 19). These values provide the foundation for integrating and aligning work processes in high-performing organizations.

Measurement, Analysis, and Knowledge Management is also called the Brain Center of an effective management system.

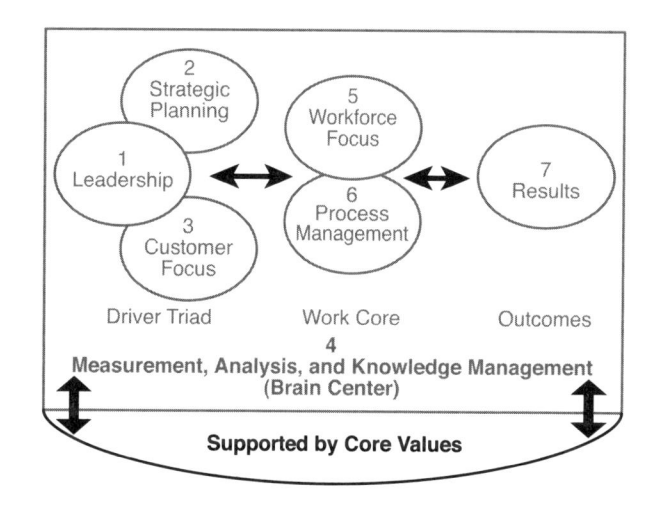

Figure 19 Core Values and Concepts.

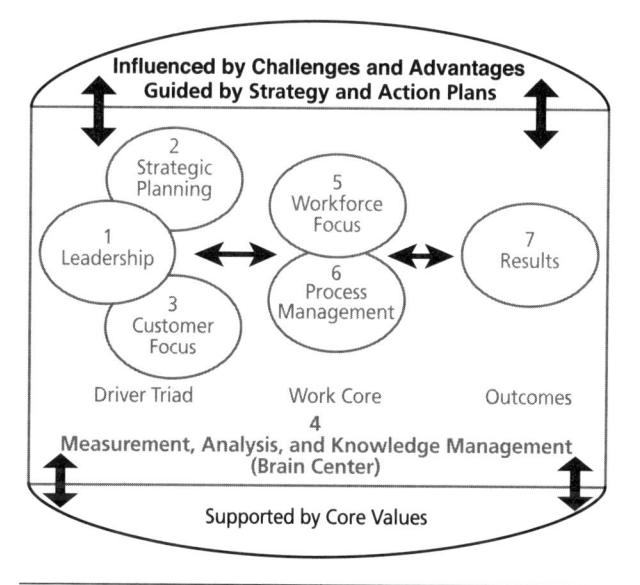

Figure 20 Guide decision making.

Guided by Strategy and Action Plans

Organizations develop effective strategic plans that are influenced by strategic challenges and advantages (including core competencies). This information helps set the direction necessary to achieve future success. Unfortunately, these plans are not always communicated and used to drive actions and the direction is not always focused. The planning process and the resulting strategy are virtually worthless if the organization does not use the plan and strategy to guide decision making at all levels of the organization (Figure 20).

When decisions are not guided by strategy, managers and other members of the workforce tend to substitute their own ideas for the correct direction. This frequently causes teams, individuals, and whole business units to work at cross-purposes, suboptimizing performance and making it more difficult for the organization to achieve desired results.

Taken together, these processes define the essential ingredients of a complex, integrated management system designed to promote and deliver performance excellence. If any part of the system is missing, the performance results suffer. If fully implemented, these processes are sufficient to enable organizations to achieve winning performance.

Award Criteria Organization

Categories

The seven Criteria Categories are subdivided into Items and Areas to Address. Figure 21 demonstrates the organization of Category 1.

Items

There are 18 Items, each focusing on a major requirement.

Areas to Address

Items consist of one or more Areas to Address (Areas). Applicants submit information in response to the specific requirements of these Areas. There are 36 Areas to Address.

Subparts

There are 82 subparts in the 2009–2010 Criteria, not counting the Organizational Profile. Areas consist of one or more subparts, where numbers are shown in parentheses. A response should be made to each subpart.

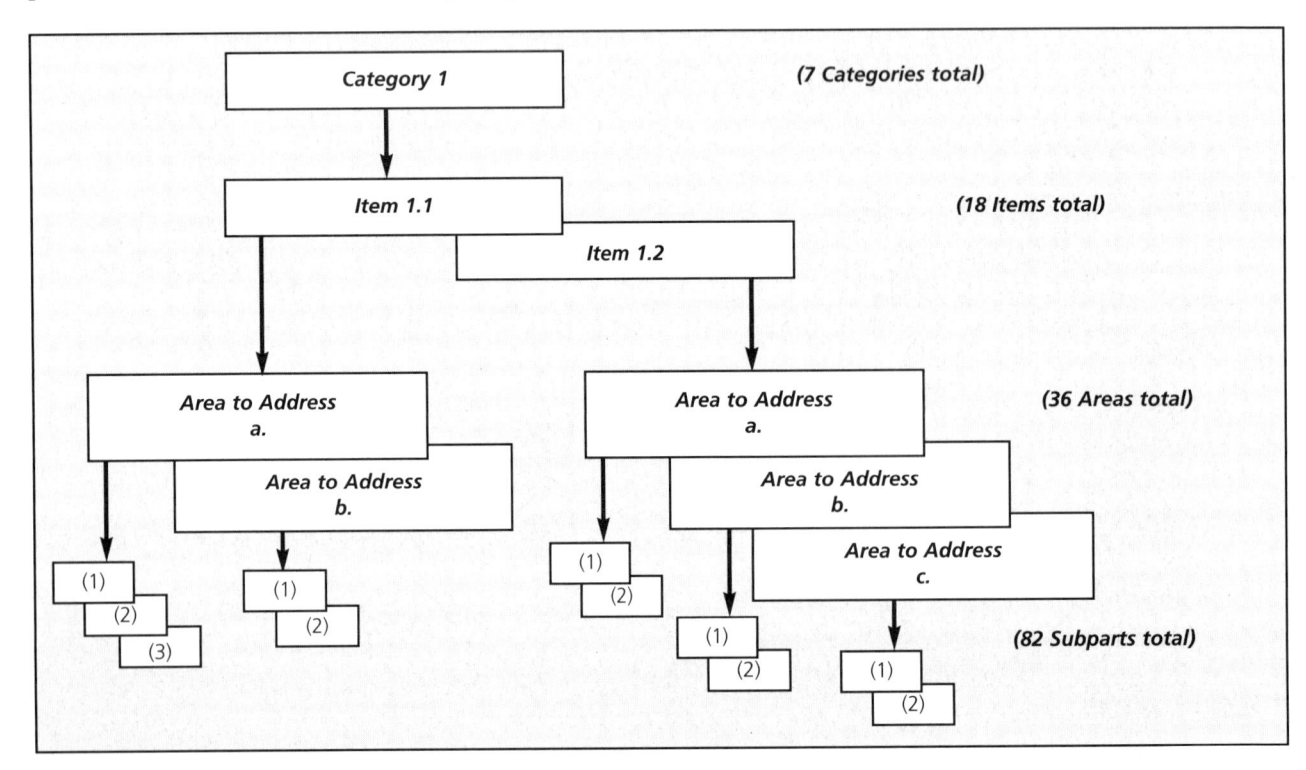

Figure 21 Organization of Category 1.

BALDRIGE AWARD CATEGORIES AND POINT VALUES

Examination Categories/Items	Maximum Points
Preface Organizational Profile	**(0 points)**
P.1 Organizational Description	0
P.2 Organizational Situation	0
1 Leadership	**(120 points)**
1.1 Senior Leadership	70
1.2 Governance and Societal Responsibilities	50
2 Strategic Planning	**(85 points)**
2.1 Strategy Development	40
2.2 Strategy Deployment	45
3 Customer Focus	**(85 points)**
3.1 Customer Engagement	40
3.2 Voice of the Customer	45
4 Measurement, Analysis, and Knowledge Management	**(90 points)**
4.1 Measurement, Analysis, and Improvement of Organizational Performance	45
4.2 Management of Information, Knowledge, and Information Technology	45
5 Workforce Focus	**(85 points)**
5.1 Workforce Engagement	45
5.2 Workforce Environment	40
6 Process Management	**(85 points)**
6.1 Work Systems	35
6.2 Work Processes	50
7 Results	**(450 points)**
7.1 Product Outcomes	100
7.2 Customer-Focused Outcomes	70
7.3 Financial and Market Outcomes	70
7.4 Workforce-Focused Outcomes	70
7.5 Process Effectiveness Outcomes	70
7.6 Leadership Outcomes	70
Total Points	**1000**

Notes

If a Note indicates the process *should* include something, examiners will interpret it as a requirement. If a Note indicates that the process *might* include something, examiners shall not treat the list as a requirement—only as an example. There are 69 Notes, not counting the Organizational Profile. A number of Items have Notes that provide additional guidance specifically for nonprofit organizations. These nonprofit-specific Notes appear at the end of the Item in *italics*.

KEY CHARACTERISTICS—2009–2010 PERFORMANCE EXCELLENCE CRITERIA

The Criteria focus on organizational performance results and the processes required to achieve them. Results are a composite of the following organizational performance areas:

- Product outcomes
- Customer-focused outcomes
- Financial and market outcomes
- Workforce-focused outcomes
- Process effectiveness outcomes, including key internal operational results
- Leadership outcomes, including governance and societal responsibility results

The use of this composite of indicators is intended to ensure that strategies are balanced—that they do not inappropriately trade off among important stakeholders, objectives, or short- and longer-term goals.

These results areas cover overall organization performance, including financial performance. The results areas also recognize the importance of suppliers and of community and national well-being.

The Criteria *do not* prescribe that the organization should or should not have any particular functions, such as departments for quality, planning, or personnel. The Criteria do not prescribe how the organization should be structured or how different units in the organization should be managed. These factors differ among organizations, and they are likely to change within an organization over time as needs and strategies evolve. The Criteria are nonprescriptive for the following reasons:

- The focus is on results, not on procedures, tools, or organizational structure. Organizations are encouraged to develop and demonstrate creative, adaptive, and flexible approaches for meeting requirements. Nonprescriptive requirements are intended to foster incremental and major ("breakthrough") improvements, which may lead to innovation.

- The selection of tools, techniques, systems, and organizational structure usually depends on factors such as business type and size, organizational relationships, the organization's stage of development, and workforce capabilities and responsibilities.

- A focus on common requirements, rather than on common procedures, fosters better understanding, communication, sharing, alignment, and integration, while supporting diversity and innovation in approaches.

The Criteria support a systems approach to maintaining organization-wide goal alignment. The systems approach to goal alignment is embedded in the integrated structure of the Core Values and Concepts, the Organizational Profile, the Criteria, the Scoring Guidelines, and the results-oriented, cause–effect linkages among the Criteria parts.

Alignment in the Criteria is built around connecting and reinforcing measures derived from the organization's processes and strategy. The measures in the Criteria tie directly to customer and stakeholder value and to overall performance that relate to key internal and external requirements of the organization. Measures serve both as a communications tool and a basis for deploying consistent performance requirements. Such alignment ensures consistency of purpose while at the same time supports speed, innovation, and decentralized decision making.

Learning Cycles and Continuous Improvement

In high-performing organizations, action-oriented learning takes place through feedback between processes and results facilitated by learning or continuous improvement cycles. The learning cycles have four clearly defined and well-established stages (Figure 22).

1. Plan—plan, including design of processes, selection of measures, and deployment of requirements
2. Do—execute plans
3. Study/Check—assess progress, taking into account internal and external results
4. Act—revise plans based on assessment findings, learning, new inputs, new requirements, and opportunities for innovation

Goal-Based Diagnosis

The Criteria and the Scoring Guidelines are the two elements that combine to make the diagnostic tool, which is part of a developmental assessment. A developmental assessment, unlike a compliance review, seeks to determine how advanced an organization is and then identify the vital few processes that need to be developed to move to the next higher level. The basic systems must be in place before they can be refined and enhanced. In a compliance review, on the other hand, all conditions or requirements must be met or the organization is *out of compliance* and may not be certified or registered. By design, compliance reviews audit against a set of minimum standards. A developmental review, such as that provided through the Baldrige Criteria, identifies continuous improvement opportunities to help the organization achieve best-in-class performance—to excel and win.

This diagnostic assessment is a useful management tool that goes beyond most performance reviews and is applicable to a variety of organizations and a wide range of strategies and management systems.

Changes from the 2008 Criteria

The Criteria for Performance Excellence continue to evolve to help senior leaders and their organizations address the dynamic environment, focus on strategy-driven performance, ensure good governance and ethics, and arrive at the key decisions driving both short-term success and long-term organizational sustainability. The Criteria continue to reinforce a comprehensive, integrated systems perspective of overall organizational performance management.

Changes over the 20 years of the Baldrige Program have been revolutionary as well—changing from a specific focus on manufacturing quality to a comprehensive strategic focus on overall organizational competitiveness and sustainability. Each year, the decision to revise the Criteria must balance two important considerations: (1) a need for Criteria that are at the leading edge of validated management practice to help users address the increasingly complex challenges they face; and (2) a desire for the Criteria to remain stable so users have continuity in their performance assessments. The 2008 Criteria contained minimal revisions, after they were significantly revised in 2007. In the ongoing efforts to balance stakeholders' needs for both currency and stability, starting in 2009, the Program will have a formal two-year revision cycle. Therefore, this current iteration becomes the 2009–2010 Criteria for Performance Excellence.

The most significant revisions in the 2009–2010 Criteria address three areas of importance: (1) customer focus, (2) organizational core competencies, and (3) sustainability and societal responsibilities.

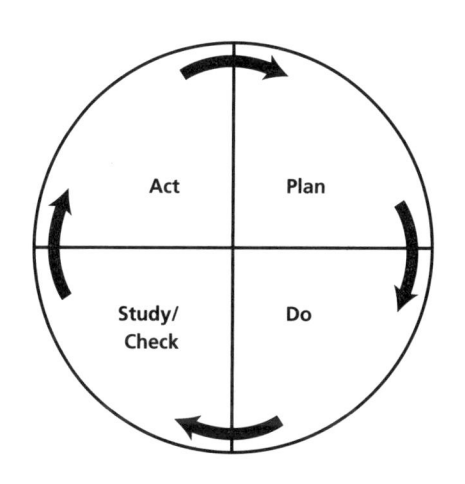

Figure 22 Continuous improvement cycle.

The concept of customer engagement has received increasing attention as organizations compete in a global marketplace and in competitive local markets. The Criteria questions probe the organization's ability to identify and deliver relevant product offerings to customers now and in the future. The questions ask about the organization's customer culture and how it contributes to customer engagement. The questions probe how the organization listens to the voice of the customer and, more importantly, how the information is used.

While core competencies were introduced as an important concept in the 2007 Baldrige Criteria, their strategic significance was not fully exploited. The Criteria questions now probe the relationship of core competencies to the organization's mission, strategy, and sustainability. Is the organization competent in the areas that will deliver its sustainability?

Leading organizations are paying increased attention to the sustainability of their environmental, social, and economic systems. The Criteria questions probe how the organization contributes to the well-being of these systems and what specific contributions have been. Is the organization fulfilling its societal responsibilities?

Substantive changes in the Criteria between 2008 and 2009 occurred in all items and are summarized as follows:

- The Preface: Organizational Profile now includes core competencies as a key characteristic of the organizational environment.
  - Item P.1, Organizational Description, now includes a question related to the organization's core competencies and their relation to the organization's mission.
    - "Products and services" in 2008 were changed to "product offerings" in 2009. However, the definition and Note 1 for P.1 define "product offerings" as "goods and services." Accordingly, the 2009 "product offerings" is virtually the same as the 2008 "products and services." A product such as a cup of coffee and the service provided by the vendor to deliver the coffee constitute the "product offering."
    - The requirement to define key supplier and customer partnering communication mechanisms [P.1b(4)] has been dropped from the Organizational Profile. Customer relationships and communication mechanisms are a multiple-level process requirement in Item 3.1a(2) where it is considered in scoring.
  - Item P.2, formerly Organizational Challenges, has been re-titled Organizational Situation to more accurately reflect the broad focus of this Item.

- Category 1, Leadership, includes an enhanced focus on sustainability and societal responsibilities and the senior leaders' role.
  - Item 1.1, Senior Leadership, requires senior leaders to enhance their personal leadership skills and participate in organizational learning.
  - Item 1.2, now Governance and Societal Responsibilities, has an enhanced focus on societal responsibilities. These responsibilities include conserving natural resources; assuming responsibility for suppliers' actions; and considering the well-being of environmental, social, and economic systems to which the organization contributes.

- Category 2, Strategic Planning, requires core competencies to be addressed as part of a strengths, weaknesses, opportunities, threats (SWOT) analysis and a description of how core competencies, strategic challenges, and strategic advantages are determined.
  - Item 2.1a(1, 2), Strategy Development, requires core competencies to be addressed as a key component of strategy development and organizational sustainability.
    - Strategic objectives [2.1b(2)] must address current and future core competencies.
  - Item 2.2, Strategy Deployment, requires the deployment of action plans to key suppliers and partners.

Numerous numbering changes were made to restructure Item 2.2 as follows:

2009	2008
2.2a(1)	2.2a(4)
2.2a(2)	2.2a(1)
2.2a(3)	2.2a(2) deleted in 2009 is the requirement to provide "adequate" resources and "Balanced" resources
2.2a(4)	2.2a(3)
2.2a(6)	2.2a(6) now requires tracking achievement and effectiveness of action plans; formerly required "tracking progress."
2.2b	2.2b deleted "How do you ensure progress to meet projections?"

- Category 3, Customer Focus, was redesigned around customer engagement and the voice of the customer. The Category has two new Items and many requirements from the 2008 Items have been redistributed within the new Category 3.

   – Item 3.1, now Customer Engagement, asks how customers are engaged to serve their needs and build relationships. It has two Areas to Address: (1) Product Offerings and Customer Support, and (2) Building a Customer Culture. Product offerings include goods and services. Customer support considers the processes for determining customer support requirements (similar to customer-contact requirements in 2008). Item 3.1b requires the use of workforce management tools [5.1a(3)] and workforce and leader development [5.1b(1, 2)] to reinforce a customer culture.

   – Item 3.2, now Voice of the Customer, asks how information from customers is obtained and used. It has three new Areas to Address: (1) Customer Listening (including complaint resolution and aggregation of complaint data for use in driving improvements), (2) Determination of Customer Satisfaction and Engagement, and (3) Analysis and Use of Customer Data to identify and anticipate customer requirements (including products and product features) and changing expectations and their relative importance to purchasing or relationship decisions (part of 3.1a(2) in 2008)

♦ Many changes between 2008 and 2009 were made in Category 3 at the detailed, multiple-requirement level. *Generally,* the following table shows the location of these requirements in 2009 versus 2008:

2009	2008
3.1a(1)	3.1a(2)
3.1a(2)	3.2a(2)
3.1a(3)	3.1b(4)
3.1b(1)	—
3.1b(2)	3.2a(1)
3.1b(3)	3.1b(4)
3.2a(1)	3.1b(2); 3.1a(2)
3.2a(2)	3.1a(2); 3.2a(2)
3.2a(3)	3.2a(3)
3.2b(1) (engaged new)	3.2b(1); 3.2a(3)
3.2b(2)	3.2b(3)
3.2b(3)	3.2b(3)
3.2c(1)	3.1a(1)
3.2c(2)	3.1a(2)
3.2c(3)	3.1a(3)

- Category 4, Measurement, Analysis, and Knowledge Management, clearly separates but emphasizes both the importance of information and knowledge management and the management of information technology and systems.

  – Item 4.1, Measurement, Analysis, and Improvement of Organizational Performance, now includes a separate Area to Address on Performance Improvement, but the requirement in 2008, 4.1b(3) to "incorporate the results of organizational performance reviews into the systematic evaluation of key processes" has moved to 6.2c.

  – Item 4.2, now Management of Information, Knowledge, and Information Technology, clarifies which Criteria requirements are related to information technology by including the term in the title of the second Area to Address, Management of Information Resources and Technology. Substantial movement of multiple-level Criteria requirements occurred in Item 4.2 between 2009 and 2008 as the following table summarizes:

2009	2008
4.2a(1)	4.2b(1)
4.2a(2)	4.2a(1)
4.2a(3)	4.2b(2)
4.2b(1)	4.2a(2)
4.2b(2)	4.2a(3)
4.2b(3)	4.2a(4)

- Category 5, Workforce Focus, was simplified to add clarity and focus to important aspects of workforce engagement.

  – Item 5.1, Workforce Engagement, still has three Areas to Address, but the number of questions in the multiple requirements was reduced to simplify and focus the requirements. Much of 5.1a(2) was eliminated, such as cooperation, skill sharing, information flow and two-way communication, and individual goal setting, empowerment, initiative, and innovation, which are all embedded as part of engagement.

- Category 6, Process Management, was reorganized for a more logical flow of the questions.

  – Item 6.1, Work Systems, was modified for a more logical flow of the questions. The three Areas to Address are now (1) Work Systems Design, (2) Key Work Processes, and (3) Emergency Readiness.

    ◆ The 2008 requirement to determine core competencies is now a part of 2.1a(1)

  – Item 6.2, now Work Processes, has three Areas to Address: (1) Work Process Design, (2) Work Process Management, and (3) Work Process Improvement. Work Process Improvement includes a question about how the results of organizational performance reviews are incorporated into the improvement of work processes, which was listed in 4.1b(3) in 2008.

- Category 7, Results, was aligned with changes in Categories 1–6 to encourage measurement of important and appropriate results.

  – Item 7.2, Customer-Focused Outcomes, is aligned with the revised Category 3, asking for results related to customer engagement.

  – Item 7.6, Leadership Outcomes, now includes a question about results for fulfillment of societal responsibilities.

- The Core Value previously related to social responsibility was re-titled and rewritten to reflect the larger sustainability concepts embodied in societal responsibility.

- Three terms were added to the Glossary of Key Terms: customer engagement, voice of the customer, and work processes. In addition, the definition of sustainability was expanded to reflect societal aspects of organizational sustainability.

- The Results Scoring Guidelines were modified to specifically address performance projection expectations in each scoring range. Also, performance projections were included in the sample results figure presented in the Guidelines for Responding to Results Items.

Organizational Profile

The **Organizational Profile** *is a snapshot of your organization, the key influences on how you operate, and the key challenges you face.*

IMPORTANCE OF THE ORGANIZATIONAL PROFILE

The Organizational Profile is critically important because:

- It is the most appropriate starting point for self-assessment in preparation for strategic planning and for writing an application.

- It helps identify potential gaps in key information and focus on key performance requirements and business results.

- It is used by the examiners and judges in all stages of application review, including the site visit, to understand the organization and what it considers important. It sets the context for the assessment.

- It may be used by itself for an initial self-assessment. By identifying topics for which conflicting, little, or no information is available, it is possible that the assessment need go no further and these topics can be used for action planning.

P.1 ORGANIZATIONAL DESCRIPTION: What are your key organizational characteristics?

Describe your organization's operating environment and your key relationships with customers, suppliers, partners, and stakeholders.

Within your response, include answers to the following questions:

a. **Organizational Environment**

(1) What are your organization's main product offerings (see Note 1 below)? What are the delivery mechanisms used to provide your products to your customers?

(2) What are the key characteristics of your organizational culture? What are your stated purpose, vision, values, and mission? What are your organization's core competencies and their relationship to your mission?

(3) What is your workforce profile? What are your workforce or employee groups and segments? What are their education levels? What are the key factors that motivate them to engage in accomplishing your mission? What are your organization's workforce and job diversity, organized bargaining units, key benefits, and special health and safety requirements?

(4) What are your major facilities, technologies, and equipment?

(5) What is the regulatory environment under which your organization operates? What are the applicable occupational health and safety regulations; accreditation, certification, or registration requirements; relevant industry standards; and environmental, financial, and product regulations?

b. **Organizational Relationships**

(1) What are your organizational structure and governance system? What are the reporting relationships among your governance board, senior leaders, and parent organization, as appropriate?

(2) What are your key market segments, customer groups, and stakeholder groups, as appropriate? What are their key requirements and expectations for your products, customer support services, and operations? What are the differences in these requirements and expectations among market segments, customer groups, and stakeholder groups?

(3) What are your key types of suppliers, partners, and collaborators? What role do these suppliers, partners, and collaborators play in your work systems and the production and delivery of your key products and customer support services? What are your key mechanisms for communicating and managing relationships with suppliers, partners, and collaborators? What role, if any, do these organizations play in your organizational innovation processes? What are your key supply chain requirements?

Notes:

N1. "Product offerings" and "products" (P.1a[1]) refer to the goods and services that your organization offers in the marketplace. Mechanisms for product delivery to your end-use customers might be direct or through dealers, distributors, collaborators, or channel partners. *Nonprofit organizations might refer to their product offerings as programs, projects, or services.*

N2. "Core competencies" (P.1a[2]) refers to your organization's areas of greatest expertise. Your organization's core competencies are those strategically important capabilities that are central to fulfilling your mission or provide an advantage in your marketplace or service environment. Core competencies frequently are challenging for competitors or suppliers and partners to imitate and provide a sustainable competitive advantage.

N3. Workforce or employee groups and segments (including organized bargaining units) (P.1a[3]) might be based on the type of employment or contract reporting relationship, location, tour of duty, work environment, family-friendly policies, or other factors.

Continued

Notes: *Continued*

N4. Customer groups (P.1b[2]) might be based on common expectations, behaviors, preferences, or profiles. Within a group there may be customer segments based on differences and commonalities within the group. Your markets might be subdivided into market segments based on product lines or features, distribution channels, business volume, geography, or other factors that your organization uses to define related market characteristics.

N5. Customer group and market segment requirements (P.1b[2]) might include on-time delivery, low defect levels, safety, security, ongoing price reductions, electronic communication, rapid response, after-sales service, and multilingual services. Stakeholder group requirements might include socially responsible behavior and community service. *For some nonprofit organizations, requirements also might include administrative cost reductions, at-home services, and rapid response to emergencies.*

N6. Communication mechanisms (P.1b[3]) should be two-way and in understandable language, and they might be in person, via e-mail, Web-based, or by telephone. For many organizations, these mechanisms may change as marketplace, customer, or stakeholder requirements change.

N7. *Customers (P.1a[1]) include the users and potential users of your products. In some nonprofit organizations, customers might include members, taxpayers, citizens, recipients, clients, and beneficiaries. Market segments might be referred to as constituencies.*

N8. *Many nonprofit organizations rely heavily on volunteers to accomplish their work. These organizations should include volunteers in the discussion of their workforce (P.1a[3]).*

N9. *For nonprofit organizations, relevant industry standards (P.1a[5]) might include industrywide codes of conduct and policy guidance. The term "industry" is used throughout the Criteria to refer to the sector in which you operate. For nonprofit organizations, this sector might be charitable organizations, professional associations and societies, religious organizations, or government entities—or a subsector of one of these.*

N10. *For some nonprofit organizations, governance and reporting relationships (P.1b[1]) might include relationships with major agency, foundation, or other funding sources.*

P.1 Key Organizational Description Item Linkages

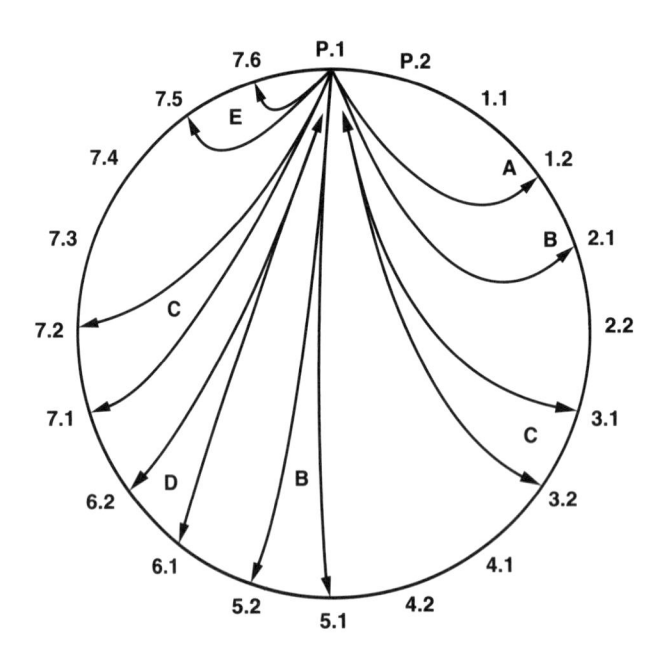

	NATURE OF RELATIONSHIP
A	The organizational structure and governance system described in P.1b(1) set the context for the review of the management systems for proper governance [1.2a(1)] and ethical behavior [1.2b(2)]. The regulatory environment described in P.1a(5) sets the context for the review of the management systems for public responsibility and should help define compliance processes and help define measures and goals. [1.2b(1)].
B	Workforce educational levels, diversity, and other characteristics [P.1a(3)] may affect the determination of human resource strengths and weaknesses as a part of the strategic planning process [2.1a(2)] and the development of key human resource plans [2.2a(5)]. Employee characteristics such as educational levels, workforce and job diversity, the existence of bargaining units, the use of contract employees, and other special requirements help set the context for determining the requirements for knowledge and skill sharing across work units, jobs, and locations [5.1a(2)], determining appropriate needs by workforce segment for building capacity and capability [5.2a(1)], leader and worker development [5.1b(1, 2)], and tailoring benefits, services, and satisfaction assessment methods for the workforce according to various types of categories [5.2b(2)].
C	The customer and market groups and their requirements reported in P.1b(2) should have been determined in 3.1a. The information in P.1b(2) helps examiners identify the kind of results, broken out by customer and market segment, that should be reported in Items 7.1 and 7.2. The product offerings that form the basis for customer support in 3.1a are described in P.1a(1). Product offerings also help determine the focus of customer listening [3.2a] and customer satisfaction and engagement [3.2b].
D	The information in P.1a(1) derives from the core competencies, work systems, and key work processes described in 6.1 and 6.2. This information helps set the context for the examiner review of those processes.
E	The regulatory and related requirements described in P.1a(5), and the key suppliers and dealers/distributors listed in P.1b(3) create an expectation that related performance results will be reported in 7.6a(4) and 7.5a(2) respectively (which should be consistent with the measures and goals in 1.2b(1)).

P.2 ORGANIZATIONAL SITUATION: What is your organization's strategic situation?

Describe your organization's competitive environment, your key strategic challenges and advantages, and your system for performance improvement.

Within your response, include answers to the following questions:

a. Competitive Environment

(1) What is your competitive position? What are your relative size and growth in your industry or markets served? What are the numbers and types of competitors for your organization?

(2) What are the principal factors that determine your success relative to your competitors? What are any key changes taking place that affect your competitive situation, including opportunities for innovation and collaboration, as appropriate?

(3) What are your key available sources of comparative and competitive data from within your industry? What are your key available sources of comparative data from outside your industry? What limitations, if any, are there in your ability to obtain these data?

b. Strategic Context

What are your key business, operational, and human resource strategic challenges and advantages? What are your key strategic challenges and advantages associated with organizational sustainability?

c. Performance Improvement System

What are the key elements of your performance improvement system, including your evaluation, organizational learning, and innovation processes?

Notes:

N1. Principal factors (P.2a[2]) might include differentiators such as your price leadership, design services, innovation rate, geographic proximity, accessibility, and warranty and product options. *For some nonprofit organizations, differentiators also might include your relative influence with decision makers, ratio of administrative costs to programmatic contributions, reputation for program or service delivery, and wait times for service.*

N2. Strategic challenges and advantages (P.2b) might relate to technology, products, your operations, your customer support, your industry, globalization, your value chain, and people.

N3. Performance improvement (P.2c) is an assessment dimension used in the Scoring System to evaluate the maturity of organizational approaches and deployment. This question is intended to help you and the Baldrige Examiners set an overall context for your approach to performance improvement. Approaches to performance improvement that are compatible with the systems approach provided by the Baldrige framework might include implementing a Lean Enterprise System, applying Six Sigma methodology, using ISO 9000 standards, or employing other process improvement and innovation tools. A growing number of organizations have implemented specific processes for meeting goals in product and process innovation.

N4. *Nonprofit organizations frequently are in a very competitive environment; they often must compete with other organizations and with alternative sources for similar services to secure financial and volunteer resources, membership, visibility in appropriate communities, and media attention.*

N5. *For nonprofit organizations, the term "business" (P.2b) is used throughout the Criteria to refer to your main mission area or enterprise activity.*

Insights to Performance Excellence 2009–2010

P.2 Key Organizational Challenges Item Linkages

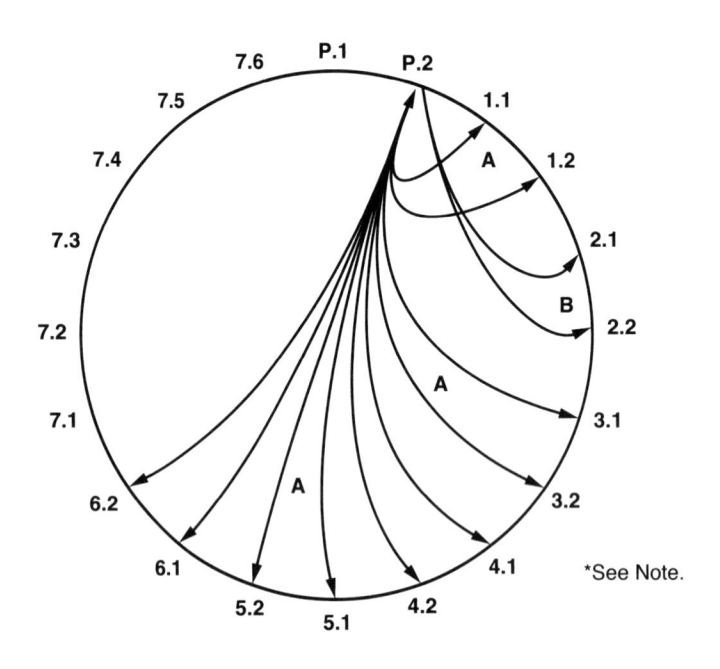

	NATURE OF RELATIONSHIP
A	Leaders [1.1a(3)] are responsible for creating an environment that drives organizational learning and sustainability, which contribute to the overall focus on performance improvement [P.2c(1)]. The overall approaches to systematic evaluation and improvement, organizational learning, and knowledge sharing identified in P.2c should be consistent with overall requirements for improvement specifically required in Items 1.2a(2) leadership effectiveness; 3.1a(3) improving customer support processes; 3.1b(3) improving customer-focused culture; 3.2c(4) improving approaches for customer listening and determining customer satisfaction, engagement, and dissatisfaction; 3.2b(4) improving processes to determine customer satisfaction; 4.1a(1, 2, 3) supporting innovation and keeping up with rapid or unexpected organizational or external changes; 4.2b(3) keeping data availability (including software and hardware) current, especially in a volatile work environment; 5.1b(1, 2) develop workers and leaders to strengthen organizational performance, technological change, and innovation; 5.1b(3) improving training and development; 5.2a(4) improving workforce capability and capacity; 5.2b(1) improving workforce health, safety, and security; and 6.2b and 6.2c improving work processes.
B	The competitive environment defined in P.2a should be examined as part of the strategy development process [2.1a(2)] and should help focus the projection of competitors' future performance in 2.2b. In addition, the strategic challenges and advantages identified in P.2b should be addressed by the strategic objectives in 2.1b(2).

*Note: To make the circle diagrams less cluttered, all of the links described in paragraph A will not be repeated on the other diagrams.

1 Leadership—120 Points

*The **Leadership** Category examines how your organization's senior leaders' personal actions guide and sustain your organization. Also examined are your organization's governance system and how your organization fulfills its legal, ethical, and societal responsibilities and supports its key communities.*

The leadership system must promote organizational core values, set performance expectations, and promote an organization-wide focus on stakeholders, customers, workforce engagement, empowerment, learning, and innovation. The Leadership Category looks at how senior leaders guide and sustain the organization; set directions and organizational vision, values, and performance expectations; enhance their personal leadership skills; participate in organizational learning and develop future leaders; measure organizational performance; and develop an environment that supports ethical behavior and high performance. Senior leaders must communicate clear values and performance expectations that address the needs of all stakeholders. The Category also looks at the how the organization practices effective governance, meets its legal, ethical, and societal responsibilities, and supports its key communities.

The Category contains two Items:

Senior Leadership

- Communicating and reinforcing clear values, performance expectations, and a focus on creating value for customers and other stakeholders.

- Reinforcing an environment for workforce engagement and innovation, and workforce and organizational learning.

- Maintaining a focus on action and a focus on creating a value for customers. (As a part of this focus, leaders drive customer engagement and a customer-focused culture—linked with 3.1 and 3.2.)

- Reviewing organizational performance and capabilities, competitiveness, and progress relative to goals to identify needed actions.

- Developing and enhancing the personal leadership skills of senior leaders.

Governance and Societal Responsibilities

- Providing effective governance that holds management accountable for the organization's actions, provides for fiscal accountability, and protects stockholder and stakeholder interests

- Ensuring accountability for management's actions, transparency in operations, and protecting stakeholder interests

- Evaluating the performance of senior leaders, the CEO, and the Board

- Evaluating and improving the effectiveness of management throughout the organization, including worker input in the process

- Addressing any adverse impacts on society caused by the organization's products, services, and operations

- Ensuring ethical business practices in all transactions

- Meeting legal, ethical, and societal responsibilities and supporting its key communities, such as improving the environment and strengthening community services, education, and health.

1.1 SENIOR LEADERSHIP: How do your senior leaders lead? (70 Pts.)   PROCESS

Describe how senior leaders' actions guide and sustain your organization. Describe how senior leaders communicate with your workforce and encourage high performance.

Within your response, include answers to the following questions:

a. Vision, Values, and Mission

(1) How do senior leaders set organizational vision and values? How do senior leaders deploy your organization's vision and values through your leadership system, to the workforce, to key suppliers and partners, and to customers and other stakeholders, as appropriate? How do senior leaders' personal actions reflect a commitment to the organization's values?

(2) How do senior leaders personally promote an organizational environment that fosters, requires, and results in legal and ethical behavior?

(3) How do senior leaders create a sustainable organization? How do they create an environment for organizational performance improvement, the accomplishment of your mission and strategic objectives, innovation, competitive or role-model performance leadership, and organizational agility? How do they create an environment for organizational and workforce learning? How do they develop and enhance their personal leadership skills? How do they participate in organizational learning, in succession planning, and in the development of future organizational leaders?

b. Communication and Organizational Performance

(1) How do senior leaders communicate with and engage the entire workforce? How do senior leaders encourage frank, two-way communication throughout the organization? How do senior leaders communicate key decisions? How do they take an active role in reward and recognition programs to reinforce high performance and a customer and business focus?

(2) How do senior leaders create a focus on action to accomplish the organization's objectives, improve performance, and attain its vision? What performance measures do senior leaders regularly review to identify needed actions? How do senior leaders include a focus on creating and balancing value for customers and other stakeholders in their organizational performance expectations?

Notes:

N1. Organizational vision [1.1a(1)] should set the context for strategic objectives and action plans, which are described in Items 2.1 and 2.2.

N2. A sustainable organization (1.1a[3]) is capable of addressing current business needs and possesses the agility and strategic management to prepare successfully for its future business and market environment. In this context, the concept of innovation includes both technological and organizational innovation to succeed in the future. A sustainable organization also ensures a safe and secure environment for the workforce and other key stakeholders. An organization's contributions to environmental, social, and economic systems beyond those of its workforce and immediate stakeholders are considered in its societal responsibilities (Item 1.2).

N3. A focus on action (1.1b[2]) considers the strategy, the workforce, the work systems, and the hard assets of your organization. It includes both innovation and ongoing improvements in productivity that may be achieved through eliminating waste or reducing cycle time, and it might use techniques such as Six Sigma and Lean. It also includes the actions to accomplish your organization's strategic objectives.

N4. Your organizational performance results should be reported in Items 7.1-7.6.

N5. *For nonprofit organizations that rely on volunteers to accomplish their work, responses to 1.1b(1) also should discuss your efforts to communicate with and engage the volunteer workforce.*

Item 1.1 examines the key aspects of senior leaders' responsibilities to set and communicate the organization's vision and values, and focuses on the need to create and sustain a high-performance organization with a business and customer focus.

To be successful, senior leaders must understand and champion the Criteria for Performance Excellence; but understanding is not enough. Effective senior leaders "mandate," through many different techniques, the use of performance excellence criteria as the way to optimize organization performance. These leaders consistently promote high performance, create and balance value for all stakeholders, set clear values and directions, and communicate them effectively to make sure all stakeholders understand their responsibilities and align work to achieve desired results.

The most successful leaders possess a strong future orientation; an organizational bias for action; a commitment to both personal and organizational improvement, innovation, and sustainability; and a disciplined, uncompromising approach to drive the necessary changes. This requires creating an environment for workforce engagement, learning, innovation, and organizational agility, as well as the means for rapid and effective application of knowledge (facts). This environment cannot be seen by the workforce as optional. Leaders should have zero tolerance for managers and workers who are not working to achieve these principles.

To be successful and sustain that success, senior leaders must commit to improving their personal leadership skills, to developing the organization's future leaders, and to the reward and recognition of the performance of members of the workforce consistent with the principles listed above. They personally participate in organizational learning and development of future leaders, and integrate that development into the organization's succession planning. Senior leaders should personally mentor and teach some leadership development courses. Senior leaders in high-performing organizations are personally involved in workforce recognition opportunities and events to demonstrate their own unwavering commitment to excellence.

Effective communication is a key theme of Item 1.1. Through their outward focus, senior leaders push values, create expectations, and align the work of the organization. In promoting high performance, senior leaders set and deploy values, short- and longer-term directions, and performance expectations and balance the expectations of customers and other stakeholders. Leaders develop and implement systems to ensure values are understood and consistently followed.

Leaders must ensure that organizational values and their own actions actually guide the behavior of the workforce (including supervisors, managers, and workers throughout the organization), or the values are meaningless. To enhance performance excellence the *right* values must be adopted. These values must include a focus on customers and other stakeholders—creating a customer culture. Since various customer and stakeholder groups often have conflicting interests, leaders must strike a balance that optimizes the interests of all groups. The failure to ensure a customer focus usually causes the organization and its workforce to focus internally. The lack of a customer focus forces workers to default to their own ideas of what customers really *need*. This increases the risk of becoming arrogant and not caring about the requirements of customers. It also increases the potential for creating and delivering products and services that customers do not want or value. That, in turn, increases rework, scrap, waste, and added cost/lower value.

Senior leaders must ensure two-way communication with subordinate leaders and other workers, key suppliers, and partners regarding organizational values, directions, and expectations. This two-way communication also provides an opportunity for senior leaders to receive feedback from others about their effectiveness as leaders. Two-way communication should help foster feedback from workers about leadership effectiveness. Accordingly, it is recommended that part of the communication with workers involve formal and informal employee and peer feedback of leader effectiveness, such as using a 360-degree feedback survey or an upward evaluation. This information could be structured to help evaluate the effectiveness of leaders at all levels, including the board of directors, as required in Item 1.2a(2).

> **An organization's failure to achieve high levels of performance can almost always be traced to a failure in leadership.**

Leaders must create an environment for workforce engagement, empowerment, and agility, as well as the means for rapid and effective application of knowledge. "Workforce capacity" refers to an organization's ability to ensure staffing levels sufficient to accomplish its work processes and successfully deliver its products and services to customers, including the ability to meet seasonal or varying demand levels. Empowerment relates to giving workers more authority over decisions about their work. Workers

1.1 Senior Leadership

Basic Approach Requirements*: Senior leaders provide leadership for the organization.

Overall Approach Requirements*: Senior leaders' actions effectively help guide and sustain the organization, communicate with the workforce, and encourage high performance.

Multiple Approach Requirements: The following diagram describes multiple approach requirements.

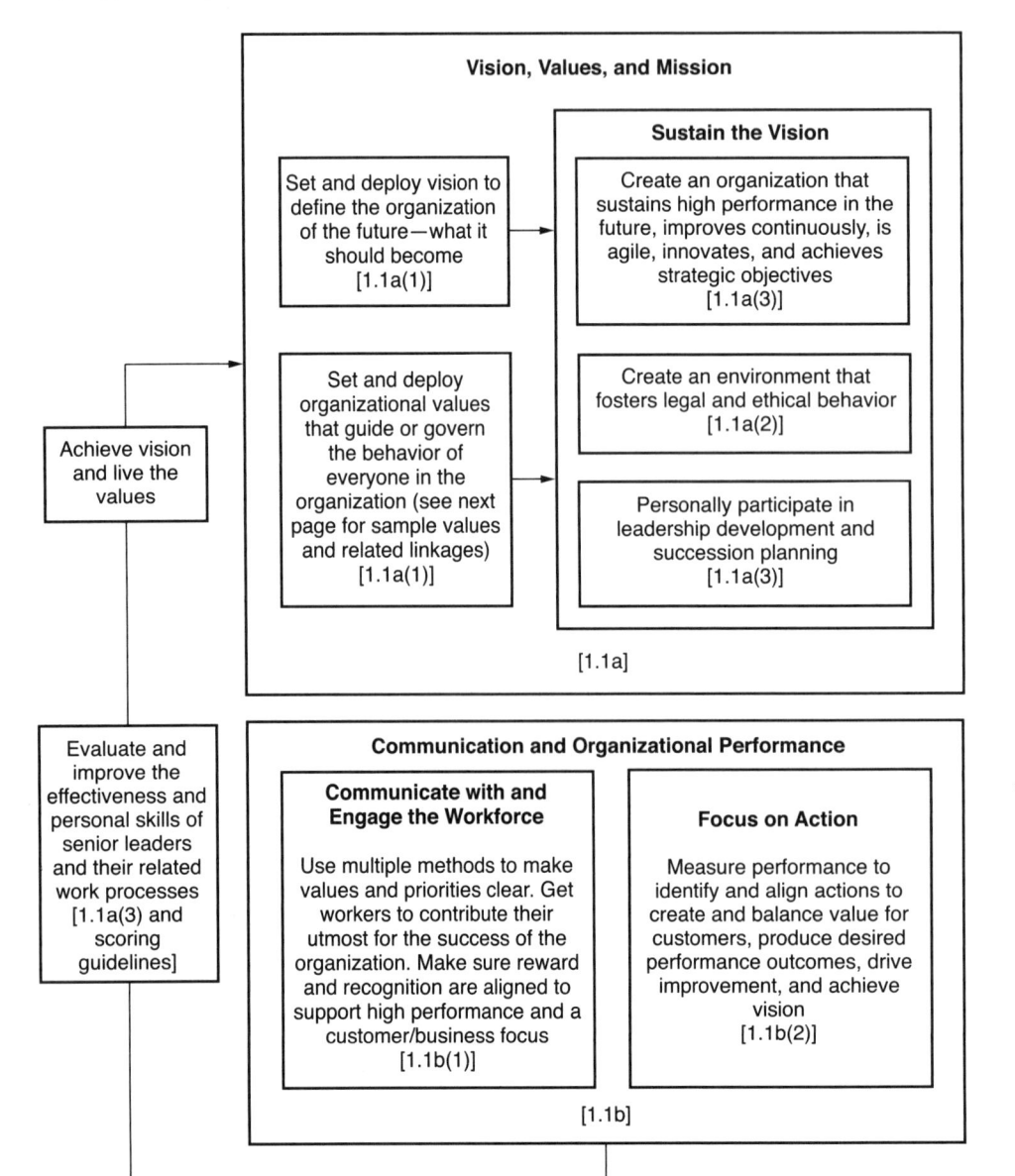

Vision, Values, and Mission

- Set and deploy vision to define the organization of the future—what it should become [1.1a(1)]
- Set and deploy organizational values that guide or govern the behavior of everyone in the organization (see next page for sample values and related linkages) [1.1a(1)]

Sustain the Vision
- Create an organization that sustains high performance in the future, improves continuously, is agile, innovates, and achieves strategic objectives [1.1a(3)]
- Create an environment that fosters legal and ethical behavior [1.1a(2)]
- Personally participate in leadership development and succession planning [1.1a(3)]

[1.1a]

Achieve vision and live the values

Evaluate and improve the effectiveness and personal skills of senior leaders and their related work processes [1.1a(3) and scoring guidelines]

Communication and Organizational Performance

Communicate with and Engage the Workforce

Use multiple methods to make values and priorities clear. Get workers to contribute their utmost for the success of the organization. Make sure reward and recognition are aligned to support high performance and a customer/business focus [1.1b(1)]

Focus on Action

Measure performance to identify and align actions to create and balance value for customers, produce desired performance outcomes, drive improvement, and achieve vision [1.1b(2)]

[1.1b]

* Multiple-level requirements usually incorporate Basic and Overall requirements. To avoid confusion, the first time a requirement appears in an Item establishes its level for scoring purposes. If the requirement first appears at the Overall Approach Level and again at the Multiple Level, the requirement should be considered an Overall-level requirement. For a more complete explanation see the chapter on Scoring System and the Scoring Calibration Guidelines.

need adequate data and the skills to interpret the data correctly, in order to make consistently good decisions. Agility generally relates to eliminating barriers and unnecessary control gates that bureaucracies and insecure leaders put in place. Unnecessary levels of review and approval make agility impossible.

Vision, Values, and Mission Linkages with Process Items

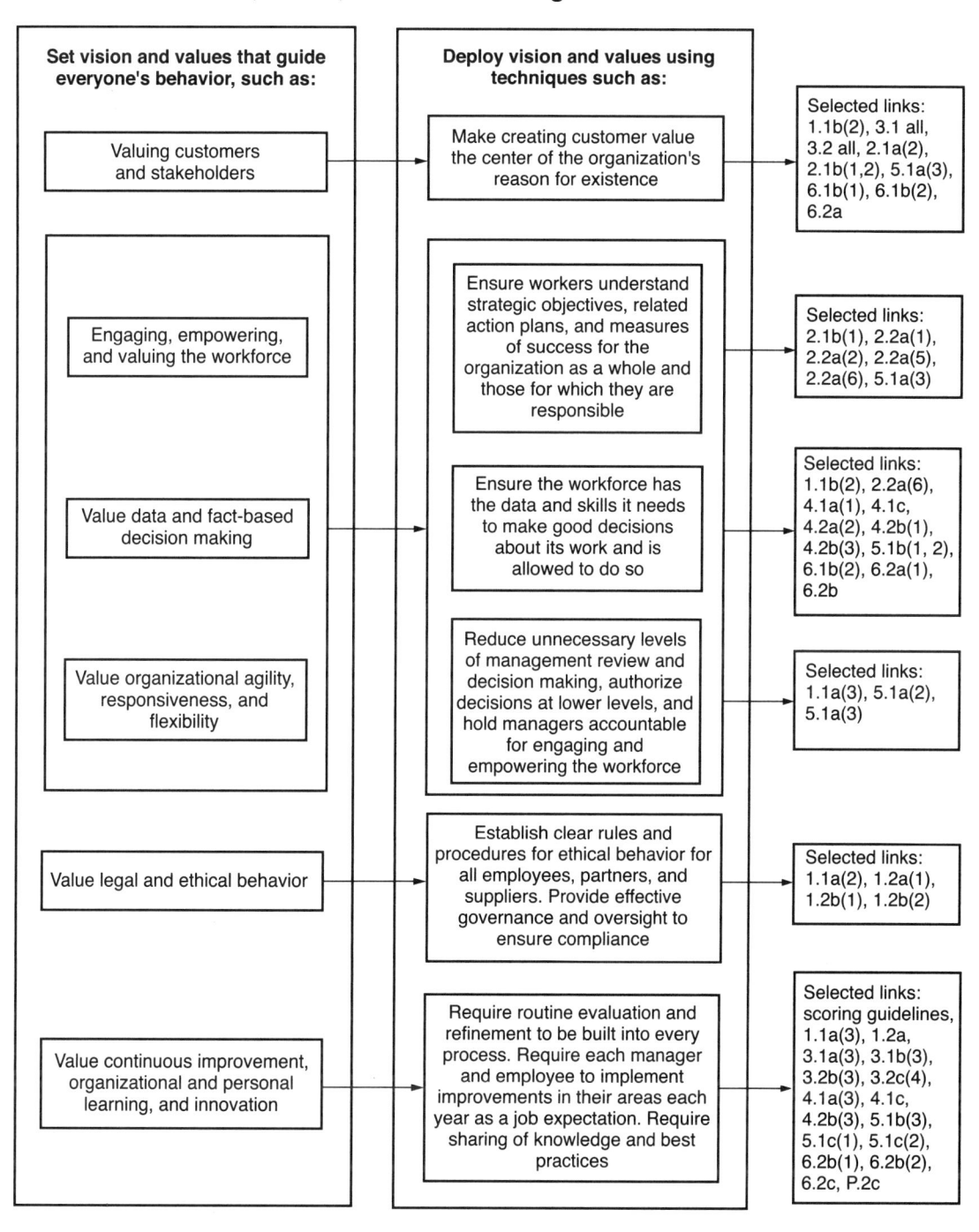

Set vision and values that guide everyone's behavior, such as:	Deploy vision and values using techniques such as:	Selected links:
Valuing customers and stakeholders	Make creating customer value the center of the organization's reason for existence	1.1b(2), 3.1 all, 3.2 all, 2.1a(2), 2.1b(1,2), 5.1a(3), 6.1b(1), 6.1b(2), 6.2a
Engaging, empowering, and valuing the workforce	Ensure workers understand strategic objectives, related action plans, and measures of success for the organization as a whole and those for which they are responsible	2.1b(1), 2.2a(1), 2.2a(2), 2.2a(5), 2.2a(6), 5.1a(3)
Value data and fact-based decision making	Ensure the workforce has the data and skills it needs to make good decisions about its work and is allowed to do so	1.1b(2), 2.2a(6), 4.1a(1), 4.1c, 4.2a(2), 4.2b(1), 4.2b(3), 5.1b(1, 2), 6.1b(2), 6.2a(1), 6.2b
Value organizational agility, responsiveness, and flexibility	Reduce unnecessary levels of management review and decision making, authorize decisions at lower levels, and hold managers accountable for engaging and empowering the workforce	1.1a(3), 5.1a(2), 5.1a(3)
Value legal and ethical behavior	Establish clear rules and procedures for ethical behavior for all employees, partners, and suppliers. Provide effective governance and oversight to ensure compliance	1.1a(2), 1.2a(1), 1.2b(1), 1.2b(2)
Value continuous improvement, organizational and personal learning, and innovation	Require routine evaluation and refinement to be built into every process. Require each manager and employee to implement improvements in their areas each year as a job expectation. Require sharing of knowledge and best practices	scoring guidelines, 1.1a(3), 1.2a, 3.1a(3), 3.1b(3), 3.2b(3), 3.2c(4), 4.1a(3), 4.1c, 4.2b(3), 5.1b(3), 5.1c(1), 5.1c(2), 6.2b(1), 6.2b(2), 6.2c, P.2c

1.1 Key Senior Leadership Item Linkages

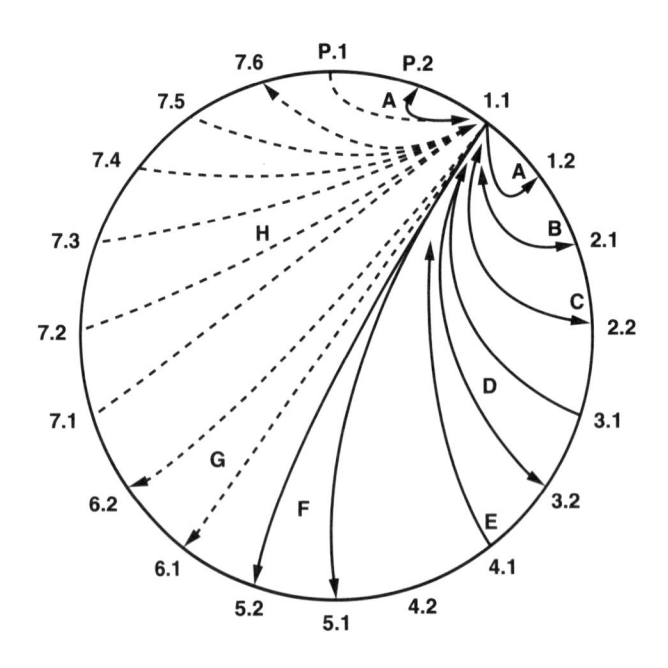

	NATURE OF RELATIONSHIP
A	Leaders in support of organizational values [1.1a(1)], create an environment that fosters, requires, and achieves ethical behavior [1.1a(2)]; role-model and support ethical and legal behavior [1.2b(2)] and organization responsibility [1.2b(1)]; and practice good citizenship [1.2c]. The organizational structure and governance system described in P.1b(1) sets the context for the review of the management systems for proper governance [1.2a] and ethical behavior [1.1a(2) and 1.2b(2)]. Leaders [1.1a(3)] are responsible for creating an environment that drives organizational learning, which in turn contributes to the overall focus on performance improvement [P.2c].
B	To effectively set organizational direction and expectations, leaders [1.1a(1)] participate in the strategic planning process [2.1]. As part of this effort, leaders [1.1b(2)] ensure that strategic objectives [2.1b(1)] create value and balance the needs of customers and stakeholders.
C	Leaders [1.1b(1)] engage, empower, motivate, and communicate clearly with the workforce at all levels throughout the organization in part to align work [2.2a(1)]. Leaders [1.1a] also approve the overall strategic objectives set forth in the plan and ensure they are consistent with vision and values based, in part, on information about the expected levels of competitor performance [2.2b]. They are also responsible for using comparative data of future projections [from 2.2b] to set meaningful goals to achieve organizational success.
D	Leaders [1.1b] use information from customers about requirements and preferences [3.1a(1)] and customer engagement, satisfaction, and dissatisfaction [3.2b] to set direction and create opportunity for the organization. Leaders [1.1b(2)] also use this information to help create and drive customer-focused value and new or expanded programs, products, and services to enhance customer engagement [3.1a], build a customer culture [3.1b], and meet customer requirements and expectations for products and support throughout the organization [3.1a(2) and 3.2b].

Continued

1 Leadership

	NATURE OF RELATIONSHIP *Continued*
E	Leaders [1.1b(2)] use analyses of data [4.1b] to monitor organizational performance and understand relationships among performance, workforce engagement and satisfaction, customers, markets, and financial success. These analyses are also used for decision making and improvement at all levels and to set priorities for action and allocate resources for maximum advantage [4.1c]. Leaders also develop a timetable for achieving strategic objectives [2.1b(1)] as a basis for defining and monitoring expected progress closely [4.1b], which means the timetable in 2.1b(1)] should define the expected levels of future performance that the leaders use during the performance reviews [4.1b] to determine if the organization is making appropriate progress against desired goals. Accordingly, if senior leaders review progress quarterly, then timelines to accomplish strategic objectives should be quarterly.
F	Leaders [1.1a(3)] create an environment for organizational sustainability, innovation, learning, competitive leadership, and agility throughout the entire organization by engaging the workforce to achieve organizational and personal success [5.1]. They ensure that the compensation and recognition system [5.1a(3)] encourages workers at all levels to achieve performance excellence in areas most critical to the organization and its customers. Leaders personally participate in reward and recognition to reinforce the importance of high performance and a customer focus [1.1b(1)]. Leaders [1.1a(3)] are also responsible for creating an environment that supports workforce learning through workforce and leader development [5.1b(1, 2)], career progression [5.1b(4)], and developing skills and competencies [5.2a(1)], as well as creating effective systems to enhance the work climate [5.2b(1, 2)].
G	Leaders [1.1a(3) and 1.1b(2)] are responsible for creating an environment that supports high performance and continuous improvement, including monitoring processes for the design of work systems [6.1a], and the design, management, and improvement of key work processes [6.2].
H	To reinforce values and vision and sustain business success, senior leaders [1.1] use performance results data [from Category 7] for many activities, including monitoring organizational performance [4.1b(1)]; deploying priority improvement areas to focus work and ensure alignment [4.1b]; strategic planning [2.1a]; setting goals and strategic objectives [2.1b(1)]; reinforcing or rewarding workforce performance [5.1a(3)]; and for improving their effectiveness and the effectiveness of senior leaders [1.1a(3)] and leaders at all levels [1.2a(2)]. In addition, key results of leadership performance, such as results related to ethical behavior and fiscal accountability, meeting strategic objectives, legal and regulatory compliance, and good citizenship in support of key communities are reported in Leadership Outcomes [7.6a].

\multicolumn{2}{c}{**IF YOU DON'T DO WHAT THE CRITERIA REQUIRE . . .**}
Item Reference	Possible Adverse Consequences
1.1a(1)	If senior leaders fail to make vision, values, and performance expectations clear (especially defining them in measurable terms), uncertainty may be created among managers and workers throughout the organization about what they must accomplish, and the direction they must follow. This may cause managers to substitute their own ideas, objectives, and directions, which may not be in alignment with those of top leadership or other managers and units. The lack of alignment may also contribute to redundancy and wasted resources. As a consequence, some parts of the organization may work at cross-purposes with other parts of the organization.
1.1a(2)	If senior leaders do not create an environment that requires and achieves legal and ethical behavior in all interactions, those who operate without regard to law and ethics will create problems for the organization that could threaten its existence and adversely affect many other organizations (consider Enron and Arthur Anderson).
1.1a(3)	Failing to put and keep systems in place to sustain high performance has caused some organizations to decline and fail...even past Baldrige Award recipients. Creating a sustainable organization requires leaders to embed values of engaging and empowering the workforce, continuous improvement (including making improvements in their personal leadership skills), fact-based decision making, and a passion for satisfying customers. To help sustain these practices, rewards and recognition systems must demand these behaviors, reinforce the use of these tools, and discipline those who fail to use them.
1.1b(1)	If senior leaders do not effectively communicate with and engage the entire workforce, they risk not leveraging the high power of a key asset—their people. As a consequence, leaders may be effectively sending a message that workers do not have the skills or ability to make decisions on their own—that micromanagement is the preferred approach within the organization. This kind of environment tends to force decision making to higher and higher levels in the organization, creating excessive delay and working against organizational agility. Unnecessary levels of review and approval may also tend to minimize innovation and creativity throughout the organization. Taken together, these problems are likely to add cost but not value—making it increasingly difficult to be successful in a highly competitive industry.
1.1b(2)	If senior leaders do not create an environment that focuses on creating value for customers and other stakeholders, workers and managers within the organization may become internally focused and risk negatively impacting the customer value on which the organization was built. An internal focus may contribute to a climate where the workforce is not primarily interested in listening to customer requirements or concerns. This may produce a high level of organizational arrogance where workers believe they know what the customers want better than the customer. This type of behavior can antagonize customers and produce high levels of customer dissatisfaction. In a related area, if senior leaders do not create an environment that focuses on balancing value for customers and other stakeholders—especially when different customer groups have competing interests—customer confidence in one group may be eroded and eventually customers may be lost. For example, end users of a product want inexpensive, reliable products, while stockholders want profits and stock price to increase. Excessive focus on one group over others makes it difficult to maximize value and keep all end users and stockholders satisfied and loyal.

1.1 SENIOR LEADERSHIP—SAMPLE EFFECTIVE PRACTICES

Perhaps most critical is that senior leaders demonstrate absolute, unwavering commitment to performance excellence—including aligning reward and recognition to provide incentives and disincentives. The best senior leaders do not tolerate a lack of aggressive commitment and urgent action from subordinates throughout the organization in support of performance excellence. They send a clear message to the workforce that the effort is serious.

A. Vision, Values, and Mission

- Leaders serve as role models (walk the talk) in leading systematic performance improvement and innovation throughout the organization.

- Leader behavior (not merely words) clearly defines what is expected of the organization and its workforce.

- All senior leaders are knowledgeable about and personally involved in performance improvement.

- Senior leaders spend a significant portion of their time on performance improvement activities.

- Senior leaders carry out many visible activities (for example, setting goals, planning, and recognizing and rewarding performance and process improvement).

- Senior leaders regularly communicate performance excellence values to managers and ensure that managers demonstrate those values in their work.

- Senior leaders participate on performance improvement teams.

- Senior leaders mentor managers and ensure that promotion criteria reflect organizational values, especially customer satisfaction.

- Senior leaders study and learn about the improvement practices of other organizations.

- Senior leaders clearly and consistently articulate values (customer focus, customer satisfaction, role model leadership, continuous improvement, workforce involvement, and performance optimization) throughout the organization.

- Senior leaders ensure that organizational values are used to provide direction to the entire workforce to help achieve the mission, vision, and performance goals.

- Senior leaders use effective and innovative approaches to reach out to all workers to spread the organization's values and align its work to support organizational goals.

- Senior leaders effectively surface problems and encourage employee risk taking.

- Roles and responsibilities of managers are clearly defined, understood by them, and used to evaluate and improve their performance.

- Job definitions with performance targets are clearly delineated for each level of the organization, objectively measured, and presented in a logical and organized structure.

- Systems and procedures are deployed that encourage cooperation and a cross-functional approach to management, team activities, and problem solving.

- Leaders monitor workforce acceptance and adoption of vision and values using annual surveys, employee focus groups, and e-mail questions.

- A systematic process is in place for evaluating and improving the integration or alignment of quality values throughout the organization.

B. Communication and Organizational Performance

- Many different techniques are used to reinforce quality values. Leaders at all levels make two-way communication easy through personal methods such as voice mail, e-mail, town hall meetings, and face-to-face meetings (which can include often-used open door access practices).

- Actions are taken to assist units that are not meeting goals or performing to plan.

- Leaders at all levels determine how well they carried out their activities (what went right or wrong and how they could be done better).
- There is evidence of adopting changes to improve leader effectiveness.
- Senior leaders require that all key processes identify internal and external customers and other stakeholders that might have competing interests; define customer and other stakeholders' specific requirements in measurable terms; and develop or assign processes to monitor customer and other stakeholders' satisfaction and correct problems quickly.

1 Leadership

1.2 GOVERNANCE AND SOCIETAL RESPONSIBILITIES: How do you govern and fulfill your societal responsibilities? (50 Pts.)   **PROCESS**

Describe your organization's governance system and approach to leadership improvement. Describe how your organization assures legal and ethical behavior, fulfills its societal responsibilities, and supports its key communities.

Within your response, include answers to the following questions:

a. Organizational Governance

(1) How does your organization review and achieve the following key aspects of your governance system?

- Accountability for management's actions
- Fiscal accountability
- Transparency in operations and selection of and disclosure policies for governance board members, as appropriate
- Independence in internal and external audits
- Protection of stakeholder and stockholder interests, as appropriate

(2) How do you evaluate the performance of your senior leaders, including the chief executive? How do you evaluate the performance of members of your governance board, as appropriate? How do senior leaders and your governance board use these performance reviews to further their development and to improve both their personal leadership effectiveness and that of your board and leadership system, as appropriate?

b. Legal and Ethical Behavior

(1) How do you address any adverse impacts on society of your products and operations? How do you anticipate public concerns with current and future products and operations? How do you prepare for these concerns in a proactive manner, including conserving natural resources and using effective supply chain management processes, as appropriate? What are your key compliance processes, measures, and goals for achieving and surpassing regulatory and legal requirements, as appropriate? What are your key processes, measures, and goals for addressing risks associated with your products and operations?

(2) How does your organization promote and assure ethical behavior in all your interactions? What are your key processes and measures or indicators for enabling and monitoring ethical behavior in your governance structure, throughout your organization, and in interactions with customers, partners, suppliers, and other stakeholders? How do you monitor and respond to breaches of ethical behavior?

c. Societal Responsibilities and Support of Key Communities

(1) How do you consider societal well-being and benefit as part of your strategy and daily operations? How do you consider the well-being of environmental, social, and economic systems to which your organization does or may contribute?

(2) How does your organization actively support and strengthen your key communities? What are your key communities? How do you identify these communities and determine areas for organizational involvement, including areas related to your core competencies? How do your senior leaders, in concert with your workforce, contribute to improving these communities?

Continued

Notes: *Continued*

N1. Societal responsibilities in areas critical to your organization's ongoing marketplace success also should be addressed in Strategy Development (Item 2.1) and in Process Management (Category 6). Key results, such as results of regulatory and legal compliance (including the results of mandated financial audits); reductions in environmental impacts through the use of "green" technology, resource-conserving activities, or other means; or improvements in social impacts, such as the global use of enlightened labor practices, should be reported as Leadership Outcomes (Item 7.6).

N2. Transparency in operations of your governance board (1.2a[1]) should include your internal controls on governance processes. *For some nonprofit organizations, an external advisory board may provide some or all of the governance board functions. For those nonprofit organizations that serve as stewards of public funds, stewardship of those funds and transparency in operations are areas of emphasis.*

N3. Leadership performance evaluation (1.2a[2]) might be supported by peer reviews, formal performance management reviews, and formal or informal workforce and other stakeholder feedback and surveys. *For some nonprofit and government organizations, external advisory boards might evaluate the performance of senior leaders and the governance board.*

N4. Measures or indicators of ethical behavior (1.2b[2]) might include the percentage of independent board members, measures of relationships with stockholder and nonstockholder constituencies, instances of ethical conduct breaches and responses, survey results on workforce perceptions of organizational ethics, ethics hotline use, and results of ethics reviews and audits. They also might include evidence that policies, workforce training, and monitoring systems are in place with respect to conflicts of interest and proper use of funds.

N5. Areas of societal contributions and community support appropriate for 1.2c might include your efforts to improve the environment (e.g., collaboration to conserve the environment or natural resources); strengthen local community services, education, and health; and improve the practices of trade, business, or professional associations.

N6. The health and safety of your workforce are not addressed in Item 1.2; you should address these workforce factors in Item 5.2.

N7. *Nonprofit organizations should report in 1.2b(1), as appropriate, how they address the legal and regulatory requirements and standards that govern fundraising and lobbying activities.*

N8. *For some charitable organizations, societal contributions and support for key communities (1.2c) may occur totally through the mission-related activities of the organization. In such cases, it is appropriate to respond with any "extra efforts" you devote to support of these communities.*

This Item [1.2] looks at the organization's governance system, how it improves its leaders, how it enables the organization to fulfill its public responsibilities, how it ensures ethical and legal behavior, and how it encourages and supports senior leaders and the entire workforce to practice good citizenship.

The first part of this Item [1.2a] looks at how the organization addresses the need for a responsible, informed, transparent, and accountable governance or advisory body that provides sound policy guidance and protect the interests of key stakeholders, such as stockholders in publicly traded companies, as well as stakeholders in private and nonprofit organizations. It should have independence in review and audit functions.

The organization must evaluate the performance and effectiveness of senior leaders, board members, and the entire leadership system. To ensure the evaluation is accurate, workers should provide feedback to the leaders and managers at all levels, which may be accomplished, in part, by the two-way communication required in Item 1.1b(1) and using tools such as 360-degree reviews and upward evaluations.

Leaders and managers at all levels should take action, based on the feedback, to improve their effectiveness. It is critical that leaders, managers, and supervisors at all levels and in all parts of the organization effectively drive and reinforce the principles of performance excellence through words and actions.

Remember, nearly every failure to achieve and sustain excellence can be traced to a failure on the part of leaders and managers. Jack Welch, former CEO of General Electric, in his last letter to stockholders emphasized the importance of rewarding and nurturing the top 20 percent of employees, and getting rid of the bottom 10 percent. The same is true of managers who do not or will not aggressively and effectively lead the effort to optimize performance excellence.

The second part of this Item [1.2b] looks at how the organization addresses current and future impacts on society in a proactive manner, and how the organization, its senior leaders, and its employees ensure ethical business practices are followed in all stakeholder transactions and interactions. The impacts and practices are expected to cover all relevant and important areas—products, services, and operations.

An integral part of performance management and improvement is proactively addressing the need for ethical behavior, legal and regulatory requirements, and risk factors. Addressing these areas requires establishing appropriate measures and/or indicators that senior leaders track in their overall performance review. The organization should be sensitive to issues of public concern, whether or not these issues are currently embodied in law or regulations. Role-model organizations seek out opportunities to exceed requirements and to excel in legal and ethical behavior. The failure to address these areas can expose the organization to future problems when it least expects them. Problems can range from a sudden decline in consumer confidence to extensive and costly litigation. In this regard, it is important to anticipate potential problems the public may have with both current and future products. Sometimes a well-intended product or service could create adverse public consequences.

For example, consider the use of automated teller machines (ATMs), or cash machines as they are called today. When these machines were first introduced, many in the industry believed that the public would never accept the machines as a surrogate for a human being. For the most part, these machines were considered an eyesore and were installed in out-of-the-way places, usually at the back of the bank building. The extraordinary success of these devices, however, resulted in hundreds of millions of people conducting cash transactions outside the relative safety of the bank building. This gave rise to more robberies, abductions, and even murder. By failing to consider the potential adverse consequence of these cash machines located in out-of-the-way places, banks were exposed to increased litigation and costs associated with relocating or providing appropriate security enclosures for the machines in an effort to reduce public risk.

Government and charitable organizations should anticipate public concerns, including the cost of products, programs, and services; timely and equitable access to products, programs, and services; and perceptions about the organization's stewardship of its resources.

The organization must also address the conservation of natural resources. These processes might include *green* technologies, replacement of hazardous chemicals with water-based chemicals, energy conservation, use of cleaner energy sources, or the recycling of by-products or wastes.

Good societal responsibility implies going beyond minimum compliance with laws and regulations. Top-performing organizations frequently serve as role models of responsibility and provide leadership in areas key to business success. For example, a manufacturing company might go beyond the requirements of the environmental protection regulations and develop innovative and award-winning systems to protect the environment and reduce pollution. This has a double benefit. Not only do high-performing organizations develop good relations with regulators (and occasionally receive the benefit of the doubt), but when regulators increase requirements, they are already in compliance, usually way ahead of competitors who only met minimum requirements.

Standards of ethical behavior should be defined (preferably in measurable terms) and everyone in the organization should understand and follow the standards. The organization must systematically monitor ethical behavior throughout the organization and with key suppliers, partners, and collaborators; and within the governance structure. Failing to follow the standards of ethical behavior should have prompt and serious consequences for every governing board member, leader, manager, employee, supplier, partner, and collaborator.

Ensuring ethical business practices are followed by all members of the workforce lessens the organization's risk of adverse public reaction as well as criminal prosecution. Programs to ensure ethical business practices typically seek to prevent activities that might be perceived as criminal or near criminal. Examples of unethical business practices might include falsifying expense reports or quality-control data, accepting lavish gifts from a contractor, or seeking kickbacks.

The third part of this Item [1.2c] looks at how the organization, its senior leaders, and its workforce identify, support, and strengthen key communities as part of good citizenship practices and consider societal well-being and benefit a routine part of strategy and operations. Social systems, the environment, and economic systems are all affected by the presence of any organization, it processes, and its workforce. To ensure sustainability, the well-being of those systems must be considered and addressed.

Good citizenship practices typically vary according to the size, complexity, and location of the organization. Larger organizations are generally expected to have a more comprehensive approach to citizenship than small organizations. However, organizations of all sizes should practice good citizenship, including encouraging and supporting community service by leaders and members of the workforce.

Examples of organizational community involvement include: influencing the adoption of higher standards in education by communicating employability requirements to schools and school boards; partnering with other businesses and health care providers to improve health in the local community by providing education and volunteer services to address public-health issues; and partnering to influence trade and business associations to engage in beneficial, cooperative activities, such as sharing best practices to improve overall U.S. global competitiveness and the environment. Examples for nonprofit organizations include partnering with other nonprofit organizations or businesses to improve overall performance and stewardship of public and charitable resources.

In addition to activities directly carried out by the organization, opportunities to practice good citizenship include workforce community service that is encouraged and supported by the organization. Frequently, the organization's leaders actively participate on community boards and support their work. Usually, organizations—like people—support causes and issues they value. Top-performing organizations are not content to simply donate money, people, and products/services to these causes without examining the impact of this support. Just as senior leaders examine the other parts of their business, they also evaluate and refine the effectiveness of community support, consistent with business strategies and objectives to get the greatest benefit from their support.

1.2 Governance and Societal Responsibilities

Basic Approach Requirements*: Provide governance and address the organization's societal responsibilities.
Overall Approach Requirements*: Provide effective governance and improve leadership. Effectively fulfill societal responsibilities and support key communities, and ensure legal and ethical behavior.
Multiple Approach Requirements: The following diagram describes multiple approach requirements.

Responsibilities to the Public

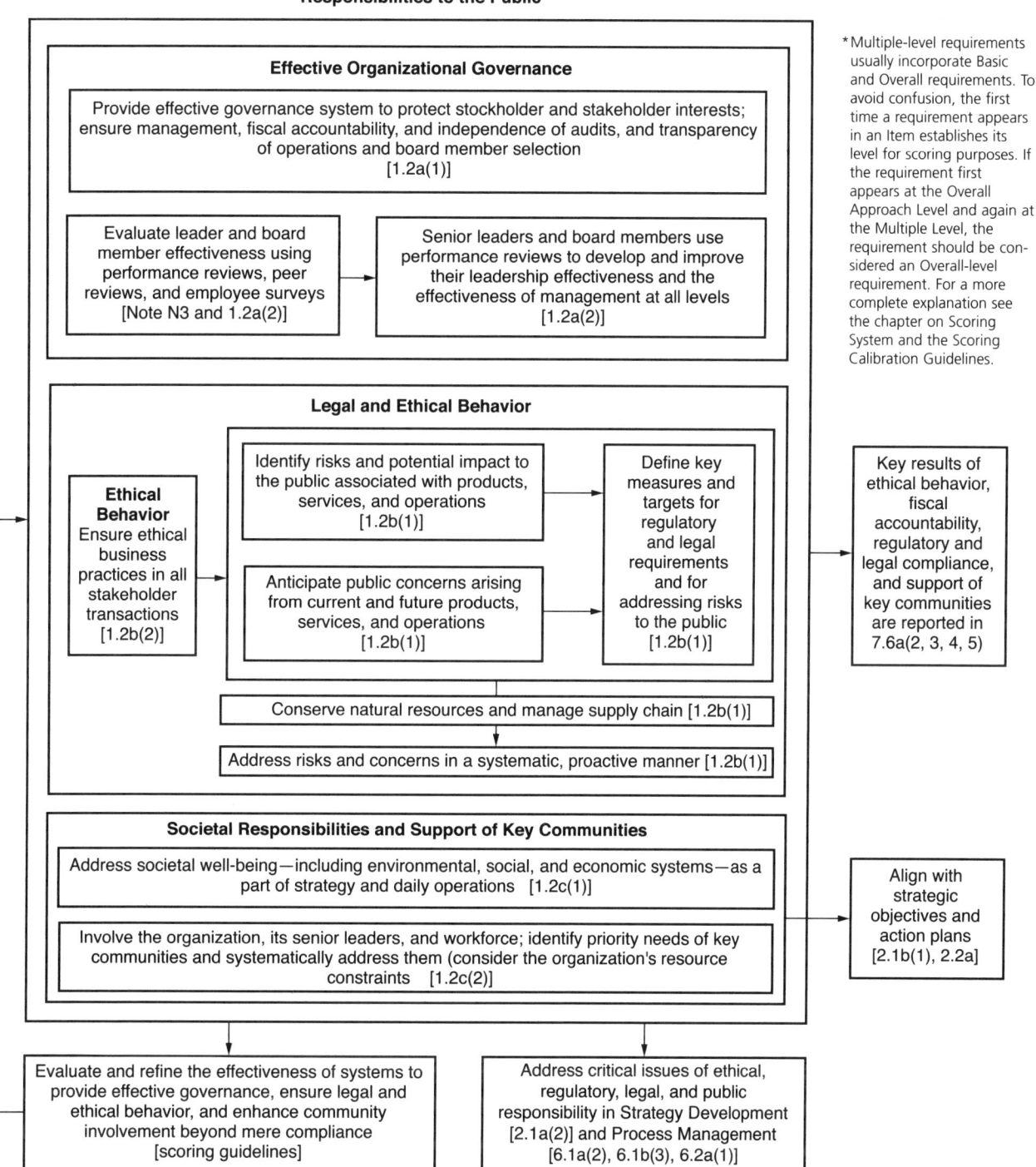

Effective Organizational Governance

Provide effective governance system to protect stockholder and stakeholder interests; ensure management, fiscal accountability, and independence of audits, and transparency of operations and board member selection [1.2a(1)]

Evaluate leader and board member effectiveness using performance reviews, peer reviews, and employee surveys [Note N3 and 1.2a(2)] → Senior leaders and board members use performance reviews to develop and improve their leadership effectiveness and the effectiveness of management at all levels [1.2a(2)]

Legal and Ethical Behavior

Ethical Behavior Ensure ethical business practices in all stakeholder transactions [1.2b(2)]

Identify risks and potential impact to the public associated with products, services, and operations [1.2b(1)]

Anticipate public concerns arising from current and future products, services, and operations [1.2b(1)]

Define key measures and targets for regulatory and legal requirements and for addressing risks to the public [1.2b(1)]

Conserve natural resources and manage supply chain [1.2b(1)]

Address risks and concerns in a systematic, proactive manner [1.2b(1)]

Societal Responsibilities and Support of Key Communities

Address societal well-being—including environmental, social, and economic systems—as a part of strategy and daily operations [1.2c(1)]

Involve the organization, its senior leaders, and workforce; identify priority needs of key communities and systematically address them (consider the organization's resource constraints [1.2c(2)]

Evaluate and refine the effectiveness of systems to provide effective governance, ensure legal and ethical behavior, and enhance community involvement beyond mere compliance [scoring guidelines]

Address critical issues of ethical, regulatory, legal, and public responsibility in Strategy Development [2.1a(2)] and Process Management [6.1a(2), 6.1b(3), 6.2a(1)]

Key results of ethical behavior, fiscal accountability, regulatory and legal compliance, and support of key communities are reported in 7.6a(2, 3, 4, 5)

Align with strategic objectives and action plans [2.1b(1), 2.2a]

*Multiple-level requirements usually incorporate Basic and Overall requirements. To avoid confusion, the first time a requirement appears in an Item establishes its level for scoring purposes. If the requirement first appears at the Overall Approach Level and again at the Multiple Level, the requirement should be considered an Overall-level requirement. For a more complete explanation see the chapter on Scoring System and the Scoring Calibration Guidelines.

Insights to Performance Excellence 2009–2010

1.2 Key Governance and Societal Responsibilities Item Linkages

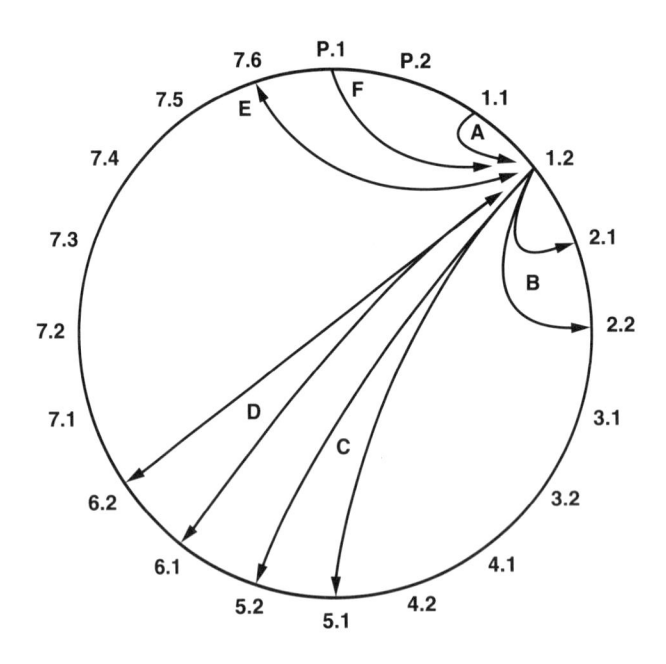

	NATURE OF RELATIONSHIP
A	Leaders [1.1a(2)] have a responsibility for setting policies and ensuring that practices and products of the organization and its workers do not adversely impact society or violate ethical standards, regulations, or law [1.2b]. They are also responsible for ensuring societal well-being and benefit are part of daily operations [1.2c(1)] and to be personally involved and to ensure that the organization and its workers strengthen key communities in areas such as local community services, education, health, the environment, and business, professional, and trade associations [1.2c(2)].
B	Public health and safety concerns, environmental protection, and waste management issues [1.2b] are important factors to consider in strategy development [2.1a(2)] and action planning [2.2a].
C	Development opportunities [5.1b] are provided to ensure all leaders and workers understand the organization's ethical business practices [1.2b] as well as the importance of ensuring societal well-being and benefit [1.2c(1)] and strengthening key communities [1.2c(2)]. In addition, recruitment and hiring [5.2a(2)] should capitalize on the ideas, culture, and thinking of key hiring and customer communities.
D	Governance, ethical, and legal rules [1.2a and b] guide the design and development of work systems [6.1a(1)] and the design and management of key work processes [6.2]. Managers at all levels have responsibility for ensuring that work practices of the organization [6.1 and 6.2] are consistent with the organization's standards of ethics and societal responsibility [1.2b and c].
E	Key results related to processes of fiscal accountability [1.2a], regulatory and legal compliance [1.2b], anticipating public concerns [1.2b(1)], legal and ethical behavior [1.2b(2)], societal responsibility and support to key communities [1.2c], are reported in Leadership Outcomes [7.6a(2, 3, 4, 5)]. In addition, these results are monitored to determine if process changes are needed. (Results in areas of workplace health and security are reported in 7.4, based on processes described in Item 5.2b. Workforce health and safety are not a part of the requirements in 1.2.)
F	The regulatory environment described in P.1a(5) sets the context for the review of the management systems for governance [1.2a] and legal/ethical behavior [1.2b].

IF YOU DON'T DO WHAT THE CRITERIA REQUIRE...

Item Reference	Possible Adverse Consequences
1.2a(1)	The adverse consequences of corrupt or incompetent organizational governance can be sudden and spectacular. One need only consider the impact of poor governance on Enron and similar companies whose businesses failed suddenly, hurting thousands of stakeholders, and tearing the economic fabric of the national economy. With increased stakeholder scrutiny and decreased trust, organizations that do not have visible and effective processes in place to ensure fiscal and management accountability and protect stockholder and stakeholder interests may find it difficult to overcome the climate of distrust that permeates the corporate sector today. Their stock prices and consumer confidence may remain flat. Intrusive government oversight may increase, which diverts leadership attention and company resources away from value-adding outcomes needed to beat competitors and satisfy customers and other stakeholders.
1.2a(2)	Even a new employee can tell the difference between an effective leader and an incompetent one. Unfortunately, an incompetent leader is too often blind to this fact. The combination of organizational performance outcomes and employee (subordinate) feedback can provide critical information to help leaders throughout the leadership system identify personal strengths and opportunities for improvement. Without this information, leaders may not be able to focus effectively on areas where improvement would be essential not only to personal growth and development but also to better organizational results. Leaders who do not receive accurate feedback about their strengths and weaknesses may not be able to keep pace with changing business needs and directions, as they are challenged to work smarter by customers, competitors, and the demands of stockholders and other stakeholders. They are not likely to lead their organization to winning levels of performance excellence.
1.2b(1)	Organizations that fail to consider the impact on the public of their products, services, and operations may be seriously impaired in the future if it is determined that these products or services cause harm. In the short term, organizations that fail to comply with regulatory and legal requirements may find themselves facing costly sanctions or be prevented from conducting business. The failure to consider risks associated with products, services, and operations may contribute to costly corrective action or litigation. Organizations that fail to anticipate and consider potential concerns that society may have with current and future products, services, and operations may be faced with costly redesign or rework. When an organization appears to treat society and the community within which it works with impunity and disregards their concerns, it becomes extremely difficult to recover trust and confidence. When the organization finds it needs public support to carry out its work or expand its operations, it may find it difficult to secure that support.
1.2b(2)	Organizations that do not ensure ethical business practices in all transactions and interactions with stakeholders (public, customers, stockholders, workers, suppliers, and so on) run the risk of violating the public trust. Accordingly, these organizations may face serious adverse consequences when their misdeeds are discovered. (One only need consider the difference between Enron and Tylenol. Both companies faced disasters that threatened their existence. Tylenol responded ethically and is still thriving.) Moreover, if the unethical practices of leaders are considered an acceptable business standard in the organization and repeated by others, they can contribute to numerous unpredictable problems that waste human and financial resources to correct.

Continued

	IF YOU DON'T DO WHAT THE CRITERIA REQUIRE... Continued
Item Reference	**Possible Adverse Consequences**
1.2c	Organizations that fail to address societal well-being and act as good corporate citizens and support its hiring and customer community may find it difficult to get support in return, especially for projects or initiatives that require local approval. For example, local communities typically provide the bulk of support for services as well as new workers. Organizations that fail to support local education or trade and professional associations may find themselves faced with a shortage of skilled workers in key areas and important services they need to conduct business.

1.2 GOVERNANCE AND SOCIETAL RESPONSIBILITIES—SAMPLE EFFECTIVE PRACTICES

A. Organizational Governance

- Independence of the board of directors is ensured by requiring that a substantial percentage of directors come from outside the organization.

- Fiscal accountability is assured by a variety of processes including independent audits and separation of consultants from auditing functions. Audit and consulting services are not provided by the same or affiliated companies.

- Stockholders approve the election slates for the board of directors and even place names on the slate.

- Board term limits enable rotating membership to ensure fresh and objective voices are present on the board.

- Board audit committees contain at least one financial expert who is independent of the organization.

- The full board of directors reviews financial statements quarterly after accuracy is certified.

- Directors with competing interests, such as key suppliers or interlocking directors, are eliminated from the board or their influence is minimized (such as becoming non-voting members).

- Dissent, debate, and open criticism are encouraged among board members.

- CEOs promote candor and meaningful discussion at board meetings by sharing relevant information with directors before meetings to permit careful analysis before deliberations begin.

- Board members formally assess their peers in writing and ask poor performing members to resign.

- A climate of trust and candor exists among board members. No secret group wields power to make back-room decisions.

- Demonstrated proficiency in the use of the Baldrige Criteria is a prerequisite for promotion to board leadership positions.

B. Legal and Ethical Behavior

- The organization's principal work activities include systems to analyze, anticipate, and minimize public hazards or risk.

- Indicators for risk areas are identified and monitored.

- Improvement strategies are used consistently, target performance levels are set, and progress is reviewed regularly and tied to recognition and reward.

- The organization considers the impact that its operations, products, and services might have on society and natural resources and considers those impacts in planning and daily operations.

- The effectiveness of systems to meet or exceed regulatory or legal requirements is systematically evaluated and improved.

- A formal system is in place to train the workforce about ethical business requirements.

- A process is in place to permit workers to file complaints about unethical or illegal behavior in the workplace or among suppliers/customers without fear of discovery or retaliation (for example, a whistleblower program).

- A process is in place to test the understanding of ethical principles for all people who must follow the principles, including the workforce, governing board members, suppliers, and partners.

- An audit process is in place to communicate and ensure ethical requirements, and practices are deployed to all levels of the organization and to key partners, suppliers, and members of the board of directors (governance group).

- The effective capability of systems to meet or exceed ethical requirements is systematically evaluated and improved.

- Senior leaders systematically and routinely check the effectiveness of their leadership activities (for example, seeking feedback at least annually from workers and peers using an upward or 360-degree evaluation), and take steps to improve.

C. Societal Responsibilities and Support of Key Communities

- As part of strategic planning and strengths, weaknesses, opportunities, threats (SWOT) analysis, issues related to environment, conservation, social systems, and economic systems are considered. Strategic plans, goals, and actions are designed to mitigate societal issues to engender maximum support from the organization's key communities.

- Senior leaders and workers at various levels in the organization are involved in professional organizations, committees, task forces, or other community activities.

- Organizational resources are allocated to support involvement in community activities outside the organization. The effectiveness of these allocations is examined to determine if expectations are met and resources are used wisely.

- Workers participate in local, state, or national quality award programs and receive recognition from the organization for doing so.

- Workers participate in professional quality- and business-improvement associations (such as the American Society for Quality).

- The effectiveness of processes to support and strengthen key communities is systematically measured, evaluated, and improved.

2 Strategic Planning—85 Points

*The **Strategic Planning** Category examines how your organization develops strategic objectives and action plans. Also examined are how your chosen strategic objectives and action plans are deployed and changed if circumstances require, and how progress is measured.*

The Strategic Planning Category looks at the organization's process for strategic and action planning, and deployment of plans to make sure everyone is working to achieve those plans. This Category examines how plans are changed if change is required, and how accomplishments are measured and sustained. Customer-driven excellence, long-term sustainability, a competitive environment, core competencies, and operational performance excellence are key strategic issues that need to be integral parts of the organization's overall planning and strategic decision making.

- Customer-driven excellence is a strategic view of quality. The focus is on the drivers of customer engagement (customer retention and loyalty), new markets, and increasing market share—key factors in competitiveness, profitability, and organizational success and sustainability.

- Operational performance improvement and innovation contribute to short- and longer-term productivity growth and cost/price competitiveness. Building operational capability—including speed, responsiveness, and flexibility—represents an investment in strengthening the organization's competitive position now and into the future.

- Organizational and personal learning are strategic considerations in today's challenging environment. The Criteria emphasize that improvement and learning must be embedded in work processes. The special role of strategic planning is to align work processes and learning initiatives with the organization's strategic directions, thereby ensuring that improvement and learning prepare organization personnel and reinforce organizational priorities.

Over the years, much debate and discussion have taken place around planning. Professors in our colleges and universities spend a great deal of time trying to differentiate strategic planning, long-term planning, short-term planning, tactical planning, operational planning, quality planning, business planning, and human resource planning, to name a few. A much simpler view, however, might serve us better.

> *Strategic objectives define in outcome-oriented, measurable terms, the things an organization must actually achieve to be successful in the future.*
>
> *Once the organization has determined what must actually be achieved to be successful in the future (the strategic objectives), it must take steps to execute that plan (the actions).*

Strategic planning helps provide a basis for aligning the organization's work processes with its strategic directions, thereby ensuring people and processes in different parts of the organization are not working at cross-purposes. To the extent that alignment does not occur, the organization's effectiveness and competitiveness are reduced.

The Strategic Planning Category looks at how the organization:

- Determines its strengths, weaknesses, opportunities, threats, and its ability to execute its strategy.

- Understands the key customer, market, and operational requirements that are essential to setting strategic directions. This helps to ensure that ongoing process improvements are aligned with the organization's strategic directions.

- Optimizes the use of resources, ensures the availability of a trained workforce, and bridges short- and longer-term requirements that may involve capital expenditures, supplier development, new workforce recruitment strategies, reengineering key processes, technology development or acquisition, new partnerships or collaborations, and other factors affecting organizational success.

- Ensures that deployment will be effective—that there are mechanisms to transmit requirements and achieve alignment on three basic levels: (1) the organization and executive level; (2) the work-system and work-process level; and (3) the work-unit and individual-job level.

The requirements for the Strategic Planning Category are intended to encourage strategic thinking and behavior—to develop a basis for achieving and maintaining a competitive position. Strategic planning requirements do not demand formalized planning departments or specific planning cycles. They also do not imply that all improvements could or should be planned in advance. They do, however, require plans and the alignment of actions to achieve those plans at all levels of the organization.

An effective improvement system combines improvements of many types and degrees of involvement. An effective system to improve performance and competitive advantage requires fact-based strategic guidance, particularly when improvement alternatives compete for limited resources. In most cases, priority setting depends heavily upon a cost rationale. However, an organization might also have to deal with critical requirements, such as public responsibilities, that are not driven by cost considerations alone.

Strategic planning consists of the planning process, the identification of goals (measurable outcome-oriented strategic objectives) and actions (activities with measures to monitor progress and completion) necessary to achieve success, and the deployment of those actions to align the work of the organization.

Although many organizations have workable strategic plans and measurable, outcome-oriented objectives, executing the strategy remains a major challenge. This is especially true if strategic objectives are vague and not outcome-oriented. A volatile environment, poor economy, and rapidly changing technologies all contribute to a heightened need for agility and focus throughout the workforce. A good strategic plan, with clear objectives and actions defined, helps make agility and focus possible.

Strategy Development

Sample elements considered during strategic planning include the following:

- Customers: market requirements and evolving expectations and opportunities

- Competitive environment and capabilities relative to competitors: industry and market

- Technologies and other innovations that might affect products and services and future business operations

- Internal strengths and weaknesses, including core competencies, workforce capabilities, capacity resource availability, and operational capabilities and needs

- Financial, societal, ethical, regulatory, and other potential risks that may affect short- and longer-term success

- Opportunities to redirect resources to higher-priority products, services, or business areas

- Changes in economic conditions (local, national, or global) that might affect the business

- Unique organizational factors such as supplier and supply chain capabilities and needs

- Clear strategic objectives with timetables that help leaders determine where the organization should be at given points in time so they can effectively monitor progress and make appropriate changes in processes or the allocation of resources

Strategy Deployment

Factors considered during strategy deployment include the following:

- Convert strategic objectives and goals into action plans and related human resource plans

- Deploy and align action plans, performance measures, and resources throughout the organization to ensure changes or improvements are sustained
- Define measures for tracking progress on action plans to ensure actions are aligned throughout the organization
- Project expected performance results, including assumptions of competitor performance increases

2.1 STRATEGY DEVELOPMENT: How do you develop your strategy? (40 Pts.) PROCESS

Describe how your organization establishes its strategy to address its strategic challenges and leverage its strategic advantages. Summarize your organization's key strategic objectives and their related goals.

Within your response, include answers to the following questions:

a. Strategy Development Process

(1) How does your organization conduct its strategic planning? What are the key process steps? Who are the key participants? How does your process identify potential blind spots? How do you determine your core competencies, strategic challenges, and strategic advantages (identified in your organizational profile)? What are your short- and longer-term planning time horizons? How are these time horizons set? How does your strategic planning process address these time horizons?

(2) How do you ensure that strategic planning addresses the key factors listed below? How do you collect and analyze relevant data and information pertaining to these factors as part of your strategic planning process:

- Your organization's strengths, weaknesses, opportunities, and threats
- Early indications of major shifts in technology, markets, products, customer preferences, competition, or the regulatory environment
- Long-term organizational sustainability, including needed core competencies
- Your ability to execute the strategic plan

b. Strategic Objectives

(1) What are your key strategic objectives and your timetable for accomplishing them? What are your most important goals for these strategic objectives?

(2) How do your strategic objectives address your strategic challenges and strategic advantages? How do your strategic objectives address your opportunities for innovation in products, operations, and your business model? How do your strategic objectives address current and future core competencies? How do you ensure that your strategic objectives balance short- and longer-term challenges and opportunities? How do you ensure that your strategic objectives consider and balance the needs of all key stakeholders?

Notes:

N1. "Strategy development" refers to your organization's approach (formal or informal) to preparing for the future. Strategy development might utilize various types of forecasts, projections, options, scenarios, knowledge (see 4.2a for relevant organizational knowledge), or other approaches to envisioning the future for purposes of decision making and resource allocation. Strategy development might involve participation by key suppliers, distributors,

Continued

> **Notes:** *Continued*
>
> partners, and customers. *For some nonprofit organizations, strategy development might involve participation by organizations providing similar services or drawing from the same donor population or volunteer workforce.*
>
> N2. The term "strategy" should be interpreted broadly. Strategy might be built around or lead to any or all of the following: new products; redefinition of key customer groups or market segments; new core competencies; revenue growth via various approaches, including acquisitions, grants, and endowments; divestitures; new partnerships and alliances; and new employee or volunteer relationships. Strategy might be directed toward becoming a preferred supplier, a local supplier in each of your major customers' or partners' markets, a low-cost producer, a market innovator, or a high-end or customized product or service provider. It also might be directed toward meeting a community or public need.
>
> N3. Your organization's strengths, weaknesses, opportunities, and threats (2.1a[2]) should address all factors that are key to your organization's future success, including the following, as appropriate: your customer and market requirements, expectations, and opportunities; your opportunities for innovation and role-model performance; your core competencies; your competitive environment and your performance relative to competitors and comparable organizations; your product life cycle; technological and other key innovations or changes that might affect your products and services and how you operate, as well as the rate of that innovation; your workforce and other resource needs; your ability to capitalize on diversity; your opportunities to redirect resources to higher-priority products, services, or areas; financial, societal, ethical, regulatory, technological, security, and other potential risks and opportunities; your ability to prevent and respond to emergencies, including natural or other disasters; changes in the national or global economy; partner and supply chain requirements, strengths, and weaknesses; changes in your parent organization; and other factors unique to your organization.
>
> N4. Your ability to execute the strategic plan (2.1a[2]) should address your ability to mobilize the necessary resources and knowledge. It also should address your organizational agility based on contingency plans or, if circumstances require, a shift in plans and rapid execution of new or changed plans.
>
> N5. Strategic objectives that address key challenges and advantages (2.1b[2]) might include rapid response, customization, co-location with major customers or partners, workforce capability and capacity, specific joint ventures, virtual manufacturing, rapid innovation, ISO quality or environmental systems registration, web-based supplier and customer relationship management, and product and service quality enhancements. Responses to Item 2.1 should focus on your specific challenges and advantages-those most important to your ongoing success and to strengthening your organization's overall performance.
>
> N6. Item 2.1 addresses your overall organizational strategy, which might include changes in product offerings and customer engagement processes. However, the Item does not address product design or customer engagement strategies; you should address these factors in Items 6.1 and 3.1, as appropriate.

This Item [2.1] looks at how the organization determines core competencies, strategic challenges, and advantages and develops measurable, outcome-oriented strategic objectives to strengthen overall performance, competitiveness, and future success.

The first part of this Item [2.1a(1)] asks the organization to describe its strategic planning process and identify the key participants, key steps, and planning-time horizons. This helps examiners understand the steps and data used in the planning process. It is a good idea to provide a flowchart of the planning process. This helps examiners understand how the planning process works without wasting valuable space in the application.

The planning process should examine all the key factors, risks, challenges, and core competencies and other advantages that might affect the organization's future opportunities and directions—taking as long-term a view as possible but requiring no specific time horizon. This approach is intended to provide a thorough and realistic context for the development of a customer- and market-focused strategy to guide ongoing decision making, resource allocation, and effective management.

The organization must consider the key factors that affect its future success. These factors encompass external and internal influences on the organization. Each factor must be addressed and should show how relevant data and information are gathered and analyzed. Although the organization is not limited to the number of factors it considers important in planning, it must address the factors identified in Item 2.1a(2) unless a valid rationale can be offered as to why the factor is not appropriate. Together, these factors will cover the most important variables for any organization's future success.

> Note to applicants: If a strategic challenge or advantage listed in P.2b is not a true challenge or advantage that must be addressed as a part of strategic planning, delete it from the P.2b list to prevent confusion within the examiner team.

This planning process should also cover all types of competitive situations, strategic issues, planning approaches, and plans. The strategic plan produces a future- and results-oriented basis for action but does not require any specific type of formalized planning, planning departments, planning cycles, or a specified way of visualizing the future. Even if the organization is seeking to create an entirely new direction, effective planning still requires setting outcome-oriented objectives to define and guide critical future actions and monitor performance to ensure appropriate progress is being made.

Achieving and sustaining a leadership position in a competitive market requires a view of the future that includes not only the markets or segments in which the organization competes but also how it competes. How it competes presents many options and requires understanding of the organization's and competitors' strengths (including core competencies) and weaknesses.

> The thrust of strategy development is finding ways to create and ensure sustained competitive leadership.

To maintain competitive leadership, an increasingly important part of strategic planning requires processes to project the future collaborative and competitive environment accurately (see 2.2b). Such projections help detect competitive threats, shorten reaction time, and identify opportunities. Depending on the size and type of organization, maturity of markets, pace of change, and competitive parameters (such as price, costs, or innovation rate), organizations might use a variety of modeling, scenario, or other techniques to project the competitive and collaborative environment.

The second part of this Item [2.1b] asks for a summary of the organization's key strategic objectives and the timetable for accomplishing them. It also asks how these objectives address the core competencies, challenges, and advantages outlined in the Organizational Profile.

Strategic objectives define the outcome or desired end state that the organization must achieve to be successful in the future. Strategic objectives do not define activities or other actions that are needed to "enable" the organization to achieve its outcomes. Many times, organizations confuse outcomes with enablers since both can be measured.

Consider the following parable. A state legislature wants to make better use of the funds it appropriates for its libraries. The legislature learned that the per capita readership in its state is among the lowest in the nation. It wants the state to be in the top ten nationally by the year 2020.

After conducting a survey of library users, the library commission determined that readership was low because existing libraries were dusty, dark, and inconvenient and because of the Internet, fewer people visited the libraries. The strategic objective they developed was "by 2010, build in a dense population center a new library with plenty of open space, light, and free parking." The design and construction of the new library had clear, measurable milestones just like a good strategic objective should. The planners were happy with the new objective until the planning consultant asked, "How do you know the new library will bring in new readers? Have you ever built a new library and found that most of the users were not new, but simply decided to go to the new library instead of the old one?" The planners frowned a little and said, "Yes, it has happened before."

As it turns out, the building of a new library—best case—is only an enabler. The planners confused the action of building a new library with the legislature's desire to improve per capita readership in the state. In addition, focusing on "building" made other ways to increase readership, such as expanding Internet access, too easy to overlook. A better strategic objective might have been "increase readership in the state from 3 per thousand to 8 per thousand by 2010." Then, the desired outcomes became clear and a more complete range of actions could be examined.

Building a library may be an appropriate action (enabler) but not an outcome (unless your organization is a construction company). Clearly it is possible to build the library on time and under budget, declare victory for having met the objective, and *still* fail to increase readership to the top ten nationally.

The danger in confusing actions or enablers with outcomes is that leaders and managers can mistakenly believe they are making appropriate progress (completing actions) and yet completely fail to achieve the desired end state (achieving outcomes). Actions are critical to help workers understand their duties, but leaders must be sure to define the true outcome. Monitoring actions is an important part of deploying and executing the strategic plan (required in Item 2.2), but completing tasks should never be confused with achieving desired results (outcomes). Success is built on achievement, not just activity.

The purpose of the timetable required by Item 2.1b(1) is to provide a basis for projecting the path that improvement should take. This enables the leaders who monitor progress to determine when performance is deviating from plan and when adjustments should be made to get back on track. Consider Figure 23. The performance goal four years into the future is to achieve a level of performance of 100. The organization's starting level is 20. At the end of year one, the organization achieved a performance level of 40, represented by the circle symbol. It appears that that level of performance is on track toward the goal of 100. However, the path from the current state to the future state is rarely a straight line. Unless the expected trajectory is known (or at least estimated), it is not possible to evaluate the progress accurately to ensure strategic objectives are integrated with other requirements of senior leader review [4.1b(1)] and priority setting [4.1b(2)]. Without timetables or trajectories, leaders are forced to default to best guess or intuition as a basis for comparing actual, measurable progress against expected progress. Based on intuition, the progress depicted in Figure 23 at the end of year one looks good.

In Figure 24, the planned trajectory is represented by the triangle symbols. When compared with the current level of performance (circle symbol), it is clear that there is a performance shortfall of approximately 30.

In Figure 25, the planned trajectory is represented by the square symbols. When compared with the current level of performance (the circle symbol), it is clear that the performance is ahead of schedule.

There are several possible decisions that leaders could make based on the information in Figure 25. It

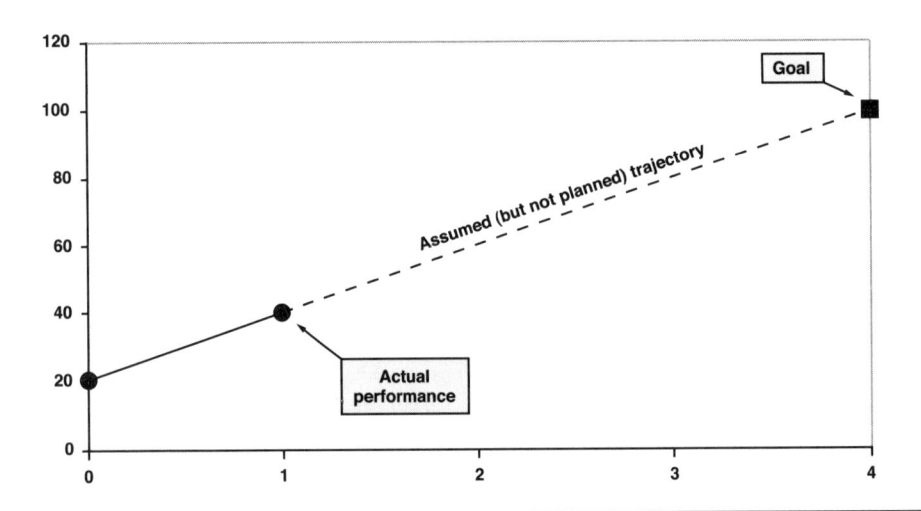

Figure 23 Assumed trajectory.

2 Strategic Planning

might mean that the original estimates/goals were low and should be reset. It might also mean that the process did not need all of the resources it had available. These resources may be better used in areas where performance is not ahead of schedule.

In any case, without knowing the expected path toward a goal, leaders are forced to guess whether the level of progress is appropriate.

The last part of this Item requires the organization to evaluate the options it considered in the strategic planning process to ensure it responded fully to the factors identified in Item 2.1a(2) that were most important to business success (including strategic challenges, advantages, and opportunities for innovation). This last step helps the organization *close the loop* to make sure the factors influencing organization success are adequately analyzed and support key strategic objectives.

Strategic plan execution is a significant challenge, especially given market demands for agility and preparation for unexpected change, such as disruptive technologies that may upset an otherwise fast-paced but more predictable marketplace. Therefore, this Item and Item 2.2 highlight the need to focus not only on developing plans but also on the capability to execute them.

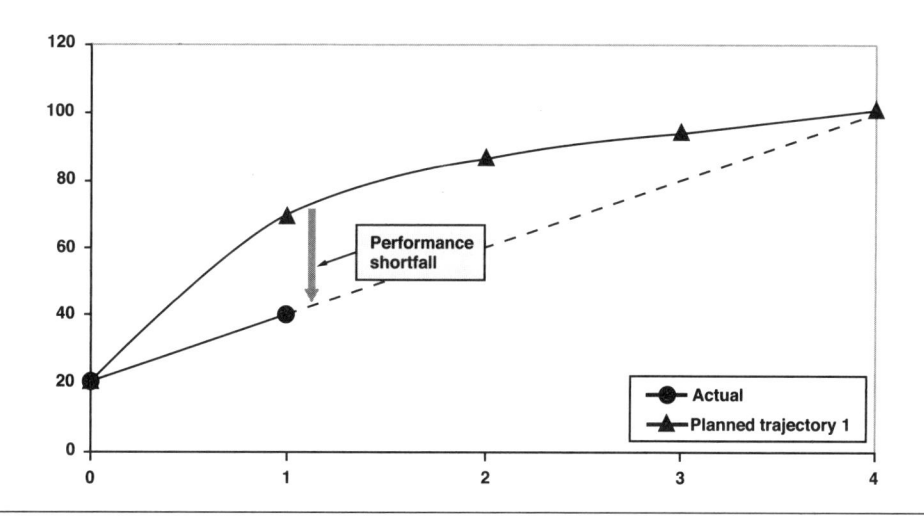

Figure 24 Planned trajectory 1—performance shortfall.

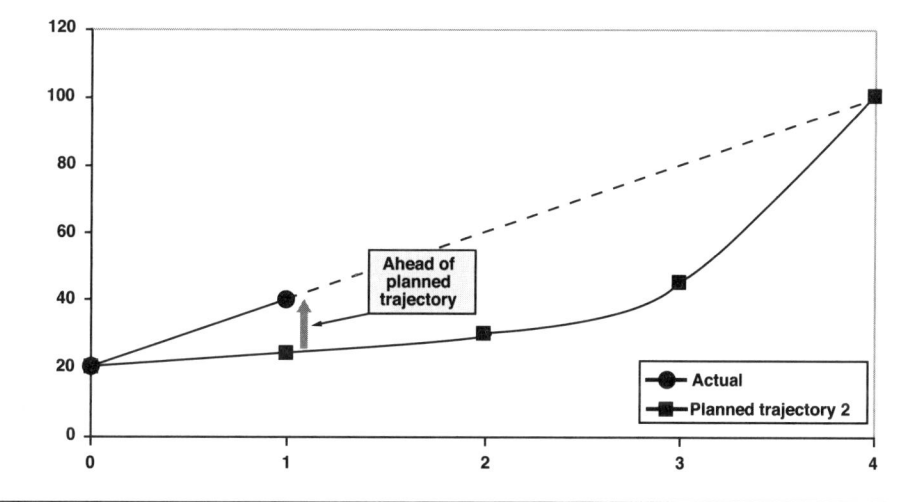

Figure 25 Planned trajectory 2—ahead of plan.

Insights to Performance Excellence 2009–2010

2.1 Strategy Development

Basic Approach Requirements*: *Develop the organization's strategy.*

Overall Approach Requirements*: *Effectively establish strategy and strategic objectives to address the organization's strategic challenges and leverage advantages. Summarize the organization's key strategic objectives and their related goals.*

Multiple Approach Requirements: *The following diagram describes multiple approach requirements.*

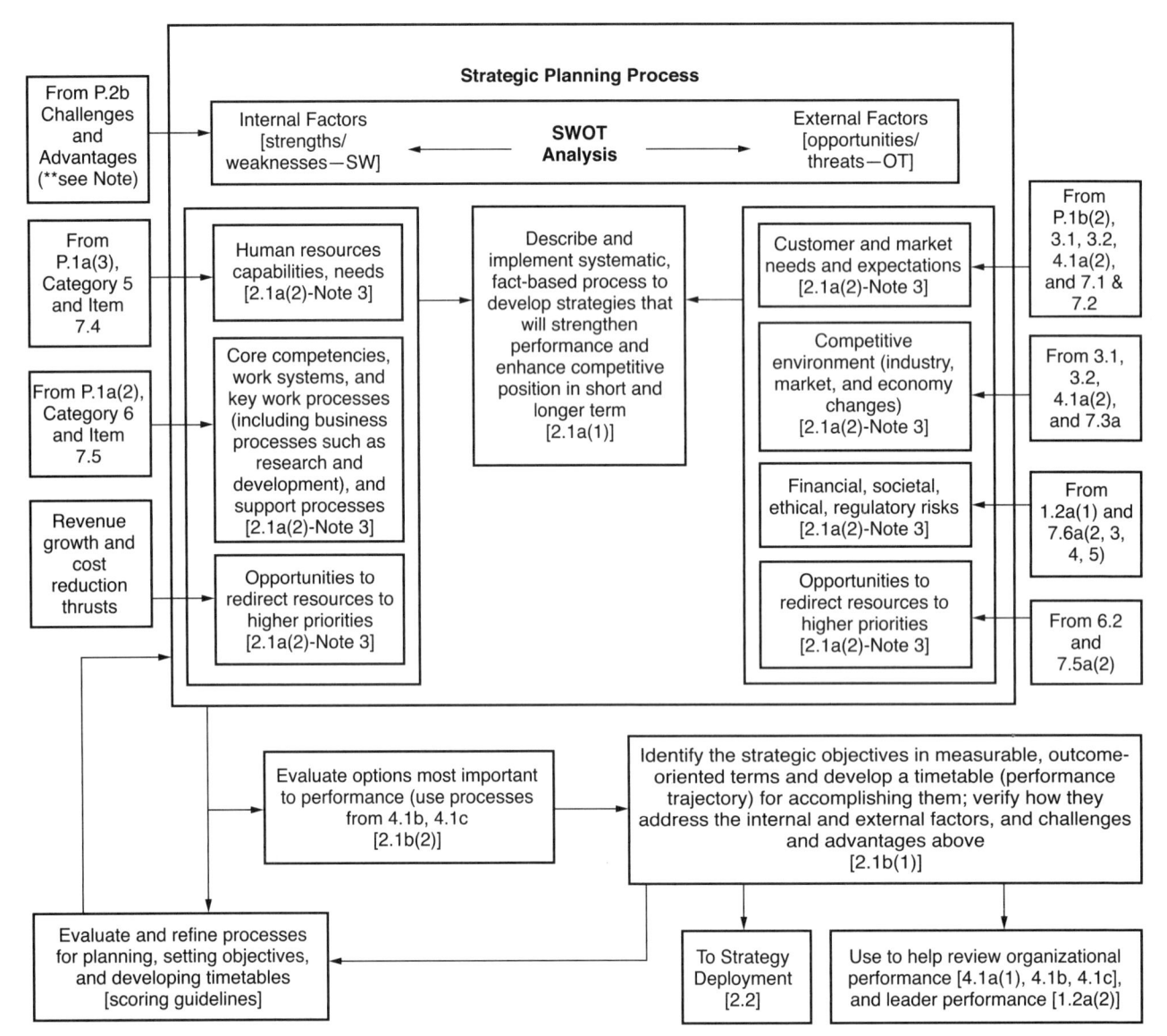

Strategic Planning Process

- From P.2b Challenges and Advantages (**see Note) → Internal Factors [strengths/weaknesses—SW] ↔ **SWOT Analysis** ↔ External Factors [opportunities/threats—OT]

- From P.1a(3), Category 5 and Item 7.4 → Human resources capabilities, needs [2.1a(2)-Note 3]

- From P.1a(2), Category 6 and Item 7.5 → Core competencies, work systems, and key work processes (including business processes such as research and development), and support processes [2.1a(2)-Note 3]

- Revenue growth and cost reduction thrusts → Opportunities to redirect resources to higher priorities [2.1a(2)-Note 3]

- Describe and implement systematic, fact-based process to develop strategies that will strengthen performance and enhance competitive position in short and longer term [2.1a(1)]

- Customer and market needs and expectations [2.1a(2)-Note 3] ← From P.1b(2), 3.1, 3.2, 4.1a(2), and 7.1 & 7.2

- Competitive environment (industry, market, and economy changes) [2.1a(2)-Note 3] ← From 3.1, 3.2, 4.1a(2), and 7.3a

- Financial, societal, ethical, regulatory risks [2.1a(2)-Note 3] ← From 1.2a(1) and 7.6a(2, 3, 4, 5)

- Opportunities to redirect resources to higher priorities [2.1a(2)-Note 3] ← From 6.2 and 7.5a(2)

↓

Evaluate options most important to performance (use processes from 4.1b, 4.1c) [2.1b(2)]

→ Identify the strategic objectives in measurable, outcome-oriented terms and develop a timetable (performance trajectory) for accomplishing them; verify how they address the internal and external factors, and challenges and advantages above [2.1b(1)]

Evaluate and refine processes for planning, setting objectives, and developing timetables [scoring guidelines]

To Strategy Deployment [2.2]

Use to help review organizational performance [4.1a(1), 4.1b, 4.1c], and leader performance [1.2a(2)]

---

*Multiple-level requirements usually incorporate Basic and Overall requirements. To avoid confusion, the first time a requirement appears in an Item establishes its level for scoring purposes. If the requirement first appears at the Overall Approach Level and again at the Multiple Level, the requirement should be considered an Overall-level requirement. For a more complete explanation see the chapter on Scoring System and the Scoring Calibration Guidelines.

**Note: "Challenges" may include internal weaknesses and external threats. Strategic objectives should mitigate or lessen their adverse impact. "Advantages" may include internal strengths and external opportunities. Strategic objectives should build on or help the organization benefit from these advantages.

2.1 Key Strategy Development Item Linkages

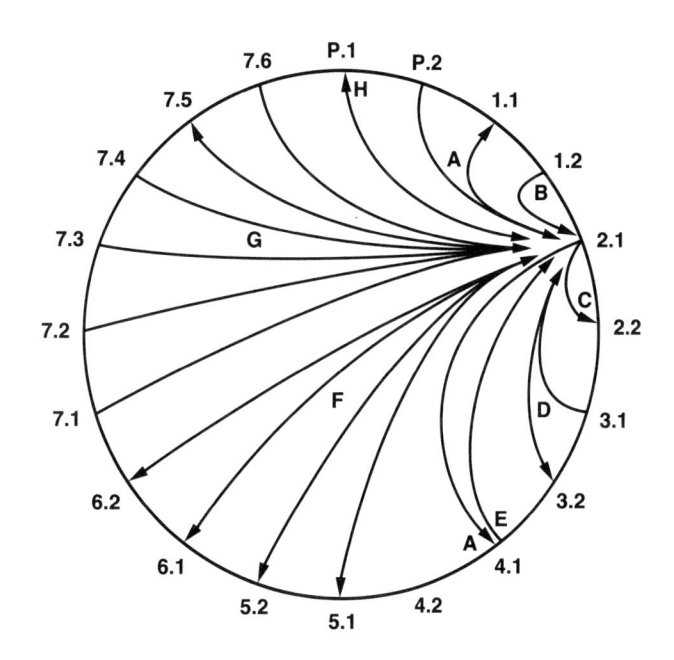

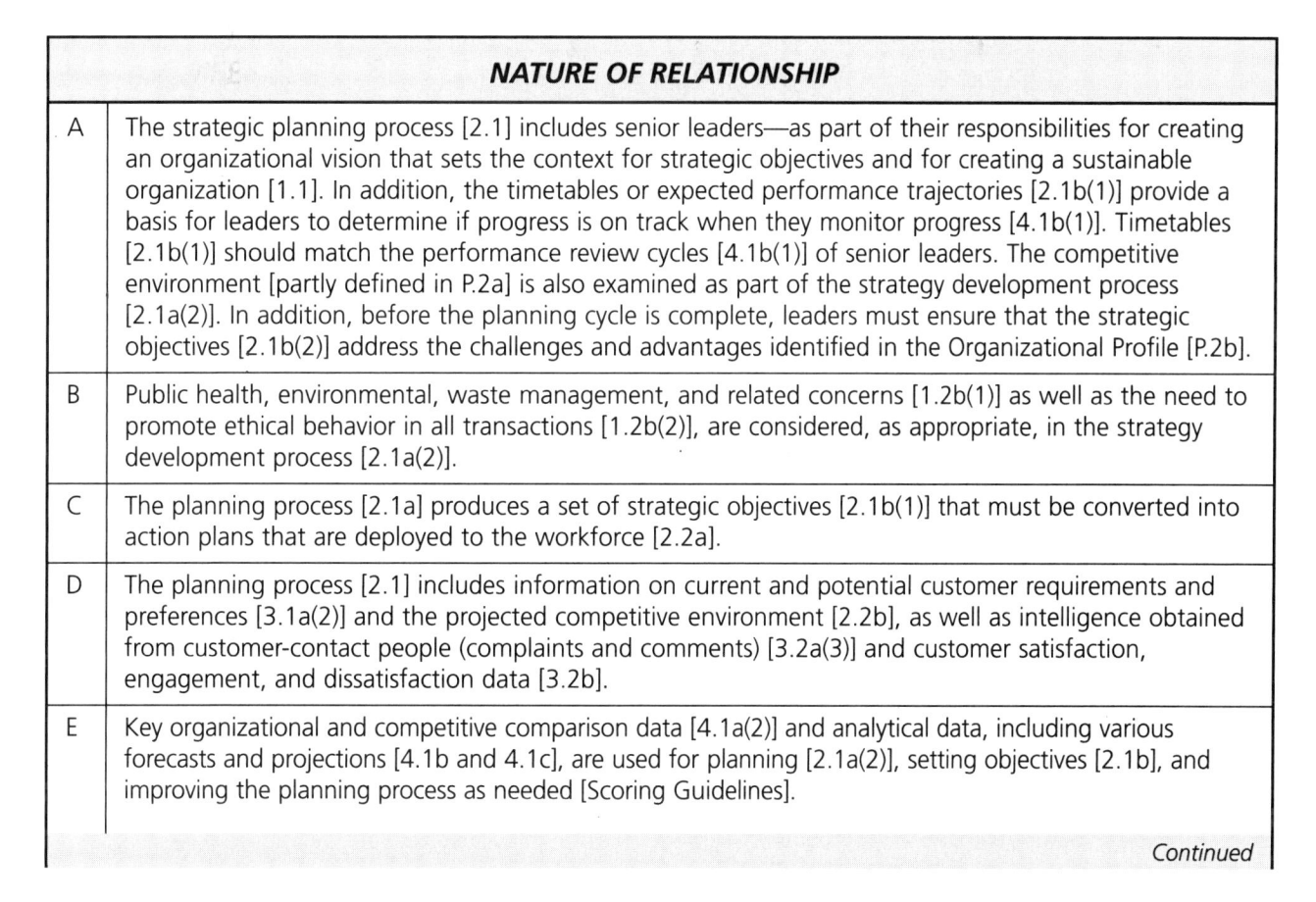

	NATURE OF RELATIONSHIP
A	The strategic planning process [2.1] includes senior leaders—as part of their responsibilities for creating an organizational vision that sets the context for strategic objectives and for creating a sustainable organization [1.1]. In addition, the timetables or expected performance trajectories [2.1b(1)] provide a basis for leaders to determine if progress is on track when they monitor progress [4.1b(1)]. Timetables [2.1b(1)] should match the performance review cycles [4.1b(1)] of senior leaders. The competitive environment [partly defined in P.2a] is also examined as part of the strategy development process [2.1a(2)]. In addition, before the planning cycle is complete, leaders must ensure that the strategic objectives [2.1b(2)] address the challenges and advantages identified in the Organizational Profile [P.2b].
B	Public health, environmental, waste management, and related concerns [1.2b(1)] as well as the need to promote ethical behavior in all transactions [1.2b(2)], are considered, as appropriate, in the strategy development process [2.1a(2)].
C	The planning process [2.1a] produces a set of strategic objectives [2.1b(1)] that must be converted into action plans that are deployed to the workforce [2.2a].
D	The planning process [2.1] includes information on current and potential customer requirements and preferences [3.1a(2)] and the projected competitive environment [2.2b], as well as intelligence obtained from customer-contact people (complaints and comments) [3.2a(3)] and customer satisfaction, engagement, and dissatisfaction data [3.2b].
E	Key organizational and competitive comparison data [4.1a(2)] and analytical data, including various forecasts and projections [4.1b and 4.1c], are used for planning [2.1a(2)], setting objectives [2.1b], and improving the planning process as needed [Scoring Guidelines].

Continued

	NATURE OF RELATIONSHIP	Continued
F	Information on workforce capability and capacity [5.2a] and work process capabilities [Category 6] is considered in the strategic planning process as part of the determination of internal strengths and weaknesses [2.1a(2)]. *To avoid cluttering diagrams in Categories 5 and 6, these linkage arrows will not be repeated in other diagrams.*	
G	Product and service [7.1], customer-focused [7.2], financial and market [7.3], workforce-focused [7.4], process effectiveness [7.5], and leadership [7.6] outcomes are used in the planning process [2.1a(2)] to set strategic objectives [2.1b(1)]. In addition, results in 7.6a(1) must specifically report on progress toward achieving the strategic objectives and are used in subsequent planning.	
H	Workforce educational levels, diversity, and other characteristics [P.1a(3)] relate to human resource strengths and weaknesses and are considered during the strategic planning process [2.1a(2)]. Plans consider the requirements of customers [P.1b(2)], and strategy [2.1] may contribute to the redefinition of key customer groups, market segments, or core competencies [P.1a(2)].	

IF YOU DON'T DO WHAT THE CRITERIA REQUIRE . . .	
Item Reference	**Possible Adverse Consequences**
2.1a(1)	Planning involves making assumptions about the future that are not always correct. Incorrect assumptions can be considered "blind spots" in the planning process. To prevent blind spots, different points of view or information are needed. Blind spots contribute to flawed plans. Without clearly defined short- and longer-term planning horizons, it may be difficult to properly align the analysis and collection of market and industry forecast data to support effective planning. The shorter the planning horizon, the easier it is to be accurate in forecasting. However, the planning horizon should be at least as long as the time it takes the organization to design, develop, and deliver new products and services required by customers and markets. For example, if the design–delivery cycle is seven years (as it was in the U.S. automobile industry in the 1970s and 1980s), then to be effective an organization must be able to forecast or anticipate customer and market requirements seven years out—which is difficult to do accurately. Alternatively, if the organization reduces its design–delivery cycle time to less than 24 months (as did the Japanese automobile industry), it will be able to reduce the required planning horizon, and more accurately anticipate customer and market requirements.
2.1a(2)	The failure to address key factors in the planning process (the organization's strengths, weaknesses, opportunities, and threats; major shifts in technology, markets, competition, or regulatory environment; organizational sustainability, core competencies, and business continuity in emergencies; or the ability to execute the strategic plan) usually result in a flawed strategic plan—a plan that has overlooked an element critical to future success. For example, an organization may fail to achieve strategic objectives if it assumed (incorrectly) that a key supplier would be able to deliver critical components at a certain time. Likewise, a strategic plan that does not adequately account for the arrival of competitive offerings or new technologies in the marketplace can be faced with major hurdles (consider the impact of the quartz watch on the traditional Swiss watch industry). Failing to consider or correctly forecast the impact of these elements may result in a strategic plan that cannot be achieved.
	Continued

	IF YOU DON'T DO WHAT THE CRITERIA REQUIRE . . . Continued
Item Reference	**Possible Adverse Consequences**
2.1b(1)	Knowing whether the strategy is unfolding as expected is critical to the successful performance of the organization and the leadership. The failure to develop a timetable with clearly defined targets for accomplishing strategic objectives that are integrated (consistent) with the performance review frequency makes it extremely difficult for leaders to monitor organizational performance effectively [as required by Items 1.1b(2) and 4.1b(1)]. Without defined milestones, leaders may be forced to guess whether the rate of progress is appropriate. Without clear time lines or trajectories for growth, leaders frequently assume the path between current state and desired state (goals) is linear. Data indicate that the actual path is almost never linear; so the assumptions of linearity that leaders make in the absence of clear time lines and trajectories are usually incorrect.
2.1b(2)	Strategy development is an ongoing, dynamic process. It is often a difficult process that takes a considerable amount of time to complete initially and then requires continual attention to address rapidly changing threats and opportunities. However, if leaders fail to ensure that planning fully addresses organizational changes and advantages it faces and ensures that the strategic objectives identify opportunities for innovation and balance the needs of all key stakeholders, the plan may be ineffective and the time it took to develop the plan may be wasted. Worse yet, these blind spots, if not addressed, may threaten the organization's sustainability. Strategic objectives should address current and future core competencies.

2.1 STRATEGY DEVELOPMENT—SAMPLE EFFECTIVE PRACTICES

A. Strategy Development Process

- Business goals, strategies, and issues are addressed and reported in measurable terms. Strategic objectives consider future requirements needed to achieve organizational leadership after considering the performance levels that other organizations are likely to achieve in the same planning time frame.

- Web-based or e-commerce initiatives are considered as part of developing new business or new markets.

- The planning and objective-setting process encourages input (but not necessarily decision making) from a variety of people at all levels throughout the organization.

- Data on customer requirements, key markets, benchmarks, suppliers and partners, workforce dynamics, and organizational capabilities (internal and external factors) are used to develop plans.

- Plans and the planning process itself are evaluated each cycle for accuracy and completeness —more often if needed to keep pace with changing business requirements.

- Opportunities for improvement in the planning process are identified systematically and carried out in each planning cycle.

- Every core competency is the subject of review to make sure potential weaknesses are eliminated.

- Refinements have been made in the process of planning, plan deployment, and receiving input from work units. Improvements in planning cycle time, resources, and accuracy are documented.

B. Strategic Objectives

- Strategic objectives are measurable, outcome-oriented results the organization must achieve to be successful in the future. Strategic objectives are then converted into actions that enable the organization to achieve its objectives—which may be expressed as a series of activities. Strategic objectives must address current and future core competencies.

- Strategic objectives are identified and a timetable (or planned growth trajectory) for accomplishing the objectives is set. The time lines match the senior leaders' review cycle. For example, if leaders review progress against goals quarterly, the time lines identify the expected level of performance for each quarter.

- Options to obtain best performance for the strategic objectives are systematically evaluated against the internal and external factors used in the strategy development process.

- The process of setting time lines or trajectories and the accuracy of the projections are analyzed and refined.

- Best practices from other providers, competitors, or outside benchmarks are identified and used to provide better estimates of trajectories.

- Strategic objectives define the desired end state, not "enablers."

2.2 STRATEGY DEPLOYMENT: How do you deploy your strategy? (45 Pts.) PROCESS

Describe how your organization converts its strategic objectives into action plans. Summarize your organization's action plans, how they are deployed, and key action plan performance measures or indicators. Project your organization's future performance relative to key comparisons on these performance measures or indicators.

Within your response, include answers to the following questions:

a. Action Plan Development and Deployment

(1) What are your key short- and longer-term action plans? What are the key planned changes, if any, in your products, your customers and markets, and how you will operate?

(2) How do you develop and deploy action plans throughout the organization to your workforce and to key suppliers and partners, as appropriate, to achieve your key strategic objectives? How do you ensure that the key outcomes of your action plans can be sustained?

(3) How do you ensure that financial and other resources are available to support the accomplishment of your action plans, while meeting current obligations? How do you allocate these resources to support the accomplishment of the plans? How do you assess and manage the financial and other risks associated with the plans?

(4) How do you establish and deploy modified action plans if circumstances require a shift in plans and rapid execution of new plans?

(5) What are your key human resource or workforce plans to accomplish your short- and longer-term strategic objectives and action plans? How do the plans address potential impacts on people in your workforce and any potential changes to workforce capability and capacity needs?

(6) What are your key performance measures or indicators for tracking the achievement and effectiveness of your action plans? How do you ensure that your overall action plan measurement system reinforces organizational alignment? How do you ensure that the measurement system covers all key deployment areas and stakeholders?

b. Performance Projection

For the key performance measures or indicators identified in 2.2a(6), what are your performance projections for both your short- and longer-term planning time horizons? How are these projections determined? How does your projected performance compare with the projected performance of your competitors or comparable organizations? How does it compare with key benchmarks, goals, and past performance, as appropriate? If there are current or projected gaps in performance against your competitors or comparable organizations, how will you address them?

Notes:

N1. Strategy and action plan development and deployment are closely linked to other Items in the Criteria. The following are examples of key linkages:

- Item 1.1 for how your senior leaders set and communicate organizational direction
- Category 3 for gathering customer and market knowledge as input to your strategy and action plans and for deploying action plans
- Category 4 for measurement, analysis, and knowledge management to support your key information needs, to support your development of strategy, to provide an effective basis for your performance measurements, and to track progress relative to your strategic objectives and action plans

Continued

Insights to Performance Excellence 2009–2010

> **Notes:** *Continued*
> - Category 5 for meeting your workforce capability and capacity needs, for workforce development and learning system design and needs, and for implementing workforce-related changes resulting from action plans
> - Category 6 for changes to core competencies, work systems, and work process requirements resulting from your action plans
> - Item 7.6 for specific accomplishments relative to your organizational strategy and action plans
>
> N2. Measures and indicators of projected performance (2.2b) might include changes resulting from new ventures; organizational acquisitions or mergers; new value creation; market entry and shifts; new legislative mandates, legal requirements, or industry standards; and significant anticipated innovations in products and technology.

The first part of this Item [2.2a] looks at how the organization translates its measurable, outcome-oriented strategic objectives (which were identified in Item 2.1b(1)) into action plans to accomplish the objectives and to enable assessment of progress relative to action plans. Overall, the intent of this Item is to ensure that strategies are converted to actions and deployed at all levels throughout the organization to align work for goal achievement.

It is important for the organization to achieve alignment and consistency—for example, via the alignment and integration of mission, vision, strategic objectives, work systems, work processes, key measurements, and reward and recognition. Leaders, managers, and other members of the workforce must develop action plans that address the key strategic objectives (which were developed using the processes in Item 2.1). Organizations must summarize key short- and longer-term action plans. Particular attention is given to products and services, customers and markets, how the organization operates, and key human resource plans that will enable accomplishment of strategic objectives and action plans.

The organization should identify the key measures/indicators it uses to track progress relative to the action plans. The organization should also use these measures or indicators to ensure organizational alignment of all key work units and stakeholders. Alignment and consistency help provide a basis for setting and communicating priorities for ongoing improvement activities—part of the daily work of all work units. Action plans should include human resource plans that support the overall strategy.

Without effective alignment, routine work and acts of improvement can be random and serve to suboptimize organizational performance. In Figure 26, the arrows represent the well-intended work carried out by the workers in organizations that lack a clear set of expectations and direction. People, managers, and work units strive diligently to achieve goals they believe are important. Each is pulling hard—but not necessarily in ways that ensure performance excellence. The lack of clear, overarching strategic objectives and action plans encourages the creation of *fiefdoms* or *silos* within organizations. The lack of clear direction from leaders forces workers to invent their own priorities.

With a clear, well-communicated strategic objective and related actions, it is easier to know when daily work is out of alignment and not integrated throughout the organization. The large arrow in Figure 27 represents the strategic plan pointing the direction the organization must take to be successful

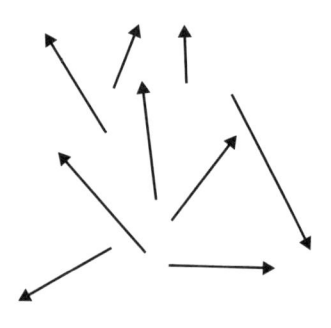

Figure 26 Nonaligned work.

and achieve its mission and vision. The strategic plan and accompanying measures make it possible to analyze work and business practices (represented by the smaller arrows) to know when they are not aligned and to help workers, including leaders, to know when adjustments are required.

A well-deployed and understood strategic plan helps everyone in the organization distinguish between random acts of improvement and aligned improvement. Random acts of improvement give a false sense of accomplishment and rarely produce optimum benefits for the organization. For example, a decision to improve a business process that is not aligned with the strategic plan (as the small bold arrow in Figure 28 represents) usually results in a wasteful expenditure of time, money, and human resources—improvement without benefiting customers or enhancing operating effectiveness.

On the other hand, by working systematically to realign or strengthen processes that are aligned with the strategic plan, the organization moves closer to achieving success, as Figure 29 indicates.

Ultimately, all processes and procedures of an organization should be aligned to maximize the achievement of strategic plans, as Figure 30 demonstrates. An alignment failure produces suboptimal performance, wastes resources, and hurts worker motivation and morale (engagement).

Adequate resources are also critical to success. The organization can perform many types of analyses to ensure that adequate financial resources are available to support accomplishment of action plans. For ongoing operations, these might include analysis of cash flow, net income statements, and current liabilities versus current assets. For investments to accomplish action plans, the organization may analyze

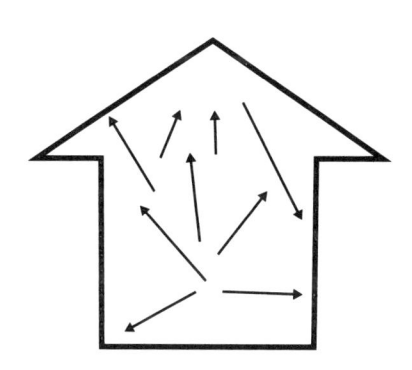

Figure 27 Strategic direction.

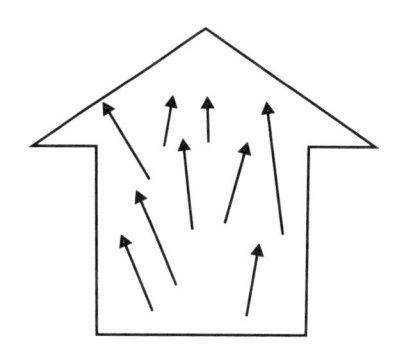

Figure 29 Moving toward alignment.

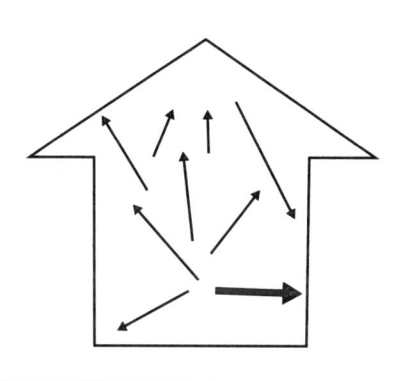

Figure 28 Random improvement.

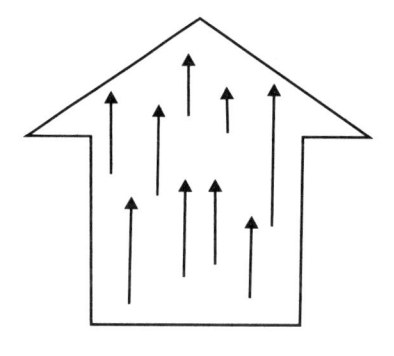

Figure 30 Systematic alignment.

discounted cash flow, return on investment (ROI), or return on invested capital (ROIC). Specific types of analyses will vary depending on the organization. These analyses should help assess the financial viability of current operations and the potential viability of and risks associated with action plan initiatives.

Critical action-plan resource requirements include human resource plans that should be put in place to support the overall strategy. Examples of possible human resource plan elements are:

- Increase in workforce engagement and empowerment, and fact-based decision making

- Initiatives to promote greater labor–management cooperation

- Initiatives to foster knowledge sharing and organizational learning

- Minimize the adverse impact of outsourcing on the workforce

- Modifying compensation and recognition systems to reflect team, organizational, stock market, customer, or other performance attributes

- Leader and workforce development initiatives, such as programs for future leaders, partnerships with universities to help ensure the future availability of an educated and skilled workforce, and establishment of training programs on new technologies critical to the organization's future success

The second part of this Item [2.2b] asks the organization to provide a projection of key performance measures and/or indicators, including key performance targets and/or goals for both short- and longer-term planning horizons. This projected performance is the basis for comparing the organization's past performance with the performance of competitors and benchmarks, as appropriate.

Projections and comparisons in this Area are intended to help the organization's leaders understand and track dynamic, competitive performance factors. Through this tracking process, they should be better prepared to take into account rate of improvement and change relative to competitors or comparable organizations and relative to their own targets or stretch goals. Such tracking serves as a key diagnostic management tool.

In addition to improvement relative to past performance and to competitors, projected performance also might include changes resulting from new business ventures, entry into new markets, e-commerce initiatives, introduction of new technologies, product or service innovations, or other strategic thrusts.

Without this comparison information, it is possible to set goals that, even if attained, may not result in competitive advantage. More than one high-performing company has been surprised by a competitor that set and achieved more aggressive goals. Consider the example represented by Figure 31. Imagine that you are ahead of your competition and committed to a 10 percent increase in profit over your base year. After eight years you are twice as profitable. To your surprise, you find that your competitor has increased 20 percent each year. You have achieved your goal, but your competitor has beaten you. After 10 years, the competitor has a significant lead. In a competitive market, it is not good enough to achieve your goals unless your goals place you in a winning position.

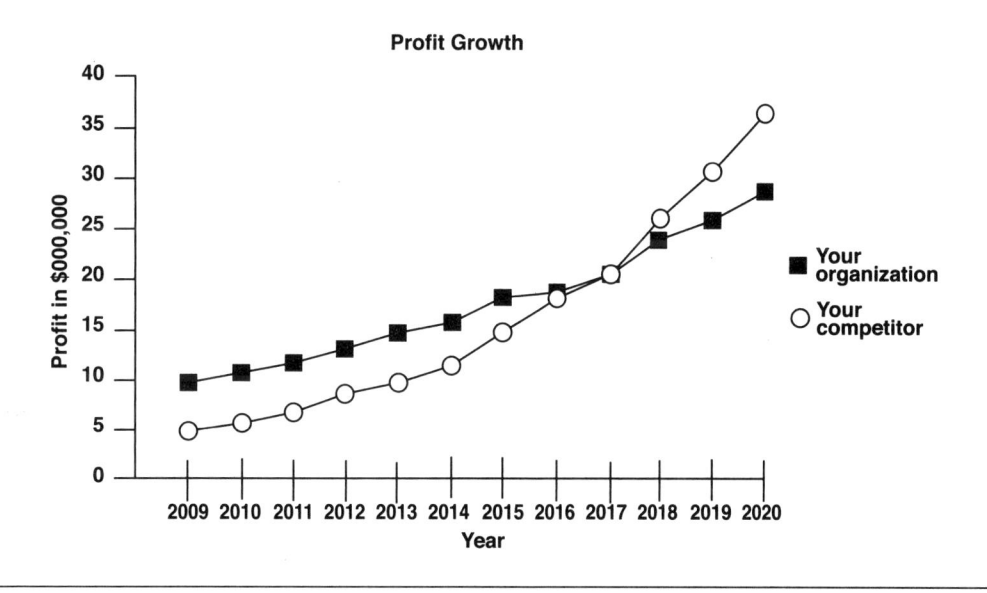

Figure 31 Projecting competitor's future performance.

2.2 Strategy Deployment

Basic Approach Requirements*:   *Deploy the organization's strategy.*

Overall Approach Requirements*:   *Effectively convert strategic objectives into action plans. Summarize the action plans, the method for deploying them, and related key performance measures or indicators. Effectively project the organization's future performance relative to key comparisons on these performance measures or indicators.*

Multiple Approach Requirements: *The following diagram describes multiple approach requirements.*

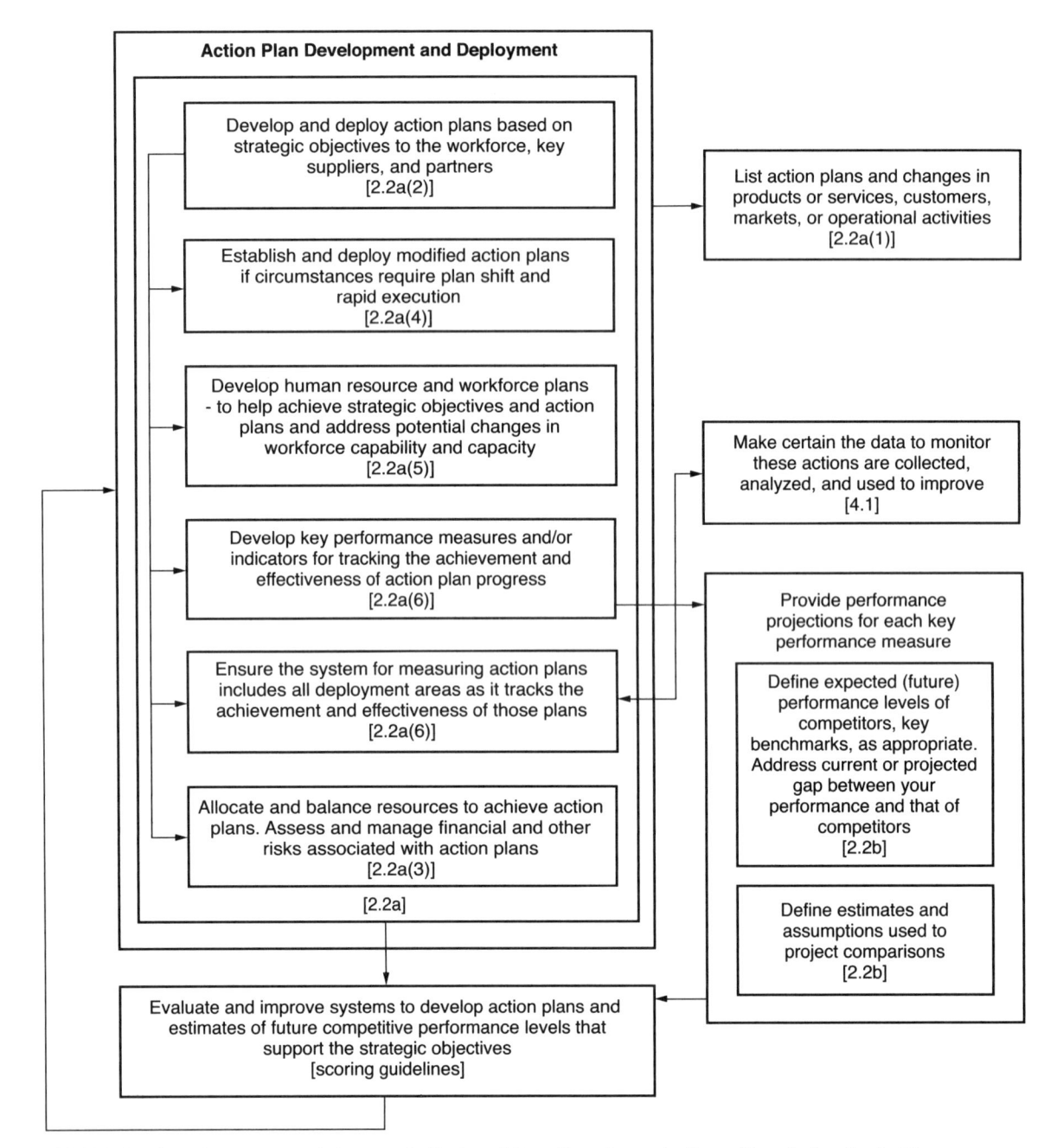

Action Plan Development and Deployment

- Develop and deploy action plans based on strategic objectives to the workforce, key suppliers, and partners [2.2a(2)]
- Establish and deploy modified action plans if circumstances require plan shift and rapid execution [2.2a(4)]
- Develop human resource and workforce plans - to help achieve strategic objectives and action plans and address potential changes in workforce capability and capacity [2.2a(5)]
- Develop key performance measures and/or indicators for tracking the achievement and effectiveness of action plan progress [2.2a(6)]
- Ensure the system for measuring action plans includes all deployment areas as it tracks the achievement and effectiveness of those plans [2.2a(6)]
- Allocate and balance resources to achieve action plans. Assess and manage financial and other risks associated with action plans [2.2a(3)]

[2.2a]

- List action plans and changes in products or services, customers, markets, or operational activities [2.2a(1)]
- Make certain the data to monitor these actions are collected, analyzed, and used to improve [4.1]
- Provide performance projections for each key performance measure
- Define expected (future) performance levels of competitors, key benchmarks, as appropriate. Address current or projected gap between your performance and that of competitors [2.2b]
- Define estimates and assumptions used to project comparisons [2.2b]

Evaluate and improve systems to develop action plans and estimates of future competitive performance levels that support the strategic objectives [scoring guidelines]

---

* Multiple-level requirements usually incorporate Basic and Overall requirements. To avoid confusion, the first time a requirement appears in an Item establishes its level for scoring purposes. If the requirement first appears at the Overall Approach Level and again at the Multiple Level, the requirement should be considered an Overall-level requirement. For a more complete explanation see the chapter on Scoring System and the Scoring Calibration Guidelines.

2.2 Key Strategy Deployment Item Linkages

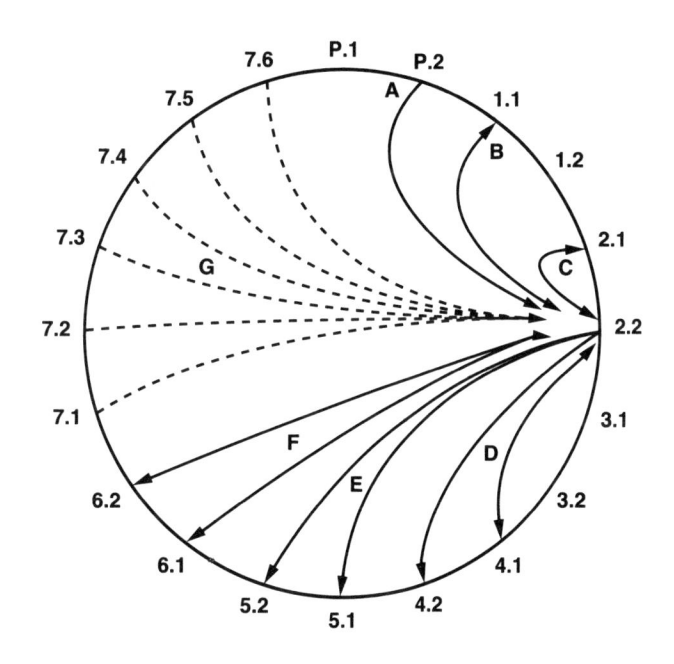

	NATURE OF RELATIONSHIP
A	The competitive environment defined in P.2a should help focus the projection of competitors' future performance in 2.2b.
B	To ensure vision is accomplished, the leadership team [1.1a] ensures that action plans are aligned throughout the organization with strategic objectives [2.2a(2)], and that resources are allocated to ensure the actions are accomplished [2.2a(3)].
C	The planning process [2.1a] develops the strategic objectives [2.1b(1)] that are converted into action plans to support these objectives [2.2a(2)]. Gaps between the organization's projected performance and that of competitors [2.2b] may cause the planning process to change [2.1a(1, 2)] and may change strategic objectives [2.1b(1)].
D	The action plans [2.2a(1)] and related performance measures [2.2a(6)] define part of the data that need to be collected [4.1a], analyzed to support decision making [4.1b], used to define improvement priorities [4.1c], and help define requirements for data availability and hardware and software reliability [4.2]. Benchmarking processes [4.1a(2)] are used to help project future performance of competitors and/or comparable organizations [2.2b].
E	Measures, action plans, and human resource plans [2.2a(1,2, 3] are used to align and develop workforce-focused processes [5.1, 5.2]. It is particularly important that action plans and measures [2.2a(1, 2, 4, 6)] are aligned with and supported by recognition and reward processes [5.1a(3)].
F	Measures and action plans [2.2a(1, 2, 4, 6)] are used to drive and align work processes to achieve improved performance [6.1, 6.2]. Feedback from work systems [6.1] and work processes [6.2] helps reinforce alignment with action plans and measures [2.2a(6)].
G	Results data [Category 7] are used to help determine performance projections for short- and longer-term goal setting [2.2b]. *To avoid clutter and make the diagrams more readable, these relationships will not be repeated on all of the Category 7 linkage diagrams.*

	IF YOU DON'T DO WHAT THE CRITERIA REQUIRE...
Item Reference	**Possible Adverse Consequences**
2.2a(1)	The inability to articulate and communicate key short- and longer-term action plans usually means those plans do not exist, or they are expressed as vague generalities. Unclear plans make it more difficult to help employees at all levels of the organization understand what work they must do to help the organization achieve future success. Again, without clear direction from the top, employees will still work hard, but their work may be unfocused as they follow their own ideas for appropriate action—everyone is not pulling in the same direction.
2.2a(2)	The failure to develop action plans to carry out strategic objectives and employ them at all levels of the organization usually means that work may not be aligned to achieve the strategy. Instead, there is a tendency for managers and other employees to focus their work on things they believe are important. This can result in significant resources being spent on activities that do not contribute to the objectives the organization's leaders have determined are critical for its future success.
2.2a(3)	The failure to allocate appropriate resources or balance resources to accomplish action plans frequently means that some plans are not accomplished due to insufficient resources, while other plans are accomplished inefficiently because of too many resources. In both cases, the value to the customer and the organization is suboptimized. Failure to assess financial risks accurately may cause leaders to overestimate available resources and overcommit operationally. This, too, may lead to poor performance.
2.2a(4)	In a fast-paced, highly competitive market, the failure to adjust plans quickly and execute them rapidly places the organization at a competitive disadvantage. It may cause significant market erosion from which recovery is difficult. For example, in the late 1990s Motorola was slow to change plans and deliver digital cellular phones to the market. They went from being the market leader to third place, and they have not yet recovered.
2.2a(5)	By definition, *plans* describe activities or actions that have not yet taken place. Many times, in order to execute plans, employees must possess skills, knowledge, or abilities that they do not currently possess. Without appropriate plans to develop, acquire, or motivate the human resources necessary to carry out desired actions, the organization may not be able to achieve its strategic objectives. Its employees may not have the skills, knowledge, or abilities to carry out the actions required for success in the future.
2.2a(6)	Without appropriate measures or indicators it is difficult for leaders, managers, and employees throughout the organization to determine if they are making appropriate progress. It is also more difficult for leaders to communicate expectations accurately. Unclear expectations increase the likelihood that employees will not understand what they are required to do to achieve strategic objectives. Consider the adage, *what gets measured gets done.* Without appropriate measures it is difficult to focus everyone on doing the right things.
2.2b	In the best-performing organizations, strategic goals are designed to enable the organization to win in competitive situations. If an organization desires to achieve a leadership position, it must understand where the competition is likely to be in the future before it sets its goals. Unless the organization's leaders understand the likely future performance levels of key competitors (in the same planning horizon), they may set an aggressive goal, achieve that goal, and still lose—finding themselves behind the competition.

2.2 STRATEGY DEPLOYMENT—SAMPLE EFFECTIVE PRACTICES

A. Action Plan Development and Deployment

- Plans are in place to optimize operational performance and improve customer focus using tools such as Lean Enterprise, ISO 9000, and Six Sigma, which can help streamline work processes and reduce cycle time.

- Actions have been defined in measurable terms, which align with strategic objectives and enable the organization to sustain leadership positions for major products and services for key customers or markets.

- Actions to achieve key organizational results (operational performance requirements) are defined and tracked at all levels of the organization.

- Planned performance and productivity levels are defined in measurable terms for all key operations.

- Planned actions are challenging, realistic, achievable, and understood by employees throughout the organization.

- Resources are available and committed to achieve the plans (minimize unfunded mandates). Capital projects are funded according to strategic plans and priorities.

- Plans are absolutely used to guide operational performance improvements. Plans drive budget and action, not the other way around.

- Incremental (short-term) tactics to achieve long-term plans are defined in measurable terms and time lines are in place to help monitor progress.

- Strategic plans, short- and long-term goals, and performance measures are understood and used to drive actions throughout the organization.

- All individuals in the organization, at all levels, understand how their work contributes to achieving organizational (or their unit) goals and plans.

- Plans are followed to ensure that resources are deployed and redeployed as needed to support goals.

- Human resource and workforce plans support strategic plans and goals. Plans show how the workforce will be developed to ensure capacity and capability exist to enable the organization to achieve its strategic goals and actions.

- Key issues of training and development, hiring, retention, workforce engagement, involvement, empowerment, and recognition and reward are addressed as a part of the human resource plan. Appropriate measures and targets for each are defined.

- Innovative human resource plans involve one or more of the following:

  - Action plans and associated performance measures provide the basis for individual worker performance management, reward, recognition, and compensation [links with processes in 5.1a(3)].

  - Redesigning work to increase worker responsibility.

  - Improving labor–management relations. (That is, prior to contract negotiations, train both sides in effective negotiation skills so people focus on the merits of issues, not on positions. A goal, for example, is to improve relations and shorten negotiation time by 50 percent.)

  - Forming partnerships with education institutions to conduct student research and develop workers and ensure a supply of well-prepared future employees.

  - Developing gain-sharing or equity-building compensation systems for all workers to increase motivation and productivity.

  - Broadening worker responsibilities; creating self-directed or high-performance work teams.

- Key performance measures (for example, workforce engagement or work-climate surveys) have been identified to gather data to manage progress. (Note: Improvement results associated with these measures are reported in 7.4.)

- The effectiveness of human resource planning and alignment with strategic plans is evaluated systematically and refined consistently.

- The process to develop action plans to support strategic objectives is systematically evaluated and subsequently improved.

B. Performance Projection

- Projections of two- to five-year changes in performance levels are developed.

- Data from competitors, key benchmarks, and/or past performance form a valid basis for comparison. The organization has valid strategies and goals in place to meet or exceed the planned levels of performance for these competitors and benchmarks.

- Expected future levels of competitor or comparison performance are used to set and validate the organization's own plans and goals.

- Future plans and projections of performance consider new acquisitions, optimum but secure growth, cost reductions through operational-excellence processes, and anticipated research and development of innovations internally or among competitors. The accuracy of these projections is mapped and analyzed. Techniques to improve accuracy are developed and used to improve future planning cycles.

3 Customer Focus—85 Points

*The **Customer Focus** Category examines how your organization engages its customers for long-term marketplace success. This engagement strategy includes how your organization builds a customer-focused culture. Also examined is how your organization listens to the voice of its customers and uses this information to improve and identify opportunities for innovation.*

This Category addresses how the organization engages its customers to meet their needs, build relationships, and develop a loyal brand and product following. Engagement is an important outcome of an effective customer-focused culture and performance excellence strategy. Customer satisfaction and dissatisfaction results provide vital information to help understand customers and the marketplace. Listening to the voice of the customer provides essential insight and useful information not only on customers' views but also on their marketplace behaviors and how these views and behaviors may contribute to long-term organizational sustainability.

This Category contains two Items. The first focuses on engaging customers to strengthen relationships and loyalty. The second focuses on listening to customers to better understand their perception of the organization's products in order to improve them.

Customer Engagement

- Determine product offerings that will meet customer requirements and exceed expectations
- Establish effective mechanisms to support customers' use of products
- Create an organization-wide culture that ensures customers have a consistently positive experience with the organization and its workforce
- Build customer relationships and loyalty
- Keep methods for creating a customer-focused culture and building customer relationships and loyalty current with changing business needs and directions

Voice of the Customer

- Listen carefully to the voice of the customer to identify opportunities for innovation
- Use complaint information and data from potential and former customers for planning process improvements, and business development
- Handle complaints effectively and responsively
- Ensure complaint data are used to eliminate causes of complaints
- Systematically measure customer satisfaction, engagement, and dissatisfaction

3.1 CUSTOMER ENGAGEMENT: How do you engage customers to serve their needs and build relationships? (40 Pts.)

PROCESS

Describe how your organization determines product offerings and mechanisms to support customers' use of your products. Describe also how your organization builds a customer-focused culture.

Within your response, include answers to the following questions:

a. Product Offerings and Customer Support

(1) How do you identify and innovate product offerings to meet the requirements and exceed the expectations of your customer groups and market segments (identified in your organizational profile)? How do you identify and innovate product offerings to attract new customers and provide opportunities for expanding relationships with existing customers, as appropriate?

(2) How do you determine your key mechanisms to support use of your products and enable customers to seek information and conduct their business with you? What are your key means of customer support, including your key communication mechanisms? How do they vary for different customers, customer groups, or market segments? How do you determine your customers' key support requirements? How do you ensure that customer support requirements are deployed to all people and processes involved in customer support?

(3) How do you keep your approaches for identifying and innovating product offerings and for providing customer support current with business needs and directions?

b. Building a Customer Culture

(1) How do you create an organizational culture that ensures a consistently positive customer experience and contributes to customer engagement? How do your workforce performance management system and your workforce and leader development systems reinforce this culture?

(2) How do you build and manage relationships with customers to:
- Acquire new customers?
- Meet their requirements and exceed their expectations in each stage of the customer life cycle?
- Increase their engagement with you?

(3) How do you keep your approaches for creating a customer-focused culture and building customer relationships current with business needs and directions

Notes:

N1. "Customer engagement" refers to your customers' investment in your brand and product offerings. Characteristics of engagement include customer retention and loyalty, customers' willingness to make an effort to do business- and to increase business-with your organization, and customers' willingness to actively advocate for and recommend your brand and product offerings.

N2. "Product offerings" and "products" refer to the goods and services that you offer in the marketplace. Product offerings (3.1a[1]) should consider all the important characteristics of products and services and their performance throughout their full life cycle and the full "consumption chain." The focus should be on features that affect customer preference and loyalty- for example, those features that differentiate your products from competing offerings or other organizations' services. Those features might include price, reliability, value, delivery, timeliness, ease of use, requirements for the use and disposal of hazardous materials, customer or technical support, and the sales relationship. Key product features also might take into account how transactions occur and factors such as customer data privacy and security. Your results on performance relative to key product features should be reported in Item 7.1, and those concerning customer perceptions and actions (outcomes) should be reported in Item 7.2.

N3. The goal of customer support (3.1a[2]) is to make your organization easy to do business with and responsive to your customers' expectations.

Continued

> **Notes:** *Continued*
>
> N4. Customer relationship building (3.1b[2]) might include the development of partnerships or alliances with customers.
>
> N5. The customer life cycle (3.1b[2]) begins in the pre-sale period and should include all stages of your involvement with the customer. This might include relationship building, the active business relationship, and an exit strategy, as appropriate.
>
> N6. For additional considerations on products, customers, and the business of nonprofit organizations, see Item P.1, Notes 1 and 7, and Item P.2, Note 5.

This Item [3.1] looks at the organization's processes for identifying and innovating product offerings that serve customers and markets [3.1a] and building a customer culture [3.1b].

Before the organization identifies or innovates its product offerings [3.1b] it should have a clear and accurate understanding of who the customers are and what they want, need, or expect.

Before developing lists of requirements, however, it is useful to divide customers into meaningful groups or segments. The various customer groups or segments should be identified in the Organizational Profile [P.1b(2)]. Within a broad customer group, several segments may be defined based on product lines, distribution channels (geography), business volume, or other factors. Within specific customer groups or segments it may be easier to determine whether common requirements exist, such as on-time delivery, low defect levels, safety, security, electronic ordering and billing, rapid response, after-sales service, and multilingual services.

The various unique and common requirements of the numerous customer groups and segments need to be addressed as the organization seeks to identify and innovate product offerings or features that will best serve and delight its customers. Dividing customers into meaningful groups or segments is done for the convenience of the organization to help it analyze, understand, design, deliver, and service the products of most value to the various customers.

Product offerings should consider all the important characteristics of products and services and their performance throughout their full life cycle and the full "consumption chain." The organization should determine the product features that affect customer preference and loyalty—for example, those features that differentiate products from competing offerings or other organizations' services. Those features might include price, reliability, value, delivery, timeliness, ease of use, and prompt and easy access to knowledgeable customer or technical support. Key product features also might take into account how transactions occur and factors such as customer data privacy and security. The organization's performance results related to the measures or characteristics of key product features should be reported in Item 7.1. Direct measures of customer perceptions and actions related to these products should be reported in Item 7.2.

Different approaches to building customer relationships may be needed for different customers, groups, or segments since one approach will not be fully effective for all. Moreover, these relationship-building approaches may need to be different during the various stages of the customer life cycle.

It is important to provide easy access for customers and potential customers to seek information or assistance and/or to comment and complain. This access makes it easier to get timely information from customers about issues that are of real concern to them. Timely information, in turn, is transmitted to the appropriate place in the organization to drive improvements or new levels of product and service. The organization should describe key communication mechanisms for customers to seek information, conduct business, and make complaints.

Customer support requirements essentially refer to customer expectations for service after the sale. Customer support requirements should be set in measurable terms to permit effective monitoring and performance review.

- A good example of a measurable customer support requirement might be the customer expectation that a malfunctioning computer would be back online within 24 hours of the request for service. Another example might be the customer requirement that a knowledgeable and polite human being is available within 10 minutes to resolve a problem with software. In both cases, clear requirements and measurable performance standards are defined.

- A bad example of a customer support standard might be "we get back to the customer as soon as we can." With this example, no standard of performance is defined. Some customer support representatives might get back to a customer within a matter of minutes. Others might take hours or days. The failure to define the contact requirement makes it difficult to allocate appropriate resources to meet that requirement consistently.

These customer support standards must be deployed to all employees who are in contact with customers. Such deployment needs to take account of all key points in the response chain—all units or individuals in the organization that make effective interactions possible. These standards then become one source of information to evaluate the organization's performance in meeting customer support requirements.

Different modes of access relate to different methods the customer might use to contact the organization: phone, e-mail, regular (snail) mail. Customers expect a response within minutes of calling, the next day when e-mailing, and many days in response to a letter.

Item 3.1 also examines mechanisms for supporting customers' use of those products and for building a customer-focused culture within the workforce. The intent of these efforts is to build relationships with customers and increase their engagement (loyalty, advocacy, and retention).

If done correctly, customer engagement processes [3.1b] should help produce such a high degree of loyalty that the customer will advocate for the organization's brand and product offerings. Engaged customers tend to remain loyal even if the organization makes mistakes—as all do, sooner or later.

Achieving such loyalty requires a customer-focused culture throughout the workforce. An effective customer-focused culture that ensures a consistently positive customer experience requires a clear understanding of the attitudes, expectations and requirements of an organization's various customers. It requires a customer service orientation among all workers and leaders.

Such a customer orientation does not develop without a systematic, integrated effort. As a start, top leaders need to ensure the organization's values include a commitment to customer engagement and service [1.1a(1)]. When setting organizational performance expectations, top leaders need to ensure there is a focus on creating and balancing value for customers and stakeholders [1.1b(2)]. These priorities should be considered as strategic planning takes place [2.1a] and should be a part of the organization's strategic objectives [2.1b(1)] and action plans [2.2a(1)]. Plans, however, are not enough. To ensure workers and leaders possess the desired traits and skills to support customers, the organization needs to hire, develop, and train its leaders and workers through the systems identified in Item 5.1a (Workforce Enrichment) and 5.1b (Workforce and Leader Development). To ensure workforce alignment with this customer focus, specific performance requirements should be included in the performance planning and appraisals of workers and leaders [5.1a(3)]. Feedback from customers [3.1 and 3.2] is used to help the organization design work systems [6.1a], select the key work processes [6.1b], and then design, execute, and improve those work processes [6.2] to produce better product results [7.1] and enhance customer satisfaction [7.2].

In the 2008 Criteria, Item 3.1 required organizations to describe the processes for identify customers, customer groups, and market segments. The 2009 Criteria do not ask for these process descriptions. Rather, the organization simply lists its market segments, customer groups, and stakeholder groups, as appropriate. Also, organizations must describe their customers' key requirements and expectations for products and customer support services and the differences in these requirements and expectations among market segments, customer groups, and stakeholder groups.

3.1 Customer Engagement

Basic Approach Requirements*: Engage customers to serve their needs and build relationships.

Overall Approach Requirements*: Determine product offerings and mechanisms to support customers' use of the products. Build a customer-focused culture.

Multiple Approach Requirements: The following diagram describes most multiple approach requirements.

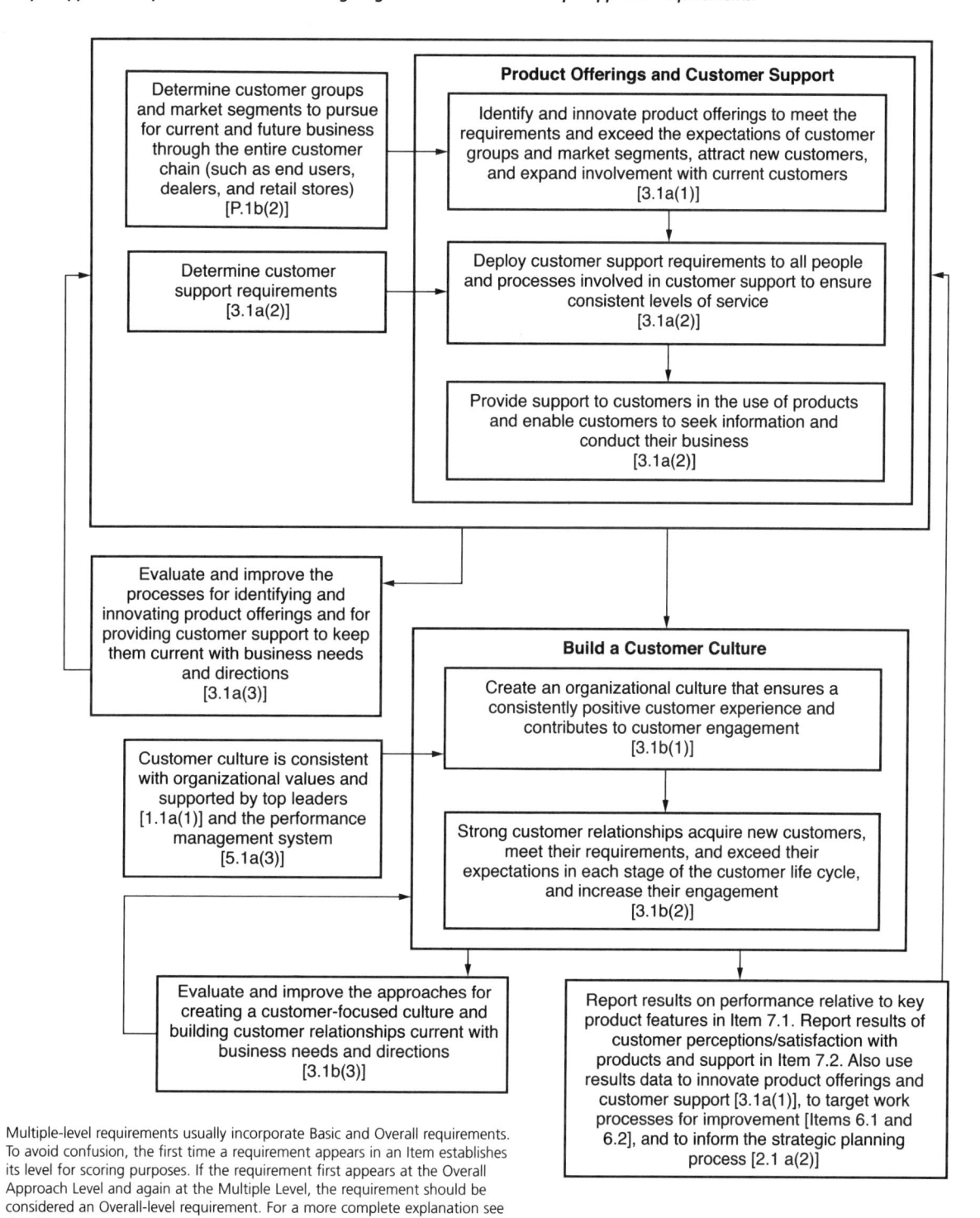

Product Offerings and Customer Support

- Determine customer groups and market segments to pursue for current and future business through the entire customer chain (such as end users, dealers, and retail stores) [P.1b(2)]
- Identify and innovate product offerings to meet the requirements and exceed the expectations of customer groups and market segments, attract new customers, and expand involvement with current customers [3.1a(1)]
- Determine customer support requirements [3.1a(2)]
- Deploy customer support requirements to all people and processes involved in customer support to ensure consistent levels of service [3.1a(2)]
- Provide support to customers in the use of products and enable customers to seek information and conduct their business [3.1a(2)]

Evaluate and improve the processes for identifying and innovating product offerings and for providing customer support to keep them current with business needs and directions [3.1a(3)]

Build a Customer Culture

- Customer culture is consistent with organizational values and supported by top leaders [1.1a(1)] and the performance management system [5.1a(3)]
- Create an organizational culture that ensures a consistently positive customer experience and contributes to customer engagement [3.1b(1)]
- Strong customer relationships acquire new customers, meet their requirements, and exceed their expectations in each stage of the customer life cycle, and increase their engagement [3.1b(2)]

Evaluate and improve the approaches for creating a customer-focused culture and building customer relationships current with business needs and directions [3.1b(3)]

Report results on performance relative to key product features in Item 7.1. Report results of customer perceptions/satisfaction with products and support in Item 7.2. Also use results data to innovate product offerings and customer support [3.1a(1)], to target work processes for improvement [Items 6.1 and 6.2], and to inform the strategic planning process [2.1 a(2)]

---

* Multiple-level requirements usually incorporate Basic and Overall requirements. To avoid confusion, the first time a requirement appears in an Item establishes its level for scoring purposes. If the requirement first appears at the Overall Approach Level and again at the Multiple Level, the requirement should be considered an Overall-level requirement. For a more complete explanation see the chapter on Scoring System and the Scoring Calibration Guidelines.

3.1 Key Customer Engagement Item Linkages

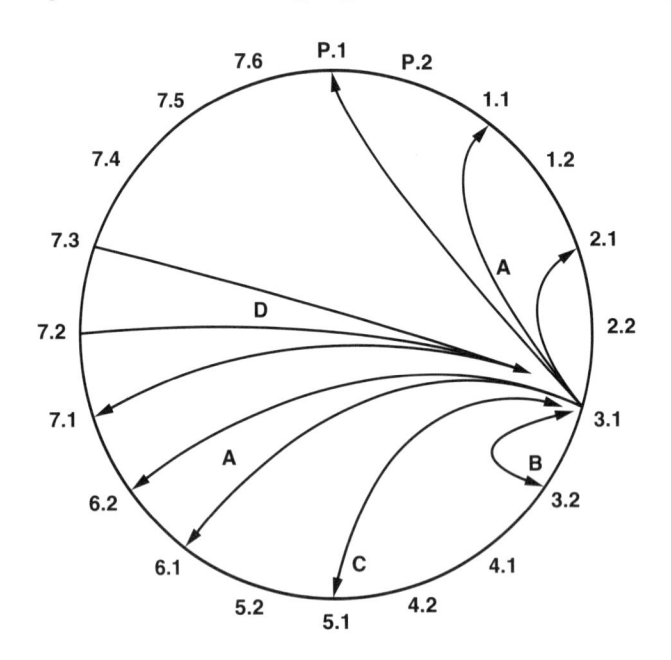

	NATURE OF RELATIONSHIP
A	Customer input and related information about engaging customers to serve their needs and build relationships [3.1a] are used for strategic planning [2.1a], to help determine and capitalize on core competencies [P.1a(2)], to plan strategically [2.1a(1)], design work systems [6.1a(2)], and design and manage work processes [6.2a, 6.2b(1)], and to help leaders set vision and directions for the organization [1.1a(1)]. Processes to identify and innovate product offerings to meet the requirements and exceed the expectations of customer groups and market segments [3.1a(1)] are central to the success of any organization. In addition, a clear definition of the product offerings is essential to guide the design of work systems [6.1a] and the design and management of key work processes [6.2].
B	Customer complaints [3.2a(3)] and customer satisfaction, engagement, and dissatisfaction data [3.2b(1, 2)] are used to help validate processes to ensure product offerings, customer support, and the customer culture are properly designed and managed to build strong customer relationships and meet their needs.
C	The workforce performance management system [5.1a(3)] and the workforce and leader development systems [5.1b(1, 2)] are aligned to support and reinforce the customer culture that ensures a consistently positive customer experience and contributes to customer engagement [3.1b(1)].
D	Customer satisfaction [7.2a(1)], product outcomes [7.1a], and market outcomes [7.3a(2)] are used to help validate customer expectations and refine requirements for customer support [3.1a(2)] and help attract new customers and expand relationships with existing customers [3.1a(1)].

3 Customer Focus

	IF YOU DON'T DO WHAT THE CRITERIA REQUIRE...
Item Reference	**Possible Adverse Consequences**
3.1a(1)	The failure to identify and innovate product offerings to meet the requirements and exceed the expectations of your customer groups and market segments will increase the likelihood that customers will not be satisfied and cause the organization to engage in excessive rework. This, in turn, increases costs, adds delay, and reduces value to customers.
3.1a(1)	The failure to identify and make innovative improvements in product offerings; to attract new customers; and to provide opportunities for expanding relationships with existing customers will eventually cause the customer base to erode. This is especially dangerous in a difficult economic climate where competitors are going to extraordinary lengths to attract a larger share of a smaller group of customers willing to purchase.
3.2a(2)	Customer support requirements (previously called customer contact requirements or service standards) help define the customers' expectations for support after the initial sale. For example, a large, direct-order computer company surveyed its customers and determined that they expected to have a technician helping solve their problem within 10 minutes of making the initial contact. By knowing the customer support requirements and the hour-to-hour call volume, the organization was able to put enough technicians in place to ensure the average response time was nine minutes or less. The failure of any worker to understand and meet customer support requirements makes it more difficult to build loyalty and learn quickly about customer problems.
3.1a(2)	Different techniques may be needed to understand the requirements of different groups of customers. The failure to listen and learn about the key customer requirements for product features and support services, especially those features that are most important to customer purchasing decisions, may make it difficult to design and develop those products that are most likely to delight (or even satisfy) customers and increase market share.
3.1a(3)	The failure to systematically keep approaches for identifying and innovating product offerings and for providing customer support current with business needs and directions increases the probability that the organization may overlook important areas for change and provide an opening for competitors to exploit. The failure to evaluate the effectiveness of the approaches used to identify and prioritize customer requirements may make it difficult to keep up with changing customer and market needs and gather critical information necessary for strategic planning [2.1a(2)] as well as the design [6.1] and management of work systems and processes [6.2].
3.1b(1)	A consistently positive customer experience is essential to promote and sustain customer engagement (loyalty, retention, and willingness to recommend and advocate for the organization and its products). Consistency requires broad commitment from the entire workforce; commitment and desire from a few are not enough. Certain attitudes and skills must be developed, and training is essential. Without such training and development, and reinforcement through the system of rewards, incentives, and compensation, the desired behaviors in support of a customer culture may be difficult to sustain. Failing to provide a positive customer experience will cause customers to go elsewhere for products and support.
3.1b(2)	The failure to build and manage lasting relationships and loyalty with customers makes it easier for customers to jump ship when problems arise. Loyal customers are twice as likely to use an organization's products and services as those who are simply satisfied. The TARP

Continued

IF YOU DON'T DO WHAT THE CRITERIA REQUIRE . . . Continued		
Item Reference	**Possible Adverse Consequences**
	Studies have found that the cost to win a new customer versus retain a current customer varies from 2:1 to 20:1.* If the organization lacks a disciplined approach for building relationships and cultivating loyalty, the benefits of having loyal customers become hit-or-miss opportunities. For example, in many manufacturing companies today, service or support is a key differentiator. Products that were once considered specialty items, such as personal computers, are now commodities. In these cases, service has become the factor that differentiates companies and cultivates loyal customers. Furthermore, since it is more costly to acquire a new customer than to keep an existing customer, organizations can avoid unnecessary expenses by building relationships and strengthening the loyalty of current customers. Loyal customers are far more likely to provide positive referrals than a dissatisfied or even minimally satisfied customer. *From J. Goodman. "Basic Facts on Customer Complaint Behavior and the Impact of Service on the Bottom Line." *Competitive Advantage* (June 1999): 1–5. The article can be read at http://www.e-satisfy.com/basicfacts.pdf.
3.1a(3)	The failure to consistently keep approaches for creating a customer-focused culture and building customer relationships current with business needs and directions increases the probability that the organization may overlook important areas for change and provide an opening for competitors to exploit. The failure to evaluate the effectiveness of the approaches used to sustain a customer culture may make it difficult to ensure a consistently positive customer experience from all workers. Not knowing what to expect and receiving inconsistent products and services adversely affects a customer's satisfaction, loyalty, and retention.

3.1 CUSTOMER ENGAGEMENT—SAMPLE EFFECTIVE PRACTICES

A. Product Offerings and Customer Support

- Key product offerings are defined in order of importance to customers. Product offerings include all important characteristics that customers want throughout the entire customer-product life cycle. Product features that bear on customer preference and loyalty—for example, those features that enhance or differentiate products and services from competing offerings—are defined in measurable terms.

- Customer requirements are identified or grouped to make it easier for the organization to plan, design, and deliver maximum value to each segment. This information is consistently used for planning, data analysis, product and service design, production, and delivery processes, and for reporting and monitoring progress.

- Customer data such as complaints and gains or losses of customers are used to support the identification or validation of key customer requirements.

- Fact-based, systematic methods are used to identify the future requirements and expectations of customers. These are tested for accuracy and estimation techniques are improved.

- Effective techniques to identify and innovate product offerings to attract new customers and improve the relationships with existing customers include:

- Close monitoring of technological, competitive, societal, environmental, economic, and demographic factors that may bear on customer requirements, expectations, preferences, or alternatives

- Focus groups with demanding or leading-edge customers

- Training of front-line employees in customer listening and using these employees to collect complaints

- Use of critical incidents in product or service performance or quality to understand key service attributes from the point of view of customers and front-line employees

- Analysis of major factors affecting key customers

• Methods to listen and learn from customers are evaluated and improved through several cycles. Examples of factors that are evaluated include:

- The adequacy and timeliness of customer-related information

- Approaches for getting reliable and timely information—surveys, focus groups, customer support personnel

- Improved aggregation and analysis of information

B. Building a Customer Culture

• Top leaders have made supporting the customer the single most important priority. It is a core value of the organization and a part of every performance appraisal. The failure to meet customer support requirements is so serious that the offender is not eligible for promotion or pay increase until the problem is resolved.

• The customer-focused culture is supported by ongoing workforce and leader training. Special training and development plans and replacement procedures exist for customer support employees to maintain consistency.

• Measurable customer support requirements (service standards) have been derived from customer expectations (for example, timeliness, courtesy, efficiency, thoroughness, and completeness).

• Requirements for building relationships are identified and may include factors such as product knowledge, employee responsiveness, and various customer support methods.

• A systematic approach is in place to evaluate and improve customer-focused decision making and customer relationships and several process improvements have been made as a result.

3.2 VOICE OF THE CUSTOMER: How do obtain and use information from your customers? (45 Pts.) — PROCESS

Describe how your organization listens to your customers and acquires satisfaction and dissatisfaction information. Describe also how customer information is used to improve your marketplace success.

Within your response, include answers to the following questions:

a. Customer Listening

(1) How do you listen to customers to obtain actionable information and to obtain feedback on your products and your customer support? How do your listening methods vary for different customers, customer groups, or market segments? How do your listening methods vary across the customer life cycle? How do you follow up with customers on the quality of products, customer support, and transactions to receive immediate and actionable feedback?

(2) How do you listen to former customers, potential customers, and customers of competitors to obtain actionable information and to obtain feedback on your products, customer support, and transactions, as appropriate?

(3) How do you manage customer complaints? How does your customer complaint management process ensure that complaints are resolved promptly and effectively? How does your customer complaint management process enable you to recover your customers' confidence, and enhance their satisfaction and engagement? How does your complaint management system enable aggregation and analysis of complaints for use in improvement throughout your organization and by your partners, as appropriate?

b. Determination of Customer Satisfaction and Engagement

(1) How do you determine customer satisfaction and engagement? How do these determination methods differ among customer groups and market segments, as appropriate? How do your measurements capture actionable information for use in exceeding your customers' expectations and securing your customers' engagement? How do your determination methods enable aggregation and analysis of data for use in improvement throughout your organization and by your partners, as appropriate?

(2) How do you obtain and use information on your customers' satisfaction relative to their satisfaction with your competitors? How do you obtain and use information on your customers' satisfaction relative to the satisfaction levels of customers of other organizations providing similar products or to industry benchmarks, as appropriate?

(3) How do you determine customer dissatisfaction? How do your measurements capture actionable information for use in meeting your customers' requirements and exceeding their expectations in the future? How do your determination methods enable aggregation and analysis of data for use in improvement throughout your organization and by your partners, as appropriate?

c. Analysis and Use of Customer Data

(1) How do you use customer, market, and product offering information to identify current and anticipate future customer groups and market segments? How do you consider customers of competitors and other potential customers and markets in this segmentation? How do you determine which customers, customer groups, and market segments to pursue for current and future products?

(2) How do you use customer, market, and product offering information to identify and anticipate key customer requirements (including products and product features) and changing expectations and their relative importance to customers' purchasing or relationship decisions? How do you identify and anticipate how these requirements and changing expectations will differ across customers, customer groups, and market segments and across the customer life cycle?

Continued

3 Customer Focus

> *Continued*
>
> (3) How do you use customer, market, and product offering information to improve marketing, build a more customer-focused culture, and identify opportunities for innovation?
>
> (4) How do you keep your approaches for customer listening; determination of customer satisfaction, dissatisfaction, and engagement; and use of customer data current with business needs and directions?
>
> **Notes:**
>
> N1. The "voice of the customer" refers to your process for capturing customer-related information. Voice-of-the-customer processes are intended to be proactive and continuously innovative to capture stated, unstated, and anticipated customer requirements, expectations, and desires. The goal is to achieve customer engagement. Listening to the voice of the customer might include gathering and integrating various types of customer data, such as survey data, focus group findings, warranty data, and complaint data that affect customers' purchasing and engagement decisions.
>
> N2. Customer listening information could include marketing and sales information, customer engagement data, win/loss analysis, and complaint data. "Actionable information" refers to specific aspects of your products and customer interactions that affect customers' future relationships with your organization.
>
> N3. Determining customer satisfaction and dissatisfaction (3.2b) might include the use of any or all of the following: surveys, formal and informal feedback, customer account histories, complaints, field reports, win/loss analysis, customer referral rates, and transaction completion rates. Information might be gathered on the Web, through personal contact or a third party, or by mail. Determining customer dissatisfaction should be seen as more than reviewing low customer satisfaction scores. Dissatisfaction should be independently determined to identify root causes of dissatisfaction and enable a systematic remedy to avoid future dissatisfaction.
>
> N4. Other organizations providing similar products (3.2b[2]) might include organizations that are not competitors but provide similar products in other geographic areas or to different populations.

This Item [3.2] looks at the organization's processes for listening to customers, determining their satisfaction, engagement, and dissatisfaction, and analyzing and using customer data to improve marketing, build a more customer-focused culture, and identify opportunities for innovation.

In Area to Address 3.2a, the voice-of-the-customer processes help an organization gain knowledge about its current and future customers and markets in order to offer relevant products and services; understand emerging customer requirements, needs, and expectations; and keep pace with changing market demands and changing business methods. Voice-of-the-customer processes required by Item 3.2 enable the organization to gather more accurate intelligence about its customers and competition. This information is intended to support marketing, business development, and planning.

Information sought should be sensitive to specific product and service requirements and their relative importance or value to the different customer groups. Close attention to the voice of the customer helps ensure this occurs. Voice-of-the-customer data should be cross-checked or verified with other types of information and data, such as complaints and gains and losses of customers.

In a rapidly changing technological, competitive, economic, and social environment, many factors may affect customer preference and loyalty, making it necessary to listen and learn on a continuous basis to ensure accuracy and completeness. To be effective, such listening and learning techniques need to have a close connection with the organization's overall business strategy. For example, if the organization customizes its products, the listening and learning process needs to identify unique and common requirements to permit accurate predictions about the nature of future customized requests.

Techniques for understanding customer preferences may include asking customers to rank their requirements in order of performance or group requirements into three categories (most important, important, least important). Another technique for determining priorities involves paired-choice or forced-choice analyses where customers are asked to state a preference of requirement A or B, A or C, A or D, B or C, B or D, and so on. Regardless of the techniques used, the organization should be able to prioritize key customer requirements and drivers of purchase decisions, which may be different for different customer groups and market segments.

It is important to obtain actionable information from customers that can be tied to key product offerings and business processes and used to support decisions, such as determining cost and revenue implications to help set improvement goals and priorities. Complaint aggregation, analysis, and root cause determination can help focus action on the elimination of the causes of complaints and help set priorities for process and product improvements.

Effective complaint management [3.2a(3)] requires the prompt and courteous resolution of complaints. This leads to recovery of customer confidence. Customer loyalty and confidence are enhanced when problems are resolved by the first person the customer contacts. Even if the organization ultimately resolves a problem, the likelihood of maintaining a loyal customer is reduced by 10 percent each time that customer is referred to another place or person in the organization. In fact, prompt resolution of problems helps to produce higher levels of loyalty than if the customer never had a problem in the first place.

The organization must also have a mechanism for learning from complaints and ensuring that design/production/delivery-process owners [Category 6] receive the information they need to improve their work processes and eliminate the causes of complaints. Effective elimination of the causes of complaints involves aggregating and analyzing complaint information from all sources to determine the root causes of the complaints. That information is then used to set priorities for specific process, product, and service improvements that will result in overall organizational improvement in both design [6.1] and work process management [6.2] stages.

Complete and accurate knowledge of customers, customer groups, market segments, former customers, and potential customers allows the organization to tailor its listening strategies and its product offerings and marketing approaches, to develop a more customer-focused workforce culture, to develop new business, and to ensure organizational sustainability.(Note: A potential customer is a customer the organization wants but is currently being served by another organization or not being served at all.)

In Area to Address 3.2b, the organization must have effective, systematic processes in place to determine customer satisfaction, engagement, and dissatisfaction. These processes provide another source of excellent information about the behavior, perceptions, and support of customers. A key aspect of customer satisfaction/dissatisfaction data is that the data permit comparative analysis with competitors, competing or alternative offerings, and/or organizations providing similar products. Such information might be derived from in-house comparative studies or from independent third-party studies. These comparison data allow leaders to better understand the factors that lead to customer preference and loyalty. These data are critical to gain an understanding of the factors that drive markets and affect longer-term competitiveness and organizational sustainability.

When trying to understand customer satisfaction, engagement, or dissatisfaction, one size does not fit all. A relationship or listening strategy may work well with some customers, but not with others. For example, focus groups are well-established and effective in the U.S. but in China public focus groups might not generate a level of trust high enough to produce accurate information. In China, anonymity using survey tools might be critical to ensure accuracy.

Because of the differences among customers, organizations are increasingly using multiple modes to gather actionable information. Some examples of listening and learning strategies include:

- Voice-of-the-customer techniques that help ensure that customer requirements, needs, and preferences are understood fully and accurately. Capturing the customer's actual words (the voice), rather than relying on summaries may reduce errors due to faulty interpretations of customer requirements

- Close integration with key customers before, during, and after products/services are delivered

- Field trials of products and services to better link research and development (R&D) and design to the market

- Close tracking of technological, competitive, and other factors that may bear upon customer requirements, expectations, preferences, or alternatives

- Defining the customers' value chains and how they are likely to change throughout the product life cycle

- Focus groups or private interviews with influential or leading-edge customers

- Use of critical incidents, such as complaints, to understand key product and service attributes from the point of view of customers and customer support employees

- Interviewing lost and potential customers to determine the factors they use in their relationship or purchase decisions

- Survey/feedback information, including information collected on the Internet

- Win/loss analysis relative to competitors and comparable organizations

- Increased use of electronic feedback and e-commerce

The organization should systematically follow up with customers regarding products, services, and recent transactions to receive feedback that is prompt and actionable. Prompt feedback enables problems to be identified quickly to help prevent them from recurring. This helps reduce future customer dissatisfaction.

The organization should determine the satisfaction levels of the customers of competitors in order to identify threats and opportunities to improve future performance. Such information might be derived from the organization's own comparative studies or from independent studies. The factors that lead to customer preference are of critical importance in understanding factors that drive markets, potentially affect longer-term competitiveness and organizational sustainability, and are particularly helpful during strategic planning.

Customers are more likely to complain right after they experience a problem. They do not tend to hold their complaint until the organization finds it convenient to ask them. Data from the complaint processes in Item 3.2a(3) are collected at the customer's convenience. However, data collected by survey or similar means, as required by Item 3.2b, produce information at the convenience of the organization.

Although the complaint-type customer feedback is timely, it is often difficult to develop reliable trend data since relatively few customers who have a problem actually complain about it to the organization. The processes in Item 3.2b make it easier to obtain accurate and reliable satisfaction data over time. Both techniques are required to fully understand customer-satisfaction dynamics that build loyalty, retention, and positive referral. To be effective, both techniques should be used to drive improvement actions. As with other elements of the Criteria, the organization must have a system in place to improve its customer-listening and learning strategies to keep current with changing business needs and directions. The organization may need to evaluate and improve its customer-listening and learning strategies more often than annually. The organization should demonstrate that it has made appropriate improvements to ensure its techniques for understanding customer requirements and priorities keep pace with changing business needs.

For long-term success, organizations should build strong relationships with customers since business development and product/service innovation increasingly depend on maintaining close relationships with customers. Organizations should keep approaches to all aspects of customer relationships current with changing business needs and directions, since approaches to and bases for relationships may change quickly.

3.2 Voice of the Customer

Basic Approach Requirements*: Obtain and use information from customers.

Overall Approach Requirements*: Listen to customers and acquire satisfaction and dissatisfaction information. Use customer information to improve marketplace success.

Multiple Approach Requirements: The following diagram describes most multiple approach requirements.

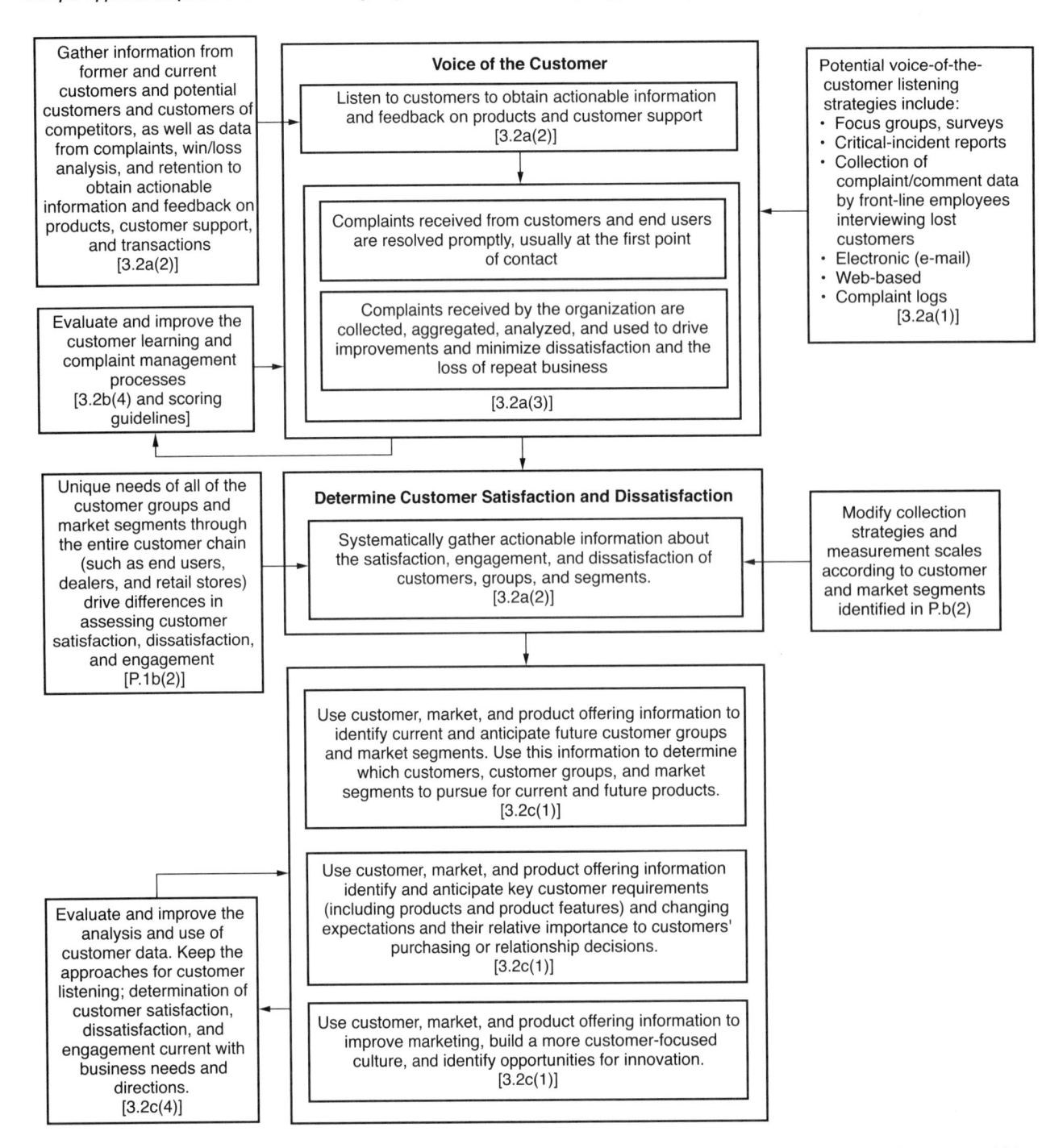

- Gather information from former and current customers and potential customers and customers of competitors, as well as data from complaints, win/loss analysis, and retention to obtain actionable information and feedback on products, customer support, and transactions [3.2a(2)]

- Evaluate and improve the customer learning and complaint management processes [3.2b(4) and scoring guidelines]

- Unique needs of all of the customer groups and market segments through the entire customer chain (such as end users, dealers, and retail stores) drive differences in assessing customer satisfaction, dissatisfaction, and engagement [P.1b(2)]

- Evaluate and improve the analysis and use of customer data. Keep the approaches for customer listening; determination of customer satisfaction, dissatisfaction, and engagement current with business needs and directions. [3.2c(4)]

Voice of the Customer
- Listen to customers to obtain actionable information and feedback on products and customer support [3.2a(2)]
- Complaints received from customers and end users are resolved promptly, usually at the first point of contact
- Complaints received by the organization are collected, aggregated, analyzed, and used to drive improvements and minimize dissatisfaction and the loss of repeat business [3.2a(3)]

Determine Customer Satisfaction and Dissatisfaction
- Systematically gather actionable information about the satisfaction, engagement, and dissatisfaction of customers, groups, and segments. [3.2a(2)]

- Use customer, market, and product offering information to identify current and anticipate future customer groups and market segments. Use this information to determine which customers, customer groups, and market segments to pursue for current and future products. [3.2c(1)]

- Use customer, market, and product offering information identify and anticipate key customer requirements (including products and product features) and changing expectations and their relative importance to customers' purchasing or relationship decisions. [3.2c(1)]

- Use customer, market, and product offering information to improve marketing, build a more customer-focused culture, and identify opportunities for innovation. [3.2c(1)]

Potential voice-of-the-customer listening strategies include:
- Focus groups, surveys
- Critical-incident reports
- Collection of complaint/comment data by front-line employees interviewing lost customers
- Electronic (e-mail)
- Web-based
- Complaint logs
[3.2a(1)]

Modify collection strategies and measurement scales according to customer and market segments identified in P.b(2)

---

* Multiple-level requirements usually incorporate Basic and Overall requirements. To avoid confusion, the first time a requirement appears in an Item establishes its level for scoring purposes. If the requirement first appears at the Overall Approach Level and again at the Multiple Level, the requirement should be considered an Overall-level requirement. For a more complete explanation see the chapter on Scoring System and the Scoring Calibration Guidelines.

3.2 Key Voice of the Customer Item Linkages

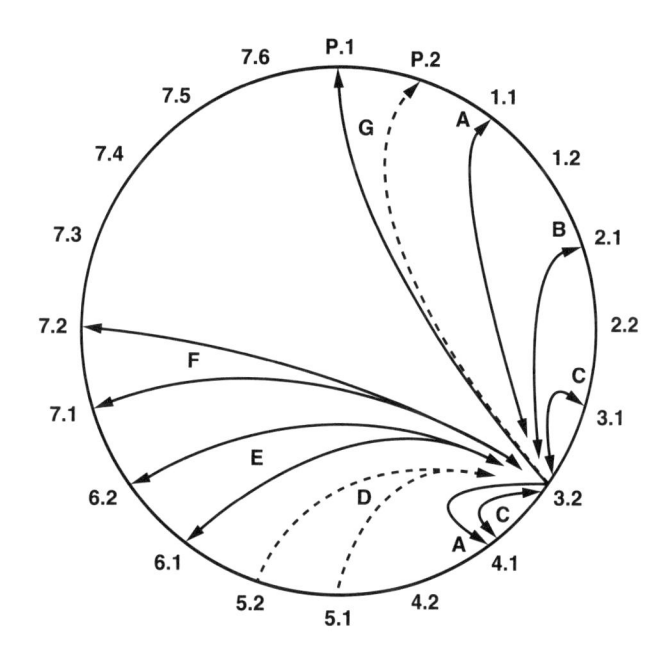

	NATURE OF RELATIONSHIP
A	The climate establishing customer-focused priorities and customer-contact requirements (service standards) for customer service personnel [3.2a(1)] is driven by top leadership [1.1b(2)]. They receive useful information from customers to improve management decision making. Customer relationships/complaint data [3.2a(3)] and satisfaction/dissatisfaction data [3.2b(1, 2)] are typically used by senior leaders to review performance [4.1b], and set priorities for action [4.1c].
B	Information about customer satisfaction [3.2b(1, 2)] and complaints [3.2a(3)] collected by customer-contact employees is used in the planning process [2.1a(2)]. In addition, strategic objectives [2.1b(1)] influence customer relationship management [3.2a] and customer satisfaction/dissatisfaction determination processes [3.2b] by identifying key focus areas.
C	Information concerning customer requirements, expectations, and preferences [3.1a(2)] and benchmark data [4.1a(2)] are used to help identify customer support requirements (service standards) [3.2a(2)]. Customer complaint data [3.2a(3)] are analyzed [4.1b] and used to help leaders ensure conclusions and decisions are valid.
D	Workforce and leader development [5.1b(1)], reward, and recognition tied to customer satisfaction [5.1a(3)] should enhance the willingness of customer-contact employees [3.2a(1)] to understand requirements and develop the capacity and capability [5.2] to resolve complaints promptly and satisfy customers [3.2a(3)].
E	Information collected from customer s [3.2)] is used to enhance design [6.1b] and management [6.2a] of work systems and key work processes.
F	Information and complaints from customer relations processes [3.2a(3)] can help in the design of customer satisfaction and dissatisfaction determination measures [3.2b(1)] and produce data on customer satisfaction outcomes [7.2] and related product and service quality outcomes [7.1]. In addition, customer satisfaction results [7.2] are used to set customer support requirements (service standards) [3.2a(1)].

Continued

Insights to Performance Excellence 2009–2010

	NATURE OF RELATIONSHIP Continued
	Improved accessibility and responsiveness in complaint management [3.2a(3)] should result in improved complaint response time, effective complaint resolution, and a higher percentage of complaints resolved on first contact. These results should be reported in 7.1 and/or 7.2.
G	Processes in Item 3.2a(2) produce information about the satisfaction of competitors' customers, which is needed to create the description for P.1b(2).

	IF YOU DON'T DO WHAT THE CRITERIA REQUIRE . . .
Item Reference	**Possible Adverse Consequences**
3.2a(1)	The failure to have effective processes to listen to customers to obtain actionable information and feedback on products and customer support, forces leaders and workers to substitute their own biases for the opinions of the customer. This is easily noticed by customers who consider the practice to be arrogant, even hostile. Failure to listen makes it difficult to consistently focus on the areas most important to customers and wastes resources designing and delivering products that do not meet requirements.
3.2a(1)	Listening methods that are not customized for different customers, customer groups, or market segments may not produce accurate, complete, or valid data to support sound decision making. Decision errors based on faulty information typically waste resources and contribute to delay and rework. Different techniques may be needed to understand the requirements of different groups of customers. The failure to listen and learn about the key customer requirements for products and services, especially those features that are most important to customer purchasing decisions may make it difficult to design and develop those products and services that are most likely to delight (or even satisfy) customers and increase market share.
3.2a(1)	If listening methods do not vary across the customer life cycle it may be difficult to capture information critical to sustaining excellence and customer support. Different methods are typically needed depending on the life cycle of the product. For example, a car manufacturer might collect information about car quality based on the number and frequency of dealer service calls. That technique might not produce accurate information after the warranty period expires because the owner may go to a local repair ship instead. It would be incorrect for the manufacturer to conclude that the car has few problems needing correction as it ages.
3.2a(1)	A natural opportunity to gather immediate and actionable customer feedback on the quality of products, customer support, and transactions occurs when customers interact with the organization. These interactions may involve placing an order, requesting support, or seeking information, to name a few. The failure to take advantage of these opportunities to acquire timely information may cause the organization to overlook a small problem and not correct it early. The longer it takes to identify a problem, the more costly it is to fix.
3.2a(2)	The failure to listen to former customers, potential customers, and customers of competitors to obtain feedback on your products, customer support, and transactions may cause the

Continued

	IF YOU DON'T DO WHAT THE CRITERIA REQUIRE . . . Continued
Item Reference	**Possible Adverse Consequences**
	organization to receive unbalanced and incomplete information. This may contribute to costly decision errors. It is said that, "If you only listen to the customers that are foolish enough to do business with you, then you will have foolish data." In addition to gathering feedback directly from former customers, the organization should collect and analyze complaint and lost customer data to gain additional insights into unmet requirements and opportunities for future work. If an organization does not know why it lost or gained customers, it is more difficult to deliver the right products and services, maintain customer engagement, and grow or sustain the business.
3.2a(3)	Once the organization learns about a customer problem, the speed and efficiency with which it resolves that problem contributes greatly to customer loyalty and willingness to make positive referrals. The failure to resolve a problem to the customer's satisfaction at the first point of contact significantly reduces the likelihood of maintaining a loyal customer. In addition, the failure to collect, aggregate, analyze, and use complaint data to drive improvements throughout the organization (and, as appropriate, to key suppliers or partners) increases the likelihood that the problem will recur.
3.2a(3)	Resolving a customer complaint and recovering customer confidence are only part of an effective complaint management system. Unless complaint data are aggregated and analyzed and root causes of problems are eliminated, the problem will recur. Customers that face repeat problems are much less likely to forgive, and engagement and loyalty will be seriously threatened, causing the customer to look elsewhere.
3.2b(1)	The failure to accurately determine customer satisfaction and engagement may make it difficult for the organization to make timely adjustments to the products and services it offers. Furthermore, if the data collection processes do not help the organization understand what drives customer behavior, the organization may not know until it is too late (the customer goes elsewhere) that they have a serious problem. The failure to predict customer behavior and the likelihood for positive referral also make it difficult to forecast demand, which may create supply chain difficulties, such as excessive inventories or excessive delays in restocking.
3.2b(1)	The failure to take into account differences in customer or market segments and adjust the techniques for collecting customer satisfaction and engagement data appropriately may cause the organization to collect inaccurate or unreliable information, which threatens the accuracy of the organization's decision making and planning. Decision error wastes resources.
3.2b(1)	Meeting customer requirements and developing loyal (engaged) customers are considered adequate, until another provider consistently exceeds expectations. Then, engagement and loyalty wane and "adequate" is no longer acceptable. Unless the organization can find ways to exceed expectations and produce more value, it may have difficulty sustaining its operations. Sustaining requires continuous improvement and innovation in a competitive market.
3.2b(1)	Raw data from individual customers is rarely sufficient to enable leaders and workers to identify areas to improve and innovate for maximum benefit. Unless customer satisfaction and engagement data are properly analyzed it will be difficult to consistently identify areas to improve for maximum benefit. Change can waste resources and create more problems than it solves unless it is properly focused.

Continued

Insights to Performance Excellence 2009–2010

	IF YOU DON'T DO WHAT THE CRITERIA REQUIRE . . . Continued
Item Reference	**Possible Adverse Consequences**
3.2b(2)	By failing to obtain information on the satisfaction of the competitors' customers, the organization may not learn what it must do differently to satisfy and acquire (win over) the customers of its competitors or other organizations providing similar products.
3.2b(3)	The failure to accurately determine customer dissatisfaction creates similar adverse consequences as the failure to determine customer satisfaction. The organization may not know until it is too late (the customer goes elsewhere) that they have a serious problem.
3.2b(3)	The failure to meet your customers' requirements and exceed their expectations in the future creates similar adverse consequences as the failure to secure your customers' engagement. Unless the organization can find ways to exceed customer expectations and produce more value, it may have difficulty sustaining its operations. Sustaining requires continuous improvement and innovation in a competitive market.
3.2b(3)	The failure to aggregate and analyze customer dissatisfaction data will make it more difficult to identify areas causing customers the most problems making it more difficult to identify the right areas to improve for maximum benefit.
3.2c(1)	Organizations group customers and markets to help plan, design, develop, and manage the array of products and support to satisfy the bulk of customers efficiently. Inappropriate grouping and segmentation may make it more difficult to deliver products and support or uncover opportunities for savings or new business. The failure to classify or group customers or markets into meaningful segments may make it difficult to identify and differentiate key requirements that may be critical to one group but not another. For example, frequent or high-volume customers may have different expectations than infrequent or low-volume customers. Dealers may have different requirements than end users. Unless these differences are understood, it may be difficult for the organization to customize information collection techniques as well as programs, products, and services according to the needs and expectations of different groups of customers.
3.2c(1)	Customers of competitors and potential customers can be defined as customers the organization desires, but they go elsewhere (or forego the product). By not considering the reasons why the desired customers are not actual customers the organization fails to acquire potentially valuable insight that could be used to change its products and support to be more attractive and build the business.
3.2c(1)	Organizations that do not have an effective process to determine which customers, customer groups, and market segments to pursue frequently misjudge (over estimate) the market and fail to reach their objectives.
3.2c(2)	The failure to anticipate key customer requirements (including products and product features), changing expectations and their relative importance to customers' purchasing or relationship decisions across the customer life cycle causes the organization to lose agility, which is usually not a serious problem if all other providers are similarly stagnant. However, if some competitors accurately and systematically anticipate emerging customer requirements, then they win the battle for the customer.
3.2c(3)	Without an ongoing system to gather customer, market, and product offering information and use it to evaluate and improve processes to build relationships and satisfy customers,

Continued

3 Customer Focus

	IF YOU DON'T DO WHAT THE CRITERIA REQUIRE... Continued
Item Reference	**Possible Adverse Consequences**
	current processes may not be able to keep up with changing business or market demands. Sooner or later, this failure will erode customer confidence and lead to a loss of customers and market share.
3.2c(4)	The failure to systematically evaluate the processes used to build relationships, resolve complaints, and prevent them from recurring may make it difficult to identify specific areas needing change. Making it easy for customers to complain but not resolving those complaints effectively and promptly may create even higher levels of dissatisfaction. Ignorance about the effectiveness of customer access and complaint resolution processes may blind the organization to a problem of its own creation, especially in a highly competitive arena where customer and market requirements can change quickly. Organizations that do not evaluate the effectiveness of their techniques to determine customer satisfaction, engagement, and dissatisfaction run the risk of making bad decisions based on misleading or even useless information. It does little good to gather customer satisfaction data unless the organization asks the right questions. Failing to ask the right questions rarely produces accurate, actionable information to support effective decision making. Moreover, the failure to evaluate the effectiveness of the approaches used to assess customer satisfaction may make it difficult to keep up with changing customer and market needs and gather critical information necessary for strategic planning as well as the development of new or improved products and services.

3.2 VOICE OF THE CUSTOMER—SAMPLE EFFECTIVE PRACTICES

A. Customer Listening

- Effective listening and learning strategies include:

    - Close monitoring of technological, competitive, societal, environmental, economic, and demographic factors that may bear on customer requirements, expectations, preferences, or alternatives

    - Focus groups with demanding or leading-edge customers

    - Training of front-line employees in customer listening and using these employees to collect complaints

    - Use of critical incidents in product or support performance or quality to understand key problems from the point of view of customers and front-line employees

    - Interviewing lost customers to determine why they left

    - Win/loss analysis relative to competitors

    - Analysis of major factors affecting key customers

- Tools such as forced- or paired-choice analysis are used (where customers select between options A and B, A and C, B and C, and so on). Using this technique, organizations quickly prioritize requirements and focus on delivering those that make the greatest impact on satisfaction and engagement (repeat business and loyalty).

- Methods to listen and learn from customers are evaluated and improved through several cycles. Examples of factors that are evaluated include:

    - The adequacy and timeliness of customer related information

    - Improvement of survey design

- Approaches for getting reliable and timely information—surveys, focus groups, customer-contact personnel
- Improved aggregation and analysis of information
- A system exists to ensure that customer complaints are resolved promptly and effectively by the first point of contact. Customer support employees have been trained and given the authority for resolving a broad range of problems.
- Requirements and satisfaction data are collected from former customers for each customer/market segment.
- Complaint data are tracked, analyzed, and used to initiate prompt corrective action to prevent the problem from recurring.
- Training and development plans and replacement procedures exist for customer support employees. These processes have been measured and refined.
- Measurable customer support requirements (service standards) have been derived from customer expectations (for example, timeliness, courtesy, efficiency, thoroughness, and completeness).
- Requirements for building relationships are identified and may include factors such as product knowledge, employee responsiveness, and various customer support methods.
- Use voice of the customer as part of Quality Function Deployment (QFD) to ensure customer needs and requirements are fully incorporated into the design and delivery of products and services.

B. Determination of Customer Satisfaction and Engagement

- Several customer-satisfaction indicators are used (for example, repeat-business measures, praise letters, and direct measures using survey questions and interviews).
- Comprehensive satisfaction, engagement, and dissatisfaction data are collected and segmented or grouped to enable the organization to predict customer behavior (likelihood of remaining a customer).
- Customer satisfaction, engagement, and dissatisfaction measurements include both a numerical rating scale and descriptors assigned to each unit in the scale. An effective (actionable) customer satisfaction and dissatisfaction measurement system provides the organization with reliable information about customer ratings of specific product and service features and the relationship between these ratings and the customers' likely market behavior.
- Customer dissatisfaction indicators include complaints, claims, refunds, recalls, returns, repeat services, litigation, replacements, performance-rating downgrades, repairs, warranty work, warranty costs, misshipments, and incomplete orders.
- Competitors' customer satisfaction is determined using external or internal studies. This information is used to refine services and product features.

C. Analysis and Use of Customer Data

- A systematic approach is in place to evaluate and improve service levels, customer-focused decision making, and customer relationships.
- The requirements of customers of competitors are identified and processes are in place to gather expectation data from potential customers.
- Various systematic methods are used to gather data and identify current requirements and expectations of customers (for example, surveys, focus groups, and the use of Web-based systems).
- Key product features are defined in order of importance to customers. Product features refer to all important characteristics and to the performance of products and services that customers experience or perceive throughout their use (life cycle). Factors that bear on customer engagement (preference and loyalty)—for example, those features that enhance or differentiate

products and services from competing offerings—are defined in measurable terms.

- Tools such as forced- or paired-choice analysis are used (where customers select between options A and B, A and C, B and C, and so on). Using this technique, organizations quickly prioritize requirements and focus on delivering those that make the greatest impact on satisfaction, repeat business, and loyalty.

- Customer requirements are identified or grouped to make it easier for the organization to plan, design, and deliver maximum value to each segment. This information is consistently used for planning, data analysis, product and service design, production, and delivery processes, and for reporting and monitoring progress.

- Customer data such as complaints and gains or losses of customers are used to support the identification or validation of key customer requirements. Fact-based, systematic methods are used to identify the future requirements and expectations of customers. These are tested for accuracy and estimation techniques are improved.

- The process of collecting complete, timely, and accurate customer-satisfaction and dissatisfaction data is regularly evaluated and improved. Customer preferences, by customer segment, are considered when designing procedures to determine satisfaction levels. Some prefer surveys, others focus groups, and others prefer face-to-face interactions. Several improvement cycles are evident.

4 Measurement, Analysis, and Knowledge Management—90 Points

*The **Measurement, Analysis, and Knowledge Management** Category examines how your organization selects, gathers, analyzes, manages, and improves its data, information, and knowledge assets and how it manages its information technology. The Category also examines how your organization reviews and uses reviews to improve its performance.*

The Measurement, Analysis, and Knowledge Management Category is the main point within the Criteria for all key information about effectively measuring, analyzing, and reviewing performance and managing organizational knowledge to drive improvement and organizational competitiveness. This Category is like the *motherboard* of a personal computer. All information flows into and out of it. Simply speaking, Category 4 is the *brain center* for the alignment of the organization's operations consistent with its strategic objectives. Such use of data and information depends on their quality and availability. Moreover, since information, analysis, and knowledge management by themselves might be sources of competitive advantage and productivity growth, the Category also may have strategic value and its capabilities should be considered as part of the strategic planning process.

Measurement, Analysis, and Knowledge Management evaluates the selection, management, and effectiveness of use of information and data to support processes, action plans, and the performance management system. Systems to analyze, review, capture, store, retrieve, and distribute data to support decision making are also evaluated.

Measurement, Analysis, and Improvement of Organizational Performance

- This Item looks at the processes associated with data collection, information, and measures (including comparative data) for planning, decision making, improving performance, and supporting action plans and operations.

- The Item also looks at the analytical processes used to make sense out of the data to ensure decision makers draw valid conclusions. In addition, it looks at how these analyses are deployed throughout the organization and used to support organization-level review, decision making, planning, and process improvement.

Management of Information, Knowledge, and Information Technology

- This Item looks at how the organization ensures that data and information are accessible to workers, suppliers and partners, and customers as needed and appropriate to support decision making. This Item also seeks to ensure that hardware and software are reliable and user-friendly throughout the organization. In many organizations, people with minimal computer skills must be able to access and use data to support decision making.

- The data system must provide for and ensure data integrity (completeness), reliability (consistency), accuracy (correctness), timeliness (available when needed), security (free from attack), and confidentiality (free from inappropriate release).

4.1 MEASUREMENT, ANALYSIS, AND IMPROVEMENT OF ORGANIZATIONAL PERFORMANCE: How do you measure, analyze, and then improve organizational performance? (45 Pts.)

PROCESS

Describe how your organization measures, analyzes, reviews, and improves its performance through the use of data and information at all levels and in all parts of your organization.

Within your response, include answers to the following questions:

a. **Performance Measurement**

(1) How do you select, collect, align, and integrate data and information for tracking daily operations and for tracking overall organizational performance, including progress relative to strategic objectives and action plans? What are your key organizational performance measures, including key short-term and longer-term financial measures? How frequently are these measures determined? How do you use these data and information to support organizational decision making and innovation?

(2) How do you select and ensure the effective use of key comparative data and information to support operational and strategic decision making and innovation?

(3) How do you keep your performance measurement system current with business needs and directions? How do you ensure that your performance measurement system is sensitive to rapid or unexpected organizational or external changes?

b. **Performance Analysis and Review**

How do you review organizational performance and capabilities? What analyses do you perform to support these reviews and to ensure that conclusions are valid? How do you use these reviews to assess organizational success, competitive performance, and progress relative to strategic objectives and action plans? How do you use these reviews to assess your organization's ability to respond rapidly to changing organizational needs and challenges in your operating environment?

c. **Performance Improvement**

How do you translate organizational performance review findings into priorities for continuous and breakthrough improvement and into opportunities for innovation? How are these priorities and opportunities deployed to work group and functional-level operations throughout your organization to enable effective support for their decision making? When appropriate, how are the priorities and opportunities deployed to your suppliers, partners, and collaborators to ensure organizational alignment?

Notes:

N1. Performance measurement [4.1a] is used in fact-based decision making for setting and aligning organizational directions and resource use at the work unit, key process, departmental, and organizational levels.

N2. Comparative data and information (4.1a[2]) are obtained by benchmarking and by seeking competitive comparisons. "Benchmarking" refers to identifying processes and results that represent best practices and performance for similar activities, inside or outside your organization's industry. Competitive comparisons relate your organization's performance to that of competitors and other organizations providing similar products and services.

N3. Organizational performance reviews (4.1b) should be informed by organizational performance measurement, performance measures reported throughout your Criteria Item responses, and performance measures reviewed by senior leaders (1.1b[2]), and they should be guided by the strategic objectives and action plans described in Items 2.1 and 2.2. The reviews also might be informed by internal or external Baldrige assessments.

Continued

> **Notes:** *Continued*
>
> N4. Analysis (4.1b) includes examining performance trends; organizational, industry, and technology projections; and comparisons, cause-effect relationships, and correlations. Analysis should support your performance reviews, help determine root causes, and help set priorities for resource use. Accordingly, analysis draws on all types of data: customer-related, financial and market, operational, and competitive.
>
> N5. The results of organizational performance analysis and review should contribute to your organizational strategic planning in Category 2.
>
> N6. Your organizational performance results should be reported in Items 7.1–7.6.

Item 4.1, Measurement, Analysis, and Review of Organizational Performance, looks at the selection, collection, alignment, integration, management, analysis, and use of data and information in support of organizational decision making, planning, and performance improvement. The processes and systems required by this Item provide a solid foundation for consistently good decision making. These processes serve as a central collection and analysis point in an integrated performance measurement and management system. These processes also enhance the organization's ability to anticipate and respond to rapid or unexpected organizational or external changes.

The first part of this Item, Performance Measurement [4.1a], requires the organization to select and use measures to track daily operations and enhance decision-making accuracy. It should also select and integrate measures for monitoring overall organizational performance.

The frequency by which measures are collected should be aligned with data needs to support decision making. For example, in Item 2.1b(1), timelines for accomplishing strategic milestones should relate to the frequency of data collection/measure in Item 4.1a(1) and the frequency of the performance review in Item 4.1b.

Data alignment and integration are key concepts for successful implementation of the performance measurement system. Measures should be aligned to link key processes throughout the organization, integrated to yield organization-wide measures, and deployed by senior leaders to track work-group and process-level performance on key measures of organization-wide success.

The organization should show how competitive comparisons and benchmarking data are selected and used to help drive performance improvement. The major reasons for using competitive and comparative information are: (1) the organization needs to know where it stands relative to competitors and comparable organizations and best practices, especially as it works to achieve top levels of performance (which may be defined by a competitor or other provider); (2) comparative and benchmarking information often provides a focus for significant (*breakthrough*) improvement or change; and (3) preparation for comparing performance information frequently leads to a better understanding of the organization's own processes and related performance. Benchmarking information also may support business analyses and decisions relating to core competencies, alliances, and outsourcing.

Effective selection of competitive comparisons and benchmarking information requires: (1) determination of needs and priorities; and (2) criteria for seeking appropriate sources for comparisons—from within and outside the organization's industry and markets. Benchmarking or comparison data and information should be used (1) to set stretch targets and to promote major or breakthrough improvements in areas most critical to the organization's competitive strategy; and (2) to demonstrate the strengths or *soundness* of the organization's performance outcomes.

Item 4.1a also looks at how the organization's performance measurement system is kept current with changing business needs. This involves ongoing, fact-based evaluation and subsequent refinements.

The second part of this Item, Performance Analysis, Review, and Measurement [4.1b], looks at how the organization analyzes data to support decision making, how leaders review performance and set priorities, and how performance results are used to drive the systematic evaluation and improvement of key processes throughout the organization.

Effective decision making usually requires leaders to understand cause–effect relationships among and between processes and performance results. Process actions and their results may have many resource implications.

High-performing organizations find it necessary to have support systems that provide an effective analytical basis for decisions because resources for improvement are limited and cause–effect relationships are often unclear. Therefore, organizations must have the ability to perform effective analyses to support senior leaders' assessments of all areas of performance and strategic planning. This includes assessment of current performance as well as how well the organization is moving toward the future. Review findings should provide a reliable means to guide both improvement and opportunities for innovation that are tied to the organization's key objectives, success factors, and measures. The results of organizational-level analysis must be effectively communicated by leaders to support decision making throughout the organization and to appropriate suppliers, partners, and key customers, and ensure those decisions are aligned with business results, strategic objectives, and action plans.

Accordingly, systematic processes must be in place for analyzing all types of data and to determine overall organizational health, including key organizational results, action plans, and strategic objectives. In addition, organizations must evaluate the effectiveness of their analytical processes and make improvements based on the evaluation.

Facts, rather than intuition, should be used to support most decision making at all levels based on the analyses conducted to make sense out of the data collected. Analyses that organizations typically conduct to gain an understanding of performance and needed actions vary widely depending on the type of organization, size, competitive environment, and other factors. These analyses help the organization's leaders understand the following:

- The extent to which product and service improvement drives customer satisfaction, customer engagement, customer retention, and market share

- The impact of customer-related problems and effective problem resolution on cost/revenue growth, repeat business, and lost customers

- Interpretation of market-share changes in terms of customer gains and losses and changes in customer satisfaction

- The impact of improvements in key operational performance areas such as productivity, cycle time, waste reduction, new-product introduction, and defect levels

- Relationships between personal/organizational learning (improvement processes) and value added per employee

- Financial benefits derived from improvements in workforce safety, absenteeism, and turnover

- Benefits and costs associated with education and training of all types, including e-learning and other distance learning methods

- Benefits and costs associated with improved organizational knowledge management and sharing of best practices

- The extent to which identifying and meeting workforce capability and capacity correlate with retention, motivation, and productivity

- Cost/revenue implications of workforce-related problems and effective problem resolution

- The relationship between knowledge management and innovation

- Individual or aggregate measures of productivity cost trends and quality relative to competitors' performance

- Relationships among product/service quality, operational-performance indicators, and overall financial-performance trends as reflected in indicators such as operating costs, revenues, asset utilization, and value added per employee

- Allocation of resources among alternative improvement projects based on cost/benefit implications or environmental/community impact

- Determination of root causes of process/product failure

- Net earnings derived from quality, operational, and workforce performance improvements

- Contributions of improvement activities to cash flow, working capital use, and shareholder value

- Profit impacts of customer retention and loss

- Cost/revenue implications of new market entry, including global market entry or expansion

- Market share versus profits

- Trends in economic, market, and shareholder indicators of value and the impact of these trends on organizational sustainability

The availability of electronic data and information of many kinds (for example, financial, operational, customer-related, accreditation/regulatory) and from many sources (for example, internal, third party, and public sources; the Internet; Internet tracking software) permits extensive analysis and correlations. Effectively using and prioritizing data and information are important to the success of top-performing organizations.

Senior leaders must review organizational performance in a disciplined, fact-based manner, and use the review findings to drive improvement and innovation [4.1b]. This organizational review should cover all areas of performance, and provide a complete and accurate picture of the *state of health* of the organization. This includes not only how well the organization is currently performing but also how well it is changing to secure future success.

- Key performance measures should focus on and reflect the key drivers of success leaders regularly review. These measures should relate to the strategic objectives necessary for success.

- Leaders should use these reviews to set priorities for focusing on improvement and change activities needed to achieve the organization's key objectives, success factors, and measures.

- Leaders must create a consistent process to translate the review findings into an action agenda, sufficiently specific for deployment throughout the organization and to suppliers and partners—people who need to take action to improve.

Finally, the results of organizational performance reviews will reveal excellent, adequate, and unacceptable levels of performance. These results help leaders identify where additional evaluation and improvement of key work processes are most needed. This analysis should help leaders identify priorities and drive improvement in critical areas throughout the organization.

4.1 Measurement, Analysis, and Improvement of Organizational Performance

Basic Approach Requirements*: Measure, analyze, and then improve organizational performance.

Overall Approach Requirements*: Effectively measure, analyze, align, review, and improve performance through the use of data and information at all levels and in all parts of the organization. Effectively and systematically use the results of these reviews to evaluate and improve processes.

Multiple Approach Requirements: The following diagram describes multiple approach requirements.

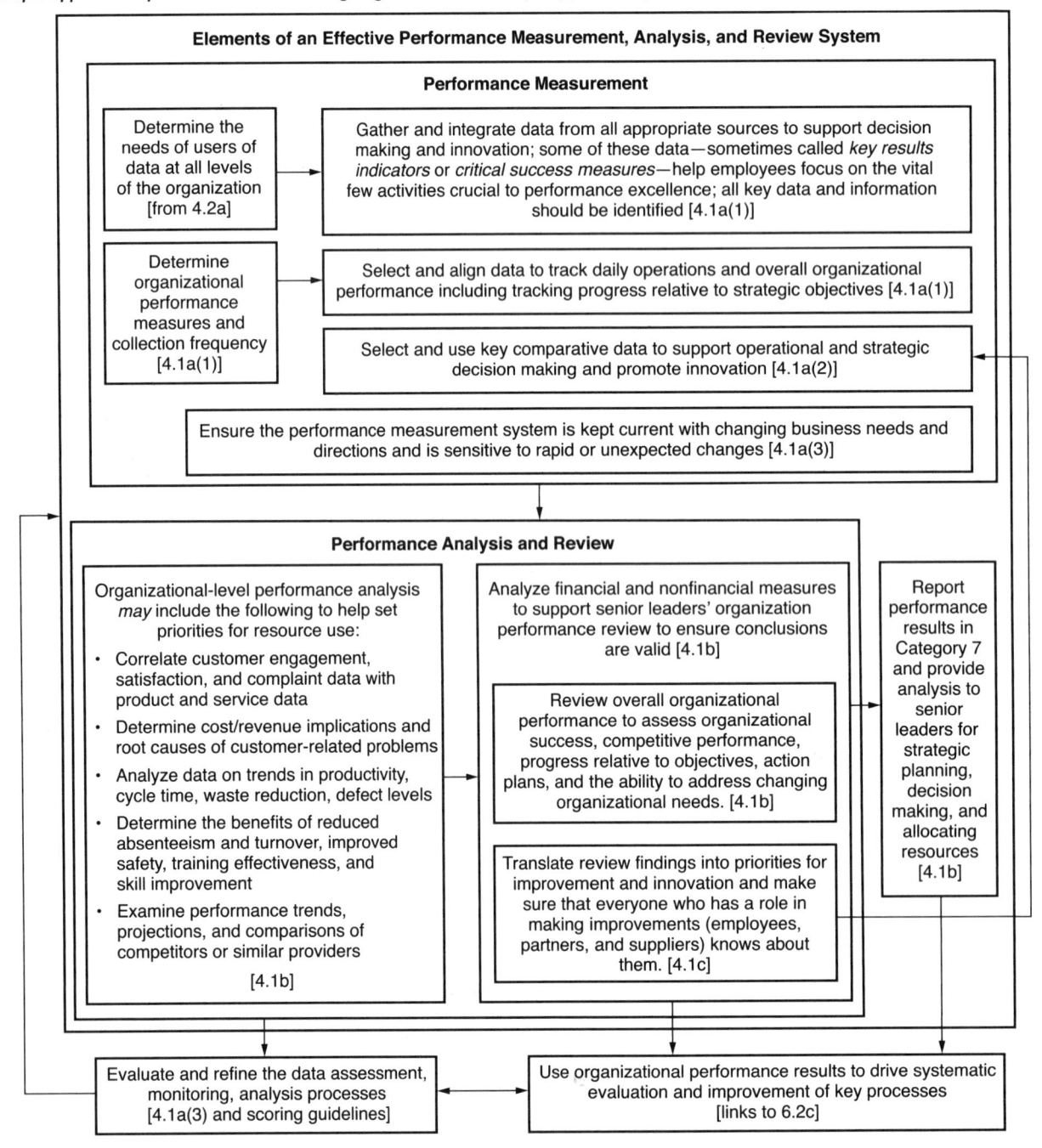

Elements of an Effective Performance Measurement, Analysis, and Review System

Performance Measurement

- Determine the needs of users of data at all levels of the organization [from 4.2a]
  → Gather and integrate data from all appropriate sources to support decision making and innovation; some of these data—sometimes called *key results indicators* or *critical success measures*—help employees focus on the vital few activities crucial to performance excellence; all key data and information should be identified [4.1a(1)]

- Determine organizational performance measures and collection frequency [4.1a(1)]
  → Select and align data to track daily operations and overall organizational performance including tracking progress relative to strategic objectives [4.1a(1)]
  → Select and use key comparative data to support operational and strategic decision making and promote innovation [4.1a(2)]

- Ensure the performance measurement system is kept current with changing business needs and directions and is sensitive to rapid or unexpected changes [4.1a(3)]

Performance Analysis and Review

Organizational-level performance analysis *may* include the following to help set priorities for resource use:
- Correlate customer engagement, satisfaction, and complaint data with product and service data
- Determine cost/revenue implications and root causes of customer-related problems
- Analyze data on trends in productivity, cycle time, waste reduction, defect levels
- Determine the benefits of reduced absenteeism and turnover, improved safety, training effectiveness, and skill improvement
- Examine performance trends, projections, and comparisons of competitors or similar providers
[4.1b]

Analyze financial and nonfinancial measures to support senior leaders' organization performance review to ensure conclusions are valid [4.1b]

Review overall organizational performance to assess organizational success, competitive performance, progress relative to objectives, action plans, and the ability to address changing organizational needs. [4.1b]

Translate review findings into priorities for improvement and innovation and make sure that everyone who has a role in making improvements (employees, partners, and suppliers) knows about them. [4.1c]

Report performance results in Category 7 and provide analysis to senior leaders for strategic planning, decision making, and allocating resources [4.1b]

Evaluate and refine the data assessment, monitoring, analysis processes [4.1a(3) and scoring guidelines]

Use organizational performance results to drive systematic evaluation and improvement of key processes [links to 6.2c]

---

* Multiple-level requirements usually incorporate Basic and Overall requirements. To avoid confusion, the first time a requirement appears in an Item establishes its level for scoring purposes. If the requirement first appears at the Overall Approach Level and again at the Multiple Level, the requirement should be considered an Overall-level requirement. For a more complete explanation see the chapter on Scoring System and the Scoring Calibration Guidelines.

4.1 Key Measurement, Analysis, and Improvement of Organizational Performance Item Linkages

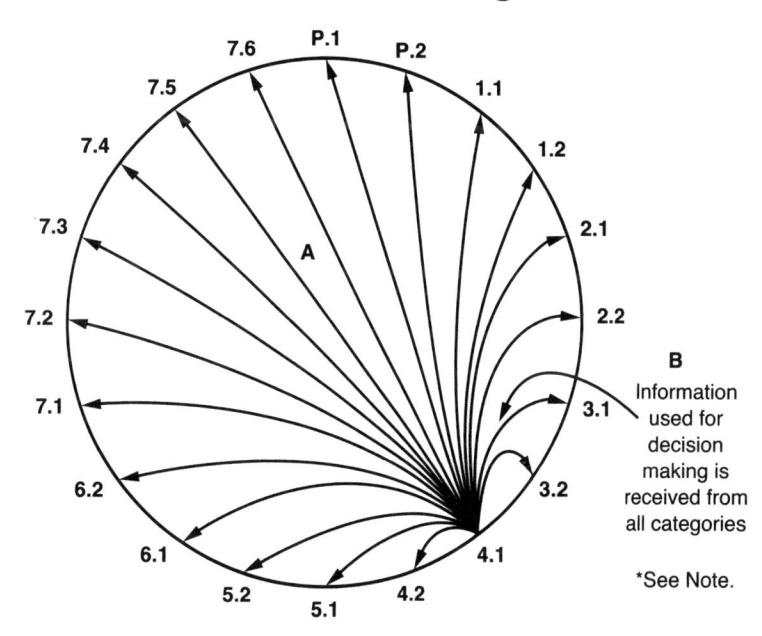

	NATURE OF RELATIONSHIP
A	Data and information are collected and analyzed [4.1] and made available [4.2] for developing the Organizational Profile [P.1 and P.2], planning [2.1a(2)], setting strategic objectives [2.1b(1)], day-to-day leadership decisions [1.1], setting and monitoring societal responsibility standards (regulatory, legal, ethical) for community involvement [1.2], reporting performance results [7.1, 7.2, 7.3, 7.4, 7.5, and 7.6], designing, managing, and improving key work systems and processes [6.1 and 6.2], workforce engagement, development, capacity, and capability systems [5.1 and 5.2], determining customer requirements and preferences [3.2], managing customer complaints and building customer relations [3.2a], and determining customer satisfaction, engagement, and dissatisfaction [3.2b].
B	Data and information used to support analysis, decision making, and continuous improvement [4.1] are received from all processes. Customer satisfaction, engagement, and dissatisfaction data [7.2] are analyzed [4.1b] and used to help determine ways to assess customer requirements [3.2a(1)], to determine appropriate standards or required levels of customer support [3.2a(1)], and to design instruments to assess customer satisfaction, engagement, and dissatisfaction [3.2b]. Data and information are received from the following areas and analyzed to support decisions: workforce engagement, capacity, capability, and climate [5.1 and 5.2]. Data are aggregated and analyzed [4.1] to improve the design of work systems [6.1] and manage key work processes [6.2] that will reduce cycle time, waste, and defect levels. Performance data from all parts of the organization are integrated and analyzed [4.1b, c] to assess and help improve performance in key Areas such as product performance [7.1], customer-related performance [7.2], process performance [7.5], financial and market performance [7.3], workforce performance [7.4], and leadership outcomes [7.6] relative to competitors or similar providers in all areas. Leaders [1.1b(2)] monitor organizational performance and understand relationships among performance, workforce engagement and satisfaction, customers, markets, and financial success. Leaders also use this information to support decision making at all levels, to set priorities for action, identify opportunities for innovation, and allocate resources for maximum advantage [4.1c]. Data are also used to drive improvements in key work processes [6.2c].

*Note: Because the information collected and used for decision making links with all other Items, all of the linkage arrows will not be repeated on the other Item maps. Only the most relevant will be repeated.

	IF YOU DON'T DO WHAT THE CRITERIA REQUIRE...
Item Reference	**Possible Adverse Consequences**
4.1a(1)	The failure to gather appropriate data and information from throughout the organization to support daily operations, organizational decision making, and track progress in achieving strategic objectives and action plans can create an environment where decisions are typically based on intuition, gut feel, or guesswork. Decisions based on intuition or guesswork tend to be highly variable and prone to error. Furthermore, in an environment where decisions are based on intuition it is usually the boss' intuition that drives the decision, which can lead to the disengagement of the workers in the organization. Decisions made in this manner erode the organization's efforts to promote workforce initiative, empowerment, and innovation [Item 1.1a(3)]. Finally, the failure to integrate data and information may make it difficult to monitor overall organizational performance. Disjointed, nonintegrated data are difficult to consolidate and report in a manageable, easy-to-understand *dashboard* to support effective decision making.
4.1a(1)	Data and information provide a basis for decision making at all levels of the organization: top leaders use the data to make decisions about the direction of the organization, and workers use data to make decisions about daily operational matters. Unless measures are selected and aligned to provide the right information, at the right time, and in the right format, the decisions of leaders and workers are likely to be suboptimized. Moreover, although the failure to gather appropriate data tends to reduce decision-making quality, spending resources to gather data and information that do not support decision making throughout the organization (useless data) adds unnecessary cost. It is difficult to collect the right data and information if the organization has failed to determine what data are needed to support decision making at all levels. In addition, the failure to collect appropriate data and information makes it more difficult to monitor performance against goals [Item 4.1b], effectively communicate expectations throughout the organization [Item 1.1a(1)], and deploy actions needed to carry out strategy [Item 2.2a].
4.1a(1)	Strategy identifies the outcomes that an organization must achieve to be successful in the future. Many actions must be taken in an organization to ensure strategic objectives are achieved. Data analysis helps leaders understand critical relationships between actions and outcomes to effectively allocate resources and achieve desired results. The failure to examine and understand the relationship between performance outcomes, action plans, and strategic objectives may cause senior leaders to make inappropriate decisions about the allocation of limited resources. This means that the organization may not realize the maximum benefit from the expenditure of those resources. For example, failing to understand the correlation between product and service quality improvement and improved customer satisfaction and retention may cause the leader to divert resources to less important activities.
4.1a(2)	The failure to collect and effectively use the right comparative data makes it difficult for the organization to learn and take appropriate action. Learning from the best helps provoke an understanding of what systems and processes may be required to make quantum leaps in performance as well as the levels that must be reached to achieve the leadership position projected during the planning process [Item 2.2b]. For example, comparisons showing that the organization's projected performance outpaces the industrial average will have little meaning

Continued

	IF YOU DON'T DO WHAT THE CRITERIA REQUIRE... Continued
Item Reference	**Possible Adverse Consequences**
	if the best competitor's rate of improvement is greater. Furthermore, if an organization collects comparative data from world-class benchmarks, but does not effectively use those data to plan [Item 2.1a(1, 2)], to identify areas needing breakthrough performance, or to set priorities for innovation [Item 4.1a(2)], then it is simply wasting resources. If an organization does not collect comparative performance outcome data, it is not able to determine if its own rate of progress is sufficient to keep it ahead of the competition or evaluate the strength of its own performance results [required by Category 7].
4.1a(3)	Organizations that fail to improve the speed and accuracy of decision making typically do not perform well in a competitive environment. Without a process to evaluate the information system and how well it responds to the needs of the business, organizations may not know they are collecting insufficient or incorrect data and information. In addition, organizations may not know if the data effectively support daily operations and organizational decision making. They may not know if the resources spent to collect benchmarking and comparison data produce appropriate benefits.
4.1b	The lack of a system to analyze and make sense out of raw data may make it difficult for senior leaders to understand cause-and-effect relationships, root causes of problems, and the impact of various processes on performance outcomes. This may make it more difficult for leaders to identify specific areas within the organization where improvement is required. It may send a message throughout the organization that performance outcomes are really not that important. If results are not important to top leaders, they may not be considered important to lower levels within the organization and workers at all levels may not contribute optimum effort to achieve these (unimportant) results. It also becomes more difficult for leaders to effectively set priorities. Consider the following examples: (a) without a cost–benefit analysis it is more difficult to determine whether project A or project B should receive support, because it is difficult to know which project is likely to be of greater benefit to the organization; (b) calculating C_{pk} (the capability of a process) helps leaders understand the extent to which their key processes are in control or need adjustment (the raw run data cannot support this kind of decision making); and (c) failing to understand root causes makes it more difficult to prevent problems from recurring, which adds cost.
4.1c	Even if senior leaders have an effective process to review organizational performance, but do not effectively use these review findings to identify priorities for improvement and targets of innovation, they may not be providing appropriate focus and alignment throughout the organization and to affected suppliers and partners. This may make it difficult for workers, managers, partners, and suppliers to make the changes needed to correct problems or comply with the new priorities for improvement, contributing to wasted resources and performance failures. The long-standing failure to identify priorities for improvement or targets of innovation may contribute to the perception that the status quo is acceptable and continuous improvement is not important. This may further contribute to organizational stagnation and may make it difficult to keep pace with competitors and increasing customer requirements.
	Continued

	IF YOU DON'T DO WHAT THE CRITERIA REQUIRE . . . Continued
Item Reference	**Possible Adverse Consequences**
4.1c	Workers and managers at all levels of the organization need useful information to support decision making. The failure to ensure that people at every level understand the impact that their work has on overall organizational performance makes it more difficult for them to identify and understand why they need to perform at certain agreed levels and why change may need to occur. Without this information, workers and managers throughout the organization must rely on intuition or incomplete data to support decision making—typically reducing the accuracy of those decisions and, in some cases, suboptimizing the overall performance of the organization.
4.1c	It is not enough to review performance results without taking steps to improve key processes that are underperforming. A key purpose of data and analysis is to support fact-based improvement to increase value and organization success.

4.1 MEASUREMENT, ANALYSIS, AND IMPROVEMENT OF ORGANIZATIONAL PERFORMANCE—SAMPLE EFFECTIVE PRACTICES

A. Performance Measurement

- Above all, data and information are favored as a decision-making support tool, rather than a quick and easy reliance on intuition or *gut feel*.

- Data collected at the individual worker level are consistent across the organization to permit consolidation and organization-wide performance monitoring.

- The cost of (poor) quality (including rework, delay, waste, scrap, errors) and other financial concerns are measured for internal operations and processes.

- Data are maintained on employee-related issues of satisfaction, morale, safety, education and training, use of teams, and recognition and reward.

- A systematic process exists for data review and improvement, standardization, and easy employee access to data. Training on the use of data systems is provided as needed.

- Data used for management decision making focus on critical success factors and are integrated with work processes for the planning, design, and delivery of products and services.

- A systematic process is in place for identifying and prioritizing comparative information and benchmark targets.

- Research has been conducted to identify best-in-class organizations, which may be competitors or noncompetitors. Critical business processes or functions are the subject of benchmarking. Activities such as those that support the organization's goals and objectives, action plans, and opportunities for improvement and innovation are the subject of benchmarking. Benchmarking also is applied to key products, services, customer satisfiers, suppliers, employees, and support operations.

- The organization reaches beyond its own business to conduct comparative studies.

- Benchmark or comparison data are used to improve the understanding of work processes and to discover the best levels of performance that have been achieved. Based on this knowledge, the organization sets goals or targets to stretch performance as well as drive innovations.

- A systematic process is in place to improve the use of benchmark or comparison data in the understanding of all work processes.

B. Performance Analysis and Review

- Systematic processes are in place for analyzing all types of data and to determine overall organizational health, including key business results, action plans, and strategic objectives. Part of the process is a method to evaluate the effectiveness of the analysis process and improve upon it.

- Facts, rather than intuition, are used to support most decision making at all levels based on the analyses conducted to make sense out of the data collected.

- The analysis process itself is analyzed to make the results more timely and useful for decision making for quality improvement at all levels.

- Analysis processes and tools, and the value of analyses to decision making, are systematically evaluated and improved.

- Analysis is linked to work groups to facilitate decision making (sometimes daily) throughout the organization.

- Analysis techniques enable meaningful interpretation of the cost and performance impact of organization processes. This analysis helps workers at all levels of the organization make necessary trade-offs, set priorities, and reallocate resources to maximize overall organization performance.

- Reviews against measurable performance standards are held frequently.

- Senior leaders base their business decisions on reliable data and facts pertaining to customers, operational processes, and worker performance and satisfaction.

- Senior leaders hold regular meetings to review performance results and use this information to set priorities to resolve problems, and evaluate and improve work processes.

- Senior leaders conduct monthly reviews of organizational performance. This requires that subordinates conduct biweekly reviews, and workers and work teams provide daily performance updates. Corrective actions are developed to improve performance that deviates from planned performance.

- Customer, performance, and financial data drive priorities for organizational improvement and innovation.

- Many processes throughout the organization have been improved or even innovated based on the analyses of the performance data.

4.2 MANAGEMENT OF INFORMATION, KNOWLEDGE, AND INFORMATION TECHNOLOGY: How do you manage your information, organizational knowledge, and information technology? (45 Pts.)

PROCESS

Describe how your organization ensures the quality and availability of needed data, information, software, and hardware for your workforce, suppliers, partners, collaborators, and customers. Describe how your organization builds and manages its knowledge assets.

Within your response, include answers to the following questions:

a. Data, Information, and Knowledge Management

(1) How do you ensure the following properties of your organizational data, information, and knowledge:
- Accuracy
- Integrity and reliability
- Timeliness
- Security and confidentiality

(2) How do you make needed data and information available? How do you make them accessible to your workforce, suppliers, partners, collaborators, and customers, as appropriate?

(3) How do you manage organizational knowledge to accomplish:
- The collection and transfer of workforce knowledge
- The transfer of relevant knowledge from and to customers, suppliers, partners, and collaborators
- The rapid identification, sharing, and implementation of best practices
- The assembly and transfer of relevant knowledge for use in your strategic planning process(1)

b. Management of Information Resources and Technology

(1) How do you ensure that hardware and software are reliable, secure, and user-friendly?

(2) In the event of an emergency, how do you ensure the continued availability of hardware and software systems, and the continued availability of data and information?

(3) How do you keep your data and information availability mechanisms, including your software and hardware systems, current with business needs and directions and with technological changes in your operating environment?

Note:

N1. Data and information access [4.2a(2)] might be via electronic or other means.

This Item examines how the organization ensures the availability of high-quality, timely data and information, software, and hardware for all the workforce, suppliers, partners, collaborators, and customers. It also examines how the organization builds and manages its knowledge assets. Top-performing organizations make data and information available and accessible to all appropriate users. The organization's hardware systems and software must be reliable and user friendly, facilitating full access and encouraging routine use. The aim of building and managing knowledge assets is to improve organizational efficiency and effectiveness and to stimulate innovation.

As the sources of data and information and the number of users within the organization grow, systems to manage information often require significant change and more resources. Top-performing organizations consider the management of information technology as a strategic imperative. The expanding use of electronic information, new organizational knowledge networks, new data from the Internet, and increasing business-to-business, organization-to-organization, and business-to-consumer communications makes it absolutely critical that the organization develop systems to ensure data reliability and availability in a user-friendly manner.

Data and information are especially important in business or organization networks, alliances, and supply chains. Information management systems should facilitate the use of data and information and should recognize the need for rapid data validation and reliability assurance.

Organizations of all types should develop plans that address how the organization will continue to provide an information technology infrastructure, data, and information in the event of either a natural or manmade disaster. These plans should consider the needs of all stakeholders, including the workforce, customers, suppliers, partners, and collaborators. Processes should be in place to protect against system failure that may damage or destroy critical data. This may require redundant systems as well as effective backup and storage of data at remote locations. Processes should be in place to protect against external threats, including attacks from hackers, viral infections, power surges, and storm-related damage. The plans should also support business continuity and ensure workplace preparedness for disasters and emergencies (see Item 6.1c).

Organizations must ensure data and information reliability since reliability is critical to good decision making, successful monitoring of operations, and successful data integration for assessing overall performance. However, data reliability or consistency alone is not sufficient. To be useful, data must also be accurate. Consistently incorrect data do not help leaders make consistently good decisions.

As with the other items required for performance excellence, the organization must systematically evaluate and improve data-availability mechanisms, software, and hardware to keep them current with changing business needs and directions.

The organization must focus on the knowledge that people need to do their work; improve processes, products, and services; keep current with changing business needs and directions; and develop innovative solutions that add value for the customer and the organization. This item addresses the properties necessary for data and information to meet user needs, including integrity (completeness—tells the whole story), reliability (consistency), accuracy (correctness), timeliness (available when needed), and appropriate levels of security and confidentiality (free from tampering and inappropriate access and release).

4.2 Management of Information, Knowledge, and Information Technology

Basic Approach Requirements*: Manage information, organizational knowledge, and information technology.

Overall Approach Requirements*: Effectively ensure the quality and availability of needed data, information, software, and hardware for the workforce, suppliers, partners, collaborators, and customers. Effectively build and manage organizational knowledge assets.

Multiple Approach Requirements: The following diagram describes multiple approach requirements.

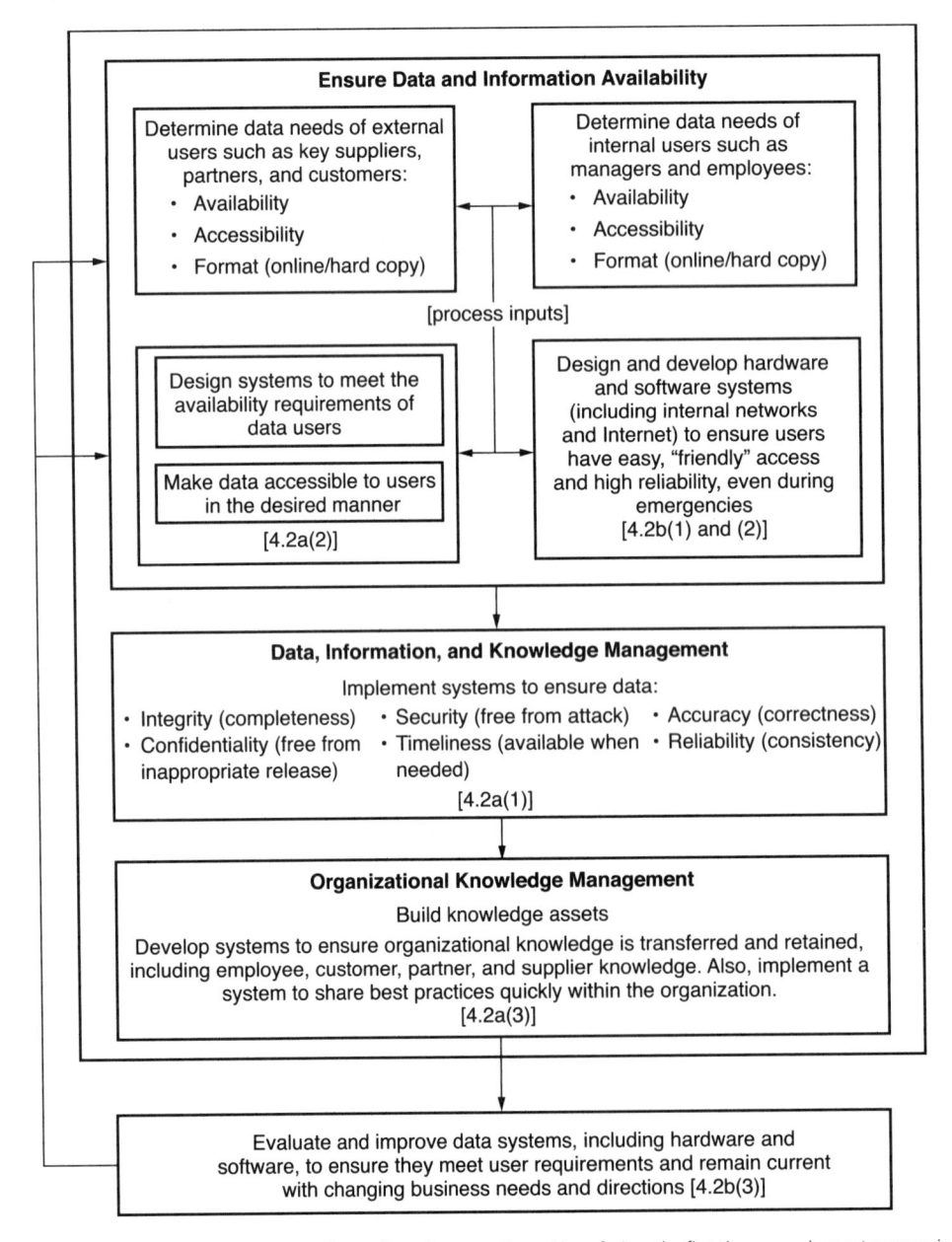

Ensure Data and Information Availability

Determine data needs of external users such as key suppliers, partners, and customers:
- Availability
- Accessibility
- Format (online/hard copy)

Determine data needs of internal users such as managers and employees:
- Availability
- Accessibility
- Format (online/hard copy)

[process inputs]

Design systems to meet the availability requirements of data users

Make data accessible to users in the desired manner
[4.2a(2)]

Design and develop hardware and software systems (including internal networks and Internet) to ensure users have easy, "friendly" access and high reliability, even during emergencies
[4.2b(1) and (2)]

Data, Information, and Knowledge Management

Implement systems to ensure data:
- Integrity (completeness)
- Confidentiality (free from inappropriate release)
- Security (free from attack)
- Timeliness (available when needed)
- Accuracy (correctness)
- Reliability (consistency)

[4.2a(1)]

Organizational Knowledge Management

Build knowledge assets

Develop systems to ensure organizational knowledge is transferred and retained, including employee, customer, partner, and supplier knowledge. Also, implement a system to share best practices quickly within the organization.
[4.2a(3)]

Evaluate and improve data systems, including hardware and software, to ensure they meet user requirements and remain current with changing business needs and directions [4.2b(3)]

---

* Multiple-level requirements usually incorporate Basic and Overall requirements. To avoid confusion, the first time a requirement appears in an Item establishes its level for scoring purposes. If the requirement first appears at the Overall Approach Level and again at the Multiple Level, the requirement should be considered an Overall-level requirement. For a more complete explanation see the chapter on Scoring System and the Scoring Calibration Guidelines.

4.2 Key Management of Information, Knowledge, and Information Technology Item Linkages

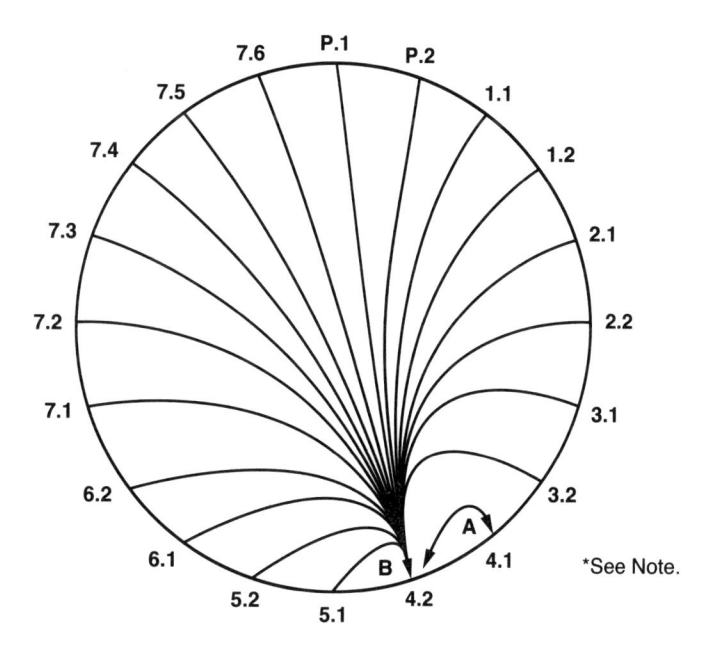

	NATURE OF RELATIONSHIP
A	Management of Information, Knowledge, and Information Technology [4.2] promotes proper data flow within the organization and indirectly interacts with all other items (similar to the relationships identified and reported in the Item 4.1 diagram). The simplest way to show these relationships is to tie this Item [4.2] with the Measurement, Analysis, and Improvement of Organizational Performance Item [4.1].
B	To ensure that hardware and software systems are reliable and user friendly [4.2b(1)], information from the following types of system users is gathered: leaders [Category 1]; planners [Category 2]; customer relationships and support staff [Category 3]; information specialists [Category 4]; human resource personnel, managers, and workers [Category 5]; operations workers, managers, suppliers, and partners [Category 6]; and people who monitor and interpret results [Category 7] for use in decision making.

*Note: Because the information collected and used for decision making links with all other Items, all of the linkage arrows will not be repeated on the other Item maps. Only the most relevant will be repeated.

	IF YOU DON'T DO WHAT THE CRITERIA REQUIRE...
Item Reference	**Possible Adverse Consequences**
4.2a(1)	Concerns about security, data loss, sophisticated hackers, and increased customer requirements for better access and availability place steadily increasing demands on hardware and software systems. The failure to keep these systems current as required by 4.2a(4) may expose them to internal or external threats. For example, the failure to update virus protections frequently and maintain up-to-date, effective firewalls can expose the computer system (and the organization) to catastrophic and costly losses. Decisions that are based on data and information may be compromised if the data are inaccurate or unreliable. For example, when a data-entry error is made and goes unnoticed (sometimes referred to as *garbage in, garbage out*), it could drive decisions to deliver the wrong product at the wrong time to the wrong customer. At the very least this is likely to cause the product to be returned and restocked, adding cost but not value. The lack of timely information may cause decisions to be delayed inappropriately. Consider, for example, an organization that conducts an employee (or customer) satisfaction survey but does not analyze or make the data available for eight months. This not only sends a message to the organization that employee (or customer) concerns are unimportant, it also makes it difficult to identify real problems that may be contributing to customer dissatisfaction, low worker morale, and poor productivity.
4.2a(2)	Getting the right information to the right people at the right time and in the right format is essential to support effective decision making. Just as different types of workers in an organization need different data to support decision making, they may need to access information in different ways. Similarly, customers and suppliers may need access to information to facilitate ordering and delivery of required products and services. The failure to provide appropriate access to data may make it more difficult for workers to make timely decisions about their work, for customers to comment, complain, seek information, or obtain products and services, or for suppliers to ensure the smooth flow of materials to support the organization's product and service delivery. Providing inappropriate access for individuals inside or outside the organization may compromise data confidentiality and security or even violate certain privacy laws.
4.2a(3)	Knowledge is of little or no use unless the people who need it, have it. Knowledge sequestered in one corner of an organization cannot benefit the entire organization unless it is transferred to other employees in other units. The same is true for knowledge held by key customers, suppliers, and partners. Knowledge withheld is knowledge (and resources) wasted. The failure to capture/transfer knowledge from long-standing employees who depart or retire is especially troublesome because they typically possess vast amounts of institutional memory.
4.2b(1)	The breadth, depth, and speed of decision making continue to increase as artificial intelligence plays an increasingly larger role. Hardware and software are at the heart of this phenomenon. More people than ever before are being asked to interact with computers. In the best-performing organizations, workers frequently use computers to access data and use them to develop relevant analyses that enable better decisions about their work. People with very little computer literacy must now enter and retrieve data from these systems. A user interface that may be easily understood by information management technicians may be incomprehensible to a line worker, customer, or supplier. The failure to make these systems

Continued

	IF YOU DON'T DO WHAT THE CRITERIA REQUIRE... *Continued*
Item Reference	**Possible Adverse Consequences**
	reliable and easy to use (user friendly) makes it difficult, if not impossible, for some people to use them effectively. This may create significant problems for organizations, particularly those venturing into areas where e-commerce plays a larger and growing role. Consider, for example, a bank that wants to expand and promote distance banking via the Internet or through home-to-bank modem connections. If the software is not reliable and very user friendly, many customers may be unwilling or unable to take advantage of these services. This may limit the organization's ability to achieve strategic and/or market-share goals that should have been considered during the strategy development process [Item 2.1a(2)].
4.2b(2)	The failure to ensure the continued availability of data, hardware, and software systems in an emergency causes reduced decision accuracy and delay at the very least. More typically, in today's world of e-commerce, information system failures can cause the organization to cease work.
4.2b(3)	In a rapidly changing world, access to information and the use of that information to provide insight and help decision making can provide a strategic advantage. Rapid data availability is becoming more and more critical for business success, especially in e-business situations. In some industries such as banking, a few seconds can make the difference between capitalizing on currency rate fluctuations or being hurt by them. As product and delivery cycle times grow shorter, the need for rapid access to information grows greater. Without evaluating the suitability of data and information systems, and making refinements based on this evaluation, the organization leaves itself open to falling behind and not being able to respond rapidly to changing business needs and directions. This Item does not require improvements in software and hardware simply for the sake of buying new gadgets. Improvements should help support changing business needs and directions—as a means to an end, not the end itself.

4.2 MANAGEMENT OF INFORMATION, KNOWLEDGE, AND INFORMATION TECHNOLOGY—SAMPLE EFFECTIVE PRACTICES

A. Data, Information, and Knowledge Management

- Users of data help determine what data systems are developed and how data are accessed.

- Every person has access to the data they need to make decisions about their work, from top leaders to individual workers or teams of workers.

- All key work processes are documented and stored in a searchable and accessible database and used to share improvements and avoid rework associated with reinventing effective processes.

- A data and knowledge exchange is in place to receive useful knowledge and information from customers, suppliers, partners and key collaborators. The system is automated for easy update and access. Face-to-face and/or electronic meetings are held regularly to share information.

- Data are protected against access and misuse from external sources through encryption and randomly changing user passwords.

- A data reliability (consistency) team periodically and randomly checks data. Systems are in place to minimize or prevent human error in data entry and analysis.

- Disciplined and automatic file backup occurs. Backup data are stored in a secure, external facility.

- Hardware and software systems have been protected against external threats from hackers, viral threats, water, and electrical damage. Protection systems are updated as appropriate (for example, viral updates are made several times daily).

B. Management of Information Resources and Technology

- A *sunset* review is conducted to determine what data no longer need to be collected and can be dropped.

- The performance measurement system is systematically evaluated and refined. Improvements have been made to reduce cycle time for data collection and to increase data access, reliability, and use.

- Procedures required to interface with the hardware and software are designed to meet the needs and capabilities of all computer users, to ensure that no one is excluded.

- Data systems are benchmarked against best-in-class systems and continually refined.

5 Workforce Focus—85 Points

*The **Workforce Focus** Category examines how your organization engages, manages, and develops your workforce to utilize its full potential in alignment with your organization's overall mission, strategy, and action plans. The Category examines your ability to assess workforce capability and capacity needs and to build a workforce environment conducive to high performance.*

Workforce Focus addresses key workforce practices—those directed toward creating a high-performance workplace and toward developing employees to enable them and the organization to adapt to change. The Category covers workforce engagement, development, and management requirements in an integrated manner, aligned with the organization's strategic directions and plans. The Category also focuses on the organization's capability and capacity needs and the workforce-support climate.

To ensure the basic alignment of workforce management with overall strategy, the Criteria also include human resource planning as part of organizational planning in the Strategic Planning Category.

Workforce Engagement

- Determine key factors that promote workforce engagement—helping workers contribute their *utmost* to the success of the organization and its customers

- Create a culture to support open communication, high-performance work, and an engaged workforce

- Support objectives for customer satisfaction, high-performance objectives, and employee and organization learning goals with performance feedback to employees and recognition and reward practices

- Develop the workforce and leaders

- Assess and improve workforce engagement

Workforce Environment

- Manage workforce capacity and capability to accomplish the work of the organization

- Recruit, hire, place, and retain employees to meet the organization's capability and capacity needs

- Ensure workplace health, safety, and security

- Assess workforce engagement and identify improvement priorities that promote key organizational results

- Provide workforce support and benefits

5.1 WORKFORCE ENGAGEMENT: How do you engage your workforce to achieve organizational and personal success? (45 Pts.)   **PROCESS**

Describe how your organization engages, compensates, and rewards your workforce to achieve high performance. Describe how members of your workforce, including leaders, are developed to achieve high performance. Describe how you assess workforce engagement and use the results to achieve higher performance.

Within your response, include answers to the following questions:

a. **Workforce Enrichment**

(1) How do you determine the key factors that affect workforce engagement? How do you determine the key factors that affect workforce satisfaction? How are these factors determined for different workforce groups and segments?

(2) How do you foster an organizational culture that is characterized by open communication, high-performance work, and an engaged workforce? How do you ensure your organizational culture benefits from the diverse ideas, cultures, and thinking of your workforce?

(3) How does your workforce performance management system support high-performance work and workforce engagement? How does your workforce performance management system consider workforce compensation, reward, recognition, and incentive practices? How does your workforce performance management system reinforce a customer and business focus and achievement of your action plans?

b. **Workforce and Leader Development**

(1) How does your learning and development system address the following factors for your workforce and your leaders:
- Your organization's core competencies, strategic challenges, and accomplishment of its action plans, both short-term and long-term
- Organizational performance improvement and innovation
- Ethics and ethical business practices
- The breadth of development opportunities, including education, training, coaching, mentoring, and work-related experiences, as appropriate

(2) How does your learning and development system address the following factors for your workforce:
- Their learning and development needs, including those that are self-identified and those identified by supervisors and managers
- The transfer of knowledge from departing or retiring workers
- The reinforcement of new knowledge and skills on the job

(3) How do you evaluate the effectiveness and efficiency of your learning and development systems?

(4) How do you manage effective career progression for your entire workforce? How do you accomplish effective succession planning for management and leadership positions?

c. **Assessment of Workforce Engagement**

(1) How do you assess workforce engagement? What formal and informal assessment methods and measures do you use to determine workforce engagement and workforce satisfaction? How do these methods and measures differ across workforce groups and segments? How do you use other indicators, such as workforce retention, absenteeism, grievances, safety, and productivity to assess and improve workforce engagement?

Continued

> *Continued*
>
> (2) How do you relate your workforce engagement assessment findings to key business results reported in Category 7 to identify opportunities for improvement in both workforce engagement and business results?
>
> **Notes:**
>
> N1. "Workforce" refers to the people actively involved in accomplishing the work of your organization. It includes your organization's permanent, temporary, and part-time personnel, as well as any contract employees supervised by your organization. It includes team leaders, supervisors, and managers at all levels. People supervised by a contractor should be addressed in Category 6 as part of your larger work systems. *For nonprofit organizations that also rely on volunteers, "workforce" includes these volunteers.*
>
> N2. "Workforce engagement" refers to the extent of workforce commitment, both emotional and intellectual, to accomplishing the work, mission, and vision of the organization.
>
> N3. The characteristics of "high-performance work" environments (5.1a[2] and 5.1a[3]) in which people do their utmost for the benefit of their customers and for the success of the organization are key to understanding an engaged workforce. These characteristics are described in detail in the definition of "high-performance work."
>
> N4. Compensation, recognition, and related reward and incentive practices (5.1a[3]) include promotions and bonuses that might be based on performance, skills acquired, and other factors. *In some government organizations, compensation systems are set by law or regulation. However, since recognition can include monetary and nonmonetary, formal and informal, and individual and group mechanisms, reward and recognition systems do permit flexibility.*
>
> N5. Your organization may have unique considerations relative to workforce development, learning, and career progression. If this is the case, your response to 5.1b should include how you address these considerations.
>
> N6. Identifying improvement opportunities (5.1c[2]) might draw on your workforce-focused results presented in Item 7.4 and might involve addressing workforce-related problems based on their impact on your business results reported in response to other Category 7 Items.

This Item [5.1] looks at the organization's systems for developing and assessing the engagement and satisfaction of the workforce, in order to enable and encourage all members of the workforce to contribute effectively and to the best of their abilities. Workforce engagement systems are intended to promote high performance, address core competencies, enhance individual and organizational learning, and enable innovation and adaptation to change, thereby contributing to organizational sustainability.

High levels of workforce engagement can have a significant, positive impact on organizational performance. Research has indicated that engagement is enhanced by performing meaningful work; having clear organizational direction, performance accountability, and an efficient work environment; and having a safe, trusting, and cooperative environment. Workers (and volunteers) in many nonprofit organizations are drawn to and derive meaning from their work, because the work is aligned with their personal values.

Although satisfaction with pay and promotion potential is important, research indicates it is not the most important driver of engagement. The most critical factors that drive workforce engagement are (a) feeling valued by supervisors, and (b) being involved. Contributors to engagement include the extent of involvement in decision making, the extent to which workers voice their ideas (and managers listen), the extent to which workers develop their knowledge, skills, and abilities, and the extent to which the organization is concerned for and supports worker health, safety, and well being.

Leader behavior helps or hinders employee engagement. To provide the environment where employees can be successful, leaders must:

- Be personally engaged, and demonstrate high energy in both their core job and supportive roles.

- Understand how each role helps support the business strategy and plan.

- Create an environment where achieving more than basic job requirements (tasks) is valued. Great leaders require workers to improve their knowledge, skills, and abilities, improve and innovate work processes, and work for the general betterment of co-workers and the organization as a whole.

Senior leaders should get their direct reports to do the same, and so forth down the chain.

Many factors adversely affect worker engagement. Factors that drain energy from leaders and workers and inhibit engagement include:

- Confusion (vague strategy, poor communication, unclear signals, conflicting or changing priorities/everything is a priority, much intuitive-based decision making)

- Distraction (non-recognition of effort, punishment for trying to improve, crisis management, initiatives such as freezes or budget reductions)

- Overwork (too many projects, too few resources, lack of closure/completion, uneven distribution of workload, lots of rework)

As these factors adversely affect leaders, the impact on workers is worse. Leaders must take action to correct poor engagement.

- If a worker lacks clarity about his or her role or is confused about what the manager and the organization needs, make sure he or she has clearly defined priorities and has the right materials, equipment, and information/data to move toward and achieve those outcomes.

- Refocus the declining worker. Reduce distractions. Consider alternative working structures such as teams.

- Examine the knowledge, skills, and abilities (KSA) required to contribute fully. Develop KSA as needed.

- Recognize the worker for moving in the desired direction. Recognition should be aligned to reinforce priorities—what the organization values. Recognition reinforces employee behaviors that reflect those values, personal development, and co-worker and organizational benefits.

Key drivers of engagement are reflected in the questions in Figure 32, which could be used to assess engagement as required by Item 5.1c(1).

Regarding worker satisfaction, high-performing organizations usually consider a variety of factors such as effective problem and grievance resolution; preparation for changes in technology; work environment; workplace safety and security; workload; effective communication, cooperation, and teamwork; job security; appreciation of the differing needs of diverse employee groups; and organizational support for serving customers.

A top-performing workforce is managed in such a way as to encourage workers to exercise optimum discretion and decision making, typically resulting in higher engagement and better performance. *In order to exercise effective decision making, workers need access to appropriate data and analyses concerning their work and must possess the knowledge and skills to interpret the data to make good decisions.* (This links to the information and knowledge management systems required in Category 4 as well as training in this Item [5.1b].) Unless workers have access to data to support effective decision making and understand how to analyze and interpret data, their decisions, by default, revert to intuition—which is highly variable. Managers are not likely to permit workers to substitute their intuition for that of managers. Without access to data to support decisions and the skill to interpret the data, worker decision making will be limited, even if managers were inclined to release decisions to subordinates. Accordingly, systems to promote workforce engagement, empowerment, and agility should ensure workers have the authority and skill to make decisions about their work, as well as data and analysis systems to support effective and consistently good decisions.

5 Workforce Focus

25 Workforce Engagement Questions		1 Never	2 Rarely	3 Sometimes	4 Often	5 Always
	Personal Contribution					
1	I understand my job and I try to exceed my manager's expectations.					
2	Nearly all of my co-workers understand their jobs and try to exceed their manager's expectations.					
3	My work gives me a feeling of achievement.					
4	My work contributes to the success of the organization.					
	Personal Capabilities					
5	My job allows me to make full use of my knowledge, skills, and abilities.					
6	In the workplace, I have good opportunities to improve my skills to excel.					
7	I have the right opportunities for career and professional growth.					
8	Someone in the organization mentors me to help me succeed.					
	Reward, Recognition, Compensation					
9	My organization evaluates and promotes employees honestly and fairly.					
10	In my organization, recognition and rewards are fair and understood by all.					
11	My work performance is appreciated and recognized.					
	Manager Attributes					
12	In the workplace, I get adequate support from my manager to succeed.					
13	My manager provides timely and accurate feedback that helps me to improve my performance (at least 2 to 3 times each year).					
14	My manager respects my thoughts, feelings, and ideas.					
15	My manager treats my opinions and suggestions seriously.					
16	Delivering customer value is a top priority for my manager.					
	Improvement, Initiative, Innovation					
17	Decisions in my organization are made at the appropriate levels.					
18	I am encouraged to make improvements in how work is done.					
19	As a part of my job, I am required to make improvements in how my work is done.					
20	During the past year, I have made or helped to make improvements in how work is done.					
	Workplace Climate					
21	This is a great place to work.					
22	I look forward to coming to work every day.					
23	I am excited about the future of my organization and I see great potential for growth here.					
24	Some of my best friends work at my organization.					
25	What questions are we not asking that are important to your workplace success? Which of the above questions are not important?					

Figure 32 Sample workforce questions.

The best organizations put in place a workforce performance management system that provides measurable feedback to workers, and ties reward, recognition, compensation, and/or incentives to the achievement of high-performance objectives and a customer and business focus. Compensation and recognition systems must be matched to support the work necessary for organizational success. Consistent with this, compensation and recognition might be tied to demonstrated skills and peer evaluations. Compensation and recognition approaches also might include profit sharing, rewarding exemplary team or unit performance, and links to customer-satisfaction and loyalty measures, achievement of organizational strategic objectives, or other essential organizational objectives.

Once the organization determines its key strategic objectives, it should review compensation, reward, and recognition systems to ensure they support those objectives. The failure to do this creates an environment where workers are focused on one set of activities (based on their compensation plan), but the organization has determined that another set of activities (the action plans to achieve the strategic objectives) is necessary for success.

All workforce and leader development and learning systems should be evaluated to determine their effectiveness and find ways to improve them. Leaders should identify specific measures of effectiveness prior to conducting an evaluation of training. Such measures might address impact on individual, unit, and organizational performance; impact on customer-related performance; and cost/benefit analysis of the training.

Organizations should ensure that workforce and leader development contribute to high performance. This may require organizations to provide training in the use of performance excellence tools. Training may focus on the use of performance measures, skill standards, quality-control methods, benchmarking, problem-solving processes, and performance improvement techniques such as Six Sigma, Lean, and the use of Balanced Scorecards, to name a few.

High-performing organizations provide mechanisms for sharing the knowledge of workers and the organization to ensure that high-performance work is maintained through personnel and organizational transitions. Accordingly, systematic processes should be designed and implemented to share information critical to the organization's operations. This is particularly important for knowledge that is stored only in the memory banks of workers.

If an objective of the organization is to enhance customer satisfaction and loyalty, it may be critical to identify job requirements for customer-contact workers and then provide them with appropriate training. Such training is increasingly important and common among high-performing organizations that seek to differentiate themselves from competitors. It frequently includes: acquiring critical knowledge and skills with respect to products, services, and customers; learning how to listen to customers; practicing recovery from problems or failures; and learning how to manage customer expectations effectively.

Workforce and leader development should also address high-priority needs such as technological change, ethical business practices, management and leadership development, orientation of new employees, successor development, safety, diversity, and performance measurement and improvement.

Unless knowledge and skills acquired in training are reinforced on the job, they are quickly and easily forgotten—even after a few days. Accordingly, leaders, managers, and supervisors throughout the organization must ensure that employees actually use the skills acquired through recent training. In fact, one of the measures of leadership effectiveness [required by Item 1.2a(2)] should consider the extent to which leaders reinforce these skills among their employees.

Developing and sustaining work systems that produce high-performance results require ongoing education and training, and information systems (see Category 4) that ensure adequate information availability. To help workers realize their full potential, many organizations use individual development plans prepared with the input of each worker and designed to address their career and learning objectives.

Workforce development needs might vary greatly depending on the nature of the organization's work, workforce responsibility, and stage of organizational and personal development. These needs might include knowledge-sharing skills, communications, teamwork, problem solving, interpreting and using data, meeting customer requirements, process analysis and simplification, waste and cycle-time reduction, and priority setting based on strategic alignment or cost/benefit analysis. Education needs might include advanced skills in new technologies as well as basic skills, such as reading, writing, language, arithmetic, and computer use.

Organizations should consider job and organizational performance in education and training design and evaluation. Education and training should tie to action plans, and balance short- and longer-term individual and organizational objectives. Workers and their supervisors should help determine training needs and contribute to the design and evaluation of education and training, because these individuals frequently are best able to identify critical needs and evaluate success.

Education and training could be delivered inside or outside the organization and could involve on-the-job, classroom, computer-based, distance learning (including Web-based instruction), or any combination of these. Apprenticeship, internship, and mentoring have proven effective techniques to deliver training and reinforce skills. Developmental assignments within or outside the organization might also be effective training.

Work and job factors important to consider include simplification of job classifications (less specialization and work isolation and more multi-skilled workers), which can be addressed by cross-training, job rotation, use of teams (including self-directed teams), and changes in work layout and location. Other important methods to combat worker isolation involve fostering communication across functions and work units, maintaining a focus on customer requirements, creating an environment of knowledge sharing and respect, and engaging all workers in making improvements to their work processes.

The organization should perform effective succession planning for senior leaders, managers, and other key personnel at all levels of the organization. The rate of new-knowledge acquisition is increasing throughout the world. Significantly more new knowledge is causing change to occur faster than ever before in history. To manage effectively in this climate of rapid change, the best organizations anticipate future leadership needs and prepare their future leaders, managers, and workers to take over. The best leaders do not wait for vacancies to occur before they take action to develop the knowledge and skills needed by successors. Succession planning enables organizations to identify future skill needs against current skill gaps, enabling them to recruit and develop the necessary human resources. Workforce hiring and career-progression planning should consider all top candidates, both internal and external, with a focus on the future sustainability and growth of the organization.

To help people realize their full potential, some organizations prepare individual development plans with all workers to address their career and learning objectives. To achieve optimum worker productivity, the organization must understand and address the factors promoting and inhibiting motivation and engagement. A better understanding of these factors could be developed through exit interviews with departing workers, as well as through feedback from surveys of the current workforce. All processes associated with education, training, and developing the full potential of workers should be systematically evaluated and ongoing refinements should be made.

High-performing organizations also use both formal and informal assessment methods and measures to determine workforce engagement and satisfaction. These methods and measures are tailored to assess the differing needs of a diverse workforce. In addition, indicators other than formal or informal workforce surveys (for example, turnover, grievances, complaints, strikes, and absenteeism) are used to support the assessment. Taken together, these methods and measures ensure that assessment findings are relevant and relate to key organizational results in order to identify key priorities for improvement.

Information and data on engagement and satisfaction are actually used in identifying improvement priorities. Priority setting might draw upon workforce-focused results reported in Item 7.4 and might involve addressing workforce problems based on the actual or potential impact on organizational performance. Factors inhibiting engagement need to be prioritized and addressed. The failure to address these factors is likely to result in even greater problems, which may not only impact workforce results (Item 7.4), but also adversely affect customer satisfaction Item 7.2), product outcomes (Item 7.1), financial performance (Item 7.3), process performance (7.5), and leadership (Item 7.6).

Insights to Performance Excellence 2009–2010

5.1 Workforce Engagement

Basic Approach Requirements*: Engage the workforce (get workers to contribute their utmost) to achieve organizational and personal success.

Overall Approach Requirements*: Effectively engage, compensate, and reward the workforce to achieve high performance. Effectively develop the workforce, including leaders, to achieve high performance. Effectively assess workforce engagement and use the results to achieve higher performance.

Multiple Approach Requirements: The following diagram describes multiple approach requirements.

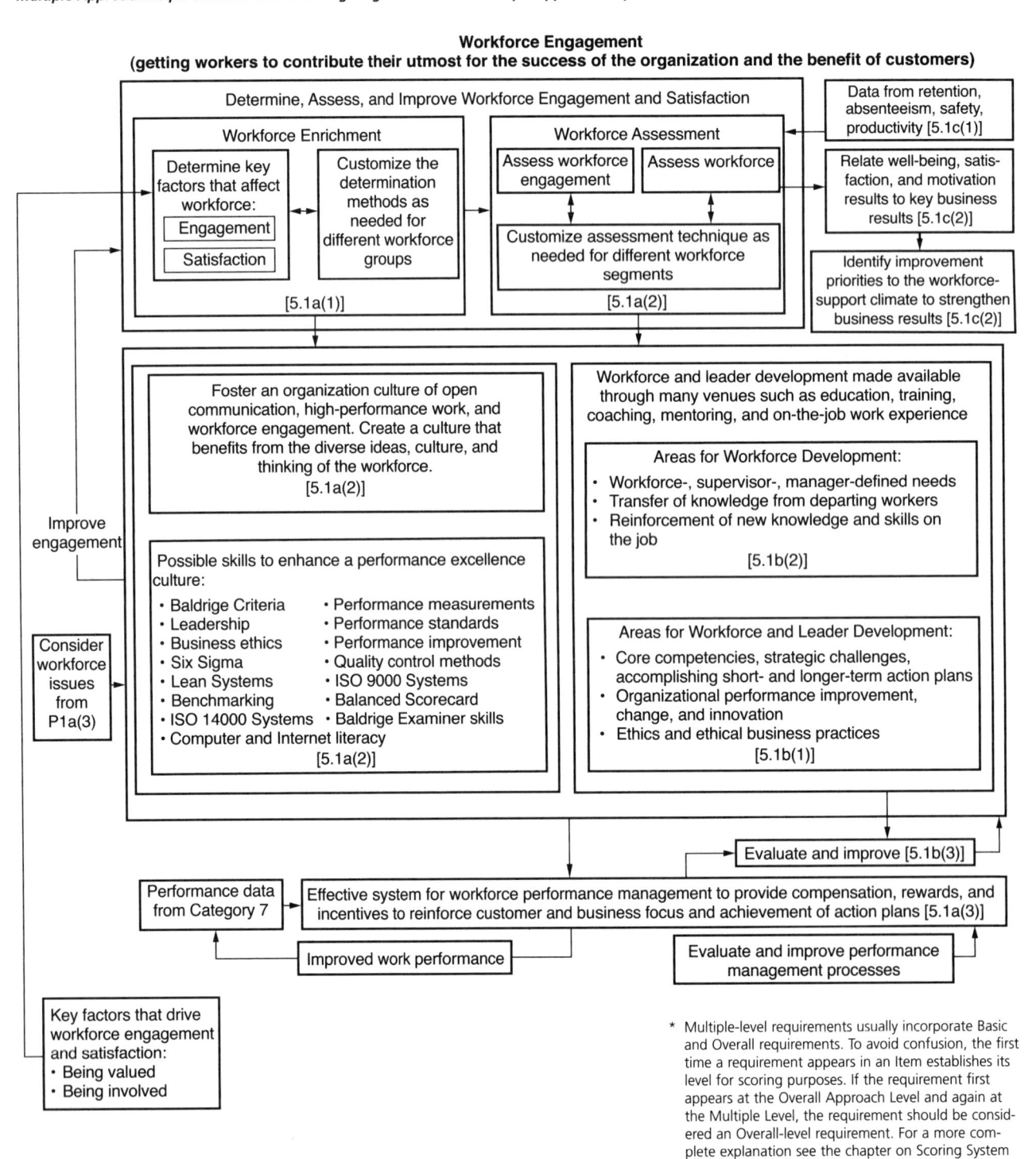

Workforce Engagement
(getting workers to contribute their utmost for the success of the organization and the benefit of customers)

```
Determine, Assess, and Improve Workforce Engagement and Satisfaction

    Workforce Enrichment                          Workforce Assessment
    ┌─────────────────┬──────────────┐          ┌──────────────┬──────────────┐
    │ Determine key   │ Customize the│          │ Assess       │ Assess       │
    │ factors that    │ determination│          │ workforce    │ workforce    │
    │ affect          │ methods as   │          │ engagement   │              │
    │ workforce:      │ needed for   │          ├──────────────┴──────────────┤
    │  Engagement     │ different    │          │ Customize assessment        │
    │  Satisfaction   │ workforce    │          │ technique as needed for     │
    │                 │ groups       │          │ different workforce         │
    │                 │              │          │ segments                    │
    │       [5.1a(1)] │              │          │               [5.1a(2)]     │
```

Data from retention, absenteeism, safety, productivity [5.1c(1)]

Relate well-being, satisfaction, and motivation results to key business results [5.1c(2)]

Identify improvement priorities to the workforce-support climate to strengthen business results [5.1c(2)]

Foster an organization culture of open communication, high-performance work, and workforce engagement. Create a culture that benefits from the diverse ideas, culture, and thinking of the workforce.
[5.1a(2)]

Workforce and leader development made available through many venues such as education, training, coaching, mentoring, and on-the-job work experience

Areas for Workforce Development:
- Workforce-, supervisor-, manager-defined needs
- Transfer of knowledge from departing workers
- Reinforcement of new knowledge and skills on the job
[5.1b(2)]

Possible skills to enhance a performance excellence culture:
- Baldrige Criteria
- Leadership
- Business ethics
- Six Sigma
- Lean Systems
- Benchmarking
- ISO 14000 Systems
- Computer and Internet literacy
- Performance measurements
- Performance standards
- Performance improvement
- Quality control methods
- ISO 9000 Systems
- Balanced Scorecard
- Baldrige Examiner skills
[5.1a(2)]

Areas for Workforce and Leader Development:
- Core competencies, strategic challenges, accomplishing short- and longer-term action plans
- Organizational performance improvement, change, and innovation
- Ethics and ethical business practices
[5.1b(1)]

Improve engagement

Consider workforce issues from P1a(3)

Evaluate and improve [5.1b(3)]

Performance data from Category 7

Effective system for workforce performance management to provide compensation, rewards, and incentives to reinforce customer and business focus and achievement of action plans [5.1a(3)]

Improved work performance

Evaluate and improve performance management processes

Key factors that drive workforce engagement and satisfaction:
- Being valued
- Being involved

* Multiple-level requirements usually incorporate Basic and Overall requirements. To avoid confusion, the first time a requirement appears in an Item establishes its level for scoring purposes. If the requirement first appears at the Overall Approach Level and again at the Multiple Level, the requirement should be considered an Overall-level requirement. For a more complete explanation see the chapter on Scoring System and the Scoring Calibration Guidelines.

5 Workforce Focus

5.1 Key Workforce Engagement Item Linkages

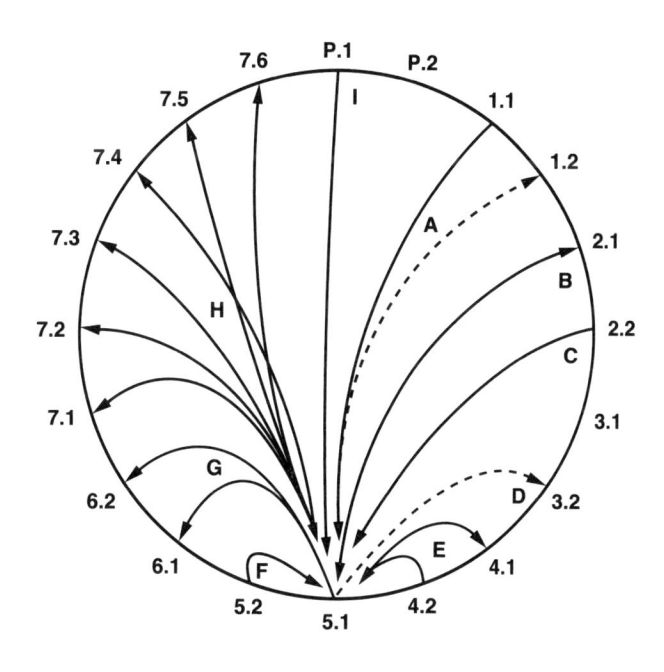

	NATURE OF RELATIONSHIP
A	Senior leaders [1.1a(3) and 1.1b(1)] (and subsequently leaders at all levels) create an environment for workforce engagement, learning, and organizational agility; set related policies; and actively role model appropriate behaviors essential to optimize worker performance and productivity [5.1a(2)]. Senior leaders must communicate effectively with the workforce (which is essential for building positive relations, trust, and clear directions) [1.1b(1)]. In addition, part of evaluating the performance of the leadership system [1.2a(2)] involves determining the extent to which leaders at all levels helped achieve increased employee engagement [5.1c(1)]. Leaders [1.1a(3)] are responsible for supporting appropriate skill development of all employees, including future leaders, through training and development systems and reinforcing learning on the job [5.1b(1, 2)]. In addition, specific training may be required to ensure employees understand governance, ethical, and regulatory requirements [1.2a, b].
B	Employee diversity, innovation, and related skills [5.1] affect human resource strengths and weaknesses—a factor that should be considered in the planning process [2.1a(2)]. Also, clear, measurable, outcome-oriented strategic objectives are defined, which are essential for setting and communicating performance expectations and establishing accountability [2.1b(1)].
C	Human resource plans [2.2a(5)] are used to help align training [5.1b(1) and (2)] to ensure employees and managers possess appropriate knowledge, skills, and ability. Human resource development plans and goals [2.2a(5)] are used to help develop leaders and the workforce [5.1b(2)], and align reward and recognition [5.1a(3)]. In addition, strategic objectives that have been converted into action plans are deployed to all employees throughout the organization (which is essential to ensure workers' understanding of achievement expectations and determining self-worth) [2.2a(1)]. Key performance measures or indicators for tracking progress on action plans must be developed (which are essential to ensure all workers are aligned, able to monitor their personal progress, and make adjustments as needed) [2.2a(6)].

Continued

	NATURE OF RELATIONSHIP *Continued*
D	A culture of workforce engagement, open communication, and high-performance work [5.1a(2)] is essential to build customer relations and engage customers [3.1 and 3.2]. Training [5.1b] can also enhance capabilities of customer-contact employees and strengthen customer engagement and relationship building [3.1 and 3.2].
E	Key benchmarking data [4.1a(2)] are used to design processes to enhance employee engagement and satisfaction. Key measures and benchmarking data [4.1a(2)] are used to improve training [5.1b]. Information regarding training effectiveness [5.1b(3)] is used to support operational decision making [4.1a], and make needed data and information available and accessible to the workforce (without timely access to correct data and information, decisions default to intuition, which introduces more variability in the decision-making process, contributing to incorrect decisions and more decisions raised to higher levels of management) [4.2].
F	A safe, secure work climate [5.2b(1)] enhances employee engagement, motivation, participation, self-direction, and initiative [5.1a] and vice versa. Effective environmental safety training [5.1b] is critical to maintaining and improving a safe, healthful work environment [5.2b(1)]. Support the workforce via policies, services, and benefits, tailored to the needs of different workers because worrying about these issues can be distracting to workers and erode engagement [5.2b(2)].
G	Engaged, skilled, motivated workers [5.1] are essential to improving core competencies, work systems, and key work processes [6.1 and 6.2] to increase customer value and organization productivity and related business processes. Effective performance feedback, compensation, and recognition [5.1a(3)] are essential to improving work process design and management [6.2]. Training [5.1b(1) and (2)] is essential to managing change and improving work process design, management effectiveness, and innovation [6.1 and 6.2]. In addition, training requirements [5.1b] are defined in part by key work process requirements and operational (in-process) measures [6.2].
H	Compensation, incentives, recognition, and rewards [5.1a(3)] are based in part on performance results [Category 7]. Improvements in workforce engagement, and communication [5.1] can result in improved performance outcomes [Category 7]. Systems that enhance workforce engagement can boost financial and market performance [7.3], product [7.1], customer satisfaction [7.2], process effectiveness [7.5], and leadership outcomes [7.6]. Specific results of workforce-focused outcomes are reported in 7.4. Results of improved training and development [5.1b] are reported in 7.4. In addition, results pertaining to product [7.1], customer satisfaction [7.2], financial and market performance [7.3], organizational effectiveness [7.5], and leadership and societal responsibility [7.6] reflect, in part, and are monitored to assess training effectiveness [5.1b(3)].
I	Workforce characteristics such as educational levels, workforce and job diversity, the existence of bargaining units, the use of contract employees, and other special requirements [P.1a(3)] help set the context for determining the requirements for knowledge and skill sharing across work units, jobs, and locations [5.1a(2)] and skills needed of employees [5.1b(1, 2)].

IF YOU DON'T DO WHAT THE CRITERIA REQUIRE...

Item Reference	Possible Adverse Consequences
5.1a(1)	Although the main drivers of engagement include being valued and involved, other factors that affect workforce engagement and satisfaction can vary significantly from organization to organization or within an organization from site to site, or among different groups of employees in the same organization at the same work site. The failure to determine the key factors affecting workforce engagement and satisfaction for each employee segment may make it difficult to identify key performance problems and take appropriate corrective action. The inability to identify and correct these problems can reduce employee morale and motivation which, in turn, hurts productivity and ultimately customer satisfaction. Failure to engage the workforce means they do not contribute their utmost to the success of the organization or its customers.
5.1a(2)	The failure to promote open communication often contributes to redundancy and working at cross-purposes. The failure to promote knowledge and skill sharing often forces the organization to duplicate efforts in the search for more effective and efficient processes. The failure to communicate also contributes to isolationism within an organization and prevents *pockets of excellence* from spreading. Frequently, employees working in a hierarchical, command-and-control environment find individual initiative, empowerment, and innovation stifled, reducing engagement and morale and further eroding productivity and responsiveness.
5.1a(2)	Failure to promote open, two-way communication among workers and supervisors inhibits trust and openness. Problems that a subordinate would raise in an open, trusting environment are not raised for discussion or even hidden from view. These problems may have serious consequences for customers (especially in critical areas such as health care and education), where fear of retaliation prevents them from expressing concerns.
5.1a(2)	The lack of workforce engagement creates an environment where workers wait for approval, do not take risks, and do not seek opportunities for innovation. This makes organizational agility nearly impossible and adversely affects productivity and motivation.
5.1a(2)	The failure to capitalize on diverse ideas, cultures, and thinking may limit the organization's ability to create an innovative and empowered workforce. This in turn may reduce productivity and limit the organization's ability to meet the challenges of today's highly competitive environment.
5.1a(3)	To optimize performance, work throughout the organization must be fully aligned to support strategic objectives, timelines [Item 2.1b(1)], and related action plans [Item 2.2a(1)]. The action plans should be deployed fully throughout the organization at all levels with appropriate quantitative measures developed to monitor progress [Item 2.2a(6)]. The work of individual employees, when taken together, should enable the organization to achieve its strategic objectives. Two questions are fundamental to the work endeavors that performance management system should address: (1) are the right things being done (the vital few); and (2) are they being done right (correctly). The failure to manage workforce performance may make it more difficult for workers to determine if they are doing the right thing in support of business strategy or if they are doing things in the right way (process discipline). It forces them to decide for themselves if they are doing a good job. The alignment of what is *expected* and what is *rewarded* sends strong messages throughout the organization about what is really

Continued

	IF YOU DON'T DO WHAT THE CRITERIA REQUIRE... Continued
Item Reference	**Possible Adverse Consequences**
	important. Failing to align appropriate compensation, recognition, rewards, and incentives with the strategic objectives also contributes to a lack of focus within the workforce, forcing employees to substitute their own ideas instead of being driven/guided by management. Many employees equate compensation with the important activities the organization wants to achieve. For example, if achieving profitability is critical for organization success, the organization typically rewards people for achieving financial goals. In this situation, everyone clearly understands the importance of *profit* because their own compensation and rewards are tied to it. Similarly, the failure to provide rewards, recognition, or compensation that support a customer focus may cause employees to behave as if customers are unimportant. Rewards (or the absence of them) drive behavior and motivate people to respond in certain ways.
5.1b(1)	Strategic objectives [Item 2.1b(1)] define what the organization must achieve to be successful in the future. Action plans [Item 2.2a(1)] define the activities or actions the organization must do to achieve the strategic objectives. If leaders and workers lack the necessary skills to carry out required actions, the strategic plan may fail. Education and training that do not contribute to closing a skill gap that is essential to the achievement of action plans may be a waste of resources.
5.1b(1)	The failure to deliver education and training using appropriate methods, consistent with the learning styles and needs of the workers, usually suboptimizes the effectiveness of training. If participants do not acquire relevant knowledge, skills, or abilities from education and training, the organization has wasted resources. If workers do learn new skills and acquire new abilities and those new skills and abilities are not used on the job, the organization has also wasted resources. If the workers use the new skills and abilities on the job and it makes no difference to organizational performance or career progression, the organization has again wasted resources.
5.1b(1)	The failure to understand and follow ethical business practices gives rise to corruption, dishonesty, and ultimate business failure (Enron, for example). The failure to develop better managers and leaders may make it more difficult to develop strategic objectives, fully engage employees, and optimize individual or organizational performance.
5.1b(1)	The lack of innovation among leaders and workers makes it difficult for organizations to keep pace with increasing customer requirements and increasing competition. It makes it impossible to achieve and sustain a competitive leadership position.
5.1b(2)	Workers and first-line supervisors who are closest to the work usually understand best what skills are required (and missing) to do the work effectively. Failing to obtain and use input from these workers (and their supervisors) may result in the development of inappropriate or ineffective education and training opportunities. Providing ineffective or inappropriate training can waste resources in several ways: (1) the cost of paying workers' salaries during training; (2) the cost of facilities and instruction; and (3) the cost to the organization of lost productivity while workers are participating in training.
5.1b(2)	If it is worth training a worker to acquire new skills and abilities, it is important to reinforce the use of those new skills when the worker returns to the job and applies this new

Continued

5 Workforce Focus

	IF YOU DON'T DO WHAT THE CRITERIA REQUIRE . . . *Continued*
Item Reference	**Possible Adverse Consequences**
	knowledge for the long term. The failure to reinforce the use of recently acquired knowledge and skills on the job may cause those new skills and abilities to become obsolete and quickly forgotten. Accordingly, the cost of training and the cost of lost productivity while the worker is receiving the training represent wasted resources. Most importantly, when the newly acquired skills are not utilized, the value of those skills and potential productivity gains are lost. Losses of this nature can materially impact an organization's rate of growth and its ability to achieve strategy objectives. A similar problem occurs when valuable organizational knowledge is lost because of employee retirement or attrition.
5.1b(2)	In all sectors of our economy, organizations of all types are beginning to lose "baby boom" workers to retirement—and the deep knowledge they possess as well. Organizations that are unable to fill behind this knowledge gap face performance shortfalls or more serious problems with quality and customer satisfaction. To help offset knowledge loss due to departing or retiring workers, organizations are finding ways to capture and record key knowledge. Some use data and process mapping, process documentation, apprenticeships programs, mentoring, job shadowing, and job sharing. Without an effective process to shelter knowledge, organizations will lose productivity and customer satisfaction as problems tend to repeat themselves.
5.1b(2)	Strategic objectives [Item 2.1b(1)] define what the organization must achieve to be successful in the future. Action plans [Item 2.2a(1)] define the things the organization must do to achieve the strategic objectives. If leaders lack the necessary skills to carry out required actions, the strategic plan may fail. Education and training that do not contribute to closing a leader skill gap that is essential to the achievement of action plans may be a waste of resources.
5.1b(3)	The failure to evaluate and improve the effectiveness of training makes it difficult to optimize individual or organizational performance. Ineffective or inefficient training and education waste resources directly (cost of training) and indirectly (cost of lost opportunity and productivity while employee is receiving training).
5.1b(4)	Managers have a responsibility to help employees attain their job- and career-progression development objectives [Item 5.1b(4)]. If managers fail to take advantage of appropriate education and training to help workers with work-related development, learning, and career progression, they run the risk of weakening morale and motivation as well as contributing to skill obsolescence. This adversely impacts job security and employability and undermines the organization's ability to maintain a viable workforce to compete effectively. In the face of worldwide shortages of highly skilled workers, an organization's failure to conduct effective succession planning for senior leaders (and for key positions throughout the organization) could threaten organizational stability in the long term and create immediate performance problems in the short term. If succession planning does not look ahead at least as far as it might take to acquire or train replacement personnel, the organization may lack the talent it needs to fulfill its promises to customers or other key stakeholders.
5.1c(1)	Because the factors that affect workforce engagement and satisfaction can vary significantly among the diverse groups of employees, if an organization fails to differentiate assessment methods and measures it may not be able to determine accurately the existence of problems and take appropriate corrective action. The failure to identify and correct a problem that

Continued

	IF YOU DON'T DO WHAT THE CRITERIA REQUIRE... Continued
Item Reference	**Possible Adverse Consequences**
	adversely affects workforce engagement or satisfaction can contribute to operational inefficiency, waste resources, and reduce product and service quality and customer satisfaction. Failing to consider data that relate to workforce engagement and satisfaction, such as absenteeism, grievances, and undesired workforce attrition, may also prevent a problem from being identified and corrected. Finally, the *one-size-fits-all* method of assessing workforce engagement and satisfaction (such as the *annual* climate survey) may fail to take into account parts of the organization that may be undergoing change and facing more turmoil than other parts of the organization. For organizations that are relatively stable, an annual survey may be appropriate. However, for organizations (or parts of organizations) that face a more volatile, unstable environment, more frequent assessments may be required. Failure to ask the right questions, at the right time, and in the right manner may prevent the organization from learning about and correcting serious problems that may adversely affect performance and productivity.
5.1c(2)	When deciding what actions to take to improve workforce engagement and business results (based on the results of appropriate surveys and related data), organizations risk wasting resources if they fail to understand the likely impact on business results of the improvement priorities they set in response to workforce engagement and satisfaction assessment findings.

5.1 WORKFORCE ENGAGEMENT—SAMPLE EFFECTIVE PRACTICES

A. Workforce Enrichment

- Leaders and managers at all levels require employees to make improvements and innovations to work processes as a basic part of job responsibility.

- Fully using the talents of all workers is a basic organizational value.

- Teams have access to data and are authorized to make decisions about their work (not just make recommendations).

- Worker opinion is sought (and obtained) regarding work design and work processes.

- Prompt and regular feedback is provided to teams and individuals regarding their performance. Feedback covers both results and processes.

- The performance management system provides feedback to workers that supports their ability to contribute to a high-performing organization.

- Compensation, recognition, and rewards/incentives are provided for generating improvement ideas. In addition, a system exists to encourage and provide rapid reinforcement for submitting improvement ideas.

- Compensation, recognition, and rewards/incentives are provided for results, such as for reductions in cycle time and exceeding target schedules with error-free products or services at less-than-projected cost.

- Workers, as well as managers, participate in creating the compensation, recognition, and rewards/incentives practices and help monitor their implementation and systematic improvement.

- The organization evaluates its approaches to workforce performance and compensation, recognition, and rewards to determine the extent to which workers are satisfied with them, the extent of worker participation, and the impact of the system on improved performance (reported in Item 7.4).

- Performance measures exist for workforce involvement, self-direction, and initiative. Goals for these measures are expressed in measurable terms. These measurable goals form at least a good part of the basis for performance recognition.

- Recognition, reward/incentives, and compensation are influenced by customer satisfaction ratings as well as other performance measures such as implementing process improvements.

- The need for diverse ideas and cultures among workers is specifically considered during the skill-mapping and recruitment process to ensure they are able to provide the perspective needed to drive innovation and creativity.

- Key workforce engagement and satisfaction opinion indicators are gathered periodically based on the stability of the organization.

B. Workforce and Leader Development

- Clear linkages exist between strategic objectives and education and training. Skills are developed based on work demands and workforce needs.

- Training plans are developed based on worker and manager input.

- Career and personal-development options, including development for leadership, diversity, and safety are enhanced through formal education and training. Some development uses on-the-job training, including rotational assignments or job exchange programs.

- The organization uses various methods to deliver training to ensure that it is suitable for workforce knowledge and skill levels.

- To minimize travel costs, all training is examined to determine if electronic or distance delivery options are viable.

- Training is linked to work requirements, which managers reinforce on the job. Just-in-time training (rather than just-in-case training) is

- preferred to help ensure that the skills will be used immediately after training.

- Worker feedback on the appropriateness of the training is collected and used to improve course delivery and content.

- The organization systematically evaluates training effectiveness on the job. Performance data are collected on individuals and groups at all levels to assess the impact of training.

- Workforce satisfaction with courses is tracked and used to improve training content, training delivery, instructional effectiveness, and the effectiveness of supervisory support for the use of training on the job.

- Training design and delivery are systematically refined and improved based on regular evaluations.

- Formal career plans are in place for each employee. Progress against these plans is evaluated and adjustments are made to ensure they remain relevant.

- Workers receive incentives such as bonuses or other rewards for developing additional career-enhancing skills.

- The organization documents or otherwise captures/stores key knowledge held by workers so that knowledge is not lost when the worker leaves the organization. Proactive sharing of personal knowledge helps preserve collective knowledge (organizational memory). Job sharing, mentoring, cross-training, job shadowing, and formal transition programs are used to transfer knowledge from departing workers.

- A formal system is in place to develop future leaders. This includes providing training and practice in high-performance leadership techniques. Leaders receive specific training and practice using Baldrige Criteria and performance-improvement systems.

- Demonstrated proficiency in the use of the Baldrige Criteria is a prerequisite to promotion to a leadership position.

- Future leaders serve as examiners in the Baldrige process, state quality award process, or internal award process.

C. Assessment of Workforce Engagement

- A systematic process is used to evaluate and improve the effectiveness and extent of workforce engagement.

- Many indicators of employee engagement exist, such as the improvements in time or cost reduction produced by teams.

- Supervisors, managers, and leaders take consistent and prompt action to improve conditions identified through workforce engagement and satisfaction surveys.

- On-demand electronic surveys are available for quick response and tabulations any time managers need workforce engagement or satisfaction feedback. Whenever the survey is completed, managers always follow up promptly to make improvements identified by the survey that relate to key business results.

- Engagement and satisfaction data are derived from worker focus groups, surveys, turnover, absenteeism, and exit interviews.

- Managers use the results of these surveys to focus improvements in work systems and enhance workforce engagement and satisfaction. Actions to improve satisfaction are clearly tied to assessments so employees understand the value of the assessment, and the improvement initiatives do not appear random or capricious.

- Workforce engagement and satisfaction indicators are correlated with drivers of business success to help identify where resources should be placed to provide maximum business benefit.

- Methods to improve assessment of workforce engagement and satisfaction are systematically evaluated and improved. Techniques to actually improve engagement and satisfaction are themselves evaluated and refined consistently.

5.2 WORKFORCE ENVIRONMENT: How do you build an effective and supportive workforce environment? (40 Pts.) **PROCESS**

Describe how your organization manages workforce capability and capacity to accomplish the work of the organization. Describe how your organization maintains a safe, secure, and supportive work climate.

Within your response, include answers to the following questions:

a. Workforce Capability and Capacity

(1) How do you assess your workforce capability and capacity needs, including skills, competencies, and staffing levels?

(2) How do you recruit, hire, place, and retain new members of your workforce? How do you ensure your workforce represents the diverse ideas, cultures, and thinking of your hiring and customer community?

(3) How do you manage and organize your workforce to accomplish the work of your organization, capitalize on the organization's core competencies, reinforce a customer and business focus, exceed performance expectations, address your strategic challenges and action plans, and achieve the agility to address changing business needs?

(4) How do you prepare your workforce for changing capability and capacity needs? How do you manage your workforce, its needs, and your needs to ensure continuity, to prevent workforce reductions, and to minimize the impact of workforce reductions, if they do become necessary?

b. Workforce Climate

(1) How do you address workplace environmental factors to ensure and improve workforce health, safety, and security? What are your performance measures and improvement goals for each of these workforce needs? What are any significant differences in these factors and performance measures or targets for different workplace environments?

(2) How do you support your workforce via policies, services, and benefits? How are these tailored to the needs of a diverse workforce and different workforce groups and segments?

Notes:

N1. "Workforce capability" (5.2a) refers to your organization's ability to accomplish its work processes through the knowledge, skills, abilities, and competencies of its people. Capability may include the ability to build and sustain relationships with your customers; to innovate and transition to new technologies; to develop new products, services, and work processes; and to meet changing business, market, and regulatory demands. "Workforce capacity" (5.2a) refers to your organization's ability to ensure sufficient staffing levels to accomplish its work processes and successfully deliver your products to your customers, including the ability to meet seasonal or varying demand levels.

N2. Workforce capability and capacity should consider not only current needs but also future requirements based on your strategic objectives and action plans reported in Category 2.

N3. Preparing your workforce for changing capability and capacity needs (5.2a[4]) might include training, education, frequent communication, considerations of workforce employment and employability, career counseling, and outplacement and other services.

This Item [5.2] looks at the organization's workforce environment, the workforce capacity and capability needs, and how those needs are met so that the work of the organization is accomplished. This Item also looks at systems the organization has in place to provide a safe, secure, and supportive work climate. The goal is an effective environment that supports the workforce and is conducive to accomplishing the organization's work.

Organizations must profile, recruit, hire, and retain employees who will meet skill requirements required to position the organization for future success. Obviously, the right workforce is a key factor in high performance. As the pool of skilled talent continues to shrink, it becomes more important than ever for organizations to specifically define the capabilities and skills needed by potential employees and create a work environment to attract them. Accordingly, it is critical to take into account characteristics of diverse populations to make sure appropriate support systems exist that make it possible to attract skilled workers.

The workforce should not only reflect the diversity of the hiring community but also the customer community. By failing to reflect the customer community, the workforce may find it more difficult to develop and support strong customer relationships and customer engagement.

Hierarchical, command-and-control management styles work against fast response and high-performance capability. Agility reflects the speed with which employees and the organization do their work, including rapid response to changing needs and requirements. Organizations that are bogged down with bureaucratic inefficiencies cannot be agile. Unnecessary layers of management approval typically add delay and cost but not value.

All organizations, regardless of size, are required to meet minimum regulatory standards for workplace safety; however, high-performing organizations will have processes in place to ensure they not only meet these minimum standards but also go beyond simple compliance. This includes designing proactive processes, with safety and security factors identified by people directly involved in the work. The organization should identify appropriate measures and targets for key workplace factors so that status and progress can be tracked. The organization should be able to show how it includes such factors in its planning and improvement activities. Important factors in this Area to Address include establishing appropriate measures and targets for worker safety, security, and health. Organizations should also recognize that work groups might experience very different environments and need different services to ensure workplace safety.

The organization must provide appropriate services, benefits, and policies to enhance worker well-being, satisfaction, and motivation. The best organizations develop a holistic view of the workforce as key stakeholders. Most organizations, regardless of size, have many opportunities to support their workforce. These organizations place special emphasis on the variety of approaches used to satisfy a diverse workforce with differing needs and expectations in order to reduce attrition and increase motivation.

Examples of services, facilities, activities, and other opportunities are: personal and career counseling; career development and employability services; recreational or cultural activities; formal and informal recognition; non-work-related education; day care; special leave for family responsibilities and/or for community service; home safety training; flexible work hours and benefits packages; outplacement services; and retiree benefits, including extended health care and ongoing access to services. Also, these services might include career-enhancement activities such as skills assessments, helping individuals develop learning objectives and plans, and conducting employability assessments.

As the workforce becomes more diverse (including workers who may work in other countries for multinational companies), it becomes more important to consider and support the needs of those members of the workforce with different services.

5 Workforce Focus

5.2 Workforce Environment

Basic Approach Requirements*: Build an effective and supportive workforce environment.

Overall Approach Requirements*: Effectively manage workforce capability and capacity to accomplish the work of the organization. Maintain a safe, secure, and supportive work climate.

Multiple Approach Requirements: The following diagram describes multiple approach requirements.

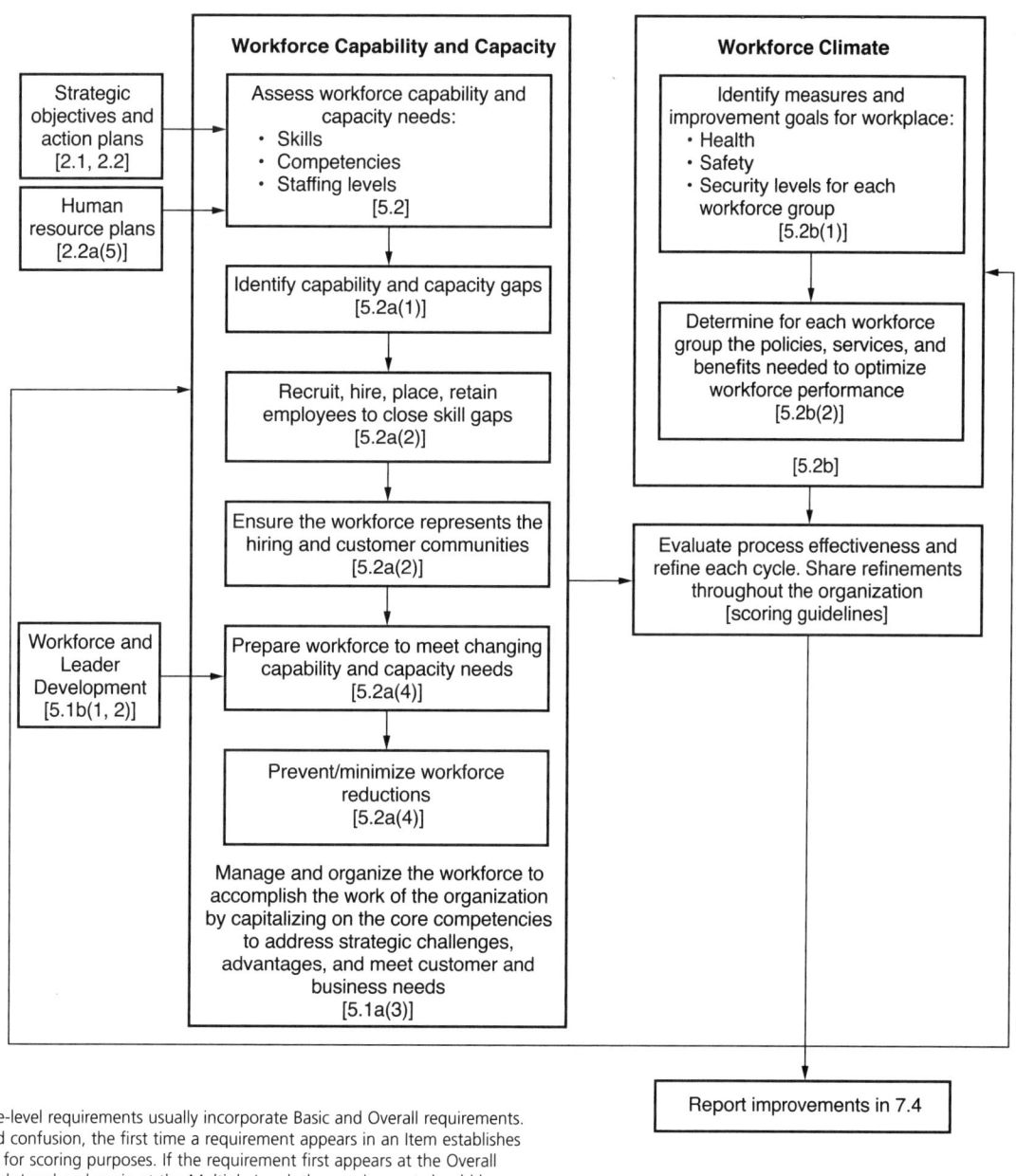

Workforce Capability and Capacity

- Strategic objectives and action plans [2.1, 2.2]
- Human resource plans [2.2a(5)]

Assess workforce capability and capacity needs:
- Skills
- Competencies
- Staffing levels
[5.2]

Identify capability and capacity gaps [5.2a(1)]

Recruit, hire, place, retain employees to close skill gaps [5.2a(2)]

Ensure the workforce represents the hiring and customer communities [5.2a(2)]

- Workforce and Leader Development [5.1b(1, 2)]

Prepare workforce to meet changing capability and capacity needs [5.2a(4)]

Prevent/minimize workforce reductions [5.2a(4)]

Manage and organize the workforce to accomplish the work of the organization by capitalizing on the core competencies to address strategic challenges, advantages, and meet customer and business needs [5.1a(3)]

Workforce Climate

Identify measures and improvement goals for workplace:
- Health
- Safety
- Security levels for each workforce group
[5.2b(1)]

Determine for each workforce group the policies, services, and benefits needed to optimize workforce performance [5.2b(2)]

[5.2b]

Evaluate process effectiveness and refine each cycle. Share refinements throughout the organization [scoring guidelines]

Report improvements in 7.4

---

* Multiple-level requirements usually incorporate Basic and Overall requirements. To avoid confusion, the first time a requirement appears in an Item establishes its level for scoring purposes. If the requirement first appears at the Overall Approach Level and again at the Multiple Level, the requirement should be considered an Overall-level requirement. For a more complete explanation see the chapter on Scoring System and the Scoring Calibration Guidelines.

Insights to Performance Excellence 2009–2010

5.2 Key Workforce Environment Item Linkages

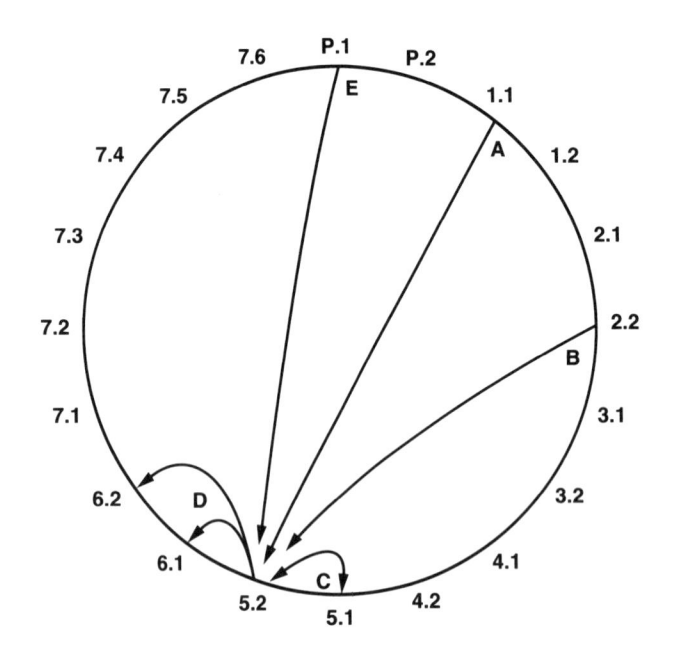

	NATURE OF RELATIONSHIP
A	Leaders [1.1a(3)] are responsible for creating a sustainable organization which requires workers with essential capability and capacity [5.2a] and effective systems to enhance employee health, safety, and security [5.2b(1)].
B	Human resource development plans [2.2a(5)] typically address or set the context for healthy, safe, and secure work systems [5.2b(1)] and future capacity and capability requirements [5.2a(1)].
C	A strong work climate with excellent benefits [5.2b(2)] enhances employee engagement, empowerment, initiative (self-direction), and innovation [5.1]; and engagement changes the work climate.
D	A safe, healthful work environment [5.2b(1)] contributes to better process management, higher performance, and productivity, with fewer errors and rework [6.1 and 6.2].
E	Workforce characteristics such as educational levels, workforce and job diversity, and other special requirements [P.1a(3)] help set the context for determining appropriate needs by workforce segment [5.2b(1)]. Employee characteristics such as educational levels, workforce and job diversity, the existence of bargaining units, the use of contract employees, and other special requirements [P.1a(3)] may help set the context for tailoring benefits and services for the workforce according to various types and categories [5.2b(2)].

5 Workforce Focus

	IF YOU DON'T DO WHAT THE CRITERIA REQUIRE . . .
Item Reference	**Possible Adverse Consequences**
5.2a(1)	Skill mapping is a process that many high-performing organizations use to compare the skills it needs to achieve strategic objectives with the skills its workforce currently possesses (capacity/capability). When a skill gap is identified, organizations are able to more effectively make better decisions as to whether they need to recruit, hire, reorganize, and/or train appropriate employees. The failure to identify the needed workforce capability and capacity levels increases the likelihood of not having appropriate staff in the right places when needed. When critical personnel shortages exist within an organization, it is frequently unable to carry out key objectives.
5.2a(2)	In a competitive labor market, slowness in recruiting and inefficiencies in hiring and placing workers in jobs may introduce delays that allow competitors to hire the best talent before your organization can act. Inefficient recruitment and bureaucratic bungling in the hiring process also provide a glimpse of the true management system and can scare off the best prospective employees. In addition, the hiring process represents a terrific opportunity to attract and hire workers with diverse ideas and cultures, without which it will be difficult to capitalize on diverse ideas, cultures, and thinking. This in turn may limit the ability of the organization's workforce to be engaged, innovative, and empowered. Productivity suffers, as does the organization's ability to meet the challenges of today's highly competitive environment.
5.2a(2)	The failure to ensure the workforce represents the thinking of the customer community makes it more difficult to build strong relationships with customers and promote solid customer engagement. This may erode customer confidence and loyalty.
5.2a(3)	The alignment of strategic objectives and the work to accomplish them is vital to the success and optimum performance of the organization. Once strategic objectives, timelines [Item 2.1b(1)], and related actions [Item 2.2a(1)] have been identified and deployed to all levels of the organization, leaders and managers can more effectively organize the workforce to carry out the necessary work. In addition, appropriate responsibilities, authorities, and other tasks should be defined to ensure the actions are aligned (consistent) at all levels and effectively carried out. If the organization and management of the workforce are not aligned to support core competencies, strategic objectives, and related actions, the organization may waste resources by failing to optimize the work that is done and may fail to meet business needs.
5.2a(4)	An organization that fails to prepare workers for changing capability and capacity needs may threaten the sustainability of the organization and waste significant resources. This waste can be classified into two categories: (1) the failure to develop existing potential and take advantage of it; and (2) the failure to use skills and abilities that already exist. Workers usually recognize when their skills are underused and their productivity suffers further erosion, or they seek job opportunities outside the organization where they can develop and advance more fully, or both. Training workers in multiple jobs, rotational assignments, and job sharing provide more flexibility among workers to meet organizational needs and maintain job security when cutbacks are unavoidable.
5.2b(1)	The failure to provide a healthy, safe, and secure workplace may increase accidents and illness, reduce employee effectiveness, and negatively impact morale and motivation. Poor working conditions distract the workforce, reduce productivity, and increase errors, rework, cycle time, and waste, to name a few. If significant variation exists in the work environment for different

Continued

	IF YOU DON'T DO WHAT THE CRITERIA REQUIRE... *Continued*
Item Reference	**Possible Adverse Consequences**
	employee groups or work units, employees are likely to face different workplace health, safety, security, and ergonomic issues. For example, carpal tunnel syndrome may be a problem for those who do substantial keypunching but not for workers on the shop floor. Those workers may be more concerned about injury from lifting heavy objects. Accordingly, the failure to define performance measures and establish targets for each key environmental factor and each distinct employee group increases the likelihood the problems will go unnoticed and those employees will be distracted from their work, suboptimizing performance.
5.2b(2)	Just as different workforce groups may have different needs for safety, different groups of workers may need different support services and benefits to keep them from being distracted in their work. When an organization fails to identify and tailor benefits and services to the needs of its diverse workforce, it may reduce optimum workforce participation and performance. Suboptimum workforce performance hurts productivity, customer satisfaction, and profitability.

5.2 WORKFORCE ENVIRONMENT—SAMPLE EFFECTIVE PRACTICES

A. Workforce Capability and Capacity

- Managers and workers conduct systematic needs analyses to ensure that skills required to perform work are routinely assessed, monitored, and maintained.

- Managers use cross-functional work teams to break down barriers, improve effectiveness, and meet goals.

- Although lower-performing organizations use teams for special improvement projects (while the *regular work* is performed using traditional approaches), higher-performing organizations use teams and self-directed workers as the way regular work is done.

- Self-directed or self-managed work teams are used throughout the organization. They have authority over matters such as budget, hiring, and team membership and roles.

- Worker skill mapping is in place to define current skills compared to an analysis of skills that are needed now and in the future. The resulting skill gap or surplus drives decisions to retrain, relocate, or recruit.

- Senior leaders build a work climate that addresses the needs of a diverse workforce. Recruitment and training are tools to enhance the work climate.

B. Workforce Climate

- Issues and concerns relating to worker health, safety, security, and workplace environment are used to design the work environment. Plans exist and processes are in place to optimize working conditions and eliminate adverse conditions.

- Root causes for health, safety, and security problems are systematically identified and eliminated. Corrective actions are communicated (shared) widely to help prevent the problem in other parts of the organization.

- Targets are set and reviewed for all key health, safety, and security factors affecting the work environment. Workers are directly involved in setting these targets.

- Special activities and services are available for workers. These are quite varied, depending on their different needs. Examples include the following:

    - Flexible benefits plan including: health care, on-site day care, dental, portable retirement, education (both work and non-work-related), maternity, paternity, and family-illness leave

    - Group-purchasing-power program where the number of participating merchants is increasing steadily

    - Facilities for worker meetings to discuss their concerns

6 Process Management—85 Points

*The **Process Management** Category examines how your organization designs its work systems and how it designs, manages, and improves its key processes for implementing those work systems to deliver customer value and achieve organizational success and sustainability. Also examined is your readiness for emergencies.*

Process Management is the focal point within the Criteria for all work systems and key work processes needed to produce products, programs, and services for customers. This Category highlights the importance of the organization's core competencies and how they are used to help achieve and sustain success. Built into the Category are the central requirements for the use of core competencies to achieve efficient and effective work process management: effective design; a prevention orientation; linkage to customers, suppliers, partners, and collaborators and a focus on value creation for all stakeholders; supply chain integration; operational and financial performance; cycle time; emergency readiness; and evaluation, continuous improvement, innovation, and organizational learning.

Organizational agility, cost reduction, and cycle-time reduction are increasingly important in all aspects of process management and organizational design. Agility refers to an organization's ability to adapt quickly, flexibly, and effectively to changing requirements. Depending on the nature of the organization's strategy and markets, agility might mean rapid changeover from one product to another, rapid response to changing demands, or the ability to produce a wide range of customized services. Delay due to unnecessary levels of review and approval inhibits agility, adds cost, and reduces workforce engagement.

Increasingly, agility involves outsourcing decisions, agreements with key suppliers, and novel partnering arrangements. Agility also involves the elimination of unnecessary levels of review and approval prior to a decision; the increased engagement and empowerment of workers to make more decisions about their work; and eliminating general bureaucratic barriers to efficiency. Flexibility might demand special strategies such as implementing modular designs, sharing components, sharing manufacturing lines, and providing specialized training.

Cost and cycle-time reduction often involves many of the same process management strategies as achieving agility, including Lean and Six Sigma process improvement techniques. Thus, it is crucial to utilize key measures for these requirements in the overall process management.

Process Management contains two Items that look at the design, management, and improvement of product and service processes (including key business processes) and support processes.

Work Systems

These are core and key business processes required to produce and deliver the organization's products and services, deliver value to customers and key stakeholders, and improve market and financial position.

- Design and innovate work systems

- Determine which processes in the organization's work systems will be done in-house and which will be outsourced to external vendors

- Determine how work systems and key work processes elate to and capitalize on core competencies

- Determine key work process requirements needed to develop and introduce products and services to meet customer requirements, operational-performance requirements, and market requirements

- Improve design processes

- Ensure continuity of operations in an emergency

Work Processes

These are processes that support value creation and business operations.

- Design key work processes
- Manage and control key work processes to meet customer requirements in support of optimum value creation, profitability, business success, and organizational sustainability
- Use customer feedback and in-process measures to control and improve the performance of these processes
- Control costs and reduce error and rework
- Improve key work processes

6.1 WORK SYSTEMS: How do you design your work systems? (35 points) — PROCESS

Describe how your organization designs its work systems and determines its key processes to deliver customer value, prepare for potential emergencies, and achieve organizational success and sustainability.

Within your response, include answers to the following questions:

a. Work Systems Design

(1) How do you design and innovate your overall work systems? How do you decide which processes within your overall work systems will be internal to your organization (your key work processes) and which will use external resources?

(2) How do your work systems and key work processes relate to and capitalize on your core competencies?

b. Key Work Processes

(1) What are your organization's key work processes? How do these processes contribute to delivering customer value, profitability or financial return, organizational success, and sustainability?

(2) How do you determine key work process requirements, incorporating input from customers, suppliers, partners, and collaborators, as appropriate? What are the key requirements for these processes?

c. Emergency Readiness

How do you ensure work system and workplace preparedness for disasters or emergencies? How does your disaster and emergency preparedness system consider prevention, management, continuity of operations, and recovery?

Notes:

N1. "Work systems" refers to how the work of your organization is accomplished. Work systems involve your workforce, your key suppliers and partners, your contractors, your collaborators, and other components of the supply chain needed to produce and deliver your products and business and support processes. Your work systems coordinate the internal work processes and the external resources necessary for you to develop, produce, and deliver your products to your customers and to succeed in your marketplace.

N2. Your key work processes (6.1b[1]) are your most important internal value creation processes and might include product design and delivery, customer support, supply chain management, business, and support processes. Your key work processes are the processes that involve the majority of your organization's workforce and produce customer, stakeholder, and stockholder value.

N3. Disasters and emergencies (6.1c) might be weather-related, utility-related, security-related, or due to a local or national emergency, including potential pandemics. Emergency considerations related to information technology should be addressed in Item 4.2.

6 Process Management

This Item [6.1] looks at core competencies, work systems, and work process decisions with the goals of maximizing customer value, ensuring emergency preparedness, and achieving organizational success and sustainability. Together, these processes can help create a competitive advantage and improve market and operational performance—necessary ingredients for sustainability.

Organizations must design work systems that include all of the work that needs to be done to deliver value to customers. The work system includes work that is both internal and external to the organization. Both types of work must be managed effectively to optimize value for customers. See Figure 33. Typically, these requirements reflect the need for increasing agility—speed and flexibility—to adapt to change and improve more quickly than competitors.

This Item looks at the organization's list of key work processes and their specific requirements to meet and exceed customer needs and expectations. In addition, this Item looks at the processes by which these key work process requirements were determined, using input from customers, suppliers, partners, and short-term collaborators.

Key work processes include both product-related processes and nonproduct business processes that are considered by senior leaders to be important to organizational success and growth. These processes frequently relate to an organization's core competencies, strategic objectives, and critical success factors.

Key business processes might include processes to promote innovation, research and development, technology acquisition, information and knowledge management, supply chain management, global expansion, supplier partnering, outsourcing, mergers and acquisitions, project management, and sales and marketing. For some nonprofit organizations, key business processes might include fundraising, media relations, and public policy advocacy. The requirements and performance characteristics among various business support processes might vary significantly.

Key work processes may include those processes that support daily operations and product delivery. Support processes might include processes for finance and accounting, facilities management, legal

Work System: All work needed to produce products and customer support services to create value for customers and achieve organization success. Some work is outsourced and the rest is internal.

Internal: Work carried out by employees and volunteers under the supervision of the organization. Work that involves the organization's core competencies and the majority of the workforce may be considered a key work process. For convenience or other reasons, the organization may elect to keep work in house, even if that work does not involve the organization's core competencies.

External: Work carried out by outside contractors, partners, suppliers, or collaborators. This work is typically outsourced because the external organization can deliver more value than if the work was done in house. Usually this work does not involve the organization's core competencies.

Key Work Process: Involves core competencies and a majority of the workforce and may include some business and support processes

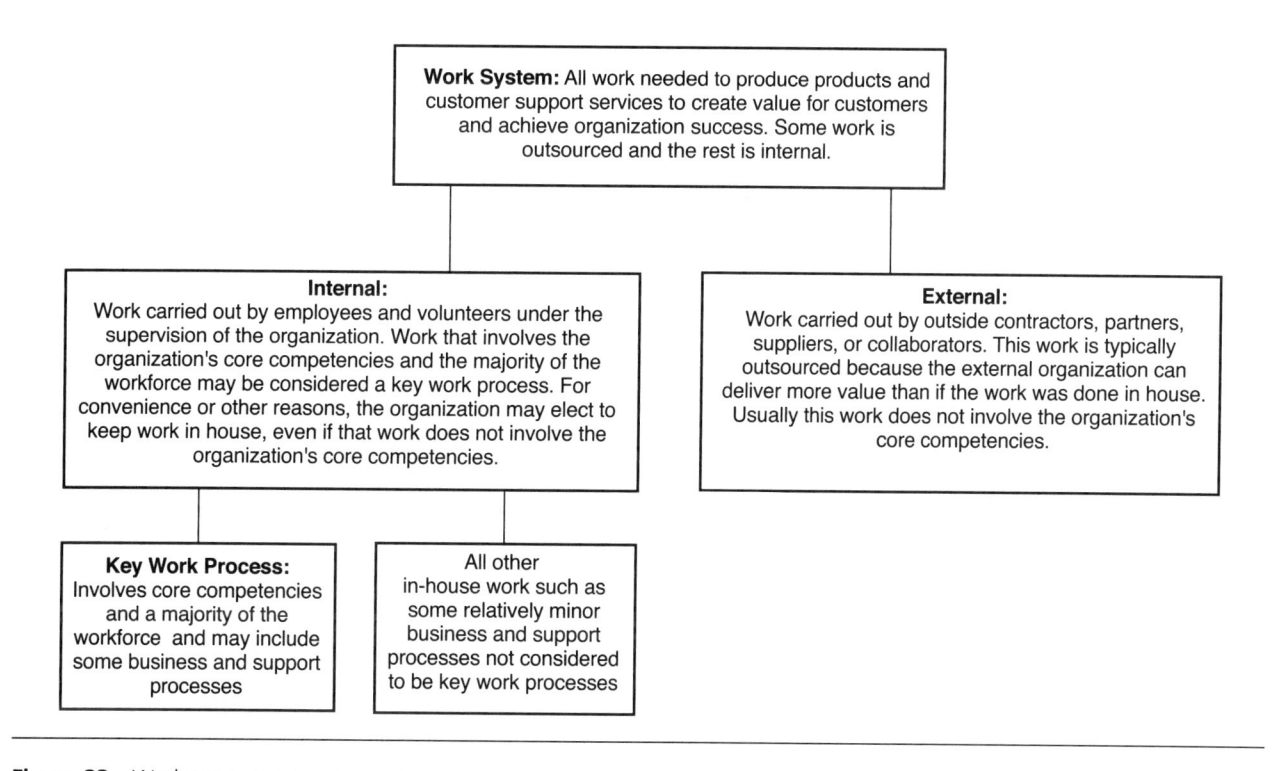

All other in-house work such as some relatively minor business and support processes not considered to be key work processes

Figure 33 Work process management.

services, human resource services, public relations, and other administrative services. Support process design requirements usually depend significantly on internal requirements, and they must be coordinated and integrated to ensure efficient and effective linkage and performance.

For many organizations, supply chain management is an important factor in achieving productivity and profitability goals and overall organizational success. Suppliers, partners, and collaborators are receiving increasing strategic attention as organizations reevaluate their core competencies to determine whether those competencies continue to provide a competitive advantage—or whether the function would be done better by an outside organization. Processes that the organization uses to interact with and manage suppliers should fulfill two purposes: to help improve the performance of suppliers and partners and to take advantage of the expertise of these outside entities to improve the organization's work systems. Supply chain management might help select better suppliers, reduce the total number of suppliers, and establish more long-standing, preferred supplier and partner agreements.

Organizations may need to define requirements for suppliers, partners, and collaborators as a part of their own work systems and work process design. To be effective, design processes must take into account all stakeholders in the value chain. If many projects are carried out in parallel or if the organization uses parts, equipment, and facilities for other products, coordination of resources should be incorporated in the design to help reduce costs an cycle time.

When developing a plan to ensure continuity of operations in an emergency, the organization should consider all facets of its operations that are needed to provide products and support services to customers, including all key work processes. The specific level of service that must be sustained will vary based on the organization's mission and its customers' needs and requirements. For example, a public utility is likely to have a higher need for services than organizations that do not provide an essential function. Nonprofit organizations whose mission is to respond to emergencies will have a high need for service readiness. Continuity of operations plans should be coordinated with processes to ensure data and information availability [Item 4.2].

6.1 Work Systems

Basic Approach Requirements*: Design work systems to accomplish the work of your organization (see Glossary for description of Work Systems).

Overall Approach Requirements*: Design work systems and determine key processes to deliver customer value, prepare for potential emergencies, and achieve organizational success and sustainability.

Multiple Approach Requirements: The following diagram describes multiple approach requirements.

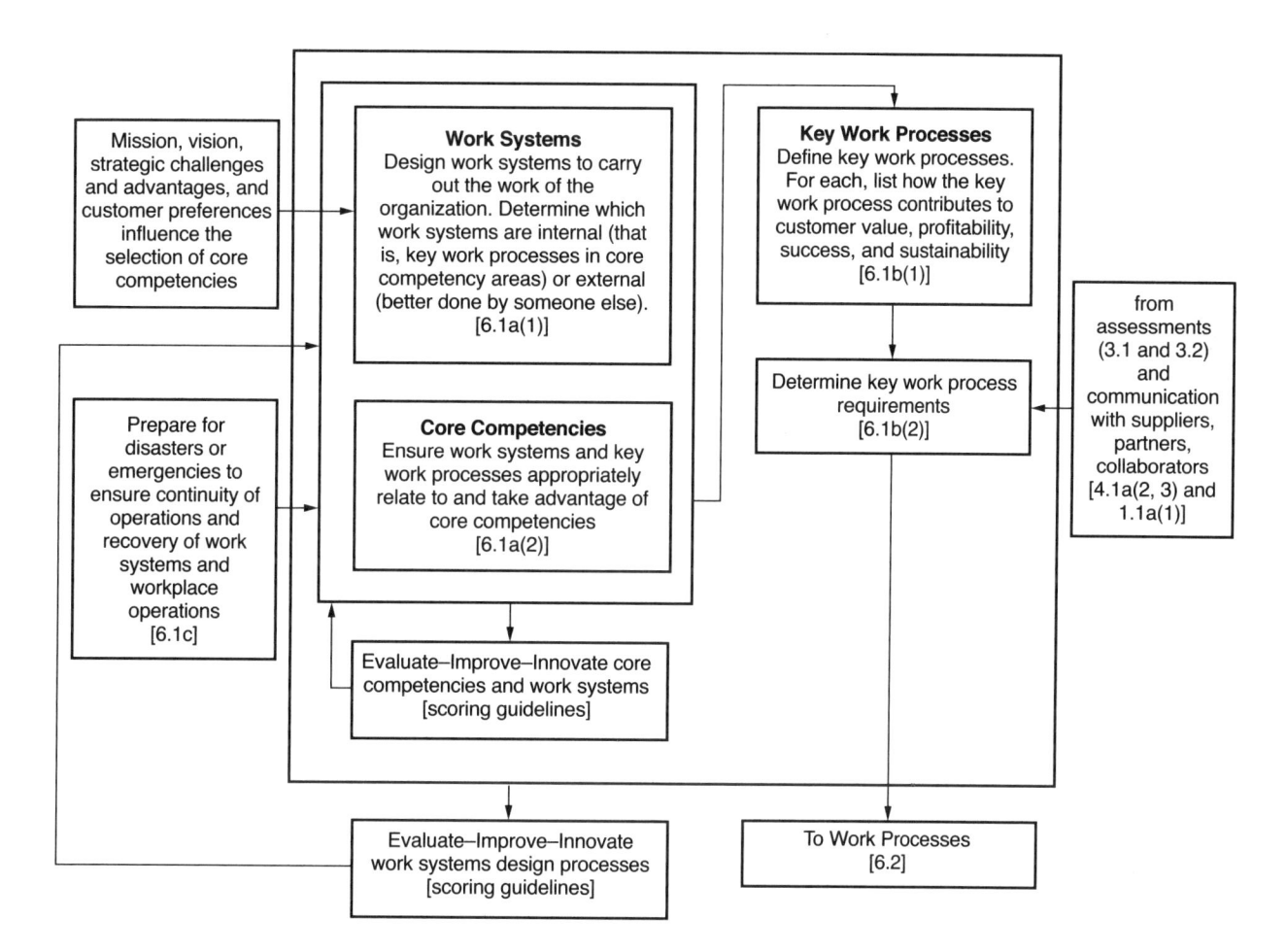

```
┌─────────────────────────────────────────────────────────────────────────────┐
│                                                                             │
│  ┌──────────────┐   ┌──────────────────┐    ┌──────────────────┐            │
│  │ Mission,     │   │   Work Systems   │    │ Key Work         │            │
│  │ vision,      │   │ Design work      │    │ Processes        │            │
│  │ strategic    │   │ systems to carry │    │ Define key work  │            │
│  │ challenges   │──▶│ out the work of  │    │ processes. For   │            │
│  │ and          │   │ the organization.│    │ each, list how   │            │
│  │ advantages,  │   │ Determine which  │    │ the key work     │            │
│  │ and customer │   │ work systems are │    │ process          │            │
│  │ preferences  │   │ internal (that   │    │ contributes to   │            │
│  │ influence    │   │ is, key work     │    │ customer value,  │            │
│  │ the          │   │ processes in     │    │ profitability,   │            │
│  │ selection    │   │ core competency  │    │ success, and     │            │
│  │ of core      │   │ areas) or        │    │ sustainability   │            │
│  │ competencies │   │ external (better │    │ [6.1b(1)]        │            │
│  └──────────────┘   │ done by someone  │    └──────────────────┘            │
│                     │ else).           │             │                      │
│                     │ [6.1a(1)]        │             ▼                      │
│                     └──────────────────┘    ┌──────────────────┐   ┌──────┐ │
│  ┌──────────────┐                           │ Determine key    │   │ from │ │
│  │ Prepare for  │   ┌──────────────────┐    │ work process     │   │assess│ │
│  │ disasters or │   │ Core             │    │ requirements     │◀──│ments │ │
│  │ emergencies  │   │ Competencies     │    │ [6.1b(2)]        │   │(3.1  │ │
│  │ to ensure    │──▶│ Ensure work      │    └──────────────────┘   │and   │ │
│  │ continuity   │   │ systems and key  │                           │3.2)  │ │
│  │ of operations│   │ work processes   │                           │and   │ │
│  │ and recovery │   │ appropriately    │                           │commu-│ │
│  │ of work      │   │ relate to and    │                           │nica- │ │
│  │ systems and  │   │ take advantage   │                           │tion  │ │
│  │ workplace    │   │ of core          │                           │with  │ │
│  │ operations   │   │ competencies     │                           │supp- │ │
│  │ [6.1c]       │   │ [6.1a(2)]        │                           │liers,│ │
│  └──────────────┘   └──────────────────┘                           │part- │ │
│         │                    │                                     │ners, │ │
│         │           ┌────────┴─────────┐                           │colla-│ │
│         │           │ Evaluate–Improve–│                           │bora- │ │
│         │           │ Innovate core    │                           │tors  │ │
│         │           │ competencies and │                           │[4.1a │ │
│         │           │ work systems     │                           │(2,3) │ │
│         │           │[scoring          │                           │and   │ │
│         │           │ guidelines]      │                           │1.1a  │ │
│         │           └──────────────────┘                           │(1)]  │ │
│         │                                                          └──────┘ │
│         │           ┌──────────────────┐    ┌──────────────────┐            │
│         │           │ Evaluate–Improve–│    │ To Work          │            │
│         └──────────▶│ Innovate work    │    │ Processes        │            │
│                     │ systems design   │    │ [6.2]            │            │
│                     │ processes        │    └──────────────────┘            │
│                     │ [scoring         │                                    │
│                     │ guidelines]      │                                    │
│                     └──────────────────┘                                    │
└─────────────────────────────────────────────────────────────────────────────┘
```

* Multiple-level approach requirements usually incorporate Basic and Overall requirements. To avoid confusion, the first time a requirement appears in an Item establishes its level for scoring purposes. If the requirement first appears at the Overall Approach Level and again at the Multiple Level, the requirement should be considered an Overall-level approach requirement. For a more complete explanation see the chapter on Scoring System and the Scoring Calibration Guidelines.

6.1 Key Work Systems Item Linkages

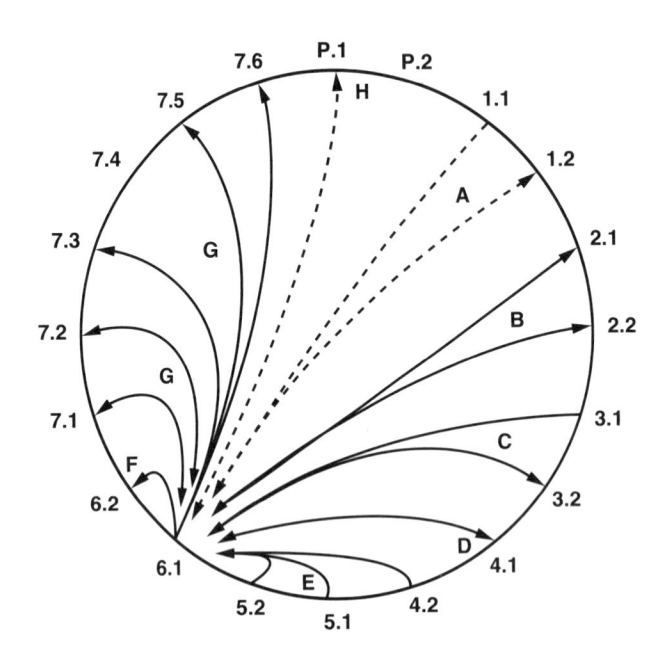

	NATURE OF RELATIONSHIP
A	Senior leaders [1.1] and the governance system [1.2a] have a responsibility for ensuring that work systems critical for growth and success are designed [6.1] consistent with the organization's vision and values, including those relating to societal responsibility and good corporate citizenship [1.2].
B	The strengths and weaknesses of core competencies and overall work systems [6.1] are considered during the planning process [2.1a(2)]. Action plans, deployed to the workforce [2.2a], are used to align actions to help ensure work processes meet all expectations [6.1b].
C	Product offerings to meet/exceed customer requirements [3.1a(1)] and mechanisms to support the use of products [3.1a(2)] must be considered in the design of work systems [6.1a] and the selection of key work processes to deliver customer value [6.1b]. Factors of key work processes that contribute to customer value [6.1b(1)] help in the design of processes to listen to the customers [3.2a] and assess satisfaction, dissatisfaction, and engagement [3.2b].
D	Core competencies [6.1b] are used to help identify benchmarking targets [4.1a(2)]. Benchmarking data are used to help decide whether work processes should be performed internally or externally [6.1a(1)].
E	A culture that promotes high-performance work [5.1a(2)], effective recognition [5.1a(3)], workforce and leader development [5.1b(1, 2)], and a safe, healthful work climate [5.2b(1)] is essential to improving related work systems [6.1].
F	Work processes [6.2] are managed to ensure all key work process requirements [6.1] are consistently met.
G	Information about product quality [7.1] and customer-focused outcomes [7.2] is used to target improvement efforts to help ensure work systems are designed to maximize customer value, profitability, success, and sustainability [6.1a(1)]. Improved work process design [6.1] can produce better customer satisfaction [7.2] and better product quality [7.1], better financial results [7.3], process efficiency [7.5a(1 and 2)], and societal responsibility/regulatory compliance [7.6a(5)].

Continued

6 Process Management

	NATURE OF RELATIONSHIP	*Continued*
H	Information in P.1a(1) about main product offerings (see P.1, Note 1) and the core competencies [P.1a(2)] should align with the design requirements [6.1] and help set the context for examiner review of these processes.	

IF YOU DON'T DO WHAT THE CRITERIA REQUIRE...

Item Reference	Possible Adverse Consequences
6.1a(1)	No organization is excellent at everything it does. Organizations that perform work through poor or mediocre work systems waste resources and reduce customer value. As work systems are designed, the organization must determine which work processes it will continue to perform internally (such as its core competencies), and which it will outsource to suppliers or partners who can perform those processes better. Thus, the organization is able to focus its resources on what it does best.
6.1a(2)	Failure to capitalize or take full advantage of core competencies makes it difficult for the organization to achieve a competitive advantage. The lack of a competitive advantage (something the organization does better than others) makes it difficult to sustain the organization or help it thrive.
6.1b(1)	Key work processes provide the core product or support service on which the organization relies to meet and exceed customer requirements and expectations. Key work processes that are not good enough to meed/exceed customer requirements erode customer confidence, loyalty, and engagement—resulting in a loss of customers and revenue.
6.1b(2)	An organization that fails to accurately identify the performance requirements of its key work processes may find it difficult to design and deliver products and support services to meet customer expectations consistently.
6.1c	Emergencies and disasters are usually difficult to predict. The stress and confusion created by a disaster or emergency can cause a normally efficient operation to become dysfunctional and fail. It is difficult to change processes *during* a disaster, which makes recovery nearly impossible until the emergency passes. Although the timing of disasters is difficult to predict, the possibility of one occurring is great enough to cause the best performing organizations to prepare, in advance, to minimize the adverse impact. Failure to prepare (in advance) increases the possibility of catastrophic failure, which many organizations may not survive.

6.1 WORK SYSTEMS—SAMPLE EFFECTIVE PRACTICES

A. Work Systems Design

- The organization has strengthened its work systems and key work processes that are essential to mission, vision, and strategic success to take advantage of its core competencies. Some of its key work processes are regarded as leading the industry. Over time, these competencies evolved to provide a sustainable advantage over its competitors.

B. Key Work Processes

- A systematic, iterative process (such as quality function deployment) is used to maintain a focus on the voice of the customer and convert customer requirements into product or service design, production, and delivery.

- Design processes are evaluated and improvements are made so that future designs are developed faster (shorter cycle time), at lower cost, and with higher quality relative to key product or service characteristics that predict customer satisfaction.

- Core competencies are systematically reviewed to improve productivity, reduce cycle time and waste, and increase quality.

C. Emergency Readiness

- A formal process exists to conduct emergency and disaster-scenario analysis and planning.

- Disaster and emergency plans are recorded and coordinated with relevant public and private organizations such as the Red Cross, local law enforcement, National Guard, Coast Guard, hospitals, utility companies, schools, and local, state, and federal agencies.

- Partnering agreements are in place to run many operations remotely, such as redundant information systems located geographically apart to minimize/localize the adverse impact of a disaster.

- A documented and tested emergency-recovery plan is in place and all employees are trained and understand the processes they will follow.

- Disaster-recovery processes are in place and serious tests (drills) are conducted to simulate emergency response to minimize problems and risks to the workforce and customers in the event of a real crisis. These procedures were developed based on benchmarking other organizations that faced crises.

6.2 WORK PROCESSES: How do you design, manage, and improve your key organizational work processes? (50 Pts.)

PROCESS

Describe how your organization designs, implements, manages, and improves its key work processes to deliver customer value and achieve organizational success and sustainability.

Within your response, include answers to the following questions:

a. Work Process Design

How do you design and innovate your work processes to meet all the key requirements? How do you incorporate new technology, organizational knowledge, and the potential need for agility into the design of these processes? How do you incorporate cycle time, productivity, cost control, and other efficiency and effectiveness factors into the design of these processes?

b. Work Process Management

(1) How do you implement and manage your work processes to ensure that they meet design requirements? How does your day-to-day operation of these processes ensure that they meet key process requirements? How is workforce, customer, supplier, partner, and collaborator input used in managing these processes, as appropriate? What are your key performance measures or indicators and in-process measures used for the control and improvement of your work processes?

(2) How do you control the overall costs of your work processes? How do you prevent defects, service errors, and rework and minimize warranty costs or customers' productivity losses, as appropriate? How do you minimize the costs of inspections, tests, and process or performance audits, as appropriate?

c. Work Process Improvement

How do you improve your work processes to achieve better performance, to reduce variability, to improve products, and to keep the processes current with business needs and directions? How do you incorporate the results of the organizational performance reviews discussed in response to Item 4.1 into the systematic evaluation and improvement of your work processes? How are work process improvements and lessons learned shared with other organizational units and processes to drive organizational learning and innovation?

Notes:

N1. To improve process performance (6.2c) and reduce variability, your organization might implement approaches such as a Lean Enterprise System, Six Sigma methodology, use of ISO quality systems standards, the Plan-Do-Check-Act methodology, or other process improvement tools. These approaches might be part of your performance improvement system described in response to P.2c in the Organizational Profile.

N2. The results of improvements in product performance should be reported in Item 7.1. All other work process performance results should be reported in Item 7.5.

This Item [6.2] examines the design, management, and improvement of key work processes. These key work processes are critical to creating value for customers and achieving organizational success and long-term sustainability. Methods to design key work processes may differ significantly depending on the nature of the organization's product offerings—whether the products are entirely new, are variants, or involve major or minor work process changes. The customers' key requirements and expectations for the products must drive the design process. Typical factors to consider in work process design include safety, long-term performance, environmental impact, "green" manufacturing, measurement capability, process capability, manufacturability, maintainability, variability in customer expectations requiring multiple product or service options, supplier capability, and documentation, to name a few. Effective design also considers the cycle time and productivity requirements of production and delivery processes. This aspect of design might require detailed mapping of manufacturing or service processes and the redesign (reengineering) of existing processes to achieve better efficiency and meet ever-changing customer requirements.

- The best-performing organizations accurately and completely define key production/delivery processes, their key performance requirements, and key performance measures. These requirements and measures provide the basis for monitoring, maintaining, and improving products, services, and production/delivery processes.

- New technology, including e-technology, could be incorporated into the design of work processes. The use of e-technology might include new ways of electronically sharing information with suppliers, partners, and collaborators; communicating with customers; and giving them continuous (24/7) access and transferring automated information.

Frequently, defective design processes require organizations to capture information from customer complaint data using the processes described in Items 3.1 and 3.2. Immediate access to customer-complaint data allows the organization to make design or production complaint changes quickly to prevent problems from recurring.

The best-performing organizations consider requirements of suppliers, partners, and collaborators early in the design stage. This minimizes the chances that important design issues are not achievable because of supplier and/or partner limitations. Similarly, effective design processes take into account all stakeholders in the value chain.

To enhance design-process efficiency, all related design and production activities should be coordinated within the organization. Coordination of design, production, and delivery processes involves all work units and/or individuals who take part in production/delivery and whose performance materially affects overall process outcome. This might include key business functions or processes such as R&D, marketing, design, product/process engineering, and key suppliers. If many design projects are carried out in parallel, or if the organization's products require parts, equipment, and facilities that are used for other products, coordination of resources frequently provides a means to significantly reduce unit costs and time to market.

Design processes should cover all key operational performance requirements and appropriate coordination and testing to ensure effective product/service launch without need for rework.

Designing key work processes includes the design of key nonproduct and nonservice processes (also called business processes) that are critical to the success and growth of the organization but do not involve actually producing products or services for end users. These key business processes frequently relate to an organization's core competencies, strategic objectives, and critical success factors.

Key business processes might include the following:

- Processes for innovation, including engaging or empowering workforce members to generate and implement new ideas.

- R&D, involving dedicated units and distributing R&D responsibility throughout the organization.

- Technology acquisition (which may involve partnering), mergers, invention, or other techniques.

- Information and knowledge management, which goes beyond traditional information technology or information-management activities. Knowledge management should support knowledge transfer and sharing among all organizational units at all levels and sites within an organization.

- Project management, to ensure on-time and consistent development of new programs, products, and services.

- Sales and marketing, to strengthen and expand new markets, including e-commerce.

- Supply-chain management, supplier partnering, and outsourcing. For many organizations, supply-chain management is an increasingly important factor in achieving productivity and profitability goals and overall organizational success. Suppliers, partners, and collaborators are receiving increasing strategic attention as organizations reevaluate and outsource their core competencies. Supply-chain management processes typically fulfill two purposes: to help improve the performance of suppliers and partners and, in turn, contribute to better internal work systems and operational performance. Supply chain management might include processes for supplier selection, with the aim of reducing the total number of suppliers and increasing preferred supplier and partnering agreements.

- For some nonprofit organizations, key business processes might include fundraising, media relations, and public policy development and analysis. Given the diverse nature of these processes, the requirements and performance characteristics might vary for different processes.

Key work processes include processes that support daily operations and product and service delivery. Support process requirements usually depend upon internal customer requirements, and they must be coordinated and integrated to ensure efficient and effective linkage and performance. Support processes might include:

- Finance and accounting
- Software or information-technology services
- Public relations
- Transportation services
- Food services
- Human resource services
- Legal services
- Plant and facilities management/maintenance
- Secretarial and other administrative services

Ensuring continuity of operations requires consideration of all facets of an organization that are needed to provide required products or services to customers as required, every time, even in emergency situations. Emergency planning should address all key work processes. The specific level of service required is usually guided by the organization's type of business and customers' needs and requirements. For example, a public utility will likely have a higher need for continuity of services than businesses that do not provide an essential function. Nonprofit organizations with missions to respond to emergencies will have a high need for service readiness. Continuity of operations efforts should also be coordinated with efforts to ensure data and information availability (Item 4.2).

High-performance work is also enhanced by systems that promote flexibility, innovation, knowledge and skill sharing, good communication and information flow, alignment with organizational objectives, customer focus, and rapid response to changing business needs and requirements of the marketplace. Work should support the achievement of organizational objectives, and the workforce should be capable of achieving high performance. Creativity and innovation from all employees should be specifically required, measured, and recognized. Suggestion boxes are not enough. The number of innovative ideas or improvements actually *implemented* per person is a better indicator of innovation and idea quality than the number of ideas *proposed*.

The organization must ensure that the day-to-day operation of its key work processes consistently meets the key performance requirements. To do this, in-process measures are defined to permit rapid identification and correction of potential problems. Work processes should incorporate mechanisms to obtain and use customer feedback to help identify problems and take prompt, corrective action.

Top organizations prevent unacceptable variability in work processes to minimize the need for inspections, tests, and audits to avoid rework and warranty costs, because they have implemented processes to prevent problems from occurring in the first place. Sometimes these processes involve error-proofing, which makes it impossible to do the wrong thing the wrong way (for example, electrical cords on today's appliances have one plug blade wider than the other and a grounding prong to prevent the plug from being inserted incorrectly into a wall outlet).

The best way to minimize the need for tests, inspections, and audits is to consistently, without fail, produce desired outcomes. To help minimize unacceptable variation (errors), organizations use key measurements, observations, or interactions at the earliest points possible in processes. Consistently achieving expected performance frequently requires setting in-process performance levels or standards to guide decision making. When deviations occur, corrective action is taken to restore the performance of the process to its design specifications. Depending on the nature of the process, the corrective action could involve technical and/or human considerations. Proper corrective action involves changes at the source (root cause) of the deviation. Effective corrective action minimizes the likelihood of this type of deviation occurring again or anywhere else in the organization. Differences among customers and how the organization interacts with customers must be considered in evaluating how well the process is performing. Specific or general contingencies might be required, depending on the customer information gathered. This is especially true of professional and personal services. The length of key process cycle times, which in some organizations may be a year or longer, can create special challenges in measuring day-to-day progress and identifying opportunities for reducing cycle times, when appropriate.

The best-performing organizations have a system in place to evaluate and improve work processes to achieve better process efficiency and better products and services. Better performance means not only better quality from the customers' perspective but also results in better financial and operational performance—such as productivity. A variety of process improvement approaches are commonly used. These approaches include:

- Sharing successful techniques across the organization to improve learning and innovation

- Process analysis and research (for example, process mapping, optimization experiments, and error-proofing)

- Technical and business research and development

- Benchmarking

- Using alternative technology

- Using information from customers of the processes—within and outside of the organization

New process improvement approaches might also involve the use of cost data to evaluate alternatives and set improvement priorities. Taken together, these approaches offer a wide range of possibilities, including complete redesign of key processes to achieve new levels of operational excellence.

6.2 Work Processes

Basic Approach Requirements*: Design, manage, and improve key organizational work processes (see Glossary for description of Work Processes).

Overall Approach Requirements*: Effectively design, implement, manage, and improve key work processes to deliver customer value and achieve organizational success and sustainability.

Multiple Approach Requirements: The following diagram describes multiple approach requirements.

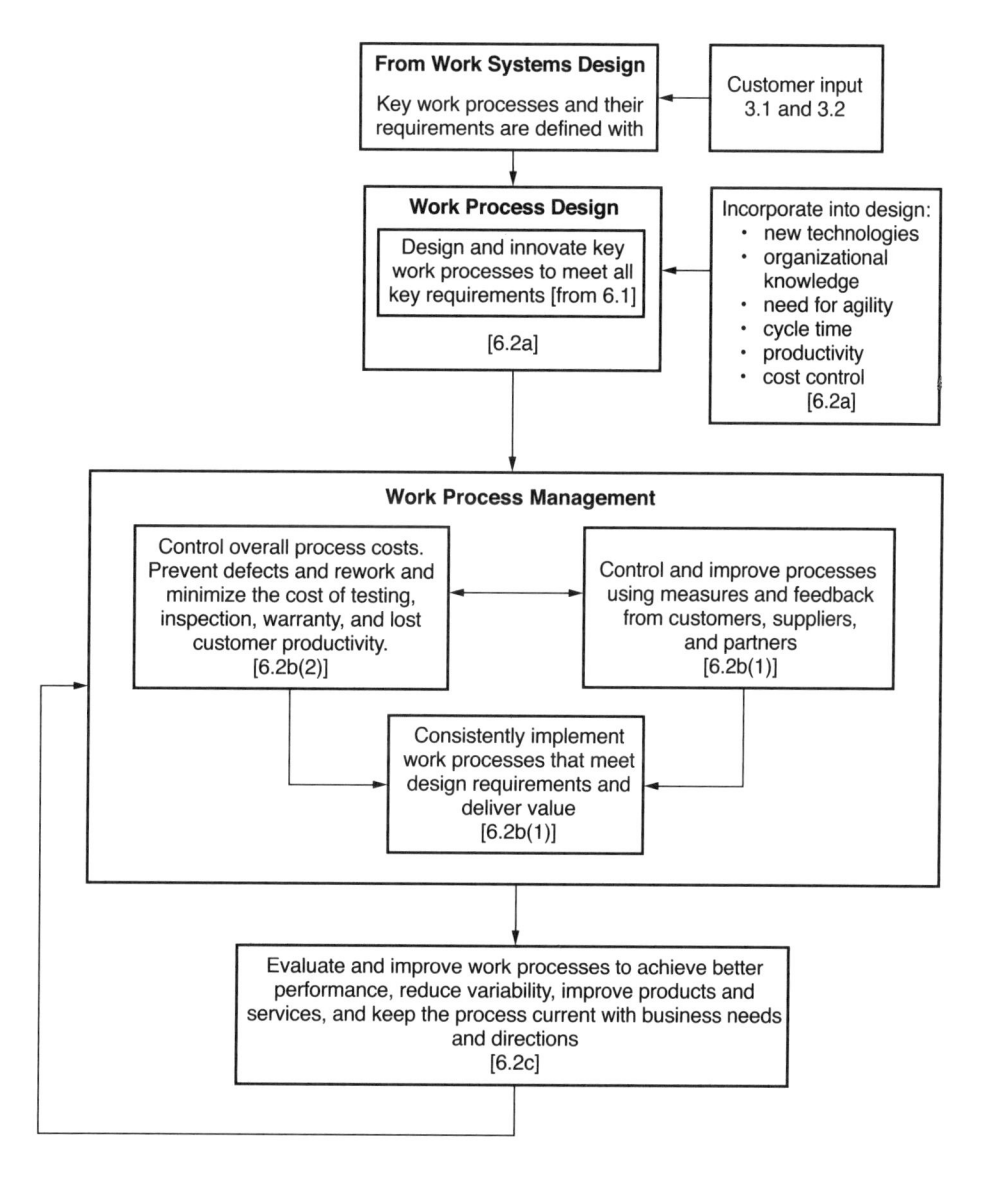

```
┌─────────────────────────────┐      ┌──────────────┐
│ From Work Systems Design    │◄─────│ Customer input│
│ Key work processes and their│      │ 3.1 and 3.2  │
│ requirements are defined with│      └──────────────┘
└─────────────────────────────┘
              │
              ▼
┌─────────────────────────────┐      ┌──────────────────────┐
│    Work Process Design      │      │ Incorporate into design:│
│ Design and innovate key     │◄─────│  • new technologies    │
│ work processes to meet all  │      │  • organizational      │
│ key requirements [from 6.1] │      │    knowledge           │
│                             │      │  • need for agility    │
│          [6.2a]             │      │  • cycle time          │
└─────────────────────────────┘      │  • productivity        │
                                     │  • cost control        │
                                     │        [6.2a]          │
                                     └──────────────────────┘
              │
              ▼
┌──────────────────────────────────────────────────────────────┐
│                   Work Process Management                    │
│  ┌─────────────────────────┐      ┌─────────────────────────┐│
│  │ Control overall process │      │ Control and improve     ││
│  │ costs. Prevent defects  │      │ processes using measures││
│  │ and rework and minimize │◄────►│ and feedback from       ││
│  │ the cost of testing,    │      │ customers, suppliers,   ││
│  │ inspection, warranty,   │      │ and partners            ││
│  │ and lost customer       │      │       [6.2b(1)]         ││
│  │ productivity.           │      └─────────────────────────┘│
│  │       [6.2b(2)]         │                                 │
│  └─────────────────────────┘                                 │
│           ┌──────────────────────────────┐                   │
│           │ Consistently implement work  │                   │
│           │ processes that meet design   │                   │
│           │ requirements and deliver     │                   │
│           │ value                        │                   │
│           │        [6.2b(1)]             │                   │
│           └──────────────────────────────┘                   │
└──────────────────────────────────────────────────────────────┘
              │
              ▼
┌──────────────────────────────────────────────────────────┐
│ Evaluate and improve work processes to achieve better    │
│ performance, reduce variability, improve products and    │
│ services, and keep the process current with business needs│
│ and directions                                           │
│                      [6.2c]                              │
└──────────────────────────────────────────────────────────┘
```

* Multiple-level requirements usually incorporate Basic and Overall requirements. To avoid confusion, the first time a requirement appears in an Item establishes its level for scoring purposes. If the requirement first appears at the Overall Approach Level and again at the Multiple Level, the requirement should be considered an Overall-level requirement. For a more complete explanation see the chapter on Scoring System and the Scoring Calibration Guidelines.

6.2 Key Work Processes Item Linkages

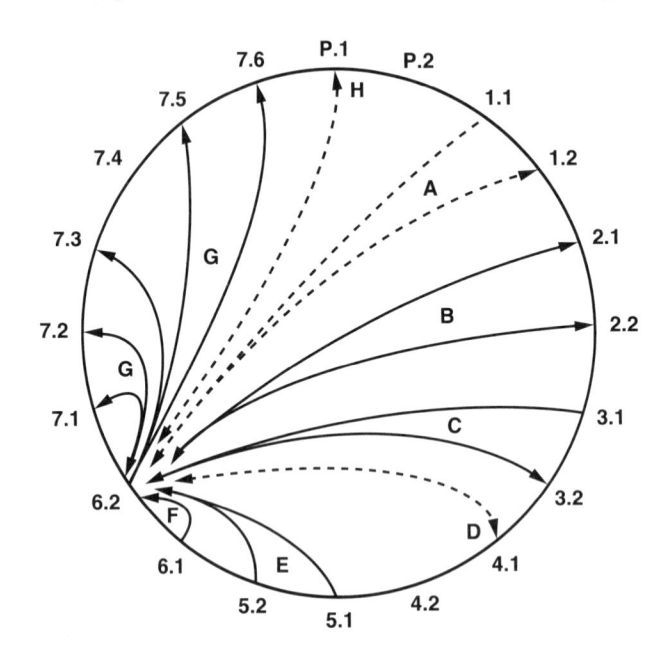

	NATURE OF RELATIONSHIP
A	Senior leaders [1.1] and the governance system [1.2a] have a responsibility for ensuring that key work processes are designed [6.2a(1)] and executed [6.2b(1)] in a manner consistent with the organization's vision and values, including those relating to ethical principles, societal responsibility, and good corporate citizenship [1.2].
B	Key work process strengths and weaknesses [6.2] are considered as part of SWOT analysis in the planning process [2.1a(2)]. Action plans, deployed to the workforce [2.2a], are used to align work to help ensure that key work processes [6.2] meet the requirements needed to carry out the action plans.
C	Product offerings to meet/exceed customer requirements [3.1a(1)] and mechanisms to support the use of products [3.1a(2)] must be considered in the design of key work processes [6.2a]. Factors of key work processes that contribute to customer value help in the design of voice-of-the-customer processes [3.2a] and to assess satisfaction, dissatisfaction, and engagement [3.2b].
D	Key work processes [6.2] are used to help identify and prioritize benchmarking targets [4.1a(2)]. Benchmarking data [4.1a(2)] are used to improve the management and control of work processes [6.2].
E	Creating a culture conducive to high performance [5.1a(2)] and effective reward/recognition [5.1a(3)], leader and workforce development [5.2b(1, 2)], and a safe, healthy, secure work climate [5.2b(1)] are essential to managing, improving, and sustaining core competencies and related key work processes [6.2].
F	Work system design processes [6.1], are used to develop key work processes and define requirements and set priorities for work processes [6.2].
G	Information about product performance [7.1] and customer-focused results [7.2] can be used to target improvement efforts in work process design [6.2a], control [6.2b], and improvement [6.2c]. Improved work processes [6.2c] result in better customer engagement and satisfaction [7.2], product quality [7.1], financial results [7.3], process effectiveness [7.5], societal responsibility [7.6a(4)], and regulatory compliance [7.6a(5)].

Continued

NATURE OF RELATIONSHIP — Continued

H	Information in P.1a(1) about main product offerings (see P.1, Note 1) and core competencies [P.1a(2) should align with the work process priorities in 6.2 and help set the context for examiner review of these processes.

IF YOU DON'T DO WHAT THE CRITERIA REQUIRE...

Item Reference	Possible Adverse Consequences
6.2a	Organizations that fail to consider all key operational performance requirements when designing key business processes find that the system they designed is not optimum. Design flaws produce undesired results, as well as nonconforming products and services. These, in turn, require even more rework to correct. The failure to identify and address all of the requirements of customers may increase the likelihood of downstream problems with the design, production, and delivery of core products and services. In today's highly competitive global economy, flexibility and agility are important factors that distinguish the best-performing organizations from the rest. The best-performing organizations provide their customers with more value at a faster pace (speed), and across a wider range of areas (agility) than their competition. The speed and agility offered by new technologies typically enhance value. Consequently, the leaders are able to distinguish their organizations in chosen markets, keeping their current customers and acquiring new ones. Increasingly, the failure to use the appropriate technologies limits the organization's ability to keep pace with aggressive competitors. These organizations may have the latest computers, but those computers may not be used effectively to accelerate delivery of the things that are important to customers. One *Fortune 500* company, learning that its customers placed a premium on accurate bills being delivered on time, acquired and implemented new technology to dramatically speed up its billing cycle. Unfortunately, the billing process itself was not capable of rendering an accurate invoice. Customers received their inaccurate invoices faster than ever. Using technology to accelerate a bad process produces unsatisfactory results faster. The failure to incorporate the technology appropriately can have significant adverse effects on an organization's ability to bring value to its customers and to operate in an efficient and effective manner. Eliminating unnecessary steps in any work process tends to reduce variation (increasing quality), reduce cycle time, and reduce cost. In addition, sharing knowledge and learning from the successes and mistakes of others help prevent workers from repeating the same problems (which add rework, waste, and delay). When designing new products and services and related production and delivery systems, the failure to consider factors such as cost control, new technology, variability, and ways to enhance productivity and efficiency typically adds unnecessary cost, delay, and rework, making it more difficult to meet increasing demands of customers and the marketplace.
6.2a	Design flaws produce undesired results and nonconforming products and services. This, in turn, requires even more rework or more people-intensive services, which can add significant delay and cost and prevent the organization from achieving its objectives. When these processes fail to meet requirements, resources are wasted and the success of the organization

Continued

	IF YOU DON'T DO WHAT THE CRITERIA REQUIRE... Continued
Item Reference	**Possible Adverse Consequences**
	may be jeopardized. The key work process requirements can vary significantly within an organization depending on the nature of the products and services required by customers. Design processes may also vary based on whether the products and services are new or only involve minor variations to current product and service offerings. In any event, a design process that fails to consider the key requirements for products and services, and other factors such as environmental impact, process capability, measurement capability, customer service expectations, supplier capability, and customer documentation requirements (such as found in ISO 9001), may make it difficult or impossible for the organization to achieve desired results (satisfy customers) in an efficient and cost-effective (profitable) manner. In an effort to ensure the design process is consistent and effective, organizations frequently develop checkpoints or *gates* that must be passed as part of bringing a new product or service into the marketplace. The gates serve a twofold purpose: (1) assuring the focus on customer requirements is maintained throughout the design process; and (2) responding to changing customer and market demands. The first deals with fully responding to customer requirements by providing value in the eyes of the customer. The second addresses the ability of the organization to do this in an efficient and effective manner. Design processes that are not capable of incorporating changing customer or market requirements into products and services in a timely fashion are not sufficiently agile and may find it difficult to remain competitive. An organization that receives customer change requirements at a faster pace than it can implement the changes can be virtually paralyzed. Unwieldy design systems often lead to frustrated workers, excessive delay, and ultimately dissatisfied customers and lost business. When faced with rapidly changing technology, customer requirements, or market demands, inflexible or cumbersome design processes can render a once-good design obsolete before it ever gets to production.

6.2b(1)	The best-performing organizations consistently deliver programs, products, and services that meet key performance requirements. They do this by identifying key processes, monitoring them regularly, and improving then continuously. The failure to ensure consistent day-to-day operation of production and delivery processes increases the likelihood of defects, which contribute to rework, waste, delay, excessive costs, and customer dissatisfaction.
	
	   Organizations can always tell if a process is producing desired results by checking to see if the end product and service meet customer and operational requirements. Unfortunately, waiting for the end of the process to learn that it has not produced desired results is time-consuming and expensive, since most costs may have already been expended. The earlier an organization determines if a process is not likely to produce desired results, the earlier it can take corrective action to minimize rework, scrap, delay, and unnecessary cost. Top-performing organizations collect in-process data to identify problems early. The failure to collect and analyze in-process data makes it more difficult for workers to know when to adjust a process to make it work better. Inappropriate or unnecessary adjustments can actually increase variation and decrease productivity and quality.
	
	   Customers are in an excellent position to determine if the products and services they receive meet (or exceed) their requirements. They can provide near-real-time feedback [3.2] that will enable workers to make adjustments to meet requirements. The failure to gather and use this information makes it more difficult for organizations to make timely changes to reduce rework costs and increase customer satisfaction.

Continued

IF YOU DON'T DO WHAT THE CRITERIA REQUIRE...		Continued
Item Reference	**Possible Adverse Consequences**	
6.2b(2)	High-performing organizations do not rely on excessive inspection and testing to determine if process requirements are met or not. Instead, these organizations design process controls that let them know how well the process is performing during each of its critical steps. They develop processes that prevent problems using tools and techniques such as error-proofing. The best that testing or inspection can hope to accomplish is to uncover and correct a problem before the customer is disrupted. Although this is better than causing problems for customers, it is still more costly to fix the problem than to prevent it from happening in the first place.	
6.2c	Organizations that fail to systematically evaluate and improve key work processes often lag behind the competition. Consider two comparable organizations, each using similar processes to develop and deliver similar products and services. Let's also assume that the organizations are equally competitive today. However, one organization has embedded into its work processes an ongoing evaluation and improvement of its design, production, and delivery systems; the other has not. As time passes the first organization begins to see the impact of improved work processes. It is able to produce goods and services faster, better, and cheaper than its competitor. It has been able to pass a portion of its cost savings on to its customers (lowering prices), keeping the rest as increased profit. As a result of better, more timely, and less-expensive products, it is acquiring greater market share—at the expense of its competitor—and making its stockholders exceedingly happy as its share price increases. In addition, the first organization has been able to accelerate performance by sharing improvements with other organizational units so they can get better as well. The organization that does not systematically improve continues to fall further and further behind in a highly competitive environment (or as the popular adage acclaims: today, if you're standing still, you're falling behind). The failure to share effective practices with other organizational support units may cause them to waste time and other resources in redundant work—work that adds cost but not value.	

6.2 WORK PROCESSES—Sample Effective Practices

A. Work Process Design

- A systematic, iterative process (such as quality function deployment) is used to maintain a focus on the voice of the customer and convert customer requirements into product or service design, production, and delivery.

- Product-design requirements are systematically translated into process specifications, with measurement plans to monitor process consistency.

- The work of various functions is coordinated to bring the product or service through the design-to-delivery phases. Functional barriers between units have been eliminated organization-wide.

- Concurrent engineering is used to operate several processes (for example, product and service planning, R&D, manufacturing, marketing, supplier certification) in parallel as much as possible, rather than operating in sequence. All activities are closely coordinated through effective communication and teamwork.

- Internal process capacity and supplier capability, using measures such as C_{pk}, are reviewed and considered before production and delivery-process designs or plans are finalized.

- Steps are taken (such as design testing or prototyping) to ensure that the production and delivery process will work as designed, and will meet customer requirements.

- Performance requirements and customer requirements are set using facts and data and are monitored using statistical or other process-control techniques.

- Design errors and subsequent corrections are monitored and verified. Improvements are shared throughout the organization.

B. Work Process Management

- Systems are in place to ensure process performance is maintained and customer requirements are met. In-process measures are defined and monitored constantly to ensure early alert of problem.

- Root causes of problems are systematically identified and corrected for processes that produce defects.

- Corrections are monitored and verified. Processes used and results obtained are systematic and integrated throughout the organization.

- Work-process simplification and performance improvement tools are applied to support processes with measurable sustained results.

- Measurable goals and related actions are used to drive higher levels of work process performance.

- Key work processes are measured and tracked. Measures (quantitative and qualitative) reflect or assess the extent to which customer requirements are met, as well as production consistency.

- For processes that produce defects (out-of-control processes), root causes are quickly and systematically identified and corrective action is taken to prevent their recurrence.

- Key business processes are systematically reviewed to improve productivity, reduce cycle time and waste, and increase quality. Improvements in these processes are shared throughout the organization.

C. Work Process Improvement

- Benchmarking, competitive comparison data, or information from customers of the process (in or out of the organization) are used to gain insight to improve processes.

- All key business processes are subject to continuous review and improvements in performance and customer satisfaction.

- Tools—such as flowcharting, work redesign, and reengineering—are used throughout the organization to evaluate and improve work processes.

- Information about customer requirements, complaints, concerns, and reactions to products and services are captured *near-real time* and used directly by workers to improve the work processes.

7 Results—450 Points

*The **Results** Category examines your organization's performance and improvement in all key areas—product outcomes, customer-focused outcomes, financial and market outcomes, workforce-focused outcomes, process effectiveness outcomes, and leadership outcomes. Performance levels are examined relative to those of competitors and other organizations with similar product offerings.*

The Results Category provides a results focus that reflects the organization's product, service, and program offerings, overall financial and market performance, workforce results, the results of all key processes and process improvement activities, and leadership system results, including legal and ethical behavior as a part of practicing good citizenship and meeting societal responsibilities.

> **The Results Category presents a balanced scorecard of organizational performance.**

Category 7 reflects timely measures of progress for evaluation and improvement of processes, products, and services, aligned with overall organizational strategy.

Historically, businesses have been far too preoccupied with budgetary and financial performance. For many, performance reviews focused almost exclusively on achieving (or failing to achieve) expected levels of financial performance. As such, these reviews were considered *unbalanced.*

In an absolute sense, all measures lag behind the event they reflect; all measures are historical. However, some measures lag behind others (lagging indicators); and some predict or influence others (leading indicators).

- Financial results are considered *lagging* indicators of business success. Financial results are the net of all the good processes, bad processes, satisfied customers, dissatisfied customers, engaged workers, disgruntled workers, effective suppliers, and sloppy suppliers, to name a few. By the time financial indicators become available, bad products and dissatisfied customers have already occurred.

- Customer satisfaction is a lagging indicator as well. Customers must experience the product or service before they are in a position to comment on their satisfaction with that product or service. As with financial results, customer satisfaction is affected by many variables including process performance, workforce engagement, and supplier performance.

- Leading indicators help organizations predict subsequent customer satisfaction and financial performance. Leading indicators include operational effectiveness and workforce engagement and satisfaction. Supplier and partner performance, because it affects an organization's own operating performance, is also a leading indicator of customer satisfaction and financial performance.

Taken together, these measures represent a balance of leading and lagging indicators and enable decision makers to identify problems early and take prompt corrective action.

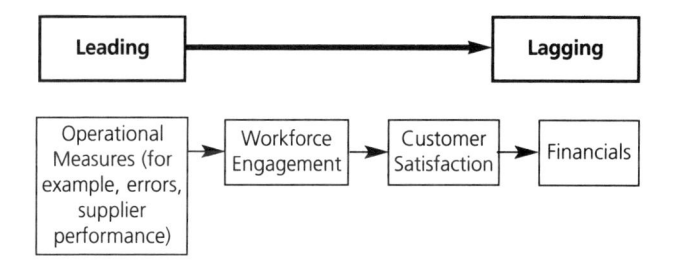

Leading → Lagging

Operational Measures (for example, errors, supplier performance) → Workforce Engagement → Customer Satisfaction → Financials

Category 7 requires organizations to report current levels and improvement trends for the following:

- Product performance important to customers, including indicators of service important to support customers

- Customer satisfaction and dissatisfaction and measures of customer engagement such as retention, customer gains and losses, and customer-perceived value broken out by appropriate customer groups and market segments

- Financial and marketplace performance, such as revenue, cash flow, business growth, earnings, new products, new markets entered, and percentage of revenue from new products or services

- Workforce performance including work systems, workforce learning, and workforce engagement and satisfaction

- Process effectiveness outcomes reflect key work processes including other processes, such as cycle time; errors; rework; time to market; Six Sigma and Lean results; productivity; supplier, partner, and collaborator performance; emergency preparedness; and innovation rates

- Leadership outcomes include the accomplishment of organizational strategy and action plans, governance, fiscal accountability, ethical behavior, regulatory and legal compliance, sanctions, contributions to societal well-being, and support of key communities

For all of these areas, organizations must include appropriate comparative data to enable examiners to define what *good* means. Otherwise, even though performance may be improving, it is difficult to determine whether the level of performance is poor, good, very good, or excellent.

Organizations should also provide projections of future performance for all key results. These projections correlate with and relate to strategic objectives, goals, and organizational sustainability.

7 Results

> **7.1 PRODUCT OUTCOMES: What are your product performance results? (100 Pts.)**   **RESULTS**
>
> Summarize your organization's key product performance results. Segment your results by product offerings, customer groups, and market segments, as appropriate. Include appropriate comparative data.
>
> Provide data and information to answer the following questions:
>
> **a. Product Results**
>
> What are your current levels and trends in key measures or indicators of product performance that are important to your customers? How do these results compare with the performance of your competitors and other organizations providing similar products offerings?
>
> **Notes:**
>
> N1. Product results reported in this Item should relate to the key product features identified as customer requirements and expectations in P.1b(2), based on information gathered in Items 3.1 and 3.2. The measures or indicators should address factors that affect customer preference, such as those included in Item P.1, Note 5, and Item 3.1, Note 2.
>
> N2. *For some nonprofit organizations, product or service performance measures might be mandated by your funding sources. These measures should be identified and reported in your response to this Item.*

Item 7.1 looks at the organization's product and service outcomes to demonstrate how well the organization has been delivering products and service quality and value that lead to customer satisfaction, engagement, and positive referral.

Organizations must provide data to demonstrate current levels, trends, and appropriate comparisons for key measures and/or indicators of product (and service) performance relating to key drivers of customers' satisfaction and engagement as well as indicators of customers' views and decisions relative to future purchases and relationships. These measures of product performance are derived from customer-related information gathered in Items 3.1 and 3.2.

The correlations between product and service performance and customer indicators are a critical tool that helps managers:

- Define and focus on key quality and customer requirements
- Identify product and service differentiators in the marketplace
- Determine cause–effect relationships between the organization's product and service attributes and evidence of customer satisfaction and loyalty, as well as positive referrals

The correlations might reveal emerging or changing market segments, the changing importance of requirements, or even the potential obsolescence of offerings.

Product/service performance results appropriate for recording in this Item might be based upon one or more of the following:

- Internal (organizational) quality measurements
- Field performance of products, defect levels, service errors, and response time.
- Data collected from customers by or for the organization.
- Attributes that cannot be accurately assessed through direct measurement (for example, ease of use) or when variability in customer expectations makes the customer's perception the most meaningful indicator (for example, courtesy and attitude).

7.1 Product Outcomes

Key product and service performance results segmented by product groups, customer groups, and market segments

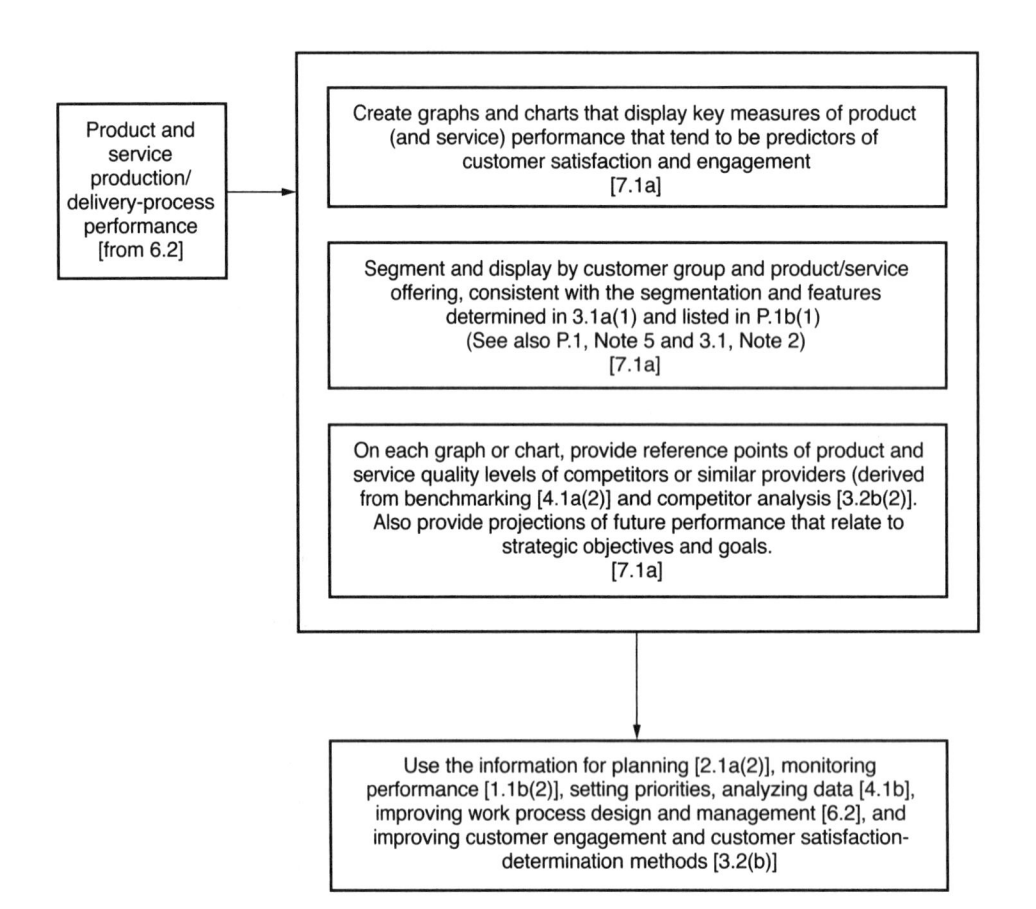

Product and service production/delivery-process performance [from 6.2]

→ Create graphs and charts that display key measures of product (and service) performance that tend to be predictors of customer satisfaction and engagement
[7.1a]

Segment and display by customer group and product/service offering, consistent with the segmentation and features determined in 3.1a(1) and listed in P.1b(1)
(See also P.1, Note 5 and 3.1, Note 2)
[7.1a]

On each graph or chart, provide reference points of product and service quality levels of competitors or similar providers (derived from benchmarking [4.1a(2)] and competitor analysis [3.2b(2)]. Also provide projections of future performance that relate to strategic objectives and goals.
[7.1a]

↓

Use the information for planning [2.1a(2)], monitoring performance [1.1b(2)], setting priorities, analyzing data [4.1b], improving work process design and management [6.2], and improving customer engagement and customer satisfaction-determination methods [3.2(b)]

7.1 Key Product Outcomes Item Linkages

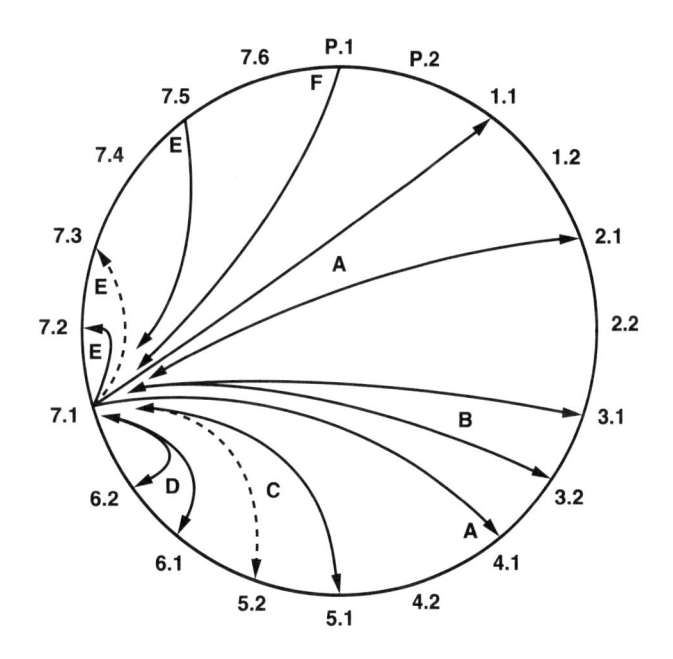

	NATURE OF RELATIONSHIP
A	Data on products [7.1] are monitored by senior leaders [1.1b(2) and 4.1b] and are used for strategic planning [2.1a(2)] and to set priorities for improvement and innovation [4.1c]. Strategic objectives and goals [2.1b] are used to help project future levels of performance in key result areas [7.1].
B	Voice-of-the-customer processes used to gather intelligence about customer requirements and preferences [3.2], strengthen customer relations [3.2a(3)], and determine customer satisfaction, dissatisfaction, and engagement [3.2b], are used to define and produce product outcomes data [7.1]. In addition, product and service quality outcomes [7.1] are used to better understand customer requirements and preferences [3.1a(1) and 3.2a(1)].
C	Recognition and rewards [5.1a(3)] should be based, in part, on product outcomes [7.1]. Innovation, empowerment, and initiative developed by effective workforce enrichment systems [5.1a] can foster better product quality [7.1] Product data [7.1] are monitored, in part, to assess development and training effectiveness [5.1b(1, 2, 3)]. In addition, results pertaining to product quality [7.1] can be improved with effective workforce development [5.1b(1, 2)]. Systems to enhance workforce engagement and satisfaction [5.1c(1, 2)] can produce higher levels of product quality [7.1]. Improved product quality can affect the rewards and recognition of workers [5.1a(3)].
D	Data on product and service quality [7.1] may be used to help design and manage [6.2] key work processes. Work system design [6.1] and key process design and delivery [6.2] can have a direct effect on product and service quality [7.1].
E	Better product results [7.1] can enhance customer satisfaction and engagement results [7.2] and can improve financial and market performance [7.3]. Better organizational effectiveness [7.5] can improve product and service results [7.1].
F	The information in P.1b(1) and P.1 Note 5) helps examiners identify the kind of product performance outcomes, broken out by customer and market segment, that should be reported in Item 7.1.

	IF YOU DON'T DO WHAT THE CRITERIA REQUIRE...
Item Reference	**Possible Adverse Consequences**
7.1	Failing to provide comparison data makes it difficult for leaders (or Baldrige examiners) to determine if the level of performance achieved is good or not. Failing to provide results data for at least most areas of importance to the organization makes it difficult to determine if performance is getting better in key areas. Finally, the failure to provide this information as part of a Baldrige Award assessment is likely to reduce the score and may even prevent an organization from receiving a site visit (during which time additional results data are usually obtained).

7.1 PRODUCT OUTCOMES—SAMPLE EFFECTIVE RESULTS

A. Product Results

- Data are presented for the most relevant product or service-quality indicators collected through the processes described in Item 3.2 (some of which may be referenced in the Organizational Profile).

- Data are presented that correlate with, and help predict, customer satisfaction. These data show consistently improving trends and levels that compare favorably with competitors and lead the industry.

- All indicators show steady improvement. (Indicators may include data collected in Item 6.2 as a part of managing key work processes, which are important to customer engagement.

- Graphs and information are accurate and easy to understand.

- Data are not missing. (For example, do not show a steady trend from 2004 to 2008, but leave out 2006.)

- Projections of expected levels of future performance are provided for all key results. These projections correlate with planned improvements or initiatives and relate to strategic objectives and goals and organizational stability.

7 Results

> **7.2 CUSTOMER-FOCUSED OUTCOMES:** What are your customer-focused performance results? (70 Pts.) **RESULTS**
>
> Summarize your organization's key customer-focused results for customer satisfaction, dissatisfaction, and engagement. Segment your results by product offerings, customer groups, and market segments as appropriate. Include appropriate comparative data.
>
> Provide data and information to answer the following questions:
>
> **a. Customer-Focused Results**
>
> (1) What are your current levels and trends in key measures or indicators of customer satisfaction and dissatisfaction? How do these results compare with the customer satisfaction levels of your competitors and other organizations providing similar products?
>
> (2) What are your current levels and trends in key measures or indicators of customer relationship building and engagement? How do these results compare over the course of your customer life cycle, as appropriate?
>
> **Notes:**
>
> N1. Customer satisfaction, dissatisfaction, relationship building, and engagement results reported in this Item should relate to the customer groups and market segments discussed in P.1b(2) and Category 3 and to the listening and determination methods and data described in Item 3.2.
>
> N2. Measures and indicators of customers' satisfaction with your products relative to customers' satisfaction with competitors and comparable organizations [7.2a(1)] might include information and data from your customers and from independent organizations.

Item 7.2 looks at the organization's customer-focused performance results to demonstrate how well the organization has been satisfying its customers and delivering products and services that lead to satisfaction, loyalty, repeat business, and positive referral.

Top-performing organizations use all relevant data to determine and help predict the organization's performance as viewed by customers. Relevant data and information include:

- Customer satisfaction and dissatisfaction
- Retention, gains, and losses of customers and customer accounts
- Customer complaints, complaint management, rapid complaint resolution, and warranty claims
- Customer-perceived value based on quality, price, convenience, and service
- Customer assessment of access and ease of use (including courtesy)
- Awards, ratings, and recognition from customers and independent rating organizations
- Customer advocacy for product offerings

This Item seeks customer-focused results that go beyond satisfaction measures because engagement measures such as loyalty, repeat business, and longer-term customer relationships are good indicators of future success in the marketplace and organizational sustainability.

Organizations should provide appropriate comparisons for key measures and/or indicators to permit the assessment of the strength or *goodness* of the organization's performance.

Organizations should also provide projections of future performance for all key results. These projections correlate with and relate to strategic objectives, goals, and organizational sustainability.

7.2 Customer-Focused Outcomes

The organization's key customer-focused results for customer satisfaction, dissatisfaction, and engagement

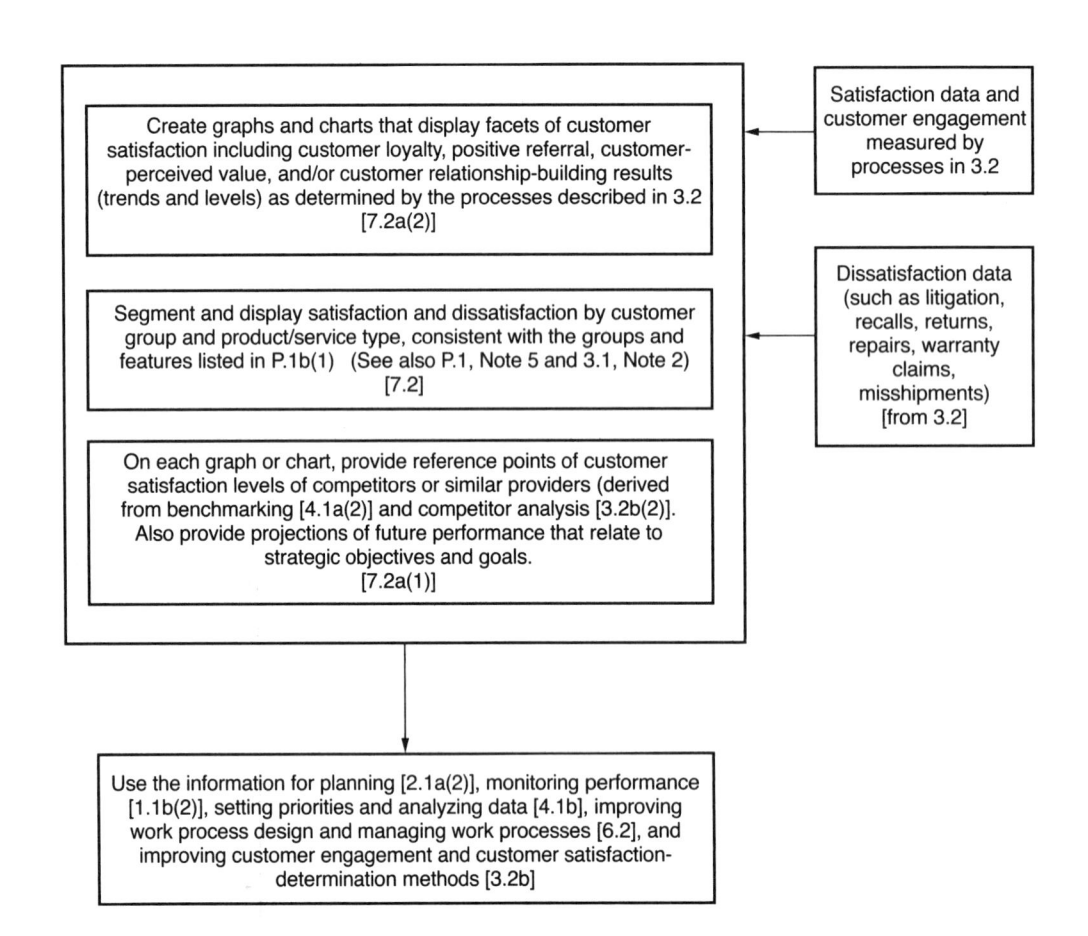

Create graphs and charts that display facets of customer satisfaction including customer loyalty, positive referral, customer-perceived value, and/or customer relationship-building results (trends and levels) as determined by the processes described in 3.2 [7.2a(2)]

Segment and display satisfaction and dissatisfaction by customer group and product/service type, consistent with the groups and features listed in P.1b(1) (See also P.1, Note 5 and 3.1, Note 2) [7.2]

On each graph or chart, provide reference points of customer satisfaction levels of competitors or similar providers (derived from benchmarking [4.1a(2)] and competitor analysis [3.2b(2)]. Also provide projections of future performance that relate to strategic objectives and goals. [7.2a(1)]

Satisfaction data and customer engagement measured by processes in 3.2

Dissatisfaction data (such as litigation, recalls, returns, repairs, warranty claims, misshipments) [from 3.2]

Use the information for planning [2.1a(2)], monitoring performance [1.1b(2)], setting priorities and analyzing data [4.1b], improving work process design and managing work processes [6.2], and improving customer engagement and customer satisfaction-determination methods [3.2b]

7.2 Key Customer-Focused Outcomes Item Linkages

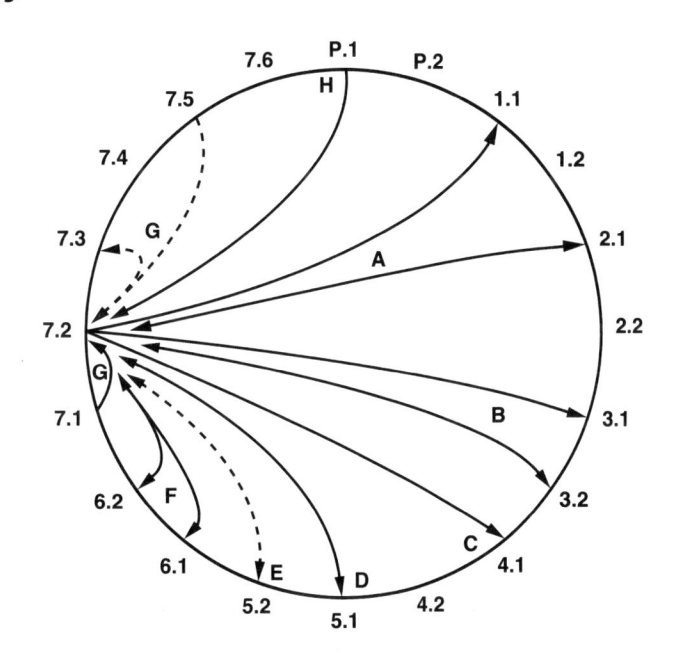

	NATURE OF RELATIONSHIP
A	Data on customer satisfaction and engagement [7.2a(2)] are used for strategic planning [2.1a(2)] and are monitored by senior leaders [1.1b(2)]. Strategic objectives and goals [2.1b(1)] are used to help project future levels of customer-focused results [7.2a].
B	Processes used to gather intelligence about current customer requirements [3.2c(2)] and support requirements [3.1a(2)], strength of customer relations [3.1b(2)], and to determine customer satisfaction [3.2b] produce customer satisfaction results data [7.2a]. In addition, customer-focused results [7.2] are used to help identify customer support requirements (service standards) [3.1a(2)] and better understand customer requirements and preferences [3.2c(2)].
C	Data on levels of satisfaction of customers [7.2] are monitored and analyzed to identify priorities for improvement [4.1b].
D	Recognition and rewards [5.1a(3)] should be based, in part, on customer-focused results [7.2].
E	Customer satisfaction and engagement data [7.2] are monitored, in part, to provide performance feedback to leaders and workers [5.1a(3)]. In addition, customer-focused results [7.2] can be improved with effective workforce and leader development [5.1b]. Systems to manage high-performance work [5.1a(3)] can produce higher levels of customer satisfaction [7.2]. Workforce innovation, empowerment, and initiative [5.1a] can foster better customer satisfaction and engagement [7.2].
F	Data on customer satisfaction, dissatisfaction and engagement [7.2a(1)] are used to help design work systems [6.1] and improve work process design and delivery [6.2]. These processes [6.1 and 6.2] have a direct effect on customer satisfaction, dissatisfaction, and engagement [7.2a].
G	Better product outcomes [7.1] and process effectiveness outcomes [7.5a] can enhance customer-focused results [7.2]. Better customer-focused results [7.2] can improve financial and market performance [7.3].
H	The information in P.1b(2) helps examiners identify the kind of results, broken out by customer and market segment, that should be reported in Item 7.2.

IF YOU DON'T DO WHAT THE CRITERIA REQUIRE . . .	
Item Reference	Possible Adverse Consequences
7.2	Failing to provide comparison data makes it difficult for leaders (or Baldrige examiners) to determine if the level of performance achieved is good. Failing to provide results data for at least most areas of importance to the organization makes it difficult to determine if performance is getting better in key areas. Finally, the failure to provide this information as part of a Baldrige Award assessment is likely to reduce the score and may even prevent an organization from receiving a site visit (during which time additional results data are usually obtained).

7.2 CUSTOMER-FOCUSED OUTCOMES—SAMPLE EFFECTIVE RESULTS

A. Customer-Focused Results

- Trends and indicators of customer satisfaction, dissatisfaction (including complaint data), and engagement—segmented by customer groups—are provided in graph and chart form for all key measures. Multiyear data are provided.

- All indicators show steady improvement. (Indicators include data collected in Area 3.2b, such as customer assessments of products and services, customer awards, and customer engagement.)

- All indicators compare favorably to competitors or similar providers.

- Graphs and information are accurate and easy to understand.

- Data are not missing. (For example, do not show a steady trend from 2004 to 2008, but leave out 2006.)

- Results data are supported by customer feedback, customers' overall assessments of products and services, customer awards, and indicators from design and production/delivery processes of products and services.

- Projections of future performance are included on charts and graphs in 7.2. These projections are supported by enhanced processes [6.1 and 6.2] and are consistent with strategic objectives and action plans.

> **7.3 FINANCIAL AND MARKET OUTCOMES: What are your financial and marketplace performance results? (70 Pts.)** **RESULTS**
>
> Summarize your organization's key financial and marketplace performance results by market segments or customer groups, as appropriate. Include appropriate comparative data.
>
> Provide data and information to answer the following questions:
>
> a. **Financial and Market Results**
>
> (1) What are your current levels and trends in key measures or indicators of financial performance, including aggregate measures of financial return, financial viability, or budgetary performance, as appropriate?
>
> (2) What are your current levels and trends in key measures or indicators of marketplace performance, including market share or position, market and market share growth, and new markets entered, as appropriate?
>
> **Notes:**
>
> N1. Responses to 7.3a(1) might include aggregate measures of financial return, such as return on investment (ROI), operating margins, profitability, or profitability by market segment or customer group. Responses also might include measures of financial viability, such as liquidity, debt-to-equity ratio, days cash on hand, asset utilization, and cash flow. Measures should relate to the financial measures reported in 4.1a(1) and the financial management approaches described in Item 2.2. For nonprofit organizations, additional measures might include performance to budget, reserve funds, cost avoidance or savings, administrative expenditures as a percentage of budget, and cost of fundraising versus funds raised.
>
> N2. For nonprofit organizations, responses to 7.3a(2) might include measures of charitable donations or grants and the number of new programs or services offered.

Item 7.3 looks at the organization's key financial and market results to provide a complete picture of financial sustainability and marketplace success and challenges.

Organizations should provide data demonstrating levels, trends, and appropriate comparisons for key financial, market, and business indicators. Measures reported in this Item are used by senior leaders to assess organization-level financial performance and viability.

- Appropriate financial measures and indicators might include:
  - Revenues (income)
  - Budgets (planned versus actual expenditures)
  - Profits or losses (reserves)
  - Cash position (cash flow)
  - Order-to-cash cycle time
  - Cost per person served
  - Debt leverage
  - Earnings per share
  - Financial returns
- Market performance measures might include:
  - Market share
  - Measures of business growth
  - New products, programs, or services and markets entered (including e-markets and exports)
  - Percent of sales from new products, programs, or services
  - Charitable donations or grants received

Organizations should provide appropriate comparisons for key measures and/or indicators to permit the assessment of the strength or *goodness* of the organization's performance.

Organizations should also provide projections of future performance for all key results. These projections correlate with and relate to strategic objectives, goals, and organizational sustainability.

7.3 Financial and Market Outcomes

Results of improvement efforts using key measures and/or indicators of financial and market performance

Financial results are derived from all organization processes (and are considered "lagging" performance indicators)

→ Create graphs and tables that display current levels and trends in key measures of financial [7.3a(1)] and market performance [7.3a(2)], such as:

- Return on investments, economic value added, profitability, liquidity [7.3 notes]
- Market share/position, business growth, and new markets entered [7.3a(2)]

↓

Each graph and table should contain comparative references so that results can be evaluated; indicate if the comparative data are considered a world-class benchmark (best in the business), an industry standard (acceptable practice), or industry norm (average performance) (derived from benchmarking [4.1a(2)]). Also provide projections of future performance that relate to strategic objectives and goals. [7.3]

← Use the information for planning [2.1a(2)], monitoring performance [1.1b(2)], setting priorities, and improving performance [4.1b, c]

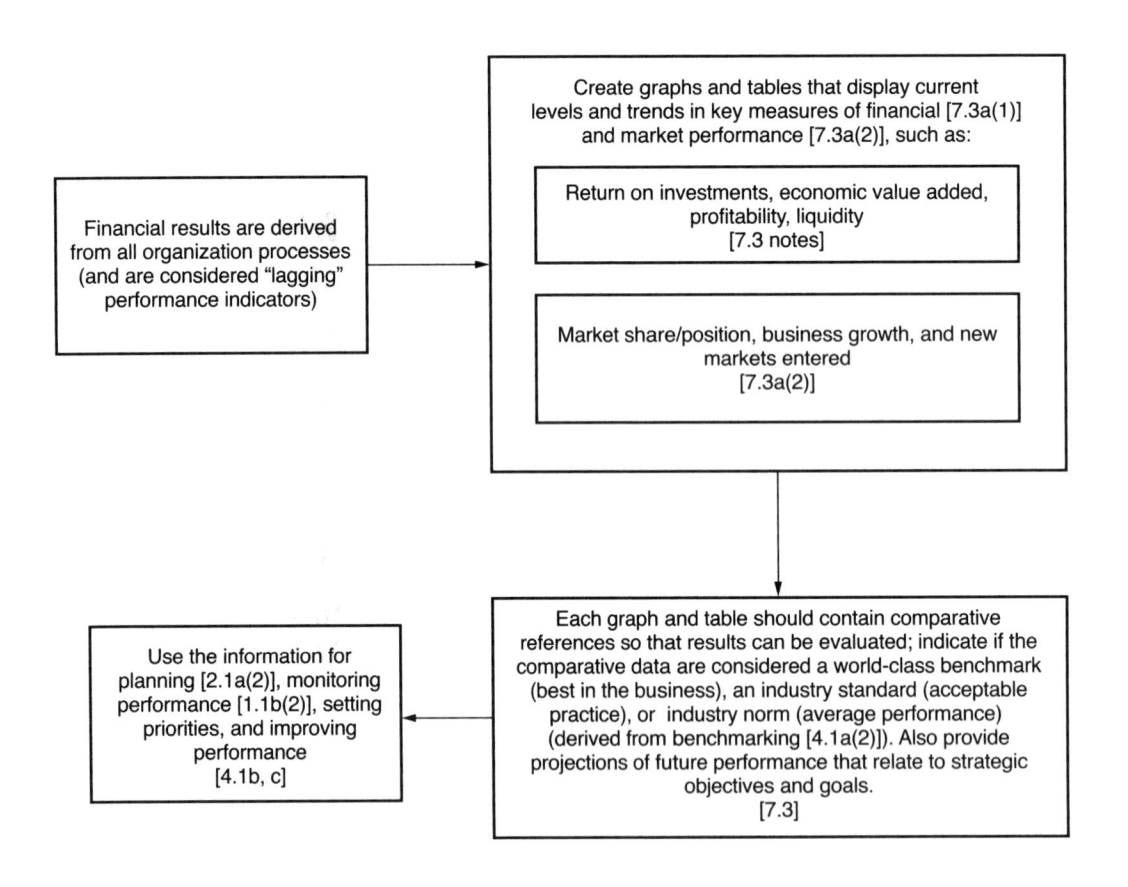

7.3 Key Financial and Market Outcomes Item Linkages

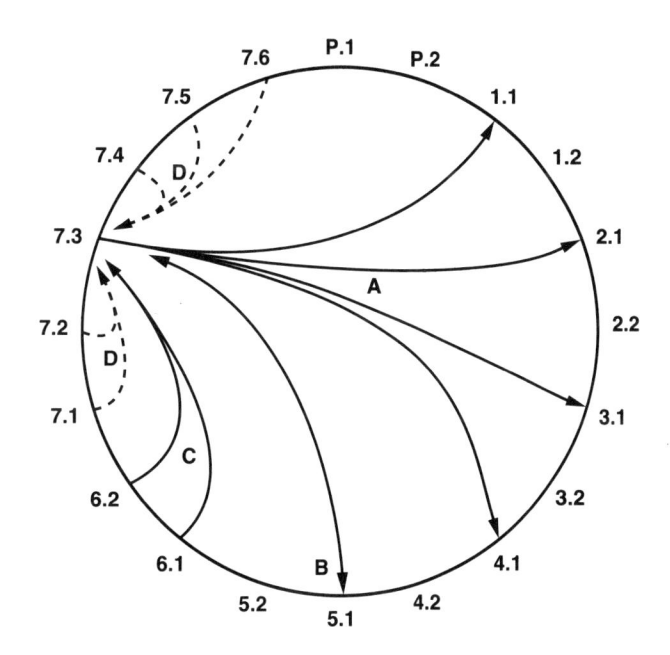

	NATURE OF RELATIONSHIP
A	Financial [7.3a(1)] and market [7.3a(2)] results are monitored by senior leaders [1.2b(2)], and used for strategic planning [2.1a(2)]; understanding market requirements and customer preferences [3.2]; and monitoring, priority setting, and analysis [4.1b].
B	Financial results [7.3a(1)] and market results [7.3a(2)] are monitored, in part, to assess training effectiveness [5.1b(1, 2)] and could be used as a partial basis for compensation, recognition, and reward [5.1a(3)]. In addition, results pertaining to financial and market performance [7.3a], reflect, in part, training effectiveness [5.1b(1, 2, 3)]. Workforce engagement and satisfaction [5.1a(1)] affect financial and market performance results [7.3a], and vice versa.
C	Financial [7.3a(1)] and market [7.3a(2)] results are enhanced by improvements in work system design [6.1] and key work processes [6.2]. Those processes may be modified or improved based on financial and market performance.
D	Better financial [7.3a(1)] and market [7.3a(2)] results (lagging indicators) can be driven by better customer satisfaction [7.2], product quality [7.1], worker engagement [7.4], operational effectiveness [7.5], and compliance with laws and regulations and good ethical behavior [7.6].

	IF YOU DON'T DO WHAT THE CRITERIA REQUIRE . . .
Item Reference	Possible Adverse Consequences
7.3	Failing to provide comparison data makes it difficult for leaders (or Baldrige examiners) to determine if the level of performance reported is good. Failing to provide results data for at least most areas of importance to the organization makes it difficult to determine if performance is getting better in key areas. Finally, the failure to provide this information as part of a Baldrige Award assessment is likely to reduce the score and may even prevent an organization from receiving a site visit (during which time additional results data are usually obtained).

7.3 FINANCIAL AND MARKET OUTCOMES—SAMPLE EFFECTIVE RESULTS

A. Financial and Market Results

- Key measures and indicators of organization market and financial performance address the following areas:
  - Effective use of materials, energy, capital, and assets
  - Asset utilization
  - Market share, business growth, new markets entered, and market shifting
  - Return on equity
  - Operating margins (income minus expenses)
  - Pre-tax profit (surplus)
  - Earnings per share
  - Generating enough revenue to cover expenses (nonprofit sector)
  - Operating within budget (nonprofit sector)
- Measures and indicators show steady improvement.
- All key financial and market data are presented.
- Comparative data include industry-best, best-competitor, and other appropriate benchmarks.
- Data are not missing. (For example, do not show a steady trend from 2004 to 2008, but leave out 2006.)
- Projections of expected levels of future performance are provided for all key results. These projections correlate with planned improvements or initiatives and relate to strategic objectives and goals and organizational stability.

7.4 WORKFORCE-FOCUSED OUTCOMES: What are your workforce-focused performance results? (70 Pts.) **RESULTS**

Summarize your organization's key workforce-focused results for workforce engagement and for your workforce environment. Segment your results to address the diversity of your workforce and to address your workforce groups and segments, as appropriate. Include appropriate comparative data.

Provide data and information to answer the following questions:

a. Workforce Results

(1) What are your current levels and trends in key measures or indicators of workforce engagement and workforce satisfaction?

(2) What are your current levels and trends in key measures or indicators of workforce and leader development?

(3) What are your current levels and trends in key measures of workforce capability and capacity, including staffing levels and appropriate skills?

(4) What are your current levels and trends in key measures or indicators of your workforce climate, including workforce health, safety, and security and workforce services and benefits, as appropriate?

Notes:

N1. Results reported in this Item should relate to processes described in Category 5. Your results should be responsive to key work process needs described in Category 6 and to your organization's action plans and human resource or workforce plans described in Item 2.2.

N2. Responses to 7.4a(1) should include measures and indicators identified in response to 5.1c(1).

N3. *Nonprofit organizations that rely on volunteers should include results for their volunteer workforce, as appropriate.*

Item 7.4 looks at the organization's workforce-focused outcomes to demonstrate how well the organization has created, maintained, and enhanced a productive, engaging, learning, and caring work environment.

Organizations should provide data demonstrating current levels, trends, and appropriate comparisons for key measures and/or indicators of workforce engagement, satisfaction, dissatisfaction, and development. Organizations should also provide data and information on the organization's workforce engagement performance and effectiveness, showing favorable comparisons with industry leaders.

Results measures reported for indicators of workforce engagement and satisfaction might include: improvement in local decision making (both decision quality and increased decision-making authority), organizational culture, and workforce or leader development.

Organization-specific factors might be those that are assessed and reported for workforce engagement and climate, and might include extent of training, re-training, or cross-training to meet capability and capacity requirements; the extent and success of self-direction; and the extent of volunteer involvement in process and program activities. Results reported might include input data, such as extent of training, but the emphasis should be on data that show effectiveness and improvement of outcomes, not inputs. For example, one measure might be productivity enhancements or cost savings realized from the redesign of work processes by work teams, new skills acquired, pre-training/post-training knowledge acquisition, and increased use of new skills on the job. Another example of an outcome measure might be increased workforce retention resulting from establishing a peer recognition program or the number of promotions that have resulted from the organization's leadership development program.

Results reported for workforce engagement and satisfaction might include generic factors such as: safety, absenteeism, turnover, satisfaction ratings of work climate, and complaints (grievances). For measures such as absenteeism and turnover, local or regional comparisons may be most appropriate. Other factors important to the workforce, such as data on wage-scale comparisons with industry standards, or perceived job security, may be important to report.

Organizations should provide appropriate comparisons for key measures and/or indicators to permit the assessment of the strength or *goodness* of the organization's performance.

Organizations should also provide projections of future performance for all key results. These projections correlate with and relate to strategic objectives, goals, and organizational sustainability.

7.4 Workforce-Focused Outcomes

Results of workforce improvement efforts using key measures and/or indicators of workforce engagement and the workforce environment

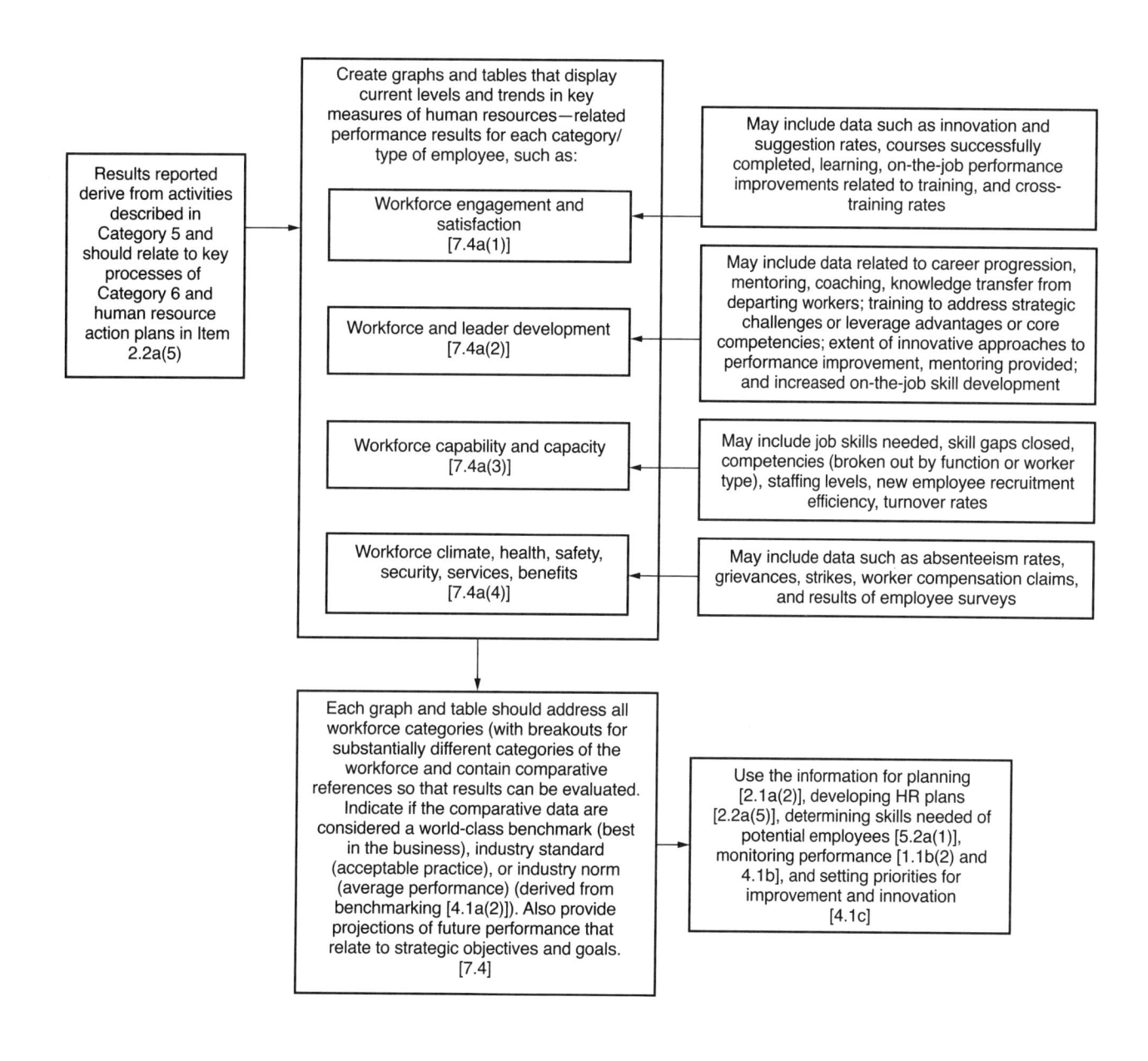

- Results reported derive from activities described in Category 5 and should relate to key processes of Category 6 and human resource action plans in Item 2.2a(5)

→ Create graphs and tables that display current levels and trends in key measures of human resources—related performance results for each category/type of employee, such as:

- Workforce engagement and satisfaction [7.4a(1)] ← May include data such as innovation and suggestion rates, courses successfully completed, learning, on-the-job performance improvements related to training, and cross-training rates

- Workforce and leader development [7.4a(2)] ← May include data related to career progression, mentoring, coaching, knowledge transfer from departing workers; training to address strategic challenges or leverage advantages or core competencies; extent of innovative approaches to performance improvement, mentoring provided; and increased on-the-job skill development

- Workforce capability and capacity [7.4a(3)] ← May include job skills needed, skill gaps closed, competencies (broken out by function or worker type), staffing levels, new employee recruitment efficiency, turnover rates

- Workforce climate, health, safety, security, services, benefits [7.4a(4)] ← May include data such as absenteeism rates, grievances, strikes, worker compensation claims, and results of employee surveys

↓

Each graph and table should address all workforce categories (with breakouts for substantially different categories of the workforce and contain comparative references so that results can be evaluated. Indicate if the comparative data are considered a world-class benchmark (best in the business), industry standard (acceptable practice), or industry norm (average performance) (derived from benchmarking [4.1a(2)]). Also provide projections of future performance that relate to strategic objectives and goals. [7.4]

→ Use the information for planning [2.1a(2)], developing HR plans [2.2a(5)], determining skills needed of potential employees [5.2a(1)], monitoring performance [1.1b(2) and 4.1b], and setting priorities for improvement and innovation [4.1c]

Insights to Performance Excellence 2009–2010

7.4 Key Workforce-Focused Outcomes Item Linkages

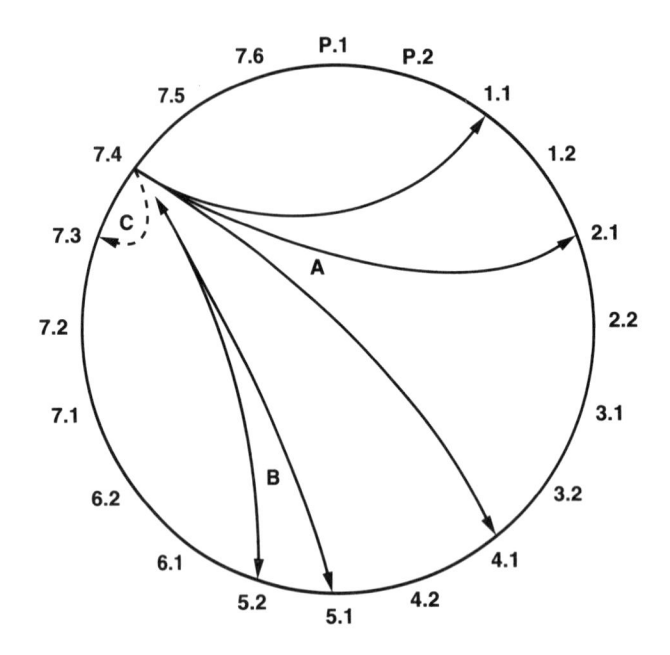

	NATURE OF RELATIONSHIP
A	Workforce-focused results [7.4] are reported and used for planning [2.1a(2)], for monitoring organizational performance [1.1b(2)], and for analysis [4.1b] and setting priorities for improvement [4.1c].
B	Workforce-focused outcomes derive from and are enhanced by stronger workforce engagement [5.1] and capacity and capability, by strengthening worker recognition systems [5.1a(3)], training and development [5.1b(3)], and engagement and satisfaction [5.1]. In addition, human resource results data [7.4] are monitored, in part, to assess training effectiveness [5.2].
C	Better financial [7.3a] and market [7.3b] results (lagging indicators) can be enhanced by better workforce engagement and satisfaction [7.4].

IF YOU DON'T DO WHAT THE CRITERIA REQUIRE...	
Item Reference	**Possible Adverse Consequences**
7.4	Failing to provide comparison data makes it difficult for leaders (or Baldrige examiners) to determine if the level of performance reported is good or not. Failing to provide results data for at least most areas of importance to the organization makes it difficult to determine if performance is getting better in key areas. Finally, the failure to provide this information as part of a Baldrige Award assessment is likely to reduce the score and may even prevent an organization from receiving a site visit (during which time additional results data are usually obtained).

7.4 WORKFORCE-FOCUSED OUTCOMES—SAMPLE EFFECTIVE RESULTS

A. Workforce Results

- The results reported in Item 7.4 are primarily aligned with activities described in Category 5 and the human resource plans from Item 2.2a(5).

- Multiyear data are provided to show sustained performance.

- All results show steady improvement.

- Data are not missing. (For example, do not show a steady trend from 2004 to 2008, but leave out 2006.) If human resource results are declared important, related data are reported.

- Comparison data for benchmark or competitor organizations are reported, and the organization compares favorably.

- Trend data are reported for employee satisfaction with working conditions, safety, retirement package, and other worker benefits. Satisfaction with management is also reported.

- Trends for declining absenteeism, grievances, worker turnover, strikes, and worker compensation claims are reported.

- Data reported are segmented for all workforce categories.

- Being recognized as one of the top organizations in America to work for provides some evidence of excellent human resource results.

- Projections of expected levels of future performance are provided for all key results. These projections correlate with planned improvements or initiatives and relate to strategic objectives and goals and organizational stability.

7.5 PROCESS EFFECTIVENESS OUTCOMES: What are your process effectiveness results? (70 Pts.) — RESULTS

Summarize your organization's key operational performance results that contribute to the improvement of organizational effectiveness, including your organization's readiness for emergencies. Segment your results by product offerings, by customer groups and market segments, and by processes and location, as appropriate. Include appropriate comparative data.

Provide data and information to answer the following questions:

a. Process Effectiveness Results

(1) What are your current levels and trends in key measures or indicators of the operational performance of your work systems, including work system and workplace preparedness for disasters or emergencies?

(2) What are your current levels and trends in key measures or indicators of the operational performance of your key work processes, including productivity, cycle time, and other appropriate measures of process effectiveness, efficiency, and innovation?

Notes:

N1. Results reported in Item 7.5 should address your key operational requirements as presented in the Organizational Profile and in Items 6.1 and 6.2. Include results not reported in Items 7.1–7.4.

N2. Results reported in Item 7.5 should provide key information for analysis and review of your organizational performance [Item 4.1]; demonstrate use of organizational knowledge (Item 4.2); and provide the operational basis for product outcomes [Item 7.1], customer-focused outcomes [Item 7.2], and financial and market outcomes [Item 7.3].

N3. Appropriate measures and indicators of work system performance (7.5a[1]) might include audit, just-in-time delivery, and acceptance results for externally provided products, services, and processes; supplier and partner performance; product, service, and work system innovation rates and results; simplification of internal jobs and job classifications; work layout improvements; changing supervisory ratios; response times for emergency drills or exercises; and results for work relocation or contingency exercises.

Item 7.5 looks at the organization's key operational performance results to demonstrate organizational effectiveness in key work processes. Organizations should provide data in this Item if they do not belong in other Category 7 Items (7.1, 7.2, 7.3, 7.4, or 7.6).

This Item encourages the organization to develop and include unique and innovative measures to track organizational development, key processes, and operational improvement. However, all key areas of organizational and operational performance should be covered by measures that are relevant and important to the organization. This includes the organization's readiness for emergencies.

Measures and/or indicators of process effectiveness and efficiency might include:

- Internal responsiveness indicators such as cycle-time reduction, production flexibility, lead times, set-up times, and time to market

- Work system performance demonstrating improved cost savings or higher productivity by using internal or external resources

- Reduced emission levels, waste stream reductions, by-product use, and recycling

- Business-specific indicators such as innovation rates and increased use of e-technology, product and process yields, Six Sigma and Lean initiative results related to quality, cost, and timeliness, and acceptable product performance at time of delivery (fit for use)

- Supply-chain indicators such as reductions in inventory and incoming inspections, increases in quality and productivity, improvements in electronic data exchange, and reductions in supply-chain management costs

- Valid third-party assessment results such as ISO 9001 audits and feedback from rigorous Baldrige-based in-company or state quality awards

- Improved performance of administrative and other support functions

Organizations should provide appropriate comparisons for key measures and/or indicators to permit the assessment of the strength or *goodness* of the organization's performance.

Organizations should also provide projections of future performance for all key results. These projections correlate with and relate to strategic objectives, goals, and organizational sustainability.

Do not report results in 7.5 that belong elsewhere. For example, if on-time product delivery is a key customer requirement, it should be reported in 7.1.

7.5 Process Effectiveness Outcomes

Results of improvement efforts that contribute to achievement of organizational effectiveness and emergency readiness

Organizational Effectiveness Results

Create graphs and tables that display current levels of sustained trends of key operational performance results that contribute to strategic objectives

Key operational performance improvement results are derived from the performance of work systems and emergency preparedness in Items 6.1, including audit, just-in-time delivery acceptance results for suppliers, work system innovation rates, job simplification and layout, changing supervisory ratios, response times for emergency drills, and results for relocation or contingency exercises.
[7.5a(1)]

Key operational performance results are derived from key work processes in Item 6.2, including productivity, cycle time, supplier and partner performance, and other efficiency and effectiveness measures important to the organization
[7.5a(2)]

Each graph and table should contain comparative references so that results can be evaluated; indicate if the comparative data are considered a world-class benchmark (best in the business), or industry norm (average performance) (derived from benchmarking [4.1a(2)]). Also provide projections of future performance that relate to strategic objectives and goals.
[7.5]

Results provide data for analysis, performance monitoring [1.1b(2)]. review, and improvement [4.1b], compensation and workforce recognition [5.1a(3)], training effectiveness evaluation [5.1b(1, 2)], and improving key work process performance [6.2c]

Insights to Performance Excellence 2009–2010

7.5 Key Process Effectiveness Outcomes Item Linkages

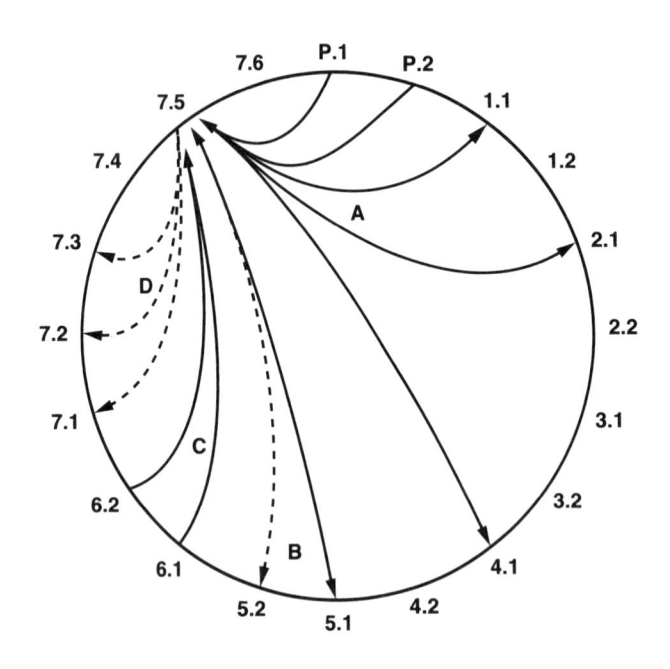

	NATURE OF RELATIONSHIP
A	Process effectiveness outcomes [7.5] are monitored by senior leaders [1.1b(2)], reported and used for planning [2.1a(2)], management improvement, performance monitoring and analysis [4.1b] and priority setting [4.1c]. Performance related to the key suppliers, partners, and other collaborators listed in P.1b(3) should be reported in 7.5a(1)].
B	Process effectiveness outcomes [7.5] are used to provide employee feedback and drive rewards and recognition [5.1a(3)] and identify areas to emphasize in workforce and leader development [5.1b(1, 2)]. Processes to improve employee engagement and worker safety, security, morale, motivation, and well-being [5.2b(1, 2)], and better align recognition and reward to desired performance outcomes [5.1a(3)] may enhance process effectiveness outcomes [7.5].
C	Designing work systems to meet customer requirements [6.1a(1)] and improving product and service delivery and consistency [6.2a(1)] should affect process effectiveness outcomes [7.5].
D	Process effectiveness outcomes [7.5] contribute to financial and market results [7.3], product performance [7.1], and customer-focused results [7.2].

IF YOU DON'T DO WHAT THE CRITERIA REQUIRE...

Item Reference	Possible Adverse Consequences
7.5	Failing to provide comparison data makes it difficult for leaders (or Baldrige examiners) to determine if the level of performance reported is good. Failing to provide results data for at least most areas of importance to the organization makes it difficult to determine if performance is getting better in key areas. Finally, the failure to provide this information as part of a Baldrige Award assessment is likely to reduce the score and may even prevent an organization from receiving a site visit (during which time additional results data are usually obtained).

7.5 PROCESS EFFECTIVENESS OUTCOMES—SAMPLE EFFECTIVE RESULTS

A. Process Effectiveness Results

- Indices and trend data are provided in graph and chart form for all operational performance measures identified in 4.1, 6.1, and 6.2, and the key business factors identified in the Organizational Profile and not reported elsewhere in Category 7. Multiyear data are reported.

- Most to all indicators show steady improvement.

- Measures and indicators address requirements such as accuracy, timeliness, and reliability. Examples include defect levels, repeat services, meeting product or service delivery or response times, and availability levels. *However, if these measures predict customer satisfaction, they should be moved to Item 7.1.*

- Operational performance measures address:

  – Productivity, efficiency, and effectiveness, such as productivity indices, and product/service design-improvement measures

  – Cycle-time reductions

- Comparative data include industry best, best competitor, industry average, and appropriate benchmarks. Data are also derived from independent surveys, studies, laboratory testing, or other sources.

- Data are not missing. (For example, do not show a steady trend from 2004 to 2008, but leave out 2006.)

- Data are not aggregated, since aggregation tends to hide poor performance by blending it with good performance. Charts and graphs break out and report trends separately.

- Projections of expected levels of future performance are provided for all key results. These projections correlate with planned improvements or initiatives and relate to strategic objectives and goals and organizational stability.

7.6 LEADERSHIP OUTCOMES: What are your leadership results? (70 Pts.)   **RESULTS**

Summarize your organization's key governance and senior leadership results, including evidence of strategic plan accomplishments, fiscal accountability, legal compliance, ethical behavior, societal responsibility, and support of key communities. Segment your results by organizational units, as appropriate. Include appropriate comparative data.

Provide data and information to answer the following questions:

a. **Leadership and Societal Responsibility Results**

  (1) What are your results for key measures or indicators of accomplishment of your organizational strategy and action plans?

  (2) What are your key current findings and trends in key measures or indicators of governance and fiscal accountability, both internal and external, as appropriate?

  (3) What are your results for key measures or indicators of regulatory and legal compliance?

  (4) What are your results for key measures or indicators of ethical behavior and of stakeholder trust in the senior leaders and governance of your organization? What are your results for key measures or indicators of breaches of ethical behavior?

  (5) What are your results for key measures or indicators of your organization's fulfillment of its societal responsibilities and your organization's support of its key communities?

Notes:

N1. Measures or indicators of strategy and action plan accomplishment [7.6a(1)] should address your strategic objectives and goals identified in 2.1b(1) and your action plan performance measures and projected performance identified in 2.2a(6) and 2.2b, respectively.

N2. Responses to 7.6a(2) might include financial statement issues and risks, important internal and external auditor recommendations, and management's responses to these matters. *For some nonprofit organizations, results of IRS 990 audits also might be included.*

N3. Regulatory and legal compliance results [7.6a(3)] should address requirements described in 1.2b. Workforce-related occupational health and safety results (for example, Occupational Safety and Health Administration (OSHA) reportable incidents) should be reported in 7.4a(4).

N4. For examples of measures of ethical behavior and stakeholder trust [7.6a(4)], see Item 1.2, Note 4.

N5. Responses to 7.6a(5) should address your organization's societal responsibilities discussed in 1.2b(1) and 1.2c(1), as well as support of the key communities discussed in 1.2c(2). Measures of contributions to societal well-being might include reduced energy consumption; the use of renewable energy resources, recycled water, and alternative approaches to conserve resources (for example, increased audio and video conferencing); and the global use of enlightened labor practices.

Item 7.6 looks at leadership and governance outcomes that reflect the behavior of a fiscally sound and ethical organization that is a good citizen in its communities. In this Item, provide data and information on key measures or indicators of organizational accountability, stakeholder trust, and ethical behavior as well as regulatory and legal compliance and citizenship.

Lack of appropriate measures can be challenging for many organizations seeking to determine their progress in accomplishing strategic objectives. Often, these progress measures can be discerned by first defining the results that would indicate success in achieving the strategic objective and then using that measure to define intermediate measures. The process described in 2.1b(1) to develop outcome-based strategic objectives and timetables for implementation are essential for leaders to monitor effectively and report meaningful progress in 7.6a(1).

Data showing progress toward achieving outcome-oriented strategic objectives should be reported. Although there is an increased focus nationally on issues of governance, ethics, and board and leadership accountability, the best-performing organizations practice and demonstrate high standards of overall conduct. The failure to do so may threaten an organization's public trust, which may threaten its long-term success, if not its survival. Boards and senior leaders should track performance measures that relate to governance and societal responsibility on a regular basis and emphasize this performance in stakeholder communications.

Measures should include legal and regulatory compliance and highlight noteworthy achievements in these areas, as appropriate. Other results worth reporting might include reduced emission levels, waste-stream reductions, by-product use, recycling, and OSHA compliance, to name a few. All sanctions or adverse audit findings should be reported.

Summarize and report any sanctions or adverse findings (including independent audit findings) under law, regulation, or contract the organization has received during the past three years, including the nature of the incidents and their current status.

Results also should include indicators of support for key communities and other public purposes. These might include charts showing increased levels of time that leaders and workers commit to volunteer activities, increased levels of support to community-based service organizations, and increased support for community health care, education, and the arts, for example.

Organizations should provide appropriate comparisons for key measures and/or indicators to permit the assessment of the strength or *goodness* of the organization's performance.

Organizations should also provide projections of future performance for all key results. These projections correlate with and relate to strategic objectives, goals, and organizational sustainability.

7.6 Leadership Outcomes

Results of governance and senior leadership efforts that contribute to achievement of strategy and action plans, fiscal accountability, ethical behavior, legal compliance, societal responsibility, and organizational citizenship

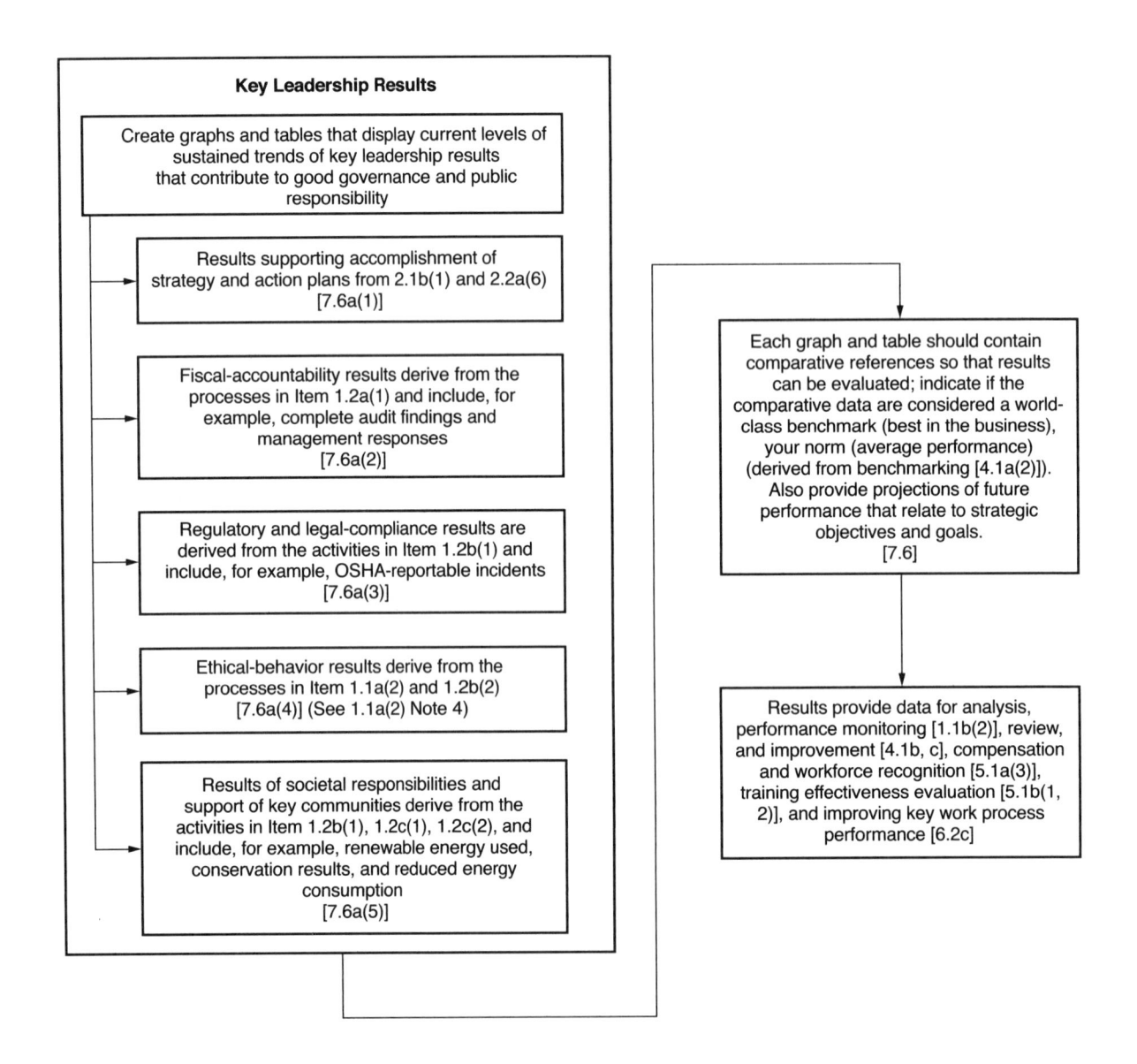

Key Leadership Results

Create graphs and tables that display current levels of sustained trends of key leadership results that contribute to good governance and public responsibility

- Results supporting accomplishment of strategy and action plans from 2.1b(1) and 2.2a(6) [7.6a(1)]
- Fiscal-accountability results derive from the processes in Item 1.2a(1) and include, for example, complete audit findings and management responses [7.6a(2)]
- Regulatory and legal-compliance results are derived from the activities in Item 1.2b(1) and include, for example, OSHA-reportable incidents [7.6a(3)]
- Ethical-behavior results derive from the processes in Item 1.1a(2) and 1.2b(2) [7.6a(4)] (See 1.1a(2) Note 4)
- Results of societal responsibilities and support of key communities derive from the activities in Item 1.2b(1), 1.2c(1), 1.2c(2), and include, for example, renewable energy used, conservation results, and reduced energy consumption [7.6a(5)]

Each graph and table should contain comparative references so that results can be evaluated; indicate if the comparative data are considered a world-class benchmark (best in the business), your norm (average performance) (derived from benchmarking [4.1a(2)]). Also provide projections of future performance that relate to strategic objectives and goals. [7.6]

Results provide data for analysis, performance monitoring [1.1b(2)], review, and improvement [4.1b, c], compensation and workforce recognition [5.1a(3)], training effectiveness evaluation [5.1b(1, 2)], and improving key work process performance [6.2c]

7 Results

7.6 Key Leadership Outcomes Item Linkages

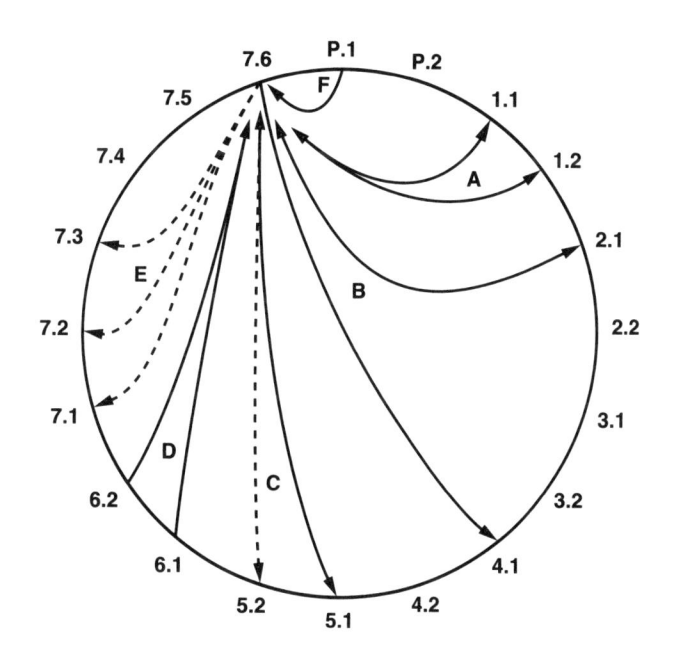

	NATURE OF RELATIONSHIP
A	Results for regulatory and legal compliance and citizenship, related to the activities in Item 1.2, should be reported in 7.5a(4). In addition, these results are monitored by senior leaders [1.1b(2)] to determine if process changes are needed.
B	Leadership results that relate to ethical behavior, fiscal accountability, and regulatory compliance [7.6a(2, 3, and 4)] are used for planning [2.1a(2)], management improvement, performance monitoring, and priority setting [4.ab] and improvement [4.1c]. Progress in addressing strategic objectives listed in 2.1b(1), should be reported in Item 7.6a(1).
C	Workforce engagement and satisfaction [5.1a(3)] affect societal responsibility results and may affect ethical behavior and regulatory compliance [7.6a(3 and 4)]. In addition, results pertaining to these key areas [7.6] should be monitored to identify needs for benefits and services [5.2b(1)] and highlight workforce and leader development needs [5.1b(1, 2)].
D	Work system design [6.1] and key work process management systems [6.2] affect regulatory compliance and possible ethical behavior [7.6a(4 and 3)].
E	Leadership results [7.6] may affect financial and market results [7.3], product performance [7.1], and customer-focused results [7.2].
F	The regulatory requirements described in P.1a(5) define the related performance results that should be reported in 7.6a(3).

	IF YOU DON'T DO WHAT THE CRITERIA REQUIRE...
Item Reference	**Possible Adverse Consequences**
7.6	Failing to provide comparison data makes it difficult for leaders (or Baldrige examiners) to determine if the level of performance reported is good. Failing to provide results data for at least most areas of importance to the organization makes it difficult to determine if performance is getting better in key areas. Finally, the failure to provide this information as part of a Baldrige Award assessment is likely to reduce the score and may even prevent an organization from receiving a site visit (during which time additional results data are usually obtained).

7.6 LEADERSHIP OUTCOMES—SAMPLE EFFECTIVE RESULTS

A. Leadership and Societal Responsibility Results

- Indices and trend data are provided in graph and chart form for all regulatory and legal compliance requirements identified in Item 1.2b(1) and P.1a(5) and relevant strategic objectives (2.1b).

- Results address public responsibilities such as environmental improvements and the increased use of technologies, materials, and work processes that are environmentally friendly.

- A large percentage of board members are independent; that is, not part of the organization's operational structure. Independent audits demonstrate full compliance with ethics rules established by the organization.

- Areas of community support demonstrate increasing efforts to strengthen local community services, education, and health care, the environment, and related trade and business associations.

- Data indicate most measures of regulatory compliance exceed requirements. Performance is leading the industry. No sanctions or violations have been reported.

- Data show sustained improvements in waste reduction and energy efficiency.

- Resources allocated to support key communities, consistent with business strategy, demonstrate positive desired results, increasing in effectiveness over time.

- Comparative data include industry best, best competitor, industry average, and appropriate benchmarks. Data are also derived from independent surveys, studies, laboratory testing, or other sources.

- Data are not missing. (For example, do not show a steady trend from 2004 to 2008, but leave out 2006.)

- Data are not aggregated, since aggregation tends to hide poor performance by blending it with good performance. Charts and graphs break out and report trends separately.

- Projections of expected levels of future performance are provided for all key results. These projections correlate with planned improvements or initiatives and relate to strategic objectives and goals and organizational stability.

Tips on Preparing a Baldrige Award Application

Applications are put together by every conceivable combination of teams, committees, and individual efforts, including consultants. There is no *right* or *best* way to do it. There are, however, lessons that have been learned and are worth considering because they contribute to people and organizations growing and improving.

Author's note: Gathering process information from across the organization is essential to prepare an accurate and complete Baldrige application. Over the past several years, I have helped many organizations conduct assessments and apply for awards. During this time, I have prepared a Microsoft Word template to help writing teams gather information and prepare to write. This application template, provided on the CD that is included with this book, facilitates the collection of critical information and makes it easier to write an accurate Baldrige application. A sample of the completed portion of the template appears in Figure 34 on the next page. Templates are available for education and health care as well.

The thoughts that follow are intended to generate conversation and learning. They are not intended to present a comprehensive treatment of the subject.

Start Writing Early

I have never worked with an applicant that complained they started too early. However, everyone seems to wish they had more time. The task of writing, editing, and publishing the application takes the least amount of time. Deciding what to write and reviewing and improving processes takes much more time. Allow four to six months of part-time effort.

Getting the Fingerprints of the Organization on the Application

How do we put together a *good* application? To be *good* from a technical perspective, it must both be accurate and respond fully to the multiple requirements of the Criteria. It must convey to examiners a succinct description of the organization's management system. It must be clear and internally consistent.

To be effective, the application must be more than technically accurate. The organization must reflect a sense of commitment and ownership for the application. Ownership requires a role for people throughout the organization as well as top leadership. The actual *putting of words on paper* can be accomplished in a variety of ways. However, ignoring this larger question of ownership exposes the organization to developing a sterile, disjointed, or unrecognizable document that diminishes its value as a vehicle of growth.

The Spirit and Values in an Application

Like it or not, many in the organization will be closely watching the team or individual that is responsible for developing an application. The people coordinating the development of the application need to be perceived as *walking the talk*. They need to be seen as believers and role models for what is being written. The application should reflect the following:

- *Continuous improvement must be fully embedded into all management and work processes.* Do not make the common mistake of only describing how the processes work today. Make sure that the methods used to evaluate each key process are briefly described. Then list the key requirements that were used to improve the process based on the evaluation. Be sure to describe innovative approaches you have developed and explain why they are perceived as innovative.

- The application describes the system used to run the business. This includes not just a description of the pieces, but also the linkages among the

Insights to Performance Excellence 2009–2010

2009 Baldrige Application Development Template*
Item 1.1a—Vision and Values

How Senior Leaders:	Set
Organizational Values	Initially set by a cross-functional working group of top leaders, board members, customers, suppliers, and workers at a planning retreat organized by the leadership team. The application of values is reviewed at quarterly progress reviews and updated annually in planning process.
Vision	Set as part of the strategic planning process (step 1) and validated by the board of directors and the executive steering committee.

How Senior Leaders:	Deploy Vision and Values through the Leadership System
To the Workforce	All-hands meetings with a discussion and examples of vision and values on the agenda. A discussion of progress toward vision during each worker performance review and during the two-way *skip-a-level* semiannual meetings.
To Key Suppliers	During the annual supplier/partner excellence forum conducted by top leaders and as needed based on performance.
To Partners/Collaborators	During the annual supplier/partner excellence forum conducted by top leaders and as needed based on performance.
To Customers	During rotating customer-appreciation meetings. Meetings with each key customer are held at least quarterly, more often for major customers. Smaller customers receive reminder tokens such as desk calendars, pens, letter openers, and so on, featuring values and vision as well as hot line access numbers.

How Personal Actions of Senior Leaders Reflect Organizational Values	Behavior/Actions
Value 1: We are Customer-focused	• Personally meet with key customers every week. • Every meeting agenda has a section relating to progress in meeting and exceeding customer requirements. • Customer satisfaction is a required key performance element for all managers and supervisors. • No manager can be considered for promotion or pay raises unless his or her customer satisfaction target has been met (both internal and external customers).
Value 2: Innovation is Everyone's Responsibility	• Have set a requirement that every manager and worker, as a part of normal work, must improve one aspect of work each year. This is a part of every performance plan and appraisal. Worker or manager cannot fully meet expectations without improving one aspect of his or her work.
Value 3: Value Workers and Promote Empowerment	• Conduct an annual review of decisions and decision authority. Require managers to develop the decision skills of subordinates and increase the number of decisions made at lower levels. This is a part of the senior leader's personal performance plan and the plan of every manager and supervisor. Top leaders monitor progress quarterly and provide counseling to managers who are not meeting expectations. • Conduct pulse survey of worker satisfaction in a different part of the organization each month and work with managers to improve weakest areas. • Personally receive worker feedback on aspects of personal leadership effectiveness including fairness, communication, commitment to values, accessibility, and openness to new ideas.

Figure 34   Example of Completed Section of the Application Development Template for Item 1.1a(1).

*Note: See the CD-ROM in the back of this book for the complete Baldrige Application Development Templates.

activities that make the organization function effectively.

- Put your best foot forward, but do not exaggerate.

Core Values and Recurring Themes

In a document as complex and fact-filled as a Baldrige Award application, make sure key messages are clearly communicated. There are 11 Core Values and the application should address and reflect all of them. The organization needs to decide at the onset what key messages reflect the drivers of business success. These key messages should be reflected in each Category and tie together the entire application. This is one of the reasons it becomes so important to design and write the Organizational Profile early and well. Too many applicants ignore the importance of the Organizational Profile as a tool for ensuring alignment and integration within the application. An effective Organizational Profile clearly identifies those things that are important to the organization, its customers and stakeholders, and future success. These selected themes guide the development of the application. We are often asked, "How many themes should an organization include?" The answer depends on how many the organization actually uses. Try starting with three.

It is important to remember that the information presented in the Organizational Profile causes examiners to *expect* certain things in the application. For example, if the organization states it has three customer groups, examiners expect to see processes the organization uses to understand the requirements of all three [3.2c(2)]; assess the satisfaction [3.2b(1)] and dissatisfaction [3.2b(3)] of all three; and report product outcomes [7.1] and satisfaction/dissatisfaction [7.2] of all three.

Interim Review and Feedback

During the development of an application, conduct *tests* periodically with two groups of people: the senior executive team and individual contributor (front-line) workers.

With senior executive teams, the issue is the rate of growth of those items undergoing intensive improvement efforts and under the direct sponsorship of senior executives. Every Baldrige application effort should use the occasion of self assessment to drive significant process improvements throughout the organization. The development of an application offers an opportunity to review and improve these initiatives. Each improvement of an existing process is a candidate for inclusion in the application to demonstrate progress.

At the front-line worker level, conduct a *reality check*. Determine whether the application as written reflects the way the organization is actually run. When people are given the opportunity to review an application during the developmental stages, several things happen:

- Front-line people can comment on how closely the write-up reflects reality. It provides the writer(s) an opportunity to calibrate those words with reality.

- It allows workers to take a top-level view—which can be a learning experience in itself.

- It forces the writers to walk in the shoes of the individual contributor—again learning.

Test the Application

As an application comes together, a question asked by everyone—particularly the leadership team—is, "How well are we doing; what's the score?" Although the real value of an application is identifying opportunities for improvement, the competitive nature of people typically comes to the forefront. After all, that spirit helps drive people to higher levels of excellence. Nurture that spirit.

The best means of getting an objective review is to have people who are expert in the Baldrige process, but unbiased with respect to the organization and its processes, examine the application. It is surprising how differently outsiders view the workings of the organization. The important aspect of this review is obviously the skill of the reviewers or examiners. The value to the organization is threefold:

- An early assessment sets expectations and eliminates surprises

- Provides opportunities for an early start on improvement initiatives

- Tests the understandability by outsiders—a test that every application ultimately has to pass

Take Time to Celebrate/ Continuously Improve

Developing an application is tough work. At the end of the day, the application represents: (1) a document highlighting the accomplishments and future aspirations of the organization; (2) a plan for getting there; and (3) an operations manual for the organization (how the organization is run).

At key milestones in the development of an application, it is important to take time to celebrate the accomplishments just achieved. The celebration should be immediate, inclusive, and visible. Such a celebration raises questions within the organization, and it raises expectations—all of which are critical when trying to change and improve the overall performance of the organization. It also presents an ideal opportunity to promote improvement initiatives.

In the words of David Kearns, former CEO of Xerox and one of the world's greatest leaders of performance excellence, "Quality is a journey without an end." Every company today is faced with the struggle to bring about change—and the pace quickens each year. The Baldrige application is a mechanism that can help focus the energy for change in a most productive manner. Used properly, it can help companies break out of restrictive paradigms and continue on the journey to top levels of performance excellence.

2009–2010 CRITERIA RESPONSE GUIDELINES

The guidelines given in this section are intended to assist Criteria for Performance Excellence users in responding most effectively to the requirements of the 18 Criteria Items. Writing an application for the Baldrige Award involves responding to these requirements in 50 or fewer pages.

The guidelines from the Baldrige Award Office are presented in three parts:

1. General guidelines regarding the Criteria booklet, including how the Items are formatted
2. Guidelines for responding to Process Items
3. Guidelines for responding to Results Items

General Guidelines

Read the Entire Criteria Booklet

The main sections of the booklet provide an overall orientation to the Criteria, including how responses are to be evaluated for self-assessment or by award examiners. Become thoroughly familiar with the following Criteria booklet sections:

- Criteria for Performance Excellence (also see the Notes below each Item and the Application Development Templates contained on the CD-ROM accompanying this book)
- Scoring System (also see the Scoring Calibration Guide on the CD-ROM)
- Glossary of Key Terms (also see the explanation of confusing terms on page 341 of this book)
- Category and Item Descriptions (also see the flow charts and linkage diagrams and sample effective practices in this book)

Review the Item Format and Understand How to Respond to the Item Requirements

The Item format shows the different parts of Items, the role of each part, and where each part is placed. It is especially important to understand the multiple requirements in the Areas to Address. Item Notes are there to help users understand the Areas.

Each Item is classified as either Process (Categories 1 through 6) or Results (Category 7), depending on the type of information required. Item requirements are presented in question format. Areas to Address include multiple questions. Responses to an Item should answer all questions (however, each question need not be answered separately). Responses to multiple questions within a single Area to Address may be grouped, as appropriate to the organization. These multiple questions serve as a guide in understanding the full meaning of the information being requested.

Carefully read the information describing the linkages, sample effective practices, and process-flow diagrams presented in this book. In particular, be certain to understand how the various requirements of the Criteria are integrated into a comprehensive management system. Then gather data using the electronic application template provided with this book on the accompanying CD-ROM.

Look at applications from Baldrige recipients. All Baldrige recipients are required to publish a sanitized copy of their applications. Some publish the entire application. Visit the Baldrige Award Web site (www.quality.nist.gov) and use the hot links to recipient organizations. These applications were all written well enough to earn a site visit from the Award Office.

Start by Preparing the Organizational Profile

The Organizational Profile is the most appropriate starting point. The Organizational Profile is intended to help everyone—including organizations using the Criteria for self-assessment, application writers, and reviewers—understand what is most relevant and important to the organization's business and mission and to its performance requirements.

Guidelines for Responding to Process Items

Although the Criteria focus on key performance results, these results by themselves offer little diagnostic value. If some results are poor or are improving at rates slower than the organization's competitors' or comparable organizations', it is important to understand why, and what might be done to accelerate improvement. The answers to the Process Item questions permit the diagnosis of the organization's most important processes—those that yield fast-paced organizational performance improvement and contribute to key outcomes or performance results. Diagnosis and feedback depend heavily on the content and completeness of Item responses. For this reason, it is important to respond to these Items by providing clear, complete key process information.

Understand the Meaning of "How"

Process Items include questions that begin with the word *how*. Responses should outline key process steps that address approach, deployment, learning, and integration. Responses lacking such process detail, or merely providing an example, are referred to in the Scoring Guidelines as *anecdotal information,* and will score very low. Describe the steps in required processes. Show process detail.

Understand the Meaning of "What"

Two types of questions in Process Items begin with the word *what*. Answers to these questions provide examiners with background information to help set a context for the assessment they are about to perform. One type of question requests basic information on the elements or components of key processes. Although it may be helpful to include *who* performs the work, merely stating *who* does not permit effective diagnosis or feedback. Another type of question may also request information on key findings, plans, objectives, goals, or measures. This type of question sets the context for showing alignment and integration in the performance management system. For example, when key strategic objectives, action plans, workforce development plans, and key performance measures are identified in Categories 1 through 6, examiners will expect to find related results reported. If these *expected* results are not presented, examiners may assume they are missing and reduce the score accordingly.

The linkage (circle) diagrams in this book will help identify the systems and processes that interrelate and should be clearly aligned in the application.

Show That Processes Are Systematic

Ensure that the response describes a systematic approach, not merely an anecdotal example. Systematic approaches are disciplined, consistent, repeatable, and predictable. At the higher scoring levels it is expected that systematic approaches involve the use of data and information for evaluation, subsequent improvement, innovations, and sharing across the organization (see *Learning* below).

Show Deployment

Ensure that the response gives clear and sufficient information on deployment in different parts of the organization. One must be able to determine from a response whether the approach described is used in one, some, most, or all parts of the organization. If the process is widely used in the organization, be sure to state where it is deployed.

Deployment can be shown compactly by using summary tables that outline what is done in different parts of the organization. *This is a particularly effective supplement when the systematic approach is described in a narrative.*

Show Evidence of Learning

Processes should include fact-based evaluation *and* improvement cycles that are based on the evaluation, as well as breakthrough change (innovation). Process improvements should be shared with other appropriate units of the organization to enable organizational learning. Each key process should include a brief explanation of how fact-based evaluations occur, what is covered, a list of refinements that have been made based on the evaluations, and how those refinements have been implemented throughout the organization, as appropriate. *It is important to describe innovative approaches that have been put in place.*

An Emphasis on Innovation

The Scoring Guidelines require, at the 50 to 65 percent level, that applicants show fact-based, systematic evaluation and improvement, *including innovation* in processes. In the past, the requirement to demonstrate innovation first appeared at the 70 to 85 percent level. This means that unless the applicant describes fact-based evaluation and improvement *and an innovative approach,* it will be difficult to score above the 65 percent level in Categories 1 through 6. Accordingly, in addition to describing fact-based systems to evaluate and improve, applicants should develop responses such as the following:

1.1 Describe innovative approaches to guide and sustain the organization, communicate with the workforce, and encourage high performance

1.2 Describe innovative approaches to provide effective governance and address societal responsibilities; ensure ethical behavior; and practice good citizenship

2.1 Describe innovative approaches to identify and address strategic challenges and advantages; leverage core competencies; and establish strategy and strategic objectives that address the challenges and leverage the advantages

2.2 Describe innovative approaches to convert strategic objectives into action plans and deploy them at all levels

3.1 Describe innovative approaches to determine product offerings, support customers' use of products, and build a customer-focused culture

3.2 Describe innovative approaches to use voice of the customer to listen, understand levels of satisfaction and dissatisfaction, and improve marketplace success

4.1 Describe innovative approaches to measure, analyze, align, review, and improve performance through the use of data and information at all levels and in all parts of the organization

4.2 Describe innovative approaches to ensure the quality and availability of needed data, the software, and hardware for your workforce, suppliers, partners, collaborators, and customers; and building and managing knowledge assets

5.1 Describe innovative approaches to engage, compensate, and reward your workforce to achieve high performance; developing the workforce and leaders to achieve high performance, and assess workforce engagement and use the results to achieve higher performance

5.2 Describe innovative approaches to manage workforce capability and capacity to accomplish the work of the organization; and maintain a safe, secure, and supportive work climate

6.1 Describe innovative approaches to design work systems to deliver customer value; prepare for potential emergencies; and achieve organizational success and sustainability

6.2 Describe innovative approaches to implement, manage, and improve key work processes to deliver customer value and achieve organizational success and sustainability

Show Integration

Integration shows process, plan, measures, and action alignment and harmonization that generate organizational effectiveness and efficiencies. For example, strategic objectives listed in 2.1b(1) must address challenges in P.2b [2.1b(2)] and timetables for implementation [2.1b(1)] must be consistent with the measures of organizational performance [4.1a(1)] and the frequency of performance reviews [4.1b]. If senior leaders review progress toward a specific customer-satisfaction objective each quarter, then customer-satisfaction data should be collected at least quarterly, and timetables in 2.1b(1) should indicate the desired progress expected each quarter. Otherwise, leaders will have no fact basis for determining whether the organization is on track or not when they meet each quarter. This lack of alignment between senior leader review frequency and projected time lines is a failure of integration.

Show Focus and Consistency

A good response demonstrates that the organization is focused on key processes and on improvements that offer the greatest potential to improve organizational performance and accomplish action plans. There are four important factors to consider regarding focus and consistency:

1. The Organizational Profile should make clear what is important

2. Strategic objective, action plans should highlight areas of greatest focus and describe how deployment is accomplished

3. Descriptions of organizational-level analysis and review (Item 4.1) should show how the organization uses performance information to set priorities for improvement

4. The Process Management Category should highlight work systems and key work processes that are essential to overall performance and show how they are used to achieve strategic objectives

Showing focus and consistency in the Process Items and tracking corresponding measures in the Results Items should help align (and possibly improve) organizational performance.

Respond Fully to Item Requirements

Ensure that the response fully addresses all important parts of each Item and each Area to Address. Missing or incomplete information will be interpreted by examiners as a system deficiency—a gap and potential opportunity for improvement. All Areas to Address should be included in the application. Individual components of an Area to Address (subparts) may be addressed individually or together. When using the Application Development Template in this book it is easy to see where gaps exist. Organizations can use this information to begin closing gaps even before the examiners conduct their analysis and prepare the feedback report.

Cross-Reference When Appropriate

Although each Item response should be self-contained, some responses to different Items might be mutually reinforcing. For example, leaders may use parts of the strategy development process to set and deploy vision [1.1a(1)]. It is best to refer to the other responses, rather than to repeat information.

Use a Compact Format

Applicants should make the best use of the 50 application pages permitted. Complete sentences are not required when lists convey the information just as well. Use flowcharts, tables, and *bulletized* text to present information concisely. *Use color to focus attention. For example, whenever an improved or innovative process is described, use blue-colored text.*

Refer to the Scoring Calibration Guidelines

The evaluation of Process Item responses is accomplished by consideration of the Criteria Item requirements and the maturity of the organization's approaches, breadth of deployment, extent of learning, and integration of other elements of the performance management system, as described in the Scoring Guidelines and clarified in the Scoring Calibration Guide contained in this book and on the accompanying CD. Therefore, applicants should consider both the Criteria and the Scoring Guidelines in preparing response*s. In particular, remember that* ***to score in the 50 to 65 percent range, organizations*** *must have in place a fact-based evaluation process and corresponding improvements including some innovations (meaningful improvements) for the key processes.* The Scoring Guidelines make this requirement applicable to all Items in Categories 1 through 6. Even if the Criteria questions for the Item do not ask for a description of evaluation, improvement, and innovation, it will help the examiners give you full credit for your processes if an explanation is provided to show how the processes are systematically evaluated, subsequently refined, and meaningfully improved (innovated). List the process improvements and innovations that have been made during the last three to four years and use a colored font to focus attention.

GUIDELINES FOR RESPONDING TO RESULTS ITEMS

The Baldrige Criteria place great emphasis (and 45 percent of the score) on results. Category 7 Items call for results related to all key requirements, stakeholders, and goals. **Examiners are likely to prepare a list of results they expect to find in Category 7 based on key factors in the Organizational Profile and process details contained in Categories 1 through 6.** *They will compare their list of expected results with the data in Category 7 to determine what is missing.* (See pages 336–337.)

Focus on Reporting the Most Critical Organizational Results

Results reported should cover the most important requirements for success highlighted in the Organizational Profile and in the Strategic Planning, Customer Focus, Workforce Focus, and Process Management Categories.

Four key requirements for effective reporting of results data include the following:

- Results show performance levels on a meaningful measurement scale

- Trends to show directions of results and rates of change, together with an indicator of the desired direction and extent of deployment

- Data to show how results compare with those of other relevant organizations

- Integration, including breadth and importance, shows that all important results are included and segmented (that is, by important customer, workforce, process, and product-line groups)

Complete Data

Be sure that results data are displayed for all relevant customer, financial, market, workforce, operational performance, and supplier-performance characteristics. If you identify relevant performance measures and goals in other parts of the analysis (for example, Categories 1 through 6), be sure to include the results of these performance characteristics in Category 7. As each relevant performance measure is identified in the assessment process, create a blank chart and label the axes. Define all units of measure, especially if they are industry-specific or unique to the applicant. As data are collected, populate the charts. If expected data are not provided in the application, examiners may assume that the trends or levels are not good. Missing data drive the score down in the same way that poor trends do.

After you complete all of the data in Category 7, review the Organizational Profile and the processes described in Categories 1 through 6. Make a list of all of the results that an examiner would expect to find in Category 7. Then, cross-check this list with the data provided in Category 7. If any *expected* data are missing, be sure to add the appropriate charts or graphs.

Actual Time Periods for Tracking Trends

No minimum period of time is required for trend data; however, a minimum of three historical data points usually are needed to determine a trend. Reporting-time intervals between data points should be meaningful for the specific measures reported. Trends might be much shorter for some of the organization's more recent improvement activities and span several years for others. Because of the importance of showing deployment and focus, new data should be included even if trends and comparisons are not yet well established. It is better to report four quarterly measures covering a one-year period than

Project Future Performance

The Scoring Guidelines for 2009, at the higher levels, expect the applicant to project future performance (and be able to validate the projection). When performance projections are provided they should be consistent with your goals and objectives in Item 2.1b(1) and projections in 2.2b. For each projection, explain briefly your supporting rationale.

Compact Presentation

Results should be reported compactly by using graphs and tables. Graphs and tables should be labeled for easy interpretation. Results over time or compared with others should be *normalized*—presented in a way (such as with the use of ratios) that takes into account various size factors. For example, reporting safety trends in terms of lost workdays per 100,000 worker-hours worked would be more meaningful than total lost workdays, if the number of workers has varied over the reporting period or if comparison organizations are different in terms of size, volume, and other key factors. When reporting cost data over many years, it may be appropriate to show constant (for example, 2001) dollars.

Integrate Results with Text

Descriptions of results and the results themselves should be in close proximity in the Award application. Trends that show a significant positive or negative change should be explained. Use figure numbers that correspond to Items. For example, the third figure for Item 7.1 should be 7.1-3 (see Figure 35).

Figure 35 illustrates data an applicant might present as part of a response to Item 7.1, Product Outcomes. In the Organizational Profile, in Item 2.1b(1), and in Item 3.1, the applicant has indicated on-time delivery as a key customer requirement.

Using the graph, the following characteristics of clear and effective data presentation are illustrated:

- A figure number is provided for reference to the graph in the text.

- Both axes and units of measure are clearly labeled.

- Trend lines report data for a key business requirement—on-time delivery.

- Results are presented for several years.

- Appropriate comparisons are clearly shown.

- The organization shows, using a single graph, that its three divisions separately track on-time delivery.

- If different segments or components exist, show each as a separate measure. Avoid aggregating data when the segments are meaningful.

- An upward-pointing arrow appears on the graph, indicating that increasing values are *good*. (A downward-pointing arrow would indicate that decreasing values are *good*.) The *desired direction* arrows may seem obvious to the authors of the application, but some desired directions are not obvious to examiners who are not familiar with certain data displays.

To help interpret the Scoring Guidelines, the following comments on the graphed results in the previous sample would be appropriate.

- The current overall organization performance level is excellent. This conclusion is supported

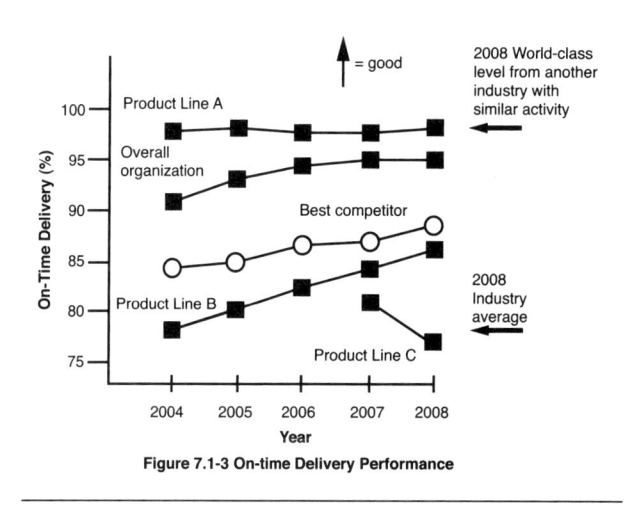

Figure 35 Linking results with text.

by the comparison with competitors and with a *world-class* level.

- The organization exhibits excellent improvement trends sustained over time.

- Product Line A is the current performance leader—showing sustained high performance and a slightly positive trend. Product Line B shows rapid improvement. Its current performance is near that of the best industry competitor but trails the world-class level.

- Product Line C—a new product—is having early problems with on-time delivery. (The applicant should analyze and explain the early problems in the application text.) Its current performance is not yet at the level of the best industry competitor.

Break Out Data

This point, mentioned earlier, bears repeating: avoid aggregating the data. Where appropriate, break data into meaningful components. If you serve several different customer groups, display performance and satisfaction data for each group. As Figure 36 demonstrates, only one of the three trends is positive, although the average is positive. Examiners will seek component data when aggregate data are reported. Presenting aggregate data instead of meaningful component data is likely to reduce the score.

Data and Measures

Comparison data are required for all Items in Category 7. These data are designed to demonstrate how well the organization is performing. To judge performance excellence, one must possess comparison data. In Figure 37, performance is represented by the line connecting the squares. Clearly the organization is improving, but how *good* is it? Without comparison data, answering that question is difficult.

Now consider the chart with comparison data added (Figure 38).

Note the position of three hypothetical comparisons, represented by the letters A, B, and C. Consider the following two scenarios:

1. If A represents the industry average and both B and C represent competitors, then examiners would conclude that your organization's performance was substandard, even though it is improving.

2. If A represents a best-in-class (benchmark) organization and B represents the industry average, then examiners would conclude that your organizational performance is very good.

In both scenarios, the organizational performance remained the same, but the examiner's perception of it changed based on changes in comparison data.

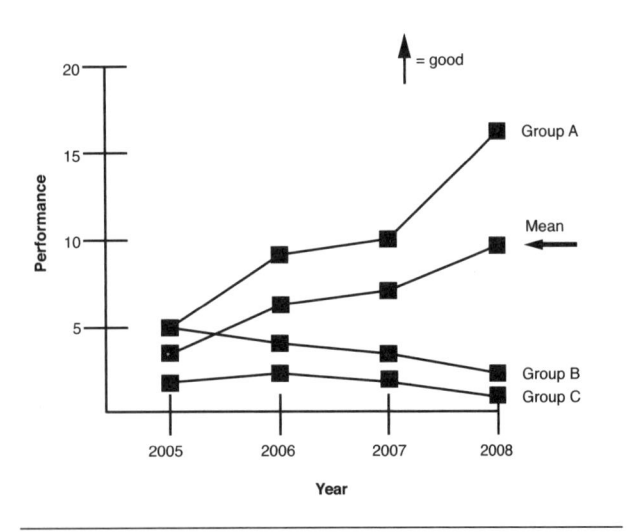

Figure 36 Breakout group data.

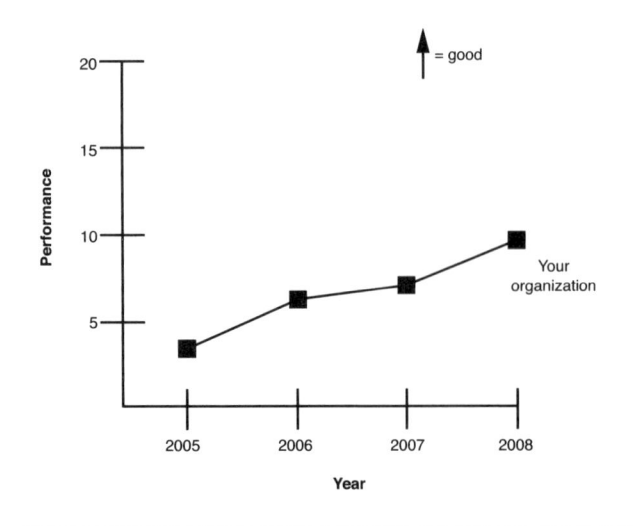

Figure 37 Getting better.

Measures

Agreeing on relevant measures is difficult for organizations in the early phases of quality and performance improvement. The task is easier if the following guidelines are considered:

- *Clearly define customer requirements.* Clear customer requirements are easier to measure. Clearly defined customer requirements require probing and suggesting. For example, the customer of a new computer wants the equipment to be reliable. After probing to find what *reliable* means, we discover that: (a) the customer expects it to work all of the time; (b) prompt appearance by a repair technician at the site if it does stop working; (c) immediate access to parts; and (d) the ability to fix it right the first time.

- *For each of the four requirements defined, identify a measure.* For example, mean time between failures is one indicator of reliability, but it does not account for all of the variation in customer satisfaction. Since the customer is concerned with run time, we must assess how long it took the repair technician to arrive at the site, diagnose the problem, and fix it. Measures include time in hours, days, weeks between failures, time in minutes between the service call and the computer regaining capability (time to fix), time in minutes waiting for parts, and the associated costs in terms of cash and worker effort.

- *Collect and report data.* Several charts might be required to display these factors, or one chart with several lines.

Refer to the Scoring Guidelines

Considerations in the evaluation of Results Item responses include the Criteria Item requirements and the significance of the results trends, actual performance levels, relevant comparative data, alignment with important elements of the performance management system, and the strength of the improvement process relative to the Scoring Guidelines. Therefore, consider both the Criteria and the Scoring Guidelines. The Scoring Calibration Guidelines in this book (pages 259–298) combine both the Criteria requirements and the Scoring Guidelines.

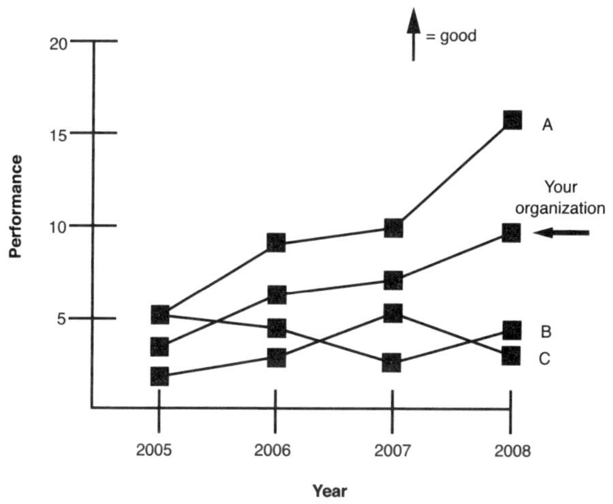

Figure 38 Comparison data.

Scoring System

Scoring dimensions are classified according to the kinds of information and/or data being reviewed. The two types of Items and their designations are:

1. Process (for the twelve Items in Categories 1 through 6)
2. Results (for the six Items in Category 7)

Applicants should furnish information relating to these dimensions. Specific factors for these dimensions are described in the following paragraphs.

Process

Process refers to the methods the organization uses and improves to address the Item requirements in Categories 1 through 6. The four factors used to evaluate process are Approach, Deployment, Learning, and Integration (A–D–L–I).

Approach (A) refers to:

- The methods used to accomplish the process
- The appropriateness of the methods to the Item requirements and the organization's operating environment.
- The effectiveness of use of the methods
- The degree to which the approach is repeatable and based on reliable data and information (for example, systematic)

The approach expected at each of the process scoring bands is further divided into basic, overall, and multiple requirements. Basic-level requirements represent a set of low-level, "introductory" requirements for each Item. The term *basic requirements* refers to the topic Criteria users need to address when responding to the most central concept of an Item. Basic requirements are the fundamental theme of that Item. In the Criteria, the basic requirements of each Item are presented as the Item title question.

Overall-level requirements represent substantially more process than the Basic level. *Overall requirements* refers to the topics Criteria users need to address when responding to the central theme of an Item. Overall requirements address the most significant features of the Item requirements. In the Criteria, the overall requirements of each Item are presented in one or more introductory sentences printed in bold, immediately following the Item title.

Multiple-level requirements represent the complex processes that the top-performing organizations have in place. The term *multiple requirement* refers to the individual questions Criteria users need to answer within each Area and Subarea to Address. These questions constitute the details of an Item's requirements. They are presented in black text under each Item's Area(s) to Address. The Scoring Calibration Guide on pages 259–298 has a more complete description.

Deployment (D) refers to the extent to which:

- The Approach is applied in addressing Item requirements relevant and important to the organization
- The Approach is applied consistently
- The Approach is used by all appropriate work units

Learning (L) refers to:

- Refining the Approach through cycles of evaluation and improvement
- Encouraging breakthrough change to the Approach through innovation
- Sharing of refinements and innovation with other relevant work units and processes in the organization

Integration (I) refers to the extent to which:

- The Approach is aligned with the organizational needs identified in the Organizational Profile and other Category or Item requirements

- The measures, information, and improvement systems are complementary across processes and work units

- The plans, processes, results, analysis, learning, and actions are harmonized across processes and work units to support organization-wide goals

For Process Items (Categories 1 through 6), Approach–Deployment–Learning–Integration (A–D–L–I) are linked to emphasize that descriptions of approach should always indicate the deployment—consistent with the specific requirements of the Item. As processes mature, their description also should indicate how cycles of learning (including innovation), as well as integration with other processes and work units, occur. Feedback to Award applicants reflects strengths and/or opportunities for improvement in any or all of these factors.

Results

Results refers to the organization's outputs and outcomes in achieving the requirements in Items 7.1–7.6. The four factors used to evaluate results include Levels, Trends, Comparisons, and Integration (LeTCI):

Levels (Le) refers to:

- Current level of performance

Trends (T) refers to:

- Rate of performance improvements or the sustainability of good performance (that is, slope of trend data)

- Breadth (how widely deployed and shared) of the organization's performance results

Comparisons (C) refers to:

- Performance relative to appropriate comparisons, such as competitors or similar organizations

- Performance relative to benchmarks or industry leaders

Integration (I) refers to the extent to which:

- Results measures (often through segmentation) address important customer, product, market, process, and action plan performance requirements identified in the Organizational Profile and in Process Items

- Results include valid indicators of future performance

- Results are harmonized across processes and work units to support organization-wide goals

Results Items call for data showing performance Levels, Trends, and relevant Comparative data for key measures and indicators of organizational performance, and Integration with key organizational requirements. Results Items also call for data on breadth of performance improvements. This is directly related to deployment and organizational learning; if improvement processes are widely shared and deployed, there should be corresponding results. A score for a Results Item is therefore a composite based upon overall performance, taking into account results factors of Levels, Trends, Comparisons, and Integration and their importance to the Item requirements and the organization's mission.

"Importance" As a Scoring Factor

The Process and Results evaluation dimensions described previously are critical to evaluation and feedback. However, another key consideration in evaluation and feedback is the *importance* of reported process and results to key business factors. The areas of greatest importance should be identified in the Organizational Profile. Key customer requirements, competitive environment, key strategic objectives, and action plans are particularly important.

Assignment of Scores

The following guidelines should be observed in assigning scores to Item responses:

- All Areas to Address should be included in Item responses. Also, responses should reflect what is important to the organization and align with mission, vision, values, customer priorities, legal and ethical principles, strategic objectives, and action plans, as appropriate.

Scoring System

- In assigning a score to an Item, examiners first decide which scoring range (for example, 50 to 65 percent) is most descriptive of the organization's achievement level as presented in the Item response. ***Most descriptive of the organization's achievement level represents the best fit and can include some gaps in one or more of the A-D-L-I (process) factors or the LeTCI (results) factors for the chosen scoring range.*** An organization's achievement level is based on a holistic view of either the four process or four results factors in aggregate and not on a tallying or averaging of independent assessments against each of the four factors. Every requirement in a scoring range does not have to be met to score in that range. Generally, all requirements in a scoring range would have to be met to score at the top of that scoring range. Assigning the actual score within the chosen range requires evaluating whether the Item response is closer to the statements in the next-higher or next-lower scoring range.

- A Process Item score of 50 to 65 percent reflects an approach where all requirements in the 30 to 45 percent scoring band and at least some requirements in the 50 to 65 percent band have been met. Examiners expect to see some of the overall requirements met to earn a score of 50 percent and all of the overall requirements met to earn a score of 65 percent. In addition, for a score of 50 to 65 percent, examiners need to see evidence that the required processes are deployed consistently to most work units covered by the Item; that is, some of the processes have been through a cycle of improvement and learning, and that the process addresses some key organizational needs (shows relevance). Higher scores reflect greater achievement, demonstrated by broader deployment, significant organizational learning, and increased integration.

- A Results Item score of 50 percent represents a clear indication of good levels of performance, beneficial trends, and appropriate comparative data for the results areas covered in the Item and important to the organization's business or mission. Performance projections are present for some high-priority results. Higher scores reflect better trends and/or levels of performance, better comparative performance, and broader coverage and integration with business or mission requirements.

Calibration Guidelines

Defining scoring terms may help reduce unnecessary variability. I have frequently asked examiners to define, in terms of percent, the meaning of *most*. Some define *most* as 51 percent. Others have a higher standard, even up to 90 percent. Defining *good* and *very good* is even more difficult. To reduce this variability, the following guidelines are suggested:

Few:	5 to 15 percent (major gaps in deployment exist)
Some:	Greater than 15 percent to 30 percent (deployed, although in the early stages)
Many:	Greater than 30 percent to 50 percent (well-deployed, although deployment may vary in some areas)
Most:	Greater than 50 percent to 80 percent (well-deployed, with no apparent gaps in most areas)
Nearly All:	Greater than 80 percent to less than 100 percent (fully deployed, with no significant gaps in any areas or work units)
All:	100 percent
Good:	*For example, better than average for competitors or similar providers; above industry average*
Very Good:	*For example, in the top quartile of competitors or similar providers*
Excellent:	*For example, at or near the top of competitors or similar providers; top 5 percent; best benchmark; better than best competitor*

Score	Baldrige Scoring Guidelines For Use With Categories 1–6 Process
0% or 5%	• No systematic approach to item requirements is evident; information is anecdotal. (A) • Little or no deployment of any systematic approach is evident. (D) • An improvement orientation is not evident; improvement is achieved through reacting to problems. (L) • No organizational alignment is evident; individual areas or work units operate independently. (I)
10%, 15%, 20%, or 25%	• The beginning of a systematic approach to the basic requirements of the Item is evident. (A) • The approach is in the early stages of deployment in most areas or work units, inhibiting progress in achieving the basic requirements of the Item. (D) • Early stages of a transition from reacting to problems to a general improvement orientation are evident. (L) • The approach is aligned with other areas or work units largely through joint problem solving. (I)
30%, 35%, 40%, or 45%	• An effective, systematic approach, responsive to the basic requirements of the Item, is evident. (A) • The approach is deployed, although some areas or work units are in early stages of deployment. (D) • The beginning of a systematic approach to evaluation and improvement of key processes is evident. (L) • The approach is in the early stages of alignment with your basic organizational needs identified in response to the Organizational Profile and other Process Items. (I)
50%, 55%, 60%, or 65%	• An effective, systematic approach, responsive to the overall requirements of the Item, is evident. (A) • The approach is well deployed, although deployment may vary in some areas or work units. (D) • A fact-based, systematic evaluation and improvement process and some organizational learning, including innovation, are in place for improving the efficiency and effectiveness of key processes. (L) • The approach is aligned with your organizational needs identified in response to the Organizational Profile and other Process Items. (I)
70%, 75%, 80%, or 85%	• An effective, systematic approach, responsive to the multiple requirements of the Item, is evident. (A) • The approach is well deployed, with no significant gaps. (D) • Fact-based, systematic evaluation and improvement and organizational learning, including innovation, are key management tools; there is clear evidence of refinement as a result of organizational-level analysis and sharing. (L) • The approach is integrated with your organizational needs identified in response to the Organizational Profile and other Process Items. (I)
90%, 95%, or 100%	• An effective, systematic approach, fully responsive to the multiple requirements of the Item, is evident. (A) • The approach is fully deployed without significant weaknesses or gaps in any areas or work units. (D) • Fact-based, systematic evaluation and improvement and organizational learning through innovation are key organization-wide tools; refinement and innovation, backed by analysis and sharing, are evident throughout the organization. (L) • The approach is well integrated with your organizational needs identified in response to the Organizational Profile and other Process Items. (I)

Score	Baldrige Scoring Guidelines For Use With Category 7 Results
0% or 5%	• There are no organizational performance results and/or poor results in areas reported. *(Le)* • Trend data either are not reported or show mainly adverse trends. *(T)* • Comparative information is not reported. *(C)* • Results are not reported for any areas of importance to the accomplishment of your organization's mission. **No performance projections are reported.** *(I)*
10%, 15%, 20%, or 25%	• A few organizational performance results are reported, and early good performance levels are evident in a few areas. *(Le)* • Some trend data are reported, with some adverse trends evident. *(T)* • Little or no comparative information is reported. *(C)* • Results are reported for a few areas of importance to the accomplishment of your organization's mission. **Limited or no performance projections are reported.** *(I)*
30%, 35%, 40%, or 45%	• Good organizational performance levels are reported for some areas of importance to the item requirements. *(Le)* • Some trend data are reported, and a majority of the trends presented are beneficial. *(T)* • Early stages of obtaining comparative information are evident. *(C)* • Results are reported for many areas of importance to the accomplishment of your organization's mission. **Limited performance projections are reported.** *(I)*
50%, 55%, 60%, or 65%	• Good organizational performance levels are reported for most areas of importance to the Item requirements. *(Le)* • Beneficial trends are evident in areas of importance to the accomplishment of your organization's mission. *(T)* • Some current performance levels have been evaluated against relevant comparisons and/or benchmarks and show areas of good relative performance. *(C)* • Organizational performance results are reported for most key customer, market, and process requirements. **Performance projections for some high-priority results are reported.** *(I)*
70%, 75%, 80%, or 85%	• Good to excellent organizational performance levels are reported for most areas of importance to the Item requirements. *(Le)* • Beneficial trends have been sustained over time in most areas of importance to the accomplishment of your organization's mission. *(T)* • Many to most trends and current performance levels have been evaluated against relevant comparisons and/or benchmarks and show areas of leadership and very good relative performance. *(C)* • Organizational performance results are reported for most key customer, market, process, and action plan requirements, and they include some projections of your future performance. *(I)*
90%, 95%, or 100%	• Excellent organizational performance levels are reported for most areas of importance to the item requirements. *(Le)* • Beneficial trends have been sustained over time in all areas of importance to the accomplishment of your organization's mission. *(T)* • Evidence of industry and benchmark leadership is demonstrated in many areas. *(C)* • Organizational performance results fully address key customer, market, process, and action plan requirements, and they include projections of your future performance. *(I)*

Note: **Bold, *italicized* text** represents changes from the 2008 Scoring Guidelines.

PROCESS TERMS

Systematic

Look for evidence of a system—a repeatable, predictable process that uses data and information to promote improvement and learning—that is used to fulfill the requirements of the Item. The application should briefly describe the system, explain how it works, how it is evaluated, and what refinements have been made as a result. The application must communicate the nature of the system to people who may not be familiar with it.

Integrated

Determine the extent to which the system is integrated or interconnected with other elements of the overall management system. Show the linkages across categories for key themes such as those displayed earlier for each Item. Consider the extent to which the work of senior leaders is integrated. For example:

1. Senior executives [Item 1.1] are responsible for shaping and communicating the organization's values and performance expectations throughout the leadership system and workforce.

2. They develop relationships with key customers [3.1] and report customer engagement, satisfaction, and dissatisfaction [7.2], related product outcomes [7.1], and operational performance outcomes [7.5].

3. With this in mind, senior executives participate in strategy development [Item 2.1] and ensure the alignment of the workforce to achieve strategic objectives and actions [Item 2.2].

4. Leaders must convert goals and strategic objectives into measurable milestones and timetables [Item 2.1b(1)] to serve as a basis for monitoring performance [Item 4.1a] and setting improvement priorities [Item 4.1c]. (Timetables [2.1b(1)] should be set to coincide with the review cycle of senior leaders [Item 4.1b]. If they review progress quarterly, then quarterly timetables or milestones should be set.)

5. This information, when properly collected and analyzed [Item 4.1], helps leaders plan and monitor progress effectively [Item 1.1b(2)] and make more informed decisions to optimize customer satisfaction and operational and financial performance.

6. Senior executives may also become involved in supporting new structures to improve workforce engagement and development [Item 5.1], ensure workforce capacity and capability and a safe, healthy, secure work environment [Item 5.2].

Similar relationships (linkages) exist between other Items. In the application, highlight these linkages using cross-references to demonstrate integration. Key linkages for each of the Items are presented in the "circle diagrams" with that Item.

Prevention-Based

Prevention-based systems are characterized by actions to minimize or prevent the existence or recurrence of problems. In an ideal world, all systems would produce perfect products and flawless service. Since that rarely happens, high-performing organizations are able to act quickly to recover from a problem (fight the fire) and then take action to identify the root cause of the problem and prevent it from surfacing again. The nature of the problem, its root cause, and appropriate corrective action are communicated to all relevant employees so that they can implement the corrective action in their area before the problem arises.

Continuous Improvement

Continuous improvement is a bedrock theme for top-performing organizations. It is the method that helps organizations establish and keep their competitive edge. Continuous improvement involves the fact-based evaluation and improvement of processes crucial to organizational success. Evaluation and improvement, including innovation, completes the high-performance management cycle. Fact-based evaluations can be complex statistical processes, or as simple as focus groups discussing and recording what went right, what went wrong, and how it could be done better. The key to optimum performance lies in the pervasive evaluation and improvement of all processes. If the organization practices systematic, pervasive, continuous improvement, time becomes its ally. Consistent fact-based evaluation and refinement practices with correspondingly good deployment and innovative approaches can drive the score to 60 percent or 70 percent, and higher. Without the beginning of a systematic approach to evaluation and refinement it is difficult to score above 40 percent.

Complete

Each Item contains one or more Areas to Address. Many Areas to Address contain several subparts. Failure to address all Areas and subparts can push the score lower. If an Area to Address or part of an Area does not apply to an organization, it is important to explain why. Otherwise, examiners may conclude that the applicant's management system is incomplete.

Anecdotal

If the application narrative describes a process or procedure that is random, *ad hoc*, or anecdotal and does not address the Criteria in a predictable, disciplined manner, it is worth very little (zero to five points).

Deployment

The extent to which processes are widely used by organization units affects scoring. For example, a systematic approach that is well-integrated, evaluated consistently, and refined routinely with evidence of an innovative approach may be worth 70 to 85 percent or more. However, if that process is not in place in all key parts of the organization, the score may be reduced, perhaps significantly, depending on the nature and extent of the deployment gap.

Major gaps are expected to exist at the 5 percent to 25 percent level. At the 30 percent and higher levels, no major gaps exist, although some units may still be at the early stages of development. At the 70 percent to 85 percent level, no major gaps exist and the approach is well-integrated with organizational needs identified in other parts of the Criteria.

Summary

For each Item examined, the process is rated as follows:

- Anecdotal: 0 to 5 percent
- Beginnings of a systematic approach to meet basic-level Item requirements (perhaps recently piloted or implemented process): 10 to 25 percent
- Effective, systematic approach in place to meet basic-level Item requirements: 30 to 35 percent
- Effective, systematic approach in place to meet basic-level Item requirements, with the beginnings (planned or piloted) of a process to evaluate and improve: 40 to 45 percent
- Effective, systematic approach in place to meet overall-level Item requirements, with fact-based evaluation process in place: 50 percent
- Effective, systematic approach in place to meet overall-level Item requirements, with fact-based evaluation process in place and a subsequent cycle of refinement with some innovation or meaningful change: 60 to 65 percent
- Effective, systematic approach in place to meet multiple-level Item requirements, with fact-based evaluation process in place and multiple cycles of refinement, innovation, and integration based on the evaluation: 80 percent to 85 percent
- Aligned: 60 to 65 percent, demonstrating linkages (alignment) among the overall-level approach requirements
- Integrated: 70 to 100 percent demonstrating numerous tight linkages (integration) among the many multiple-level approach requirements
- Refined and innovative: 60 to 100 percent
- Widely used, with no significant gaps in deployment: 70 percent or greater

Systematic, integrated, prevention-based, and continuously improved systems that are widely used are generally easier to describe than undeveloped systems. Moreover, describing activities or anecdotes does not convince examiners that an integrated, systematic process is in place. In fact, simply describing activities and anecdotes suggests that an integrated system does not exist. However, by tracing critical success threads through the relevant Items in the Criteria, the organization demonstrates that its system is integrated and fully deployed.

To demonstrate system integration, pick several critical success factors and show how they work together. For example, trace the leadership focus on performance.

- Identify performance-related data that are collected to indicate progress against goals [Item 4.1] and strategic objectives [2.1b(1)] and action plan measures [2.2a(6)].

- Show how senior leaders analyze and review performance data [Item 4.1b], and use them to set priorities for work and resources [Item 4.1b]. Show how review findings are used to evaluate and improve [4.1c]. (Be sure to highlight the process improvements that have been made based on these evaluations.)

- Show how performance effectiveness is considered in the planning process [Item 2.1a] and how work at all levels is aligned to increase performance [Item 2.2a] and competitiveness [2.2b].

- Demonstrate the impact of workforce engagement [Item 5.1a] and development [Item 5.1b] on performance and show how both tie to the strategy and workforce plans [Item 2.2a(5)].

- Show how work systems [Item 6.1] and key work processes [Item 6.2] are enhanced to improve results. Demonstrate innovative approaches.

- Report the results of improved performance outcomes [Items 7.1, 7.2, 7.3, 7.4, 7.5, and 7.6] and be sure key results are reported with key comparative or benchmark data included to demonstrate good to excellent levels of performance.

- Show that improved product performance [Item 7.1] affects customer engagement and satisfaction/dissatisfaction levels [Item 7.2].

- Show how customer requirements and preferences [P.1b(2)] are used to drive the selection of key measures [Item 4.1] and impact design and delivery processes [Items 6.1 and 6.2].

Note that the application is limited to 50 pages, not including the five-page Organizational Profile. This may not be sufficient to describe in great detail the process, results, integration, and refinement of all systematic critical success factors, goals, or processes. Thus, it is better to pick the most important few, indicate them as such, and then thoroughly describe the threads and linkages throughout the application.

Clarifying the Baldrige Scoring Requirements

INTRODUCTION

The Baldrige Criteria, together with the Scoring Guidelines, are intended to help Examiners identify the key strengths and vital few areas needing improvement to help leaders focus their resources on the steps needed to get to the next developmental level. Unfortunately, for several years, national and State Examiners have tended to "nit-pick" applicants by citing minute, inconsequential opportunities for improvement—even when basic or fundamental processes were not in place. Because of the tendency to select trivial issues as opportunities for improvement, scores were inappropriately low and comments were not properly focused.

To avoid this problem, the Baldrige Award office redefined the Scoring Guidelines to focus attention on a hierarchy of requirements moving from "basic" to "overall" to "multiple." The purpose of this hierarchy was to keep Examiners focused on the most important factors each applicant needed to put in place to get to the next level and not turn the examination process into a compliance checklist.

In other words, the strengths comments were supposed to describe the processes and systems an applicant had in place that supported or justified the score assigned. The opportunities for improvement were supposed to identify the processes or systems that were not in place that kept the organization from moving to the next higher level. By focusing on insignificant issues (nits) in the feedback report, an applicant might spend resources fixing a problem that had relatively low impact and overlook a key area essential for growth and improvement.

I believe that the Baldrige Award office was correct in identifying the need to keep Examiners focused on the vital few issues. To achieve this objective, *it is essential that all Examiners reviewing applications for a State, regional, or "in-house" Baldrige-based recognition program interpret the Criteria and scoring guidelines consistently.* Unfortunately, the process and definitions presented in the 2003 to 2009 Criteria and Scoring Guidelines do not help the less experienced Examiners achieve this objective.

From my experience in training thousands of Examiners on the use of the Baldrige criteria, I have found that the greatest source of unacceptable variation is caused by Examiners who each believe different aspects of the Criteria are "most important." The lack of clarity in defining precisely what systems and/or processes are required for each scoring level and for each Item forces examiners to decide for themselves the elements of each Item they deem more critical than others. With Examiners holding many different opinions as to what constitutes basic and overall requirements, their comments and scores have not been consistent, either from team to team or Examiner to Examiner. For example, in recent Examiner training classes conducted, I asked the Examiners to follow the Baldrige definitions and list the factors they would look for as a basic requirement of "Senior Leadership" [Item 1.1] of the business criteria. Each class generated a list similar to the following.

The applicant organization and its senior leaders must have in place processes to:

- *Set vision and values*
- *Deploy vision and values*
- *Communicate with the workforce*
- *Focus on customers*
- *Deploy values to key partners, suppliers, and customers*

- *Require and achieve legal and ethical behavior*
- *Promote workforce learning*
- *Encourage 2-way communication throughout the organization*
- *Make sure their actions match their values*
- *Ensure steady performance improvement, innovation, and agility throughout the organization*
- *Personally participate in succession planning*
- *Develop future leaders*
- *Reinforce high performance and a customer and business focus by actively rewarding and recognizing employees*
- *Focus on improving performance*
- *Balance value for customers and stakeholders*

The list of "basic" requirements that the individual Examiners produced (required for a score of 10 to 45 percent), more accurately defines most of the *multiple* level requirements (needed for a score of 70 to 100 percent). With this kind of variation in defining the "basic" requirements of Item 1.1, a relatively straightforward Item, imagine the differences a team of 6 to 10 examiners will have interpreting the requirements of the 12 Process Items in Categories 1 through 6. It is difficult to conduct a consistently accurate assessment when each Examiner's interpretation of the *basic* and *overall* requirements is so varied.

During the past six years, many State and in-house organizational award programs tested and subsequently implemented an approach to scoring that produces more consistently accurate assessments. This technique provides examiners with a more precise and consistent definition of "basic" and "overall" requirements for each Item (the multiple level requirements are already precise).

Having been provided clearer definitions of Criteria requirements for the "Approaches" at the basic and overall levels, Examiners are able to more accurately and consistently assess, score, and provide meaningful feedback to award applicants.

Official Baldrige Definitions

This section presents the actual "Approach" definitions (in bold italic type) from the Baldrige Award office that created the confusion.

Basic Requirements

The term "basic requirements" refers to the topic Criteria users need to address when responding to the most central concept of an Item. Basic requirements are the fundamental theme of that Item (for example, your approach for strategy development for Item 2.1). In the Criteria, the basic requirements of each Item are presented as the Item title question.

Only meeting the basic requirements of the Item could result in a score at the 10 to 45 percent levels, depending on the level of development of the basic systems and on the extent of deployment of those systems.

Accordingly, for Item 1.1, an organization can meet the *basic* requirements by providing *Senior Leadership* (the Item title question of Item 1.1). For Item 2.1, the organization must have a process for *Strategy Development* (also undefined). What do these terms mean? What does "strategy development process" include? There is simply not enough information presented by these terms to ensure a consistent review, which is critical to ensure appropriate feedback and an accurate score.

Overall Requirements

The term "overall requirements" refers to the topics Criteria users need to address when responding to the central theme of an Item. Overall requirements address the most significant features of the Item requirements. In the Criteria, the overall requirements of each Item are presented in one or more introductory sentences printed in bold.

Meeting the overall requirements of the Item could result in a score at the 50, 55, 60 or 65 percent level depending on the maturity of the overall systems, the extent of deployment of those systems, and the extent of systematic evaluation and refinement, and integration of those systems.

More detail is provided in the Criteria to define the *overall* level approach than is provided for the *basic* level approach. However, the explanation is still too limited in many Items to enable Examiners to provide a consistent review, appropriate feedback, and an accurate score.

For example, the "overall" level of Item 4.1, requires the *organization to measure, analyze, align, review, and improve its performance through the use of data and information at all levels and in all parts of the organization*. Ask any five people what systems and processes might be appropriate to meet these requirements and you will receive five different answers.

Multiple Requirements

The term "multiple requirements" refers to the individual questions Criteria users need to answer within each Area to Address. These questions constitute the details of an Item's requirements. They are presented in black text under each Item's Area(s) to Address.

Meeting the multiple requirements of the Item could result in a score at the 70 to 100 percent levels, depending on the maturity of the multiple systems, the extent of deployment of those systems, and the extent of systematic evaluation, refinement, innovation, and improved integration of those systems.

Unlike the *basic* and *overall* definitions, sufficient detail is provided in the *multiple* level definitions to enable Examiners to identify the elements of management systems and processes that must be in place to score at the 70 percent or higher level.

Importance As a Scoring Factor

Examiners must determine the extent to which the management systems and processes are responsive to the organization's *key business requirements* and *changing business needs* (especially at the 50 percent and higher scoring bands). Accordingly, examiners should consider the extent to which processes support or respond to key business needs that were expressed in the Organizational Profile and in Items such as:

- 2.1 Strategic objectives

- 2.2 Action plans and measures that derive from the strategic objectives and are deployed to all levels of the organization

- 3.1 and 3.2 The definition of customer segments, their requirements, and their preferences for products and services that are most likely to enhance loyalty

- 5.1 Workforce engagement to align workforce feedback, reward, recognition, and compensation to achieve high performance, business, and customer-focused objectives

- 6.1 and 6.2 Design and manage work systems and Key Work Processes to deliver customer value and achieve organizational success and sustainability

Key customer requirements, the competitive environment, strategic objectives, and action plans are important to consider when determining the relevance of the systems and processes described in the application.

Clarifications for Scoring

The definitions on the following pages are intended to help improve consistency of interpretation and are offered as guidelines only. Prior to using these clarifying statements, the staff, judges, and senior examiners of the award program should reach consensus that the Basic, Overall, and Multiple requirements listed on the following pages appropriately capture the levels and meaning of the Criteria. Remember that the notes at the end of each Item provide additional clarification about information that is expected as part of the review. The full version of the Scoring Calibration Guide, which is on the CD-ROM included with this book, includes cross-referenced Notes for each Criteria Item.)

- The word *should* creates an expectation that the process is in place. For example, Note 1 for Item 1.1 indicates that, "Organizational vision [1.1a(1)] *should* set the context for strategic objectives and action plans, which are described in Items 2.1 and 2.2." This means that examiners expect to find these linkages.

- The word *might* is meant to suggest alternatives or examples, but not establish the expectation that the process is required. For example, Note 3 in 1.1 indicates that "A focus on action [1.1b(2)] considers the strategy, the workforce, the work systems, and the hard assets of your organization. It includes both innovation and ongoing improvements in productivity that may be achieved through eliminating waste or reducing cycle time, and it *might* use techniques such as Six Sigma and Lean. It also includes the actions to accomplish your organization's strategic objectives." This means that examiners can give credit for but not require Six Sigma and Lean, and they must not write an Opportunity for Improvement comment or lower the score if the organization does not use such approaches.

To make the following clarifying tables more complete, for the process Items in Categories 1 through 6 the Best Fit Scoring Guidelines are presented in the first column as a reminder of the key points in the scoring for each level. The process-scoring guidelines for the 70 to 85 percent level and the 90 to 100 percent levels have been grouped together in the tables because these scoring levels all require the multiple-level requirements to be met. For results Items in Category 7, the overall requirements of each Item are presented, followed by the scoring calibration statements and corresponding actual scoring guidelines that apply to all the Category 7 Items.

Remember, the following analysis is presented only as a guideline that state, local, and in-house recognition programs may want to consider in order to help their examiners provide more consistent and meaningful scoring and feedback to applicants.

	1.1 Senior Leadership *(70 points possible)*
Best Fit Scoring Guidelines	**Expected Findings**
0–5% If examiners observe the applicant is not responsive to the requirements of an Item or provides no relevant information, the score should be zero (0%). If the applicant provides some anecdotal information addressing Item requirements (even though no systematic approach has begun), the score should be 5%.	*0–5% Scoring Band: No Systems to Meet Requirements* **1.1 Senior Leadership.** Senior leaders have no effective processes to lead the organization (such as providing clear direction or guidance) [1.1a(1)] *(A)*. *The guidance that senior leaders provide has not been deployed (D). Reacting to problems is the normal way of approaching work and no consistent effort is made to prevent problems (L). There is no effective alignment in the organization among leaders related to values and direction and people and/or units seem to operate independently (I).*
10–25% If examiners observe the applicant is barely doing some of the things required in the 10–25% Beginning scoring band, the score should be in the lower part of this band. If they observe the applicant is doing everything required in the 10–25% Beginning band, but nothing in the higher bands, the score should be 25%.	*10–25% Scoring Band: Beginning to Meet Basic Requirements* **1.1 Senior Leadership.** *Senior leaders are in the beginning stages of establishing effective processes to lead the organization, which may include providing clear direction or guidance* [1.1a(1)] *(A). The leadership/guidance that senior leaders provide is not widely deployed or understood by the workforce (D). Reacting to problems is widespread and senior leaders are not focused on improvement (L). Some joint problem-solving activities are sometimes used to help promote alignment within the organization (I).*
30–45% If examiners observe the applicant is doing everything required in the 10–25% Beginning scoring band, and a few additional things in the higher bands, the score should be in the lower part of the 30–45% Basic band. If they observe the applicant is doing everything required in the 30–45% Basic band, but nothing in the higher bands, the score should be 45%.	*30–45% Scoring Band: Systematically Meeting Basic Requirements* **1.1 Senior Leadership.** *Senior leaders have effective, systematic processes in place to lead the organization, which may include providing clear direction or guidance* [1.1a(1)] *(A). The leadership/guidance that senior leaders provide is generally understood by the workforce (D). Senior leaders are beginning to evaluate some of their leadership processes and may or may not have made improvements based on the evaluation (L). The directions and guidance of senior leaders are generally consistent with organization priorities such as those set forth in the Organizational Profile (for example, values and vision) and basic requirements of other Process Items (for example, strategy development [2.1], societal responsibilities [1.2], and customer engagement [3.1]) (I).*
50–65% If examiners observe the applicant is doing everything required in the 30–45% Basic scoring band, and a few additional things in the higher bands, the score should be in the lower part of the 50–65% Overall band. If they observe the applicant is doing everything in the 50–65% Overall band, but nothing in the next higher 70–85% band, the score should be 65%.	*50–65% Scoring Band: Systematically Meeting Overall Requirements* **1.1 Senior Leadership.** Senior leaders have effective, systematic processes in place to do the following: a. **Vision and Values.** Through personal actions, effectively guide the organization (for example by establishing clear direction and values) [1.1a(1)] and sustain organizational success (by ensuring it is capable of addressing current business needs and preparing for future challenges) [1.1a(3)] *(A)*. b. **Communication and Organizational Performance.** Communicate with the workforce and encourage high performance throughout most of the organization [1.1b(1)] *(A)*. *Some relatively minor gaps may exist in the deployment of these processes in some parts of the organization (D). A systematic, fact-based process is in place to evaluate the efficiency/ effectiveness of some of the key elements of (a) and/or (b) above; and—for scores of 65%— evidence of at least one cycle of improvement* **and some innovation (meaningful change)** *within one or more of these elements (L). The leadership processes are generally aligned with organizational needs set forth in the Organizational Profile (for example, mission,*

Continued

Insights to Performance Excellence 2009–2010

	1.1 Senior Leadership *(70 points possible)* Continued
Best Fit Scoring Guidelines	**Expected Findings**
	vision, values, customer requirements, and workforce characteristics and needs), and the requirements of other Process Items (for example, strategic objectives [2.1b(1)], action plans and their performance measures [2.2a(1, 6)], governance and societal responsibilities [1.2], and leadership development [5.1b(1)]) (I).
70–85% If examiners observe the applicant is doing everything required in the 50–65% Overall scoring band, and a few additional things in the 70–100% Multiple scoring band, the score should be in the lower part of the Multiple scoring band (for example, 70–75%). If they observe the applicant is meeting many to most requirements in the 70–100% Multiple scoring band, the score should be 85%. **90–100%** If examiners observe the applicant fully addressing the multiple Approach requirements and most of the Deployment, Learning, and Integration requirements described in the 70–100% Multiple scoring band, the score should be 90–95%. If examiners observe the applicant is meeting all of the requirements in the 70–100% Multiple band, the score should be 100%. **Note**: A score of 100% is possible only if *all* requirements are met and no Opportunities for Improvement can be identified. In addition, to score in the 90% to 100% band, examiners must observe full deployment, extensive and ongoing evaluation, improvement, organizational learning, innovation, and knowledge sharing throughout the organization. Required approaches must be well integrated with organizational needs identified in response to most other Criteria Items.	**70–85% and 90–100% Scoring Bands: Multiple Requirements** *1.1 Senior Leadership (70 pts.)* Senior leaders effectively guide and sustain the organization, communicate with the workforce, and encourage high performance. *a. Vision and Values* 1. Senior leaders have an effective, systematic process in place to set and deploy organizational vision and values through the leadership system, to the workforce, key suppliers and partners, customers, and other stakeholders, as appropriate. Their personal actions consistently reflect a commitment to the organization's values. 2. Senior leaders have an effective, systematic process in place to promote an organizational environment that fosters, requires, and results in legal and ethical behavior. 3. Senior leaders have an effective, systematic process in place to create a sustainable organization (by ensuring, for example, the organization is able to address current business needs and possesses the agility and strategic management to prepare successfully for future business, market, and operating environments). Senior leaders have created an environment for organizational performance improvement, accomplishment of mission and strategic objectives, innovation, competitive or role model performance leadership, organizational agility, and organizational and workforce learning. They develop and enhance their personal leadership skills. They personally participate in organizational learning, succession planning, and the development of future organizational leaders. *b. Communication and Organizational Performance* 1. Senior leaders have an effective, systematic process in place to communicate with and engage the entire workforce. They have an effective process in place to encourage frank, two-way communication throughout the organization and to communicate key decisions. They take an active role in reward and recognition programs to reinforce high performance and a customer and business focus. 2. Senior leaders have an effective, systematic process in place to create a focus on action to accomplish the organization's objectives, improve performance, and attain the organization's vision. They review clearly defined performance measures to keep informed about actions they might need to take. They focus on creating and balancing value for customers and other stakeholders in their organizational performance expectations. *The approach is well deployed with no significant gaps (D). A systematic, fact-based process is in place to evaluate and improve elements of (a) and (b) above, with clear evidence of ongoing innovation, organizational learning, and organization-level sharing and analysis, which results in refinements and improved integration throughout the organization (L). Organizational learning about (a) and (b) above and systematic evaluation and improvement of (a) and (b) above are key management tools. The approach is integrated with the organizational needs set forth in the Organizational Profile and other Process Items (for example, governance, improving the leadership system, and societal responsibility [1.2], strategic objectives [2.1b(1)], action plans and their performance measures [2.2a(1, 6)], and leadership development [5.1b(1)] succession planning for management and leadership positions [5.1b(4)]) (I).*

1.2 Governance and Societal Responsibilities *(50 points possible)*

Best Fit Scoring Guidelines	Expected Findings
0–5% If examiners observe the applicant is not responsive to the requirements of an Item or provides no relevant information, the score should be zero (0%). If the applicant provides some anecdotal information addressing Item requirements (even though no systematic approach has begun), the score should be 5%.	**0–5% Scoring Band: No Systems to Meet Requirements** **1.2 Governance and Societal Responsibilities.** The organization has no effective processes to provide governance [1.2a(1)] and meet its societal responsibilities [1.2b(1)] *(A)*. The processes to promote effective governance and meet societal responsibilities have not been deployed *(D)*. Reacting to problems is the normal way of approaching work and no consistent effort is made to prevent problems *(L)*. There is no effective alignment in the organization related to governance and meeting societal responsibilities and people and/or units seem to operate independently *(I)*.
10–25% If examiners observe the applicant is barely doing some of the things required in the **10–25%** Beginning scoring band, the score should be in the lower part of this band. If they observe the applicant is doing everything required in the 10–25% Beginning band, but nothing in the higher bands, the score should be 25%.	**10–25% Scoring Band: Beginning to Meet Basic Requirements** **1.2 Governance and Societal Responsibilities.** The organization is in the beginning stages of establishing processes to provide effective governance (such as ensuring management accountability (or other key aspects of governance) [1.2a(1)] and to meet its societal responsibilities (such as complying with laws and regulations) [1.2b(1)] *(A)*. Major gaps exist where the processes do not provide effective governance or ensure compliance with key regulatory or legal requirements in most parts of the organization *(D)*. Reacting to problems related to governance and societal responsibility is common, and working to prevent problems is in the beginning stages *(L)*. Some joint problem-solving activities are generally used to help promote alignment within the organization *(I)*.
30–45% If examiners observe the applicant is doing everything required in the 10–25% Beginning scoring band, and a few additional things in the higher bands, the score should be in the lower part of the 30–45% Basic band. If they observe the applicant is doing everything required in the 30–45% Basic band, but nothing in the higher bands, the score should be 45%.	**30–45% Scoring Band: Systematically Meeting Basic Requirements** **1.2 Governance and Societal Responsibilities.** The organization has systematic processes in place to provide effective governance (such as ensuring management accountability or other key aspects of governance) [1.2a(1)] and meet its societal responsibilities (such as complying with laws and regulations) [1.2b(1)] *(A)* in most parts of the organization *(D)*. The organization is beginning to evaluate some of these processes and may or may not have made improvements based on the evaluation *(L)*. The governance and societal responsibility processes are generally consistent with organization priorities, such as those set forth in the Organizational Profile (values and vision) and basic requirements of other Process Items (for example strategy [2.1] and senior leadership priorities [1.1]) *(I)*.
50–65% If examiners observe the applicant is doing everything required in the 30–45% Basic scoring band, and a few additional things in the higher bands, the score should be in the lower part of the 50–65% Overall band. If they observe the applicant is doing everything in the 50–65% Overall band, but nothing in the next higher 70–85% band, the score should be 65%.	**50–65% Scoring Band: Systematically Meeting Overall Requirements** **1.2 Governance and Societal Responsibilities.** The organization has effective, systematic processes in place to do the following: a. **Organizational Governance.** Govern the organization (to ensure, for example, accountability for management actions and protection of stakeholder interests) [1.2a(1)] and has approaches in place to improve the leadership system [1.2a(2)] *(A)*. b. **Legal and Ethical Behavior.** Assures legal [1.2b(1)] and ethical behavior [1.2b(2)] and fulfills its societal responsibilities [1.2c(1)] (for example, meeting regulatory and legal requirements [1.2b(1)], and promoting ethical behavior throughout the organization) [1.2b(2)] *(A)*. c. **Societal Responsibilities and Support of Key Communities.** Fulfills its societal responsibilities (for example considering societal well-being as part of operations) [1.2c(1)] and supporting key communities) [1.2c(2)] *(A)*. Some relatively minor gaps may exist in the deployment of these processes in some parts of the organization *(D)*. A systematic, fact-based process is in place to evaluate the efficiency/effectiveness of some of the key elements of (a), (b), and/or (c) above; and—for scores of 65%—evidence of at least one cycle of improvement **and some innovation (meaningful change)** within one or more of these elements. *(L)*. The governance and

Continued

1.2 Governance and Societal Responsibilities (50 points possible)	Continued
Best Fit Scoring Guidelines	**Expected Findings**
	societal responsibility processes are generally aligned with organizational needs set forth in the Organizational Profile (for example, mission, vision, values, customer requirements, and workforce characteristics and safety needs), and the requirements of other Process Items (for example, strategic objectives [2.1b(1)], action plans and their performance measures [2.2a(1, 6)], leadership development [5.1b(1)], and work process management [6.2b(1)]) (I).
70–85% If examiners observe the applicant is doing everything required in the 50–65% Overall scoring band, and a few additional things in the 70–100% Multiple scoring band, the score should be in the lower part of the Multiple scoring band (for example, 70–75%). If they observe the applicant is meeting many to most requirements in the 70–100% Multiple scoring band, the score should be 85%. **90–100%** If examiners observe the applicant fully addressing the multiple Approach requirements and most of the Deployment, Learning, and Integration requirements described in the 70–100% Multiple scoring band, the score should be 90–95%. If examiners observe the applicant is meeting all of the requirements in the 70–100% Multiple band, the score should be 100%. **Note**: A score of 100% is possible only if *all* requirements are met and no Opportunities for Improvement can be identified. In addition, to score in the 90% to 100% band, examiners must observe full deployment, extensive and ongoing evaluation, improvement, organizational learning, innovation, and knowledge sharing throughout the organization. Required approaches must be well integrated with organizational needs identified in response to most other Criteria Items.	**70–85% and 90–100% Scoring Bands: Multiple Requirements** *1.2 Governance and Societal Responsibilities.* The organization has a clearly defined governance system and approaches for improving the leadership system. The organization effectively assures legal and ethical behavior, fulfills its societal responsibilities, and supports its key communities: *a. Organizational Governance* 1. The organization governance system effectively and systematically reviews and achieves the following: - Accountability for management's actions - Fiscal accountability - Transparency in operations of, election of, and disclosure policies for governance board members, as appropriate - Independence in internal and external audits - Protection of stakeholder and stockholder interests, as appropriate 2. The organization effectively and systematically evaluates the performance of senior leaders, including the chief executive and members of the governance board, as appropriate. Senior leaders and the governance board use these performance reviews to further develop and improve both their personal leadership effectiveness and that of the governing board and entire leadership system, as appropriate. *b. Legal and Ethical Behavior* 1. The organization effectively and systematically addresses adverse impacts on society that may result from the organization's products, services, and operations. It anticipates public concerns with current and future products, services, and operations, and prepares for these concerns in a proactive manner, including conserving natural resources and using effective supply chain management processes as appropriate. The organization establishes key compliance processes, measures, and goals for achieving and surpassing regulatory and legal requirements and for addressing risks associated with its products, services, and operations, as appropriate. 2. The organization effectively and systematically promotes and assures ethical behavior in all interactions. It has established key processes and measures or indicators for enabling and monitoring ethical behavior in the governance structure, throughout the organization, and in interactions with customers, partners, suppliers, and other stakeholders. The organization effectively and systematically monitors and responds to breaches of ethical behavior. *c. Societal Responsibilities and Support of Key Communities* 1. The organization considers societal well-being and benefit as part of its strategy and daily operations. It considers the well-being of environmental, societal, and economic systems to which it contributes.

Continued

1.2 Governance and Societal Responsibilities *(50 points possible)* — Continued

Best Fit Scoring Guidelines	Expected Findings
	2. The organization actively supports and strengthens key communities. It identifies and defines (lists) key communities, and systematically determines areas of emphasis for organizational involvement, including areas related to core competencies. Senior leaders, along with the workforce, contribute to improving these communities. *The approach to organizational governance and societal responsibility is well deployed with no significant gaps (D). A systematic, fact-based process is in place to evaluate and improve elements of (a), (b) and (c) above, with clear evidence of ongoing innovation, organizational learning, and organization-level sharing and analysis, which results in refinements and improved integration throughout the organization. Organizational learning about (a), (b) and (c) above and systematic evaluation and improvement of (a), (b) and (c) above are key management tools (L). The approach is integrated with the organizational needs set forth in the Organizational Profile and other Process Items (for example, governance, improving the leadership system, and societal responsibility [1.2], strategic objectives [2.1b(1)], action plans and their performance measures [2.2a(1, 6)], and leadership development [5.1b(1)] succession planning for management and leadership positions [5.1b(4)]) (I).*

2.1 Strategy Development *(40 points possible)*

Best Fit Scoring Guidelines	Expected Findings
0–5% If examiners observe the applicant is not responsive to the requirements of an Item or provides no relevant information, the score should be zero (0%). If the applicant provides some anecdotal information addressing Item requirements (even though no systematic approach has begun), the score should be 5%.	**0–5% Scoring Band: No Systems to Meet Requirements** **2.1 Strategy Development.** The organization has no effective processes to develop its strategy for future success (sometimes called strategic plans) [2.1a(1)] *(A)*. Strategies that may exist are incomplete *(D)*. *Reacting to problems is the normal way of approaching work and no consistent effort is made to prevent problems (L). There is no effective alignment in the organization related to the development of strategic plans and people and/or units seem to operate independently (I).*
10–25% If examiners observe the applicant is barely doing some of the things required in the 10–25% Beginning scoring band, the score should be in the lower part of this band. If they observe the applicant is doing everything required in the 10–25% Beginning band, but nothing in the higher bands, the score should be 25%.	**10–25% Scoring Band: Beginning to Meet Basic Requirements** **2.1 Strategy Development.** The organization is in the beginning stages of establishing effective processes for systematically developing its strategy for future success (sometimes called strategic plans) [2.1a(1)] *(A)*. Major gaps exist where the strategy development process does not consider most business requirements that are key to future business success and essential to effective strategic planning *(D)*. *Reacting to problems in the planning process is widespread; working to prevent problems is in the beginning stages (L). Alignment within the planning process is accomplished generally by the use of joint problem solving (I).*

Continued

2.1 Strategy Development (40 points possible)	Continued
Best Fit Scoring Guidelines	**Expected Findings**
30–45% If examiners observe the applicant is doing everything required in the 10–25% Beginning scoring band, and a few additional things in the higher bands, the score should be in the lower part of the 30–45% Basic band. If they observe the applicant is doing everything required in the 30–45% Basic band, but nothing in the higher bands, the score should be 45%.	**30–45% Scoring Band: Systematically Meeting Basic Requirements** *2.1 Strategy Development.* The organization has effective, systematic processes in place to develop its strategy for future success (sometimes called strategic plans) [2.1a(1)] *(A)*. The planning process considers many issues that are key to future business success and essential to effective strategic planning (D). The organization is beginning to evaluate some of these processes and may or may not have made improvements based on the evaluation (L). The strategy development processes are generally consistent with organization priorities such as those set forth in the Organizational Profile (for example, values, vision, mission, core competencies, workforce characteristics, and key customer requirements) and basic requirements of other Process Items (for example, strategy deployment [2.1] and measures of success [4.1]) (I).

50–65% If examiners observe the applicant is doing everything required in the 30–45% Basic scoring band, and a few additional things in the higher bands, the score should be in the lower part of the 50–65% Overall band. If they observe the applicant is doing everything in the 50–65% Overall band, but nothing in the next higher 70–85% band, the score should be 65%.	**50–65% Scoring Band: Systematically Meeting Overall Requirements**
	
	2.1 Strategy Development. The organization has effective, systematic processes in place to do the following:
	
	   a. Strategy Development Process. Determine strategic challenges and advantages and develop an overall strategy that will lead to future success [2.1a(1)] *(A)*.
	
	   b. Strategic Objectives. Develop and summarize clear strategic objectives and related quantifiable goals or targets [2.1b(1)] that address important organizational challenges and enhance its advantages [2.1b(2)]. Strategic objectives are measurable, outcome-oriented, and define what the organization must achieve to be successful) *(A)*.
	
	Some relatively minor gaps may exist in the process of determining strategic challenges and advantages, and planning and setting strategic objectives (D). A systematic, fact-based process is in place to evaluate the efficiency/effectiveness of some of the key elements of (a) and/or (b) above; and—for scores of 65%—evidence of at least one cycle of improvement **and some innovation (meaningful change)** *within one or more of these elements (L). The planning processes are generally aligned with organizational needs set forth in the Organizational Profile (for example, mission, vision, values, culture, product offerings, customer groups/segments and requirements, core competencies, challenges and advantages, workforce characteristics and needs, technologies, equipment, regulatory environment, key suppliers, partners, and collaborators, and the competitive environment) and the requirements of other Process Items (for example, strategic objectives [2.1b(1)], action plans and their performance measures [2.2a(1, 6)], governance and societal responsibilities [1.2], leadership development [5.1b(1)] and measures and analysis of performance [4.1]) (I).*

70–85% If examiners observe the applicant is doing everything required in the 50–65% Overall scoring band, and a few additional things in the 70–100% Multiple scoring band, the score should be in the lower part of the Multiple scoring band (for example, 70–75%). If they observe the applicant is meeting many to most requirements in the 70–100% Multiple scoring band, the score should be 85%.	**70–85% and 90–100% Scoring Bands: Multiple Requirements**
	
	2.1 Strategy Development. The organization effectively determines its strategic challenges and advantages and establishes a strategy and strategic objectives to address these challenges and enhance its advantages. The organization's strategic objectives and related goals are clearly defined.
	
	   a. Strategy Development Process
	   1. The organization effectively and systematically conducts strategic planning, with key process steps and key participants clearly defined. It uses this process to identify potential blind spots. The organization determines core competencies, strategic challenges and advantages as identified in the Organizational Profile. It sets and addresses short- and longer-term planning time horizons,

Continued

2.1 Strategy Development *(40 points possible)*	Continued
Best Fit Scoring Guidelines	**Expected Findings**

90–100% If examiners observe the applicant fully addressing the multiple Approach requirements and most of the Deployment, Learning, and Integration requirements described in the 70–100% Multiple scoring band, the score should be 90–95%. If examiners observe the applicant is meeting all of the requirements in the 70–100% Multiple band, the score should be 100%. **Note**: A score of 100% is possible only if *all* requirements are met and no Opportunities for Improvement can be identified. In addition, to score in the 90% to 100% band, examiners must observe full deployment, extensive and ongoing evaluation, improvement, organizational learning, innovation, and knowledge sharing throughout the organization. Required approaches must be well integrated with organizational needs identified in response to most other Criteria Items.	and is able to explain how these horizons are set, and addressed through the strategic planning process. 2. The organization effectively and systematically ensures that strategic planning addresses the key factors listed below. In addition, it collects and analyzes relevant data and information pertaining to these factors as part of the strategic planning process: • Organizational strengths, weaknesses, opportunities, and threats • Early indications of major shifts in technology, markets, products, customer preferences, competition, or the regulatory environment • Long-term organizational sustainability, including needed core competencies • The organization's ability to execute the strategic plan **b. Strategic Objectives** 1. The organization clearly defines key strategic objectives and the timetable for accomplishing them, and lists the most important quantifiable goals or targets for these strategic objectives. 2. Strategic objectives effectively address strategic challenges and advantages and opportunities for innovation in products, operations, and the business model. The organization ensures strategic objectives address current and future core competencies. The organization ensures that strategic objectives balance short- and longer-term challenges and opportunities, and balance the needs of all key stakeholders. *The approach to strategy development is well deployed with no significant gaps (D). A systematic, fact-based process is in place to evaluate and improve elements of (a) and (b) above, with clear evidence of innovation, organizational learning, and organization-level sharing and analysis, which results in ongoing refinements and improved integration throughout the organization (L). Organizational learning about (a) and, (b) above and systematic evaluation and improvement of (a) and (b) above are key management tools. The approach is integrated with organizational needs set forth in the Organizational Profile (for example, mission, vision, values, culture, product offerings, customer groups/segments and requirements, core competencies, challenges and advantages, workforce characteristics and needs, technologies, equipment, regulatory environment, key suppliers, partners, and collaborators, and the competitive environment) and the requirements of other Process Items (for example, action plans and their performance measures [2.2a(1, 6)], governance and societal responsibilities [1.2], measures and analysis of performance [4.1], reward and recognition of performance [5.1a(3)], leadership and workforce development [5.1b(1)], and process management [6.1, 6.2]) (I).*

Insights to Performance Excellence 2009–2010

\multicolumn{2}{c}{**2.2 Strategic Deployment** (45 points possible)}
Best Fit Scoring Guidelines	**Expected Findings**
0–5% If examiners observe the applicant is not responsive to the requirements of an Item or provides no relevant information, the score should be zero (0%). If the applicant provides some anecdotal information addressing Item requirements (even though no systematic approach has begun), the score should be 5%.	**0–5% Scoring Band: No Systems to Meet Requirements** **2.2 Strategy Deployment.** The organization has no effective processes to deploy its strategy (usually involving a process to convert its strategic objectives into action plans and implement them) [2.2a(1)] *(A)*. Day-to-day work actions are generally ad hoc *(D)*. Reacting to problems is the normal way of approaching work and no consistent effort is made to prevent problems *(L)*. There is no effective alignment in the organization related to strategy deployment and people and/or units seem to operate independently *(I)*.
10–25% If examiners observe the applicant is barely doing some of the things required in the 10–25% Beginning scoring band, the score should be in the lower part of this band. If they observe the applicant is doing everything required in the 10–25% Beginning band, but nothing in the higher bands, the score should be 25%.	**10–25% Scoring Band: Beginning to Meet Basic Requirements** **2.2 Strategy Deployment.** The organization is in the beginning stages of establishing effective processes for systematically developing action plans to deploy its strategy (usually involving a process to convert its strategic objectives into action plans and implementing them) [2.2a(1)] *(A)*. Major gaps exist where the action plans do not cover most elements essential to effective deployment of strategic objectives *(D)*. Reacting to problems in deploying strategic plans and actions is widespread; working to prevent problems is in the beginning stages *(L)*. Alignment of action plans is accomplished generally by the use of joint problem solving *(I)*.
30–45% If examiners observe the applicant is doing everything required in the 10–25% Beginning scoring band, and a few additional things in the higher bands, the score should be in the lower part of the 30–45% Basic band. If they observe the applicant is doing everything required in the 30–45% Basic band, but nothing in the higher bands, the score should be 45%.	**30–45% Scoring Band: Systematically Meeting Basic Requirements** **2.2 Strategy Deployment.** The organization has effective, systematic processes in place to develop action plans to deploy its strategy (usually involving a process to convert its strategic objectives into action plans and implement them) [2.2a(1)] *(A)*. Action plans for key elements of its strategic plan have been deployed to most key areas in the organization *(D)*. The organization is beginning to evaluate some of the processes to deploy action plans and may or may not have made improvements based on the evaluation *(L)*. The action plans are generally consistent with organization priorities such as those set forth in the Organizational Profile (for example, values and vision) and basic requirements of other Process Items (for example, strategy [2.1], measures of success [4.1]), and engaging the workforce [5.1]) *(I)*.
50–65% If examiners observe the applicant is doing everything required in the 30–45% Basic scoring band, and a few additional things in the higher bands, the score should be in the lower part of the 50–65% Overall band. If they observe the applicant is doing everything in the 50–65% Overall band, but nothing in the next higher 70–85% band, the score should be 65%.	**50–65% Scoring Band: Systematically Meeting Overall Requirements** **2.2 Strategy Deployment.** The organization has effective, systematic processes in place to do the following: a. **Action Plan Development and Deployment.** Convert its strategic objectives into action plans [2.2a(2)]. Action plans [2.2a(1)], how they are deployed [2.2a(2)], and related performance measures or indicators [2.2a(6)] are summarized *(A)*. b. **Performance Projection.** Project the organization's future performance levels relative to key comparisons for most of the key performance measures or indicators identified in 2.2a(6) [2.2b] *(A)*. Some relatively minor gaps may exist in the deployment of these processes in some parts of the organization *(D)*. A systematic, fact-based process is in place to evaluate the efficiency/effectiveness of some of the key elements of (a) and/or (b) above; and—for scores of 65%—evidence of at least one cycle of improvement **and some innovation (meaningful change)** within one or more of these elements *(L)*. Action plans are generally aligned with organizational needs set forth in the Organizational Profile (for example, mission, vision, values, culture, product offerings, customer groups/segments and requirements, core competencies, challenges

Continued

Clarifying the Baldrige Scoring Requirements

267

Best Fit Scoring Guidelines	2.2 Strategic Deployment *(45 points possible)* Continued Expected Findings
	and advantages, workforce characteristics and needs and the competitive environment) and the requirements of other Process Items (for example, strategic objectives [2.1b(1)], governance and societal responsibilities [1.2a, c], leadership development [5.1b(1)], measures and analysis of performance [4.1], data used by senior leaders to review organizational progress [1.1b(2) and 4.1b], and the performance management system [5.1a(3)]) (I).
70–85% If examiners observe the applicant is doing everything required in the 50–65% Overall scoring band, and a few additional things in the 70–100% Multiple scoring band, the score should be in the lower part of the Multiple scoring band (for example, 70–75%). If they observe the applicant is meeting many to most requirements in the 70–100% Multiple scoring band, the score should be 85%. **90–100%** If examiners observe the applicant fully addressing the multiple Approach requirements and most of the Deployment, Learning, and Integration requirements described in the 70–100% Multiple scoring band, the score should be 90–95%. If examiners observe the applicant is meeting all of the requirements in the 70–100% Multiple band, the score should be 100%. **Note**: A score of 100% is possible only if *all* requirements are met and no Opportunities for Improvement can be identified. In addition, to score in the 90% to 100% band, examiners must observe full deployment, extensive and ongoing evaluation, improvement, organizational learning, innovation, and knowledge sharing throughout the organization. Required approaches must be well integrated with organizational needs identified in response to most other Criteria Items.	***70–85% and 90–100% Scoring Bands: Multiple Requirements*** **2.2 Strategy Deployment.** The organization has effective processes in place to convert its strategic objectives into action plans . The organization has clearly defined these action plans, how they are deployed, and the key action plan performance measures or indicators are summarized. The organization has projected its future performance relative to key comparisons on these key performance measures or indicators. *a. Action Plan Development and Deployment* 1. The organization identifies key short- and longer-term action plans and any key planned changes to products, customers and markets and how it will operate. 2. The organization effectively and systematically develops and deploys action plans throughout the organization to the workforce and to key suppliers and partners, to achieve its key strategic objectives. It ensures that the key outcomes of action plans can be sustained. 3. The organization effectively and systematically ensures that adequate financial and other resources are available to support the accomplishment of its action plans while meeting current obligations. It allocates resources in a way that supports the accomplishment of these plans. The organization assesses and manages the financial and other risks associated with the plans. 4. The organization establishes and deploys modified action plans promptly if circumstances require a shift in plans and rapid execution of new plans. 5. The organization effectively and systematically develops key human resource plans to accomplish short- and longer-term strategic objectives and action plans. These plans address potential impacts on the organization's workforce, as well as any potential changes to workforce capability and capacity. 6. The organization effectively and systematically develops a list of key performance measures or indicators that are used for tracking the achievement and effectiveness of its action plans. It ensures that the organization's overall action plan measurement system reinforces organizational alignment and covers all key deployment areas and stakeholders. *b. Performance Projection.* The organization has defined both short- and longer-term performance projections for the key performance measures or indicators identified in 2.2a(6). —These projections are determined in a systematic and clearly defined way —The projections are determined in a systematic and clearly defined way —The organization has assessed how its projected performance compares with the projected performance of its competitors or comparable organizations, and with its own key benchmarks, goals, and past performance, as appropriate —The organization has a system in place to ensure that it is making progress to meet its performance projections *Organizational strategies have been converted to action plans and are well deployed with no significant gaps (D). A systematic, fact-based process is in place to evaluate*

Continued

2.2 Strategic Deployment *(45 points possible)* — Continued

Best Fit Scoring Guidelines	Expected Findings
	and improve elements of (a) and (b) above, with clear evidence of ongoing innovation, organizational learning, and organization-level sharing and analysis, which results in refinements and improved integration throughout the organization (L). Organizational learning about (a) and, (b) above and systematic evaluation and improvement of (a) and (b) above are key management tools. The approach is integrated with organizational needs set forth in the Organizational Profile (for example, vision, customer groups/segments and requirements, core competencies, challenges and advantages, workforce characteristics and needs and the competitive environment) and the requirements of other Process Items (for example, strategic objectives [2.1b(1)], governance and societal responsibilities [1.2a, c], leadership development [5.1b(1)], measures and analysis of performance, including benchmarking comparison organizations [4.1], data used by senior leaders to review organizational progress [1.1b(2) and 4.1b], and the performance management system [5.1a(3)]) (I).

3.1 Customer Engagement *(40 points possible)*

Best Fit Scoring Guidelines	Expected Findings
0–5% If examiners observe the applicant is not responsive to the requirements of an Item or provides no relevant information, the score should be zero (0%). If the applicant provides some anecdotal information addressing Item requirements (even though no systematic approach has begun), the score should be 5%.	**0–5% Scoring Band: No Systems to Meet Requirements** **3.1 Customer Engagement.** The organization has no effective processes to engage customers to serve their needs and build relationships [3.1a(1)] *(A)*. *Efforts to learn about customer engagement and building relationships are ad hoc (D). Reacting to problems is the normal way of approaching work and no consistent effort is made to prevent problems related to customer or market knowledge (L). There is no effective alignment in the organization related to understanding customer and market requirements and people and/or units seem to operate independently (I).*
10–25% If examiners observe the applicant is barely doing some of the things required in the 10–25% Beginning scoring band, the score should be in the lower part of this band. If they observe the applicant is doing everything required in the 10–25% Beginning band, but nothing in the higher bands, the score should be 25%.	**10–25% Scoring Band: Beginning to Meet Basic Requirements** **3.1 Customer Engagement.** The organization is in the beginning stages of establishing effective processes to engage customers to serve their needs [3.1a(1)] and build relationships [3.1b(2)] *(A). Major gaps exist where the processes to serve customers needs and build relationships do not cover most customer segments or groups (D). Reacting to problems related to understanding customer and market requirements is widespread; working to prevent problems is in the beginning stages (L). Alignment of customer requirements with organization priorities and work is accomplished generally by the use of joint problem solving (I).*

Continued

3.1 Customer Engagement *(40 points possible)* — Continued

Best Fit Scoring Guidelines	Expected Findings
30–45% If examiners observe the applicant is doing everything required in the 10–25% Beginning scoring band, and a few additional things in the higher bands, the score should be in the lower part of the 30–45% Basic band. If they observe the applicant is doing everything required in the 30–45% Basic band, but nothing in the higher bands, the score should be 45%.	**30–45% Scoring Band: Systematically Meeting Basic Requirements** **3.1 Customer Engagement.** The organization has effective, systematic processes in place for engaging customers to serve their needs [3.1a(1)] and to build relationships [3.1b(2)] *(A)*. Some gaps exist where engaging customers and building relationships do not cover some customer segments or groups to effectively understand their requirements *(D)*. The organization is beginning to evaluate some of these processes and may or may not have made improvements based on the evaluation *(L)*. The processes to engage customers and build relationships are generally consistent with organization priorities, such as those set forth in the Organizational Profile (for example, values, vision, customer groups and their requirements) and basic requirements of other Process Items (for example, strategy [2.1] related action plans [2.2], and obtaining and using customer information [3.2]) *(I)*.
50–65% If examiners observe the applicant is doing everything required in the 30–45% Basic scoring band, and a few additional things in the higher bands, the score should be in the lower part of the 50–65% Overall band. If they observe the applicant is doing everything in the 50–65% Overall band, but nothing in the next higher 70–85% band, the score should be 65%.	**50–65% Scoring Band: Systematically Meeting Overall Requirements** **3.1 Customer Engagement.** The organization has effective, systematic processes in place to do the following: **a. Product Offerings and Customer Support.** Determine product offerings and mechanisms to support customers' use of the organization's products [3.1a(1)] *(A)*. **b. Building a Customer Culture.** Build a customer-focused culture that ensures a positive customer experience [3.1b(1)] *(A)*. *Some relatively minor gaps may exist in the use of these processes in some parts of the organization and the processes may not fully consider all customer or market segments (D). A systematic, fact-based process is in place to evaluate the efficiency/effectiveness of some of the key elements of (a) above; and—for scores of 65%—evidence of at least one cycle of improvement* **and some innovation (meaningful change)** *within one or more of these elements (L). The customer engagement processes are generally aligned with organizational needs set forth in the Organizational Profile (for example, mission, vision, values, culture, product offerings, customer groups/segments and requirements, core competencies) and the requirements of other Process Items (for example, strategic objectives [2.1b(1)], action plans and their performance measures [2.2a(1, 6)], measures and analysis of performance [4.1], and work systems [6.1] and work process design and management to deliver customer value [6.2]) (I).*
70–85% If examiners observe the applicant is doing everything required in the 50–65% Overall scoring band, and a few additional things in the 70–100% Multiple scoring band, the score should be in the lower part of the Multiple scoring band (for example, 70–75%). If they observe the applicant is meeting many to most requirements in the 70–100% Multiple scoring band, the score should be 85%.	**70–85% and 90–100% Scoring Bands: Multiple Requirements** **3.1 Customer Engagement.** The organization effectively determines product offerings and mechanisms to support customers' use of the organization's products. The organization builds a customer-focused culture. **a. Product Offerings and Customer Support** 1. The organization effectively and systematically identifies and innovates product offerings to meet the requirements and exceed the expectations of customer groups and market segments (identified in the organizational profile). The organization identifies and innovates product offerings to attract new customers and provides opportunities for expanding relationships with existing customers, as appropriate. 2. The organization effectively and systematically determines key mechanisms to support the use of its products and to enable customers to seek information and conduct business with the organization. The organization identifies its key means

Continued

3.1 Customer Engagement *(40 points possible)*	Continued
Best Fit Scoring Guidelines	**Expected Findings**

90–100% If examiners observe the applicant fully addressing the multiple Approach requirements and most of the Deployment, Learning, and Integration requirements described in the 70–100% Multiple scoring band, the score should be 90–95%. If examiners observe the applicant is meeting all of the requirements in the 70–100% Multiple band, the score should be 100%.

Note: A score of 100% is possible only if *all* requirements are met and no Opportunities for Improvement can be identified. In addition, to score in the 90% to 100% band, examiners must observe full deployment, extensive and ongoing evaluation, improvement, organizational learning, innovation, and knowledge sharing throughout the organization. Required approaches must be well integrated with organizational needs identified in response to most other Criteria Items.

of customer support, including key communication mechanisms and how they vary for different customers, customer groups, or market segments. The organization determines its customers' key support requirements and ensures they are deployed to all people and processes involved in customer support.

3. The organization effectively and systematically keeps its approaches for identifying and innovating product offerings for providing customer support current with business needs and directions.

b. Building a Customer Culture

1. The organization has effective, systematic approaches in place to create an organization culture that ensures a consistently positive customer experience and contributes to customer engagement. The organization's workforce performance management system and workforce and leader development systems reinforce this culture.
2. The organization builds and manages relationships with customers to:
   - Acquire new customers
   - Meet their requirements and exceed their expectations in each stage of the customer life cycle
   - Increase their engagement with the organization
3. The organization effectively and systematically keeps its approaches for creating a customer-focused culture and building customer relationships current with business needs and direction.

The approach to ensuring customer engagement and building relationships is well deployed with no significant gaps (D). A systematic, fact-based process is in place to evaluate and improve elements of customer engagement with clear evidence of innovation, organizational learning, and organization-level sharing and analysis, which results in ongoing refinements and improved integration throughout the organization (L). Organizational learning about customer engagement and building relationships through the systematic evaluation and improvement of the processes related to gaining this knowledge are key management tools. The approach is integrated with organizational needs set forth in the Organizational Profile (for example, mission, vision, values, culture, product offerings, customer groups/segments and requirements, core competencies) and the requirements of other Process Items (for example, strategic objectives [2.1b(1)], action plans and their performance measures [2.2a(1, 6)], customer requirements, preferences and changing expectations [3.2], measures and analysis of performance [4.1], transferring knowledge to customers [4.2a(3)], and work systems selection and design incorporating information from customers [6.1] and work process design and management to deliver customer value with input from customers [6.2]) (I).

Best Fit Scoring Guidelines	3.2 Voice of the Customer (45 points possible) Expected Findings
0–5% If examiners observe the applicant is not responsive to the requirements of an Item or provides no relevant information, the score should be zero (0%). If the applicant provides some anecdotal information addressing Item requirements (even though no systematic approach has begun), the score should be 5%.	**0–5% Scoring Band: No Systems to Meet Requirements** ***3.2 Voice of the Customer.*** The organization has no effective processes for obtaining [3.2a(1)] and using information [3.2c(1)] from customers *(A)*. *Efforts to obtain and use information are ad hoc (D). Reacting to problems is the normal way of approaching work and no consistent effort is made to prevent problems related to building customer relationships or determining levels of satisfaction (L). There is no effective alignment in the organization related to listening to customers and determining levels of satisfaction; people and/or units seem to operate independently (I).*
10–25% If examiners observe the applicant is barely doing some of the things required in the 10–25% Beginning scoring band, the score should be in the lower part of this band. If they observe the applicant is doing everything required in the 10–25% Beginning band, but nothing in the higher bands, the score should be 25%.	**10–25% Scoring Band: Beginning to Meet Basic Requirements** ***3.2 Voice of the Customer.*** The organization is in the beginning stages of obtaining [3.2a(1)] and using information [3.2c(1)] from customers *(A)*. *Major gaps exist where obtaining and using information do not cover most customer segments/groups and/or products and services (D). Reacting to problems with customer relationships and satisfaction is widespread; working to prevent problems is in the beginning stages (L). The organization generally relies on joint problem-solving teams to align activities to listen to customers and understand customer satisfaction levels (I).*
30–45% If examiners observe the applicant is doing everything required in the 10–25% Beginning scoring band, and a few additional things in the higher bands, the score should be in the lower part of the 30–45% Basic band. If they observe the applicant is doing everything required in the 30–45% Basic band, but nothing in the higher bands, the score should be 45%.	**30–45% Scoring Band: Systematically Meeting Basic Requirements** ***3.2 Voice of the Customer.*** The organization has effective, systematic processes in place to obtain [3.2a(1)] and use information [3.2c(1)] from its customers *(A)*. *Some gaps exist where obtaining and using information do not cover many important customer segments or groups (D). The organization is beginning to evaluate some of these processes and may or may not have made improvements based on the evaluation (L). The processes for listening to customers and determining satisfaction and engagement are generally consistent with organization priorities such as those set forth in the Organizational Profile (for example, values, vision, and customer groups and requirements) and basic requirements of other Process Items (for example, engaging customers and building relationships [3.1], strategy development [2.1], engaging the workforce [5.1], and managing work processes [6.2b]) (I).*
50–65% If examiners observe the applicant is doing everything required in the 30–45% Basic scoring band, and a few additional things in the higher bands, the score should be in the lower part of the 50–65% Overall band. If they observe the applicant is doing everything in the 50–65% Overall band, but nothing in the next higher 70–85% band, the score should be 65%.	**50–65% Scoring Band: Systematically Meeting Overall Requirements** ***3.2 Voice of the Customer.*** The organization has effective, systematic processes in place to do the following: **a. Customer Listening.** Listen to customer [3.2a(1)] *(A)*. **b. Determination of Customer Satisfaction and Engagement.** Acquires customer satisfaction [3.2b(1)] and dissatisfaction information [3.2b(3)] *(A)*. **c. Analysis and Use of Customer Data.** Use Customer information to improve marketplace success. *Some relatively minor gaps may exist in the use of these processes in some parts of the organization (D). A systematic, fact-based process is in place to evaluate the efficiency/effectiveness of some of the key elements of (a) and/or (b) above; and—for scores of 65%—evidence of at least one cycle of improvement **and some innovation (meaningful change)** within one or more of these elements (L). The processes for listening to customers, determining satisfaction and engagement, and using that information for improvement are generally aligned with organizational needs set forth in the*

Continued

	3.2 Voice of the Customer *(45 points possible)*	Continued
Best Fit Scoring Guidelines	**Expected Findings**	
	Organizational Profile (for example, mission, vision, values, culture, product offerings, customer groups/segments and requirements, core competencies) and the requirements of other Process Items (for example, strategic objectives [2.1b(1)], action plans and their performance measures [2.2a(1, 6)], managing workforce performance [5.1a(3)], developing the workforce and leaders [5.1b], measures and analysis of performance [4.1], work systems identification and design [6.1], and implement, manage, and improve work processes to deliver customer value [6.2]) (I).	
70–85% If examiners observe the applicant is doing everything required in the 50–65% Overall scoring band, and a few additional things in the 70–100% Multiple scoring band, the score should be in the lower part of the Multiple scoring band (for example, 70–75%). If they observe the applicant is meeting many to most requirements in the 70–100% Multiple scoring band, the score should be 85%. **90–100%** If examiners observe the applicant fully addressing the multiple Approach requirements and most of the Deployment, Learning, and Integration requirements described in the 70–100% Multiple scoring band, the score should be 90–95%. If examiners observe the applicant is meeting all of the requirements in the 70–100% Multiple band, the score should be 100%. **Note**: A score of 100% is possible only if *all* requirements are met and no Opportunities for Improvement can be identified. In addition, to score in the 90% to 100% band, examiners must observe full deployment, extensive and ongoing evaluation, improvement, organizational learning, innovation, and knowledge sharing throughout the organization. Required approaches must be well integrated with organizational needs identified in response to most other Criteria Items.	**70–85% and 90–100% Scoring Bands: Multiple Requirements** **3.2 Voice of the Customer.** The organization effectively listens to customers and acquires satisfaction and dissatisfaction information. The organization describes how customer information is used to improve marketplace success. **a. Customer Listening** 1. The organization has effective systems in place to listen to customers to obtain actionable information and to obtain feedback on its products and customer support. Listening methods vary for different customers, customer groups, or market segments and vary across the customer life cycle. The organization follows up with customers on the quality of products, customer support, and transactions to receive immediate and actionable feedback. 2. The organization has effective systems in place to listen to former customers, potential customers, and customers of competitors to obtain actionable information and to obtain feedback on its products, customer support, and transactions, as appropriate. 3. The organization has effective systems in place to manage customer complaints. The customer complaint management process ensures that complaints are resolved promptly and effectively and allows the organization to recover its customers' confidence, and enhance their satisfaction and engagement. The complaint management system enables the aggregation and analysis of complaints for use in improvement throughout the organization and by partners, as appropriate. **b. Determination of Customer Satisfaction and Engagement** 1. The organization effectively and systematically determines customer satisfaction and engagement. These determination methods differ among customer groups and market segments, as appropriate. The organization's measurements capture actionable information for use in exceeding customers' expectations and securing customers' engagement. Determination methods enable the aggregation and analysis of data for use in improvement throughout the organization and by partners, as appropriate. 2. The organization effectively and systematically obtains and uses information on its customers' satisfaction relative to their satisfaction with competitors. It obtains and uses information on customers' satisfaction relative to the satisfaction levels of customers of other organizations providing similar products or to industry benchmarks, as appropriate. 3. The organization effectively and systematically determines customer dissatisfaction. Measurements capture actionable information for use in meeting customers' requirements and exceeding their expectations in the future. These methods enable the aggregation and analysis of data for use in improvement throughout the organization and by partners, as appropriate.	
		Continued

Best Fit Scoring Guidelines	3.2 Voice of the Customer *(45 points possible)* Continued **Expected Findings**
	c. Analysis and Use of Customer Data 1. The organization effectively and systematically uses customer, market, and product offering information to identify current and anticipate future customer groups and market segments. It considers customers of competitors and other potential customers and markets in this segmentation. It determines which customers, customer groups, and market segments to pursue for current and future products. 2. The organization effectively and systematically uses customer, market, and product offering information to identify and anticipate key customer requirements (including products and product features) and changing expectations and their relative importance to customers' purchasing or relationship decisions. It identifies and anticipates how these requirements and changing expectations will differ across customers, customer groups, and market segments and across the customer life cycle. 3. The organization effectively and systematically uses customer, market, and product offering information to improve marketing, build a more customer-focused culture, and identify opportunities for innovation. 4. The organization effectively and systematically keeps its approaches for customer listening; determination of customer satisfaction, dissatisfaction, and engagement; and use of customer data current with business needs and directions. *The approaches to listening to customers and determining customer satisfaction, engagement, and dissatisfaction are well deployed with no significant gaps (D). A systematic, fact-based process is in place to evaluate and improve elements of (a) and (b) above, with clear evidence of ongoing innovation, organizational learning, and organization-level sharing and analysis, which results in refinements and improved integration throughout the organization (L). Organizational learning about customer relationships and satisfaction, and systematic evaluation and improvement of the related processes are key management tools. The approach is integrated with organizational needs set forth in the Organizational Profile (for example, mission, vision, values, culture, product offerings, customer groups/segments and requirements, core competencies) and the requirements of other Process Items (for example, strategic objectives [2.1b(1)], action plans and their performance measures [2.2a(1, 6)], managing workforce performance [5.1a(3)], measures and analysis of performance [4.1], work systems identification and design with input from customers [6.1], and implement, manage, and improve work processes to deliver customer value [6.2]) (I).*

4.1 Measurement, Analysis, and Improvement of Organizational Performance *(45 points possible)*	
Best Fit Scoring Guidelines	**Expected Findings**
0–5% If examiners observe the applicant is not responsive to the requirements of an Item or provides no relevant information, the score should be zero (0%). If the applicant provides some anecdotal information addressing Item requirements (even though no systematic approach has begun), the score should be 5%.	*0–5% Scoring Band: No Systems to Meet Requirements* *4.1 Measurement, Analysis, and Improvement of Organizational Performance.* The organization has no effective processes to measure, [4.1a(1)], analyze [4.1b], and improve organizational performance [4.1c] *(A). Efforts to gather, analyze, and use data to support decision making and performance improvement are not consistent throughout the organization (D). Intuition, "gut feel," and guess work are usually used rather than data to drive decisions and make improvements; reacting to problems is the normal way of approaching work (L). There is no effective alignment between the data, information, and analyses that are used to support organization strategic objectives (2.1), mission, vision, and values (1.1), reward and recognition (5.1), and people and/or units seem to operate independently (I).*
10–25% If examiners observe the applicant is barely doing some of the things required in the 10–25% Beginning scoring band, the score should be in the lower part of this band. If they observe the applicant is doing everything required in the 10–25% Beginning band, but nothing in the higher bands, the score should be 25%.	*10–25% Scoring Band: Beginning to Meet Basic Requirements* *4.1 Measurement, Analysis, and Improvement of Organizational Performance.* The organization is in the beginning stages of establishing effective processes for measuring [4.1a(1)], analyzing [4.1b], and improving organizational performance [4.1c] *(A). Major gaps exist where the measures and reviews do not cover many elements essential to organization performance (D). Reacting to problems with ineffective data and analyses to support decision making and process improvement is widespread; working to prevent problems is in the beginning stages (L). The organization generally relies on joint problem solving to promote organization alignment of measurement, analysis, and improvement processes (I).*
30–45% If examiners observe the applicant is doing everything required in the 10–25% Beginning scoring band, and a few additional things in the higher bands, the score should be in the lower part of the 30–45% Basic band. If they observe the applicant is doing everything required in the 30–45% Basic band, but nothing in the higher bands, the score should be 45%.	*30–45% Scoring Band: Systematically Meeting Basic Requirements* *4.1 Measurement, Analysis, and Improvement of Organizational Performance.* The organization has effective, systematic processes in place for measuring [4.1a(1)], analyzing [4.1b], and improving organizational performance [4.1c] *(A). Measures, analyses, and improvement activities cover some areas essential to organization performance (D). The organization is beginning to evaluate some of these processes and may or may not have made improvements based on the evaluation (L). These processes are generally consistent with organization priorities such as those set forth in the Organizational Profile (for example, values and vision) and basic requirements of other Process Items (for example, strategy development [2.1], strategy deployment [2.2], and engaging the workforce [5.1b]) (I).*
50–65% If examiners observe the applicant is doing everything required in the 30–45% Basic scoring band, and a few additional things in the higher bands, the score should be in the lower part of the 50–65% Overall band. If they observe the applicant is doing everything in the 50–65% Overall band, but nothing in the next higher 70–85% band, the score should be 65%.	*50–65% Scoring Band: Systematically Meeting Overall Requirements* *4.1 Measurement, Analysis, and Improvement of Organizational Performance.* The organization has effective, systematic processes in place to do the following: a. **Performance Measurement.** Measure (gather), align, and use data and information to support effective decision making to improve organizational performance at all levels and in all parts of the organization [4.1a(1)] *(A).* b. **Performance Analysis and Review.** Analyzes performance through the use of data and information at all levels and in all parts of the organization. [4.1b)] *(A).* c. **Performance Improvement.** Improves performance through the use of data and information at all levels and in all parts of the organization. [4.1c] *Some relatively minor gaps may exist in the deployment or use of these processes in some parts of the organization (D). A systematic, fact-based process is in place to evaluate the efficiency/effectiveness of some of the key elements of (a), (b), and/or*

Continued

4.1 Measurement, Analysis, and Improvement of Organizational Performance (45 points possible) Continued

Best Fit Scoring Guidelines	Expected Findings
	(c) above; and—for scores of 65%—evidence of at least one cycle of improvement *and some innovation (meaningful change)* within one or more of *these elements (L). The measurement, analysis, and improvement processes are generally aligned with organizational needs set forth in the Organizational Profile (for example, mission, vision, values, culture, product offerings, customer and workforce groups/segments and requirements, core competencies) and the requirements of other Process Items (for example, strategic objectives [2.1b(1)],, action plans and their performance measures [2.2a(1, 6)], information and knowledge management [4.2], workforce reward and recognition [5.1a(3)], work systems selection and design [6.1], and work process design, management, and improvement [6.2]) (I).*
70–85% If examiners observe the applicant is doing everything required in the 50–65% Overall scoring band, and a few additional things in the 70–100% Multiple scoring band, the score should be in the lower part of the Multiple scoring band (for example, 70–75%). If they observe the applicant is meeting many to most requirements in the 70–100% Multiple scoring band, the score should be 85%. **90–100%** If examiners observe the applicant fully addressing the multiple Approach requirements and most of the Deployment, Learning, and Integration requirements described in the 70–100% Multiple scoring band, the score should be 90–95%. If examiners observe the applicant is meeting all of the requirements in the 70–100% Multiple band, the score should be 100%. Note: A score of 100% is possible only if *all* requirements are met and no Opportunities for Improvement can be identified. In addition, to score in the 90% to 100% band, examiners must observe full deployment, extensive and ongoing evaluation, improvement, organizational learning, innovation, and knowledge sharing throughout the organization. Required approaches must be well integrated with organizational needs identified in response to most other Criteria Items.	**70–85% and 90–100% Scoring Bands: Multiple Requirements** *4.1 Measurement, Analysis, and Improvement of Organizational Performance.* The organization measures, analyzes, aligns, reviews, and improves its performance through the use of data and information at all levels and in all parts of the organization. *a. Performance Measurement* 1. The organization effectively selects, collects, aligns, and integrates data and information to track daily operations and overall organizational performance, including progress relative to strategic objectives and action plans. Key organizational performance measures and the frequency of those measures, including key short- and longer-term financial measures, are clearly defined. These data and information are used consistently to support decision making and innovation throughout the organization. 2. The organization effectively and systematically selects and ensures the effective use of key comparative data and information to support operational and strategic decision making and innovation. 3. The organization effectively and systematically keeps the performance measurement system current with business needs and directions. The performance measurement system is sensitive to rapid or unexpected organizational or external changes (e.g., able to identify the need to change plus have the flexibility and responsiveness to make the changes needed in a timely manner so the needs of data users continue to be met). *b. Performance Analysis and Review* Organizational performance and capabilities are systematically reviewed. Appropriate analyses are used to support these reviews and ensure conclusions are valid. These reviews are used to assess organizational success, competitive performance, and progress relative to strategic objectives and action plans, and the organization's ability to respond rapidly to changing organizational needs and challenges in its operating environment. *c. Performance Improvement* The organization effectively uses organizational performance review findings to identify priorities for continuous and breakthrough improvement, and opportunities for innovation. These priorities for improvement and opportunities for innovation are deployed to work groups and functional-level operations throughout the organization to support their decision making. The organization also deploys these priorities and opportunities to appropriate suppliers, partners, and collaborators to ensure organizational alignment.

Continued

4.1 Measurement, Analysis, and Improvement of Organizational Performance *(45 points possible)* Continued	
Best Fit Scoring Guidelines	**Expected Findings**
	The approaches to measurement, analysis, review, and improvement of organization performance are well deployed with no significant gaps (D). A systematic, fact-based process is in place to evaluate and improve elements of (a), (b), and (c) above, with clear evidence of ongoing innovation, organizational learning, and organization-level sharing and analysis, which results in refinements and improved integration throughout the organization (L). Organizational learning about, as well as systematic evaluation and improvement of (a), (b), and (c) above, are key management tools. The approach is integrated with organizational needs set forth in the Organizational Profile (for example, mission, vision, values, culture, product offerings, customer and workforce groups/segments and requirements, core competencies) and the requirements of other Process Items (for example, strategic objectives [2.1b(1)],. action plans and their performance measures [2.2a(1, 6)], information and knowledge management [4.2], workforce reward and recognition [5.1a(3)], work systems selection and design [6.1], and work process design, management, and improvement including the use of in-process measures [6.2]) (I).

4.2 Management of Information, Knowledge, and Information Technology *(45 points possible)* Continued	
Best Fit Scoring Guidelines	**Expected Findings**
0–5% If examiners observe the applicant is not responsive to the requirements of an Item or provides no relevant information, the score should be zero (0%). If the applicant provides some anecdotal information addressing Item requirements (even though no systematic approach has begun), the score should be 5%.	**0–5% *Scoring Band: No Systems to Meet Requirements*** **4.2 *Management of Information, Knowledge, and Information Technology.*** The organization has no effective processes to manage its organizational information [4.2a(2)] and knowledge [4.2a(3)], or its information technology [4.2b(1)] *(A)*. *Efforts to make needed information and/or knowledge available to support organizational decision making and/or learning are ad hoc (D). Reacting to problems through intuition and guess work is the normal way of approaching work and no consistent effort is made to prevent problems (L). There is no effective alignment in the organization related to information technology, data availability, or knowledge management, and people and/or units seem to operate independently (I).*
10–25% If examiners observe the applicant is barely doing some of the things required in the 10–25% Beginning scoring band, the score should be in the lower part of this band. If they observe the applicant is doing everything required in the 10–25% Beginning band, but nothing in the higher bands, the score should be 25%.	**10–25% *Scoring Band: Beginning to Meet Basic Requirements*** **4.2 *Management of Information, Knowledge, and Information Technology.*** The organization is in the beginning stages of establishing effective processes to manage organizational information [4.2a(2)], knowledge [4.2a(3)], and information technology [4.2b(1)] (ensuring their availability to support decision making) *(A)*. *Major gaps exist where essential information, knowledge, and information technology are not available when and where needed to support organizational decision making (D). Reacting to problems related to poor data availability is widespread; working to prevent problems is in the beginning stages (L). The organization generally relies on joint problem solving to promote alignment of information technology, information, and knowledge management needs (I).*

Continued

4.2 Management of Information, Knowledge, and Information Technology *(45 points possible)* Continued	
Best Fit Scoring Guidelines	**Expected Findings**
30–45% If examiners observe the applicant is doing everything required in the 10–25% Beginning scoring band, and a few additional things in the higher bands, the score should be in the lower part of the 30–45% Basic band. If they observe the applicant is doing everything required in the 30–45% Basic band, but nothing in the higher bands, the score should be 45%.	**30–45% Scoring Band: Systematically Meeting Basic Requirements** *4.2 Management of Information, Knowledge, and Information Technology.* The organization has effective, systematic processes in place to manage organizational information [4.2a(2)], knowledge [4.2a(3)], and information technology [4.2b(1)], (ensuring their availability to support decision making) *(A)* for some areas essential to effective organizational decision making (D). *The organization is beginning to evaluate some of these processes and may or may not have made improvements based on the evaluation (L). Information technology, information, and knowledge management processes are generally consistent with organization priorities such as those set forth in the Organizational Profile (for example, values and vision) and basic requirements of other Process Items (for example, needs related to measuring and analyzing organizational performance [4.1] and work process management [6.2]) (I).*
50–65% If examiners observe the applicant is doing everything required in the 30–45% Basic scoring band, and a few additional things in the higher bands, the score should be in the lower part of the 50–65% Overall band. If they observe the applicant is doing everything in the 50–65% Overall band, but nothing in the next higher 70–85% band, the score should be 65%.	**50–65% Scoring Band: Systematically Meeting Overall Requirements** *4.2 Management of Information, Knowledge, and Information Technology.* The organization has effective, systematic processes in place to do the following: *a. Data, Information, and Knowledge Management.* Ensure the availability of needed data and information [4.2a(2)] and build and manage knowledge assets [4.2a(3)] to support the decision making of its workforce, suppliers, partners, collaborators, and customers *(A)*. *b. Management of Information Resources and Technology.* Ensure data quality [4.2a(1)] and availability of software and hardware to its workforce, suppliers, partners, collaborators, and customers [4.2b(1)] *(A)*. *Some relatively minor gaps may exist in the deployment of these processes in some parts of the organization (D). A systematic, fact-based process is in place to evaluate the efficiency/effectiveness of some of the key elements of (a) and/or (b) above; and— for scores of 65%—evidence of at least one cycle of improvement* **and some innovation (meaningful change)** *within one or more of these elements (L). Processes to manage information, knowledge and information technology are generally aligned with organizational needs set forth in the Organizational Profile (for example, mission, vision, values, product offerings) and the requirements of other Process Items (for example, strategic objectives [2.1b(1)], action plans and their performance measures [2.2a(1, 6)], measurement, analysis, and knowledge management [4.1], workforce and leader development [5.1b], disaster or emergency contingency plans [6.1c], and work process design, management, and improvement [6.2]) (I).*
70–85% If examiners observe the applicant is doing everything required in the 50–65% Overall scoring band, and a few additional things in the 70–100% Multiple scoring band, the score should be in the lower part of the Multiple scoring band (for example, 70–75%). If they observe the applicant is meeting many to most requirements in the 70–100% Multiple scoring band, the score should be 85%.	**70–85% and 90–100% Scoring Bands: Multiple Requirements** *4.2 Management of Information, Knowledge, and Information Technology.* The organization ensures the quality and availability of needed data, information, software, and hardware for its workforce, suppliers, partners, collaborators, and customers. It effectively builds and manages its knowledge assets. *a. Data, Information, and Knowledge Management* 1. The organization has systems in place to ensure its organizational data, information and knowledge possess the following properties: • Accuracy (correctness) • Integrity (completeness) and reliability (consistency) • Timeliness (available when needed) • Security (free from attack) and confidentiality (free from inappropriate release)

Continued

Insights to Performance Excellence 2009–2010

4.2 Management of Information, Knowledge, and Information Technology *(45 points possible)* Continued	
Best Fit Scoring Guidelines	**Expected Findings**
90–100% If examiners observe the applicant fully addressing the multiple Approach requirements and most of the Deployment, Learning, and Integration requirements described in the 70–100% Multiple scoring band, the score should be 90–95%. If examiners observe the applicant is meeting all of the requirements in the 70–100% Multiple band, the score should be 100%. **Note**: A score of 100% is possible only if *all* requirements are met and no Opportunities for Improvement can be identified. In addition, to score in the 90% to 100% band, examiners must observe full deployment, extensive and ongoing evaluation, improvement, organizational learning, innovation, and knowledge sharing throughout the organization. Required approaches must be well integrated with organizational needs identified in response to most other Criteria Items.	2. The organization has systems in place to make needed data and information available and accessible to its workforce, suppliers, partners, collaborators, and customers, as appropriate. 3. Organizational knowledge is effectively managed to accomplish the following: • The collection and transfer of workforce knowledge • The transfer of relevant knowledge from and to customers, suppliers, partners, and collaborators • The rapid identification, sharing, and implementation of best practices • The assembly and transfer of relevant knowledge for use in the organization's strategic planning process **b. Management of Information Resources and Technology** 1. The organization has systems in place to ensure that hardware and software are reliable, secure, and user-friendly. 2. The organization has systems in place to ensure the continued availability of hardware and software systems, as well as the continued availability of data and information, in the event of an emergency. 3. The organization has systems in place to keep data and information availability mechanisms, including software and hardware systems, current with business needs and directions and with technological changes in the operating environment. *The approach to the management of information, information technology, and knowledge is well deployed with no significant gaps (D). A systematic, fact-based process is in place to evaluate and improve elements of (a) and (b) above, with clear evidence of ongoing innovation, organizational learning, and organization-level sharing and analysis, which results in refinements and improved integration throughout the organization (L). Organizational learning about, as well as systematic evaluation and improvement of (a) and (b) above, are key management tools. The approach is integrated with organizational needs set forth in the Organizational Profile (for example, mission, vision, values, product offerings) and the requirements of other Process Items (for example, strategic objectives [2.1b(1)], action plans and their performance measures [2.2a(1, 6)], measurement, analysis, and knowledge management [4.1], workforce and leader development [5.1b], disaster or emergency contingency plans [6.1c], and work process design, management, and improvement including requirements for in-process measures [6.2]) (I).*

Clarifying the Baldrige Scoring Requirements

5.1 Workforce Engagement *(45 points possible)*	
Best Fit Scoring Guidelines	**Expected Findings**
0–5% If examiners observe the applicant is not responsive to the requirements of an Item or provides no relevant information, the score should be zero (0%). If the applicant provides some anecdotal information addressing Item requirements (even though no systematic approach has begun), the score should be 5%.	**0–5% Scoring Band: No Systems to Meet Requirements** *5.1 Workforce Engagement.* The organization has no effective processes to engage the workforce to achieve organizational and personal success (which are usually defined by strategic objectives, related action plans, and workforce development plans) [parts of 5.1a(2, 3) and 5.1b(1, 2)] *(A). Efforts to ensure the workforce is engaged to achieve high levels of performance are ad hoc (D). Reacting to problems is the normal way of approaching work (L). There is no effective alignment of systems to engage the workforce with strategic objectives, action plans or other organization priorities, and people and/or units seem to operate independently (I).*
10–25% If examiners observe the applicant is barely doing some of the things required in the 10–25% Beginning scoring band, the score should be in the lower part of this band. If they observe the applicant is doing everything required in the 10–25% Beginning band, but nothing in the higher bands, the score should be 25%.	**10–25% Scoring Band: Beginning to Meet Basic Requirements** *5.1 Workforce Engagement.* The organization is in the beginning stages of establishing effective processes to engage the workforce to achieve organizational success (which is usually defined by strategic objectives and related action plans) [parts of 5.1a(2)] and personal success (which is usually defined by workforce development plans) [5.1a(3) and 5.1b(1, 2)] *(A). Major gaps exist where the engagement processes do not help most employees achieve organizational or personal success (D). Reacting to employee performance problems is widespread; working to prevent problems is in the beginning stages (L). The organization generally relies on joint problem solving to align and engage the workforce (I).*
30–45% If examiners observe the applicant is doing everything required in the 10–25% Beginning scoring band, and a few additional things in the higher bands, the score should be in the lower part of the 30–45% Basic band. If they observe the applicant is doing everything required in the 30–45% Basic band, but nothing in the higher bands, the score should be 45%.	**30–45% Scoring Band: Systematically Meeting Basic Requirements** *5.1 Workforce Engagement.* The organization has effective, systematic processes in place to engage the workforce to achieve organizational success (which is usually defined by strategic objectives and related action plans) [parts of 5.1a(2)] and personal success (which is usually defined by workforce development plans) [5.1a(3) and 5.1b(1, 2)] *(A). Work engagement processes in some parts of the organization support (or are beginning to support) organizational and personal success (D). The organization is beginning to evaluate some of these processes and may or may not have made improvements based on the evaluation (L). Systems to engage the workforce are generally consistent with organization priorities such as those set forth in the Organizational Profile (for example, values, vision, and workforce motivators) and basic requirements of other Process Items (for example, leadership [1.1], strategy development [2.1] strategy deployment, [2.2], the management of organizational knowledge [4.2], and workforce environment [5.2]) (I).*
50–65% If examiners observe the applicant is doing everything required in the 30–45% Basic scoring band, and a few additional things in the higher bands, the score should be in the lower part of the 50–65% Overall band. If they observe the applicant is doing everything in the 50–65% Overall band, but nothing in the next higher 70–85% band, the score should be 65%.	**50–65% Scoring Band: Systematically Meeting Overall Requirements** *5.1 Workforce Engagement.* The organization has effective, systematic processes in place to do the following: **a. Workforce Enrichment.** Engage, compensate, and reward its workforce to achieve high performance [5.1a(2, 3)] *(A).* **b. Workforce and Leader Development.** Develop its workforce, including leaders, to achieve high performance [5.1b(1, 2)] *(A).* **c. Assessment of Workforce Engagement.** Assess workforce engagement and use the results to achieve higher performance [5.1c(1, 2)] *(A).* *Some relatively minor gaps may exist in the deployment of these processes in some parts of the organization (D). A systematic, fact-based process is in place to evaluate the efficiency/effectiveness of some of the key elements of (a), (b), and/or (c)*

Continued

5.1 Workforce Engagement *(45 points possible)*	Continued
Best Fit Scoring Guidelines	**Expected Findings**
	above; and—*for scores of 65%—evidence* of at least one cycle of improvement ***and some innovation (meaningful change)*** within one or more of *these elements (L). Systems for engaging, enriching, developing, and assessing the workforce are generally aligned with organizational needs set forth in the Organizational Profile (for example, mission, vision, values, culture, workforce groups/segments and requirements) and the requirements of other Process Items (for example, senior leadership communication with the workforce and encouraging high performance [1.1], societal responsibility, legal and ethical behavior [1.2], strategic objectives [2.1b(1)], action plans and their performance measures [2.2a(1, 6)], information and knowledge management [4.2], workforce climate [5.2], and work process design, management, and improvement [6.2]) (I).*
70–85% If examiners observe the applicant is doing everything required in the 50–65% Overall scoring band, and a few additional things in the 70–100% Multiple scoring band, the score should be in the lower part of the Multiple scoring band (for example, 70–75%). If they observe the applicant is meeting many to most requirements in the 70–100% Multiple scoring band, the score should be 85%. **90–100%** If examiners observe the applicant fully addressing the multiple Approach requirements and most of the Deployment, Learning, and Integration requirements described in the 70–100% Multiple scoring band, the score should be 90–95%. If examiners observe the applicant is meeting all of the requirements in the 70–100% Multiple band, the score should be 100%. **Note**: A score of 100% is possible only if *all* requirements are met and no Opportunities for Improvement can be identified. In addition, to score in the 90% to 100% band, examiners must observe full deployment, extensive and ongoing evaluation, improvement, organizational learning, innovation, and knowledge sharing throughout the organization. Required approaches must be well integrated with organizational needs identified in response to most other Criteria Items.	**70–85% and 90–100% Scoring Bands: Multiple Requirements** *5.1 Workforce Engagement.* The organization effectively engages, compensates, and rewards the workforce to achieve high performance; develops the workforce and its leaders to achieve high performance; and assesses workforce engagement and uses the results of the assessments to achieve higher performance. *a. Workforce Enrichment* 1. The organization determines key factors affecting workforce engagement and workforce satisfaction for its different workforce groups and segments. 2. An organizational culture conducive to high performance exists that is characterized by open communication, high performance work, and an engaged workforce; and benefits from the diverse ideas, cultures, and thinking of its workforce. 3. The workforce performance management system supports high-performance work and workforce engagement. The workforce performance management system considers workforce compensation, reward, recognition, and incentive practices that effectively reinforce a customer and business focus, as well as achievement of organizational action plans. *b. Workforce and Leader Development* 1. The organization's *workforce* and leader development and learning system effectively addresses the following: • The organization's core competencies, strategic challenges, and accomplishment of action plans, both short- and longer-term • Organizational performance improvement and innovation • Ethics and ethical business practices • The full range of development opportunities, including education, training, coaching, mentoring, and work-related experiences, as appropriate 2. The organization's workforce development and learning system effectively addresses the following: • Learning and development needs, including those that are self-identified and those identified by supervisors and managers. • Transfer of knowledge from departing or retiring workers • Reinforcement of new knowledge and skills on the job 3. The organization systematically evaluates the effectiveness of its learning and development systems. 4. The organization manages effective career progression for its entire workforce and ensures effective succession planning for management and leadership position.

Continued

Clarifying the Baldrige Scoring Requirements

281

Best Fit Scoring Guidelines	5.1 Workforce Engagement (45 points possible) *Continued* Expected Findings. *Assessment of Workforce Engagement*
	1. The organization systematically uses formal and informal assessment methods and measures to determine workforce engagement and workforce satisfaction for its different workgroups and segments. Additionally, it uses other indicators, such as workforce retention, absenteeism, grievances, safety, and productivity to assess and improve workforce engagement. 2. The organization relates assessment findings to key business results reported in Category 7 to identify opportunities for improvement in both workforce engagement and business results. *The approach to workforce engagement is well deployed with no significant gaps (D). A systematic, fact-based process is in place to evaluate and improve elements of (a), (b), and (c) above, with clear evidence of innovation, organizational learning, and organization-level sharing and analysis, which results in refinements and improved integration throughout the organization (L). Organizational learning about, as well as systematic evaluation and improvement of (a), (b), and (c) above, are key management tools. The approach is integrated and consistent with organizational needs set forth in the Organizational Profile (for example, mission, vision, values, culture, workforce groups/segments and requirements) and the requirements of other Process Items (for example, senior leadership communication with the workforce and encouraging high performance [1.1], societal responsibility, legal and ethical behavior [1.2], strategic objectives [2.1b(1)], human resource plans [2.2a(5)], action plans and their performance measures [2.2a(1, 6)], information and knowledge management [4.2], workforce capability, capacity, structure, policies, services, and benefits [5.2], and work process design, management, and improvement [6.2]) (I).*

Best Fit Scoring Guidelines	5.2 Workforce Environment (40 points possible) Expected Findings
0–5% If examiners observe the applicant is not responsive to the requirements of an Item or provides no relevant information, the score should be zero (0%). If the applicant provides some anecdotal information addressing Item requirements (even though no systematic approach has begun), the score should be 5%.	**0–5% Scoring Band: No Systems to Meet Requirements** **5.2 Workforce Environment.** The organization has no processes to build an effective and supportive workforce environment (which may include managing and organizing the workforce to achieve strategic objectives and action plans) [5.2a(3)] and maintaining a supportive work climate [5.2b(2)] *(A). The work environment does not support the work of the organization (D). Reacting to problems is the normal way of approaching employee learning and motivation (L). There is no effective alignment between learning processes and employee needs or strategic or other business priorities in the organization and people and/or units seem to operate independently (I).*
10–25% If examiners observe the applicant is barely doing some of the things required in the 10–25% Beginning scoring band, the score should be in the lower part of this band. If they observe the applicant is doing everything required in the 10–25% Beginning band, but nothing in the higher bands, the score should be 25%.	**10–25% Scoring Band: Beginning to Meet Basic Requirements** **5.2 Workforce Environment.** The organization is in the beginning stages of establishing processes to build an effective workforce environment (which may include managing and organizing the workforce to achieve strategic objectives and action plans) [5.2a(3)] and maintaining a supportive work climate [5.2b(2)]) *(A). Major gaps exist where the workforce environment does not support the work of the organization (D). Reacting to problems in the workforce environment is a common approach; working to prevent problems is in the beginning stages (L). The organization generally relies on joint problem solving to promote alignment of workforce climate issues with other organization needs (I).*

Continued

5.2 Workforce Environment *(40 points possible)*		Continued
Best Fit Scoring Guidelines	**Expected Findings**	

Best Fit Scoring Guidelines	Expected Findings
30–45% If examiners observe the applicant is doing everything required in the 10–25% Beginning scoring band, and a few additional things in the higher bands, the score should be in the lower part of the 30–45% Basic band. If they observe the applicant is doing everything required in the 30–45% Basic band, but nothing in the higher bands, the score should be 45%	**30–45% Scoring Band: Systematically Meeting Basic Requirements** **5.2 Workforce Environment.** The organization has effective, systematic processes in place to build an effective workforce environment (which may include managing and organizing the workforce to achieve strategic objectives and action plans) [5.2a(3)] and maintaining a supportive work climate [5.2b(2)]) *(A). Processes to build an effective workforce environment support (or are just beginning to support) performance objectives in some parts of the organization (D). The organization is beginning to evaluate some of these processes and may or may not have made improvements based on the evaluation (L).* Workforce environment processes are generally consistent with organization priorities such as those set forth in the Organizational Profile (for example, values, vision, and workforce safety requirements) and basic requirements of other Process Items (for example, strategy development [2.1, strategy deployment, [2.2 , and workforce engagement [5.1]) *(I).*
50–65% If examiners observe the applicant is doing everything required in the 30–45% Basic scoring band, and a few additional things in the higher bands, the score should be in the lower part of the 50–65% Overall band. If they observe the applicant is doing everything in the 50–65% Overall band, but nothing in the next higher 70–85% band, the score should be 65%.	**50–65% Scoring Band: Systematically Meeting Overall Requirements** **5.2 Workforce Environment.** The organization has effective, systematic processes in place to do the following: a. **Workforce Capability and Capacity.** Manage workforce capability and capacity to accomplish the work of the organization (which may include managing and organizing the workforce to achieve strategic objectives and action plans). [5.2a(3)] *(A)*. b. **Workforce Climate.** Maintain a safe, secure, and supportive work climate [5.2b(1, 2)] *(A)*. *Some relatively minor gaps may exist in the deployment of these processes in some parts of the organization (D). A systematic, fact-based process is in place to evaluate the efficiency/effectiveness of some of the key elements of (a) and/or (b) above; and— for scores of 65%—evidence of at least one cycle of improvement* **and some innovation (meaningful change)** *within one or more of these elements (L).* Workforce environment processes are generally aligned with organizational needs set forth in the Organizational Profile (for example, mission, vision, values, culture, workforce groups/segments and requirements) and the requirements of other Process Items (for example, societal responsibility, legal and ethical behavior [1.2], strategic objectives [2.1b(1)], action plans and their performance measures [2.2a(1, 6)], information and knowledge management [4.2], workforce engagement [5.1], and work process design, management, and improvement [6.2]) *(I)*.

70–85% If examiners observe the applicant is doing everything required in the 50–65% Overall scoring band, and a few additional things in the 70–100% Multiple scoring band, the score should be in the lower part of the Multiple scoring band (for example, 70–75%). If they observe the applicant is meeting many to most requirements in the 70–100% Multiple scoring band, the score should be 85%.	**70–85% and 90–100% Scoring Bands: Multiple Requirements**
	
	5.2 Workforce Environment. The organization effectively manages workforce capability and capacity, in order to accomplish the work of the organization. The organization maintains a safe, secure, and supportive work climate.
	a. **Workforce Capability and Capacity**
	  1. The organization systematically and effectively assesses workforce capability and capacity needs, including skills, competencies, and staffing levels.
	  2. The organization has effective processes in place to recruit, hire, place, and retain new members of the workforce. It ensures that the workforce represents the diverse ideas, cultures, and thinking of its hiring and customer community.
	  3. The organization effectively manages and organizes its workforce to accomplish the work of the organization, capitalize on the organization's core competencies, reinforce a customer and business focus, exceed performance expectations,

Continued

Clarifying the Baldrige Scoring Requirements

5.2 Workforce Environment (40 points possible)	Continued
Best Fit Scoring Guidelines	**Expected Findings**
90–100% If examiners observe the applicant fully addressing the multiple Approach requirements and most of the Deployment, Learning, and Integration requirements described in the 70–100% Multiple scoring band, the score should be 90–95%. If examiners observe the applicant is meeting all of the requirements in the 70–100% Multiple band, the score should be 100%. **Note**: A score of 100% is possible only if *all* requirements are met and no Opportunities for Improvement can be identified. In addition, to score in the 90% to 100% band, examiners must observe full deployment, extensive and ongoing evaluation, improvement, organizational learning, innovation, and knowledge sharing throughout the organization. Required approaches must be well integrated with organizational needs identified in response to most other Criteria Items.	address its strategic challenges and action plans, and achieve the agility to address changing business needs. 4. The organization effectively prepares its workforce for changing needs related to capability and capacity. It manages the workforce and its needs to ensure continuity, prevent workforce reductions, and if they do become necessary, minimize the impact of workforce reductions. **b. Workforce Climate** 1. The organization effectively addresses workplace environmental factors to ensure and improve workplace health, safety, and security. It also has a system in place to identify performance measures or targets for workplace health, safety and security for its different workplace environments. Where significant differences exist, performance measures and targets for the different workplace environments are identified. 2. The organization effectively supports its workforce via policies, services, and benefits that are tailored to the needs of a diverse workforce and different workforce groups and segments. *The approach to the Items mentioned above is well deployed with no significant gaps (D). A systematic, fact-based process is in place to evaluate and improve elements of (a) and (b) above, with clear evidence of ongoing innovation, organizational learning, and organization-level sharing and analysis, which results in refinements and improved integration throughout the organization (L). Organizational learning about, as well as systematic evaluation and improvement of (a) and (b) above are key management tools. The approach is integrated and consistent with organizational needs set forth in the Organizational Profile (for example, mission, vision, values, culture, workforce groups/segments and requirements) and the requirements of other Process Items (for example, societal responsibility, legal and ethical behavior [1.2], strategic objectives [2.1b(1)], action plans and their performance measures [2.2a(1, 6)], information and knowledge management [4.2], workforce engagement [5.1], and work process design, management, and improvement [6.2]) (I).*

6.2 Work Systems (35 points possible)	
Best Fit Scoring Guidelines	**Expected Findings**
0–5% If examiners observe the applicant is not responsive to the requirements of an Item or provides no relevant information, the score should be zero (0%). If the applicant provides some anecdotal information addressing Item requirements (even though no systematic approach has begun), the score should be 5%.	**0–5% Scoring Band: No Systems to Meet Requirements** **6.1 Work Systems.** The organization has no effective process to design work systems to deliver value to customers [6.1a(1)] *(A). Efforts to design products to deliver value are ad hoc (D). Reacting to problems is the normal way of approaching work (L). There is no effective alignment in the organization of work systems, core competencies, and key business processes to deliver value to customers. People and/or units seem to operate independently (I).*

Continued

6.1 Work Systems (35 points possible)	Continued
Best Fit Scoring Guidelines	**Expected Findings**
10–25% If examiners observe the applicant is barely doing some of the things required in the 10–25% Beginning scoring band, the score should be in the lower part of this band. If they observe the applicant is doing everything required in the 10–25% Beginning band, but nothing in the higher bands, the score should be 25%.	**10–25% Scoring Band: Beginning to Meet Basic Requirements** **6.1 Work Systems.** The organization is in the beginning stages of establishing effective processes to design work systems [6.1a(1)] (which typically coordinate the work processes used to deliver value to customers) *(A)*. *Major gaps exist where key work system design processes essential to business success and growth are not in place (D). Reacting to problems with work system design processes is widespread; working to prevent problems is in the beginning stages (L). The organization generally relies on joint problem solving to promote alignment of work system design processes with organization priorities (I).*
30–45% If examiners observe the applicant is doing everything required in the 10–25% Beginning scoring band, and a few additional things in the higher bands, the score should be in the lower part of the 30–45% Basic band. If they observe the applicant is doing everything required in the 30–45% Basic band, but nothing in the higher bands, the score should be 45%.	**30–45% Scoring Band: Systematically Meeting Basic Requirements** **6.1 Work Systems.** The organization has effective, systematic processes in place to design work systems [6.1a(1)] (which typically coordinate the work processes used to deliver value to customers) *(A)*. *Work system design processes in some parts of the organization may be just beginning to support customer requirements and key business needs (D). The organization is beginning to evaluate some of these processes and may or may not have made improvements based on the evaluation (L). Work system design processes are generally consistent with organization priorities such as those set forth in the Organizational Profile (for example, product delivery mechanisms, values, vision, and core competencies) and basic requirements of other Process Items (for example, strategy development [2.1], strategy deployment [2.2], identifying product offerings to meet customer needs [3.1], and managing work processes [6.2]) (I).*
50–65% If examiners observe the applicant is doing everything required in the 30–45% Basic scoring band, and a few additional things in the higher bands, the score should be in the lower part of the 50–65% Overall band. If they observe the applicant is doing everything in the 50–65% Overall band, but nothing in the next higher 70–85% band, the score should be 65%.	**50–65% Scoring Band: Systematically Meeting Overall Requirements** **6.1 Work Systems.** The organization has effective, systematic processes in place to do the following: a. **Work Systems Design.** Determine core competencies [6.1a(1)] and work systems [6.1a(2)] essential to delivering customer value *(A)* b. **Key Work Processes.** Identify and design key processes that relate to core competencies to deliver customer value and achieve organizational success and sustainability [6.1b(1, 3)] *(A)* c. **Emergency Readiness.** Ensure work systems and workplace preparedness for potential emergencies [6.1c] (which helps to support organizational sustainability) *(A)*. *Some relatively minor gaps may exist in the identification of core competencies, design of work systems, and preparation of emergency plans in some parts of the organization (D). A systematic, fact-based process is in place to evaluate the efficiency/effectiveness of some of the key elements of (a), (b), and/or (c) above; and—for scores of 65%—evidence of at least one cycle of improvement and some innovation within one or more of these elements (L). The work system design processes are generally aligned with mission and values (1.1), strategic objectives (2.1), action plans (2.2), and requirements set forth in the Organizational Profile and other Process Items (I).*

Continued

6.1 Work Systems *(35 points possible)*	Continued
Best Fit Scoring Guidelines	**Expected Findings**

<table>
<tr><td>

70–85% If examiners observe the applicant is doing everything required in the 50–65% Overall scoring band, and a few additional things in the 70–100% Multiple scoring band, the score should be in the lower part of the Multiple scoring band (for example, 70–75%). If they observe the applicant is meeting many to most requirements in the 70–100% Multiple scoring band, the score should be 85%.

90–100% If examiners observe the applicant fully addressing the multiple Approach requirements and most of the Deployment, Learning, and Integration requirements described in the 70–100% Multiple scoring band, the score should be 90–95%. If examiners observe the applicant is meeting all of the requirements in the 70–100% Multiple band, the score should be 100%.

Note: A score of 100% is possible only if *all* requirements are met and no Opportunities for Improvement can be identified. In addition, to score in the 90% to 100% band, examiners must observe full deployment, extensive and ongoing evaluation, improvement, organizational learning, innovation, and knowledge sharing throughout the organization. Required approaches must be well integrated with organizational needs identified in response to most other Criteria Items.

</td><td>

70–85% and 90–100% Scoring Bands: Multiple Requirements

6.1 Work Systems. The organization effectively *designs* its work systems and *determines* key processes to deliver customer value, prepare for potential emergencies, and achieve organizational success and sustainability.

a. Work Systems Design
1. The organization effectively and systematically designs and innovates its overall work systems, clearly identifying which of its key processes are internal (the key work processes) and which use external resources.
2. The organization's work systems and key work processes effectively relate to and capitalize on its core competencies.

b. Key Work Processes
1. The organization has clearly defined the key work processes and how they contribute to delivering customer value, profitability or financial return, organizational success, and sustainability.
2. The organization has effective, systematic processes in place to determine key work process requirements, incorporating input from customers, suppliers, partners, and collaborators, as appropriate. Key requirements for these work processes are clearly defined.

c. Emergency Readiness. The organization has effective, systematic processes in place to ensure work system and workplace preparedness for disasters and emergencies. These processes consider prevention, management, continuity of operations, and recovery during and after disasters and emergencies.

The approach to Work Systems Design is well deployed with no significant gaps (D). A systematic, fact-based process is in place to evaluate and improve elements of (a), (b), and (c) above, with clear evidence of innovation, organizational learning, and organization-level sharing and analysis, which results in refinements and improved integration throughout the organization (L). Organizational learning about, as well as systematic evaluation and improvement of (a), (b), and (c) above are key management tools. The approach is integrated with organizational needs set forth in the Organizational Profile (for example, mission, vision, values, culture, customer and workforce groups/segments and requirements, core competencies, challenges and advantages) and the requirements of other Process Items (for example, senior leadership actively guiding and enhancing organizational sustainability and encouraging high performance [1.1], societal responsibility, legal and ethical behavior [1.2], strategic objectives [2.1b(1)], action plans and their performance measures [2.2a(1, 6)], measurement, analysis, and improvement [4.1], information and knowledge management including preparation for emergencies [4.2], workforce engagement [5.1], workforce environment [5.2], and work process design, management, and improvement [6.2]) (I).

</td></tr>
</table>

Continued

6.2 Work Processes (50 points possible)	
Best Fit Scoring Guidelines	**Expected Findings**
0–5% If examiners observe the applicant is not responsive to the requirements of an Item or provides no relevant information, the score should be zero (0%). If the applicant provides some anecdotal information addressing Item requirements (even though no systematic approach has begun), the score should be 5%.	**0–5% Scoring Band: No Systems to Meet Requirements** *6.2 Work Processes.* The organization has no effective processes to design [6.2a], manage [6.2b(1)] or improve [6.2c] key organizational work processes *(A)*. Efforts to manage key work processes are ad hoc *(D)*. Reacting to problems is the normal way of approaching these processes *(L)*. There is no alignment of key work processes with organization priorities and people and/or units seem to operate independently *(I)*.
10–25% If examiners observe the applicant is barely doing some of the things required in the 10–25% Beginning scoring band, the score should be in the lower part of this band. If they observe the applicant is doing everything required in the 10–25% Beginning band, but nothing in the higher bands, the score should be 25%.	**10–25% Scoring Band: Beginning to Meet Basic Requirements** *6.2 Work Processes.* The organization is in the beginning stages of establishing effective processes to design [6.2a], manage (ensure consistent quality) [6.2b(1)] and improve [6.2c] key organizational work processes *(A)*. Major gaps exist where work processes essential to business success and growth have not been developed *(D)*. Reacting to problems with the management of work processes is widespread; working to prevent problems is in the beginning stages *(L)*. The organization generally relies on joint problem solving to promote alignment of key work processes *(I)*.
30–45% If examiners observe the applicant is doing everything required in the 10–25% Beginning scoring band, and a few additional things in the higher bands, the score should be in the lower part of the 30–45% Basic band. If they observe the applicant is doing everything required in the 30–45% Basic band, but nothing in the higher bands, the score should be 45%.	**30–45% Scoring Band: Systematically Meeting Basic Requirements** *6.2 Work Processes.* The organization has effective, systematic processes in place to design [6.2a], manage (ensure consistent quality) [6.2b(1)] and improve [6.2c] key organizational work processes *(A)*. *Key work processes in some parts of the organization may be just beginning to support customer requirements and key business needs (D). The organization is beginning to evaluate some of these processes and may or may not have made improvements based on the evaluation (L). Key work processes are generally consistent with organization priorities such as those set forth in the Organizational Profile (for example, product delivery mechanisms, values, vision, and core competencies) and basic requirements of other Process Items (for example, societal responsibilities [1.2], strategy development [2.1], strategy deployment [2.2], identifying product offerings to meet customer needs [3.1], supportive workforce environment [5.2], designing work systems [6.1], and measuring, analyzing, and improving organizational performance [4.1]) (I).*

50–65% If examiners observe the applicant is doing everything required in the 30–45% Basic scoring band, and a few additional things in the higher bands, the score should be in the lower part of the 50–65% Overall band. If they observe the applicant is doing everything in the 50–65% Overall band, but nothing in the next higher 70–85% band, the score should be 65%.	**50–65% Scoring Band: Systematically Meeting Overall Requirements**
	
	6.2 Work Processes. The organization has effective, systematic processes in place to do the following:
	  a. Work Process Design. Design key work processes to deliver customer value and achieve organizational success and sustainability [6.2a] *(A)*.
	  b. Work Process Management. Implement and manage (control) key work processes to deliver more customer value and achieve higher levels of organizational success and sustainability [6.2b(1)] *(A)*.
	  c. Work Process Improvement. Improve key work processes to deliver customer value and achieve organizational success and sustainability [6.2c].
	Some relatively minor gaps may exist in the deployment of these processes in some parts of the organization (D). A systematic, fact-based process is in place to evaluate the efficiency/effectiveness of some of the key elements of (a), (b) and/or (c) above; and—for scores of 65%—evidence of at least one cycle of improvement **and some innovation (meaningful change)** *within one or more of*

Continued

Clarifying the Baldrige Scoring Requirements

6.2 Work Processes (50 points possible)	Continued
Best Fit Scoring Guidelines	**Expected Findings**

	these elements (L). *The processes to manage and improve the core work of the organization are generally aligned with organizational needs set forth in the Organizational Profile (for example, mission, vision, values, culture, customer and workforce groups/segments and requirements, core competencies, challenges and advantages) and the requirements of other Process Items (for example, senior leadership actively enhancing organizational sustainability and encouraging high performance [1.1], societal responsibility, legal and ethical behavior [1.2], strategic objectives [2.1b(1)], action plans and their performance measures [2.2a(1, 6)], measurement, analysis, and improvement [4.1], information and knowledge management [4.2], workforce engagement [5.1], workforce environment [5.2], and work system design [6.1]) (I).*

70–85% If examiners observe the applicant is doing everything required in the 50–65% Overall scoring band, and a few additional things in the 70–100% Multiple scoring band, the score should be in the lower part of the Multiple scoring band (for example, 70–75%). If they observe the applicant is meeting many to most requirements in the 70–100% Multiple scoring band, the score should be 85%.
 	
90–100% If examiners observe the applicant fully addressing the multiple Approach requirements and most of the Deployment, Learning, and Integration requirements described in the 70–100% Multiple scoring band, the score should be 90–95%. If examiners observe the applicant is meeting all of the requirements in the 70–100% Multiple band, the score should be 100%.
 	
Note: A score of 100% is possible only if *all* requirements are met and no Opportunities for Improvement can be identified. In addition, to score in the 90% to 100% band, examiners must observe full deployment, extensive and ongoing evaluation, improvement, organizational learning, innovation, and knowledge sharing throughout the organization. Required approaches must be well integrated with organizational needs identified in response to most other Criteria Items.
	70–85% and 90–100% Scoring Bands: Multiple Requirements
	
	6.2 Work Processes. The organization effectively designs, implements, manages, and improves key work processes in order to deliver customer value, and achieve organizational success and sustainability.
	
	   a. Work Process Design. The organization effectively and systematically designs work processes to meet all the key requirements, to include the incorporation of new technology, organizational knowledge, and the potential need for agility. It also incorporates cycle time, productivity, cost control, and other efficiency and effectiveness factors into the design of these processes.
	
	   b. Work Process Management
	    1. The organization effectively implements and manages work processes to ensure they meet design requirements. Subsequent day-to-day operations of these processes ensure process requirements are met. The organization effectively uses workforce, customer, supplier, partner, and collaborator input to manage these processes, as appropriate. Clearly defined key performance measures or indicators and in-process measures are consistently and effectively used to control and improve work processes.
	    2. The organization has effective systems in place to control the overall costs of work processes. The organization effectively prevents defects, service errors, and rework, and minimizes warranty costs or customers productivity losses, as appropriate. These systems minimize overall costs associated with inspections, tests, and process or performance audits.
	
	   c. Work Process Improvement. The organization effectively and systematically improves work processes to achieve better performance, to reduce variability, to improve products, and to keep the processes current with business needs and directions. The results of organizational performance reviews [4.1] are incorporated into the systematic evaluation and improvement of work processes. Improvements and lessons learned are shared with other organizational units and processes to drive organizational learning and innovation.
	
	The approach to Work Processes is well deployed with no significant gaps (D). A systematic, fact-based process is in place to evaluate and improve elements of (a), (b), and (c) above, with clear evidence of innovation, organizational learning, and organization-level sharing and analysis, which results in refinements and improved integration throughout the organization (L). Organizational learning about, as well as systematic evaluation and improvement of (a) and (b) above are key management tools. The approach is integrated and consistent with

Continued

6.2 Work Processes *(50 points possible)*	Continued
Best Fit Scoring Guidelines	**Expected Findings**
	organizational needs set forth in the Organizational Profile (for example, mission, vision, values, culture, customer and workforce groups/segments and requirements, core competencies, challenges and advantages) and the requirements of other Process Items (for example, senior leadership actively enhancing organizational sustainability and encouraging high performance [1.1], societal responsibility, legal, and ethical behavior [1.2], strategic objectives [2.1b(1)], action plans and their performance measures [2.2a(1, 6)], measurement, analysis, and improvement [4.1], information and knowledge management [4.2], workforce engagement [5.1], workforce environment [5.2], and work system design [6.1]) (I).

7.1 Product Outcomes *(100 points possible)*	

7.1 Performance outcomes are provided for the organization's key product and service performance results. Results are segmented by appropriate customer groups and markets. Appropriate comparative data are provided.

  a. **Product Results**

  Data show current levels and trends in key measures or indicators of product performance that are important to customers. For the measures or indicators above, comparative data demonstrate how well the organization's results compare with the performance of competitors and other organizations providing similar products and services.

Scoring Calibration Statement	Scoring Calibration Guidelines
0 or 5% If the examiners observe there are no business results for any areas of importance to the organization's mission or only poor results in areas reported, the score should be zero. If any trend data are reported that are positive, the score should be at least 5%. Comparative information is not expected.	• There are no organizational performance results and/or poor results reported for product performance important to customers. (Le) • Trend data either are not reported or show mainly adverse trends. (T) • Comparative information is not reported. (C) • Results are not reported for any areas of importance to the accomplishment of the organization's mission. *No performance projections are reported for customer-focused outcomes.* (I)
10–25% If no comparative data and only a few results are reported with some improvements and/or early good performance levels in a few areas, the score should be at the bottom of this band. If, in addition, comparative data and/or trend data are reported for a few areas of importance to the organization's mission, the score should be in the upper part of this band. No performance projections may be provided.	• A few organizational performance results are reported, and early good performance levels are evident in a few areas of product performance important to customers. (Le) • Some trend data are reported, with some adverse trends evident. (T) • Little or no comparative information is reported. (C) • Product performance results are reported for a few areas of importance to the accomplishment of the organization's mission. Limited or no performance projections are reported. *Limited or no performance projections are reported for customer-focused outcomes.* (I)

Continued

7.1 Product Outcomes *(100 points possible)* Continued	
Scoring Calibration Statement	**Scoring Guidelines**
30–45% If all of the requirements of the 10–25% scoring band have been met, and if some trend data and/or good performance levels are reported for many areas of importance to the item requirements and organization's mission, the score should be at least 30%. If, in addition to these trend data, comparative data are reported that show a few good levels of performance, the score should be in the higher part of this band (40–45%).	• Good organizational performance levels are reported for some areas of product performance important to customers. (Le) • Some trend data are reported, and a majority of the trends presented are beneficial. (T) • Early stages of obtaining comparative information are evident. (C) • Product performance results are reported for many areas of importance to the accomplishment of the organization's mission. *Limited performance projections are reported for product performance outcomes.* (I)
50–65% If all of the requirements of the 30–45% scoring band have been met, and if improvement trends and/or good performance levels are reported for most areas of importance to the item requirements and most key customer, market, and process requirements (as appropriate), the score should be at least 50%. If, in addition, no pattern of adverse trends and no poor performance levels are reported, the score should be higher (55%). Furthermore, if some trends and/or current performance levels—evaluated against relevant comparisons and/or benchmarks—show areas of good to very good relative performance, the score should be in the upper part of the band (60–65%).	• Good organizational performance levels are reported for most areas of product performance important to customers. (Le) • Beneficial trends are evident in areas of importance to the accomplishment of the organization's mission. (T) • Some current performance levels have been evaluated against relevant comparisons and/or benchmarks and show areas of good relative performance. (C) • Product performance results are reported for most key customer, market, and process requirements related to product outcomes. *Performance projections for some high-priority product performance outcomes are reported.* (I)
70–85% If all of the requirements of the 50–65% scoring band have been met and if current performance is good to excellent in most areas of importance to the item requirements and most key customer, market, and process requirements (as appropriate), the score should be at least 70–75%. If, in addition, data show that most improvement trends and/or current performance levels are sustained, and many to most reported trends and/or current performance levels—evaluated against relevant comparisons and/or benchmarks—show areas of leadership and very good relative performance and they include some projections of future expected performance, the score should be higher (80–85%).	• Good to excellent organizational performance levels are reported for most areas of product performance important to customers. (Le) • Beneficial trends have been sustained over time in most areas of importance to the accomplishment of the organization's mission. (T) • Many to most trends and current performance levels have been evaluated against relevant comparisons and/or benchmarks and show areas of leadership and very good relative performance. (C) • Product performance results are reported for most key customer, market, process, and action plan requirements related to product outcomes, and they include some projections of the organization's future product performance. (I)
90–100% If all of the requirements of the 70–85% scoring band have been met and if current performance is excellent in most areas of importance to the item requirements and fully address key customer, market, and process requirements (as appropriate), the score should be at least 90%. If, in addition, excellent improvement trends and/or sustained excellent performance levels are reported in most areas and they include some projections of future expected performance, the score should be higher (95%). Finally, if there is also evidence of industry and benchmark leadership demonstrated in many areas important to business success, the score could be higher.	• Excellent organizational performance levels are reported for most areas of product performance important to customers. (Le) • Beneficial trends have been sustained over time in all areas of importance to the accomplishment of the organization's mission. (T) • Evidence of industry and benchmark leadership is demonstrated in many areas. (C) • Product results fully address key customer, market, process, and action plan requirements related to product and service outcomes, and they include projections of the organization's future product performance. (I)

7.2 Customer-Focused Outcomes *(70 points possible)*

7.2 *Performance outcome data are provided for the organization's key customer-focused results, including customer satisfaction, dissatisfaction, and engagement. Results are segmented by appropriate product offerings, customer groups and markets. Appropriate comparative data are provided.*

a. Customer-Focused Results

1. Data show current levels and trends in key measures or indicators of customer satisfaction and dissatisfaction. The results compare favorably with the customer satisfaction levels of competitors and other organizations providing similar products and services.
2. Data show current levels and trends in key measures or indicators of customer relationship building and engagement. The results compare favorably over the course of the customer life cycle, as appropriate.

For the measures or indicators above, comparative data demonstrate how well the organization's results compare with competitors' performance, including competitors' levels of customer satisfaction.

Scoring Calibration Statement	Scoring Guidelines
0 or 5% If the examiners observe there are no business results for any areas of importance to the organization's mission or only poor results in areas reported, the score should be zero. If any trend data are reported that are positive, the score should be at least 5%. Comparative information is not expected.	• There are no organizational performance results and/or poor results in the areas of customer satisfaction, dissatisfaction, and engagement. (Le) • Trend data either are not reported or show mainly adverse trends. (T) • Comparative information is not reported. (C) • Customer-focused results are not reported for any areas of importance to the accomplishment of the organization's mission. No performance projections are reported for customer-focused outcomes. (I)
10–25% If no comparative data and only a few results are reported with some improvements and/or early good performance levels in a few areas, the score should be at the bottom of this band. If, in addition, comparative data and/or trend data are reported for a few areas of importance to the organization's mission, the score should be in the upper part of this band. No performance projections may be provided.	• A few organizational performance results are reported, and early good performance levels are evident in a few areas of customer satisfaction, dissatisfaction, and engagement. (Le) • Some trend data are reported, with some adverse trends evident. (T) • Little or no comparative information is reported. (C) • Customer-focused results are reported for a few areas of importance to the accomplishment of the organization's mission. Limited or no performance projections are reported for customer-focused outcomes. (I)
30–45% If all of the requirements of the 10–25% scoring band have been met, and if some trend data and/or good performance levels are reported for many areas of importance to the item requirements and organization's mission, the score should be at least 30%. If, in addition to these trend data, comparative data are reported that show a few good levels of performance, the score should be in the higher part of this band (40–45%).	• Good organizational performance levels are reported for some areas customer satisfaction, dissatisfaction, and engagement. (Le) • Some trend data are reported, and a majority of the trends presented are beneficial. (T) • Early stages of obtaining comparative information are evident. (C) • Customer-focused results are reported for many areas of importance to the accomplishment of the organization's mission. Limited performance projections are reported for customer-focused outcomes. (I)
50–65% If all of the requirements of the 30–45% scoring band have been met, and if improvement trends and/or good performance levels are reported for most areas of importance to the item requirements and most key customer, market, and process requirements (as appropriate), the score should be at least 50%. If, in addition, no pattern of adverse trends and no poor performance levels are reported, the score should be higher (55%). Furthermore, if some trends and/or current performance levels—evaluated against relevant comparisons and/or benchmarks—show areas of good to very good relative performance, the score should be in the upper part of the band (60–65%).	• Good organizational performance levels are reported for most areas customer satisfaction, dissatisfaction, and engagement (Le) • Beneficial trends are evident in areas of importance to the accomplishment of the organization's mission. (T) • Some current performance levels have been evaluated against relevant comparisons and/or benchmarks and show areas of good relative performance. (C) • Customer-focused results are reported for most key customer, market, and process requirements. Performance projections are reported for some high priority customer-focused results. (I)

Continued

Clarifying the Baldrige Scoring Requirements

7.2 Customer-Focused Outcomes *(70 points possible)* *Continued*	
Scoring Calibration Statement	**Scoring Guidelines**
70–85% If all of the requirements of the 50–65% scoring band have been met and if current performance is good to excellent in most areas of importance to the item requirements and most key customer, market, and process requirements (as appropriate), the score should be at least 70–75%. If, in addition, data show that most improvement trends and/or current performance levels are sustained, and many to most reported trends and/or current performance levels—evaluated against relevant comparisons and/or benchmarks—show areas of leadership and very good relative performance and they include some projections of future expected performance, the score should be higher (80–85%).	• Good to excellent organizational performance levels are reported for most areas customer satisfaction, dissatisfaction, and engagement. (Le) • Beneficial trends have been sustained over time in most areas of importance to the accomplishment of the organization's mission. (T) • Many to most trends and current performance levels have been evaluated against relevant comparisons and/or benchmarks and show areas of leadership and very good relative performance. (C) • Customer-focused results are reported for most key customer, market, process, and action plan requirements related to customer-focused outcomes, and they include some projections of the organization's future customer-focused performance. (I)
90–100% If all of the requirements of the 70–85% scoring band have been met and if current performance is excellent in most areas of importance to the item requirements and fully address key customer, market, and process requirements (as appropriate), the score should be at least 90%. If, in addition, excellent improvement trends and/or sustained excellent performance levels are reported in most areas and they include some projections of future expected performance, the score should be higher (95%). Finally, if there is also evidence of industry and benchmark leadership demonstrated in many areas important to business success, the score could be higher.	• Excellent organizational performance levels are reported for most areas of customer satisfaction, dissatisfaction, and engagement. (Le) • Beneficial trends have been sustained over time in all areas of importance to the accomplishment of the organization's mission. (T) • Evidence of industry and benchmark leadership is demonstrated in many areas. (C) • Customer-focused results fully address key customer, market, process, and action plan requirements related to customer-focused outcomes, and they include projections of the organization's future customer-focused performance. (I)

7.3 Financial and Market Outcomes *(70 points possible)*

7.3 *Performance outcome data are provided for the organization's key financial and marketplace performance results. These results are broken out by appropriate customer and market segments. Appropriate comparative data are provided.*

  a. Financial and Market Results

  1. Data show current levels and trends in key measures or indicators of financial performance, including aggregate measures of financial return, financial viability, or budgetary performance, as appropriate.
  2. Data show current levels and trends in key measures or indicators of marketplace performance, including market share or position, market and market share growth, and new markets entered, as appropriate.

For the measures or indicators above, comparative data demonstrate how well the organization's results compare with competitors' performance.

Scoring Calibration Statement	Scoring Guidelines
0 or 5% If the examiners observe there are no business results for any areas of importance to the organization's mission or only poor results in areas reported, the score should be zero. If any trend data are reported that are positive, the score should be at least 5%. Comparative information is not expected.	• There are no organizational performance results and/or poor results in areas of financial and marketplace performance. (Le) • Trend data either are not reported or show mainly adverse trends. (T) • Comparative information is not reported. (C) • Financial and marketplace performance results are not reported for any areas of importance to the accomplishment of the organization's mission. No financial and market place performance projections are reported. (I)

Continued

7.3 Financial and Market Outcomes *(70 points possible)* Continued	
Scoring Calibration Statement	**Scoring Guidelines**
10–25% If no comparative data and only a few results are reported with some improvements and/or early good performance levels in a few areas, the score should be at the bottom of this band. If, in addition, comparative data and/or trend data are reported for a few areas of importance to the organization's mission, the score should be in the upper part of this band. No performance projections may be provided.	• A few organizational performance results are reported, and early good performance levels are evident in a few areas of financial and marketplace performance. (Le) • Some trend data are reported, with some adverse trends evident. (T) • Little or no comparative information is reported. (C) • Financial and marketplace performance results are reported for a few areas of importance to the accomplishment of the organization's mission. *Limited or no financial or marketplace performance projections are reported.* (I)
30–45% If all of the requirements of the 10–25% scoring band have been met, and if some trend data and/or good performance levels are reported for many areas of importance to the item requirements and organization's mission, the score should be at least 30%. If, in addition to these trend data, comparative data are reported that show a few good levels of performance, the score should be in the higher part of this band (40–45%).	• Good organizational performance levels are reported for some areas of financial and marketplace performance. (Le) • Some trend data are reported, and a majority of the trends presented are beneficial. (T) • Early stages of obtaining comparative information are evident. (C) • Financial and marketplace performance results are reported for many areas of importance to the accomplishment of the organization's mission. *Limited financial or marketplace performance projections are reported.* (I)
50–65% If all of the requirements of the 30–45% scoring band have been met, and if improvement trends and/or good performance levels are reported for most areas of importance to the item requirements and most key customer, market, and process requirements (as appropriate), the score should be at least 50%. If, in addition, no pattern of adverse trends and no poor performance levels are reported, the score should be higher (55%). Furthermore, if some trends and/or current performance levels—evaluated against relevant comparisons and/or benchmarks—show areas of good to very good relative performance, the score should be in the upper part of the band (60–65%).	• Good organizational performance levels are reported for most areas of financial and marketplace performance. (Le) • Beneficial trends are evident in areas of importance to the accomplishment of the organization's mission. (T) • Some current performance levels have been evaluated against relevant comparisons and/or benchmarks and show areas of good relative performance. (C) • Financial and marketplace performance results are reported for most key customer, market, and process requirements related to financial and marketplace outcomes. *Performance projections are reported for some high-priority financial and marketplace performance results.* (I)
70–85% If all of the requirements of the 50–65% scoring band have been met and if current performance is good to excellent in most areas of importance to the item requirements and most key customer, market, and process requirements (as appropriate), the score should be at least 70–75%. If, in addition, data show that most improvement trends and/or current performance levels are sustained, and many to most reported trends and/or current performance levels—evaluated against relevant comparisons and/or benchmarks—show areas of leadership and very good relative performance and they include some projections of future expected performance, the score should be higher (80–85%).	• Good to excellent organizational performance levels are reported for most areas of financial and marketplace performance. (Le) • Beneficial trends have been sustained over time in most areas of importance to the accomplishment of the organization's mission. (T) • Many to most trends and current performance levels have been evaluated against relevant comparisons and/or benchmarks and show areas of leadership and very good relative performance. (C) • Financial and marketplace performance results are reported for most key customer, market, process, and action plan requirements related to financial and market outcomes, and they include some projections of the organization's future financial and marketplace performance. (I)

Continued

Clarifying the Baldrige Scoring Requirements

7.3 Financial and Market Outcomes *(70 points possible)* — Continued

Scoring Calibration Statement	Scoring Guidelines
90–100% If all of the requirements of the 70–85% scoring band have been met and if current performance is excellent in most areas of importance to the item requirements and fully address key customer, market, and process requirements (as appropriate), the score should be at least 90%. If, in addition, excellent improvement trends and/or sustained excellent performance levels are reported in most areas and they include some projections of future expected performance, the score should be higher (95%). Finally, if there is also evidence of industry and benchmark leadership demonstrated in many areas important to business success, the score could be higher.	• Excellent organizational performance levels are reported for most areas of financial and marketplace performance. (Le) • Beneficial trends have been sustained over time in all areas of importance to the accomplishment of the organization's mission. (T) • Evidence of industry and benchmark leadership is demonstrated in many areas. (C) • Financial and marketplace performance results fully address key customer, market, process, and action plan requirements related to financial and marketplace outcomes, and they include projections of the organization's future financial and marketplace performance. (I)

7.4 Workforce-Focused Outcomes *(70 points possible)*

7.4 *Performance outcomes are provided for the organization's key workforce-focused results for workforce engagement and for workforce environment. Results address the diversity of the workforce and workforce groups and segments, as appropriate. Appropriate comparative data are provided.*

  a. **Workforce Results**

  1. Data show current levels and trends in key measures or indicators of workforce engagement and workforce satisfaction.
  2. Data show current levels and trends in key measures or indicators of leader and workforce development.
  3. Data show current levels and trends in key measures of workforce capability and capacity, including staffing levels and appropriate skills.
  4. Data show current levels and trends in key measures or indicators of workforce climate, including workplace health, safety, and security and workforce services and benefits, as appropriate.

For the measures or indicators above, comparative data demonstrate how well the organization's results compare with competitors' performance.

Scoring Calibration Statement	Scoring Guidelines
0 or 5% If the examiners observe there are no business results for any areas of importance to the organization's mission or only poor results in areas reported, the score should be zero. If any trend data are reported that are positive, the score should be at least 5%. Comparative information is not expected.	• There are no organizational performance results and/or poor results reported for workforce-focused performance. (Le) • Trend data either are not reported or show mainly adverse trends. (T) • Comparative information is not reported. (C) • Workforce-focused results are not reported for any areas of importance to the accomplishment of the organization's mission. *No performance projections are reported for workforce-focused results.* (I)

Continued

7.4 Workforce-Focused Outcomes *(70 points possible)*	Continued
Scoring Calibration Statement	**Scoring Guidelines**
10–25% If no comparative data and only a few results are reported with some improvements and/or early good performance levels in a few areas, the score should be at the bottom of this band. If, in addition, comparative data and/or trend data are reported for a few areas of importance to the organization's mission, the score should be in the upper part of this band. No performance projections may be provided.	• A few organizational performance results are reported, and early good performance levels are evident in a few key areas of workforce-focused performance. (Le) • Some trend data are reported, with some adverse trends evident. (T) • Little or no comparative information is reported. (C) • Workforce-focused results are reported for a few areas of importance to the accomplishment of the organization's mission. *Limited or no performance projections are reported for workforce-focused results.* (I)
30–45% If all of the requirements of the 10–25% scoring band have been met, and if some trend data and/or good performance levels are reported for many areas of importance to the item requirements and organization's mission, the score should be at least 30%. If, in addition to these trend data, comparative data are reported that show a few good levels of performance, the score should be in the higher part of this band (40–45%).	• Good organizational performance levels are reported for some key areas of workforce-focused performance. (Le) • Some trend data are reported, and a majority of the trends presented are beneficial. (T) • Early stages of obtaining comparative information are evident. (C) • Workforce-focused results are reported for many areas of importance to the accomplishment of the organization's mission. *Limited performance projections are reported for workforce-focused results.* (I)
50–65% If all of the requirements of the 30–45% scoring band have been met, and if improvement trends and/or good performance levels are reported for most areas of importance to the item requirements and most key customer, market, and process requirements (as appropriate), the score should be at least 50%. If, in addition, no pattern of adverse trends and no poor performance levels are reported, the score should be higher (55%). Furthermore, if some trends and/or current performance levels—evaluated against relevant comparisons and/or benchmarks—show areas of good to very good relative performance, the score should be in the upper part of the band (60–65%).	• Good organizational performance levels are reported for most key areas of workforce-focused performance. (Le) • Beneficial trends are evident in areas of importance to the accomplishment of the organization's mission. (T) • Some current performance levels have been evaluated against relevant comparisons and/or benchmarks and show areas of good relative performance. (C) • Workforce-focused results are reported for most key customer, market, and process requirements related to workforce outcomes. *Performance projections are reported for some high-priority workforce-focused results.* (I)
70–85% If all of the requirements of the 50–65% scoring band have been met and if current performance is good to excellent in most areas of importance to the item requirements and most key customer, market, and process requirements (as appropriate), the score should be at least 70–75%. If, in addition, data show that most improvement trends and/or current performance levels are sustained, and many to most reported trends and/or current performance levels—evaluated against relevant comparisons and/or benchmarks—show areas of leadership and very good relative performance and they include some projections of future expected performance, the score should be higher (80–85%).	• Good to excellent organizational performance levels are reported for most key areas of workforce-focused performance. (Le) • Beneficial trends have been sustained over time in most areas of importance to the accomplishment of the organization's mission. (T) • Many to most trends and current performance levels have been evaluated against relevant comparisons and/or benchmarks and show areas of leadership and very good relative performance. (C) • Workforce-focused results are reported for most key customer, market, process, and action plan requirements related to workforce outcomes, and they include some projections of the organization's future workforce-focused performance. (I)

Continued

7.4 Workforce-Focused Outcomes *(70 points possible)* — Continued

Scoring Calibration Statement	Scoring Guidelines
90–100% If all of the requirements of the 70–85% scoring band have been met and if current performance is excellent in most areas of importance to the item requirements and fully address key customer, market, and process requirements (as appropriate), the score should be at least 90%. If, in addition, excellent improvement trends and/or sustained excellent performance levels are reported in most areas and they include some projections of future expected performance, the score should be higher (95%). Finally, if there is also evidence of industry and benchmark leadership demonstrated in many areas important to business success, the score could be higher.	• Excellent organizational performance levels are reported for most key areas of workforce-focused performance. (Le) • Beneficial trends have been sustained over time in all areas of importance to the accomplishment of the organization's mission. (T) • Evidence of industry and benchmark leadership is demonstrated in many areas. (C) • Workforce-focused results fully address key customer, market, process, and action plan requirements related to workforce outcomes, and they include projections of the organization's future workforce-focused performance. (I)

7.5 Process Effectiveness Outcomes *(70 points possible)*

7.5 Performance outcomes are provided for the organization's key operational performance results that contribute to the improvement of organizational effectiveness, including the organization's readiness for emergencies. These results are broken out by product offerings, by customer groups and market segments, and by processes and locations, as appropriate. Appropriate comparative data are provided.

a. *Process Effectiveness Results*

1. Data show current levels and trends in key measures or indicators of the operational performance of work systems, including work system and workplace preparedness for disasters or emergencies.
2. Data show current levels and trends in key measures or indicators of the operational performance of key work processes, including productivity, cycle time, and other appropriate measures of process effectiveness, efficiency, and innovation.

For the measures or indicators above, comparative data demonstrate how well the organization's results compare with competitors' performance.

Scoring Calibration Statement	Scoring Guidelines
0 or 5% If the examiners observe there are no business results for any areas of importance to the organization's mission or only poor results in areas reported, the score should be zero. If any trend data are reported that are positive, the score should be at least 5%. Comparative information is not expected.	• There are no *operational* performance results and/or poor results reported. (Le) • Trend data either are not reported or show mainly adverse trends. (T) • Comparative information is not reported. (C) • Results are not reported for any areas of importance to the accomplishment of the organization's mission. *No performance projections are reported for process effectiveness results.* (I)
10–25% If no comparative data and only a few results are reported with some improvements and/or early good performance levels in a few areas, the score should be at the bottom of this band. If, in addition, comparative data and/or trend data are reported for a few areas of importance to the organization's mission, the score should be in the upper part of this band. No performance projections may be provided.	• A few *operational* performance results are reported, and early good performance levels are evident for a few key operational performance requirements. (Le) • Some trend data are reported, with some adverse trends evident. (T) • Little or no comparative information is reported. (C) • *Operational* performance results are reported for a few areas of importance to the accomplishment of the organization's mission. *Limited or no performance projections are reported for process effectiveness results.* (I)

Continued

7.5 Process Effectiveness Outcomes *(70 points possible)* Continued	
Scoring Calibration Statement	**Scoring Guidelines**
30–45% If all of the requirements of the 10–25% scoring band have been met, and if some trend data and/or good performance levels are reported for many areas of importance to the item requirements and organization's mission, the score should be at least 30%. If, in addition to these trend data, comparative data are reported that show a few good levels of performance, the score should be in the higher part of this band (40–45%).	• Good *operational* performance levels are reported for some key *operational* performance requirements. (Le) • Some trend data are reported, and a majority of the trends presented are beneficial. (T) • Early stages of obtaining comparative information are evident. (C) • Operational performance results are reported for many areas of importance to the accomplishment of the organization's mission. *Limited performance projections are reported for process effectiveness results.* (I)
50–65% If all of the requirements of the 30–45% scoring band have been met, and if improvement trends and/or good performance levels are reported for most areas of importance to the item requirements and most key customer, market, and process requirements (as appropriate), the score should be at least 50%. If, in addition, no pattern of adverse trends and no poor performance levels are reported, the score should be higher (55%). Furthermore, if some trends and/or current performance levels—evaluated against relevant comparisons and/or benchmarks—show areas of good to very good relative performance, the score should be in the upper part of the band (60–65%).	• Good *operational* performance levels are reported for most key *operational* performance requirements. (Le) • Beneficial trends are evident in areas of importance to the accomplishment of the organization's mission. (T) • Some current performance levels have been evaluated against relevant comparisons and/or benchmarks and show areas of good relative performance. (C) • *Operational* performance results are reported for most key customer, market, and process requirements related to process effectiveness outcomes. *Performance projections are reported for some high-priority process effectiveness results.* (I)
70–85% If all of the requirements of the 50–65% scoring band have been met and if current performance is good to excellent in most areas of importance to the item requirements and most key customer, market, and process requirements (as appropriate), the score should be at least 70–75%. If, in addition, data show that most improvement trends and/or current performance levels are sustained, and many to most reported trends and/or current performance levels—evaluated against relevant comparisons and/or benchmarks—show areas of leadership and very good relative performance and they include some projections of future expected performance, the score should be higher (80–85%).	• Good to excellent *operational* performance levels are reported for most key *operational* performance requirements. (Le) • Beneficial trends have been sustained over time in most areas of importance to the accomplishment of the organization's mission. (T) • Many to most trends and current performance levels have been evaluated against relevant comparisons and/or benchmarks and show areas of leadership and very good relative performance. (C) • *Operational* performance results are reported for most key customer, market, process, and action plan requirements related to process effectiveness outcomes, and they include some projections of the organization's future operational performance. (I)
90–100% If all of the requirements of the 70–85% scoring band have been met and if current performance is excellent in most areas of importance to the item requirements and fully address key customer, market, and process requirements (as appropriate), the score should be at least 90%. If, in addition, excellent improvement trends and/or sustained excellent performance levels are reported in most areas and they include some projections of future expected performance, the score should be higher (95%). Finally, if there is also evidence of industry and benchmark leadership demonstrated in many areas important to business success, the score could be higher.	• Excellent *operational* performance levels are reported for most key *operational* performance requirements. (Le) • Beneficial trends have been sustained over time in all areas of importance to the accomplishment of the organization's mission. (T) • Evidence of industry and benchmark leadership is demonstrated in many areas. (C) • *Operational* performance results fully address key customer, market, process, and action plan requirements related to process effectiveness outcomes, and they include projections of the organization's future operational performance. (I)

7.6 Leadership Outcomes *(70 points possible)*

7.6 *Performance outcomes are provided for the organization's key governance and senior leadership results, including evidence of strategic plan accomplishment, fiscal accountability, legal compliance, ethical behavior, societal responsibility, and support of key communities. These results are broken out by organizational units, as appropriate. Appropriate comparative data are provided.*

a. **Leadership and Societal Responsibility Results**

1. Data show key measures or indicators of accomplishment of organizational strategy and action plans.
2. Data show key current findings and trends in key measures or indicators of governance and fiscal accountability, both internal and external, as appropriate.
3. Data show key measures or indicators of regulatory and legal compliance.
4. Data show key measures or indicators of ethical behavior and of stakeholder trust in the senior leaders and governance of the organization. Data also show key measures or indicators of breaches of ethical behavior, if any.
5. Data show key measures or indicators of the organization's fulfillment of its societal responsibilities and its support of key communities.

For the measures or indicators above, comparative data demonstrate how well the organization's results compare with competitors' performance.

Scoring Calibration Statement	Scoring Guidelines
0 or 5% If the examiners observe there are no business results for any areas of importance to the organization's mission or only poor results in areas reported, the score should be zero. If any trend data are reported that are positive, the score should be at least 5%. Comparative information is not expected.	• There are no organizational performance results and/or poor results reported in areas of governance and leadership performance. (Le) • Trend data either are not reported or show mainly adverse trends. (T) • Comparative information is not reported. (C) • Results are not reported for any areas of importance to governance and leadership related to the accomplishment of the organization's mission. *No performance projections are reported for governance and leadership performance results.* (I)
10–25% If no comparative data and only a few results are reported with some improvements and/or early good performance levels in a few areas, the score should be at the bottom of this band. If, in addition, comparative data and/or trend data are reported for a few areas of importance to the organization's mission, the score should be in the upper part of this band. No performance projections may be provided.	• A few organizational performance results are reported and early good performance levels are evident in a few areas of governance and leadership performance. (Le) • Some trend data are reported, with some adverse trends evident. (T) • Little or no comparative information is reported. (C) • Results are reported for a few areas of importance to governance and leadership related to the accomplishment of the organization's mission. *Limited or no performance projections are reported for governance and leadership performance results.* (I)
30–45% If all of the requirements of the 10–25% scoring band have been met, and if some trend data and/or good performance levels are reported for many areas of importance to the item requirements and organization's mission, the score should be at least 30%. If, in addition to these trend data, comparative data are reported that show a few good levels of performance, the score should be in the higher part of this band (40–45%).	• Good organizational performance levels are reported for some areas of governance and leadership performance. (Le) • Some trend data are reported, and a majority of the trends presented are beneficial. (T) • Early stages of obtaining comparative information are evident. (C) • Results are reported for many areas of importance to governance and leadership related to the accomplishment of the organization's mission. *Limited performance projections are reported for governance and leadership performance results.* (I)

Continued

7.6 Leadership Outcomes *(70 points possible)*	Continued
Scoring Calibration Statement	**Scoring Guidelines**
50–65% If all of the requirements of the 30–45% scoring band have been met, and if improvement trends and/or good performance levels are reported for most areas of importance to the item requirements and most key customer, market, and process requirements (as appropriate), the score should be at least 50%. If, in addition, no pattern of adverse trends and no poor performance levels are reported, the score should be higher (55%). Furthermore, if some trends and/or current performance levels—evaluated against relevant comparisons and/or benchmarks—show areas of good to very good relative performance, the score should be in the upper part of the band (60–65%).	• Good organizational performance levels are reported for most areas of governance and leadership performance. (Le) • Beneficial trends are evident in areas of importance to the accomplishment of the organization's mission. (T) • Some current performance levels have been evaluated against relevant comparisons and/or benchmarks and show areas of good relative performance. (C) • Organizational performance results are reported for most key customer, market, and process requirements related to governance and leadership outcomes. *Performance projections are reported for some high-priority governance and leadership performance results.* (I)
70–85% If all of the requirements of the 50–65% scoring band have been met and if current performance is good to excellent in most areas of importance to the item requirements and most key customer, market, and process requirements (as appropriate), the score should be at least 70–75%. If, in addition, data show that most improvement trends and/or current performance levels are sustained, and many to most reported trends and/or current performance levels—evaluated against relevant comparisons and/or benchmarks—show areas of leadership and very good relative performance and they include some projections of future expected performance, the score should be higher (80–85%).	• Good to excellent organizational performance levels are reported for most areas of governance and leadership performance. (Le) • Beneficial trends have been sustained over time in most areas of importance to the accomplishment of the organization's mission. (T) • Many to most trends and current performance levels have been evaluated against relevant comparisons and/or benchmarks and show areas of leadership and very good relative performance. (C) • Organizational performance results are reported for most key customer, market, process, and action plan requirements related to governance and leadership outcomes, and they include some projections of the organization's future governance and leadership performance. (I)
90–100% If all of the requirements of the 70–85% scoring band have been met and if current performance is excellent in most areas of importance to the item requirements and fully address key customer, market, and process requirements (as appropriate), the score should be at least 90%. If, in addition, excellent improvement trends and/or sustained excellent performance levels are reported in most areas and they include some projections of future expected performance, the score should be higher (95%). Finally, if there is also evidence of industry and benchmark leadership demonstrated in many areas important to business success, the score could be higher.	• Excellent organizational performance levels are reported for most areas of governance and leadership performance. (Le) • Beneficial trends have been sustained over time in all areas of importance to the accomplishment of the organization's mission. (T) • Evidence of industry and benchmark leadership is demonstrated in many areas. (C) • Organizational performance results fully address key customer, market, process, and action plan requirements related to governance and leadership outcomes, and they include projections of the organization's future governance and leadership performance. (I)

Self-Assessments of Organizations and Management Systems

Baldrige-based self-assessments of organization performance and management systems take several forms, ranging from rigorous and time-intensive to simple and superficial. This section discusses the various approaches to organizational self-assessment and the pros and cons of each. Curt Reimann, the first director of the Malcolm Baldrige National Quality Award Office and the closing speaker for the 10th Quest for Excellence Conference, spoke of the need to streamline assessments to get a good sense of strengths, opportunities for improvement, and the vital few areas to focus leadership and drive organizational change. Three distinct types of self-assessment will be examined: the written narrative, the Likert-scale survey, and the behaviorally anchored survey.

Full-Length Written Narrative

The Baldrige application development process is the most time-consuming organizational self-assessment process. To apply for the Baldrige Award, applicants must prepare a 50-page written narrative to address the requirements of the performance excellence Criteria. In the written self-assessment, the applicant is expected to describe the processes and programs it has in place to drive performance excellence. The Baldrige application process serves as the vehicle for self-assessment in most state-level quality awards. The process has not changed significantly since the national quality award program was created in 1987 (except for reducing the maximum page limit from 85 pages to 50 pages). (Author's note: *The CD-ROM attached to the back cover of this book contains an application development template document designed to facilitate the collection of information within an organization to serve as a basis for a complete and thorough written application.*)

Over the years, three methods have been used to prepare the full-length, comprehensive written narrative self-assessment.

1. The most widely used technique involves gathering a team of people to prepare the application. The team members are usually assigned one of the seven Categories and asked to develop a narrative to address the Criteria requirements of that Category. The Category writing teams are frequently subdivided to prepare responses by Item. After the initial draft is complete, an oversight team consolidates the narrative and tries to ensure processes are linked and integrated throughout. Finally, top leaders review and *scrub* the written narrative to put the best spin on the systems, processes, and results reported.

2. Another technique is similar to that described previously. However, instead of subdividing the writing team according to the Baldrige Categories, the team remains together to write the entire application. In this way, the application may be more coherent and the linkages between business processes are easier to understand. This approach also helps to ensure consistency and integrity of the review processes. With fewer people involved, however, the natural *blind spots* of the team may prevent a full and accurate analysis of the management system. Finally, as with the method described previously, top leaders review and scrub the written narrative.

3. The third method of preparing the written narrative is the least common and involves one person writing for several days to produce the application. Considering the immense amount of knowledge and work involved, it is easy to understand why the third method is used so rarely.

External experts are usually involved with all three methods. Nearly all Baldrige Award recipients reported they hired consultants to help them finalize their application by sharpening its focus and clarifying linkages.

Pros:

- Baldrige Award-winning organizations report that the discipline of producing a full-length written self-assessment (Baldrige application) helped them learn about their organization and identify opportunities for improvement before the site-visit team arrived. The written narrative self-assessment process clearly helped focus leaders on their organization's strengths and opportunities for improvement—provided that a complete and honest assessment was made.

- The written narrative self-assessment also provides rich information to help examiners conduct a site visit (the purpose of which is to verify and clarify the information contained in the written self-assessment).

Cons:

- Written narrative self-assessments are extremely time and labor intensive. Organizations that use this approach for Baldrige or state applications or for internal organizational review report that it requires between approximately 2000 and 4000 person-hours of effort—sometimes much more. People working on the self-assessment are diverted from other tasks during this period.

- Because the application is closely scrutinized and carefully scrubbed, and because of page limits, it may not fully and accurately describe the actual management processes and systems of the organization. Decisions based on misleading or incomplete information may take the organization down the wrong path.

- Although the written self-assessment provides information to help guide a site visit, examiners cannot determine the depth of deployment because only a few points of view are represented in the narrative.

- Finally, and perhaps most importantly, the discipline and knowledge required to write a meaningful narrative self-assessment are usually far greater than that possessed within the vast majority of organizations. Many Baldrige Award recipients have hired expert consultants to help them prepare and refine their written narratives.

Short Written Narrative

Two of the most significant obstacles to writing a useful full-length written narrative self-assessment are poor knowledge of the performance excellence Criteria and the time required to produce a meaningful assessment. If people do not understand the Criteria, it takes significantly longer to prepare a written self-assessment. In fact, the amount of time required to write an application/assessment is inversely related to the writers' knowledge of the Criteria. The difficulty associated with writing a full-length narrative has prevented many organizations from participating in state, local, or national award programs.

To encourage more organizations to begin the performance improvement journey, many state award programs developed progressively higher levels of recognition, ranging, for example, from *commitment* at the low end, through *demonstrated progress,* to *achieving excellence* at the top of the range. Even with progressive levels of recognition, however, the obstacle of preparing a 50-page written narrative discouraged many from engaging in the process. To help resolve this problem, several state programs permit applicants who seek recognition at the lower levels to submit a 7- to 20-page *short* written narrative self-assessment. The short form ranges from requiring a one-page description per Category to one page per Item (hence the 7- to 20-page range in length). The very short (one page per Category) applications have not provided sufficient detail for examiners, and many states now require longer applications.

Pros:

- It clearly takes less time to prepare the short form.

- Because of the reduced effort required to complete the self-assessment, more organizations are beginning the process of assessing and improving their performance.

Cons:

- The short form provides significantly less information to help examiners prepare for the site visit. In some cases, the very short, seven-page version provides examiners with no useful information.

- The short form is usually as closely scrutinized and carefully scrubbed as its full-length cousin.

This reduces accuracy and value to both the organization and examiners.

- The knowledge required to write even a short narrative prevents organizations in the beginning stages from preparing an accurate and meaningful assessment.

- Finally, not enough information is presented in the short form to understand the extent of deployment of the systems and processes covered by the Criteria.

The Survey Approach

Just about everyone is familiar with a Likert-scale survey. These surveys typically ask respondents to rate, on a scale of one to five, the extent to which they strongly disagree or strongly agree with a comment. The following is an example of a simple Likert-scale survey item from the *Are We Making Progress as Leaders* survey released in February 2004 by the Baldrige Award Office of NIST:

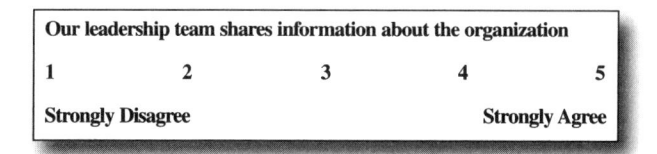

Our leadership team shares information about the organization				
1	2	3	4	5
Strongly Disagree				Strongly Agree

A variation on the simple Likert-scale survey item has been developed in an attempt to improve consistency among respondents. Brief descriptors have been added at each level as shown in this descriptive Likert-scale survey item:

Senior leaders effectively share information about the organization				
1	2	3	4	5
Not Evident	Beginning	Effective	Mature	Advanced

Pros:

- The Likert-scale survey is quick and easy to administer. People from all functions and levels within the organization can provide their opinion.

Cons:

- Both the simple and the descriptive Likert-scale survey items are subject to wide ranges of interpretation. One person's rating of *two* and another person's rating of *four* may actually describe the same systems or behaviors. This problem of scoring reliability raises serious questions about the usefulness of both the simple and the word-descriptor survey techniques for conducting accurate organizational self-assessments. After all, a quick and easy survey that produces inaccurate data still has low value. That is the main reason why states have not adopted the brief Likert-scale survey as a tool for conducting the self-assessments, even for organizations in the beginning stages of the quality journey.

The Behaviorally Anchored Survey

A behaviorally anchored survey contains elements of a written narrative and a survey approach to conducting a self-assessment. The method is simple. Instead of brief descriptors such as *strongly agree/strongly disagree* or *none–few–some–many–most*, a more complete behavioral description is presented for each level of the survey scale. Respondents simply identify the behavioral description that most closely fits the activities in the organization. In addition, by asking the respondent to describe briefly the processes used by the organization to do what the Baldrige Criteria require, we can simulate the kind of information collected on a site visit, checking deployment and process integration. A sample is shown on the next page.

Since the behavioral descriptions in the survey combine the requirements of the Criteria with the standards from the scoring guidelines, it is possible to produce accurate Baldrige-based scores for Items and Categories for the entire organization and for any subgroup or division.

Figure 39 provides sample scores for the entire organization. The chart shows the percent scores, on a zero to 100 scale, for each Item. This helps users determine, at a glance, the relative strengths and weaknesses.

Figure 40 shows the ratings by job-classification subgroup, in this case, positions of senior leaders and other members of the workforce. In Figure 39, Item 1.1, Leadership System reflected a rating of 50 percent. According to the breakout in Figure 40, however, senior leaders believe the processes are much

1E Organizational Governance: Review and Achieve Management Accountability, Protect Stakeholder Interests, and Improve Leader Effectiveness **Baldrige Reference [1.2a(1, 2)]**	
To what extent are senior leaders and managers held accountable for their actions? How well do senior leaders improve their own effectiveness?	
1 **Not Evident** ☐	Effective processes are not in place to ensure management and fiscal accountability. The organization does not have processes, policies or practices in place to hold senior leaders and managers accountable for their actions. The organization does not have processes in place to identify and mitigate potential conflicts of interest.
2 **Beginning** ☑	The organization is beginning to identify and implement processes to govern effectively. The processes are not effective since they are not consistently or widely used. The processes are not evaluated to check effectiveness or to see how they could be improved.
3 **Basically Effective** ☐	The organization has basic systems in place to govern effectively (for example, leaders are generally held accountable for fraud, waste or abuse violations). The organization is starting to gather data about the effectiveness of some of these processes.
4 **Mature** ☐	The organization has well-deployed processes in place to in place to govern effectively (for example, leaders are consistently held accountable for fraud, waste or abuse violations). To protect against fraud, waste and abuse, inspections and/or audits are conducted. The organization sometimes checks the effectiveness of these processes. Leaders may have made some changes as a result of feedback from inspections and/or audits.
5 **Advanced** ☐	The organization has effective processes in place to govern effectively. These processes ensure accountability for management actions, fiscal accountability, and protection of stakeholder interests. Internal control procedures and independent inspections and/or audits help protect against fraud, waste and abuse. Most leaders receive performance evaluations that include accountability for their performance against the organization's goals and may include other feedback from peers and workers. Many leaders and managers use this information to improve their personal leadership style and leadership system processes. Leaders may have used this information to make some improvements to processes involving the accountability of management actions and/or financial operations; and to the leadership system of the organization.
6 **Role Model** ☐	The organization has effective processes in place to ensure accountability for management actions, fiscal accountability, transparency in operations and conflict of interest disclosure policies for senior officers, and protection of stakeholder interests. Internal control procedures and independent inspections and/or audits are widely used to protect against fraud, waste and abuse. Nearly all leaders receive performance evaluations (which include feedback from peers and workers) that address their performance against the organization's goals, strategic objectives, and action plans. Most senior leaders, managers, and supervisors throughout the organization use this information to improve leadership processes and their personal effectiveness. Ongoing improvements are made to these processes as a result of this information. Innovative processes are routinely developed and shared as appropriate across the organization.
? or Not Applicable ☐	I do not have enough information to answer this question or it is not applicable to my organization.
How are senior leaders and managers held accountable for their actions? Describe how independent audits and inspections are used to protect against fraud, waste, and abuse. How have senior leaders improved their personal effectiveness, the leadership system, or management and fiscal accountability? How widely is this done? What innovations have been made and shared throughout the organization?	

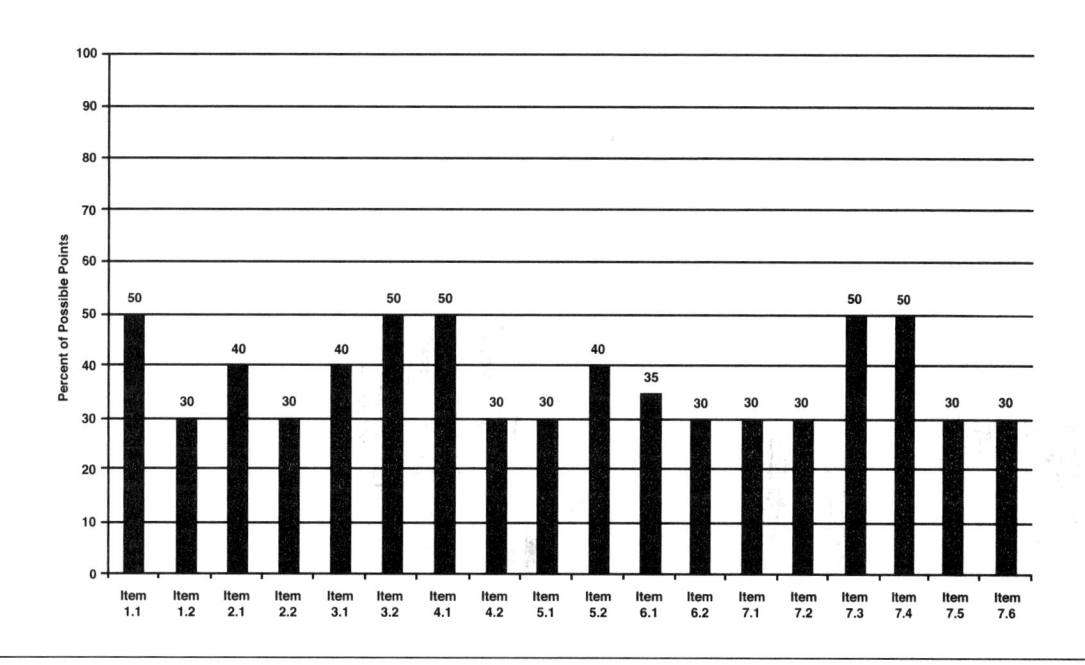

Self-Assessments of Organizations and Management Systems

Figure 39 Sample organization overall percent scores by Item.

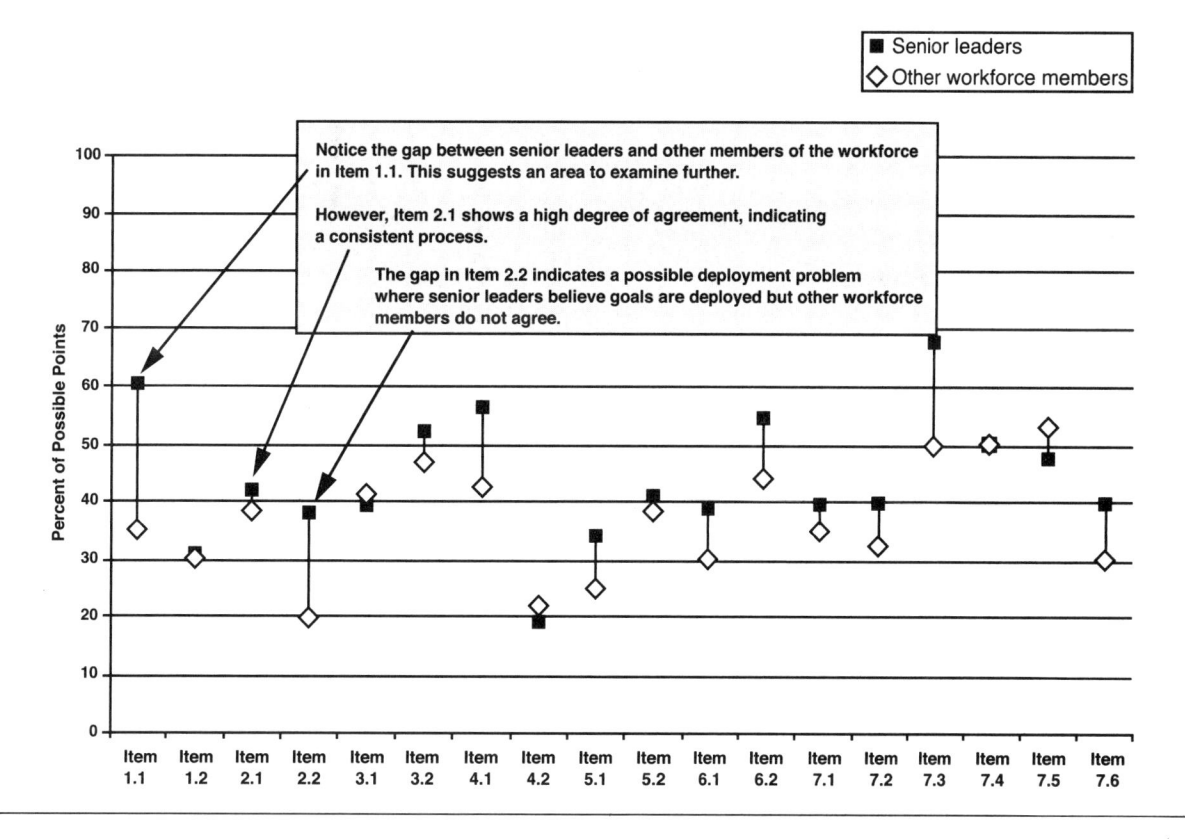

Figure 40 Sample organization position percent scores by Item and job classification.

stronger (more than 60 percent) than other workforce members (less than 35 percent). This typically indicates incomplete systems development or poor deployment of existing systems and processes required by the Item.

The Pareto diagram in Figure 41 presents data reflecting the areas respondents believed were most in need of improvement. Continuing with the leadership example, it is clear that respondents believe that leaders need to do a better job of empowerment, motivation, taking action to improve performance, creating customer value (theme D), holding management accountable, protecting stakeholder interests, improving leader effectiveness (theme E), and following laws and regulations and addressing public risks and concerns (theme F). This helps examiners focus on which areas in leadership may present the most important opportunities for improvement.

Figure 42 allows examiners to determine what type of workforce member identified the various improvement priorities. Look at D in Figure 41 and you will see that workforce members identified the need to improve D by more than a 2 to 1 margin over managers/supervisors. This tends to indicate a deployment gap.

Finally, a complete report of the comments and explanations of the respondents can be prepared

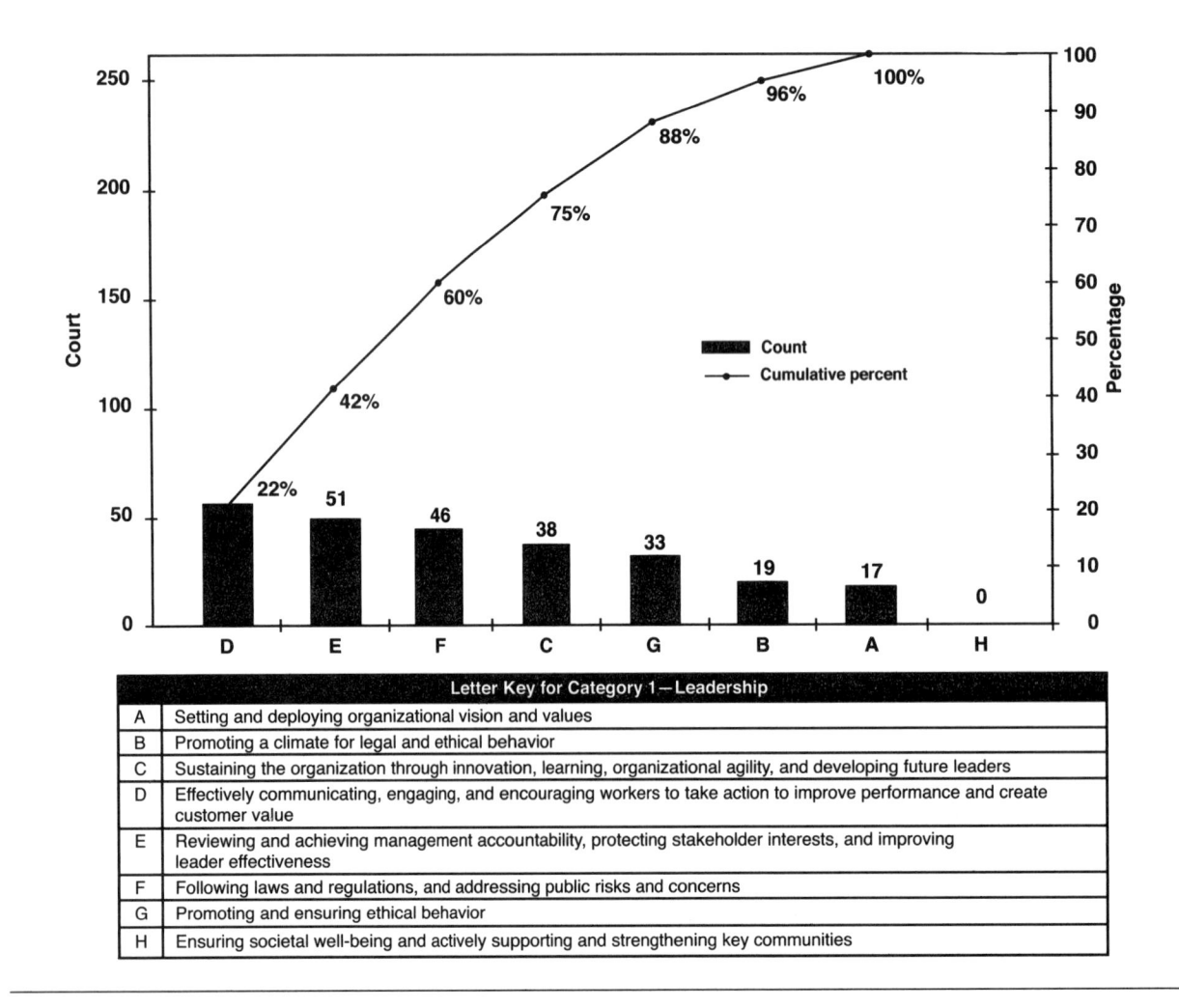

	Letter Key for Category 1—Leadership
A	Setting and deploying organizational vision and values
B	Promoting a climate for legal and ethical behavior
C	Sustaining the organization through innovation, learning, organizational agility, and developing future leaders
D	Effectively communicating, engaging, and encouraging workers to take action to improve performance and create customer value
E	Reviewing and achieving management accountability, protecting stakeholder interests, and improving leader effectiveness
F	Following laws and regulations, and addressing public risks and concerns
G	Promoting and ensuring ethical behavior
H	Ensuring societal well-being and actively supporting and strengthening key communities

Figure 41   Category 1—Leadership: analysis of areas most needing improvement.

1. Leadership

Count

	D	E	F	C	G	B	A	H	Total
Workers	41	22	22	19	20	6	5	0	135
Managers/Supervisors	15	29	24	19	13	12	13	0	125
Total	56	51	46	38	33	19	17	0	260

Percentage (See chart below)

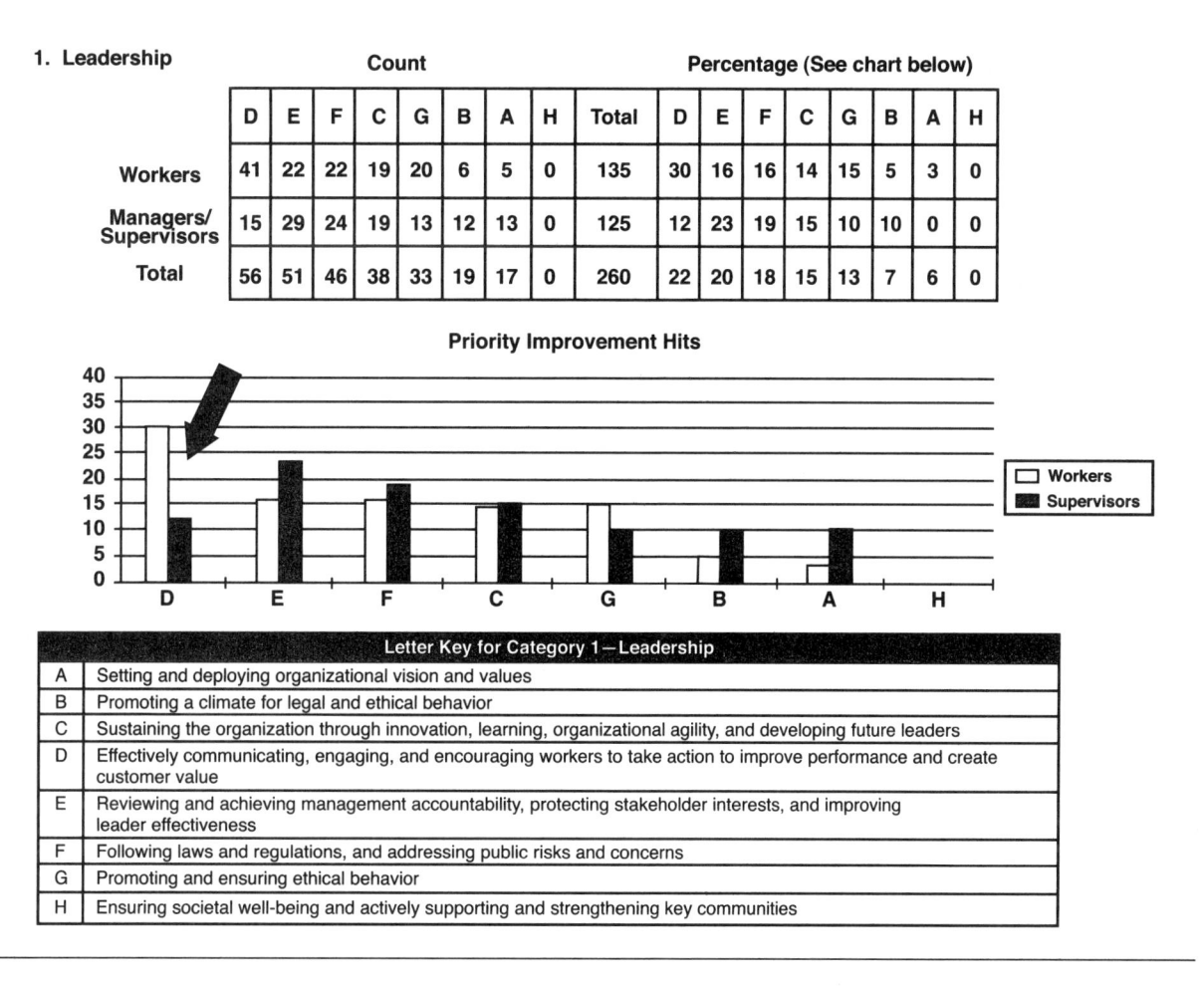

	D	E	F	C	G	B	A	H
Workers	30	16	16	14	15	5	3	0
Managers/Supervisors	12	23	19	15	10	10	0	0
Total	22	20	18	15	13	7	6	0

Priority Improvement Hits (bar chart: Workers vs Supervisors across D, E, F, C, G, B, A, H)

	Letter Key for Category 1—Leadership
A	Setting and deploying organizational vision and values
B	Promoting a climate for legal and ethical behavior
C	Sustaining the organization through innovation, learning, organizational agility, and developing future leaders
D	Effectively communicating, engaging, and encouraging workers to take action to improve performance and create customer value
E	Reviewing and achieving management accountability, protecting stakeholder interests, and improving leader effectiveness
F	Following laws and regulations, and addressing public risks and concerns
G	Promoting and ensuring ethical behavior
H	Ensuring societal well-being and actively supporting and strengthening key communities

Figure 42 Priority improvement counts and percentages—by position for the Leadership Category.

and used by examiners and organization leaders for improvement planning.

Pros:

- Descriptive behavioral anchors increase the consistency of rating. That is, one respondent's rating of *two* is likely to reflect the same observed behaviors as another respondent's rating of *two*.

- Although completing a behaviorally anchored survey requires more reading than a Likert-scale survey, the amount of time and cost required to complete it is still less than 10 percent of the time and cost required to prepare a written narrative.

- Because it is easy and simple to use, the behaviorally anchored survey does not impose a barrier to participation as does the written narrative. States and companies that use surveys with properly written behavioral anchors find the accuracy of the assessment to be as good and in many cases better than that achieved by the full-length narrative self-assessment, and significantly better than Likert-scale or short-narrative assessments. A performance profile can be developed by obtaining input from a cross section of functions, locations, and grade levels throughout the organization. The profile not only identifies strengths and opportunities for improvement, but deployment gaps as well—something the written-narrative assessments rarely provide.

- For organizations doing business throughout the world, the behaviorally anchored survey—translated into the native language of respondents—

permits far greater input than the written narrative.

- Modern techniques involving surveying through Internet access can facilitate an easier way to survey a large, global company.

- Accurate survey data, based on behavioral anchors, can be used to compare or benchmark organizations within and among industries, and can also support longitudinal performance studies.

- Finally, examiners report that the effort required to analyze survey data and plan a site visit is about 50 percent less than the amount of effort required to analyze and prepare for a site visit based on a written narrative. Moreover, they report better information regarding deployment.

Cons:

- Organizations with highly developed performance management systems that seek to apply for top state or national recognition may prefer to practice developing the full-length narrative self-assessment because it is usually required.

- Examiners who are comfortable with the Baldrige application review process, which requires 25 to 40 or more hours to conduct an individual review of a full-length narrative self-assessment, initially find it disconcerting to develop comments and plan a site visit based on data gathered from a survey. Different training for examiners is required to develop skills at using survey data to prepare feedback and plan site visits.

Note: The preceding report summary is of a behaviorally anchored organizational self-assessment written by Quantum Performance Group (QPG) and used with its permission. This behaviorally anchored assessment tool is administered by the National Council for Performance Excellence (NCPE) under a license from QPG. Readers may contact them by calling 802-655-1922 or by writing to NCPE, 480 Hercules Drive, Colchester, VT 05446. Several state quality awards and many private-sector organizations are using this type of assessment as an alternative to the written-narrative form of evaluation.

In conclusion:

- The full-length written-narrative self-assessment is costly. It provides useful information both to examiners and the organizations completing it. The process of completing the written self-assessment can help more advanced organizations to focus and work together as a team.

- The usefulness of the short-form written self-assessment is marginal, especially for beginning organizations; little useful information is provided to examiners and managers/workforce members of the organization. Because the short-form written self-assessment takes less time to complete, one barrier to participation is lowered.

- Concerns over the accuracy and inter-rater reliability of the simple and descriptive Likert scales make their use in conducting effective organizational assessments of management systems marginal.

- The behaviorally anchored survey with comments from respondents combines the benefits of survey speed with the accuracy and completeness of a well-developed written-narrative self-assessment. In addition, the behaviorally anchored survey can identify gaps in deployment unlike the written-narrative self-assessment and is less costly and quicker to administer than the written narrative.

In addition to the business assessment presented in this book, NCPE administers organizational self-assessments in education, health care, and nonprofit organizations including government agencies. More information about business, education, and health care surveys can be obtained from the National Council for Performance Excellence, 480 Hercules Drive, Colchester, VT 05446, (802-655-1922). Its Web site is: http://www.PerformanceExcellence.com.

Following is a sample of a behaviorally anchored survey originally developed by Mark Blazey in 1992 and revised each year since then.

2009 Baldrige Business

Organizational Self-Assessment, Behaviorally Anchored Version

Customized Demographic Profile

Each participating organization completes a customized demographic profile (a generic sample follows). In this way, survey data can be analyzed by these variables to help pinpoint specific areas needing improvement. This allows the extent of use (deployment) of management systems to be examined.

Please circle one selection from each column below to indicate your position within the organization.

Position	Location	Function	Org.	Years of Service
• Executive • Manager • Supervisor • Technician • Individual Contributor	• North • South • East • West • HQ	• Engineering • Sales • Human Resources • Finance Marketing • Manufacturing • Supply Management • Info Technology • Other	• 1 • 2 • 3 • 4 • 5 Other	• 0 < 1 • 1 < 3 • 3 < 5 • 5 < 10 • 10 +

BALDRIGE IN-DEPTH FOR BUSINESS INSTRUCTIONS

This survey consists of 44 themes or questions that relate to the 2009–2010 Baldrige Performance Excellence Criteria. It is organized into seven *sections*, one for each of the seven Performance Excellence Criteria Categories.

- To the best of your knowledge, select a rating (1 to 6) that describes the level of development in your organization. Note that *all* of the elements of a statement must be true before you can select that level. If one or more is not true, you must go to a lower level. After you have selected the rating level, please enter the value in the empty box to the right of the row of statements.

▶ Accuracy tip: The rating scale involves your assessment about the extent of use of the required management processes. The following definitions should help you rate this consistently:

✔ Few	less than 15%
✔ Some	15% to less than 30%
✔ Many	30% to less than 50%
✔ Most	50% to less than 80%
✔ Nearly All	80% to less than 99%
✔ All	100%

➣ Time-saving tip: Start reading at level 3. If all parts of the statement are true, go to level 4, if not, drop back to read level 2. After a few answers, save even more time by starting at the number you select most often. Don't waste time by reading from row 1 each time (unless most of your answers are 1).

- If you do not know an answer, enter NA (Not Applicable/Does Not Apply) or ? (Don't Know). If you are unsure of the meaning of a word or phrase, please check the glossary at the end of this booklet.

- After all statements in each Category have been rated, you will be directed to identify two areas you believe are the most important to improve in your organization now. Then, go back to the space below each row of statements you identified as vital to improve and describe briefly the activities your organization conducts that relate to the topic. Also, please suggest steps that your organization or its leaders could take to improve the processes. Your thoughtful comments are as helpful as the rating itself. If you want to comment on more themes, please do so.

- Continue in the same way to complete all seven Categories.

- ➡ Accuracy Tip: Begin the survey with the Category you know best. You do not have to start with Category 1.

SUMMARY OF CATEGORY 1: LEADERSHIP

This sample assessment looks at one question in the Leadership Category (see sample question at Figure 43). The full-length assessment of Leadership contains eight themes: The first part looks at how senior leaders guide and sustain the organization by setting organizational vision and values and deploying these through the organization to all members of the workforce, and key suppliers and partners. Senior leaders need to communicate openly with the workforce and set high performance expectations. Their personal actions must reflect the values they communicate. In addition, they must promote an environment that fosters and achieves legal and ethical behavior as well as promote strategic objectives, innovation, organizational agility, and performance improvement. Senior leaders must engage the workforce to achieve high performance through customer and business focus.

- You are asked to comment on the extent to which senior leaders guide and sustain the organization through clear values, vision, and setting of high performance expectations. This includes how leaders create an environment for innovation, learning, knowledge sharing, and organizational agility. You are asked how senior leaders create an environment that fosters legal and ethical behavior. You are also asked how senior leaders personally participate in succession planning and develop future leaders.

- You are asked how senior leaders communicate with and engage the workforce while encouraging frank, two-way communications. This includes taking an active role in reward and recognition to encourage high performance. You are asked how they focus on creating and balancing value for customers and other stakeholders.

The second part looks at how well the organization's governance system works to address its societal responsibilities.

- You are asked to comment on management accountability and governance-system effectiveness in protecting interests of stakeholders and stockholders, and how senior leaders and members of the governance board are evaluated and how the system has improved.

- You are asked to comment on how well the organization ensures its behavior addresses impacts on the public and complies with legal and other regulatory requirements, as well as acts ethically in business interactions.

- Finally, you are asked to comment on the extent to which the organization meets its societal responsibilities and supports its communities.

Self-Assessments of Organizations and Management Systems

Communication and Organizational Performance: Effectively Communicating, Engaging, and Encouraging Workers to Take Action to Improve Performance and Create Customer Value [Baldrige reference: 1.1b(1, 2)]

1D. How well do senior leaders communicate with workers, and engage them to do their best at all times to achieve high performance and meet customer needs?

Not Evident
1. Senior leaders do not talk to or share ideas with workers. Leaders usually wait for communication and performance problems to become serious before taking action.

Beginning
2. A few senior leaders discuss work priorities with workers. Leaders give clear direction to employees in a few parts of the organization. Senior leaders do not check how well they communicate with employees.

Basically Effective
3. Some senior leaders discuss work priorities with some workers. Leaders give clear direction to employees in some parts of the organization Senior leaders are starting to check how well they communicate with employees.

Mature
4. Many senior leaders provide clear direction to employees in many parts of the organization. Leaders stress the need for high performance to meet the organization's objectives and actions plans required for success in the future. Senior leaders sometimes check how well they are communicating with workers and may have made some changes as a result.

Advanced
5. Senior leaders effectively communicate with and motivate most workers to do their best to meet high performance objectives. Most senior leaders make sure that honest, two-way communication occurs with workers in most parts of the organization. Most senior leaders participate in award programs that recognize workers for meeting high performance objectives and customer needs. Most senior leaders inspire action to achieve the organization's objectives and vision and improve performance. Senior leaders regularly check how well they communicate with workers and encourage high performance. They sometimes make improvements based on this information. Leaders sometimes make sure that good ideas and practices are shared across the organization.

Role Model
6. Senior leaders effectively communicate with, engage, empower, and motivate nearly all workers to do their best to meet high performance objectives. Nearly all senior leaders make sure that honest, two-way communication occurs with workers throughout the organization. Nearly all senior leaders actively participate in award programs that recognize workers for meeting high performance objectives, action plans, and customer needs. Nearly all senior leaders inspire action to achieve the organization's objectives and vision and improve performance. Senior leaders almost always check to see how well they communicate with workers and encourage high performance. Leaders usually make ongoing improvements based on this information. Senior leaders have developed creative (innovative) approaches in these areas. Leaders almost always make sure that good ideas and practices are shared across the organization.

Figure 43 Sample Leadership question.

SUMMARY OF CATEGORY 2: STRATEGIC PLANNING

This sample assessment looks at one question in the Strategic Planning Category (see sample question at Figure 44). The full-length assessment of Strategic Planning contains six themes.

The first part looks at how the organization develops its strategic plans. The Category stresses that customer-driven quality and operational-performance excellence are key strategic challenges that need to be integral parts of the organization's overall planning.

The second part looks at the way the organization converts its strategic objectives into action to align work to support the organization's strategic directions, and make sure that priorities are carried out. The organization must translate its strategic objectives into action plans to accomplish the objectives. The organization must also be able to assess the progress of action plans. The aim is to ensure that strategies are understood and followed by everyone in the organization to help achieve goals.

Strategic Objectives: Developing Clear Strategic Objectives and Timetables for Meeting the Objectives [Baldrige ref: 2.1b(1)]

2B. Does the organization have measurable strategic objectives in place? Is there a timetable (schedule) for meeting the objectives?

Not Evident
1. The organization does not have clear objectives in place. The organization usually waits until problems caused by unclear objectives become serious (that is, parts of the organization are not working against the common goals) before fixing the problem.

Continued

Continued

Beginning

2. The organization is beginning to develop strategies for success; but most do not provide clear direction. The method(s) used to develop strategies that provide clear guidance are not very effective and are not evaluated to see how they could be improved.

Basically Effective

3. The organization has a process in place to develop strategies for success. The strategies identify activities the organization will take. The organization has started to check whether its strategies are clear and well understood by some managers and workers.

Mature

4. The organization has measurable, outcome-based objectives in place. The objectives are not a list of activities, but rather reflect many areas of performance the organization must achieve to ensure its future success. The organization sometimes checks whether its objectives are clear and understood by many managers and workers. Based on this information, some changes to the organization's objectives may have been made.

Advanced

5. The organization has developed measurable, outcome-based strategic objectives that reflect areas important to the organization's competitive position, overall performance, and future success. There are specific timetables with numerical targets for carrying out most objectives. The organization regularly checks whether its objectives and timetables are clear, understood and used by most managers and workers to support decision making and progress reviews. Improvements to objectives and timetables are sometimes made. Some sharing of good ideas/practices related to setting objectives and timetables takes place within the organization.

Role Model

6. The organization has developed measurable, outcome-based strategic objectives that reflect areas important to the organization's vision, values, competitive position, overall performance, and future success. There are specific timetables with numerical targets for carrying out nearly all objectives. The timetables match the leaders' performance review cycles (for example, quarterly milestones/timetables support quarterly senior leader reviews). The organization regularly checks whether its objectives and timetables are clear, understood and used by nearly all managers and workers to support decision making and match the cycle of progress reviews. Ongoing improvements to the objectives and timetables are made. Creative (innovative) approaches to developing and communicating outcome-based objectives and timetables have been made. Good ideas and best practices are nearly always shared across the organization.

Figure 44 Sample Strategic Planning question.

SUMMARY OF CATEGORY 3: CUSTOMER FOCUS

This sample assessment looks at one question in the Customer Focus Category (see sample question at Figure 45). The full-length assessment of Customer and Market Focus contains seven themes.

The first part looks at how the organization identifies product offerings to meet customer requests and exceed expectations; and support the customers' uses of products. This part also examines systems to create a customer culture. The second part looks at systems to use the voice of the customer to understand their requirements and learn about their levels of satisfaction, engagement, and dissatisfaction.

Analysis and Use of Customer Data: Becoming More Customer Focused [Baldrige ref: 3.2c]

3C. How well does the organization use voice-of-the-customer information and feedback to verify customer needs and become more customer-focused?

Not Evident

1. The organization does not use direct customer information or feedback to improve marketplace success. Rather than proactively understanding customer needs, expectations, and preferences, the organization usually waits until customer problems become serious before taking action.

Beginning

2. The organization is beginning to obtain and use information on a few customers. The customer information is of little use since it is not consistently or widely used. Processes used to obtain information are not evaluated to see how they could be improved.

Basically Effective

3. The organization has effective processes in place to obtain and use customer information to improve marketplace success. The organization has started to check some of these processes to determine if they are collecting meaningful customer data.

Mature

4. The organization effectively listens to many customers to ensure its products and services are likely to meet customer requirements, improve marketing, and build a more customer-focused culture. The organization sometimes gathers data on these processes to determine

Continued

> *Continued*
>
> if they are collecting meaningful and accurate customer data. The organization may have made some improvements as a result of this information.
>
> *Advanced*
> 5. The organization regularly uses customer, market, and product feedback to identify and anticipate requirements and changing expectations, better satisfy their needs/desires, and identify opportunities for meaningful change. The organization regularly checks its voice-of-the-customer processes to ensure the information they collect is accurate and complete. Based on this evaluation, the organization sometimes improves these processes. Some sharing of improved practices takes place within the organization.
>
> *Role Model*
> 6. The organization frequently uses customer, market, and product feedback to identify and anticipate requirements and changing expectations, better satisfy customer needs and desires, and identify opportunities for meaningful change. The organization regularly checks its voice-of-the-customer processes to ensure the information they collect is meaningful, accurate, and complete. Based on this information, the organization makes ongoing improvements to its process to analyze and use customer data. Nearly all parts of the organization have put in place new or creative (innovative) approaches resulting in a greater focus on meeting the current and future needs of the customer throughout the customer life cycle. Good ideas and best practices are nearly always shared across the organization.

Figure 45 Sample Customer Focus question.

SUMMARY OF CATEGORY 4: MEASUREMENT, ANALYSIS, AND KNOWLEDGE MANAGEMENT

This sample assessment looks at one question in the Measurement, Analysis, and Knowledge Management Category (see sample question at Figure 46). The full-length assessment of Measurement, Analysis, and Knowledge Management contains seven themes.

Measurement, Analysis, and Knowledge Management is the *brain center* of an effective management system. Appropriate information and analysis are used to improve decision making at all levels to achieve high levels of performance. Effective measures, properly deployed, help align the organization's operations to achieve its strategic goals as well as protect organizational knowledge.

The first part looks at the selection, collection, alignment, review, and integration of data and information to support effective decision making at all levels. Data and information guide decision making to help the organization achieve key business results and strategic objectives. Measurement, Analysis, and Knowledge systems serve as a key foundation for achieving innovation and sustaining peak performance.

The second part looks at how the organization ensures the quality and availability of data and information to support effective decision making for employees and appropriate suppliers, partners, and customers. It also examines building and managing knowledge assets.

> **Performance Analysis and Review: Systematically Evaluating and Improving Key Processes and Translating Performance Review Findings into Priorities for Improvement and Innovation. Communicating the Priorities to Support Decision-Making [Baldrige ref: 4.1c]**
>
> **4D.** How well does the organization use results (findings) from performance reviews to identify priorities for improvement? How are these priorities communicated throughout the organization to help workers make good decisions?
>
> *Not Evident*
> 1. The organization does not use information from performance reviews to help workers make good decisions. The organization usually waits until performance problems become serious before taking action.
>
> *Beginning*
> 2. A few workers and managers are beginning to use measures from organizational performance reviews to support better decision making and improve performance. The results from performance reviews are of little value since they are not consistently or widely used to support good decision making. The use of measures to make better decisions is not evaluated to see how such use could be improved.
>
> *Basically Effective*
> 3. Some workers and managers use measures from performance reviews to support better decision making and improve performance. The organization has started to evaluate whether performance reviews support good
>
> *Continued*

> *Continued*
>
> decision making. The organization may or may not have made improvements to these processes.
>
> *Mature*
>
> 4. Many workers and managers use performance review findings to help align work and support decision making and improve performance throughout the organization. The organization sometimes evaluates the whether performance reviews support effective (good) decision making. Based on this information, the organization has made some improvements to these processes.
>
> *Advanced*
>
> 5. Most workers, managers, and senior leaders use performance review findings to help prioritize action, align work, identify improvement priorities, and support decision making throughout the organization. Priorities and targets for improvement are clearly communicated to most leaders, managers and workers. The organization regularly evaluates how well performance reviews support effective (good) decision making. Based on this information, the organization sometimes makes improvements to these processes. Some sharing of improved analysis and decision-making processes takes place within the organization.
>
> *Role Model*
>
> 6. Nearly all workers, managers, and senior leaders use performance review findings to help prioritize action, align work, identify improvement priorities and opportunities for innovation, and to support decision making throughout the organization. Priorities and targets for improvement are clearly communicated to nearly all leaders, managers, and workers. The organization regularly checks the effectiveness of these processes and makes ongoing improvements. Some new and creative (innovative) solutions to the processes for analyzing and improving performance have been made and best practices are shared across the organization.

Figure 46 Sample Measurement, Analysis, and Knowledge Management question.

SUMMARY OF CATEGORY 5: WORKFORCE FOCUS

This sample assessment looks at one question in the Workforce Focus Category (see sample question at Figure 47). The full-length assessment of Workforce Focus contains six themes.

The first part looks at how well the organization's systems for workforce engagement, enrichment, development, and assessment help all employees reach peak performance.

The second part looks at how well all parts of the organization check and improve workforce capability and capacity, including the skills, competencies, and staffing levels needed to accomplish the organization's work and provide a safe, secure, and healthful workplace.

> **Assessment of Workforce Engagement: Assessing and Improving Workforce Engagement and Satisfaction**
> [Baldrige ref: 5.1c(1. 2)]
>
> **5D.** How well does the organization evaluate the commitment (involvement/engagement) of its employees to the organization, determine their levels of satisfaction, and the affect these factors have on organizational performance?
>
> *Not Evident*
>
> 1. The organization does not have processes in place to assess the commitment or satisfaction of its workers. Managers and supervisors usually wait until worker motivation and satisfaction problems become serious before taking action.
>
> *Beginning*
>
> 2. The organization is beginning to assess the commitment of its workers to do their very best work. Processes to assess levels of commitment/satisfaction are of little value since they are not consistently or widely used. The assessment processes are not evaluated to see how they could be improved.
>
> *Basically Effective*
>
> 3. The organization provides effective feedback and recognition to some employees to enable them to achieve high-performance objectives. The organization has started to evaluate the effectiveness of some of these processes.
>
> *Mature*
>
> 4. The organization has effective processes in place to assess whether the workforce contributes its very best efforts to help the organization succeed (such as using surveys and other data). The assessments of employee commitment have been used in some areas to improve worker performance. The organization sometimes checks how well these assessment processes measure worker commitment and may have made some improvements to the assessment process.
>
> *Advanced*
>
> 5. The organization has effective processes in place to assess most factors of workforce engagement and satisfaction. The organization accurately determines
>
> *Continued*

Self-Assessments of Organizations and Management Systems

Continued

whether workers, managers, and leaders contribute their very best efforts to the success of the organization. The organization uses surveys and other data such as retention, absenteeism, grievances, safety, and productivity to assess workforce engagement and satisfaction. Some improvements in workforce engagement have been made, resulting in some higher performance. The organization regularly checks the methods it uses to assess workforce engagement and satisfaction, and sometimes makes improvements. Some sharing of improved practices takes place across the organization.

Role Model

6. The organization has effective processes in place to assess nearly all factors of workforce engagement and satisfaction. The organization accurately determines whether nearly all workers, contract employees, supervisors, managers, and leaders contribute their very best efforts to the success of the organization. The organization uses surveys and other data such as retention, absenteeism, grievances, safety, and productivity to measure workforce engagement and satisfaction. Many improvements in workforce engagement and satisfaction have been made based on how they affect business results. These improvements have produced even higher levels of performance. The organization regularly checks the methods it uses to determine workforce engagement and satisfaction, and makes ongoing improvements. Some creative (innovative) improvements to these processes have been made and best practices are shared across the organization.

Figure 47 Sample Workforce Focus question.

SUMMARY OF CATEGORY 6: PROCESS MANAGEMENT

This sample assessment looks at one question in the Process Management Category (see sample question at Figure 48). The full-length assessment of Process Management contains five themes.

Process Management is the focal point for all key work processes. The first part looks at the organization's work systems and the systems to design work processes to create customer value, business success, and growth.

The second part examines how the organization designs, manages, and controls its work processes to improve overall operational performance. Key work processes must meet design requirements constantly.

Work Process Management: Implement and Control Work Processes to Ensure They Consistently Meet Requirements [Baldrige ref: 6.2b(1) and 6.2c]

6D. How well does the organization implement its work processes to ensure that they meet design requirements? How does the day-to-day operation of these processes ensure that they meet key process requirements?

Not Evident

1. Effective systems are not in place to manage and improve key work processes. Managers and supervisors usually wait until process problems become serious before taking action.

Beginning

2. The organization has started to use systematic approaches to manage and improve a few work processes. They may include the use of Lean, Six Sigma, plan-do-check-act, or other process improvement tools. The approaches are not effective since they are not consistently or widely used. The approaches are not evaluated to see how they could be improved.

Basically Effective

3. Effective systems are in place to manage and improve some work processes. These systems may include the use of Lean, Six Sigma, plan-do-check-act, or other process improvement tools. The organization has started to gather data about the effectiveness of some of these processes.

Mature

4. The organization systematically implements many of its key work processes to ensure that they meet both design and key process requirements. Key performance measures or indicators and in-process measures used to control and improve many work processes. Control and improvement techniques may include Lean, Six Sigma, plan-do-check-act, or other process improvement tools. The organization sometimes evaluates the effectiveness of these processes and may have made some changes as a result.

Advanced

5. The organization systematically implements most of its key work processes to ensure that they usually meet both design and key process requirements. Appropriate input from customers, suppliers, partners, and collaborators input is often used in managing these processes. This input may be obtained from complaint data, satisfaction surveys, and other methods. Key performance outcome measures and in-process measures used to control and improve most work processes. Control and improvement techniques may include Lean, Six Sigma, plan-do-check-act, or other process improvement tools. The organization regularly checks the effectiveness of these processes and makes ongoing improvements. Some innovations to these processes have been made and best practices are shared across the organization.

Continued

> *Continued*
>
> ***Role Model***
> 6. The organization systematically implements nearly all of its key work processes to ensure that they meet both design and key process requirements. Appropriate input from customers, suppliers, partners, and collaborators input is nearly always used in managing these processes. This input may be obtained from complaint data, satisfaction surveys, and other methods. Key performance outcome measures and in-process measures used to control and improve nearly all work processes. Control and improvement techniques may include Lean, Six Sigma, plan-do-check-act, or other process improvement tools. The organization regularly checks the effectiveness of these processes and makes ongoing improvements. Some innovations to these processes have been made and best practices are shared across the organization.

Figure 48 Sample Process Management question.

SUMMARY OF CATEGORY 7: RESULTS

This sample assessment looks at one theme in the Results Category (see sample question at Figure 49). The full-length assessment of the Results Category contains six themes.

The Results Category looks for the results produced by the management systems described in Categories 1 through 6. Results range from lagging performance outcomes such as product and service performance, customer satisfaction, market share, and financial performance to predictive or leading outcomes such as internal operating measures and human resource results. Together, these lagging and leading results create a set of balanced indicators of organizational health, commonly called a *balanced scorecard*.

- Question 7A looks at looks at product outcomes that lead to customer satisfaction, loyalty, and positive referral such as on-time delivery.

- Question 7B looks at how well the organization has been satisfying customers and building stronger customer engagement and relations.

- Question 7C looks at the strength of the organization's financial and market results.

- Question 7D looks at how well the organization has been creating and maintaining a positive, productive, learning, and engaging work environment.

- Question 7E looks at the organization's key operational performance results to achieve high levels of process effectiveness.

- Question 7F looks at key results in the areas of leadership, governance, and societal responsibilities; accomplishment of strategy and action plans, organizational citizenship, ethical behavior, and compliance with applicable laws and regulations.

> **Customer-Focused Outcomes: Trends, Levels, and Comparisons [Baldrige ref: 7.2a(1, 2)]**
>
> 7B. What are the levels of the organization's customer-focused performance results? What are the trends of these key measures? How do levels and trends compare with those of competitors, similar organizations, or organizations providing similar products/services?
>
> ***Not Evident***
> 1. To my knowledge, the organization does not have customer satisfaction results OR its customer satisfaction ratings are poor.
>
> ***Beginning***
> 2. A few results for customer satisfaction and loyalty, retention, and value exist. A few customer-focused results show the beginning of improvement trends. A little comparative information is reported.
>
> ***Basically Effective***
> 3. Customer-focused results, such as customer satisfaction, loyalty, retention, and value exist for many products and services and customer groups. Many customer-focused results show improvement trends and/or good performance levels. The organization has reported some comparative data.
>
> ***Mature***
> 4. Customer-focused results, such as customer satisfaction, dissatisfaction, and engagement exist for most products and customer groups. Most of these results show steady improvement trends. Some show good to very good levels of performance when compared to industry standards. Limited projections of future performance are available.
>
> ***Advanced***
> 5. Customer-focused results such as customer satisfaction, dissatisfaction, and engagement are reported for most products and customer groups. Most of these results,
>
> *Continued*

> *Continued*
>
> when compared to top-performing competitors or benchmarks, show sustained good to excellent performance. Unless the actual level of performance is already near the top levels, many to most trends in areas important to the organization customers continue to improve. Projections of future performance are provided for some high-priority areas.
>
> *Role Model*
>
> 6. Customer-focused results such as customer satisfaction, dissatisfaction, loyalty, retention, positive referral, and value are reported for most products and services and customer groups. Most of these results, when compared to top-performing competitors or benchmarks, show sustained excellent performance. Unless the actual level of performance is already near the top levels, most trends in areas important to the organization customers continue to improve. No pattern of unfavorable trends and no poor performance levels are evident in areas important to the organization. The results lead the industry (or similar providers) in many areas. Some projections of future performance are reported that reflect strategic objectives.

Figure 49 Sample Results question.

The Site Visit

INTRODUCTION

Many examiners and organizations have asked about how to prepare for site visits. This section is intended to help answer those questions and prepare the organization for an on-site examination. It includes rules of the game for examiners and what they are taught to look for. The best preparation for this type of examination is to see things through the eyes of the trained examiner.

Before an organization can be recommended to receive the Malcolm Baldrige National Quality Award, it must receive a visit from a team of organizational assessment experts from the National Board of Examiners. Approximately 25 percent to 30 percent of organizations applying for the Baldrige Award in recent years have received these site visits. Although the panel of judges does not have a pre-determined scoring minimum for site-visit candidates, generally a score of 550 points or more is needed.

The Baldrige Award site-visit team usually includes two to five senior examiners—one of whom is designated as team leader—and three to eight other examiners. In addition, the team is accompanied by a representative of the National Quality Award Office and a "process monitor" from the American Society for Quality (ASQ), which provides administrative services under contract to the Baldrige Award Office.

The site-visit team usually gathers at a hotel near the organization's headquarters on the day immediately preceding the site visit launch. During the day, the team makes final preparations and plans for the visit.

Each examiner is assigned lead responsibility for one or more categories of the Award Criteria. Each examiner is usually teamed with one other examiner for most interviews during the site visit. These examiners usually conduct the visit in pairs to ensure the accurate interpretation and recording of information.

Site visits usually begin on a Monday morning and last one week. By Wednesday afternoon or Thursday morning, most site-visit teams will have completed their on-site review. (Geographically diverse organizations may require more time.) They retire to the nearby hotel to confer and write their reports. By the end of the site visit, the team must reach consensus on the findings and prepare a final report for the panel of judges.

Purpose of Site Visits

Site visits help clarify uncertain points and verify self-assessment (that is, application) accuracy. During the site visit, examiners investigate areas most difficult to understand from self-assessments, such as the following:

- Deployment: How widely a process is used throughout the organization

- Integration: Whether processes fit together to support performance excellence

- Process ownership: Whether processes are broadly owned, simply directed, or micromanaged

- Workforce member involvement: The extent to which workers' participation in managing processes of all types is optimized

- Continuous improvement maturity (learning): The number and extent of improvement cycles and resulting refinements in all areas of the organization and at all levels.

Characteristics of Site-Visit Issues

Examiners look at issues that are an essential component of scoring and role-model determination. They have a responsibility to:

- Clarify information that is missing or vague and verify significant strengths identified from the self-assessment
- Verify deployment of the practices described in the self-assessment

Examiners will:

- Concentrate on cross-cutting issues
- Examine data, reports, and documents
- Interview individuals and teams
- Receive presentations from the applicant organization

Examiners may not conduct their own focus groups or surveys with customers, suppliers, or dealers. Conducting focus groups or surveys would violate confidentiality agreements as well as be statistically unsound.

Discussions with the Applicant Prior to the Site Visit

Prior to the official Baldrige Award site visit, all communication between the applicant organization and its team must be routed through their respective single points of contact. Only the team leader may contact the applicant on behalf of the site-visit team prior to the site visit. This helps ensure consistency of message and communication for both parties. It prevents confusion and misunderstandings. The team leader should provide the applicant organization with basic information about the process. This includes schedules, arrival times, and equipment and meeting room needs.

Applicant organizations usually provide the following information prior to the site-visit team's final planning meeting at the hotel on the day before the site visit starts:

- List of key contacts
- Organization chart
- Facility layout
- Performance data requested by examiners

TYPICALLY IMPORTANT SITE-VISIT ISSUES

- Role of senior management in leading and serving as a role model
- Independence of governance system to protect stakeholder interests and hold managers accountable
- Degree of involvement and self-direction of members of the workforce below upper management
- Comprehensiveness and accessibility of the information system
- Extent that facts and data are used in decision making at all levels
- Degree of emphasis on customer satisfaction; effective use of voice of the customer
- Extent of systematic approaches to work processes
- Workforce and leadership development effectiveness
- Use of compensation, recognition, and rewards to reinforce and align work to high-performance objectives
- Extent that strategic plans align organizational work
- Extent of the use of measurable goals at all levels in the organization
- Evidence of evaluation and improvement cycles in all work processes and in system effectiveness
- Improvements in cycle times and other operating processes
- Extent of integration of all processes—operational and support
- Extent and use of benchmarking

The team leader, on behalf of team members, will ask for supplementary documentation to be compiled (such as results data brought up to date) to avoid placing an undue burden on the organization at the time of the site visit. The team will select sites that allow them to examine key issues and check deployment in key areas. This information may or may not be discussed with the applicant prior to the site visit. Examiners will need access to all areas of the organization.

Conduct of Site-Visit Team Members (Examiners)

Examiners are not allowed to discuss findings with anyone but team members. Examiners may not disclose the following to the applicant:

- Personal or team observations and findings
- Conclusions and decisions
- Observations about the applicant's performance systems, whether complimentary or critical

Examiners may not discuss the following with anyone:

- Observations about any applicants
- Names of other award program applicants

Examiners may not accept trinkets, gifts, or gratuities of any kind (coffee, cookies, rolls, breakfast, and lunch are okay), so applicant organizations should not offer them. At the conclusion of the site visit, examiners are not permitted to leave with any of the applicant's materials including logo items or catalogs—not even items usually given to visitors. Examiners will dress in appropriate business attire unless instructed otherwise by the applicant organization.

Opening Meeting

An opening meeting will be scheduled to introduce all parties and set the structure for the site visit. The meeting is usually attended by senior executives and the self-assessment writing team. The opening meeting usually is scheduled first on the initial day of the site visit (8:30 AM or 9:00 AM). The team leader generally starts the meeting, introduces the team, and opens the site visit. When multiple site visits are conducted it is usually a good idea to prepare a set of talking points or a script for the team leader to use so a common message is communicated by all teams.

The applicant organization usually has one hour to present any information it believes important for the examiners to know. This includes time for a tour, if necessary.

Immediately after the meeting, examiners usually meet with senior leaders and those responsible for preparing sections of the self-assessment (application), since those people are likely to be at the opening meeting.

Conducting the Site Visit

The team will follow the site-visit plan, subject to periodic adjustments according to its findings. The site-visit team will need a private room to conduct frequent caucuses. Applicant representatives are not present at these caucuses. The team will also conduct evening meetings at the hotel to review the findings of the day, reach consensus, write comments, and revise the site-visit report.

If, during the course of the site visit, someone from the applicant organization believes the team or any of its members are missing the point, the designated point of contact should inform the team leader or the Baldrige Award Office monitor. Also, someone who believes an examiner behaved inappropriately should inform the designated point of contact, who will inform the team leader or the award office monitor.

Members of the workforce should be instructed to mark every document given to examiners with the name and work location of the person providing the document. This will ensure that it is returned to the proper person. Records should be made of all material given to team members. Organization personnel may not ask examiners for opinions and advice. Examiners are not permitted to provide any information of this type during the site visit.

GENERIC SITE-VISIT QUESTIONS

Examiners must verify or clarify the information contained in an application, whether they have determined a process to be a strength or an opportunity for improvement. Examiners must verify the existence of strengths as well as clarify the nature of each opportunity for improvement in the final feedback report.

Before and during the site-visit review process, examiners formulate a series of questions based on the Baldrige Criteria. This chapter identifies a series of questions that examiners are likely to ask during the site-visit process, based on the Baldrige Criteria. Of course, during a site visit, actual questions should be tailored to the specific key factors of the organization deemed to be most relevant. The questions in the following section are presented to help prepare applicants and examiners for the site-visit process.

Leaders and workforce members are usually focused on the process they have in place today. **They often fail to describe how they systematically refined the process and show how it evolved to the process of today.** *Therefore, after learning how the process works, all examiners should ask the following questions: "Have you always done it this way? How did you do it before? Why did you change? Do you have additional improvements in the works?" If examiners do not ask these questions, each member of the workforce should offer the answer as if they were asked.*

Category 1—Leadership

1. (To top leaders) How do you set vision and values to guide the organization? Please share with us the values of your organization. [1.1a(1)]

    - What are your top priorities to achieve vision?
    - How do you ensure that your entire workforce knows these priorities?
    - How do you know how effective you and your subordinates are at communicating these values to the workforce, customers, partners, and suppliers?
    - How do you know your messages to your workforce are understood as you intended?

2. (To leaders) What actions do you take that prove to your workforce, customers, and suppliers that you fully embrace the values you mentioned?

    - (To the workforce) What are the values and priorities of the organization? What does your leader do to show you that he or she actually believes these values are important? [1.1a(1)]

3. What do you (the leader) do personally to make sure everyone in the organization behaves in a legal and ethical manner? What are ethical rules that must not be violated (zero tolerance)? What happens when someone—even a senior manager—breaks these rules? Ask members of the workforce the same question. [1.1a(2)]

    - What are some of the most important ethical principles? What processes have you put in place to achieve the desired ethical behavior? How well do these processes work? How do you know? What has been done to improve them?

4. What does it mean to you (senior leader) to create a sustainable organization? How do you make sure that your organization will continue to excel even after you leave? (Note: "I do not plan to leave" is not an acceptable answer. Follow this answer with "What might happen if you were hit by a bus or otherwise incapacitated?") [1.1a(3)]

5. What do you do to increase learning (continuous improvement) throughout the organization, with all units and the entire workforce? What are some examples of new knowledge they have acquired? [1.1a(3)]

6. What techniques have you put in place to ensure the strategic goals or objectives are attained and the organization achieves winning levels of leadership in your industry or sector? [1.1a(3)]

7. The Criteria ask how you "create an environment for" several things such as performance improvement, achieving your strategic objectives, innovation, role model performance leadership, and organizational agility. What do you do to make certain that your entire workforce does these things? [1.1a(3)]

8. What does innovation mean for you? For your workforce? For your organization? What process have you put in place to encourage innovation? What innovative approaches have you personally implemented? Your workers? [1.1a(3)]

    - What does organizational agility mean to you? What barriers to this agility have you identified in the organization? Pick some barriers and ask, what have you done to overcome this barrier? [1.1a(3)]

    - What processes have you put in place to ensure that innovations and other knowledge are effectively shared throughout the organization to appropriate managers and members of the workforce? How well do these processes work? How do you know? What has been done to improve them? [1.1a(3)]

9. What processes do you use to help you improve your personal leadership skills? Provide examples of improvements you have made in your own leadership skills.

10. Please describe the methods you use to prepare people for leadership roles. What is your role in this effort? How do you know this process is working? What improvements have you made in it? [1.1a(3)]

11. What does two-way communication mean to you (the leader)? What do you do to promote two-way communication? How widely is the process actually used? [1.1b(1)] To check deployment, ask members of the workforce about how this two-way communication works and whether they have used it.

12. What are the ways you communicate throughout the organization and to key partners and suppliers? What kind of information do you communicate? When do you do this? [1.1b(1)]

    - What kinds of communication or feedback do you receive from members of the workforce and partners/suppliers? What do you do with this information? How well do these processes work? How do you know? What has been done to improve them? [1.1b(1)]

13. What is your role in supporting processes to ensure performance excellence (high performance)? [1.1b(1)]

    - How do you encourage innovation and workforce engagement and empowerment? Give me some examples of improved empowerment throughout the organization as a result of your efforts. (Follow up on these examples with other members of the workforce.) [1.1b(1)]

    - How do you ensure that middle managers and other subordinates promote workforce engagement and innovation throughout the organization? [1.1b(1)]

14. What steps have you (senior leader) taken to focus the organization on actions to achieve your objectives, missions, and vision? What actions have you taken to improve performance? What performance data do you use to determine whether you are successful or whether other actions are needed? [1.1b(2)]

15. Do your various customer segments have different priorities or value different things? If yes, pick some of the differences and ask, how do you make sure that your organization balances these different requirements and delivers what the customers want? [1.1b(2)]

16. What are your key customer or stakeholder segments? [3.1a(1), 1.1a(1), 1.1b(2)]

    - Pick one and ask, what does this customer/stakeholder group value?

    - Are the requirements or value expected of this customer group different from any other group? If so, what are the differences, and how have you ensured that your organization is addressing the different or competing interests of these groups? [1.1b(2)]

17. How independent is your board of directors? [1.2a]

    - What percentage of the board is not affiliated with your organization in any way (other than being a board member)?

    - How does your audit function ensure objectivity and independence?

- Have problems existed in the past where stakeholder interests were threatened? If so, what was done to prevent the possibility of those problems recurring?

- How does the board make sure managers behave properly and account for their actions in the organization?

- How would you rate the board's climate of trust? To what extent are dissension and disagreement among board members tolerated? Encouraged?

- What policies are in place to ensure the board remains alert to management problems in the organization?

- What type of fiscal oversight does the board provide? What problems or issues have emerged in the past three to five years? Pick some and ask, what was the board's reaction to this issue? How was it resolved? What steps were taken to prevent the problem from happening again?

- What processes have you put in place to ensure the board effectively protects stockholder and shareholder value? How well do these processes work? How do you know? What has been done to improve them?

18. How do your senior leaders check the effectiveness of the leadership system? How is your own personal leadership effectiveness checked? [1.2a(2)]

    - How do you include or use workforce feedback from the two-way communication (if done) in the evaluation?

    - Please identify specific examples where you and the leadership system have improved as a result of these evaluations. How do managers evaluate and improve their personal leadership effectiveness? How are data from organizational performance reviews used here?

19. What are the criteria for promoting and rewarding leaders within the organization? [1.2a(2); 5.1a(3)]

    - How are you making leaders and top managers accountable for performance improvement, workforce-involvement, and customer-satisfaction objectives? (Look at some samples of managers' evaluations [chosen at random] and check to see if they reflect refinements based on organizational performance review findings and worker feedback.) [1.2a(2); 5.1a(3)]

    - How have you improved the process of evaluating managers over the years? [1.2a(2); 5.1a(3)]

    - What processes have been put in place to evaluate and improve the effectiveness of the board of directors as a whole and individual board members? How well do these processes work? How do you know? What has been done to improve them? [1.2a(2); 5.1a(3)]

20. How do you anticipate public concerns over the possible impact of your organization? How do you determine what risks the public faces because of your current and/or future products, services, and operations? What are some examples of risks you have identified? Pick some risks at random and ask, what have you done to reduce the risk or threat to the public? How do you know you are successful in these areas? How do you measure progress? [1.2b(1)]

    - What goals have been developed to identify and reduce risks to the public? [1.2b(1)]

    - How do you know that your processes for protecting the public from risks associated with your products, services, and programs are effective? How have you improved these processes? [1.2b(1)]

21. What processes are in place to conserve natural resources? How did you determine what areas of conservation were important? How effective are these conservation processes? How do you know? [1.2b(1)]

22. What are some ways your organization ensures that members of the workforce and key partners act in an ethical manner in all business and stakeholder transactions? How is this measured and monitored to ensure compliance? [1.2b(2)]

23. What are the biggest environmental issues your organization faces? As a corporate citizen, what

is your process for contributing to and improving the environment and society? [1.2c(1)]

24. As a part of strategy and daily operations, what processes are in place to help you address your impact on societal well-being? How do your operations contribute to and benefit economic, environmental, and social systems? [1.2c(1)]

25. What support does your organization provide to local communities? Why do you provide this support? How does this support align with organizational priorities and the strategy? [1.2c(2)]

    - How do you know that the processes you have in place for identifying and supporting key communities are appropriate?

    - How do you know the resources allocated for these purposes are appropriately used? Have you always provided this type of support?

    - What do you (senior leaders) do personally to contribute to improving local community organizations?

    - What have workers done to strengthen or support local community organizations?

    - What has been done to improve your efforts to support these communities?

Category 2—Strategic Planning

1. When was the strategic plan last updated? Were you involved in the strategic planning process? What was your role? Who else was involved and what did each person do? [2.1a(1)]

    - How far out does your planning look? Why? Why not shorter or longer? [2.1a(1)]

    - How does the overall process for developing strategy work? (If people were involved in the planning process, ask them to recite how the process works without referring to written documentation. We must determine whether a consistent planning process is in place that meets the requirements of the Criteria—we are not testing the ability of senior leaders to read a written document.)

    - What flawed assumptions have been made in previous planning cycles? What have you done to check the accuracy of planning assumptions and projections you used in the past to develop your strategic plan? What have you done to eliminate flawed assumptions (blind spots)?

2. Please give some examples of how your planning process has helped you to identify problems, trouble areas, challenges or threats that you might not have known about otherwise. [2.1a(1)]

3. What challenges does the organization face that might hurt future success? What advantages do you have that might help your competitive position and enhance your future?

4. What are your organization's core competencies? (You may have to ask, "what are the things you do well that provide you with an advantage in the market place, among other providers? What sets you above the rest?") [2.1a(1)]

    - Show me how you consider these core competencies as you develop your strategic plans, objectives, and goals?

5. What factors do you consider when you analyze organizational strengths, weaknesses, opportunities, and threats? Please show the data you use to help you understand the issues. [2.1a(2)]

6. What data, information, or other factors did you consider in the development of your strategic plan? [2.1a(2)] The following bulletized questions relate to 2.1 Note 3.

    - Does your organization depend on key suppliers or partners to be successful? If so, which ones? Examiners should pick some from their list and ask, how did you consider the needs and capabilities of these suppliers/partners during the process of developing your strategic plan?

    - Does your organization have key competitors that affect your ability to be successful? Which ones? Pick some and ask, what abilities does this competitor possess that may create a problem for your organization? How did you consider the threats posed by this key competitor during the process of developing your strategic plan? How has your plan addressed these potential problems or threats?

- Do new technologies help or hurt your organization? Which ones? Pick some and ask, how did you consider these new technologies during the process of developing your strategic plan?

- How do you consider the needs of all key customers (or other appropriate stakeholders) in the development of the strategic plan? How do you handle customer requirements that conflict with each other?

- What future regulatory, legal, financial, economic, or ethical risks does your organization face? Pick some and ask, how did you determine this was a risk? How did your planning process consider the potential problems presented by this risk when developing your plan?

7. What have you done to improve the accuracy and effectiveness of your planning process? What refinements have you made during the past few years? [Scoring Guidelines]

8. How often do you review progress of your key strategic objectives? Please show me the time lines or projections for achieving each objective. How did you develop the projected or expected levels of future performance for each strategic objective (also called time lines)? [2.1b(1)]

9. Review the list of strategic challenges and advantages the organization provided in P2. Pick one, then ask: Please show me how you check your objectives to be sure this strategic challenge or advantage was addressed. Then repeat the process for another challenge or advantage. [2.1b(2)]

10. Can you tell from this information where you expect to be on each objective when you next review performance? Next quarter? Next year? In two years? (Note: the frequency of review should be consistent with the review processes described in Item 4.1b. For example, if the senior leadership team reviews progress toward achieving the customer-satisfaction objectives quarterly, then quarterly time lines or milestones should be defined to permit effective review. In addition, the time lines reported under 2.1b(1) should identify the measurable, outcome-based levels of performance that are expected during these reviews, not just a list of activities.)

- How did you determine the appropriate frequency or period to review progress for these objectives?

11. Describe your long- and short-term plans. What changes are planned in your products or services, your customers or markets, or your operations to achieve your strategic objectives? [2.2a(1)]

12. What is the process you use to identify the actions that need to be taken throughout the organization in order to meet your goals or strategic objectives? [2.2a(2)]

13. How do you break the strategic objectives into actions that drive work at all levels of the organization? [2.2a(2)]

14. How do you make sure that every member of the workforce knows what work he or she must do to achieve his or her part of the plan? [2.2a(2)]

15. Ask to see an old plan. Pick an action that drove improvement. Determine the extent to which the changes that were put in place have been sustained. If the change was not sustained, determine what process changes were made to ensure that future changes can be sustained. In other words, determine what they learned from the failure and what they did with that knowledge. [2.2a(2)]

16. What process is used to figure out what resources are needed to do this work? How are resources allocated to make sure the actions can be completed on schedule? How effective are these processes? How do you know? What improvements in the processes of converting plans to actions and assigning resources have been made in the past few years? [2.2a(3)]

17. How do you ensure that organizational, work unit, and individual actions and resources are aligned at all levels?

- Pick a strategy that the leader has indicated is important to organizational success. Then ask the leader what actions they have determined are critical to achieve the strategy.

- From the list of actions, pick one or two and ask the leader to explain specifically how resources were allocated to ensure these plans would be accomplished.

- Then ask how the leader checks to determine if appropriate resources were allocated.

- Ask if any improvements have been made in this process over the past few years. Repeat this line of questioning at different levels in the organization to check alignment. [2.2a(3)]

18. What are some examples of resource allocations that you made that allowed you to accomplish your action plans and, at the same time, meet your other obligations?

19. How do you make sure that goals, objectives, and action plans are understood and used throughout the organization to drive and align work? [2.2a(4)]

20. Have circumstances changed in your organization that required a change of action plans? If yes, ask how you made sure that everyone involved understood and took appropriate action to make the change. If no, ask what process they have in place to make sure that everyone involved understood and took appropriate action to make the change. [2.2a(4)]

21. Have any changes been made in key products, customers, markets, or operations since the Baldrige application was submitted? If no, go to the next issue. If yes, how were actions required by these changes identified and deployed to appropriate units and people to implement? Follow the action trail to determine if those who need to take action know about the changes, how they learned about them, when, and what action they are taking. [2.2a(4)]

22. How do you determine what people and skills you will need to carry out your strategic objectives and related action plans? What changes have been made in your workforce plan during the past few years to help you achieve your strategic objectives and related action plans? How effective and accurate have your workforce plans been? [2.2a(5)]

23. Summarize the organization's workforce plans that are needed to carry out the strategic objectives and related action plans. How do these plans ensure the workforce has sufficient skills and staffing levels? [2.2a(5)]

- What are examples of changes to the workforce plans based on inputs from the strategic planning in the following areas: recruitment, training, compensation, rewards, incentives, fringe benefits, and other programs, as appropriate?

24. Please show me a list of the measures you use to determine if your strategic objectives and actions are being accomplished as planned. [2.2a(6)]

- (Pick an action or strategic objective.) Please show me how this particular objective or action is measured. Who has responsibility for doing the work to achieve the objective or action?

25. What is (summarize) your process for evaluation and improvement of the strategic planning and plan deployment processes, including workforce planning?

26. What are examples of improvements made as a result of these evaluation processes? Where and when did they occur?

- Why did you decide to focus on these improvements?

- What facts helped with your decisions on what to improve and how to improve the planning process? [Scoring Guidelines]

27. How did you determine that the goals or objectives you set were appropriate? How do you know that achieving this goal will make you a leader in the industry or sector? [2.2b]

28. Who do you consider to be your top competitors? How did you determine who your top competitors are? How do your planned future performance levels (goals) compare to their expected future performance levels? [2.2b]

- At what level do you expect your key competitors or other similar providers to perform during the same period as your plan covers? How did you figure this out?

- How accurate have your past estimates of your competitor's future performance been? What have you done to make these projections more accurate?

- What gaps have you identified where the competitor is ahead? What are you doing to close the gap?

Category 3—Customer Focus

1. What does "voice of the customer" mean to you? Please provide specific examples of techniques you use to acquire information that has helped you determine customer requirements and expectations. [3.1a(1), 3.2c(2)]

2. After you figure out what your customers require, how do you identify and innovate product features to meet these requirements and exceed their expectations? [3.1a(1)]

    - Provide a specific example of an innovation in your product offerings that helped attract new customers. [3.1a(1)]

    - Overall, how successful were these innovations in attracting new customers or in strengthening the relationships you have with existing customers.

3. How do you make it easy for your customers to contact you, get information and assistance, or complain? What process did you use to figure this out? [3.1a(2)]

4. What do you learn from customer questions, comments, and complaints? Please provide examples. [3.1a(2)]

5. What are the customer-support requirements or service standards you identified? Do they vary for the different customer groups or segments? If so, please explain how, and give examples. [3.1a(2)]

    - Are customer-support requirements the same for customer inquiries made by phone, e-mail, and postal services? Why or why not? [3.1a(2)]

6. How do you make sure that every member of the workforce involved with customer support understands and works to meet or exceed these customer support requirements? How do you know the customer-support requirements (standards) are consistently met for all customers throughout the organization? [3.1a(2)]

7. What processes do you use to evaluate and improve your methods for innovating product offerings and customer support? [3.1a(3)]

    - What meaningful improvements or innovations have been made as a result of your evaluation/improvement process? [3.1a(3)]

8. What does customer engagement mean to your organization? [3.1b(1)]

9. What steps does your organization take to maximize customer engagement? [3.1b(1)]

10. What actions or mechanisms are in place to help create an organizational culture that ensures a consistently positive customer experience? [3.1b(1)]

11. For one of your key customer groups or market segments, what are the major stages in the customer life cycle? (Note: The customer life cycle covers all interactions from initial inquiries, to purchase, delivery, service, repair and use, and discard or replacement. Each of these stages may pose differing challenges for the customer and the organization and require different customer support options and processes.) [3.1b(2)]

12. What steps does your organization take to build better relationships to acquire new customers and increase engagement? [3.1b(2)] How long has this process been in place? What have you done to evaluate the effectiveness and take steps to improve it [3.1b(3)]

    - What are some improvements that have been made to the way you strengthen customer relationships and loyalty? How did you decide what changes were important to make, and when they should have been made? [3.1b(3)]

13. Describe your process for listening to customers to get information from them about your products and customer support activities. [3.2a(1)]

14. What do you do with the feedback you solicit from customers regarding products and services? What triggers follow-up action? [3.2a(1)]

15. Describe your process for following-up with customers after they have contacted the organization or used its products and services. [3.2a(1)]

16. What customer-satisfaction information do you have about your competitors or benchmarks? What do you do with this information? [3.2a(2)]

    - How do members of the workforce use this information in their regular work? What action do they take as a result? Please provide some examples. [3.2a(2)]

17. What processes are in place to encourage customer complaints? How do you handle customer complaints? What occurs between receiving the complaint and resolving the complaint? [3.2a(3)] (Ask to see some sample complaints and follow the data trail. Determine how the data are analyzed and used to drive improvements in the work process that produced the error.) [3.2a(3)]

18. What does prompt and effective resolution of a complaint mean to your organization? [3.2a(3)]

19. What processes do you have in place to ensure complaints are resolved by the first person in your organization to receive the complaint? What skills and authority do your customer-support workers need to resolve complaints promptly and effectively? How do you check to determine if your complaint-resolution processes are effective or not? [3.2a(3)] What improvements have you made in these processes over the past few years? [3.2c(4)]

20. What are your key measures for customer satisfaction and engagement? [3.2b(1)]

21. Do you measure satisfaction and engagement and for all key customer groups/segments? If yes, do your methods vary according to customer group? If yes, please tell me how they are different and why. What do you do with the information? [3.2b(1)]

22. How do you aggregate (compile) and analyze customer data to identify areas for improvement within the organization and by key partners? Please give specific examples of using customer data to make improvements. (Ask to see the data and follow the trail. Pick a particular finding and follow the aggregation, analysis, and improvement of the work processes (or supplier) that caused the complaint.) [3.2b(1)]

23. How do you learn about your customers' satisfaction relative to their satisfaction with your competitors or other organizations providing similar products? How do you use this information? [3.2b(2)]

    - Please provide some examples of how this information has helped you identify areas needing improvement; and the nature of the improvement you subsequently made.[3.1b(2)]

24. Who are your key customers, customer groups, or market segments? [3.2c(1)]

25. What was your reason for grouping them this way? [3.2c(1)]

26. Which customers/groups/market segments do you want to attract for future business? How did you make this determination? What data or decision process did you use? Have you always done it this way? Why or why not? [3.2c(1)]

27. How did you figure out what your customers expect of you? [3.2c(2)]

    - Do you use the same techniques for all customer groups? Why or why not? [3.2c(2)]

28. Are the requirements of potential customers different from the requirements of the customers you presently serve? If so, how are they different? [3.2c(2)]

29. What is most important to the different customer groups you serve or want to serve? What features of products and services are most important to getting them and keeping them happy? How did you determine this? How do you separate the most important customer requirements from less important requirements? [3.2c(2)]

30. How do you anticipate new or emerging customer requirements? What do you do with this

information? How do you use customer feedback? Help me understand how customer data and feedback are used to better satisfy their needs (check for voice-of-the-customer tools or processes). [3.2c(2)]

31. How do you use information from customers to improve marketing, improve the organization's customer-focused culture, or develop new business? [3.2c(3)]

32. How do you evaluate and improve processes for determining customer requirements? Provide some examples of improvements that you have made in the past few years. [3.2c(4)]

33. How do you go about checking and improving the way you determine customer satisfaction, engagement, and dissatisfaction? Please provide some examples of how you have improved these techniques over the past several years. [3.2c(4)]

34. How do you know you are asking customers and right questions when trying to determine satisfaction and engagement? [3.2c(4)]

Category 4—Measurement, Analysis, and Knowledge Management

1. What kind of decisions do you have to make in your job? Show me the data that are collected to help you make these decisions. [4.1a(1)]

    - What are the major performance indicators critical to your job?

2. How do you determine whether the information you collect and use for decision making is appropriate for tracking your daily work and (to leaders) the performance of the entire organization? [4.1a(1)]

    - What criteria do you use for data selection? How do you ensure that all data collected meet these criteria?

3. What is the process you use to determine the relevance of the information used to support strategic planning? [4.1a(1)]

4. You have told us what your top priorities are. How do you benchmark against these? [4.1a(2)]

- Please describe how needs and priorities for selecting comparisons and benchmarking are determined.
- Show us samples of comparative studies and how the resulting information was used to support innovation throughout the organization. Picking some at random, ask:
    - Why was the area selected for benchmarking?
    - How did you use competitive or comparative performance data?
    - How are the results of your benchmarking efforts used to set appropriate goals, make better decisions about work, and set priorities for improvement or innovation?
    - How are the results of your benchmarking efforts used to improve work processes?
    - How do you evaluate and improve your benchmarking processes to make them more efficient and useful?

5. Describe how you obtain feedback from the workforce, suppliers, and customers who use this information to support their decision making. How is this feedback used to make improvements in the data and information you collect and analyze? [4.1a(3)]

6. Please share with us an example of analysis of information important to organizational performance review and strategic planning. [4.1b]

    - How are data analyzed to determine relationships between customer information and financial performance; operational data and financial performance; or operational data and workforce requirements and/or performance? [4.1b]
    - What information or data do you use to check if adequate progress in achieving strategic objectives is being made? [4.1b]

7. What data and analyses do you use to understand your people, your customers, your competitors, and your market to help with strategic planning? Show how the following types of

analyses are used to support decision making and innovation or improvements:

- Technology projections
- Cause–effect relationships
- Root-cause analysis
- Descriptive analyses such as statistical process control, central tendencies, Pareto analysis, histograms
- Other statistical tools such as correlation analysis, regression and factor analyses, and tests of significance (t-tests, f-tests)[4.1b]
- What are you doing to improve the analysis process and make it more useful for organizational and operational decision making? [4.1b]

8. What is the process used to monitor the performance of your organization? How does it relate to the organization's strategic business plan? [4.1b]

    - What measurable goals exist? How are they monitored? How often? How well do these monitoring processes work? How do you know? Have you always done it this way? What has been done to improve them?
    - What are the key success factors (or key result areas, critical success factors, key business drivers) for your organization, and how do you use them to drive performance excellence?
    - What percentage of your time is spent on performance review and improvement activities? How do you review performance to assess the organization's health, competitive performance, and progress against key objectives? What key performance measures do you and other senior leaders regularly review?

9. Please show me how you use organizational review findings to identify priorities for innovation. Have you set or changed priorities for innovation and resource allocation? Please give examples of how this is done. [4.1c]

    - How do you ensure that these priorities and opportunities for innovation are understood and used throughout the organization to align work? (After you identify a top priority for innovation, ask the leaders to provide specific examples of how they ensure these priorities are implemented and aligned throughout the organization, as appropriate.) To what extent do these priorities and innovation opportunities involve support from key suppliers and/or partners? (Pick one example of a priority and ask the leader to help you understand how the organization works with affected suppliers or partners.) [4.1c]

10. What do you do to make sure the data that support decision making are complete and tell the whole story (data integrity)? [4.2a(1)]

11. What kind of reliability problems have you experienced with your hardware and software? How have you resolved them? What have you done to prevent these types of problems from happening again? [4.2a(1)]

12. How do you make sure that data, information, and analysis needed to support decision making at all levels of the organization are available, timely, and accurate? [4.2a(1)]

13. How do you make sure relevant knowledge and information are appropriately shared throughout the organization and with appropriate suppliers, partners, and customers? [4.2a(2)]

14. How are worthy processes and work practices shared among all appropriate members of the workforce quickly and effectively? (These processes and practices are also known as best practices, exemplary practices, role-model practices or, in Minnesota, pretty good practices.) [4.2a(3)]

15. How do you make sure that your hardware and software systems meet the needs of all users? How do you determine whether the software and hardware are user friendly? (Ask what groups use the hardware/software system. Randomly pick a group and ask how the organization makes sure these people can easily use the hardware and software. Then randomly ask some

people in a group how their user-friendliness requirements were identified and met.) [4.2b(1)]

16. What are the data-security requirements you believe are critical to your system? (For example, certain statutes and regulations, such as the Family and Education Rights and Privacy Act, may require certain levels of security and data protection.) How do you guarantee data and system security and confidentiality? [4.2b(1)]

17. Please walk me through the process you use to make sure data and information systems (both hardware and software) will continue to be available during an emergency. [4.2b(2)]

18. Please show how you ensure software and hardware are current. What drives decisions to change or upgrade systems? [4.2b(3)]

19. Show me what knowledge or information you developed and sent for use in strategic planning. [4.2b(3)]

Category 5—Workforce Focus

1. What factors are most important to workforce engagement in your organization? [5.1a(1)]

    - How did you determine these were the most important? Are they the same for all groups or segments of the workforce?

2. What are the key elements, conditions, or factors that help or hurt workforce satisfaction? [5.1a(1)]

    - How did do you determine that these were the key elements? Are the elements the same for all groups within the workforce? If not, how do they differ? [5.1a(1)]

    - Please show us how your workforce-assessment tools (for example, surveys) reflect the key factors you identified that affect workforce engagement and satisfaction. [5.1c(1)]

3. What authority do members of the workforce have to direct their own actions and make decisions about their work? [5.1a(2)]

    - (To members of the workforce) What authority do you have to make decisions about your work, such as resolving problems and improving work processes? What have managers done to demonstrate they value the contribution of workers? [5.1a(2)]

    - (To managers) How do you engage the workforce? What do you do to encourage initiative and self-directed responsibility among members of the workforce in their regular work and jobs? What have you done to increase engagement in areas such as worker innovation, where members of the workforce actually make improvements, not just suggestions? Show examples of actions taken and improvements made. When were they made? [5.1a(2)]

4. What different cultural groups do you employ? What have you done to draw out and use ideas and thinking of these diverse cultures and types of workers? [5.1a(2)]

5. What do you do to ensure open, effective communication among members of the workforce and work units (unit-to-unit, not top-down communication)? [5.1a(2)]

    - How do you break down barriers to effective sharing and communication? Show me some examples. [5.1a(2)]

    - How do you know the communication among members of the workforce and work units is understood correctly? What have you done to check understanding and improve communication? [5.1a(2); scoring guidelines]

6. Describe your approach to workforce recognition and compensation. [5.1a(3)]

    - What specific reward and recognition programs are in place? Is the reward and recognition the same for all members of the workforce? Why are they the same (or different)? [5.1a(3)]

    - How does the organization link recognition, reward, and compensation to achieve high performance objectives (which are usually stated as strategic objectives or goals)? [5.1a(3)]

- How do compensation, recognition, and related reward and incentive systems reinforce, strengthen, or support customer-focus objectives (for example, customer satisfaction and customer engagement)? [5.1a(3)]

- (General question for members of the workforce) What do you get rewarded for around here? What recognition is offered and why? Are the reward and recognition systems consistent? Fair? Can you show me how your reward and recognition supports strategic objectives or action plans? [5.1a(3)]

7. After you determine the key groups or segments of the organization's workforce, ask the following question: What training and development do you provide to ensure that you meet the education and training needs of all categories of the workforce? [5.1b(1)]

8. How do you integrate worker, supervisor, and manager feedback into the design and delivery of your training program? (Ask related follow-up questions to supervisors, managers, and members of the workforce to determine the extent to which their needs for development, learning, and career progression were identified and considered when designing the education and training approach.) [5.1b(2)]

9. What methods are used to determine what training should be offered to members of the workforce? [5.1b(2)]

10. How do you make sure that the knowledge and skills acquired during training are actually used and reinforced on the job? Provide some examples (then select from this list and follow up with workforce members and their supervisors to determine how skills are reinforced on the job). [5.1b(2)]

11. How does your training program affect operational-performance goals? How do you know your training improves your business results? What evaluation of training effectiveness has been done? How often? What improvements were made as a result? Show examples. [5.1b(3)]

12. What is your system for improving training? Please give us some examples of improvements made and when they were made. [5.1b(3)]

13. To what extent is training provided to enhance workforce motivation, career development, and progression? What do you (senior leaders, managers, and supervisors) do to develop the full potential of members of the workforce? Give specific examples. [5.1b(4)]

14. What development and/or replacement strategy or process do you have in place for key leaders and workforce members/workforce groups throughout the organization? (For example, if the organization knows key senior leaders or a group of engineers/technicians are scheduled to retire, determine what it is doing to fill the resulting gap.) [5.1b(4)]

15. How do you assess workforce engagement and satisfaction? [5.1c(1)]

- If a survey is used, ask how they know they are asking the right questions on the survey. Unless they have already told you, ask for some specific examples about how they use other information such as worker retention, absenteeism, grievances, safety, and productivity data to assess and improve worker engagement and satisfaction.

16. What do you do with the workforce engagement and satisfaction information? Provide examples. [5.1c(1)]

17. What do you do to improve workforce engagement and satisfaction? [5.1c(2)]

- Describe the process you use to analyze workforce-engagement and satisfaction data and other indicators to determine what problems exist that may disrupt or hurt organization performance outcomes?

- When was the last assessment? How quickly or effectively do you use this information to drive improvements? [5.1c(2)]

18. How do you ensure that managers throughout the organization work to improve the climate for

worker engagement and satisfaction? [5.1c(2)] [Links to 1.1a(3)]

19. When you identify the priorities for improving workforce engagement and satisfaction, what factors do you consider? [5.2c(2)]

    • What are the top three or four improvement priorities? (Pick one and ask the leader.)

    • What specific finding from the workforce engagement or satisfaction assessment tool did the organization use to identify this priority action? How is this priority for improving work environment likely to affect key business results? How did you determine the potential impact on business results? [5.1c(2)]

20. What improvements have you made in the process of assessing workforce engagement and satisfaction, and then actually improving the work climate? [Scoring Guidelines].

21. How do you figure out what workforce knowledge, skills, and abilities are needed by your organization now and in the future (capability)? [5.2a(1)]

    • What areas of shortfall (surplus) have you identified? What actions did you take to address the issue?

22. How do you figure out what workforce staffing levels are needed by your organization now and in the future (capacity)? [5.2a(1)]

    • What areas of shortfall (surplus) have you identified? What actions did you take to address the issue?

23. How do you attract workers with the right skills your organization needs to be successful? How do you make sure that the workforce represents the diversity of the general community from which you hire? What diverse workers do you recruit and why? How does this recruitment help you get the right mix of diverse ideas, culture, and thinking? [5.2a(2)]

24. How do you make sure these skills, diverse ideas, and cultures are used to maximum advantage within your organization? [5.2a(2)]

25. How do you organize your workforce to:

    • Carry out the work and achieve mission (for example, self-directed work teams, cross-functional teams)

    • Take advantage of core competencies (sustain the advantages that the core competencies offer)

    • Reinforce a customer and business focus (customer culture)

    • Exceed performance expectations and meet strategic challenges and action plans (use process improvement tools such as ISO 9000, Baldrige Criteria, Lean Six Sigma)

    • Be agile enough to address changing business needs (promote employee engagement, initiative, empowerment, reduce layers of non-value-added decision making that cause delay)) [5.2a(3)]

26. What system is in place to prepare your workforce for changing capability and capacity needs? (Note: such systems might include cross training, job sharing, shadowing, training, education, career counseling, and outplacement services) [5.2a(4)]

27. What processes have been put in place to manage the workforce to ensure continuity of operations and prevent or minimize the impact of workforce reductions? (Note: such systems might also include cross training, job sharing, training, formal education, career counseling, and outplacement services.) [5.2a(4)]

28. What training is provided for your leaders and members of the workforce? [5.2b(1)]

    • (From the action plans identified in 2.2, pick some and ask) What training and development are provided to support the achievement of (the selected action plan)? How was it determined that these training and development opportunities were needed?

29. What are your standards, performance measures, and targets for workforce health, security, and safety? [5.2b(1)]

- How do you make sure that your approach to health and safety addresses the needs of all workforce groups? [5.2b(1)]

30. How do you determine that you have a safe and healthy work environment? How do you measure this? [5.2b(1)]

    - What are your procedures for systematic evaluation and improvement of workplace health, safety, and security? [5.2b(1)]

    - What have you done to improve workplace health, safety, and security? [5.2b(1)]

31. What are the benefits and services you provide your workforce to enhance motivation and satisfaction? [5.2b(2)]

    - To what extent are these customized for different workforce types or groups? How did you determine what changes in the benefits and services should be offered to the different groups? [5.2b(2)]

Category 6—Process Management

1. What innovative work systems have you designed and developed over the years? (Note: "Work systems" refers to how the work of your organization is accomplished. Work systems coordinate ALL of the internal work processes and the external resources needed to develop, produce, and deliver products to customers and succeed in the marketplace.) [6.1a(1)]

2. How do you decide which work processes you will keep in-house (key work processes) and which you will contract out (outsource)? [6.1a(1)]

3. (Note: Core competencies include the things your organization does that give it an advantage over other providers or competitors) Describe how the work systems (external support such as suppliers) and internal key work processes take advantage of the organization's core competencies. What key work processes help your organization make good use of its advantages in the marketplace? [6.1a(2)]

4. What are your key work processes? [6.1b(1)]

5. (Pick one and ask) How does this key work process help the organization deliver customer value, profit (financial return), organizational success, and sustainability? (Then, pick another key work process and ask the question again.) [6.1b(1)]

6. (Based on the list of key work processes, pick one and ask) What are the customer requirements that this work process must meet? How did you determine these requirements? What input did you receive from customers? From suppliers or partners? Once these requirements were identified, what happened next? [6.1b(2)]

7. What kinds of emergencies or disasters have occurred in your area? What are you doing to ensure these kinds of things do not disrupt your operations? That customer needs continue to be met? [6.1c]

8. What processes or systems have you put in place to prepare for emergencies or disasters that may affect your workplace? [6.1c]

    - How do you know these systems work as intended?

    - What kinds of disruptions have you faced in the past?

    - What was the impact on the workplace, your workforce, and your customers?

    - What have you put in place to reduce the possible impact of such disasters or emergencies? [6.1c]

9. How do you make sure that your products (goods and services) will perform as expected and meet all customer and operational requirements? What have you done to prevent errors in the design process? What have you done to consider cycle time, productivity, and cost control in designing these processes? Provide examples.

10. What new key work process (program, product, or service) have you designed in the past few years? (Pick one from their list and ask.) What is your process for designing this new or revised program, product, or service to ensure that customer requirements are met and value is created for the

customers, the organization, or other stakeholders? Please walk us through the steps. [6.2a]

11. What new design technologies, including e-technology, have you used in recent product/service and production/delivery or support-service projects? [6.2a] What kinds of problems or troubles have you had with past introductions of new products and services? Provide examples of how you have learned from these problems and prevented them in subsequent product/service designs. [6.2a and Scoring Guidelines]

12. Please give an example of how a customer request or complaint resulted in an improvement of a current process or the establishment of a new process. How often do customers change their requirements? How do you respond to these changes? How has this process been refined to respond more quickly, especially when customer requirements change more often? [6.2b(1)]

13. Please share with us your list of key work processes, requirements, and associated performance measures, including in-process measures. For example, if supply-chain management is designated as a key work process, the following series of questions may be useful: What process is in place for managing your supplier chain? Who are your most important [key] suppliers? How do you establish and communicate to your key suppliers the requirements they must meet so your needs are met? What are the key performance requirements? Please explain how you measure your suppliers' performance and provide feedback to help them improve. [6.2b(1)]

14. What kinds of tests, audits, or inspections do you routinely conduct to ensure products and services are defect-free and require no rework? Show how you have reduced the need for these tests, audits, or inspections and still eliminated defects and rework. [6.2b(2)]

15. What steps have you taken to improve the effectiveness/efficiency of key work processes, including cycle time? [6.2c]

16. Once you determine that a process may not be meeting measurement goals or performing according to expectations, what process do you use to determine root cause and make needed process improvements? [6.2c]

17. How do you evaluate and improve key work processes and make meaningful and innovative improvements? Please provide some examples of improvements and when they were made. [6.2c]

- How widely are process improvements carried out in the organization?

- What innovations have been made in work processes?

- What process do you have in place to make sure that lessons learned in one part of the organization (or from past improvement efforts) are transferred to others in the organization to save time and prevent rework? [6.2c]

Category 7—Results

Normally, applicants are eager to display good results and sometimes neglect to report results that are not as good. The scoring guidelines penalize applicants for failing to provide results that are important to the organization's key business requirements.

To score accurately, examiners must be able to determine what results should be reported in the application that are important to the organization's success. To evaluate Category 7 properly, examiners first develop a list of the results that they expect to be provided in Category 7 based on what the organization reported was important to its success. Then, by comparing the list of expected results to the results actually provided in the application, examiners can determine what important results are missing.

Usually a description of important results can be found in the Organizational Profile, strategic goals [Item 2.1b], the list of actions and measures required to achieve strategic objectives [Item 2.2a(1, 6)], the priority customer requirements [Item 3.1a(1), 3.2c(2)], or other places in the application.

Figure 50 represents the type of information that might be presented by an applicant in the Organizational Profile [P.1b(2)], listing Customer

The Site Visit

Segments and Requirements. Note that three customer segments were identified, each with multiple requirements.

This information serves as a basis for expecting results related to the satisfaction of these customers with the important product and service features. Accordingly, note that in Figure 50, the first column identifies where these results should be reported [Item 7.2]. The second column lists the customer segments and the specific requirements of each segment as found in the Organizational Profile (Figure 51). The third column simply identifies the place in the application that the examiner found the reference to expected results. (In case another examiner on the team did not find the expected requirement, little time will be wasted searching for it.) The fourth column indicates whether results were actually reported in 7.2, where they can be found (figure reference), and whether results are improving. Column five indicates whether benchmark/comparative data were reported (as required) and how favorably the applicant's performance compares with the benchmark data.

In this way, examiners can easily determine if few, some, many, or most important results were reported. Applicants should prepare a similar table to make sure the actual results are aligned with the important results.

Most of the site-visit work for Category 7 involves studying reports containing raw data as well as trend and comparison data. All relevant results that were reported in the application should be updated to reflect current conditions.

Comparison data and the rationale for offering the comparison data should be examined to determine if the comparisons are appropriate and relevant. Comparisons are relevant if the applicant is able to present a plausible explanation or link between the comparison data and the data the applicant has reported.

1. What are the product performance levels at this time? [Links to P.1, Note 5, and Item 3.1, Note 2 and Items 3.1, 3.2, and 6.1] [7.1]

   - Show a breakout of data by customer group or segment.
   - Provide current levels and trends for how customers perceive your products and service performance.
   - Provide the performance results for key products that are most critical to customer satisfaction.
   - Bring results up to date and close any information gaps that may have been noted in your application.
   - Show how these trends and levels compare with those of competitors or similar providers.

2. What are the customer satisfaction and dissatisfaction [7.2a(1)] and customer relationship building and engagement [7.2a(2)] trends and levels at this time? [Links to P.1b(2) and the requirements in Items 3.1 and 3.2] [7.2]

   - Provide a breakout of data by customer group or segment.
   - Provide current levels and trends for customer engagement such as loyalty, positive referral, customer-perceived value, and relationship building.
   - Bring your customer satisfaction, dissatisfaction, and related results up to date and close

Customer Segments (As Reported by the Applicant)	Key Customer Requirements (As Reported by the Applicant)
Individual End Users	Reliability, prompt repair, friendly service, value
Dealers	Reliable vehicles, order accuracy, parts availability, billing accuracy
Commercial/Fleet users	Speedy access to service, reliability, value, loaner vehicles

Figure 50 Example of applicant customer segments and corresponding key requirements provided in the Organizational Profile.

any information gaps that may have been noted in your application.

- Show how these trends and levels compare with those of competitors or similar providers.

3. What are the current levels and trends showing financial and marketplace performance or economic value? [7.3]

- Provide data on key financial measures, such as return on investment (ROI), operating profits (or budget reductions as appropriate), or economic value added.

- Provide data on market share or business growth, as appropriate. Identify new markets entered and the level of performance in those markets.

- Provide a breakout of data by customer and market group or segment.

- Bring financial and marketplace performance results up to date and close any information gaps that may have been noted in your application.

- Show how these trends and levels compare with those of competitors or similar providers.

4. What are the current levels and trends showing the effectiveness of your workforce practices? [Links to processes in Category 5] [7.4]

- Provide data on workforce engagement and satisfaction (including data such as absenteeism, undesired attrition, grievances, and litigation as well as engagement and satisfaction survey data). [7.4a(1)]

- Provide data showing levels of workforce and leader development. [7.4a(2)]

Expected Results Matrix *(Figure 51)*

Prepare a List of Critical Organizational Results

When examiners review an application for a Baldrige or State quality award, they typically develop a list of the most critical organizational results that they expect to find in Category 7. The Expected Results Matrix on the opposite page is an example of such a list. The first three columns in the matrix are completed by examiners as they read the Organizational Profile, strategic objectives, and action plans and learn about factors important to organizational success. The first column describes a name of the expected result, such as *End User Customer Satisfaction*. The second column identifies the location in the application where the expected result was described, such as a section in the Organizational Profile [P1b(2)]. The third column lists the area in Category 7 where the result is expected to be reported.

The remaining nine columns describe the results that were actually reported in Category 7 that related to the expected result.

- The *Time Frame* column identifies the time period for which data are reported.
- *Segmentation* identifies any subdivisions of the data that were reported. Such subdivisions may also be identified as an expected result in column 1.
- The *Level/Trend* column identifies whether the applicant provided current levels and/or trend data.
- The *Direction* column identifies whether the level and or trend is favorable (+), flat (=), uneven (^), or unfavorable (U).
- The *Comparison* column identifies what type of comparison data have been presented by the applicant. Comparison data may be best in class (B), a Baldrige recipient (D), an industry average (A), a key competitor (K), or no data (N).
- The *Performance Against Comparison* column identifies the strength of the applicant's data against the comparisons mentioned in the previous column. For example the applicant could be leading (L) (better than) the performance of a Baldrige recipient. The applicant could be strong (S) relative to an industry average (for example, top quartile), *good* (about average). The applicant could be lagging (L) a key competitor.

Some examiners may use other headings for the columns in the Expected Results Matrix, but these are the most common. If applicants prepare their own Expected Results Matrix, they can make certain that the results contained in Category 7 completely align with areas of importance described in the Organizational Profile and Categories 1 through 6.

The Site Visit

Name of Expected Result	Source Reference	Cat 7 Reference	Results found in Fig. #	Time Frame	Segmentation	Level/ Trend	Direction: + favorable = flat ^ uneven U unfavorable	Comparison: Best in class, BalDrige, Industry Average, Key Competitor, None	Performance Against Comparison: Leading Strong Good Lagging	Process Item Linkages	Gaps
End User Customers											
End user customer satisfaction (Overall)	P1b(2)	7.2a(1)	7.2-3	2004–2008	By vehicle type	Current Level and Trend	+	D	S	2.1b(1) 3.2b(1) 3.2b(2) 3.2b(3)	None
Vehicle reliability/ safety							+	A	L		
Prompt repair							+	B	L	3.2a(3)	
Friendly, knowledgeable service techs							=	A	G		
Value / economy							=	A	G		
Dealer Customers											
Dealer customer satisfaction (Overall)	P1b(2)	7.2a(1)	7.2-4	2004–2008	By dealer size (small, medium, large)	Current Level and Trend	=	A/K	A	3.2b(1)	None
Vehicle reliability							+	A/K	G		
Order accuracy							+	A/K	G		
Parts availability							=	A/K	G		
Service support							=	B	A		
Commercial/Fleet Customers											
Commercial/Fleet Customer Satisfaction	P1b(2)	7.2a(1)	7.2-5	2004–2008	By vehicle type (full size car, premium car, small truck)	Trend	+	None	NA	3.2b(1) 3.2b(2)	Comp Data Missing
Speedy access to service							+	None			
Value							=	None			
Loaner vehicles							+	None			

Figure 51 Table of expected results.

- Provide data showing levels of workforce capability (skills) and capacity (staffing levels). [7.4a(3)]

- Provide data on key indicators of workplace climate, such as safety/accident record. [7.4a(4)]

- Bring your workforce results up to date and close any information gaps that may have been noted in your application.

- How does performance on these key indicators compare to your competitors, other providers, or benchmarks?

5. What are the current levels and trends showing the effectiveness of your work systems and key work processes? [Links to Items 6.1 and 6.2] [7.5]

- Show current levels and trends for operational performance of work systems, including work system and workplace preparedness for disasters or emergencies. [7.5a(1)]

- Show current levels and trends for operational performance of key work processes, including productivity, cycle time, and other appropriate measures of process effectiveness, efficiency, and innovation. [7.5a(1)]

- Provide current levels and trends for production and cycle time for delivery and production (such as defect/error rate, rework, waste, scrap, process improvements, and the results of innovative processes).

- Bring your data about organizational effectiveness up to date and close any information gaps that may have been noted in your application.

- Show how performance on these key indicators compares to your competitors, other providers, or benchmarks?

6. What are the current levels and trends showing the effectiveness of leadership and societal responsibility processes? [7.6]

- Provide key measures or indicators of accomplishment of your organizational strategy and action plans [7.6a(1)]

- Provide performance results related to governance and fiscal accountability. [7.6a(2)]

- Bring your Leadership and Societal Responsibility Results up to date and close any information gaps that may have been noted in your application. [7.6a(2)]

- Provide performance data related to regulatory and legal compliance. [7.6a(3)]

- Provide results for ethical behavior and of stakeholder trust in the senior leaders and governance of your organization. Also provide results reflecting breaches of ethical behavior. [7.6a(4)]

- Provide results reflecting the organization's fulfillment of its societal responsibilities and support of its key communities. [7.6a(5)]

- Show how your performance on these key indicators compares to your competitors, other providers, or benchmarks.

General Cross-Cutting Questions to Ask Members of the Workforce

- What are the organization's mission, vision, and values? [Links to 1.1a(1) and 2.1a(1)]

- What is the strategic plan for the organization? What are the organization's goals, and what role do you play in helping to achieve the goals? [Links to 2.1b(1) and 2.2a]

- What kind of training have you received? Was it useful? Who decided what training you should receive? What kind of on-the-job support did you get for using the new skills you learned during training? [Links to 5.1b]

- What kinds of decisions do you usually make about your work and the work of the organization? What data or information do you use to help make these decisions? Is this information readily available to help make decisions easier? [Links to 1.1b(1), 4.1b, 4.2a, 5.1a, 5.1c(1)]

- What activities or work are recognized or rewarded? Is achieving customer satisfaction a critical part of your job? Are your rewards and/or recognition determined in part on achieving certain customer-satisfaction levels? If so, explain how this works. [Links to 5.1a(3)]

- What does your organization do best? What sets it above other organizations that do similar work? [Links to P.1a(2), Core Competencies]

- Remember to ask the worker how processes are improved and innovated. Are improvements and innovations based on factual evaluations or are they random? Be sure to ask if the process you are examining has been improved. Ask how the improvement was identified. Ask what steps are being taken to continue to evaluate and improve the process.

Clarifying Confusing Terms

Comparative Information versus Benchmarking

Comparative information includes benchmarking and competitive comparisons. Benchmarking refers to collecting information and data about processes and performance results that represent the best practices and performance for similar activities inside or outside the organization's business or industry. Competitive comparisons refer to collecting information and data on performance relative to direct competitors or similar providers.

For example, a personal computer manufacturer, ABC Micro, must store, retrieve, pack, and ship computers and replacement parts. ABC Micro is concerned about shipping response time, errors in shipping, and damage during shipping. To determine the level of performance of its competitors in these areas, and to set reasonable improvement goals, ABC Micro would gather competitive comparison data from similar providers (competitors). However, these performance levels may not reflect best practices for storage, retrieval, packing, and shipping.

Benchmarking would require ABC Micro to find organizations that execute these processes better than any other organization, such as the catalog company L.L. Bean, and examine both their processes and performance levels.

Benchmarking seeks best-practices information. Competitive comparisons look at competitors, whether or not they are the best.

Customer-Contact Employees

Customer-contact employees are any members of the workforce who are in direct contact with customers. They may be direct-service providers or answer complaint calls. They may be volunteers or contract workers. Whenever a customer makes contact with an organization, either in person or by phone or other electronic means, that customer forms an opinion about the organization and its employees. Employees who come in contact with customers are in a critical position to influence customers for the good of the organization or to its detriment.

Customer Satisfaction versus Customer Dissatisfaction

One is not the inverse of the other. The lack of complaints does not indicate satisfaction, although the presence of complaints can be a partial indicator of dissatisfaction. Measures of customer dissatisfaction can include direct measures through surveys as well as complaints, product returns, and warranty claims.

Customer satisfaction and dissatisfaction are complex areas to assess. Customers are rarely *thoroughly* dissatisfied, although they may dislike a feature of a product or an aspect of service. There are usually degrees of satisfaction and dissatisfaction.

Data versus Information

Information can be qualitative and quantitative. Data lend themselves to quantification and statistical analysis. For example, an incoming inspection might produce a count of the number of units accepted, rejected, and total shipped. This count is considered data. These counts add to the base of information about supplier quality.

Education versus Training

Training refers to learning about and acquiring job-specific skills and knowledge. Education refers to the general development of individuals. An organization might provide training in equipment maintenance for its workers, as well as support the education of workers through an associate degree program at a local community college.

Engagement, Empowerment, and Involvement

Engagement refers to a condition where workers contribute their utmost to the success of the organization and its customers. Empowerment generally refers to processes and procedures designed to provide individuals and teams the tools, skills, and authority to make decisions that affect their work—decisions traditionally reserved for managers and supervisors. Empowerment is a tool used to enhance engagement. The most powerful drivers of engagement are feeling valued and involved.

Empowerment as a concept has been misused in many organizations. For example, managers may appear to extend decision-making authority under the guise of chartering teams and individuals to make recommendations about their work, while continuing to reserve decision-making authority for themselves.

This practice has given rise to another term—involvement—which describes the role of workers who are asked to become involved in decision making, without necessarily making decisions. Involvement is a practice that many agree is better than not involving workers at all, but still does not optimize their contribution to initiative, flexibility, and fast response.

Consider the metaphor of a clutch in an automobile. The clutch is considered "engaged" when it is fully in place and providing maximum pull or torque. During the process of becoming fully engaged, the clutch is slowly extended, causing some slippage before it is locked in. This slippage is an act of partial involvement or empowerment.

Measures and Indicators

The Award Criteria do not make a distinction between measures and indicators. However, some users of these terms prefer the term indicator: (1) when the measurement relates to performance but is not a direct or exclusive measure of such performance, for example, the number of complaints is an indicator of dissatisfaction, but not a direct or exclusive measure of it; and (2) when the measurement is a predictor (leading indicator) of some more significant performance, for example, gain in customer satisfaction might be a leading indicator of market share gain.

Product Performance, Operational Performance, and Predictors of Customer Satisfaction

Product performance [7.1] can generally predict customer satisfaction. Operational-performance measures can reflect issues that concern customers but most may not. Operational-performance measures are used by the organization to assess effectiveness and efficiency.

In the example of the coffee shop, freshness is a key customer requirement. One predictor of customer satisfaction might be the length of time, in minutes, between brewing and serving to guarantee freshness and good aroma. The standard might be five minutes or less to ensure satisfaction. Coffee more than five minutes old would be discarded. A product-performance standard would be length of time (in minutes) between brewing and serving.

A measure of operational effectiveness might be how many cups were discarded (waste) because the coffee was too old. The customer does not care if the coffee shop discards stale coffee, and therefore, that measure is not a predictor of satisfaction. However, pouring out coffee does affect profitability and should be measured and minimized because the organization cares.

Ideally, an organization should be able to identify enough measures of product (and service) quality to predict customer satisfaction accurately *and* monitor operating effectiveness and efficiency.

Performance Requirements versus Performance Measures

Performance requirements are an expression of customer requirements, expectations, and preferences. Sometimes performance requirements are expressed as design requirements or engineering requirements. They are viewed as a basis for developing measures to enable the organization to determine whether the customer is likely to be satisfied.

Performance measures can also be used to assess efficiency, effectiveness, and productivity of a work process. Process-performance measures might include variance to standard, cycle time, error rate, or throughput.

Customer Engagement versus Customer Satisfaction

Customer engagement refers to the level that customers are vested in an organization's brand and product offerings. Factors that contribute to customer engagement include loyalty, retention, willingness to make an effort to do business and increase business, and the willingness to actively advocate for and recommend the organization's product offerings. Similar to engaged workers, engaged customers will put forth an extra effort to support the organization. Customer that are merely satisfied may not exert this special level of support—and would not be considered "engaged."

Teams and Natural Work Units

Natural work units reflect the people who normally work together because they are a part of a formal work unit. For example, on an assembly line, three or four people may naturally work together to install a motor in a new car. Hotel employees who prepare food in the kitchen might constitute another natural work unit.

Teams may be formed of people within a natural work unit or may cross existing (natural) organization boundaries. To improve room service in a hotel, for example, certain members of several natural work units, such as the switchboard, kitchen workers, and waiters, may form a special team. This team would not be considered a natural work unit. It might be called a cross-functional work team because its members come from different functions within the organization.

Workforce Engagement versus Workforce Satisfaction

Workforce engagement involves getting the workers to contribute their utmost to the success of the organization and its customers. Workforce satisfaction refers to the degree the workforce feels positive about the organization, the workplace, supervisors, and co-workers. It is possible, even likely, that a worker can be highly satisfied with his or her work and be almost fully disengaged. Some workers can be fully satisfied doing little for the organization—but they are not engaged.

Glossary

This glossary defines and briefly describes key terms used throughout the Criteria that are important to performance management and assessment.

action plans—specific actions that respond to short- and longer-term strategic objectives. Action plans include details of resource commitments and time horizons for accomplishment. Action plan development represents the critical stage in planning when strategic objectives and goals are made specific so that effective, organization-wide understanding and deployment are possible. In the Criteria, deployment of action plans includes creating aligned measures for all departments and work units. Deployment also might require specialized training for some employees or recruitment of personnel.

An example of a strategic objective for a supplier in a highly competitive industry might be to develop and maintain a price-leadership position. Action plans could entail designing efficient processes and creating an accounting system that tracks activity-level costs, aligned for the organization as a whole. Deployment requirements might include unit and/or team training in setting priorities based upon costs and benefits. Organizational-level analysis and review likely would emphasize productivity growth, cost control, and quality. See the definition of *strategic objectives* for the description of this related term.

alignment—consistency of plans, processes, information, resource decisions, actions, results, and analysis to support key organization-wide goals. Effective alignment requires a common understanding of purposes and goals. It also requires the use of complementary measures and information for planning, tracking, analysis, and improvement at three levels: the organizational level, the key process level, and the work-unit level. See the definition of *integration* for the description of this related term.

analysis—assessments performed by an organization or its work units to provide a basis for effective decisions. Every organization must analyze data to support effective decision making. The types and amount of analysis depend on the complexity and decision needs of the organization, its leaders, and employees. Overall organizational analysis guides process management toward achieving key business results and toward attaining strategic objectives.

Despite their importance, individual facts and data do not usually provide an effective basis for actions or setting priorities. Actions depend upon understanding cause/effect relationships. Understanding such relationships comes from analysis of facts and data. Examples of these analyses include, but are not limited to, the following:

- How product and service-quality improvement correlates with key customer indicators such as customer satisfaction, customer retention, and market share

- Cost/revenue implications of customer-related problems and problem-resolution effectiveness

- Interpretation of market-share changes in terms of customer gains and losses and changes in customer satisfaction

- Improvement trends in key operational performance indicators such as productivity, cycle time, waste reduction, new-product introduction, and defect levels

- Relationships between workforce/organizational learning and value added per employee

- Financial benefits derived from improvements in workforce safety, absenteeism, and turnover

- Benefits and costs associated with education and training
- Benefits and costs associated with improved organizational-knowledge management and sharing
- How the ability to identify and meet workforce requirements correlates with workforce retention, motivation, and productivity
- Cost/revenue implications of workforce-related problems and effective problem resolution
- Individual or aggregate measures of productivity and quality relative to competitors
- Cost trends relative to competitors
- Relationships between product/service quality, operational-performance indicators, and overall financial-performance trends as reflected in indicators such as operating costs, revenues, asset utilization, and value added per employee
- Allocation of resources among alternative improvement projects based on cost/revenue implications and improvement potential
- Net earnings derived from quality/operational/workforce performance improvements
- Comparisons among business units showing how quality and operational-performance improvement affect financial performance
- Contributions of improvement activities to cash flow, working-capital use, and shareholder value
- Profit impacts of customer retention
- Cost/revenue implications of new-market entry, including global-market entry or expansion
- Cost/revenue, customer, and productivity implications of engaging in and/or expanding e-commerce
- Market share versus profits
- Trends in economic, market, and shareholder indicators of value

anecdotal—process information that lacks specific methods, measures, deployment mechanisms, and evaluation/improvement/learning factors. Anecdotal information frequently uses examples and describes individual activities rather than systematic processes.

An anecdotal response to how senior leaders deploy performance expectations might describe a specific occasion when a senior leader visited all company facilities. On the other hand, a systematic process might describe the communication methods used by all senior leaders to deliver performance expectations on a regular basis to all workforce locations, the measures used to assess effectiveness of the methods, and the tools and techniques used to evaluate and improve the communication methods.

analytical tools—tools for analyzing data may include brainstorming, Pareto charts, cause-and-effect diagrams, scatter diagrams, correlation and regression analysis, and histograms, to name a few.

approach—the methods used by an organization to address the Baldrige Criteria Item requirements. Approach includes the appropriateness of the methods to the Item requirements and the effectiveness of their use. Approach is one of the dimensions considered in evaluating Process Items.

basic requirements—the topic Criteria users need to address when responding to the most central concept of an Item. Basic requirements are the fundamental theme of that Item. In the Criteria, the basic requirements of each Item are presented as the Item title question. Examiners should refer to the *Scoring System* and *Clarifying Baldrige Scoring Requirements* chapters in this book for a detailed explanation of basic, overall, and multiple requirements.

benchmarks—processes and results that represent best practices and performance for similar activities, inside or outside an organization's industry. Organizations engage in benchmarking as an approach to understand the current dimensions of world-class performance and to achieve discontinuous (nonincremental) or breakthrough improvement.

Benchmarks are one form of comparative data. Other comparative data organizations might use include industry data collected by a third party (frequently industry averages), data on competitors' performance, and comparisons with similar organizations in the same geographic area or that provide similar products and services in other geographic areas.

collaborators—those organizations or individuals who cooperate with the organization to support a particular activity or event or who cooperate on an intermittent basis when mutual short-term goals exist. Typically, collaborations do not involve formal agreements or arrangements.

continuous improvement—the ongoing improvement of products, programs, services, or processes by small increments or major breakthroughs, including innovation and reengineering.

core competencies—the organization's areas of greatest expertise. The organization's core competencies are those strategically important capabilities that provide an advantage in the marketplace or service environment. Core competencies frequently are challenging for competitors or suppliers and partners to imitate, and they provide a sustainable competitive advantage.

Core competencies may involve technology expertise, unique service offerings, a marketplace niche, or a particular business acumen (for example, business acquisitions).

cross purposes—actions taken by different people or units in an organization that do not support the overall mission and objectives of the organization. For example, to improve customer contact and satisfaction, the Information Technology unit installs a new phone system but neglects to work with the Training unit to ensure everyone understands and can use the system. Customers become angry when their calls go unanswered, resulting in lower customer satisfaction and loyalty than with the old system.

customer—actual and potential users of the organization's products, programs, or services (referred to as "products" in the Criteria). Customers include the end users of the organization's products, as well as others who might be the immediate purchasers or users of its productss, such as wholesale distributors, agents, or organizations that further process the product as a component of their product. The Criteria address customers broadly, referencing current and future customers, as well as customers of competitors.

See the definition of *stakeholders* for the relationship between customers and others who might be affected by the organization's products.

customer-driven excellence—the Baldrige core value embedded in the beliefs and behaviors of high-performance organizations. Customer focus impacts and integrates an organization's strategic directions, its value creation processes, and its business results.

customer chain—usually several entities that are involved as customers at different stages of the life of a program, product, or service. In the example of the automobiles (see definition of *end user*), the original equipment manufacturer (car maker) sells to dealers, the first segment of the customer chain. When the dealer resells the car to a cab company, that company becomes the next customer in the chain as *car owner*. Finally, the ultimate users of the car, the cab driver and passengers, become the users. Customer chains can be considered to extend through the life cycle of the product. In the case of automobiles, the secondary market of used cars begins and used-car dealers and their customers may extend the customer chain. Each customer in the chain may have different requirements that must be met.

customer-interaction process—the process by which an organization approaches, responds to, and follows up with customers. It builds ongoing business and learns about customer needs and expectations. The process of interacting with an organization can be by many methods including phone, fax, e-mail, and face-to-face meetings. Attending to these interactions is important because customers frequently make decisions about the organization based on one interaction.

customer engagement—the customers' investment in or commitment to the organization's brand and product offerings. It is based on the ongoing ability to serve their needs and build relationships so they will continue using the organization's products. Characteristics of customer engagement include customer retention and loyalty, customers' willingness to make an effort to do business with the organization, and customers' willingness to actively advocate for and recommend the organization's brand and product offerings.

cycle time—the amount of time required to complete a defined process from end to end. For example, the time required from the beginning of design to the delivery of product can be measured as the *design-to-delivery cycle time*. Additionally, each component of this cycle can be also measured. The design phase can have one cycle time, the production phase can have another, and the delivery phase a third. Organizations are responsible for defining work cycles in meaningful terms. These defined cycles must make sense to the organization and help its workers measure and monitor the processes in the cycles in order to drive improvements. Time measurements play a major role in the assessment because of the great importance of time performance to improving competitiveness and overall performance. Time-related terms in common use are setup time, customer response time, lead-time, changeover time, delivery time, order-fulfillment time, time to market, changeover time, and other key process times.

data validity and utility—data are numerical information. They are used as a basis for reasoning, discussion, determining status, decision making, and analysis. Data proven to measure a particular construct or characteristic are *valid data*. Data *utility* (usefulness) is determined by the customers of the data—the people who must use them.

deployment—the extent to which an organization's approach is applied to the requirements of a Baldrige Criteria Item. Deployment is evaluated on the basis of the breadth and depth of application of the approach to relevant work units throughout the organization. Deployment is one of the dimensions considered in evaluating Process Items.

diversity—valuing and benefiting from personal differences. These differences address many variables including race, religion, color, gender, national origin, disability, sexual orientation, age and generational preferences, education, geographic origin, and skill characteristics, as well as differences in ideas, thinking, academic disciplines, and perspectives.

The Baldrige Criteria refer to the diversity of workforce hiring and customer communities. Capitalizing on both provides enhanced opportunities for high performance; customer, workforce, and community satisfaction; and customer and workforce engagement.

effective—how well a process or a measure addresses its intended purpose. Determining effectiveness requires the evaluation of how well a need is met by the approach taken and its deployment or by the outcome of the measure used.

empowerment—giving people the authority and responsibility to make decisions and take actions. Empowerment results in decisions being made closest to the *front line*, where work-related knowledge and understanding reside.

Empowerment is aimed at enabling people to satisfy customers on first contact, to improve processes and increase productivity, and to improve the organization's performance results. An empowered workforce requires information to make appropriate decisions; therefore, an organizational requirement is to provide that information in a timely and useful way.

end user—the ultimate user of the programs, products, or services an organization produces and delivers. For example, a manufacturer of automobiles sells to a network of dealers. However, except for the cars the dealer actually uses, it is not considered an end-user. The end-user is the person at the end of the customer chain actually using the car (see definition of *customer chain*). A dealer may resell the car to a taxi company. The taxi company (car owner) hires people to drive the car. The cab driver and passengers may be considered end users until the car is resold.

engagement—see *workforce engagement* or *customer engagement*, as applicable.

ethical behavior—how an organization ensures that all its decisions, actions, and stakeholder interactions conform to the organization's moral and professional principles. These principles should support all applicable laws and regulations. They are the foundation for the organization's culture and values and define *right* from *wrong*.

Senior leaders should act as role models for these principles of behavior. The principles apply to all individuals involved in the organization, from temporary members of the workforce to members of the board of directors, and need to be communicated and reinforced on a regular basis. Although there is no universal model for ethical behavior, senior leaders should ensure that the organization's mission and vision are aligned with its ethical principles. Ethical behavior should be practiced with all stakeholders, including the workforce, shareholders, customers, partners, suppliers, and the organization's local community.

While some organizations may view their ethical principles as boundary conditions restricting behavior, well-designed and clearly articulated ethical principles should empower people to make effective decisions with great confidence.

goals—a future condition or performance level that one intends to attain. Goals can be both short-term and longer-term. Goals are ends that guide actions. Quantitative goals, frequently referred to as *targets*, include a numerical point or range. Targets might be projections based on comparative data and/or competitive data. The term *stretch goals* refers to desired major, discontinuous (nonincremental), or breakthrough improvements, usually in areas most critical to the organization's future success.

Goals can serve many purposes, including clarifying strategic objectives and action plans to indicate how success will be measured, fostering teamwork by focusing on a common end, encouraging *out-of-the-box* thinking to achieve a stretch goal, and providing a basis for measuring and accelerating progress.

governance—the system of management and controls exercised in the stewardship of the organization. It includes the responsibilities of the organization's owners/shareholders, board of directors, and senior leaders. Corporate or organizational charters, bylaws, and policies document the rights and responsibilities of each of the parties and describe how the organization will be directed and controlled to ensure accountability to owners/shareholders and other stakeholders, transparency of operations, and fair treatment of all stakeholders. Governance processes may include approving strategic direction, monitoring and evaluating CEO performance, succession planning, financial auditing, establishing executive compensation and benefits, managing risk, disclosure, and reporting to shareholders. Ensuring effective governance is important to stakeholders' and the larger society's trust and to organizational effectiveness.

groupings and segments—ways in which the organization clusters or subdivides various people and organizations with which it interacts. Groupings are formed for the convenience of the organization and are defined by the organization. Sometimes the organization will group or segment customers with similar requests, such as high volume, low volume, high risk, or geographical regions. Workforce elements may be grouped as well for the convenience of the organization (for example, hourly, salary, manufacturing, technical, physicians, nurses, technicians, and so on).

high-performance work—work processes used to systematically pursue ever-higher levels of overall organizational and individual performance, including quality, productivity, innovation rate, and cycle-time performance. High-performance work results in improved service for customers and other stakeholders.

Approaches to high-performance work vary in form, function, and incentive systems. High-performance work focuses on workforce engagement. It frequently includes cooperation between management and the workforce, which may involve workforce bargaining units; cooperation among work units, often involving teams; the empowerment of people, including self-directed responsibility; employee input to planning; individual and organizational skill building and learning; learning from other organizations; flexibility in job design and work assignments; a flattened organizational structure, where decision making is decentralized and decisions are made closest to the *front line*; and effective use of performance measures, including comparisons. Many high-performance work systems use monetary and nonmonetary incentives based upon factors such as organizational performance, team and/or individual contributions, and skill building. Also, high-performance work processes usually seek to align the organization's structure, core competencies, work, jobs, workforce development, and incentives.

how—the systems and processes that an organization uses to accomplish its mission requirements. In responding to *how* questions in the Process Item requirements, process descriptions should include information such as approach (methods and measures), deployment, learning, and integration factors.

innovation—making meaningful change to improve products, programs, processes, or organizational effectiveness, and to create new value for stakeholders. *Innovation involves the adoption of an idea, process, technology, product, or business model that is either new or new to its proposed application.* The outcome of innovation is a discontinuous or breakthrough change in results, products, or processes.

Successful organizational innovation is a multistep process that involves development and knowledge sharing, then a decision to implement, followed by implementation, evaluation, and learning. Although innovation is often associated with technological innovation, it is applicable to all key organizational processes that would benefit from change, whether through breakthrough improvement or change in approach or outputs. It could include fundamental changes in organizational structure or business model to more effectively accomplish the organization's work.

indicators and measures—is relevant when two or more measurements are required to provide a more complete picture of performance. Indicators (measures) are input, output, and performance dimensions of processes, products, programs, services, and the overall organization. Indicators and measures might be simple (derived from one measurement) or composite. Some users of these terms prefer the term indicator: (1) when the measurement relates to performance, but is not a direct or exclusive measure of such performance (for example, the number of complaints is an indicator of dissatisfaction, but not a direct or exclusive measure of it); and (2) when the measurement is a predictor (*leading indicator*) of some more significant performance, for example, gain in customer satisfaction might be a leading indicator of market-share gain.

inspection and testing—assessments of product or service suitability, checks to determine if requirements are met, or whether defects exist. Counting the number of bubbles in a glass lens is an end-process inspection since it is conducted after the glass is made. The term *testing* refers to determining whether the product or service works as intended. The same lens might be tested by shining a light through it and measuring the refraction or distortion of the light. The components of a computer can be inspected to ensure they are all in place. The computer is tested by turning it on and performing calculations. In the education sector testing is used to assess levels of education progress, student achievement, or knowledge mastery.

integration—the harmonization of plans, processes, information, resource decisions, actions, results, analysis, and learning to support key organization-wide goals. Effective integration goes beyond alignment and is achieved when the individual components of a performance management system operate as a fully interconnected unit. See the definition of *alignment* for the description of this related term. Integration is one of the dimensions considered in evaluating Process Items.

key—the major or most important elements or factors, those that are critical to achieving the intended outcome. The Baldrige Criteria, for example, refer to key challenges, key plans, key work processes, key measures—those that are most important to the organization's success. They are the essential elements for pursuing or monitoring a desired outcome.

key communities—defined by the organization, *key communities* refers to elements of the public that may be affected by the work of the organization. Key communities for a local public school may include organizations such as the local library, volunteer organizations, and education or professional associations. Key communities for a large corporate manufacturer may include organizations in local areas where the company maintains facilities or conducts business. Key communities may include schools, colleges, health care organizations, charitable organizations, or any group the organization believes key to its business objectives. A key community may also include individuals who are affected by the process, products, services, and processes of the organization. Residents in the vicinity of an industrial facility might be considered a key community since they may impact the organization and its ability to expand or conduct business.

knowledge assets—the accumulated intellectual resources of the organization. It is the knowledge possessed by the organization and its workforce in the form of information, ideas, learning, understanding, memory, insights, cognitive and technical skills, and capabilities. The workforce, software, patents, databases, documents, guides, policies and procedures, and technical drawings are repositories of an organization's knowledge assets.

Knowledge assets are held not only by an organization but reside within its customers, suppliers, and partners as well. Knowledge assets are the *know-how* that the organization has available to use, to invest, and to grow. Building and managing its knowledge assets are key components for the organization to create value for its stakeholders and to help sustain competitive advantage.

leadership system—how leadership is exercised, formally and informally, throughout the organization—the basis for and the way key decisions are made, communicated, and carried out. It includes structures and mechanisms for decision making; two-way communications, selection and development of leaders and managers; and reinforcement of values, ethical behavior, directions, and performance expectations.

An effective leadership system respects the capabilities and requirements of the workforce and other stakeholders, and it sets high expectations for performance and performance improvement. It builds loyalties and teamwork based on the organization's vision and values and the pursuit of shared goals. It encourages and supports initiative and appropriate risk taking, subordinates organization structure to purpose and function, and avoids chains of command that require long, cumbersome decision paths. An effective leadership system includes mechanisms for the leaders to conduct self-examination, receive feedback, and improve.

learning—new knowledge or skills acquired through evaluation, study, experience, and innovation. The Baldrige Criteria include two distinct kinds of learning: organizational and personal. Organizational learning is achieved through research and development, evaluation and improvement cycles, workforce and stakeholder ideas and input, best-practice sharing, and benchmarking. Personal learning is achieved through education, training, and developmental opportunities that further individual growth.

To be effective, learning should be embedded in the way an organization operates. Learning contributes to a competitive advantage for the organization and its workforce. For further description of organizational and personal learning, see the related Core Value and Concept on page 23 of this book.

Learning is one of the dimensions considered in evaluating Process Items.

levels—numerical information that places or positions an organization's results and performance on a meaningful measurement scale. Performance levels permit evaluation relative to past performance, projections, goals, and appropriate comparisons.

measures and indicators—numerical information that quantifies input, output, and performance dimensions of processes, products, programs, projects, services, and the overall organization (outcomes). Measures and indicators might be simple (derived from one measurement) or composite.

The Criteria do not make a distinction between measures and indicators. However, some users of these terms prefer the term *indicator:* (1) when the measurement relates to performance but is not a direct measure of such performance (for example, the number of complaints is an indicator of dissatisfaction but not a direct measure of it), and (2) when the measurement is a predictor (*leading indicator*) of some more significant performance (for example, increased customer satisfaction might be a leading indicator of market-share gain).

mission—the overall function of an organization. The mission answers the question, "What s this organization attempting to accomplish?" The mission might define customers or markets served, distinctive or core competencies, or technologies used.

multiple requirements—the individual questions Criteria users need to answer within each Area to Address. These questions constitute the details of an Item's requirements. Multiple requirements are presented in black text under each Item's Area(s) to Address. Examiners should refer to the *Scoring System* and *Clarifying Baldrige Scoring Requirements* chapters in this book for a detailed explanation of basic, overall, and multiple requirements.

objective—usually considered to be a subset of goals. A goal may relate to financial success. One of the short-term objectives needed to meet this goal may be a monthly sales target. (See outcome-based strategic objectives)

organization—a group of people with common goals and mission. The group may be any size, formal or informal, ad hoc or permanent.

organizational agility—the ability of the organization to act quickly or change quickly. Speed of response of all aspects of organizational operations is increasingly important as organizations experience less tolerance from customers and stakeholders for slow, plodding service and bureaucratic inefficiency. Organizational agility, like the agility demonstrated by an Olympic gymnast, suggests the ability to move quickly and bend the organization to adapt to changing requirements and environmental constraints.

organization leaders and senior leaders—the leaders—executives and top managers—in the organization being reviewed by the Baldrige process. At a bank, senior leaders could include the president, vice presidents, branch managers, and staff managers. For a company, senior leaders could include the chief executive officer and his or her direct reports. If the unit under review is a division of a larger organization, the division manager and direct reports are considered *senior leaders*. If the unit under review is a government organization or subdivision, the leaders might include top officials, members of policy boards, workforce-development boards, and city or county commissions.

outcome-based strategic objectives—(also called *results-oriented* or *results-based* strategic objectives) defines in measurable terms the outcomes or results that the organization must achieve to be successful in the future. To achieve Outcome-Based Strategic Objectives the organization must engage in activities but it should be outcome achievement not activity completion that is used to measure success. Since it is possible to carry out the assigned activity and still fail to achieve the desired outcome, strategic objectives define the outcome required for success, not the activities to be carried out.

overall requirements—the topics Criteria users need to address when responding to the central theme of an Item. Overall requirements address the most significant features of the Item requirements. In the Criteria, the overall requirements of each Item are presented as one or more introductory sentences printed in bold. Examiners should refer to the *Scoring System* and *Clarifying Baldrige Scoring Requirements* chapters in this book for a detailed explanation of basic, overall, and multiple requirements.

partners—those key organizations or individuals who are working in concert with the organization to achieve a common goal or to improve performance. Typically, partnerships are formal arrangements for a specific aim or purpose, such as to achieve a strategic objective or to deliver a specific product or service.

Formal partnerships are usually for extended periods of time and involve a clear understanding of the individual and mutual roles and benefits for the partners.

performance—output results and their outcomes obtained from processes, products, and customers that permit evaluation and comparison relative to goals, standards, past results, and other organizations. Performance might be expressed in nonfinancial and financial terms. The Baldrige Criteria address four types of performance: (1) product, (2) customer-focused, (3) financial and marketplace, and (4) operational.

Product performance refers to performance relative to measures and indicators of product and service characteristics important to customers. Examples include product reliability, on-time delivery, customer-experienced defect levels, and service-response time. These are considered *indirect* measures of customer satisfaction since the organizations are using measures or indicators of product and service quality to *predict* what the customer is likely to think without actually asking the customer or waiting for the customer to leave. For nonprofit organizations, *product performance* examples might include program and project performance in areas of rapid response to emergencies, at-home services, or multilingual services. In the Criteria these results are reported in Item 7.1.

Customer-focused performance refers to performance relative to measures and indicators of customers' perceptions, reactions, and behaviors. Examples include customer retention, complaints, and customer-survey results. These are considered *direct* measures of customer satisfaction since they are *telling* organizations directly about their levels of satisfaction or dissatisfaction. In the Criteria these results are reported in Item 7.2.

Financial and marketplace performance refers to performance relative to measures of cost, revenue, and market position, including asset utilization, asset growth, and market share. Examples include returns on investments, value added per employee, debt-to-equity ratio, returns on assets, operating margins, performance to budget, amount of reserve funds, cash-to-cash cycle time, other profitability and liquidity measures, and market gains. In the Criteria these results are reported in Item 7.3.

Operational performance refers to workforce, leadership, organizational, and ethical performance relative to effectiveness, efficiency, and accountability measures and indicators. Examples include cycle time, productivity, waste reduction, workforce turnover, workforce cross-training rates, regulatory compliance, fiscal accountability, and community involvement. Operational performance might be measured at the work-unit level, key-process level, and organizational level. In the Criteria these results are reported in Items 7.4, 7.5, and 7.6.

performance excellence—an integrated approach to organizational-performance management that results in: (1) delivery of ever-improving value to customers and stakeholders, contributing to organizational sustainability; (2) improvement of overall organizational effectiveness and capabilities; and (3) organizational and personal learning. The Baldrige Criteria for Performance Excellence provide a framework and an assessment tool for understanding organizational strengths and opportunities for improvement and thus for guiding planning efforts.

performance projections—estimates of future performance or goals for future results. Projections may be inferred from past performance, may be based on competitors' or similar organizations' performance that must be met or exceeded, may be predicted based on changes in a dynamic environment, or may be goals for future performance. Projections integrate estimates of the organization's rate of improvement and change, and they may be used to indicate where breakthrough improvement or change is needed. While performance projections may be set to attain a goal, they also may be predicted levels of future performance that indicate the challenges your organization faces in achieving a goal. Thus, performance projections serve as a key management-planning tool.

prevention-based intervention—determining the root cause of a problem and preventing its recurrence rather than just solving the problem and waiting for it to happen again (reactive posture).

process—linked activities with the purpose of producing a product or service for a customer (user) within or outside the organization. Generally, processes involve combinations of people, machines, tools, techniques, materials, and improvements in a defined series of steps or actions. Processes rarely operate in isolation and must be considered in relation to other processes that impact them. In some situations, processes might require adherence to a specific sequence of steps, with documentation (sometimes formal) of procedures and requirements, including well-defined measurement and control steps.

In many service situations, particularly when customers are directly involved in the service, process is used in a more general way; that is, to spell out what must be done, possibly including a preferred or expected sequence. If a sequence is critical, the service needs to include information to help customers understand and follow the sequence. Service processes involving customers also require guidance to the providers of those services on handling contingencies related to customers' likely or possible actions or behaviors.

In knowledge work such as strategic planning, research, development, and analysis, process does not necessarily imply formal sequences of steps. Rather, process implies general understandings regarding competent performance such as timing, options to be included, evaluation, and reporting. Sequences might arise as part of these understandings.

In the Baldrige Scoring System, process-achievement level is assessed. This achievement level is based on four factors that can be evaluated for each of an organization's key processes: Approach, Deployment, Learning, and Integration.

productivity—measures of the efficiency of resource use. Although the term often is applied to single factors such as the workforce (labor productivity), machines, materials, energy, and capital, the productivity concept applies as well to the total resources used in producing outputs. The use of an aggregate measure of overall productivity allows a determination of whether the net effect of overall changes in a process—possibly involving resource trade-offs—is beneficial.

purpose—the fundamental reason that an organization exists. The primary role of purpose is to inspire an organization and guide its setting of values. Purpose is generally broad and enduring. Two organizations in different businesses could have similar purposes, and two organizations in the same business could have different purposes.

results—outputs and outcomes achieved by an organization in addressing the requirements of a Baldrige Criteria Item. Results are evaluated on the basis of current performance; performance relative to appropriate comparisons; the rate, breadth, and importance of performance improvements; and the relationship of results measures to key organizational performance requirements.

rework and defects—problems associated with not doing things right the first time. In manufacturing, rework (doing the job again) typically results when the inspector notices that a product has flaws (is defective or contains defects). This forces the organization to make the product again. Since the work must be done again, it is considered rework. Other examples of rework caused by defective processes might include remedial education, rewriting a sentence to correct typographical or grammatical errors, repealing faulty legislation and passing new or replacement legislation, or repairing an incisional hernia caused by faulty (or defective) surgical procedures. The list of defects which cause work to be done again is virtually endless.

root cause—the original or basic cause or reason for a condition. The root cause of a condition is that cause which, if eliminated, ensures that the condition will not recur.

segment—a part of an organization's overall customer, market, product offering, or workforce base. Segments typically have common characteristics that can be logically grouped. In Results Items, the term refers to disaggregating results data in a way that allows for meaningful analysis of an organization's performance. It is up to each organization to determine the specific factors that it uses to segment its customers, markets, products, and workforce.

Understanding segments is critical to identifying the distinct needs and expectations of different customer, market, and workforce groups and to tailoring product offerings to meet their needs and expectations. As an example, market segmentation might be based on geography, distribution channels, business volume, or technologies employed. Workforce segmentation might be based on geography, skills, needs, work assignments, or job classification.

senior leaders—an organization's senior management group or team. In many organizations, this consists of the head of the organization and his or her direct reports.

societal risk—potential dangers to the community and society at large that might be created by an organization. For example, speculative investing by a bank may pose a risk to the public as well as the customers of the bank.

stakeholders—all groups that are or might be affected by an organization's actions and success. Examples of key stakeholders include customers, the workforce, partners, collaborators, governing boards, stockholders, donors, suppliers, taxpayers, regulatory bodies, policy makers, funders, and local and professional communities.

strategic advantages—those marketplace benefits that exert a decisive influence on an organization's likelihood of future success. These advantages frequently are sources of an organization's current and future competitive success relative to other providers of similar products. Strategic advantages generally arise from either or both of two sources: (1) core competencies, through building and expanding on an organization's internal capabilities, and (2) strategically important external resources, which are shaped and leveraged through key external relationships and partnerships. When an organization realizes both sources of strategic advantage, it can amplify its unique internal capabilities by capitalizing on complementary capabilities in other organizations.

See the definitions of *strategic challenges* and *strategic objectives* for the relationship among strategic advantages, strategic challenges, and the strategic objectives an organization articulates to address its challenges and advantages.

strategic challenges—those pressures that exert a decisive influence on an organization's likelihood of future success. These challenges frequently are driven by an organization's future competitive position relative to other providers of similar products. Strategic challenges generally, but not exclusively, are externally driven. However, in responding to externally driven strategic challenges, an organization may face internal strategic challenges.

External strategic challenges may relate to customer or market needs or expectations; product or technological changes; or financial, societal, and other risks or needs. Internal strategic challenges may relate to an organization's capabilities or its human and other resources. See the definition of *strategic advantages* and *strategic objectives* for the relationship between strategic challenges, strategic advantages, and the strategic objectives organizations create to address key challenges and advantages.

strategic objectives—an organization's articulated aims or responses to address major change or improvement, competitiveness, social issues, or business advantages. Strategic objectives generally are focused both externally and internally and relate to significant customer, market, product, service, or technological opportunities and challenges (strategic challenges). Broadly stated, they are what an organization must achieve to remain or become competitive and ensure the organization's long-term sustainability. Strategic objectives set an organization's longer-term directions and guide resource allocations and redistributions. See the definition of *action plans* for the relationship between strategic objectives and action plans and for an example of each.

supplier and partner capability—the ability of suppliers and partners to provide products and services as required. If an organization fails to consider the capability of its key suppliers and partners when planning or designing new products or services, the ability of that organization to deliver may be threatened.

sustainability—an organization's ability to address current business needs and to have the agility and strategic management to prepare successfully for future business, market, and operating environments. Both external and internal factors need to be considered. The specific combination of factors might include industry-wide and organization-specific components. Sustainability considerations might include workforce capability and capacity, resource availability, technology, knowledge, core competencies, work systems, facilities, and equipment.

In addition to an organization's ability to respond to changes in the business and financial markets, legal and regulatory requirements, and operating environment, sustainability also has a component related to preparedness for real-time or short-term emergencies.

system versus process—a *system* is a set of disciplined, consistent, well-defined, and well-designed *processes* for meeting the organization's quality and performance requirements. For example, the Leadership System refers to processes by which leadership is exercised throughout the organization and includes all people exercising leadership, from top executives to managers, to supervisors. Everything done in an organization is a process but not all processes are part of a system and not all processes are systematic.

systematic—approaches that are well-ordered, consistent, disciplined, and repeatable, and use data and information so learning is possible. Approaches are systematic if they include the opportunity for evaluation, improvement, and sharing, thereby permitting a gain in maturity.

timetable—a *timetable* for accomplishing strategic objectives sets forth the expected levels of achievement that leaders use to monitor progress toward achieving the outcome-based strategic objectives. To be aligned with strategic objectives, each objective should have a corresponding set of milestones to track progress. To be well-integrated, the timetable should be aligned and the intervals in the timetable should match the review cycle of the leaders. For example, if leaders review progress each quarter, then milestones should be developed that identify the level of progress that is expected to be made each quarter. Without timetables that predict the desired level of achievement, it is difficult for leaders to know if progress is on track or adjustments need to be made.

trends—numerical information that shows the direction and rate of change for an organization's results. Trends provide a time sequence of organizational performance.

A minimum of three historical (not projected) data points generally is needed to begin to ascertain a trend. More data points are needed to define a statistically valid trend. The time period for a trend is determined by the cycle time of the process being measured. Shorter cycle times demand more frequent measurement, while longer cycle times might require longer periods before meaningful trends can be determined.

Examples of trends called for by the Criteria include data related to product and service performance, customer and workforce satisfaction and dissatisfaction results, financial performance, marketplace performance, and operational performance, such as cycle time and productivity.

value—the perceived worth of a product, service, process, asset, or function relative to cost and to possible alternatives.

Organizations frequently use value considerations to determine the benefits of various options relative to their costs, such as the value of various product and service combinations to customers. Organizations need to understand what different stakeholder groups value and then deliver value to each group. This frequently requires balancing value for customers and other stakeholders, such as the workforce, stockholders, and the community.

value creation—processes that produce benefit for the organization's customers and for the organization. They are the processes most important to *running the business*—those that involve the majority of the workforce and generate products, services, and positive business results for stockholders and other key stakeholders.

values—the guiding principles and behaviors that embody how the organization and its people are expected to operate. Values reflect and reinforce the desired culture of the organization. Values support and guide the decision making of every workforce member, helping the organization to accomplish its mission and attain its vision in an appropriate manner. Examples of values might include ensuring integrity and fairness in all interactions, exceeding customer expectations, valuing individuals and diversity, protecting the environment, and demonstrating performance excellence every day.

vision—the desired future state of the organization. The vision describes where the organization is headed, what it intends to be, or how it wishes to be perceived.

voice of the customer—the process for capturing customer-related information. Voice-of-the-customer processes are intended to be proactive and continuously innovative to capture stated, unstated, and anticipated customer requirements, expectations, and desires. The goal is to achieve customer engagement. Listening to the voice of the customer might include gathering and integrating various types of customer data, such as survey data, focus group findings, warranty data, and complaint data, that affect customers' purchasing and engagement decisions.

work processes—the most important internal value creation processes. They might include product design and delivery, customer support, supply chain management, business, and support processes. They are the processes that involve the majority of the organization's workforce and produce customer, stakeholder, and stockholder value.

Key work processes frequently relate to core competencies, to the factors that determine success relative to competitors, and to the factors considered important for business growth by senior leaders.

work systems—how the work of the organization is accomplished. Work systems involve the workforce, key suppliers and partners, contractors, collaborators, and other components of the supply chain needed to produce and deliver products and business and support processes. Work systems coordinate the internal work processes and the external resources necessary to develop, produce, and deliver products to customers and to succeed in the marketplace.

Decisions about work systems are strategic. These decisions involve protecting and capitalizing on core competencies and deciding what should be procured or produced outside the organization in order to be efficient and sustainable in the marketplace.

workforce—all people who contribute to the delivery of an organization's products and services, including paid employees (such as permanent, part-time, temporary, and telecommuting employees as well as contract employees supervised by the organization). The workforce includes team leaders, supervisors, and managers at all levels. For purposes of Baldrige review, the workforce may include volunteers who provide essential services to the organization. Contract employees supervised by a contractor are covered by the requirements of business or support processes in Category 6.

workforce capability—an organization's ability to accomplish its work processes through the knowledge, skills, abilities, and competencies of its people. Capability may include the ability to build and sustain relationships with customers; to innovate and transition to new technologies; to develop new products and work processes; and to meet changing business, market, and regulatory demands.

workforce capacity—an organization's ability to ensure sufficient staffing levels to accomplish its work processes and successfully deliver products and services to customers, including the ability to meet seasonal or varying demand levels.

workforce engagement—the extent of workforce commitment, both emotional and intellectual, to accomplishing the work, mission, and vision of an organization. Organizations with high levels of workforce engagement are often characterized by high-performing work environments in which people are motivated to do their utmost for the benefit of their customers and for the success of the organization.

In general, members of the workforce feel engaged when they find personal meaning and motivation in their work and when they receive positive interpersonal and workplace support. An engaged workforce benefits from trusting relationships, a safe and cooperative environment, good communication and information flow, empowerment, and performance accountability. Key factors contributing to engagement include training and career development, effective recognition and reward systems, equal opportunity and fair treatment, and family friendliness.

About the Author

Mark L. Blazey, EdD

Mark Blazey is the president of Quantum Performance Group, a management consulting and training firm specializing in organization assessment and high-performance systems development. Dr. Blazey has an extensive background in quality systems. For five years he served as a senior examiner for the Malcolm Baldrige National Quality Award. He also served as the lead judge for Baldrige-based awards for the U.S. Army Communities of Excellence Award, New York State, Vermont, Delaware, and Aruba, and a judge for the Wisconsin Forward Award. Dr. Blazey has participated on and led numerous site-visit teams for national, state, and company quality awards and audits over the past 17 years.

Dr. Blazey has trained thousands of quality award examiners and judges for state and national quality programs including the Alabama Quality Award, Delaware Quality Award, Illinois Lincoln Award for Excellence, Kentucky Quality Award, Minnesota Quality Award, New York State Quality Award, Pennsylvania Quality Leadership Awards, Nebraska Quality Award, Vermont Quality Award, Wisconsin Forward Award, Aruba Quality Award, Costa Rica Quality Award, the Army Communities of Excellence Award, the Army Performance Excellence Award, and the national Workforce Excellence Network Award, as well as managers and examiners for schools, health care organizations, major businesses, and government agencies. He has set up numerous Baldrige-based programs to enhance and assess performance excellence for all sectors and types of organizations, many of which have subsequently received State and Baldrige recognition.

Dr. Blazey has written many books and articles on quality, including the ASQ Quality Press best-seller *Insights to Performance Excellence,* and co-authored *Baldrige in Brief: A Guide to the Baldrige Performance Excellence Criteria.* He is a senior member and a certified quality auditor of the American Society for Quality.

Dr. Blazey may be contacted via e-mail at authors@asq.org or Blazey@QuantumPerformance.com, or by telephone at 585-394-3700. He encourages feedback, recommendations, and questions about this book.

Index

Note: Italicized page numbers indicate illustrations.

A

accountability, 3, 21, 42–43, 46, 83, 167, 231, 302, 308
action plans, 3, 29, 31, 33–36, *68–69,* 71, 75–75, 103–05, 115–17, 120–24, 128, 147, 150, 165–66, 170–77, 208, 216, 221, 230, 232, 239–41, 248, 257, 266–67, 309, 314, 325, 331–32, 336, 338, 349
   definition, 345
actionable information, 134–36, 138, 140, 143, 272
agility, 23, 25, 85–87, 104, 109, 168, 182, 189, 191 256, 308, 320–21, 352, 355
agility, as core value, 26–27
alignment, 29–31, 33–34, 72, 128, 149, 170, 199, 237, 240, 245, 252, 311, 325, 350
   definition, 345
   of work management, 3, 103-04, 116–17, *116–17, 147,* 165, 188, 239, 241
anecdotal, 239, 253, 346
application,
   2009 Application template, CD-ROM
   eligibility certification, CD-ROM
   instructions, CD-ROM
   optional worksheet, CD-ROM
   preparation for, 235–45
application development templates, CD-ROM
award categories, and point values, 71
award criteria
   organization of, 70–71, *70*
   See also Baldrige criteria; criteria
award criteria framework, 69–70, *69–70*
award winners, 7–15

B

Baldrige criteria
   2009–2010 Award criteria, CD-ROM
   alignment with Six Sigma, Lean Thinking, and Balanced Scorecard, CD-ROM
   business case for using, 2–7
   changes from 2008 criteria, 73–76
   economic impact, 15
   worldwide use, 15
   See also award criteria; criteria
beginning implementation, 4
behaviorally anchored survey, 299, 301, 305–06
   sample, 307–15
benchmarking, 24, 36, 47, 148–49, 170, 174, 194, 200, 202, 206, 318, 328, 310, 341, 346, 351
brain center, 68–69, *68–69,* 147, 311
business results, 5, 6, 37, 43, 50, 77, 150, 311, 313, 332, 345, 347, 356

C

calibration guidelines, 241, 245, 249
competition, 7, 15, 37, 39, 42, 67, 118, 135
competitive comparison, 149, 206, 341
complaint information, 125, 136
compliance model, versus maturity/excellence model, CD-ROM
contephobia, 46–47
continuous improvement, 16, 23, 26, 30–31, 37, 43–44, 52, 59, 61–62, 66, 73, *73,* 189, 235, 252–53, 317, 320, 347
core competencies, 25, 29–30, 33, 36, 70, 73–74, 76, 78. 103–07, 149, 167, 189–196, *191, 198,* 240, 323, 332–34, 350, 352, 355, 357
   definition, 347
core values, 22–30
   agility, 26–27
   customer-driven excellence, 22–23
   focus on results and creating value, 29
   focus on the future, 26
   management by fact, 27–28
   managing for innovation, 26–27
   organizational and personal learning, 23–24
   societal responsibility, 28
   systems perspective, 29–30
   valuing workforce members and partners, 24–25
   visionary leadership, 22
cost reduction, 189
criteria
   changes from 2008, 73–76
   key characteristics of, 72
   worldwide use of, 15
   See also award criteria; Baldrige criteria
customer engagement, 34, 45, 49, 74–76, 83, 103, 125, 128, 182, 252, 254, 314, 326, 331, 335, 343, 357
   definition, 347
customer focus, 16, 45, 59, 67, 73, 85, 128, 199, 326, 347
   criteria framework, 68, *68–69*
   lessons, 45–46
Customer Focus, Category 68, *68–69,* 71, 75, 125–45, 242, 310, *310–11*
   site visit questions, 326–28
   3.1 Customer Engagement, 125, 126–33
      Adverse Consequences, 131–32
      Approach/Deployment, 129
      Criteria, 126–27
      discussion, 127–28
      Item Linkages, 130
      Sample Effective Practices, 132–33
   3.2 Customer, Voice of the, 125, 134–45
      Adverse Consequences, 140–43
      Approach/Deployment, 138
      Criteria, 134–35
      discussion, 135–37
      Item Linkages, 139–40
      Sample Effective Practices, 143–45
customer requirements, *16,* 17, 19, 25, 34, 37, 49, 59–61, 63, 68, 75, 125, 135–37, 170–71, 189–90, 198–99, 209, *236,* 245, 248, 254, 257, 324, 327–28, 333–35, 342, 357
customer satisfaction, 1–2, 5–6, 34, 37, 45, 47–48, 50, 59–66, 75, 125, 128, 136, 150, 165, 170–71, 207–09, *207,* 213, 241, 245, 252, 314, 318, 324, 327–28, 335–36, *337,* 339, 341–43, 347, 353
customer-driven excellence, as core value, 22–23
customer-focus champion, 34–35
cycle-time reduction, 170, 189, 229

D

dashboard, to monitor progress, 20, 154, *19–20*
data alignment, 149

361

data analysis, 132, 145, 154
Deming, W. Edwards, 39
deployment, 33–34, 55, *55,* 73–74, 103–04, 114, 120, 212, 123, 128, 151, 239, 241–42, 247–49, 253, 256–57, 300–01, 305–07, 317–19, 345, 348, 350, 354
   definition, 348
dot-coms, 1
DRIP, 47
driver triad, 68, *68*

E

economic impact, 15
eligibility forms, CD-ROM
eligibility guidelines, CD-ROM
employee feedback, 32, 43, 51, 228
employee satisfaction, 5–6, 50, 225
expected results, 239, 335–36, *337*

F

fear, 46, 48
focus on results and creating value, as core value, 29
focus on the future, as core value, 26

G

global competition, 37, 42
glossary, 345–57
good citizenship, 28, 88, 94, 96, 207, 240
governance, 22, 27–28, 32, 50, 72–73, 83, 94–95, 208, 231, 240, 308, 314, 318, 338
   definition, 349
guidelines, for criteria response, 239, 242
   data and measures, 244–45
   general, 238–39
   Process Items, 239–42
   Results Items, 242–45

H

Hendricks, Kevin B., 2–6

I

implementation cycle, of quality management, 4
information technology, 76, 147, 159
innovation, 2, 21, 26–27, 32, 34, 36, 42, 47, 48, 51, 59, 72–73, 76, 83, 85, 103–04, 107, 109, 118, 125, 135, 137, 150–51, 159, 167, 189, 191, 198–200, 226, 240, 242, 247–48, 252–53, 256–58, 308, 320–21, 326, 328-30, 334, 347, 349, 351
   definition, 350
innovation, managing for, as core value, 26–27
integrated management system, 16–20, *16–20*
   consequences of missing elements, 21
integrated system, 20, 74, 254
integrated structure, 72
International Organization for Standardization (ISO), 43, 332, CD-ROM
ISO 9001, CD-ROM
   comparison to Baldrige, CD-ROM.

J

K

L

leadership, 2, 19, *20,* 22, 30–32, 39–44, 47–48, 50, 51–53, 56, *56,* 59–67, 68, *68–69,* 72, 83, 85, 95, 107, 170, 231, *236,* 237, 252, 299, *304–05,* 318, 320–22, 351, 353
Leadership, Category, 83–101
   1.1 Senior Leadership, 83, 84–92
      Adverse Consequences, 90
      Approach/Deployment, 86–87
      Criteria, 84
      discussion, 85–87
      Item Linkages, 88–89
      Sample Effective Practices, 91–92
   1.2 Governance and Societal Responsibility, 83, 93–101
      Adverse Consequences, 99–100
      Approach/Deployment, 97
      Criteria, 93–94
      discussion, 94–96
      Item Linkages, 98
      Sample Effective Practices, 100–01
leadership lessons, 42–44
leadership practices, 51
learning, organizational and personal, as core value, 23–24
lessons learned, 37–50
   customer focus, 45–46
   measurement, analysis, and knowledge management, 46–47
   leadership, 42–44
   process management, 49
   results, 49–50
   strategic planning, 44–45
   workforce focus, 47–48
Likert scale survey, 299, 301, 305–06
Link, Albert N., 15

M

Malcolm Baldrige National Quality Award (MBNQA)
   economic impact of, 15
   establishment of, CD-ROM
   Improvement Act of 1987, CD-ROM
management by fact, as core value, 27–28
Management Effectiveness Survey, 56, *57–58*
managing for innovation, as core value, 26–27
manufacturing, 1, 3–4, 37, 39–40, 73, 95, 189, 197–98, 307, 354
mature implementation, 4
measurement, analysis, and knowledge management, 30, 35, 37, 46, *68–69,* 76, 147, 311, *311–12,* 328
Measurement, Analysis, and Knowledge Management, Category 147–64
   4.1 Measurement, Analysis, and Improvement of Organizational Performance, 147, 148–57
      Adverse Consequences, 154–56
      Approach/Deployment, 152
      Criteria, 148–49
      discussion, 149–51
      Item Linkages, 153
      Sample Effective Practices, 156–57
   4.2 Management of Information, Knowledge, and Information Technology, 147, 158–64
      Adverse Consequences, 162–63
      Approach/Deployment, 160
      Criteria, 158
      discussion, 159
      Item Linkages, 161
      Sample Effective Practices, 164
measurement, analysis, and knowledge management champion, 35–36
measurement, analysis, and knowledge management lessons, 46–47
motivated people, *17,* 19
must-do practices, 51–53

N

"The Nation's CEOs Look to the Future," 3
nonprofit-specific notes, 72

Index

O

optimum performance, 1, 16–17, 31–32, 252
organizational and personal learning, as core value, 23–24
organizational leadership champion, 31–32
Organizational Profile, 77–82
    importance of, 77
    P.1 Organizational Description, 78–80
        Criteria, 78–79
        Item Linkages, 80
    P.2 Organizational Situation, 81–82
        Criteria, 81
        Item Linkages, 82

P

performance excellence standards, 59–66
performance improvement council, 30–37
    council expertise, 31
    council membership, 30–31
    customer focus champion, 34–35
    measurement, analysis, and knowledge management champion, 35–36
    organizational leadership champion, 31–32
    process management champion, 36–37
    results champion, 37
    strategic planning champion, 33–34
    workforce focus champion, 36
performance standards, for managers, 59, 63–66
plan–do–check–act (PDCA), 73, *73*
point values, and award categories, 71
prevention-based systems, 252
Process Management, Category 6, 189–206
    6.1 Work Systems, 190–196
        Adverse Consequences, 195
        Approach/Deployment, 193
        Criteria, 190
        discussion, 191–92
        Item Linkages, 194–95
        Sample Effective Practices, 196
    6.2 Work Processes, 197–206
        Adverse Consequences, 203–05
        Approach/Deployment, 201
        Criteria, 197
        discussion, 197–200
        Item Linkages, 202–03
        Sample Effective Practices, 205–06
process-management champion, 36–37
process management lessons, 49
processes, efficient, 18–19, *18,* 345
promising practice, 1

Q

quality, use of word, 43

R

requirements, scoring, 255–99, 346, 352
    basic, 247, 250, 253, 256–57, 346
    multiple, 74–76, 235, 238, 247, 250, 253, 255–58, 352
    overall, 247–250, 253, 255–58, 352
research study, Hendricks and Singhal, 2–6
results, 16–20, *16–20,* 29, 37, 42–43, 50, 52–56, 61, 68–70, *68–69,* 72–73, 76, 105, 107–08, 125, 127–28, 165, 171, 207–09, 213, 217, 221–22, 226–27, 231, 238–43, *243,* 245, 247–49, 251, 254, 258, 299, 314, *315,* 334–36, *337,* 338, 352–56
    definition, 354
Results, Category 207–234
    7.1 Product Outcomes, 209–12
        Adverse Consequences, 212
        Approach/Deployment, 210
        Criteria, 209
        discussion, 209
        Item Linkages, 211
        Sample Effective Results, 206
    7.2 Customer-Focused Outcomes, 213–16
        Adverse Consequences, 216
        Approach/Deployment, 214
        Criteria,
        discussion, 213
        Item Linkages, 215
        Sample Effective Results, 216
    7.3 Financial and Market Outcomes, 217–20
        Adverse Consequences, 220
        Approach/Deployment, 218
        Criteria, 217
        discussion, 217
        Item Linkages, 219
        Sample Effective Results, 220
    7.4 Workforce-Focused Outcomes, 221–25
        Adverse Consequences, 225
        Approach/Deployment, 223
        Criteria, 221
        discussion, 221–22
        Item Linkages, 224
        Sample Effective Results, 225
    7.5 Process Effectiveness Outcomes, 226–229
        Adverse Consequences, 229
        Approach/Deployment, 227
        Criteria, 226
        discussion, 226–27
        Item Linkages, 228
        Sample Effective Results, 229
    7.6 Leadership Outcomes, 230–34
        Adverse Consequences, 234
        Approach/Deployment, 232
        Criteria, 230
        discussion, 231
        Item Linkages, 233
        Sample Effective Results, 234
results, focus on, as core value, 29
results champion, 37
results lessons, 49–50

S

scoring calibration guide, 241, 245, 247, 257, 259–99, CD-ROM
scoring, clarifications, 257
scoring guidelines, 2, 72–73, 76, 239–43, 245, 250–51, 255, 258, 301, 334
    by category, 259–99
    expected findings, 259–99
scoring requirements, 255–99, 346, 352
    basic, 247, 250, 253, 256–57, 346
    multiple, 74–76, 235, 238, 247, 250, 253, 255–58, 352
    overall, 247–250, 253, 255–58, 352
scoring system, 238, 247–54, 354
    Approach/Deployment Items, 247
    dimensions, 247–48, 346, 348, 350–51
    process, 247–48, 250
    results, 248–49, 251
Scott, John T., 15
self-assessments, 299–315
    behaviorally anchored survey, 299, 301, 305–06
    full-length written narrative, 299–300, 306
    sample organizational self-assessment, 307–15
    short written narrative, 300
    survey approach, 301
seven must-do practices, 51–53
Singhal, Vinod R., 2–6
site visit, 317–339
    characteristics of, 318
    conduct of examiners, 319
    conducting, 319
    expected results matrix, 336–37
    general workforce questions, 339
    generic questions, by category, 320–338

preceding discussions, 318–19
purpose of, 317
typically important issues, 318
societal responsibility, as core value, 28
stakeholders, 3, 7, 26, 32, 36, 43, 72–73, 83, 85, 94, 116, 128, 159, 182, 189, 192, 198, 237, 242, 256, 308, 324, 334, 349, 349, 351–53, 356
    definition, 355
Strategic Planning, Category 103–24
    2.1 Strategy Development, 104, 105–14
        Adverse Consequences, 112–13
        Approach/Deployment, 110
        Criteria, 105
        discussion, 106–09
        Item Linkages, 111–12
        Sample Effective Practices, 114
    2.2 Strategy Deployment, 104, 115–24
        Adverse Consequences, 122
        Approach/Deployment, 120
        Criteria, 115–16
        discussion, 116–19
        Item Linkages, 121
        Sample Effective Practices, 123–24
strategic planning champion, 33–34
strategic planning lessons, 44–45
strategies, execution of, 3
strategy, 20, *20*, 22, 30, 33–36, 67–68, *68–69*, 70, 72, 74, 96, 103–04, 107, 116, 118, 125, 165, 168, 189, 207–08, 240–41, 254, 256, 258, 323–25, 338
supply chain, 104, 159, 189, 191–92, 198–99, 227, 334, 357
sustainability, 33, 34, 36, 73–74, 76, 85, 96, 103, 125, 136–37, 151, 167, 171, 188–91, 197, 208, 213, 217, 222, 227, 231, 240, 248, 257, 333, 353, 355
    definition, 355

organizational, 34, 73–75, 125, 136–37, 151, 167, 190, 208, 213, 217, 222, 227, 231, 353
system vs process, 356
systems, 1,–2, 7, 21, 29–38, 42–43, 46–48, 51, 53, 60–61, 67, 69, 72–74, 85, 116, 128, 147, 149–150, 159, 167–68, 170, 182, 239–41, 252–58, 299–301, 304, 306, 319, 333, 338, 350, 357
systems, work, 2, 6, 25, 27, 29, 47, 80, 116, 128, 170, 189, 191–96, 199, 208, 240–41, 254, 257–58, 313, 333, 338, 355
systems perspective, as core value, 29–30

T

table of expected results, 242, 336, *337*
terms, clarification of, 341–43
training, 4, 16–17, 24–25, 31, 34, 39–42, 44, 47–48, 50, 52–54, 59–62, 65, 118, 150, 168, 170–71, 182, 189, 221, 331, 339
    education vs, 341–42
trends, in business environments, 3

U

U.S. Congress, 15
upward evaluation, 55, 85, 94

V

valuing workforce members and partners, as core value, 24–25
visionary leadership, as core value, 22
voice of the customer, 23, 45, 49, 74–77, 125, 138–39, 143, 196, 202, 205, 211, 240, 271–73, 310, *310–311*, 318, 326, 357
    3.2 Voice of the Customer, 134–36

W

well-being, societal, 28, 72, 74, 96–98, 100, 208, 323
well-being, workforce, 24, 54
work core, 68, *68–69*
work results, 16
work systems, 2, 6, 25, 27, 29, 47, 80, 116, 128, 170, 189, 191–96, 199, 208, 240–41, 254, 257–58, 313, 333, 338, 355
    definition, 357
workforce engagement, 47–48, 59–62, 65–66, 76, 83, 85–86, 118, 165–68, 171–80, 189, 207–08, 221–22, 240, 252, 254, 257, 312–13, 321, 330–32, 336, 343, 348–49
    definition, 357
workforce environment, 165, 182,
workforce, worker feedback, 180, 257, 322
Workforce Focus, Category 5, 165–87
    5.1 Workforce Engagement, 165, 166–80
        Adverse Consequences, 175–78
        Approach/Deployment, 172
        Criteria, 166–67
        discussion, 167–71
        Item Linkages, 173–74
        Questions, *169*
        Sample Effective Practices, 177–80
    5.2 Workforce Environment, 165, 181–87
        Adverse Consequences, 185–86
        Approach/Deployment, 183
        Criteria, 181
        discussion, 182
        Item Linkages, 184
        Sample Effective Practices, 187
workforce focus champion, 36
workforce focus lessons, 47–48
workforce performance management, 170

Belong to the Quality Community!

Established in 1946, ASQ is a global community of quality experts in all fields and industries. ASQ is dedicated to the promotion and advancement of quality tools, principles, and practices in the workplace and in the community.

The Society also serves as an advocate for quality. Its members have informed and advised the U.S. Congress, government agencies, state legislatures, and other groups and individuals worldwide on quality-related topics.

Vision

By making quality a global priority, an organizational imperative, and a personal ethic, ASQ becomes the community of choice for everyone who seeks quality technology, concepts, or tools to improve themselves and their world.

ASQ is…

- More than 90,000 individuals and 700 companies in more than 100 countries
- The world's largest organization dedicated to promoting quality
- A community of professionals striving to bring quality to their work and their lives
- The administrator of the Malcolm Baldrige National Quality Award
- A supporter of quality in all sectors including manufacturing, service, healthcare, government, and education
- YOU

Visit www.asq.org for more information.

ASQ Membership

Research shows that people who join associations experience increased job satisfaction, earn more, and are generally happier*. ASQ membership can help you achieve this while providing the tools you need to be successful in your industry and to distinguish yourself from your competition. So why wouldn't you want to be a part of ASQ?

Networking

Have the opportunity to meet, communicate, and collaborate with your peers within the quality community through conferences and local ASQ section meetings, ASQ forums or divisions, ASQ Communities of Quality discussion boards, and more.

Professional Development

Access a wide variety of professional development tools such as books, training, and certifications at a discounted price. Also, ASQ certifications and the ASQ Career Center help enhance your quality knowledge and take your career to the next level.

Solutions

Find answers to all your quality problems, big and small, with ASQ's Knowledge Center, mentoring program, various e-newsletters, Quality Progress magazine, and industry-specific products.

Access to Information

Learn classic and current quality principles and theories in ASQ's Quality Information Center (QIC), ASQ Weekly e-newsletter, and product offerings.

Advocacy Programs

ASQ helps create a better community, government, and world through initiatives that include social responsibility, Washington advocacy, and Community Good Works.

Visit www.asq.org/membership for more information on ASQ membership.

*2008, The William E. Smith Institute for Association Research